Environmental Ethics and Forestry
A Reader

In the series
Environmental Ethics, Values, and Policy,
edited by Holmes Rolston III

Environmental Ethics and Forestry

A Reader

EDITED BY Peter C. List

TEMPLE UNIVERSITY PRESS

PHILADELPHIA

Temple University Press, Philadelphia 19122
Copyright © 2000 by Temple University
All rights reserved
Published 2000
Printed in the United States of America

⊗ The paper used in this publication meets the requirements
of the American National Standard for Information Sciences—Permanence
of Paper for Printed Library Materials, ANSI Z39-48.1984

Library of Congress Cataloging-in-Publication Data

Environmental ethics and forestry : a reader / edited by Peter C. List
    p. cm.— (Environmental ethics, values, and policy)
    Includes bibliographical references (p.) and index.
    ISBN 1-56639-784-7 (alk. paper)—ISBN 1-56639-785-5 (pbk. : alk. paper)
    1. Forests and forestry—Moral and ethical aspects.   2. Environmental ethics.
   I. List, Peter C.   II. Series.
SD387.E78 E58 2000
179'.1—dc21   00-025421

To Judy, Julia, Chris, Dave, Matt, Theo, Isabella, and Nicholas—family all

The Poplar Field by William Cowper

The poplars are fell'd, farewell to the shade
And the whispering sound of the cool colonnade;
The winds play no longer and sing in the leaves,
Nor Ouse on his bosom their image receives.

Twelve years have elapsed since I first took a view
Of my favourite field, and the bank where they grew:
And now in the grass behold they are laid,
And the tree is my seat that once lent me a shade.

The blackbird has fled to another retreat
Where the hazels afford him a screen from the heat;
And the scene where his melody charm'd me before
Resounds with his sweet-flowing ditty no more.

My fugitive years are all hasting away,
And I must ere long lie as lowly as they,
With a turf on my breast and a stone at my head,
Ere another such grove shall arise in its stead.

'Tis a sight to engage me, if anything can,
To muse on the perishing pleasures of man;
Short-lived as we are, our enjoyments, I see,
Have a still shorter date; and die sooner than we.

Contents

Preface xi

Acknowledgments xix

General Introduction 1

Part I: Ethical Systems in Forestry 11

1. THE ECONOMIC RESOURCE MODEL OF FORESTS AND FORESTRY 23

Bernhard Fernow
Forest and Forestry Defined 26

Gifford Pinchot
Principles of Conservation 32

Gifford Pinchot
The Use of the National Forests 36

2. JOHN MUIR ON THE PRESERVATION OF THE WILD FORESTS OF THE WEST 41

John Muir
The American Forests 44

3. ALDO LEOPOLD'S LAND ETHIC IN FORESTRY 53

Aldo Leopold
The Land Ethic 57

Part II: Two Philosophical Issues in Forestry Ethics 69

4. MULTIPLE VALUES IN FORESTS 73

Holmes Rolston III
Values Deep in the Woods 75

Holmes Rolston III
Aesthetic Experience in Forests 80

5. THE RIGHTS OF TREES AND OTHER NATURAL OBJECTS 93

Robin Attfield
The Good of Trees 98

Lawrence E. Johnson
Holistic Entities—Species 114

Lawrence E. Johnson
Ecointerests and Forest Fires 117

Part III: Contemporary Forestry Ethics 121

6. BASIC PRINCIPLES IN FORESTRY ETHICS 125

Michael McDonald
First Principles for Professional Foresters 128

Paul M. Wood
"The Greatest Good for the Greatest Number": Is This a Good Land-Use Ethic 145

James E. Coufal
Environmental Ethics: Cogitations and Ruminations of a Forester 152

The Ecoforestry Declaration of Interdependence 160

7. CODES OF ETHICS IN FORESTRY, FISHERIES, AND WILDLIFE BIOLOGY 163

Code of Ethics for Members of the Society of American Foresters 167

Code of Ethics and Standards for Professional Conduct for Wildlife Biologists, The Wildlife Society 169

Code of Practices, American Fisheries Society 171

Code of Ethics, Oregon Chapter, American Fisheries Society 173

A Code of Ethics for Government Service 176

The Ecoforester's Way 177

8. ADOPTING A LAND ETHIC IN THE SOCIETY OF AMERICAN FORESTERS 179

James E. Coufal
The Land Ethic Question 184

Norwin E. Linnartz, Raymond S. Craig, and M. B. Dickerman
Land Ethic Canon Recommended by Committee 186

Holmes Rolston III and James Coufal
A Forest Ethic and Multivalue Forest Management: The Integrity of Forests and of Foresters Are Bound Together 189

Raymond S. Craig
Further Development of a Land Ethic Canon 196

Raymond S. Craig
Land Ethic Canon Proposal: A Report from the Task Force 199

9. ADVOCATING NEW ENVIRONMENTAL ETHICS IN PUBLIC NATURAL RESOURCE AGENCIES 205

Kristin Shrader-Frechette
Ethics and Environmental Advocacy 209

Inner Voice 221

AFSEEE Vision: Strategy for Forest Service Reform 225

Jeff DeBonis
Speaking Out: A Letter to the Chief of the U.S. Forest Service 227

F. Dale Robertson
Chief Robertson Responds 235

On Speaking Out: Fighting for Resource Ethics in the BLM 237

Whistleblower Spills Beans on North Kaibab 240

A Combat Biologist Calls It Quits: An Interview with Al Espinosa 243

Tongass Employees Speak Out 247

Cheri Brooks
Enough Is Enough! A Tongass Timber Beast Puts His Foot Down 248

10. ETHICAL ISSUES IN GLOBAL FORESTRY 253

James L. Bowyer
Responsible Environmentalism: The Ethical Features of Forest Harvest and Wood Use on a Global Scale 259

Alastair S. Gunn
Environmental Ethics and Tropical Rain Forests: Should Greens Have Standing? 264

Doug Daigle
Globalization of the Timber Trade 280

11. NEW FORESTRY, NEW FOREST PHILOSOPHIES 289

Alan G. McQuillan
Cabbages and Kings: The Ethics and Aesthetics of New Forestry 293

Stephanie Kaza
Ethical Tensions in the Northern Forest 319

Alan Drengson and Duncan Taylor
An Overview of Ecoforestry: Introduction 333

EPILOGUE 345

Kathleen Dean Moore
Traveling the Logging Road, Coast Range 346

Selected Bibliography 351

Index 358

Preface

The social movements of the 1950s and 1960s in the United States have had a powerful influence on many aspects of American public life. The Civil Rights movement turned public attention to the evils of discrimination and racism, and stimulated Congress and the White House to create new federal legislation that guaranteed equal legal rights to all citizens regardless of race or ethnic status. Environmentalists followed the lead of civil rights activists and raised public concerns about deteriorating conditions in the North American environment. They helped to move Congress to enact groundbreaking legislation in the late 1960s and 1970s that was designed to ensure more significant protection and better management of our many natural resources on public lands.[1] Along with concerns about such issues as the conduct of the Vietnam War and the status of women in our society, these movements also had an effect on university research and teaching. Ecology and other environmental sciences became popular university subjects, and there was unprecedented scholarly focus on environmental issues in such disciplines as philosophy, history, sociology, and religious studies.[2]

As a result of these social developments, forestry as well has come under increasing public and scholarly scrutiny in the United States. In fact, it is reasonable to say that during the past twenty-five years, American forestry has experienced a vigorous critical assault on its basic assumptions, methods, and practical outcomes by the environmental movement, environmental scientists, public interest groups, and many members of the public.[3] Critics have expressed concern about a number of issues, including the increasing exploitation of public and private forests

---

1. This includes such landmark federal laws as the Wilderness Act of 1964, the Wild and Scenic Rivers Act of 1968, the National Environmental Policy Act of 1969, the Endangered Species Act of 1973, the National Forest Management Act of 1976, and the Federal Land Policy and Management Act of 1976.

2. Roderick Nash, *The Rights of Nature: A History of Environmental Ethics* (Madison: University of Wisconsin Press, 1989).

3. Criticism of forestry or forest practices in the United States has waxed and waned throughout the twentieth century, and the behavior of natural resource corporations that have wasted or destroyed forest resources has been a part of public dialogue about the American landscape since at least the mid-nineteenth century when George Perkins Marsh published his classic contribution to conservation, *Man and Nature*, in 1864. However, beginning in the early 1970s and continuing into the 1980s and 1990s, critical reviews of forest management have risen to a crescendo. Forestry has been evaluated by individuals representing various professions, groups, and

for timber production at the expense of other uses and values; the reduction and elimination of old-growth habitats along with their associated animal and plant species; the degradation of public grasslands used for grazing; the lack of sufficient attention to recreation on public forest lands; the silvicultural methods that foresters have used in their eagerness to "get out the cut" such as clearcutting, slashburning, and the use of pesticides and herbicides; and the

---

resource philosophies, including not only environmental and conservation groups but forester and also resource extraction groups as well. This history is discussed by scholars and historians in such classics as John Ise, *The United States Forest Policy* (New Haven: Yale University Press, 1920); Samuel Trask Dana, *Forest and Range Policy: Its Development in the United States* (New York: MacGraw-Hill Book Company, 1956); Samuel P. Hays, *Conservation and the Gospel of Efficiency: The Progressive Conservation Movement, 1890–1920* (Cambridge, Mass.: Harvard University Press, 1959); Michael Frome, *Whose Woods These Are: The Story of the National Forests* (Garden City, N.Y.: Doubleday, 1962); Roderick Nash, *Wilderness and the American Mind* (New Haven, Conn.: Yale University Press, 1967); John F. Reiger, *American Sportsmen and the Origins of Conservation* (New York: Winchester Press, 1975); Harold K. Steen, *The U.S. Forest Service: A History* (Seattle: University of Washington Press, 1976); Stephen H. Pyne, *Fire in America: A Cultural History of Wildland and Rural Fire* (Princeton, N.J.: Princeton University Press, 1982); Thomas Cox et al., *The Well-Wooded Land: Americans and Their Forests from Colonial Times to the Present* (Lincoln: University of Nebraska Press, 1985); David A. Clary, *Timber and the Forest Service* (Lawrence: University of Kansas Press, 1986); Michael Williams, *Americans and Their Forests: A Historical Geography* (Cambridge, U.K.: Cambridge University Press, 1989); Paul Hirt, *A Conspiracy of Optimism: Management of the National Forests since World War Two* (Lincoln: University of Nebraska Press, 1994); Steven Lewis Yaffee, *The Wisdom of the Spotted Owl: Policy Lessons for a New Century* (Washington, D.C.: Island Press, 1994); Nancy Langston, *Forest Dreams, Forest Nightmares: The Paradox of Old Growth in the Inland West* (Seattle: University of Washington Press, 1995); and Richard A. Rajala, *Clearcutting the Pacific Rain Forest: Production, Science, and Regulation* (Vancouver, B.C.: University of British Columbia Press, 1998). Critical discussions of North American forestry and forest debates, published in the past thirty years and written mostly by nonforesters, include Pete Gunter, *The Big Thicket: A Challenge for Conservation* (Austin, Tex.: Jenkins Publishing Company, 1971); Daniel R. Barney, *The Last Stand: Ralph Nader's Study Group Report on the National Forests* (New York: Grossman Publishers, 1974); Ray Raphael, *Tree Talk: The People and Politics of Timber* (Covelo, Calif.: Island Press, 1981); Chris Maser, *The Redesigned Forest* (San Pedro, Calif.: R. & E. Miles, 1988); K. A. Soderberg and Jackie DuRette, *People of the Tongass: Alaska Forestry under Attack* (Bellvue, Wash.: The Free Enterprise Press, 1988); Keith Ervin, *Fragile Majesty: The Battle for North America's Last Great Forest* (Seattle, Wash.: The Mountaineers, 1989); Edward C. Fritz, *Clearcutting: A Crime Against Nature* (Austin, Tex.: Eakin Press, 1989); Ian Mahood and Ken Drushka, *Three Men and a Forester* (Madeira Park, B.C.: 1990); Elliott A. Norse, *Ancient Forests of the Pacific Northwest* (Washington, D.C.: Island Press, 1990); Grace Herndon, *Cut and Run: Saying Goodbye to the Last Great Forests in the West* (Telluride, Colo.: Western Eye Press, 1991); Richard Manning, *Last Stand* (Salt Lake City, Utah: Gibbs Smith Publishers, 1991); William Dietrich, *The Final Forest: The Battle for the Last Great Trees of the Pacific Northwest* (New York: Simon & Schuster, 1992); Mitch Lansky, *Beyond the Beauty Strip: Saving What's Left of Our Forests* (Gardiner, Maine: Tilbury House Publishers, 1992); David Seideman, *Showdown at Opal Creek: The Battle for America's Last Wilderness* (New York: Carroll & Graf Publishers, 1993); Ron MacIsaac and Anne Champagne, eds., *Clayoquot Mass Trials: Defending the Rainforest* (Gabriola Island, B.C.: New Society Publishers, 1994); Ray Raphael, *More Tree Talk: The People, Politics, and Economics of Timber* (Washington, D.C.: Island Press, 1994); David Dobbs and Richard Ober, *The Northern Forest* (White River Junction, Vt.: Chelsea Green Publishing Company, 1995); David Harris, *The Last Stand: The War between Wall Street and Main Street over California's Ancient Redwoods* (New York: Times Books, Random House, 1995); Robert Leo Heilman, *Overstory Zero: Real Life in Timber Country* (Seattle: Sasquatch Books, 1995); Charles E. Little, *The Dying of the Trees: The Pandemic in America's Forests* (New York: Viking Penguin, 1995); Katy Durbin, *Tree Huggers: Victory, Defeat and Renewal in the Northwest Ancient Forest Campaign* (Seattle: The Mountaineers, 1996); Joan Dunning, *From the Redwood Forest, Ancient Trees and the Bottom Line: A Headwaters Journey* (White

exportation of industrial forestry to other parts of the world by large timber companies. The fragmentation of forest habitats as a consequence of managing forests primarily for timber production has been a more recent focal point for debate because this management practice has threatened and endangered many wild animal and plant species, including numerous fish species and a variety of mammal and bird populations.[4] Efforts by government and university scientists to document species loss in public and private forests have solidified understanding of the ecological consequences of forest management, and the federal government has been spurred on to list a number of forest and forest-related species as either endangered or threatened under the 1973 Endangered Species Act.[5] Moreover, some critics have suggested that federal forest management is a losing proposition on the national forests, in economic terms, once all of the publicly subsidized costs, such as road building for timber management, are figured into the total cost and benefit equation.[6]

As new public interest groups have gained increasing power in our political system and their use of the tools of political change has become more sophisticated and effective, conventional forest management has been scrutinized and found wanting. Because the environmental values of environmentalist critics have coincided more closely with those of the public while the values of foresters have traditionally been more aligned with those of the timber industry, many foresters

---

River Junction, Vt.: Chelsea Green Publishing Company, 1998); Elisabeth May, *At the Cutting Edge: The Crisis in Canada's Forests* (San Francisco: Sierra Club Books, 1998); Jane Claire Dirks-Edmunds, *Not Just Trees: The Legacy of a Douglas-fir Forest* (Pullman: Washington State University Press, 1999) and Bill Shoaf, *The Taking of the Tongass: Alaska's Rainforest* (Sequin, Wash.: Running Wolf Press, 2000).

4. The causes of species loss on forest lands are of course more varied than this, and logging is not the only culprit. This is evident in the Pacific Northwest where such factors as the damming of major rivers; human intrusions into formerly wild forest habitats for housing and other urban development; changing conditions in the Pacific Ocean; and agricultural, industrial, and municipal practices near streams have affected riverine species. But such forest practices as cutting all trees next to creeks and streams, and on steep slopes, removing large volumes of wood and woody debris over large acreages, building extensive networks of forest roads, and disturbing the forest floor with heavy logging machinery in sensitive forest areas have all had serious and negative consequences, some long-term, on stream and water quality, fish survival, and the viability of other forest species as well. The 1993 "FEMAT Report" prepared by a phalanx of federal experts in forestry, fisheries, biology, wildlife, and other environmental and social sciences, and published by six different federal agencies responsible for federal land management, documents the effects of these practices on biodiversity in Pacific Northwest forests. See *Forest Ecosystem Management: An Ecological, Economic, and Social Assessment*, Report of the Forest Ecosystem Management Assessment Team, USDA, Forest Service et al., July 1993. The concern about fragmentation and its serious consequences for biodiversity in forests of the Douglas fir region of western North America was stimulated by the work of many forest and wildlife scientists including Larry D. Harris, *The Fragmented Forest: Island Biogeography Theory and the Preservation of Biodiversity* (Chicago: University of Chicago Press, 1984).

5. For an account of the history of scientific research into old-growth forests, centered at the H. J. Andrews Experimental Forest near Blue River, Oregon, in the Central Oregon Cascade Mountains, read Jon R. Luoma, *The Hidden Forest: The Biography of an Ecosystem* (New York: Henry Holt and Company, 1999).

6. There are a number of forest interest groups that have taken this tack, including taxpayer groups and environmental groups such as the Wilderness Society, but a few economists have been making this argument for some years now. See, e.g., Randall O'Toole, *Reforming the Forest Service* (Washington, D.C.: Island Press, 1988). It has been noted as well that the road system in the national forests is now larger than the massive interstate highway system in the United States, and that construction of forest roads into formerly roadless areas has been the entering wedge to fragment forests and endanger forest biodiversity.

have discovered that their presumed "contract" with society to manage forests using their best professional judgment has been undermined.[7] Comfortable assumptions by foresters about the benefits of "scientific" forest management and about the needs and demands of the public for wood have been challenged at nearly every turn.[8]

At a time of crisis, some practitioners and critics of a craft turn their attention to fundamentals and begin to look for different ways to think about traditional practices, methodologies, concepts, and philosophies. This self-reflective process can sometimes produce radically new ideas that significantly reshape the activities of practitioners. In other cases it can lead to retrenchment and reaction, and a desire to return to customary ways of doing things. More typically it results in incremental modifications in old ways of thinking that make for a more modest evolution in those

---

7. The similarities and differences between the values of Forest Service employees, on the one hand, and commercial users of national forests and environmentalists, on the other, has been studied for some years now. Some social scientists and historians have argued that there has been a strong value bias in the U.S. Forest Service in favor of commercial timber production and against environmental protection. They argue that in contrast to the perception within the Forest Service—for example in the 1980s that the agency represented a balance between these competing interests—it was actually closer to the interests of the timber industry. For this view, consult Ben W. Twight and Fremont J. Lyden, "Measuring Forest Service Bias," *Journal of Forestry* 87(5) (May 1989); William B. Robbins, *Lumberjacks and Legislators* (College Station: Texas A&M Press, 1982). See also William B. Robbins, *American Forestry: A History of National, State and Private Cooperation* (Lincoln: University of Nebraska Press, 1985); and David Clary, *Timber and the Forest Service* (Lawrence: University of Kansas Press, 1986). More recent studies conclude that this value bias is changing, as a result of various factors, and is a time and generationally dependent phenomenon, among other things. Thus the values and attitudes of some Forest Service employees are becoming more congruent with noncommodity aspects of forests and with environmental concerns, and are moving away from a more strictly utilitarian land ethic. Aside from its connection to cultural changes, for example changes in public environmental values, this appears to be a consequence of such factors as changes in the demographics of newer generations of Forest Service employees, changes in the mix of disciplines within the service itself with a greater diversity of nonforester specialities in the agency since the 1970s, and changes in attitudes as a result of interdisciplinary planning in the agency. See, e.g., Catherine McCarthy, Paul Sabatier, and John Loomis, "Attitudinal Change in the Forest Service: 1960–1990," paper for the 1991 Annual Meeting of the Western Political Science Association, Seattle, Washington, March 21–23, 1991; Lori A. Cramer, James J. Kennedy, Richard S. Krannich, and Thomas M. Quigley, "Changing Forest Service Values and Their Implications for Land Management Decisions Affecting Resource-Dependent Communities," *Rural Sociology* 58(3) (1993): 475–91; and Greg Brown and Chuck Harris, "Professional Foresters and the Land Ethic, Revisited," *Journal of Forestry* 96 (1) (January 1998): 4–8. Recent changes made at the top level of Forest Service management during the Clinton Administration have moved the Forest Service toward ecosystem management and toward management of public forest lands for such values as ecosystem health; this represents another step away from the discredited "timber first" approach.

8. One recurring idea among professional foresters is that forest management is a technical matter that should be left to the experts and that the experts can adequately manage forest lands for all of the values that the public now holds dear. While it is understandable that foresters should champion this view and it is true that some aspects of forest management are quite technical, the public distrust of expertise in the United States has grown and deepened consistently since the 1950s, and so this idea is bound to be received with skepticism by the public. Moreover, there is considerable evidence that the public places a very high value on its own involvement in forest management, particularly on public lands, and seeks "more inclusive" forms of forest decision processes. The practical difficulty then is to determine how forest management can emerge from a broader dialogue that involves the public in a direct and meaningful way. See Bruce Shindler and Lori A. Cramer, "Shifting Public Values for Forest Management: Making Sense of Wicked Problems," *Western Journal of Applied Forestry*, 14(1) (January 1999): 28–34.

practices. In any event, it can cause people in a field to rethink comfortable beliefs about their standard practices and to find new ones on which to base different ways of doing things. This reexamination is occurring now in forestry in the United States, and environmental ethics and environmental philosophy are part of the self-reflective process. Ethical issues, ethical codes, and in particular the ethics of professional behavior are now being discussed in the applied environmental sciences like seldom before in the history of these disciplines. There is a new recognition in many environmental fields that the scientific applications of forestry, fisheries, botany, wildlife science, zoology, biology, and ecology to environmental and natural resource management are not always ethically neutral or unbiased. Moreover, while there is a developing belief that such management should be more "science-based" than in the past, there is also a correlative awareness that our ecological understanding of nature leaves much to be desired. These new attitudes have led scientists, natural resource agency personnel, environmental philosophers, representatives of public interest groups, and citizens to advocate new forms of environmental ethics and forest management for public and private forest lands. While much of the focus of this is directed at federal forestry and the national forests, some of the leading ideas have been applied to other kinds of forestry as well, such as state-based forestry, large corporate industrial operations, and small-scale private forestry.

In order to help this self-reflective process along, this anthology aims to reveal to a wider audience, particularly to students of the environmental and natural resource sciences, some examples of these new ideas about the ethical dimensions of forestry and associated environmental sciences. Included are samples of the writings of the original shapers of public forestry in America, such as Gifford Pinchot; the ideas of important thinkers in the field of environmental ethics, such as Aldo Leopold and Holmes Rolston III; and also some philosophically-minded foresters and environmental scientists. Readers and students will be able to judge how much the ideas of these more recent contributors to national and regional discussions about the ethical aspects of forestry amount to either conceptual evolution or revolution, and how useful these ideas are in advancing the cause of forest conservation and preservation. This book presupposes that such contributors' ideas are valuable sources for the intellectual reassessment of forestry and merit serious study and reflection.

Readers should keep in mind that the aim of this collection is not to provide a technical manual for forest or environmental management, an account of current research in the forest-related environmental sciences, a treatise on forest policy, a history of environmentalism and its critique of forestry, or a sociological and political tract on the social and political forces that affect forests and other natural resources. Moreover, this anthology does not include detailed "pro and con" selections on such issues as the ethical dimensions of clearcutting or public involvement in forest planning. Those issues are already covered elsewhere in the forestry literature. Instead, the goal of the book is, first, to give readers a sampling of environmental ethics and environmental philosophy as these new disciplines have been applied very directly to forestry and forest issues by environmental philosophers and, second, to acquaint readers with several important ethical issues that have been the focus of public and academic debate about forests. The book especially aims to give readers a better understanding of how environmental philosophers have formulated some important ethical questions about the management of forests, the conduct of foresters, and the treatment of forest organisms and ecosystems whether by foresters or forest users, though it is not a comprehensive survey of all such topics. I hope the collection will be particularly useful to college students in courses that deal directly with the social and ethical dimensions of natural resource issues and forestry. It is best that it be used in conjunction with other sources, such as more technical documents and writings in the applied environmental sciences, including forestry.

My interest in putting together this anthology goes back to May 1990 when I was asked by Steve Radosevich, a professor of forest science at Oregon State University, to join a new faculty group on campus, the Sustainable Forestry Program. The goal of the program was to devise interdisciplinary research projects that could bring foresters together with social scientists and humanists in an effort to produce new and useful conclusions about sustaining forests and human forest communities. After many lengthy discussions of the meaning of sustainability in forestry and of the methods, perspectives, and vocabularies of the academic disciplines represented in the group, a number of the group members split into research teams to pursue research that would implement this general goal. As I personally sought to feel my way into the unfamiliar territory of technical forestry, I learned that my contributions to group discussion and research could most profitably center on environmental ethics, a subject I had been teaching at the university since the early 1970s. Aldo Leopold's land ethic had long intrigued me, enough to make it one focus of my philosophical interests in environmental ethics and my philosophy teaching, because after over fifty years Leopold's ethical ideas still have significant implications for the natural resource disciplines such as agriculture, forestry, fisheries, and the environmental sciences that are prevalent in land grant universities around the country.[9]

Because of these personal concerns, I joined a small group of researchers in the Sustainable Forestry Program who decided to do survey research in Oregon and nationwide on public attitudes and values with regard to human ethical relationships to forests and to federal forest management—something that, at the time, was largely ignored by most social scientists. Other interdisciplinary research and writing projects evolved from the first, such as an analysis of the causes and consequences of forest land-use changes on public and private forests in the Central Oregon Cascade Mountains, a study of public attitudes about adaptive management areas in national forests of the Pacific Northwest, and a recent project on attitudes and expectations about the involvement of front-line, ecological scientists in natural resource management.[10] It was clear to me in doing this research with colleagues that worldviews and environmental values help to shape forest uses and land-use changes, and that philosophy and environmental ethics thus have something useful to say about these matters. Consequently, I began to search the philosophy literature for philosophical contributions to forestry, particularly articles and essays that directly address forestry and forest issues; sifted out what I thought was valuable for my

---

9. Applicable passages from Leopold's writings can be found in Curt Meine and Richard L. Knight, editors, *The Essential Aldo Leopold: Quotations and Commentaries* (Madison: University of Wisconsin Press, 1999).

10. Bruce Shindler, Peter List, and Brent Steel, "Managing Federal Forests: Public Attitudes in Oregon and Nationwide," *Journal of Forestry* 91(7) (1993): 36–42; Brent Steel, Peter List, and Bruce Shindler, "Conflicting Values about Federal Forests: A Comparison of National and Oregon Publics," *Society and Natural Resources* 7 (1994): 137–53; and Bruce Shindler, Brent Steel, and Peter List, "Public Judgements of Adaptive Management," *Journal of Forestry* 94(6) (1996): 4–12. The last project was supported by a grant from the National Science Foundation and is a joint effort by Peter List, Bruce Shindler, Denise Lach, and Brent Steel, all of Oregon State University.

students; and eventually compiled a collection of writings that helped clarify the issues and would be useful for teaching students in the natural resource disciplines—such as in several of the interdisciplinary courses I teach with my colleagues. I also located some valuable materials on ethics and ethical issues written by foresters, environmental scientists, and representatives of professional science organizations. I was guided in this by the efforts of other philosophers to do the same for other applied science areas, such as agriculture and engineering—two fields where philosophical thinking has proven useful in examining some of the underlying dimensions of technical disciplines and technological practices.[11]

---

11. For example, R. J. Baum and A. Flores, eds., *Ethical Problems in Engineering,* Vols. 1 and 2 (Troy, N.Y.: Center for the Study of the Human Dimensions of Science and Technology, Rensselaer Polytechnic Institute, 1978); Charles V. Blatz, ed., *Ethics and Agriculture: An Anthology of Current Issues* (Moscow: University of Idaho Press, 1991).

Acknowledgments

In putting this collection together, I have used my own research and experience, and take responsibility for the result, but I have also been helped by many others. First and foremost are several members of the Sustainable Forestry Program at Oregon State University, particularly Steve Radosevich, professor of forest science, who has been an invaluable colleague, friend, and forestry confidant the past few years, and Bruce Shindler, Brent Steel, Sheila Cordray, Court Smith, and Denise Lach, compatriots in the social assessment of forestry. This also includes Dave Perry, Jim Boyle, Dick Clinton, Sally Duncan, Perry Brown, Phil Sollins, Dick Gale, Mark Brunson, Steve Daniels, Chris Anderson, Jean Panek, Lori Cramer, Mary Lynn Roush, Eric Swanson, and David Brooks. Several of these individuals reviewed and criticized the original manuscript plan, as did J. Baird Callicott of the University of North Texas. Michael McDonald, director of the Centre for Applied Ethics at the University of British Columbia in Vancouver, helped solicit contributions to the anthology early in its formative stage. In addition, I have benefitted significantly from my relationships with Scott Reed, George Stankey, Fred Swanson, Warren Cohen, and Art McKee, forest researchers and thinkers of no slight ability. Many thanks also to George Brown, recently retired dean of the College of Forestry at Oregon State University, who generously supported interdisciplinary research in the Sustainable Forestry Program and also other interdisciplinary projects that have led to stimulating collaborations between foresters and nonforesters.

Additionally, I would like to especially thank Courtney Campbell, director of the Program for Ethics, Science and the Environment (PESE) in the Philosophy Department at Oregon State University (OSU), and Kathleen Moore, chair of the Philosophy Department, for significant financial support to make this project succeed. Sandra Shockley of PESE, and Rachel MacVean and especially Maria-Isabel Deira, OSU graduates, have helped immensely with manuscript preparation. In 1996, John Reisenweber, graduate student in the environmental policy masters program at Oregon State University, located some useful library bibliographic resources on ethical issues in the environmental sciences. Students in several of my courses in environmental ethics and natural resource ethics at Oregon State University have also been very helpful in a number of ways—as readers and evaluators as well as sources of ideas and insight for some of the readings included in this anthology. They have usually been frank about the value of what they have been asked to digest. Al Levno, USDA Forest Service, graciously allowed me access to Forest Service photo files. Several people at Temple University Press have been instrumental in getting the collection published, including Jane Cullen, former acquisitions editor, who enthusiastically supported the project early on; David M. Bartlett, former director; and Lois Patton, current director. In the past few years, Doris Braendel, Senior Acquisitions Editor, has very patiently nudged me along and also assisted with a great variety of editorial matters; Tamika L. Hughes and Jennifer French have also lent their able support. Finally, Holmes Rolston III of Colorado State University, an inspiration for many of us who teach environmental ethics and a series editor for Temple, has strongly supported the idea of the collection, made many useful editorial suggestions, and generally been encouraging. The product is better for the involvement of all of these people, just as forestry has benefitted from the visions and perceptions of many observers, both the naive and the expert.

General Introduction

Environmental Crisis and Environmental Ethics

Since the rise of environmental consciousness and activism in the United States during the 1960s, the call for a new environmental ethic has been made increasingly by many individuals and groups in our society. Establishing such an ethic has been seen as at least a partial solution to the environmental problems that we have brought upon ourselves. The assumption behind this perception is that our philosophical beliefs and attitudes make a difference in how we behave; if there is to be real change in our environmental behavior, then there must be real change in the way we think about the earth and its many ecosystems, including forests. This means changes in our ideas about our ethical relationships to each other and to the land.[1]

The historical reasons behind this call for a new ethic are obvious on the surface: beginning in the 1960s, Americans became more aware of widespread abuses of the American environment because of media attention given to the problems of pesticide overuse, air and water pollution, rapid population growth, large-scale and ugly land development including visual pollution of our cities, roadways, and countryside; increasing consumption of consumer goods and resultant solid waste disposal quandaries; and encroachments on our wilder natural areas.[2] Public concern about environmental matters continues to this day and has intensified in the past twenty

---

1. In scientific, social, and philosophical literature, there is a lack of scholarly consensus about the human causes of environmental change. Paul Stern and his colleagues have identified five different types of social variables or "driving forces" that have been proposed in the literature; these include population change, economic growth, technological change, political-economic institutions, and attitudes and beliefs. All have their adherents and supporting evidence, but I believe that our understanding of change is still too incomplete to decisively argue that one type of variable is causally superior to another. What is likely is that complex interactions between these variables, interacting with biophysical factors, explain specific instances of environmental change, but the causal picture is still cloudy. Obviously environmental philosophers are more impressed with the power of philosophical attitudes and beliefs, though they usually recognize that these are more likely to be accompanied by other variables. For a review of the research on this issue, see Paul C. Stern, Oran R. Young, and Daniel Druckman, eds., *Global Environmental Change, Understanding the Human Dimensions* (Washington, D.C.: National Academy Press, 1992).

2. Rachel Carson's book, *Silent Spring* (Boston: Houghton Mifflin Company, 1962), had a deep and widespread effect on public environmental consciousness in the 1960s.

years because of a series of environmental disasters around the world, such as Chernobyl and Bhopal, and also reports about such global problems as tropical rain forest destruction and deforestation, desertification in Africa, drift netting and overfishing in many of our ocean systems, the disappearance of many wild species of plants and animals all over the world, acid rain in North America, global warming, and of course excessive logging and forest land conversion in Southeast Asia, Latin America, Central America, and North America. The extensive logging and clearing of both original and regenerated forests in such places as Indonesia, Malaysia, Thailand, Australia, the Philippines, British Columbia, Mexico, the Pacific Northwest of the United States, Southeast Alaska, Maine, the Himalayan region, and some parts of Africa, Argentina, Chile, and Brazil, to name some examples, has become a matter of public concern in many parts of the world, and future threats to the original forests in such areas as Patagonia and Siberia promise more of the same.

Given the seriousness of the environmental crisis, it is no wonder that beginning in the 1960s, scholars in the United States and other countries began to study intellectual and cultural history for ideas that could form the basis of new practices toward the environment. The general feeling was that our philosophies about nature are at the root of the crisis, and if it is to be resolved we need new forms of philosophical thinking. As a result, new intellectual mentors were identified whose ideas about nature have since been enthusiastically discussed and embraced by many individuals sympathetic to the development of a new "ecological ethic." The growth of environmentalism as a political force is certainly another cause of this rise in public environmental awareness and concern. The 1960s and 1970s witnessed the most significant increase in the political and social influence of environmental groups in the United States since the 1890s and the 1930s, when the first two "waves" of conservation swept the country. Moreover, this last contemporary wave of environmental concern has not died out at it did in the earlier cases. Some social scientists argue that environmentalism has widened and deepened its character and its political influence during the past thirty years in the United States, unlike any other period in our history, and has achieved the status of a successful social movement, at least ideologically speaking.[3] In fact, the vast majority of Americans now describe themselves as environmentalists,[4] though they obviously mean many different things by this term, and this deepening of public environmental awareness and concern is present in all regions of the world.[5]

3. See Riley E. Dunlap and Angela G. Mertig, "The Evolution of the U.S. Environmental Movement from 1970 to 1990: An Overview," *Society and Natural Resources* 4 (1991): 209–21; also Riley E. Dunlap, "Trends in Public Opinion toward Environmental Issues: 1965–1990," *Society and Natural Resources* 4 (1991): 285–312; and Riley E. Dunlap and Rik Scarce, "The Polls—Poll Trends, Environmental Problems and Protection," *Public Opinion Quarterly* 55 (1991): 651–72. However, Dunlap and Mertig suggest that this movement has not succeeded in its goal of putting a stop to the destruction of the environment.

4. For example, in 1991 the Gallup organization reported that 78 percent of Americans considered themselves environmentalists. See *The Gallup Poll Monthly*, no. 307 (April 1991), p. 6. While this figure has varied in recent polls, and what is meant by "environmentalist" obviously differs greatly, a large majority of Americans still accept this description of themselves.

5. There is a high level of citizen awareness of environmental deterioration and widespread support for environmental protection in many nations of the world, in all regions of the world, whether "rich" or "poor." Evidence for this can be found in several worldwide environmental value studies. See Riley Dunlap, George Gallup, Jr., and Alec Gallup, *The Health of the Planet Survey* (Princeton, N.J.: Gallup International Institute,

Along with growth in environmentalism, environmental groups, and public environmental concern, the fields of environmental ethics and environmental philosophy began to blossom in universities and colleges by the mid-1970s and to become the focus of philosophical and religious reflection about human relationships to nature. Some academics and other writers and thinkers turned their attention to the environmental crisis and, inevitably, to forestry and forests. They applied systematic philosophical thinking to fundamental questions about humans and nature, and to the ethics of managing and using natural resources. In time, an academic specialty developed in these subjects and a large body of literature was produced. Some novel approaches to traditional ethical systems were constructed and new theories about human responsibilities to nature were developed.[6]

Global Deforestation and Land Conversion

The destruction, deforestation, and conversion of the earth's forests for such purposes as agriculture, human settlement, and economic activity has now become a global issue, not just a local or regional one. While the United States and some other industrialized countries in the temperate zone may be better off than others with regard to forest conservation, the problems associated with the loss of forest cover in the world are now generally acknowledged to be serious.[7] This includes depletion of necessary fuel-wood supplies for heating and cooking, severe flooding,

---

1992); and Ronald Inglehart, *Culture Shift in Advanced Industrial Society* (Princeton, N.J.: Princeton University Press, 1991), and *Modernization and Postmodernization: Cultural, Economic and Political Changes in Forty-Three Societies* (Princeton, N.J.: Princeton University Press, 1997).

6. This paragraph briefly indicates some of the central themes of environmental ethics, especially as an academic discipline. For further explanation of what environmental ethics is, see Joseph R. Des Jardins, *Environmental Ethics: An Introduction to Environmental Philosophy*, 2d ed., (Belmont, Calif.: Wadsworth Publishing Company, 1997). Since "an environmental ethic" is one product of "environmental ethics" as a field, refer to Holmes Rolston III, *Environmental Ethics: Duties to and Values in the Natural World* (Philadelphia: Temple University Press, 1988), for guidance on the nature of an environmental ethic.

7. A 1997 report by the World Resources Institute states that about half of the Earth's original forest cover is gone, and much of this has been destroyed in the past thirty years. Today about one-fifth of the world's original forest cover remains in large tracts of relatively undisturbed forests, what the World Resources Institute calls "frontier forest." Some 40 percent of the Earth's forest cover qualifies as frontier forest, and about 39 percent of it is threatened by logging, clearing, and other human activities, largely in the temperate regions of the world but also in boreal areas. See Dirk Bryant et al., *The Last Frontier Forests: Ecosystems and Economies on the Edge* (World Resources Institute, 1997). A recent United Nations FAO (Food and Agriculture Organization) report estimates that the world's forests cover approximately 3.5 billion hectares of land, almost half of which are in four countries: the Russian Federation, Brazil, Canada, and the United States. Between 1980 and 1995 world forests decreased by 180 million hectares. Forest cover increased in some developed countries but decreased in many developing countries, especially in the tropics where forests have been reduced by half of their original extent in the past fifty years. See Norman Myers, "The World's Forests: Need for a Policy Appraisal," *Science* 268 (May 12, 1995): 823–24. The area of Central and North America is the largest industrial wood consuming region in the world, accounting for about 40 percent of the total world roundwood consumption in 1994. See Food and Agricultural Organization of the United Nations, *State of the World's Forests* (Rome, Italy: FAO, 1997).

The developing countries are the major consumers of wood for fuel, while the developed countries use wood mostly for industrial purposes. A recent study indicates that "more than half of the global wood harvest is for

accelerated loss of soils and soil productivity, and encroachment of deserts, in addition to the many social costs that result, such as the destruction of indigenous cultures that depend on forests for survival. Some scholars and scientists argue that the current situation is critical, but the worst is yet to come with regard to the world's forests, particularly those in tropical and boreal regions.[8] They predict that if deforestation continues at current rates globally, many of the world's native or "frontier" forests will disappear in the next twenty years and with them a considerable source of the earth's natural habitat and biodiversity.[9] Others, mostly economists, argue optimistically that this may not amount to a global crisis from an economic point of view if more intense management of the world's native and artificial forests occurs, though such intensification inevitably raises both policy and technical questions of its own because of the environmental and social tradeoffs that result.[10]

It has also been noted that people in the developed world face future threats from deforestation and forest land conversion in the tropics as well, because the deterioration in Amazonian forests, for example, may exacerbate the greenhouse effect and cause global climate changes, given the function of such forests in the global carbon and hydrologic cycles. Global climate changes in turn could require costly economic adjustments in the wealthier nations.[11] Within the forests

---

energy purposes," particularly for heating homes and housing, and "critical shortages" of fuel wood exist for a large portion of the world's population. Moreover, the demand on forests for industrial wood and wood products is increasing and likely to continue to increase, though this prospect is not altogether clear and the rate of increase may be "moderate." See B. Solberg, ed., *Long-term Trends and Prospects in World Supply and Demand for Wood and Implications for Sustainable Management* (Joensuu, Finland: European Forest Institute, Research Report No. 6, 1996). Some argue that the consumption of industrial wood in developed countries could remain constant or actually decrease if economic growth slows and prices increase. The consumption of forest products also is affected by changes in the mix of products, efficiencies in manufacturing, the use of recovered and recycled wood fibre, and substitution of other nonwood materials in markets. These factors could also lead to a slower rate of increase in wood consumption. But many observers believe that even if there are temporary reductions in wood demand, the long-term prospect is for increasing demand and thus increasing pressure on existing forest resources, because of such factors as population growth.

8. Nigel Dudley, Jean-Paul Jeanrenaud, and Francis Sullivan, *Bad Harvest? The Timber Trade and the Degradation of the World's Forests* (London: Earthscan Publications, 1995, chap. 2). M. Patricia Marchak evaluates the location and extent of global deforestation in *Logging the Globe* (Montreal: McGill-Queen's University Press, 1995).

9. Thomas E. Lovejoy is one prominent scientist who has connected the accelerating process of deforestation and habitat destruction in tropical forests with significant decreases in biodiversity and consequent increases in extinction of plant, animal, and invertebrate species. He argues that "we are clearly in the initial stages of what could be a major transformation of the biology of the planet." See his discussion, "Deforestation and the Extinction of Species," in D. B. Botkin, M. F. Caswell, J. E. Estes, and A. A. Orio, eds., *Changing the Global Environment, Perspectives on Human Involvement* (Boston: Academic Press, 1989, pp. 91–98). Research by Daniel Nepstad of Woods Hole Research Center and his colleagues at the Institute of Environmental Research in Belem, Brazil, confirms that Brazil's Amazon rain forest is being destroyed and damaged more than twice as fast as formerly thought. They conclude that this amounts to at least 16 percent of the original rain forest, and that this estimate is "quite conservative." See D. C. Nepstad, A. Berissimo, and V. Brooks, "Large-Scale Impoverishment of Amazonian Forests by Logging and Fire," *Nature* 398(6727) (April 8, 1999): 505–07.

10. B. Solberg, *Long-term Trends and Prospects in World Supply and Demand for Wood and Implications for Sustainable Management*, pp. 10–11.

11. See Lester Brown's foreword to John Perlin's book, *A Forest Journey: The Role of Wood in Civilization* (Cambridge, Mass.: Harvard University Press, 1989); and Edward Goldsmith and Caspar Henderson, "The Economic Costs of Climate Change," *The Ecologist* 29(2) (March–April 1999): 98.

of the industrialized Western world, there are also some serious problems of forest health that have resulted from faulty forest management and industrial pollution, such as chronic insect and pathogen infestations, and dying trees. Moreover, the conversion of native forests to industrial tree plantations is thought to exact a cumulative ecological toll on forests and forest biodiversity in the industrialized world as well, though it can also serve to relieve pressures on forests that have been set aside for recreation and other nontimber uses.[12]

Forests and Deforestation in Ancient Societies

Historians now recognize that deforestation and forest land conversion for such purposes as agriculture is an old story in human civilization and began many thousands of years ago. The consumption of wood for fuel, building materials, and other purposes made it possible for many ancient societies to thrive, and the practice of cutting down forests and using trees for wood products permanently altered the ecological and social landscapes of many regions of the world. John Perlin records the history of the process of forest destruction, showing that some ancient writers were aware of the close relationship between the development and growth of human civilization and the loss of forests.[13] He documents how many ancient cultures—Sumeria, Assyria, Egypt, China, Mycenae, classical Greece and Rome, western Europe, and North America—could not have emerged without the vast supplies of wood that were cut from forests under their control.[14] Some of these cultures were able to sustain themselves by finding other sources of raw materials, by using former forest lands for agriculture or by technological changes and advances. According to J. V. Thirgood, still other societies, especially in the modern era in northern Europe, realized what was happening to their wood supplies and introduced the techniques of forest management and tree planting in order to reconstruct their forests, though land-clearing made the reforestation of some native species impossible.[15] However, some civilizations declined socially and politically as their forest lands were depleted or as they turned formerly productive forest lands into deserts. In some cases the loss of forest cover led to serious soil erosion, flooding, and declines in soil productivity. Unable to maintain indigenous agricultural systems and support their citizens, economic systems collapsed and societies suffered for lack of wood for fuel, manufacturing, and fiber, Perlin argues.

Perlin also believes, paradoxically, that as societies decline, forests have tended to regenerate, though, I would add, obviously at different rates of regrowth and species composition, and in different or more impoverished ecological conditions. J. V. Thirgood has confirmed the existence of this phenomenon but like other scholars notes, wisely enough, that social declines may occur for various reasons, including episodes of warfare or disease that can decimate human populations

---

12. David Perry, *Forest Ecosystems* (Baltimore: Johns Hopkins University Press, 1994).
13. John Perlin, *A Forest Journey: The Role of Wood in the Development of Civilization* (Cambridge, Mass.: Harvard University Press, 1989). J. V. Thirgood asserts that "clearing and modification of forested land has been a familiar phase in the development of all major civilizations" and suggests that such a widespread phenomenon must surely have some merits. See "Man's Impact on the Forests of Europe," *Journal of World Forest Resource Management*, 4 (1989): 127–67.
14. See Perlin, chap. 1.
15. Thirgood, "Man's Impact on the Forests of Europe."

and reduce demands on forests. The forests in some parts of Europe have been cleared and regenerated with different species several times by different cultures in the same locations over the past two thousand years, and a great number of political regimes have come into existence and died out in this period of time.[16] Thirgood maintains that Europe was largely forested at the dawn of written history but thereafter suffered through various periods of extensive forest clearing, reversion, and reclamation. He argues that despite a "long history of uncontrolled use, excessive demand, maltreatment and clearance," it is remarkable that so much European forest remains, and he suggests that this is due to such factors as the capacity of forests to recover and also to the growth of intensive forest management in the past three hundred years. Forest destruction inevitably results in social change, but it need not lead to social catastrophe, he concludes.[17] As wood resources are depleted, the societies that depend on them for raw material can thus also be destroyed, though the relationship is not always as linear and direct as Perlin would suggest. Others argue that intensive forestry itself can be abused and lead to negative environmental and social consequences in industrial societies.[18] In any event, one lesson to be learned from the historical record is that forest destruction or deforestation can have very grave effects on the prospects and the viability of the human cultures and economies that depend on forests, especially if suitable material substitutes for wood cannot be found and there is no effort to regenerate or conserve forests.

The Importance of Forests in United States Culture

Because forests have been a major feature of our geography and environment in the United States, they have played a central role in our social and political history, just as they have in ancient societies, and have had a critical impact on our economic fortunes. The geographical historian Michael Williams has done a massive study of the spatial and visual aspects of forests in American life, and he argues that other than cities, "possibly the greatest single factor in the evolution of the American landscape has been the clearing of the forest that covered nearly half of the country" in the sixteenth century.[19] This is not to imply, however, that the United States

16. For interesting accounts of the transformation of European forests since preindustrial times and the relationships between deforestation and European societies, see Jost Hermand, " 'The Death of Trees Will Be the End of Us All': Protests against the Destruction of German Forests 1780–1950," *The Idea of the Forest: German and American Perspectives on the Culture and Politics of Trees*, eds. Karla L. Schultz and Kenneth S. Calhoon (New York: Peter Lang, 1996); see also Thirgood, "Man's Impact on the Forests of Europe."

17. Thirgood, "Man's Impact on the Forests of Europe." Thirgood also documents the history of forest clearing in northwest Africa, where deforestation, overcropping, overgrazing, and rapid soil erosion have transformed a formerly densely forested landscape rather dramatically in the past four thousand years, particularly since European intervention in the nineteenth century. Even there, he argues, in an arid and semiarid region, there are vast, biologically productive areas that could yield substantial benefits through forestry and other environmental programs. See "The Barbary Forests and Forest Lands, Environmental Destruction and the Vicissitudes of History," *Journal of World Forest Resource Management* 2 (1986): 137–84.

18. Steve Radosevich, Professor of Forest Science, Oregon State University, lecture on "ecological forestry" for FS 591: Sustainable Forestry, Multiple Perspectives; Oregon State University, Fall 1991.

19. Michael Williams, *Americans and Their Forests: A Historical Geography* (Cambridge, U.K.: Cambridge University Press, 1989), p. xvii.

will also follow the path of those ancient cultures that declined because of the depletion of their original forests. While native forests in A.D. 1600 accounted for roughly one-half of the total land area in the United States, or about 1.1 billion acres, including Alaska, and have now been significantly reduced, it has been estimated that about one-third of the country, or approximately 737 million acres, was still forested in 1990.[20] Moreover, some argue that forest conditions in the United States, such as forest growth rates and tree planting, have actually improved since 1900 and that professional forest management in this country is among the best in the world, though our forests represent a "substantially transformed legacy" if you compare them to the condition they were in when Europeans wrested them from native Americans.[21]

Social Issues in American Forestry

The problems of forestry in the United States, then, do not currently center so much on how much forest exists now or how much will exist in the future, though there are some worries about the latter.[22] Instead, they concern what kind and quality of forests and forest ecosystems will exist, what original or native forests and forest remnants will endure, and how public and private forests will be managed and used in the future. How much forest land should be allocated to different land uses? For example, how much should be "set aside" for nonextractive uses such as recreation, wild species protection, and aesthetics? How much more forest land should be turned into tree farms or plantations? How much should be harvested and converted for housing and other urban development purposes? Further, should foresters continue to use all of the techniques of conventional forestry, such as clearcutting and even-age management, on public and private forests?[23] Or should they shift toward more variety in their methods, such as the use of selective

20. Doug MacCleery, "What in the World Have We Done to Our Forests? A Brief Overview on Conditions and Trends of U.S. Forests." In *Culture and Natural Resources*, The 1992 Starker Lecture, compiled by Bo Shelby and Sandie Abrogast (Corvallis, Ore.: College of Forestry, Oregon State University), p. 48. See also *U.S. Forests: Facts and Figures 1995*, American Forest and Paper Association. Definitions of "old growth" and "ancient forest" differ, in some cases dramatically, but in the Pacific Northwest the amount of old-growth forest has declined significantly since World War II and what little remains—anywhere from 3 to 10 percent—has been highly fragmented in the past twenty years. Consult T. A. Spies, W. J. Ripple, and G. A. Bradshaw, "Dynamics and Pattern of a Managed Coniferous Forest Landscape in Oregon," *Ecological Applications* 4(3) (1994): 555–68; T. A. Spies and J. F. Franklin, "The Diversity of Management of Old-Growth Forests," in *Biodiversity in Managed Landscapes*, eds. R. C. Szaro and D. W. Johnson (New York: Oxford University Press, 1995); and Thomas Spies, "Forest Stand Structure, Composition, and Function," in *Creating a Forestry for the 21st Century*, eds. Kathryn A. Kohm and Jerry F. Franklin (Washington, D.C.: Island Press, 1997), pp. 12 and 25.

21. MacCleery, p. 59. It isn't sufficient just to note increases in these quantitative factors, however, since the quality of the lumber produced from regenerated forests—for example, its strength for such purposes as building construction—can suffer, depending on the species and rotation age.

22. For example, worries about the acceleration of logging in the hardwood forests of the eastern United States are expressed in Ralph D. Nyland, "Exploitation and Greed in Eastern Hardwood Forests: Will Foresters Get Another Chance?" *Journal of Forestry* 90(1) (January 1992): 33–37. Similar concerns are being raised about accelerated logging in the oak and pine forests of the southern states.

23. It is interesting to note that public ballot initiatives to ban clearcutting have failed in such states as Oregon and California, but several large corporate timber firms are turning away from this practice in North America.

harvesting and uneven-age management?[24] And, what will the short- and long-term biological and social consequences be of the management choices that are made now and the techniques that are currently used for harvesting trees, preserving forested wildernesses, or providing for additional forest recreation? For example, what consequences will different forest practices and techniques have on currently healthy, threatened, and endangered species? Moreover, what local, regional, national, and global effects will intensified timber management on public and private forests have for future generations of Americans and citizens in other countries? And, will these choices, land allocations, and effects be acceptable to our grandchildren? Additionally, what role should foresters, resource managers, the forest industry, scientists, environmentalists, other forest interest groups, and the public play in managing and preserving forests? Who should participate in forest management and how? Further, do we need new forestry ethics that are more sensitive to the ecological conditions of forests and their role in the earth's ecosystem processes? Or can we make do with the ethics that we have now, tinkering with them as we go along? All of these questions and others have been raised by observers of forestry in the United States, as environmentalists and environmental philosophers, both within and outside of forestry, have voiced their concerns about forest practices and the sustainability of forests.[25]

For example, MacMillan Bloedel, Canada's largest forest products company, announced in 1998 that it would be phasing out clearcutting in all of its British Columbia operations and using a harvesting method called "variable retention" that would enable it to protect biodiversity and original forests in variously-sized stands and clusters. See *The Forestry Source* 3(7) (July/August 1998): 1, 13, a publication of the Society of American Foresters. When the Weyerhauser Corporation bought out MacMillan Bloedel in 1999, there was some question about whether this new policy would be continued, but in July 1999 Weyerhauser agreed to do so; see *The Forestry Source,* 4 (8) (September 1999): 1.

24. "Even-aged management" means that all trees in a forested area or forest "stand" are of roughly the same age and are either cut in one final harvest at the same time or harvested in several segments in a relatively short period of time. The idea is "to regenerate and maintain a stand in a single age class." A larger forest area managed in this manner may result in a mosaic of forest stands of different ages. Uneven-aged management, in comparison, means that all ages of trees exist in smaller areas of a forest, and harvests are more partial and frequent. Here larger trees may be selected for harvest and smaller trees cut to maintain a mixture of trees of various ages. The idea here is "to regenerate and maintain a multiaged structure by removing some trees in all size classes either singly, in small groups, or in strips." "Clearcutting" or "clearfelling" refers to the practice of completely clearing all trees from an area of a forest or the forest itself. It is most commonly used to convert "unmanaged" forests to "managed" ones, and is also the most common method of harvest used in forests managed for timber production around the world. Useful guides to understanding these and other forestry concepts include Hamish Kimmins, *Balancing Act: Environmental Issues in Forestry* (Vancouver, B.C.: UBC Press, 1992); and John A. Helms, ed., *The Dictionary of Forestry* (Bethesda, Md.: The Society of American Foresters, 1998).

25. "Sustainable forestry" has become a rallying concept for new ways of thinking about managing forests in some parts of the world, including Europe and North America, and various international timber conventions have identified general criteria for sustainable forest management in recent years. In the United States, sustainable forestry is being promoted by a number of academic, professional, industrial, and other groups associated with forestry. This has spawned a "forest certification" process that is gaining a foothold among North American companies that grow trees and market wood products at the retail level, though certification has been more successful in Europe. There are now many sources published on these topics, but Richard Gale and Sheila Cordray identify the variety of meanings involved in "What Should Forests Sustain? Eight Answers," *Journal of Forestry* 89(5) (May 1991): 31–36. An overview of sustainable forestry developments can be found in Roger A. Sedjo et al., *Sustainability of Temperate Forests* (Washington, D.C.: Resources for the Future, 1998). Consult

It may appear to some readers that these kinds of questions should be answered primarily by professionally trained foresters, economists, biologists, and other scientists, but these are not exclusively technical, scientific, or economic issues. Many of them are, fundamentally, questions of value.[26] The technical and scientific disciplines, whether biophysical or social, are important in the valuation process because there are biophysical and social effects of forest management that must be understood, and forest management must at least partly be based on the sciences. But it is society at large and our political system—specifically members of public and private organizations in addition to individual citizens—who decide the values and principles that determine, ultimately, how most of these questions will and should be answered.[27] The fields of philosophy and environmental ethics become important, then, because they focus very systematically on basic questions about how the natural world should be valued and what this implies about our relationships with natural objects such as forests.[28] Therefore, it is essential to turn to these sources, specifically to discussions of values as they affect forestry, to get a better sense of how these questions might best be answered.

In this book, the ethical dimensions of forest value questions are examined from different points of view, some of which have been influential in forestry while others have only recently begun to receive attention. However, just as cultural diversity is being stressed as an important ingredient in our political system, new forms of philosophy and ethics are being advocated for forest lands. The new voices for change represent powerful, long-term cultural trends in our society,[29] but it remains to be seen how much they will become the harbingers of new ways of doing things in forestry proper. This will depend in part on how seriously foresters, natural resource managers, and environmental scientists assess their relevance and value.

---

also the collection of articles edited by Gregory H. Aplet et al., *Defining Sustainable Forestry* (Washington, D.C.: Island Press, 1993). An explanation of certification occurs in Eric Hansen, "Forest Certification and Marketing," *Forest Products Journal* 47(3) (1997): 16–22.

26. Some foresters have made this point as well. For example, N. Taylor Gregg, "Sustainability and Politics: The Cultural Connection," *Journal of Forestry* 90(7) (July 1992): 17–21.

27. For a more extended justification of this point, see Mark Sagoff, *The Economy of the Earth: Philosophy, Law, and The Environment* (Cambridge, U.K.: Cambridge University Press, 1988).

28. One of the best examples of a serious philosophical effort to develop a system of environmental ethics can be found in Holmes Rolston III, *Environmental Ethics: Duties to and Values in the Natural World* (Philadelphia: Temple University Press, 1988).

29. For a review of value changes in American society, consult the work of Ronald Inglehart cited in note 5. The implications of these changes for American forestry are considered by Brent Steel and others in Brent S. Steel, ed., *Public Lands Management in the West: Citizens, Interest Groups, and Values* (Westport, Conn.: Praeger, 1997).

Part I

Ethical Systems in Forestry

New Attitudes about Forest Values

Answers to critical questions about forestry lie partly in the attitudes and values humans have about forests and their proper management and use, and these attitudes have been changing, over time, as American society has urbanized and become more affluent.[1] In contrast with the prevalent attitudes of native Americans, the forests and forest "wildernesses" of North America were originally seen by European settlers to be barriers to progress and threats to survival on a physical level, and also as locations for "savagery" and immorality, as they understood these eurocentrically-biased notions.[2] But forests were also basic sources of food, fuel, land, lumber, and other useful products that people needed to survive. In fact, until well into the twentieth century, trees provided "the most valuable raw material in American life and livelihood: wood," and wood manufacturing was one of the most important manufacturing industries in the United States as late as 1920. Aside from the milling of lumber, wood was used in a great variety of ways for quite an immense number of domestic and industrial products, ranging from construction materials to chemicals.[3] As recently as 1980 wood still accounted for "one-quarter of all the industrial raw materials used in the country," though this picture has now changed because of such factors as the rise of other forms of manufacturing and the use of other materials such as steel and plastic.[4] Moreover, forests have served other valuable purposes in our economy such as preventing floods and maintaining a cleaner and more constant flow of water for domestic water supplies, irrigation, and hydroelectric

---

1. Ronald Inglehart, *Cultural Shift in Advanced Industrial Society* and *Modernization and Postmodernization*, referred to above in note 5, General Introduction.
2. Chapter 2 in Roderick Nash, *Wilderness and the American Mind*, 3d rev. ed., 1982.
3. Williams, *Americans and Their Forests*, p. 5.
4. Ibid., p. 8.

power generation. In short, it is hard to imagine how our economic system could have prospered originally or could prosper today without forests and the material resources they provide.

Environmental historians conclude that these earlier colonial attitudes about forests began to change in the United States during the nineteenth century.[5] New ideas about the value of forests became important as old ideas about wilderness began to change. Forests came to be appreciated as more than sources of raw materials and valuable wood products; they were seen also as places of great natural beauty and spiritual inspiration and, later in the century, as locations for recreation and rejuvenation of the body and spirit. Under the influence of the theology of deism, protestant religious leaders, for example, began to emphasize the idea that, after all, since God had created and designed nature, wild forests were thus a reflection of God's very existence, not to mention his power and purposes. American novelists and artists such as Henry David Thoreau and the Hudson River painters began to glorify forested landscapes in their "natural" state, finding forests to be sublime aesthetically and a joy to behold even when not altered by human labor for commercial and agricultural purposes.[6] Later in the century, as the country began to urbanize and more and more people lived away from forests and wilder forest landscapes, city residents began to think of forests in more romantic terms and as places to visit for nonmaterialistic reasons. Moreover, as more and more of the midwestern and western forests in the last quarter of the nineteenth century were raided for their timber resources by large land and resource corporations, including railroad and timber companies, and as government officials, conservation groups, and private citizens began to call attention to this fact and to the possibility of a "timber famine," a strong forest conservation movement developed in the 1880s that had as its aim the reservation of forests for both economic and noneconomic purposes.[7]

Foundation Forest Philosophies

By 1900, two different philosophical conceptions about the nature and purposes of forests and the directions of forest management took hold and competed for public attention. On the one hand, the resource conservation philosophy became important in government forestry and resource management, under the vigorous shepherding of such public foresters as Bernhard Fernow and Gifford Pinchot. On the other hand, the forest preservation movement developed behind the direction of such national figures

---

5. Nash, *Wilderness and the American Mind;* see also Joseph M. Petulla, *American Environmental History* (San Francisco: Boyd and Fraser Publishing Company, 1977).

6. Barbara Novak, *Nature and Culture: American Landscape and Painting, 1825–1875* (New York: Oxford University Press, 1980).

7. Fears about a timber famine in the United States, in the late nineteenth century and later, are discussed by David A. Clary in *Timber and the Forest Service* (Lawrence: University Press of Kansas, 1986).

as Frederich Law Olmstead, perhaps America's most famous landscape architect, and John Muir, founder of the Sierra Club, wilderness theologian, and advocate for the cause of wild forest protection.[8]

To the resource conservationists like Pinchot, forests were to be reserved for utilitarian economic purposes; they were to become "fountains of timber" that would supply the wood manufacturing industry in perpetuity and produce material products that the current and succeeding generations of Americans would need to sustain themselves over time. The idea was that the greatest benefit for society would come from the orderly development and use of forests to yield products such as wood and grass and also returns on capital.[9] Forest preservationists like Muir, on the other hand, promoted the reservation of forests primarily for their scenic, recreational, and psychic benefits. Such conservationists obviously valued forests as habitats for animals and plants, but their preservation rationales were based on the aesthetic, spiritual, and recreational values in forests.[10] Most of them were not opposed to commercial exploitation of forests at some level of extraction, but they did believe that forests should become "garden[s] for the recreation of the lover of nature," to use the words of one of America's first conservationists, George Perkins Marsh.[11] In so doing, they championed a different way of thinking about forests and forest management, though one that was consistent with earlier European ideas about forest uses.[12] Because these two strains of philosophy are deeply embedded in our normal reactions to forests, and because we need forests for both kinds of purposes, these philosophies have had a major impact ever since on the thinking of Americans about what forests are and how they should be used. The two philosophies have significantly affected the management and use of forests, parks, and wilderness areas on federal, state, and other lands in all parts of the country, and were basic motivations behind the creation of both the national forest and the national park systems.

Philosophical and ethical notions about forests have a way of evolving over time, however, to incorporate new realities and new beliefs about nature. One such change occurred in the first half of the twentieth century, as evolutionary theory and the

8. Max Oelschlaeger does a masterful job of explaining Muir's significance as a wilderness thinker in *The Idea of Wilderness: From Prehistory to the Age of Ecology* (New Haven: Yale University Press, 1991).

9. Gifford Pinchot, *A Primer of Forestry, Part II: Practical Forestry* (USDA Bureau of Forestry, Washington, D.C.: Government Printing Office, 1905), p. 11.

10. J. Baird Callicott, "Current Concepts in Conservation," paper presented at the Program for Ethics, Science and the Environment, Oregon State University, May 1997.

11. See Nash, *Wilderness and the American Mind*, p. 105.

12. Bryan Norton does an illuminating comparison of the conservation ideas of Pinchot and Muir, arguing that they were both well within the "anthropocentric" camp of nature valuers with regard to the national forests and that their ideas lay on different ends of a single value continuum. Thus Muir accepted that forests had to be used for economic purposes, and Pinchot believed that forests had aesthetic and recreational value; however, they diverged in regard to the emphases they placed on these values. See Norton's book, *Toward Unity among Environmentalists* (New York: Oxford University Press, 1991).

new science of ecology began to influence the thinking of biologists, foresters, wildlife scientists, environmental scientists, and philosophers of many stripes. These scientific developments came to be seen as fundamental for understanding nature and for interpreting the ethical responsibilities of humans in nature. One thinker who helped to spearhead this process was Aldo Leopold, because of the land ethic he proposed in several of his scientific publications in the 1930s and later in his seminal work *A Sand County Almanac*, published in 1949, a year after his death.[13]

Leopold's relationship to forests and forestry is clear enough; he was trained as a forester at the new graduate school of forestry at Yale University, from 1906 to 1909, then was employed, off and on, by the newly organized U.S. Forest Service in the Southwest and Upper Midwest. He had responsibilities as a forester, forest supervisor, and forest administrator and also, later on, as an academic forester and wildlife management expert. By the time of his death in 1948 he had developed an international reputation as a wildlife ecologist and had been elected president of the Ecological Society of America. He helped found the Wilderness Society, served on the state game commission in Wisconsin, and became an influential professor at the University of Wisconsin and speaker in academic and nonacademic circles around the country. Because he was respected for his deeper thoughts about conservation, he was often given free reign to publish more literary and persuasive pieces in science journals, and not only articles that recorded his scientific research. He was well aware of the ideological leanings of forestry and its roots in Pinchotian conservation, and sought to steer it in new, more ecologically sensitive directions in the 1930s and 1940s.

For nearly twenty years, *A Sand County Almanac* went largely unnoticed by the public until it was republished in several inexpensive editions just before environmental fervor reached one of its recent peaks on Earth Day 1970. Leopold's ethical ideas at first had a more significant impact on a small group of individuals who were either leaders in the environmental movement or knowledgeable about his work as a result of their own scientific and professional activities. Then, through their enthusiasm and promotion, the land ethic idea became known to so many mainstream environmentalists that *A Sand County Almanac* was seen eventually as "the new testament" of the environmental movement in the early 1970s, not just as a call for a new kind of forestry and wildlife science.[14] Leopold's land ethic achieved this status because it elegantly tied together diverse ideas from ecology, natural history, ethics, the natural resource sciences such as wildlife management and forestry, and Leopold's field observations into a novel, holistic philosophy about the conservation and preservation of "the biotic community." Leopold argued for new values and attitudes that would harmonize our personal behavior and

---

13. Aldo Leopold, *A Sand County Almanac* (New York: Oxford University Press, 1949).
14. This is Nash's term in his book, *The Rights of Nature* (1989).

environmental practices, including forestry, with the ecological systems of nature, and he managed to delineate in a coherent manner some of the important ingredients of the ecological ethic that many in our society thought we so badly needed. As one historian has noted, more than any other writing, Leopold's classic signaled the arrival of the "Age of Ecology." It combined "a scientific approach to nature, a high level of ecological sophistication, and a biocentric, communitarian ethic that challenged the dominant economic attitude toward land use" that was embodied in resource conservation thinking and commercial ideology in our society at large.[15]

Leopold's land ethic has also had a significant impact on the thinking of academic, environmental philosophers, including some who have made efforts to devise new systems of environmental ethics or to develop the implications of the land ethic itself. Leopold was not a professional philosopher, and his writings raise philosophical issues that require interpretation and further explanation. While his ethic may be serviceable for his followers, professional philosophers are more fussy, intellectually, and demand that an ethic be more fully defensible. Thus, some of Leopold's basic ideas, such as his ecological holism[16] and his assumptions about the foundations of ethics, particularly the assumption that ecological science can provide moral directives, have not always fared well in environmental philosophy.[17] But his ethic did help to crystallize and inspire the thinking of such environmental philosophers as J. Baird Callicott and Holmes Rolston III, two leading representatives of the "holistic" branch of environmental ethics, and George Sessions, one of the more influential American deep ecologists.[18] Callicott has spent considerable intellectual effort to, in his words, "flesh out the arguments which Leopold himself only evoked and to connect his ideas, especially his ethical ideas, with the antecedents in the history of Western philosophy echoing in his rich literary allusions."[19]

---

15. Donald Wooster, *Nature's Economy: The Roots of Ecology* (Garden City, New York: Anchor Books, 1979), p. 284.

16. Ecological holism in environmental ethics is the view that the biotic community or biosphere as a whole is a primary object of moral consideration, moral respect, or inherent worth. Some philosophers argue that this means the biosphere itself is to take priority over its component species, ecosystem processes, and individuals, such as members of the human race.

17. An example of a philosopher critic of holism is Paul W. Taylor in his landmark of environmental philosophy, *Respect for Nature: A Theory of Environmental Ethics* (Princeton, NJ: Princeton University Press, 1986). Kristin Shrader-Frechette of the University of Notre Dame, another important figure in environmental ethics, has also led the attack on holism. See K. Shrader-Frechette and E. D. McCoy, *Method in Ecology: Strategies for Conservation* (Cambridge, U.K.: Cambridge University Press, 1993).

18. See, e.g., J. Baird Callicott, *In Defense of the Land Ethic* (Albany, N.Y.: SUNY Press, 1989); and Holmes Rolston III, *Environmental Ethics: Duties to and Values in The Natural World* (Philadelphia: Temple University Press, 1988).

19. Callicott, *In Defense of the Land Ethic*, p. 6. See also J. Baird Callicott, ed., *Companion to A Sand County Almanac: Interpretive and Critical Essays* (Madison: The University of Wisconsin Press, 1987).

Some Recent Forms of Radical Environmental Philosophy

The founding philosophies of American forestry were all constructed with forests and forestry very directly in mind. They were created by applied scientists and designed to provide very general ethical guidelines that would undergird public forest management.[20] Deep ecology and ecofeminism, in contrast, are two recent and much discussed environmental philosophies that have different origins and a more broad social orientation. They draw on philosophical traditions more purposively and make their ethical foundations and norms more explicit. Both were formulated to a large degree by philosophers instead of scientists, and both recognize, as Leopold did, the central importance of reshaping philosophical beliefs and attitudes if society is to practice true conservation. Moreover, they are an outgrowth of public worries about the environmental crisis that emerged in the 1960s, and they respond to social concerns of the day. In agreement with Leopold, they argue that there is a need for a completely novel form of environmental consciousness in industrialized nations, something in fact that is unprecedented in the dominant intellectual traditions of modern industrial culture. They propose a radical reshaping of personal attitudes and social institutions, rather than only reform in our basic worldview, in our typical attitudes toward nature, or in our social practices. At the same time, these two philosophical systems are an outgrowth of somewhat different philosophical and social traditions, are buoyed by somewhat different central concepts, and have somewhat different implications for human behavior in nature.

If these philosophies are to be implemented, forestry and the other applied environmental sciences must dramatically change their principles and practices, as must most humans in industrialized countries. Both philosophies have been critical of the subservience of forestry to the goals of industrial capitalism, though they have rarely been taken seriously or evaluated in any detail by mainline foresters and by the academic disciplines that deal directly with forests. They have found enthusiastic acceptance by some of the most vocal environmentalist critics of forestry, such as adherents of the Sierra Club, Earth First, and other forest interest groups that are influential in the radical branch of the environmental movement. Moreover, deep ecology is now being used to provide philosophical support for the budding "ecoforestry movement" and thus for new kinds of forestry and forest ethics.[21]

---

20. While John Muir was not employed as a scientist, he did receive some scientific education at the University of Wisconsin and obviously was accomplished in natural history, particularly in botany. He later developed a scientific account of glaciation in the Sierras that was based on his own observations and his desire to correct what he thought were false scientific accounts by geologists about the history of Sierra land formation. He successfully argued, for example, that glaciation was a major factor in the formation of the Yosemite Valley. His knowledge of geology impressed Joseph LeConte, a leading geologist at the time, and LeConte was at least partially convinced of the truth of Muir's glaciation theory, against its rivals. Other geologists dismissed his explanation, however. See Frederick Turner, *Rediscovering America: John Muir in His Time and Ours* (New York: Viking, 1985).

21. For an account of their influence on environmentalism, see the introduction to Peter List, ed., *Radical Environmentalism: Philosophy and Tactics* (Belmont, Calif.: Wadsworth Publishing Company, 1993).

Deep Ecology

Deep ecology is an environmental philosophy that is one of the biocentric inheritors of Leopold's land ethic.[22] Aside from its influence on ecoforesters, it has had some appeal to forest biologists and ecologists because of its focus on biotic health and the preservation of forest biodiversity, and also because of its emphasis on deep respect for nature. In popularized versions it has been promoted by public educational groups as well, such as the Northwest Earth Institute in Portland, Oregon.[23]

Formulated first by the Norwegian philosopher Arne Naess in the early 1970s, this form of environmental thinking emphasizes the intrinsic value of all natural things, the biocentric equality of all the earth's species, the idea that humans should develop a broader self and submerge their narrow egos into a larger, natural self, and the central need to preserve the earth's natural diversity. It advocates a radical rethinking of the "anthropocentric" traditions of Western culture and philosophy, those that make humans and the human species more important morally than other parts of nature and that elevate human needs, desires, interests, and wants over those of other species. In this regard, it affirms the meaning of Leopold's famous dictum that humans need to stop thinking of themselves as conquerors of the earth and come to see themselves as plain members and citizens of the biotic community.

To deep ecologists, the environmental crisis is a crisis of consciousness and culture, not just a matter of environmental degradation of the earth's systems or a technological, political, or social crisis. The basis of their beliefs is the idea that humans must learn to refashion their ways of thinking and feeling about the earth if they are to begin to transform their societies on any mass scale. Central to this is the rejection of any form of human-centered conservation ethic, for—as they argue—anthropocentric morality is not consistent with the realities of nature. Humans are not the only locus of value, and the members of other species have interests and lives of their own that often have very little and sometimes nothing to do with human life and society.

In 1972, Naess distinguished between two kinds of ecological thinking, the "deep" and the "shallow," and argued that the shallow was the most powerful current approach to the environmental crisis but that it needed to be replaced by the deep. The shallow emphasizes the need to eliminate the crisis because of concerns about its effects on the health and living conditions of people in industrial countries. It accepts the premises of the dominant Western worldview while also assuming that reform of industrial systems will be sufficient to eliminate the environmental crisis. The deep, on the other hand,

---

22. Bill Devall and George Sessions, *Deep Ecology: Living as if Nature Mattered* (Salt Lake City: Peregrine Smith Books, 1985), chap. 6.

23. The Northwest Earth Institute is devoted to the study and practice of deep ecology and simplified living. The institute has organized a large number of seminars on these topics for employees in business corporations, public agencies, education institutions, and other nonprofit organizations throughout the Pacific Northwest. The Northwest Earth Institute was founded by Dick and Jeanne Roy of Portland, Oregon.

is based on a "minority tradition" of thought in Eastern and Western cultures, both religious and philosophical, and advocates a more global and biocentered worldview that consists of various norms and intuitions about how humans should fit into nature and organize themselves in their societies. If people begin to adopt the principles of the deep ecology platform and put these individual philosophies (or "ecosophies") into practice, our relationships with the environment will be radically different over time, they predict.[24]

Arne Naess is the founding thinker of deep ecology philosophy, but Bill Devall and George Sessions, two American academics, and such individuals as Delores LaChapelle, Alan Drengson, Freya Mathews, David Rothenberg, Warwick Fox, Gary Snyder, David Abram, and Michael Zimmerman, have all contributed to the deep ecology movement, helping to explain and rationalize its basic principles and practical directions.[25] Devall and Sessions have spent countless hours interpreting and expanding the deep ecology philosophy, and their book *Deep Ecology* has long been recognized as one of the best sources for understanding its basic principles.[26] They have also applied deep ecology to natural resource conservation and management, contrasting the exploitative ideology and practices of Pinchot's form of management ideology with the "hands-off" approach that results from pursuing Muir's form of "righteous management" and deep ecology principles.[27] In their analysis, Pinchotian forestry is the embodiment of what is wrong, philosophically, with forestry in this country; it makes the underlying and erroneous assumptions that humans are "the central figures and actors in history" and that all of nature is a "resource" for human consumption, use, and manipulation.[28] It thus stresses the development of forest resources rather than the true conservation of forests and forest biodiversity. Because Pinchot instilled this philosophical rationale in the U.S. Forest Service and Pinchotism has been taught in schools of forestry and also enacted in various federal land use laws and regulations, Pinchotian forestry has been so deeply entrenched in the land management hierarchy in the United States that it is taken for granted. As the deep ecologists argue, only when these assumptions and their consequences for forestry and forests are addressed will forest degradation and destruction be reversed.

Bill Devall, Alan Drengson, and many others on the Pacific Coast of North America have all worked to apply the philosophy of deep ecology to forestry, and to find a

---

24. Arne Naess, "The Shallow and the Deep, Long-Range Ecology Movement: A Summary," *Inquiry* 16 (Spring 1973): 95–100.

25. Michael Tobias, ed., *Deep Ecology* (San Diego: Avant Books, 1985); Alan Drengson and Yuichi Inoue, eds., *The Deep Ecology Movement: An Introductory Anthology* (Berkeley: North Atlantic Books, 1995); David Abram, *The Spell of the Sensuous* (New York: Random House, 1996).

26. Devall and Sessions, *Deep Ecology: Living as if Nature Mattered*.

27. Ibid., chap. 8.

28. Ibid.

practical alternative to the standard form of industrial forestry that is used by large forest corporations and government forest agencies. They call this approach to forestry "wholistic, ecosystem-based forest management" or "natural selection ecoforestry." Ecoforestry is an outgrowth of deep dissatisfactions with the destructive ecological and human effects of industrial forestry and is designed to provide a novel philosophical vision and a comprehensive set of forest practices; as such, ecoforestry presents a logical alternative to the dominant traditions of forestry in North America since Pinchot's day. The practical dimensions of ecoforestry have been pursued for some years now by a small minority of forest landowners in the Pacific Northwest and elsewhere.[29] But this form of forestry is just beginning to come to the attention of the profession of forestry in North America.

Ecofeminism

Another form of contemporary environmental ethics that has acquired some cachet in the environmental movement and some appeal to environmentalists and academic thinkers is "ecofeminism." Like deep ecology, ecofeminism is a radical philosophical outgrowth of environmentalism during the 1960s that has been informed by feminism and feminist critiques of social arrangements and personal interrelationships in Western patriarchal societies.[30] Its effects on foresters and forestry in the United States are still minimal, since forestry has traditionally been, and continues to be, the paragon of a male-dominated profession and culture. Nevertheless, it has some adherents in forestry and, in some of its versions, has affected environmental criticism of public forestry.[31]

---

29. Ecoforestry is explained in detail in Alan Drengson and Duncan Taylor, eds., *Ecoforestry: The Art and Science of Sustainable Forest Use* (Gabriola Island, B.C.: New Society Publishers, 1997); and Bill Devall, ed., *Clearcut: The Tragedy of Industrial Forestry* (San Francisco: Sierra Club Books and Earth Island Press, 1993), a publication sponsored by the Foundation for Deep Ecology.

30. Charlene Spretnak discusses some of roots of this philosophy in "Ecofeminism: Our Roots and Flowering," in *Reweaving the World: The Emergence of Ecofeminism*, eds. Irene Diamond and Gloria Feman Orenstein (San Francisco: Sierra Club Books, 1990).

31. One of the more interesting applications of ecofeminism to forestry can be found in the work of Vandana Shiva, a scientist in India who has written extensively on feminist issues. In her writing Shiva attacks certain Western biases about productivity, nature, and non-Western societies, arguing, for example, that in "Western patriarchy" natural forests are thought to be unproductive and in need of replacement by monocultural plantations of commercial species. This kind of forest "development" is claimed to be beneficial for societies such as hers, Shiva says, but is really equivalent to "maldevelopment—development deprived of the feminine, the conserving, the ecological principle." She states that "when commodity production as the prime economic activity is introduced as development, it destroys the potential of nature and women to produce life and goods and services for basic needs." When the heavy demand for wood is allowed to dictate forest management practices, this can damage the regenerative capacity of forests and the ecological processes they sustain. This in turn can make it difficult for women in these countries to carry on their work of collecting water, fodder, and fuel. See her article "Development as a New Project of Western Patriarchy," in *Reweaving the World, The Emergence of Ecofeminism*, eds. Irene Diamond and Gloria Feman Orenstein (San Francisco: Sierra Club Books, 1990).

Also like deep ecology, ecofeminism has produced considerable variety in philosophy and practical belief, but it is based on the core idea that there are important connections between the oppression or domination of nature, including forests, and the oppression or domination of women in patriarchal societies. Understanding these connections is important, ecofeminists argue, if we are to learn how to live in harmony with nature and practice a different kind of forestry.[32] Though ecofeminism is grounded in many sources, one of the inspirations for ecofeminists has been the "Chipko" tree-hugging actions by women in India in the 1970s. When small-village women with a deep commitment to preserving their local environment and homes felt threatened by floods and landslides from forest clearing, they successfully used nonviolent methods to prevent trees from being cut for manufacturing purposes and other kinds of economic development.[33]

Though ecofeminism agrees with some of the basic ideas of deep ecology, particularly the idea that humans need a radical change in their consciousness about nature and a totally new form of environmental philosophy and ethics that is more biocentered in orientation, the form of consciousness and philosophy advocated by ecofeminists is still quite different in key respects. "Liberal feminists" probably have the most in common with advocates of Leopold's land ethic or of deep ecology, while the more radical ecofeminists would find less to agree with in these philosophies.[34] The connection between the domination of women and nature has not been a key principle in deep ecology, and although adherents of both philosophies are sympathetic to the other, some ecofeminists have posed critical challenges to the land ethic and to deep ecology on feminist grounds.[35] This does not mean that ecofeminist and deep ecologist activists have dissimilar critical attitudes about forestry, but it does mean that they do not always

---

32. Some classics of ecofeminist philosophy include Rosemary Radford Reuther, *New Woman, New Earth: Sexist Ideologies and Human Liberation* (New York: The Seabury Press, 1975); Susan Griffin, *Women and Nature: The Roaring Inside Her* (New York: Harper and Row, 1978); Elizabeth Dodson Gray, *Green Paradise Lost* (Wellesley, Mass.: Roundtable Press, 1979); Leonie Caldecott and Stephanie Leland, eds., *Reclaim the Earth: Women Speak Out for Life on Earth* (London: The Women's Press, 1983); and Carolyn Merchant, *The Death of Nature: Women, Ecology and the Scientific Revolution* (New York: Harper and Row, 1983).

33. See, e.g., Pamela Philipose, "Women Act: Women and Environmental Protection in India," in *Healing the Wounds: The Promise of Ecofeminism*, ed. Judith Plant (Philadelphia: New Society Publishers, 1989), pp. 67–75. A scholarly account of the Chipko movement can be found in Ramachandra Guha, *The Unquiet Woods: Ecological Change and Peasant Resistance in the Himalaya* (Berkeley: University of California Press, 1989).

34. A set of categories for understanding the varieties of ecofeminism can be found in Carolyn Merchant, "Ecofeminism and Feminist Theory," in *Reweaving the World: The Emergence of Ecofeminism*, eds. Irene Diamond and Gloria Feman Orenstein (San Francisco: Sierra Club Books, 1990), pp. 100–5.

35. Some examples of this are Ariel Kay Salleh, "Deeper Than Deep Ecology: The Eco-Feminist Connection," *Environmental Ethics* 6 (Winter 1984): 339–45 and Michael E. Zimmerman, "Deep Ecology and Ecofeminism: The Emerging Dialogue," in Diamond and Orenstein, *Reweaving the World*, pp. 138–54. An ecofeminist critique of Leopold's land ethic can be found in Marti Kheel, "Ecofeminism and Deep Ecology: Reflections on Identity and Difference," ibid., 128–37.

see eye-to-eye on the causes of forest degradation and the best methods of changing forest practices.

As this brief review implies, systems of environmental ethics and philosophy are moving away from Pinchot and resource conservation toward new ways of thinking about nature and natural resource management. Leopold's land ethic and other developments in science and philosophy have set the stage for a more biocentered approach to philosophical reflection about human ethical relationships with other species. Additionally, the great growth in ecology and the environmental sciences and concern about the deteriorating global environment have strengthened the belief among scientists, environmental policymakers, and environmental philosophers that the preservation of biological or ecological diversity must be the first priority of conservation, in forestry and elsewhere. It has been noted before that Americans began to value wilderness as wilderness began to vanish under their feet, and the same phenomenon appears to be operating with regard to forest biodiversity.[36] Paradoxically, the more we destroy, alter, and convert our original forests for our own economic purposes instead of conserving them for other species and future generations, the more we appear to value them for their noneconomic qualities and emphasize their importance. Oddly, while our systems of environmental ethics move in a more biocentered direction, our environmental behavior now threatens the biosphere itself. This may be one reason why Leopold is so appealing to so many; his land ethic allows us to be more radical in our environmental philosophy than in our environmental behavior. Unlike the deep ecologists and ecofeminists, Leopold was not a critic of culture and politics so much as he was a scientist with strong ethical convictions who set out to transform scientific and conservation practices in agriculture, forestry, and the other applied environmental sciences. This is also why deep ecology, ecofeminism, and ecoforestry are more fundamental challenges to customary natural resource management and forestry: they tackle both the behavioral and attitudinal sides of our industrial culture, viewing them as necessarily intertwined. They may remain minority movements in their direct effects on the dominant schools of forestry and forest management, but they do raise crucial questions about the assumptions behind forest management on both public and private lands. Moreover, the environmentalist adherents of these philosophies began to have more influence in the environmental movement in the early 1980s, and thus on the way in which the critique of public forestry and public forest management, in particular, has proceeded. Instead of business as usual, the philosophies embolden their practitioners with new ways of thinking and acting, and thus may in time bring more significant changes in mainstream forestry.[37]

36. Nash, *Wilderness and the American Mind*.
37. The effects that radical environmental activism has had on federal and state forestry in the United States are still somewhat unclear, but there is little doubt that environmental protests of forest policies and practices

since the early 1980s by environmental groups, radical and otherwise, have found a sympathetic public ear and have sometimes succeeded in moving the U.S. Forest Service and some private forestry operators to change the way they do business in public and private forests. The same phenomenon is occurring in Canada, where protests in British Columbia, for example at Clayoquot Sound on Vancouver Island, have helped to move government officials toward more sustainable forest policies (e.g., consult *Sustainable Ecosystem Management in Clayoquot Sound: Planning and Practices,* prepared by the 1995 Scientific Panel for Sustainable Forest Practices in Clayoquot Sound, British Columbia, mentioned in chapter 4 of this book). Moreover, mainstream environmental groups have slowly become more radical in their own outlooks, and this can be attributed partly to the more widespread dispersion of such philosophies as deep ecology, not to mention public recognition of the destructive effects of government and private forestry on forest biodiversity. The Clinton Administration has also been significantly affected by environmental protest—considering, for example, the main directions of the 1994 Clinton Forest Plan for the Pacific Northwest compared to the region's timber management policies in the 1980s, a decade some call the "decade of excess" in federal forest management. Protestors have also occasionally been able to stop forest cutting in other locations around the country. While these reductions in timber harvests on public lands are not sufficient to satisfy adherents of such groups as Earth First! and the Sierra Club, and are unpalatable to many legislators in Congress and also to supporters of traditional resource policies who seek a return to higher levels of timber extraction, it is clear that the American public is ready for a more holistic, ecosystem-based form of federal forest management that places less emphasis on timber harvesting. On this point see research done by Bruce Shindler, Peter List, and Brent Steel reported in "Managing Federal Forests: Public Attitudes in Oregon and Nationwide," *Journal of Forestry* 91(7) (1993): 36–42; and also Brent S. Steel, Peter List, and Bruce Shindler, "Conflicting Values about Federal Forests: A Comparison of National and Oregon Publics," *Society and Natural Resources* 7 (1994): 137–53. Recent shifts toward ecosystem management on federal lands, under the leadership of natural resource administrators in the Clinton Administration, are clearly a move in this direction.

CHAPTER I

The Economic Resource Model of Forests and Forestry

Though there are several competing philosophical conceptions about the nature of forests and the purposes of forestry in American history, as this anthology will illustrate, one of the most important and dominant conceptions in public forestry had its roots in concerns about the economic effects of timber exploitation in the nineteenth century. Because of the importance of forests in our economy and due to mounting destruction and conversion of forest lands in the United States, fears about a timber shortage were expressed as early as 1849. Assaults on the native forests of the Upper Midwest, the South, and the West made forest conservation into a national issue in the 1870s and 1880s.[1] By the end of the century, professional forestry had begun to develop as a serious profession to help Americans understand how to more efficiently manage their forests.[2]

In the last quarter of the nineteenth century, foresters thus rather naturally turned to philosophical ideas about forests and forestry that emphasized the economic values and uses of forests for human society. These "anthropocentric" or human-centered models and their associated conservation mandates were in turn derived mainly from European forestry sources, though various American scientists, such as George Perkins Marsh and Franklin B. Hough, also had a hand in promoting forest conservation and developing forestry as a profession in the United States. In some cases European foresters provided our first leadership in public forestry, and some important early professional foresters, such as Gifford Pinchot, went to Europe for professional forestry education, something that was unavailable in the United States before 1898.[3] Thus

---

1. Samuel Trask Dana, *Forest and Range Policy: Its Development in the United States* (New York: McGraw-Hill, 1956), chap. 4.
2. Williams, *Americans and Their Forests*, 1989.
3. In 1898, the first professional education in forestry in the United States was established with the creation of the New York State College of Forestry at Cornell University. Bernhard Fernow was its director. The first graduate program in forestry began with the founding of the School of Forestry at Yale in 1900. Pinchot persuaded his wealthy parents to set up an endowment for the Yale School. See Samuel Trask Dana, *Forest and Range Policy*, p. 134, and Harold Pinkett, *Gifford Pinchot: Private and Public Forester* (Urbana: University of Illinois Press, 1970), p. 86.

Carl Schurz, a German immigrant who was familiar with some of the methods of "scientific forestry" practiced in Europe, served as Secretary of the Interior from 1877 to 1881, and in that role advocated the need to reserve forest lands and manage them in a rational manner.[4] The most influential European forester in the federal bureaucracy at the time was another German immigrant, Bernhard E. Fernow, who was appointed third chief of the Division of Forestry in the Department of Agriculture in 1886.[5] Fernow is a key figure in helping to make forestry both a science and a profession in the United States before World War I and in focusing American forestry on the utilitarian and economic aspects of forests. While there is some disagreement among scholars as to the exact impact of Fernow's "Prussian forestry" in America, particularly his influence in developing the U.S. Forest Service in comparison with Gifford Pinchot, there is little doubt that he did much to "plant the idea of forestry in the fertile American soil." He is sometimes referred to as the "father of American forestry" and as the "founder and dean of forestry education in America."[6]

While Fernow worked the field before Gifford Pinchot, Pinchot has clearly had more lasting philosophical and practical influence on American forestry, and his ideas are still cited as important for understanding the purposes that public forests should serve, such as the multiple-use doctrine.[7] Pinchot is considered to be "America's first trained forester," meaning that he was the first native-born citizen to study forestry in Europe and then to set up shop in the United States as a private forestry consultant whose expertise was for sale at a fee.[8] In 1900 he had a powerful role in helping to create the Society of American Foresters, the most important professional association of scientifically-trained foresters in the country, and in establishing a School of Forestry at Yale University. He was also appointed head of the Division of Forestry in 1898 and served as first chief of the U.S. Forest Service when the forest reserves of the country were transferred to the Department of Agriculture in 1905.[9] Pinchot had the ear of President Theodore Roosevelt, an ardent sportsman and lover of nature, and as Roosevelt's adviser on natural resource issues, Pinchot helped to formulate and promote the new philosophy of "conservation" that earlier scientists such as Marsh and Fernow had advocated before him. To

---

4. See his *Annual Report of the Secretary of the Interior on the Operations of the Department for the Fiscal Year Ended June 30, 1877* (Washington, D.C.: Government Printing Office, 1877).

5. The Division of Forestry was established by Congress in a bill that was approved in 1876. The first two chiefs were Franklin B. Hough and Nathaniel H. Egleston, neither of whom had professional qualifications in forestry, though Hough was an outstanding forestry leader whose work as chief was instrumental in making forest conservation a national issue. See Dana, *Forest and Range Policy*, chap. 4.

6. Page 24 of Char Miller, "The Prussians Are Coming! The Prussians Are Coming!: Bernhard Fernow and the Roots of the USDA Forest Service," *Journal of Forestry*, 89 (March 1991): 23–27, 42; see also Ben W. Twight, "Bernhard Fernow and Prussian Forestry in America: Building Support for Federal Forestry," *Journal of Forestry* 88 (February 1990): 21–25; Andrew Denny Rodgers III, *Bernhard Eduard Fernow: A Story of North American Forestry* (Princeton, N.J.: Princeton University Press, 1951); and M. Nelson McGeary, *Gifford Pinchot: Forester, Politician* (Princeton, N.J.: Princeton University Press, 1960).

7. For example, Alan G. McQuillan, "Is National Forest Planning Incompatible with a Land Ethic?", *Journal of Forestry* 88 (May 1990): 31–37; J. E. DeSteiguer, "Can Forestry Provide the Greatest Good of the Greatest Number?", *Journal of Forestry* 92 (September 1994): 22–25; David A. Clary, *Timber and the Forest Service* (Lawrence: University Press of Kansas, 1986).

8. McGeary, *Gifford Pinchot*, 1960.

9. Dana, *Forest and Range Policy*, chap. 6.

Pinchot, conservation served as a unifying idea in managing forests, waterways, range lands, and minerals on federal and private lands, and he did much to explain and rationalize this philosophy in government and public circles. Pinchot's brand of resource conservation became the dominant conservation ideology in government agencies for many years and has strongly affected the way public forests are managed and conserved in the United States.

In the following selections, Fernow and Pinchot articulate some of the basic elements of this "economic resource" conception of the purposes of forests, which includes the idea that trees are crops that lend themselves to the methods of agriculture. Fernow's classic text, *Economics of Forestry,* used for many years in schools of forestry in this country, defines the nature of forestry and the primary purpose of "forest growth," namely, to provide us with "wood material." A secondary function, he indicates, is to regulate water flow and climate. Forestry is a combination of personal strategy, science, art, and business, and a forester is a technically-educated "man" who uses his knowledge of tree growth and production to manage a forest for the "highest attainable revenue."

In the selections from Pinchot's writings, Pinchot reviews the essential principles of conservation as they apply to forests and other resources, and also makes clear that the national forests should be reserved for "the best use" of the people of the United States. In agreement with Fernow, this means wood for the economy, primarily, but also includes water regulation for such purposes as irrigation and forage land for grazing. Other uses such as recreation and hunting are "incidental" to these, he suggests. The pursuit of forest conservation, he argues, leads to "national efficiency" and thus gives the United States an advantage in the international commercial competition between nations. In short, professional forest conservation serves the interests of the capitalist economy of America in domestic and foreign markets.

Bernhard Fernow

Forest and Forestry Defined

Etymology, linguistic sense, and as we believe actual usage, especially in the literature of later times, since the subject of forests and forestry has become prominent, would warrant us to define, more precisely, *woodland* as the general or generic term for land naturally covered with woody growth in contradistinction to land not so covered; *forest* as the restricted or specific term, namely, woodland whether of natural growth or planted by man, considered in relation to the economic interests of man and from the standpoint of national economy, as an *object of man's care,* a woodland placed under management for *"forest purposes,"* and, we may also add, exhibiting *"forest conditions."* These last limitations are important ones and lead to the necessity of further definition.

By the first restriction we exclude at once those lands covered with trees or woody growth, which serve other than forest purposes, such as coffee plantations, orchards, which are grown for fruit, roadside plantings and parks, which are planted or kept for shade and ornament, wind-breaks consisting of single rows of trees, which, although like the other conditions of tree growth mentioned may answer some functions of a forest growth, are not primarily intended to fulfil forest purposes and lack what we have called "forest conditions."

The first and foremost purpose of a forest growth is to supply us with *wood material;* it is the *substance of the trees* itself, not their fruit, their beauty, their shade, their shelter, that constitute the primary object of this class of woodland.

With the settlement of the country and the growing needs of civilization this use must and will attach as an essential predicate, a fundamental requisite, to any woodland left as such, whatever other purposes it may or may not be designed to subserve, temporarily or continuously.

Thus if the state of New York withdraws from such use a large woodland area in the Adirondacks to subserve solely other purposes, this can be only a temporary withdrawal from its main purpose which time and intelligent conception of rational economy will reverse.

Just so, if a private individual sets apart for the purpose of a game preserve a piece of woodland, and keeps out the axe which

---

Bernhard Fernow, "Forestry and Forestry Defined," pp. 84–91 and 94–103 from chapter 4 of Bernhard E. Fernow, *Economics of Forestry.* New York: Thomas Y. Crowell, 1902.

would utilize in part the useful timber, he frustrates the primary object of the forest growth temporarily and commits an economic mistake.

Occasionally it is not the wood but some other part of the tree itself that is the main object of the harvest, as for instance the bark for tanning purposes or the resinous contents which are transformed into naval stores. Yet, as a rule, the wood too is utilized and at least forest conditions are maintained in the production of the crop. But when it comes to a maple sugar orchard, expressly grown for the purpose, or the cork oak plantation, managed for the cork, the primary object not only begins to vanish, but also the second criterion of a forest, namely, forest conditions, is absent, and this kind of woodland ceases to fall properly under the term "forest," the designation of orchard or plantation being more appropriate.

Besides the great primary object of forest growth, that of furnishing useful materials either of wood or parts of the wood substance, there has been recognized indistinctly through all ages, more clearly during the last century and with greater precision during the last thirty to forty years, that forest growth serves an object in the economy of nature and of man which under certain conditions may become equally if not more important than this direct primary one.

We have learned that in general all conditions in nature are interrelated, and in particular that the condition of the surface cover of the ground not only influences more or less potently the condition of the soil and meteorological factors under the cover, but that this influence reaches even beyond the limits of the cover to its neighborhood; and, with the recognition of this influence upon soil, temperature, and water conditions a new important forest use, namely, as a protective cover and climatic factor, has become established, so that we may distinguish, according to whether the one or the other purpose becomes more prominent, *supply forests* and *protection forests,* although the latter invariably also furnish supplies, and finally, when pleasure and game cover are the main objects, we may speak of *luxury forests.*

To fulfil either or both of the first two, more important functions satisfactorily or continuously, to furnish most useful material and to act as a protective cover, it is needful that the woodland designated as forest exhibit what we have called "*forest conditions.*"

A forest in the sense in which we use the term, as an economic factor, is by no means a mere collection of trees, but an *organic whole* in which all parts, although apparently heterogeneous, jumbled together by accident as it were and apparently unrelated, bear a close relation to each other and are as interdependent as any other beings and conditions in nature.

Not only is there interrelation between plant and climate and between plant and soil conditions, but also an interrelation between the individuals composing the forest growth based on definable laws, and finally an interrelation between the arborescent growth and the lower vegetation; the whole being a result of reactions of plant life to all surrounding influences and reciprocally of influences on all elements of its environment. Even the seemingly lawless mixture of species which we find in the virgin forest is not altogether fortuitous, but a result of such reactions.

Out of these reactions and interrelations result conditions which we call *forest conditions,* and which not only distinguish the forest from other collections of trees or woodlands, but also impart a particular individuality and character to the forest growth of each locality. Even the virgin woodlands may lack what we conceive as ideal forest conditions, when in the struggle for existence other forms of vegetation have still the advantage over the arborescent growth and hence forest purposes are imperfectly performed, or when the latter has not yet been able to fully establish itself under unfavorable soil and climatic conditions. In such cases, which are frequent in the arid and sub-arid and the arctic regions, the single stragglers of trees, the park-like open stand, their stunted and scrubby appearance may leave it doubtful whether the term "forest," with its economic significance, is applicable to these woodlands, or may exempt them from consideration under the term.

Forest conditions, then, imply a more or less exclusive occupancy of the soil by arborescent growth, a close stand of trees, as a consequence of which a form of individual tree development results unlike that produced in the open stand, and a more or less dense shading of the ground which excludes largely the lower vegetation.

By so much as these conditions are deficient, by so much does the forest fail to fulfil its economic functions, as a source of useful material and as a factor in influencing climatic and soil conditions.

With regard to the first function, it must be understood that it is not wood simply that is required for the industries of man, but wood of certain qualities and sizes, such as are fit to be cut into lumber, as boards, planks, joists, scantlings, or into timber as beams, sills, and posts, into bolts free from blemish, which can be advantageously manufactured into the thousands of articles that are indispensable to human civilization. Such sizes and qualities combined are not as a rule produced by trees in open stand. Their production requires the close stand, by which the trees are forced to reach up for light in order to escape the shade of their neighbors and all growth energy is utilized in the bole or trunk, the most useful part to man, instead of being dissipated in the growth of branches. The useful forest tree is the one that has grown up with close neighbors, which have deprived it of side light and thereby forced it to form a long cylindrical shaft, to shed its side branches early, which if persisting would have produced knotty lumber, to confine its branch growth to the crown alone.

Such conditions are also the most favorable in fulfilling the second function of the forest as regulator of waterflow and climate, for it is the shaded condition of the soil and the effective barrier to sun and winds, results of a dense stand, by which the forest exercises these regulatory functions.

The history of the woodlands has been the same in all parts of the world, progressing according to the cultural development of the people. First the forest was valued as a harbor of game; then it appeared as an impediment to agricultural development, and relentless war was waged against it, while at the same time the value of its material stores made it an object of greedy exploitation, and only in a highly civilized nation and in a well-settled country does the conception of the relation of forests to the future welfare of the community lead to a rational treatment of forests as such for continuity and to the application of the principles embodied in the science of forestry.

• • •

In the pioneer days of a newly settled country, which is forest-covered like the eastern United States, man by necessity must remove a part of the forest growth for the purpose of gaining ground for food production. That part which is not cleared for such purpose he exploits, usually regardless of the conditions in which he leaves it, cutting out the best trees of the most useful species or else cutting off the entire growth and leaving nature to take care of the future.

When this crude forest exploitation and destructive process has gone on so long that virgin supplies are nearly exhausted, that the effects of inconsiderate clearing or forest devastation becomes visible in soil washes, in high and low water stages of rivers, more frequent and more destructive floods, etc., then he begins to consider more carefully the relation which the forest and its continuance bears toward the further development of society, toward the conditions of his surroundings; he realizes that he may not continue to disturb the balance of nature unpunished, nay, that he must be active in improving the methods of nature, and weight that side of the balance which is favorable to him and his pursuits; he begins to bring more rational method into his use of the forest, he attempts to apply knowledge and care in its treatment, he makes it an object of economic thought, in other words he arrives at a first conception of and applies *forestry,* which may be most comprehensively defined as the *rational treatment of forests for forest purposes.* First he determines upon a rational policy for his further conduct toward the forest, and then, having studied the manner in which forests grow, having become familiar with the *science* of forestry, he develops superior positive methods in treatment and perpetuation of the forest and applies the *art* of forestry; and, adding the financial aspect in the application of the art, he practises the *business* of forestry.

In its broadest sense thus the term "forestry," according to the point of view, represents a policy, a science, an art, a business. A policy is a general plan of behavior, a general line of conduct with reference to our affairs, embodying the philosophy, the motives and object of our programme. By determining upon a policy with reference to a resource like the forest, we assign it a place in our political or domestic economy, we make up our mind as to *what* to do with it. It is from this point of view that this volume proposes to discuss the subject.

Such a policy we naturally base on knowledge or science which furnishes us the reason for our policy, the *why* to do. This science of forestry comprises all the knowledge regarding forest growth,—its component parts, the life history of the species, and their behavior under varying conditions, its development and dependence upon natural conditions, its retroactive influence upon those natural conditions, in short its place in the economy of nature and of man.

When we come to formulate our knowledge into rules of procedure and apply the same to the treatment of forest areas specifically, we begin to practise the *art* of forestry—we learn *how* to do; and finally, applying this art systematically for the purpose for which all technical arts are carried on, namely, for money results, we come to practise the *business* of forestry.

Like agriculture, forestry is concerned in the use of the soil for crop production; as the agriculturist is engaged in the production of food-crops, so the forester is engaged in the production of wood-crops, and finally both are carrying on their art for the practical purpose of a revenue.

Forest crop production is the business of the professional forester.

A *forester* then is not, as the American public has been prone to apply the word, one who knows the names of trees and flowers, a botanist; nor even one who knows their life history, a dendrologist; nor one who, for the love of trees, proclaims the need of preserving them, a propagandist; nor one who makes a business of planting parks or orchards, an arboriculturist, fruit grower, landscape gardener, or nurseryman; nor one who cuts down trees and converts them into lumber, a woodchopper or a lumberman; nor one set to prevent forest fires or depredations in woodlands, a forest guard; nor even one who knows how to produce and reproduce wood-crops, a silviculturist; but in the fullest sense of the term, a forester is a technically educated man who, with the knowledge of the forest trees and their life history and of all that pertains to their growth and production, combines further knowledge which enables him to manage a forest property so as to produce certain conditions resulting in the highest attainable revenue from the soil by wood-crops.

The virgin forest grows where it pleases, and as it pleases, without reference to the needs of man. It covers the rich agricultural soils as well as the dry and thin soils of the mountain slope and top; it may encumber the ground which can more profitably be employed in the production of food-materials, and it may be absent where its protection is needed for human comfort or for successful agriculture.

Nature produces weeds—tree weeds—and useful species side by side; she does not care for the composition of the crop; tree growth, whatever the kind, satisfies her laws of development; nor has she concern with the form of the component trees,—they may be branched and crooked, short and tapering. In time, in a long time, she too may produce long clear shafts, but by her methods such results will only be accomplished in centuries; nature takes no account of time or space, both of which are lavishly at her command. The area of virgin forest which we harvest today has produced a tithe of the useful material which it is capable of producing, and has taken two to threefold the time which it would take under skilful direction to secure better results, quantitatively and qualitatively.

It is in the application of the economic point of view, in relegating forest growth to non-agricultural soils, in influencing its composition and its development toward usefulness, in securing its reproduction in a manner more satisfactory to human wants and human calculations, than nature's fitful performances promise, that the forester's forest differs.

Forestry in more or less developed form is begun when this economic point of view is applied, when care, however slight, is bestowed upon the virgin wood to secure its improvement and continuance.

Before the finer methods of forest management become practicable under such economic conditions as surround us, a common-sense management may be possible, which consists in more careful utilization of the natural forest, protecting it against fire, fostering young volunteer growth of the better kinds, by keeping out cattle, and in general avoiding whatever prevents a satisfactory reproduction of the natural woods. For large sections of this country, this will for some time to come be the only forestry that is practicable, namely, wherever distance from market for inferior material makes finer methods unprofitable or impracticable.

Finally, however, the art in its fullest and finest development will become applicable through the length and breadth of our country, just as in the old countries.

As in every productive industry, so in the forestry industry we can distinguish two separate yet necessarily always closely interdependent branches, namely, the technical art which concerns itself with the production of the material, and the business art which concerns itself with the orderly, organized conduct of the industry of production.

Since the materials and forces of nature are the source of the mighty processes of organic life which find expression in forest growth, the art of forest crop production naturally relies mainly upon a knowledge of natural sciences, by which the forester may be enabled to direct and influence nature's forces into more useful production, than its unguided activity would secure.

The nature of the plant material, its biology, its relation to climate and soil, must be known to secure the largest, most useful, and most valuable crop; that portion of botany which may be segregated as dendrology—the botany of trees in all its ramifications—must form the main basis of the forester's art. To study such a segregated portion of the large field of botanical science presupposes, to be sure, a sufficient amount of general botanical knowledge. In order to know, recognize, and classify his materials the methods of classification, the general anatomy and histology, must be familiar to him, as well as general physiology and biology; finally, he must specialize and become an expert on biological dendrology, *i.e.* a knowledge of the life history, the development, and dependence upon surroundings, the ecology, of trees, in individuals as well as in communities,—a very special study, to which few botanists have as yet given much attention. *Forest crop production,* or *silviculture,* in its widest sense, may be called applied dendrology. And the forester is not satisfied only to know the general features of the biology of the species, their development from seed to maturity, their requirements regarding soil and light conditions, but as he is a producer of material for revenue, he is most emphatically interested in the amount of production and the rate at which this production takes place. Far different from the agriculturist's crop, his is not an annual one, but requires many years of accumulations, and as each year's waiting increases the cost of production by tying up the capital invested, it is of importance not only to know the likely progress of the crop, the mathematics of accretion, but also how its progress may be influenced.

In this connection the study of geology and meteorology, of soil and climate, the factors of site, is required, as far as necessary to understand the relationship of plant life to surroundings, and teach the chemico-physical basis for wood production. The protection of his crop not only against climatic ills, but against enemies of the animal and plant world, requires studies in that direction, and finally to harvest his crop and bring it to market and dispose of it to best advantage calls for engineering knowledge and acquaintance with wood technology.

The business side of the forestry industry, which we call *forest economy,* relies mainly upon mathematical calculations and the application of principles of political economy. The fact that the time from the start of the crop to the harvest may be fifty, one hundred, or more years—the time it takes to grow a useful size of timber—necessitates a more thoroughly premeditated and organized conduct, more complicated profit calculations, more careful plans, than in any other business which deals with shorter time periods.

In this connection one of the first and most important mathematical problems for the forester to settle, is when his crop is ripe. This is not as with agricultural crops and fruits determined by a natural period, but by the judgment of the harvester, based upon mathematical and financial calculations.

There are various principles which may be followed in determining the maturity of a stand, or what is technically called the rotation, *i.e.* the time within which a forest, managed as a unit, shall be cut over and reproduced; but all rely finally upon measurements of the quantity of production as basis of the business calculation, and hence forest mensuration has been developed into a special branch of mathematics and many methods have been developed, by which not only the volume and rate of growth of single trees, but of whole stands, can be more or less accurately determined. Similarly, finance calculations have been more fully developed in the forestry business than are usually practised in any other business excepting perhaps Life Insurance.

Gifford Pinchot

Principles of Conservation

The principles which the word Conservation has come to embody are not many, and they are exceedingly simple. I have had occasion to say a good many times that no other great movement has ever achieved such progress in so short a time, or made itself felt in so many directions with such vigor and effectiveness, as the movement for the conservation of natural resources.

Forestry made good its position in the United States before the conservation movement was born. As a forester I am glad to believe that conservation began with forestry, and that the principles which govern the Forest Service in particular and forestry in general are also the ideas that control conservation.

The first idea of real foresight in connection with natural resources arose in connection with the forest. From it sprang the movement which gathered impetus until it culminated in the great Convention of Governors at Washington in May, 1908. Then came the second official meeting of the National Conservation movement, December, 1908, in Washington. Afterward came the various gatherings of citizens in convention, come together to express their judgment on what ought to be done, and to contribute, as only such meetings can, to the formation of effective public opinion.

The movement so begun and so prosecuted has gathered immense swing and impetus. In 1907 few knew what Conservation meant. Now it has become a household word. While at first Conservation was supposed to apply only to forests, we see now that its sweep extends even beyond the natural resources.

The principles which govern the conservation movement, like all great and effective things, are simple and easily understood. Yet it is often hard to make the simple, easy, and direct facts about a movement of this kind known to the people generally.

The first great fact about conservation is that it stands for development. There has been a fundamental misconception that conservation means nothing but the husbanding of resources for future generations. There could be no more serious mistake. Conservation does mean provision for the future, but it means also and first of all the recognition of the right of the present generation to the fullest necessary use of all the resources with which this country is so abundantly blessed. Conservation

---

Gifford Pinchot, "Principles of Conservation," pp. 40–52 from *The Fight for Conservation*. New York: Doubleday, Page & Col, 1910.

demands the welfare of this generation first, and afterward the welfare of the generations to follow.

The first principle of conservation is development, the use of the natural resources now existing on this continent for the benefit of the people who live here now. There may be just as much waste in neglecting the development and use of certain natural resources as there is in their destruction. We have a limited supply of coal, and only a limited supply. Whether it is to last for a hundred or a hundred and fifty or a thousand years, the coal is limited in amount, unless through geological changes which we shall not live to see, there will never be any more of it than there is now. But coal is in a sense the vital essence of our civilization. If it can be preserved, if the life of the mines can be extended, if by preventing waste there can be more coal left in this country after we of this generation have made every needed use of this source of power, then we shall have deserved well of our descendants.

Conservation stands emphatically for the development and use of water-power now, without delay. It stands for the immediate construction of navigable waterways under a broad and comprehensive plan as assistants to the railroads. More coal and more iron are required to move a ton of freight by rail than by water, three to one. In every case and in every direction the conservation movement has development for its first principle, and at the very beginning of its work. The development of our natural resources and the fullest use of them for the present generation is the first duty of this generation. So much for development.

In the second place conservation stands for the prevention of waste. There has come gradually in this country an understanding that waste is not a good thing and that the attack on waste is an industrial necessity. I recall very well indeed how, in the early days of forest fires, they were considered simply and solely as acts of God, against which any opposition was hopeless and any attempt to control them not merely hopeless but childish. It was assumed that they came in the natural order of things, as inevitably as the seasons or the rising and setting of the sun. Today we understand that forest fires are wholly within the control of men. So we are coming in like manner to understand that the prevention of waste in all other directions is a simple matter of good business. The first duty of the human race is to control the earth it lives upon.

We are in a position more and more completely to say how far the waste and destruction of natural resources are to be allowed to go on and where they are to stop. It is curious that the effort to stop waste, like the effort to stop forest fires, has often been considered as a matter controlled wholly by economic law. I think there could be no greater mistake. Forest fires were allowed to burn long after the people had means to stop them. The idea that men were helpless in the face of them held long after the time had passed when the means of control were fully within our reach. It was the old story that "as a man thinketh, so is he"; we came to see that we could stop forest fires, and we found that the means had long been at hand. When at length we came to see that the control of logging in certain directions was profitable, we found it had long been possible. In all these matters of waste of natural resources, the education of the people to understand that they can stop the leakage comes before the actual stopping and after the means of stopping it have long been ready at our hands.

In addition to the principles of development and preservation of our resources there is a third principle. It is this: The natural resources must be developed and preserved for the benefit of the many, and not merely for the profit of a few. We are coming to understand in this country that public action for public benefit has a very much wider field to cover and a much larger part to play than was the case when there were resources enough for every one, and before certain constitutional provisions had given so tremendously strong a position to vested rights and property in general.

A few years ago President Hadley, of Yale, wrote an article which has not attracted the attention it should. The point of it was that by reason of the xivth amendment to the Constitution, property rights in the United States occupy a stronger position than in any other country in the civilized world. It becomes then a matter of multiplied importance, since property rights once granted are so strongly entrenched, to see that they shall be so granted that the people shall get their fair share of the benefit which comes from the development of the resources which belong to us all. The time to do that is now. By so doing we shall avoid the difficulties and conflicts which will surely arise if we allow vested rights to accrue outside the possibility of governmental and popular control.

The conservation idea covers a wider range than the field of natural resources alone. Conservation means the greatest good to the greatest number for the longest time. One of its great contributions is just this, that it has added to the worn and well-known phrase, "the greatest good to the greatest number," the additional words "for the longest time," thus recognizing that this nation of ours must be made to endure as the best possible home for all its people.

Conservation advocates the use of foresight, prudence, thrift, and intelligence in dealing with public matters, for the same reasons and in the same way that we each use foresight, prudence, thrift, and intelligence in dealing with our own private affairs. It proclaims the right and duty of the people to act for the benefit of the people. Conservation demands the application of common-sense to the common problems for the common good.

The principles of conservation thus described—development, preservation, the common good—have a general application which is growing rapidly wider. The development of resources and the prevention of waste and loss, the protection of the public interests, by foresight, prudence, and the ordinary business and home-making virtues, all these apply to other things as well as to the natural resources. There is, in fact, no interest of the people to which the principles of conservation do not apply.

The conservation point of view is valuable in the education of our people as well as in forestry; it applies to the body politic as well as to the earth and its minerals. A municipal franchise is as properly within its sphere as a franchise for water-power. The same point of view governs in both. It applies as much to the subject of good roads as to waterways, and the training of our people in citizenship is as germane to it as the productiveness of the earth. The application of common-sense to any problem for the Nation's good will lead directly to national efficiency wherever applied. In other words, and that is the burden of the message, we are coming to see the logical and inevitable outcome that these principles, which arose in forestry and have their bloom in the conservation of natural resources, will have their fruit in the increase and promotion of national efficiency along other lines of national life.

The outgrowth of conservation, the inevitable result, is national efficiency. In the great commercial struggle between nations which is eventually to determine the welfare of all, national efficiency will be the deciding factor. So from every point of view conservation is a good thing for the American people.

The National Forest Service, one of the chief agencies of the conservation movement, is trying to be useful to the people of this nation. The Service recognizes, and recognizes it more and more strongly all the time, that whatever it has done or is doing has just one object, and that object is the welfare of the plain American citizen. Unless the Forest Service has served the people, and is able to contribute to their welfare, it has failed in its work and should be abolished. But just so far as by cooperation, by intelligence, by attention to the work laid upon it, it contributes to the welfare of our citizens, it is a good thing and should be allowed to go on with its work.

The Natural Forests are in the West. Headquarters of the Service have been established throughout the Western country, because its work cannot be done effectively and properly without the closest contact and the most hearty cooperation with the Western people. It is the duty of the Forest Service to see to it that the timber, water-powers, mines, and every other resource of the forests is used for the benefit of the people who live in the neighborhood or who may have a share in the welfare of each locality. It is equally its duty to cooperate with all our people in every section of our land to conserve a fundamental resource, without which this Nation cannot prosper.

Gifford Pinchot

The Use of the National Forests

What They Are For: The Whole Result

Taking it altogether, then, it will be seen that a National Forest does not act like a wall built around the public domain, which locks up its lands and resources and stops settlement and industry. What it really does is to take the public domain, with all its resources and most of its laws, and make sure that the best possible use is made of every bit of it. And more than this, it makes these vast mountain regions a great deal more valuable, and *keeps* them a great deal more valuable, simply by using them in a careful way, with a little thought about the future.

What They Are For: In General

Use. National Forests are for use by all the people. Their resources are now used in such a common-sense way that instead of being *used up* they *keep coming.* They are for present

---

Gifford Pinchot, "The Use of the National Forests" from *The Use of the National Forests,* USDA Forest Service publication, June 14, 1907, pp. 15–24.

use, for use a few years ahead, and for use a long time ahead. It is easy to draw a picture of the West, say twenty-five or fifty years from now. The picture will show a great increase in population, in the cities and in the country; it will show innumerable homes, now almost unthought of; it will show a wonderful growth in agriculture and the cultivation of vast areas now unproductive; it will show great strides in manufacturing and in all kinds of industry. This means an enormous increase in the demand upon its natural resources. Without enough wood, water, and forage it would be a very poor kind of country. If these great resources should become scarce or hard to get, future growth and prosperity would be severely handicapped.

National Forests keep these resources coming in abundance by using them wisely at present.

Production. The permanent wealth of a country comes from the soil. To insure permanent wealth the soil must be kept productive. Agricultural lands are managed so as to produce the most valuable crops, year after year, without a break. Forest lands also should be managed so as to produce the most valuable crops of timber and wood, year after year, without interruption. Without a plentiful, cheap, and continuous supply of wood, agriculture and all its dependent industries must suffer. And in regions of little rainfall, without a plentiful and steady flow of water for irrigation, agriculture is either impossible or unprofitable.

National Forests from their own soil produce always the greatest possible amounts and the most valuable kinds of timber, wood, and forage; and the Forests themselves make the soil of the surrounding country produce the largest and most useful agricultural crops by supplying it with a steady flow of water for irrigation and by furnishing its settlers with an abundance of timber, and wood, and forage, for home and local business use.

Homes. Homes are of vital importance to the West, and to the whole country. A land without homes is not worth living in. What the West needs is people who come to stay. The man who skins the land and moves on does the country more harm than good. He may enrich himself and a few others for a very brief time, but he kills the land. He cares nothing for this, because he does not stay in the country, but moves on to new fields and repeats the skinning process. It is he who is the greatest enemy of the home builder.

National Forests are made, first of all, for the lasting benefit of the real home builder. They make it impossible for the land to be skinned. They benefit the man with a home and the man who seeks to build one by insuring protection and wise use of the timber and grass and by conserving the water. In considering what National Forests are for and how they affect the resources of the western mountains, the fact should never be lost sight of that they are for the home builder first, and that their resources are protected and used for his special welfare before everything else.

To Protect and Grow Wood for Use

The National Forests occupy high mountain lands, rough and rocky, and which will always be of value chiefly for the production of timber and wood. The first thing that is made sure is that the timber is not burnt up; the next, that it is used, though not used up. Before there were any National Forests enormous quantities of the people's timber on the public domain every year went up in smoke. Forests which covered districts as large as the State of Rhode Island were completely wiped out in the course of a few days. It meant losses to the people of millions and millions of dollars. Fire destroys quickly; trees grow slowly. It often takes a hundred years to make good the damage done by a single day's fire.

In National Forests there is a force of men on the ground whose business it is to look out for fire. They have been remarkably successful in keeping it down. Since the fire patrol was started less than one-third of 1 per cent of the total area of the Forests has been burned over, and the money loss has been insignificant. This is a wonderful improvement over the old conditions on the open public domain, where fires were incessant and enormously destructive.

Hundreds of millions of feet of timber are sold from the National Forests each year. That is why the Forest is protected. The timber is for use. The cuttings do not damage the Forest, because the lumbering operations are so carefully done that the stand is left in first-class condition for a second crop, and after that a third crop and any number of future crops. Fire is kept out of the cut-over lands to give the young growth a fair chance. By wise use the timber crop is made perpetual, and its quality is improved by encouraging a new and better growth of the most useful kinds of trees.

The actual results on private lands where

the owners do not care what happens after they have skinned them, are quite different. These lands are usually cut over with the sole object of getting everything possible out of them at one stroke. They are stripped of timber, while the slashings which are left on the ground make good fire traps. Very soon the whole area burns over and the ground becomes a nonproductive waste. A glance from a car window in Michigan, Wisconsin, or Minnesota shows the now absolutely ruined lands which but a short time ago produced magnificent stands of white pine. Think of the great wealth which the people of these States might have made permanent, simply by using the Forests wisely.

Then, again, wood is so very essential in everyday life that it seems unwise to let it be monopolized by individuals or corporations. Actual results show that when public timber lands pass out of the Government's hands they eventually, and often very quickly, fall into the hands of big concerns, which rarely show the slightest tendency to handle them for the greatest good of the people in the long run.

On a National Forest the present and future *local* demand is always considered first. The Government tries to see that there shall always be enough timber and wood on hand for use by the home builder, the prospector, the miner, the small mill man, the stockman, and all kinds of local industries. If local needs promise to consume it all, nothing is allowed to be shipped out of the country. If it were in the hands of individual or corporate owners, it would very likely be shipped out, regardless of local needs. It would seek the best market. If it were sold locally, the users would have to pay whatever price the owner might demand, and this price might be very unfair.

This is especially important to the mining industry. All mining operations require a great deal of timber. It must be accessible, of suitable quality, fairly cheap, and always on hand. When timber for mines has to be shipped in from a distance at great expense it often makes the operations so costly as to be unprofitable. If the local supply is burned up, the mines suffer. In mining districts one of the chief objects of National Forests is to protect the timber and keep it on hand ready for use in the mines at all times.

To Keep the Water Flow Steady

It should be clearly understood that in regions of heavy rainfall—for example, on the Pacific slopes in Washington, Oregon, northern California, and Alaska—National Forests are not made for the purpose of regulating the water flow for irrigation. In these localities there is plenty of water to spare. The Forests here are created and maintained to protect the timber and keep it in the people's hands for their own present and future use and to prevent the water from running off suddenly in destructive floods.

In other parts of the West, however, in all the great arid regions of the Rockies and the eastern Pacific slopes, one of the most vital reasons for making and maintaining the National Forests is to save every drop of water and to make it do the most effective work.

No one has yet proved that forests increase the rainfall to any great extent. What they do, and this no one of experience disputes, is to nurse and conserve the rain and snow after they have fallen. Water runs down a barren, hard surface with a rush, all at once. It runs down a spongy, soft surface much more slowly, little by little. A very large part of the rain and snow of the arid regions falls upon the great mountain ranges. If these were bare of soil and vegetation, the waters would rush down to the valleys below in floods. But the forest cover—the trees, brush, grass, weeds, and vegetable litter—acts like a big sponge. It soaks up the water, checks it from rushing down all at once, and brings about an even flow during the whole season.

In irrigation it is very important to have an even flow throughout the growing season, especially toward the end. That is where the trouble usually comes. As a rule the rancher has more water than he can use at the beginning of the season and not enough at the end. The flood waters in the spring can not be used; they run off and go to waste. In order to save these flood waters the Government is now constructing many great reservoirs and canals throughout the West, at enormous cost. These reservoirs store up the flood waters and hold them for use when most needed. That is precisely what the forests of the mountains do, although, of course, in a different way.

The forest cover is also very important in preventing erosion and the washing down of silt. If the slopes were bare and the soil unprotected, the waters would carry down with them great quantities of soil, gradually filling up the reservoirs and canals and causing immense damage to the great irrigation systems. The Government engineers who are building these reservoirs and canals say that their work will be unsuccessful unless the drainage basins at the headwaters of the streams are protected by the National Forests.

The home builder, more than anybody else, is vitally interested in a steady flow of water for irrigation. Often his existence depends upon it.

To Keep the Range in Good Condition

The use of the range by live stock enters unavoidably into the management of National Forests. All through the western mountains the range goes with the timber; it can not be separated from it. It is a great resource, and of course ought to be used. The way in which it is used has a great deal to do with the growth of young timber and the flow of water. If it is not wasted or used up, but wisely used, it neither harms the forest growth nor has a bad effect on the water flow. If it is over-grazed or destroyed, the young tree growth is stamped down or eaten off, and the soil is left bare and unprotected, to be washed down the slopes into the canals and reservoirs below.

In the use of the range National Forests work first to protect the settler and home builder. They make sure, before everything else, that he has what range he needs for his own stock. Before the Forests were made the settler was at the mercy of the big stockman, who often drove his herds in from a distance and completely grazed off the settler's range right at his own door. This can not happen in a National Forest, because the man with a home is sure of the range near by for his own use, and the big men from a distance are kept away from him.

In allotting the range the small local owners are considered first; then the larger local owners who have regularly used it; then the owners who live at a distance, but who have been regular occupants; and lastly, if there is any room left after these have been provided for, the owners of transient stock.

Special effort is being made to keep down wild animals which damage stock, and the Forests officers, when requested, help to enforce the State and Territorial live-stock laws.

A small fee is charged for grazing on the National Forests, because when any man gets for his own special use any property maintained for the use of the whole people, he ought to pay for it. Most people are quite willing to pay the cost of restoring the range and keeping it in good condition, especially when such control does away with the old conflicts of all kinds and assures each man of getting his rights. The men who use the range are not the kind who think they ought to get something for nothing.

National Forests, then, are not made for the special purpose of controlling the livestock business; they are concerned with it incidentally, and help to regulate the use of the range because the people want it regulated.

To Use Well All the Land

There are many other incidental uses which National Forests help to bring about and greatly assist. Of course the land itself should be put to the best use. As already mentioned, it is used as sites for all kinds of commercial enterprises, and is open to improvements such as the construction of railroads, wagon roads, trails, canals, reservoirs, and telephone and power lines. All kinds of development work are benefited by National Forests, because they make sure, so far as can be, that timber and wood are kept on hand ready for use instead of being burned up or shipped out of the country, and that the flow of water is kept even and steady for power and other purposes. The conservation (which means simply the wise use) of all the various resources of the Forests, especially of the water, means a great gain in dollars and cents to many commercial enterprises, the water-power companies in particular. The protection of the forest at the heads of streams means a prosperous life to such companies, for it assures them a steady and clear flow of water. The destruction or misuse of the Forest means failure, for it carries with it flood, silt, and drought. Here, again, it is considered that valuable rights which belong to all the people and are protected at Government expense should not be given away free of charge when they are sought for commercial use. It would seem doubly unwise to do this when the corporations which are benefited show a tendency to form great monopolies. So a reasonable charge is made for the value received. The charge is not made for the water, but for the conservation of the water.

Playgrounds. Quite incidentally, also, the National Forests serve a good purpose as great playgrounds for the people. They are used more or less every year by campers, hunters, fishermen, and thousands of pleasure seekers from the near-by towns. They are great recreation grounds for a very large part of the people of the West, and their value in this respect is well worth considering.

Game. The Forest officers are often appointed as State and Territorial game wardens, to protect the game under State and Territorial laws. As a consequence game is usually more abundant and better looked after within the National Forests than outside of them. Although the services of Forest officers in this respect are wholly incidental to their other work, because they are acting for the States and Territories and not as Federal officials, much good has been accomplished, and the arrangement has met with general approval. The people want the game preserved. In many cases it means a good money return to the locality concerned.

CHAPTER 2

John Muir on the Preservation of the Wild Forests of the West

At the same time that Fernow and Pinchot were helping to promote the need for more efficient forest management to serve economic goals and were putting their forest conservation ideas to work in the federal resource bureaucracy, John Muir was roaming the forested wildernesses of the eastern and western United States in search of the deeper meaning of wild nature. Born in Scotland in 1838, Muir's family moved to Wisconsin in 1849 for religious reasons and also to carve out a pioneer farm. Muir worked on the family farm until, at the age of twenty-two in 1860, his mechanical inventions attracted attention at the state agricultural fair in Madison and he was invited to enroll in the state university. After studying science and the humanities for several years, and hiking through neighboring states and Canada with friends, he left the university and eventually worked successfully in several machine shops. An accident in one of them caused him to temporarily lose sight in one eye, and this shocked him into realizing that he should give up his manufacturing work and devote himself to the works of nature. So in 1867 he hiked by himself to Florida and the Gulf of Mexico, and in the following year took a boat to California to explore the western wilderness. Arriving in San Francisco, he saw nothing but ugliness on Market Street, took the ferry to Oakland, and set out on foot for the Sierra mountains, eventually ending up in Yosemite Valley. Working as a sawyer and guide for several years, he did much hiking, exploring, and guiding in the region and, in the early 1870s, began to write about the mountains and wild areas of California and to publish his observations about nature in various popular magazines. He also became alarmed about destructive use of the forests by sheepherders and lumbermen, and resolved to do something about it.

In time Muir wandered through many other areas of the western United States, including Utah, Nevada, the Pacific Northwest, the Puget Sound area, and Alaska, exclaiming in his writings, in poetically descriptive language, about the natural beauty that he discovered in the woods and mountains. In 1880 he settled down in Martinez, California, got married, and turned some of his energies to orchard farming for his father-in-law and to various conservation battles of the day. He fought for the preservation of the Yosemite Valley and Yosemite Park, the Mariposa Big Tree Grove, and King's Canyon and Sequoia National Parks in California. He became one of the founders of the Sierra Club in 1892 and published his first book, *The Mountains of California*, in 1894. This book was an immediate national success and helped to rally conservation sentiment behind the creation of new national forest reserves. It was at this time that he also wrote the article "The American Forests," in which he expresses his more public views about the wonders and also the human depredations of the western forests. One of his last conservation battles centered on the proposal to dam a large valley in the Yosemite National Park, the Hetch Hetchy Valley, to supply water for the city of San Francisco. Muir vigorously opposed this plan and spent a good deal of personal energy rallying public support for his position. Though Congress eventually decided to favor the project in 1913, much to his disgust, and Muir died shortly thereafter in 1914, his efforts did lead to compensating legislation in the creation of the National Park Service in 1916.[1]

Muir was not completely opposed to some of the uses of forests that Pinchot advocated, but he did have a parting of the ways with Pinchot over grazing in the national forests and also the damming of Hetch Hetchy, and he was associated most closely with a wilderness philosophy or "theology" that favored the preservation and protection of forests for noneconomic and noncommercial purposes.[2] Muir was concerned about maintaining most of the American forests in a wild state because he located somewhat different values in wild nature than Fernow and Pinchot. He focused his energies on understanding the spiritual meaning of wilderness, characterizing the western forests as "cathedrals" erected by God not only for human use but also for use by animal and plant "kinfolk." He had a special gift for describing the aesthetic qualities of forested landscapes, and for expressing his delight in the many beauties of wild nature in all of its shapes and forms. To him, it was as if a supreme artist had painted the forests of the West in perfect condition, no matter how they appeared to the naive eye, and the role of humans was to appreciate them for what they were in themselves. He was also interested in the value of forests for renewing and rejuvenating our souls and providing physical challenges for the weary denizens of cities.

The following reading, excerpted from Muir's essay "The American Forests," is less a poetic than a polemical piece and gives a good introduction to Muir's views about why the wild forests of the country needed the immediate attention of the federal government. The essay was originally published in the *Atlantic Monthly* in 1897, before Muir had a falling out with Pinchot over

---

1. This information on Muir is drawn from the following sources: Michael P. Cohen, *The Pathless Way: John Muir and the American Wilderness* (Madison: University of Wisconsin Press, 1984); Linnie Marsh Wolfe, *Son of the Wilderness: The Life of John Muir* (New York: Alfred A. Knopf, 1945); Joseph M. Petulla, *American Environmental History* (San Francisco: Boyd & Fraser, 1977); and Frederick Turner, *Rediscovering America: John Muir in His Time and Ours* (New York: Viking Penguin, 1985).

2. Max Oelschlaeger, *The Idea of Wilderness*, chap. 6, explains Muir's wilderness theology. For a quick review of Muir's various wilderness thoughts, see Edwin Way Teale, ed., *The Wilderness World of John Muir* (Boston: Houghton Mifflin, 1954). The idea that Muir was at least a partial supporter of wood extraction for such purposes as home and ship construction is explained by Bryan Norton in *Toward Unity among Environmentalists* (New York: Oxford University Press, 1991).

grazing in the national forest reserves; it was then republished in his book, *Our National Parks*, in 1901. In it he urges Uncle Sam to do what God apparently could not do, namely, save the western forests from the "fools" that were exploiting them. In hindsight, it is interesting to see that he had so much confidence in the federal government to manage forests for uses other than timber production. But more vigorous federal management was one of the only real conservation alternatives of the day, for "progressive conservation" of forests was clearly not noticeable in the actions and ideas of timber and resource extraction businessmen, rural entrepreneurs, or local and state politicians in the West. Consequently, Muir had to ally himself with various scientists, urban citizens, eastern politicians, and citizen environmentalists to promote the goal of forest protection and preservation.[3]

---

3. An interesting and influential interpretation of the progressive conservation movement can be found in Samuel P. Hays, *Conservation and the Gospel of Efficiency: The Progressive Conservation Movement 1890–1920* (Cambridge, Mass.: Harvard University Press, 1959). Hays argues that it was not only large corporations and a corporate land monopoly that exploited the land in the nineteenth century, as the progressive conservationists argued, but Americans in all walks of life, including small farmers. Some large corporations actually supported conservation measures, once they were proposed, while many smaller operators opposed them. Hays asserts that this movement was part of an effort to transform U.S. society from a "decentralized, nontechnical, loosely organized society, where waste and inefficiency run rampant into a highly organized, technical, and centrally planned and directed social organization which could meet a complex world with efficiency and purpose." This effort was led by President Theodore Roosevelt, implemented by many key professional scientists and scientific bureaucrats such as Pinchot, and supported by the American urban middle-class.

John Muir

The American Forests

The forests of America, however slighted by man, must have been a great delight to God; for they were the best he ever planted. The whole continent was a garden, and from the beginning it seemed to be favored above all the other wild parks and gardens of the globe. To prepare the ground, it was rolled and sifted in seas with infinite loving deliberation and forethought, lifted into the light, submerged and warmed over and over again, pressed and crumpled into folds and ridges, mountains, and hills, subsoiled with heaving volcanic fires, ploughed and ground and sculptured into scenery and soil with glaciers and rivers,—every feature growing and changing from beauty to beauty, higher and higher. And in the fullness of time it was planted in groves, and belts, and broad, exuberant, mantling forests, with the largest, most varied, most fruitful, and most beautiful trees in the world. Bright seas made its border, with wave embroidery and icebergs; gray deserts were outspread in the middle of it, mossy tundras on the north, savannas on the south, and blooming prairies and plains; while lakes and rivers shone through all the vast forests and openings, and happy birds and beasts gave delightful animation. Everywhere, everywhere over all the blessed continent, there were beauty and melody and kindly, wholesome, foodful abundance.

These forests were composed of about five hundred species of trees, all of them in some way useful to man, ranging in size from twenty-five feet in height and less than one foot in diameter at the ground to four hundred feet in height and more than twenty feet in diameter,—lordly monarchs proclaiming the gospel of beauty like apostles. For many a century after the ice-ploughs were melted, nature fed them and dressed them every day,—working like a man, a loving, devoted, painstaking gardener; fingering every leaf and flower and mossy furrowed bole; bending, trimming, modeling, balancing; painting them with the loveliest colors; bringing over them now clouds with cooling shadows and showers, now sunshine; fanning them with gentle winds and rustling their leaves; exercising them in every fibre with storms, and pruning them; loading them with flowers and fruit, loading them with snow, and ever making them more beautiful as the

---

John Muir, "The American Forests," excerpts from chapter 10 of *Our National Parks*, pp. 331–37, 340–46, 349–52, 356–37, and 359–65. Boston: Houghton Mifflin, 1901.

years rolled by. Wide-branching oak and elm in endless variety, walnut and maple, chestnut and beech, ilex and locust, touching limb to limb, spread a leafy translucent canopy along the coast of the Atlantic over the wrinkled folds and ridges of the Alleghanies,—a green billowy sea in summer, golden and purple in autumn, pearly gray like a steadfast frozen mist of interlacing branches and sprays in leafless, restless winter.

To the southward stretched dark, level-topped cypresses in knobby, tangled swamps, grassy savannas in the midst of them like lakes of light, groves of gay, sparkling spice-trees, magnolias and palms, glossy-leaved and blooming and shining continually. To the northward, over Maine and Ottawa, rose hosts of spiry, rosiny evergreens,—white pine and spruce, hemlock and cedar, shoulder to shoulder, laden with purple cones, their myriad needles sparkling and shimmering, covering hills and swamps, rocky headlands and domes, ever bravely aspiring and seeking the sky; the ground in their shade now snow-clad and frozen, now mossy and flowery; beaver meadows here and there, full of lilies and grass; lakes gleaming like eyes, and a silvery embroidery of rivers and creeks watering and brightening all the vast glad wilderness.

Thence westward were oak and elm, hickory and tupelo, gum and liriodendron, sassafras and ash, linden and laurel, spreading on ever wider in glorious exuberance over the great fertile basin of the Mississippi, over damp level bottoms, low dimpling hollows, and round dotting hills, embosoming sunny prairies and cheery park openings, half sunshine, half shade; while a dark wilderness of pines covered the region around the Great Lakes. Thence still westward swept the forests to the right and left around grassy plains and deserts a thousand miles wide: irrepressible hosts of spruce and pine, aspen and willow, nut-pine and juniper, cactus and yucca, caring nothing for drought, extending undaunted from mountain to mountain, over mesa and desert, to join the darkening multitudes of pines that covered the high Rocky ranges and the glorious forests along the coast of the moist and balmy Pacific, where new species of pine, giant cedars and spruces, silver firs and Sequoias, kings of their race, growing close together like grass in a meadow, poised their brave domes and spires in the sky, three hundred feet above the ferns and the lilies that enameled the ground; towering serene through the long centuries, preaching God's forestry fresh from heaven.

Here the forests reached their highest development. Hence they went wavering northward over icy Alaska, brave spruce and fir, poplar and birch, by the coasts and the rivers, to within sight of the Arctic Ocean. American forests! the glory of the world! Surveyed thus from the east to the west, from the north to the south, they are rich beyond thought, immortal, immeasurable, enough and to spare for every feeding, sheltering beast and bird, insect and son of Adam; and nobody need have cared had there been no pines in Norway, no cedars and deodars on Lebanon and the Himalayas, no vine-clad selvas in the basin of the Amazon. With such variety, harmony, and triumphant exuberance, even nature, it would seem, might have rested content with the forests of North America, and planted no more.

So they appeared a few centuries ago when they were rejoicing in wildness. The Indians with stone axes could do them no more harm than could gnawing beavers and browsing moose. Even the fires of the Indians and the fierce shattering lightning seemed to work together only for good in clearing spots here and there for smooth garden prairies, and openings for sunflowers seeking the light. But when the steel axe of the white man rang out on the startled air their doom was sealed. Every tree heard the bodeful sound, and pillars of smoke gave the sign in the sky.

I suppose we need not go mourning the buffaloes. In the nature of things they had to give place to better cattle, though the change might have been made without barbarous wickedness. Likewise many of nature's five hundred kinds of wild trees had to make way for orchards and cornfields. In the settlement and civilization of the country, bread more than timber or beauty was wanted; and in the blindness of hunger, the early settlers, claiming Heaven as their guide, regarded God's trees as only a larger kind of pernicious weeds, extremely hard to get rid of. Accordingly, with no eye to the future, these pious destroyers waged interminable forest wars; chips flew thick and fast; trees in their beauty fell crashing by millions, smashed to confusion, and the smoke of their burning has been rising to heaven more than two hundred years. After the Atlantic coast from Maine to Georgia had been mostly cleared and scorched into melancholy ruins, the overflowing multitude of bread and money seekers poured over the Alleghanies into the fertile middle West, spreading ruthless devastation ever wider and farther over the rich valley of the Mississippi and the vast shadowy pine region about the Great Lakes. Thence still westward, the invading horde of destroyers called settlers made its fiery way over the broad Rocky Mountains, felling and burning more fiercely than ever, until at last it has reached the wild side of the continent, and entered the last of the great aboriginal forests on the shores of the Pacific.

Surely, then, it should not be wondered at that lovers of their country, bewailing its baldness, are now crying aloud, "Save what is left of the forests!" Clearing has surely now gone far enough; soon timber will be scarce, and not a grove will be left to rest in or pray in. The remnant protected will yield plenty of timber, a perennial harvest for every right use, without further diminution of its area, and will continue to cover the springs of the rivers that rise in the mountains and give irrigating waters to the dry valleys at their feet, prevent wasting floods and be a blessing to everybody forever.

Every other civilized nation in the world has been compelled to care for its forests, and so must we if waste and destruction are not to go on to the bitter end, leaving America as barren as Palestine or Spain. In its calmer moments, in the midst of bewildering hunger and war and restless over-industry, Prussia has learned that the forest plays an important part in human progress, and that the advance in civilization only makes it more indispensable. It has, therefore, as shown by Mr. Pinchot, refused to deliver its forests to more or less speedy destruction by permitting them to pass into private ownership. But the state woodlands are not allowed to lie idle. On the contrary, they are made to produce as much timber as is possible without spoiling them. In the administration of its forests, the state righteously considers itself bound to treat them as a trust for the nation as a whole, and to keep in view the common good of the people for all time.

. . .

It seems, therefore, that almost every civilized nation can give us a lesson on the management and care of forests. So far our government has done nothing effective with its forests, though the best in the world, but is like a rich and foolish spendthrift who has inherited a magnificent estate in perfect order, and then has left his fields and meadows, forests and parks, to be sold and plundered and wasted at will, depending on their inexhaustible abundance. Now it is plain that the forests are not inexhaustible, and that quick measures must be taken if ruin is to be avoided. Year by year the remnant is growing smaller before the axe and fire, while the laws in existence provide neither for the protection of the timber from destruction nor for its use where it is most needed.

As is shown by Mr. E. A. Bowers, formerly Inspector of the Public Land Service, the foundation of our protective policy, which has never protected, is an act passed March 1, 1817, which authorized the Secretary of the Navy to reserve lands producing live-oak and cedar, for the sole purpose of supplying timber for the navy of the United States. An extension of this law by the passage of the act of March 2, 1831, provided that if any person should cut live-oak or red cedar trees or *other timber* from the lands of the United States for any other purpose than the construction of the navy, such person should pay a fine not less than triple the value of the timber cut, and be imprisoned for a period not exceeding twelve months. Upon this old law, as Mr. Bowers points out, having the construction of a wooden navy in view, the United Stated government has to-day chiefly to rely in protecting its timber throughout the arid regions of the West, where none of the naval timber which the law had in mind is to be found.

By the act of June 3, 1878, timber can be taken from public lands not subject to entry under any existing laws except for minerals, by *bona fide* residents of the Rocky Mountain states and territories and the Dakotas. Under the timber and stone act, of the same date, land in the Pacific States and Nevada, valuable mainly for timber, and unfit for cultivation if the timber is removed, can be purchased for two dollars and a half an acre, under certain restrictions. By the act of March 3, 1875, all land-grant and right-of-way railroads are authorized to take timber from the public lands adjacent to their lines for construction purposes; and they have taken it with a vengeance, destroying a hundred times more than they have used, mostly by allowing fires to run in the woods. The settlement laws, under which a settler may enter lands valuable for timber as well as for agriculture, furnish another means of obtaining title to public timber.

With the exception of the timber culture act, under which, in consideration of planting a few acres of seedlings, settlers on the treeless plains got 160 acres each, the above is the only legislation aiming to protect and promote the planting of forests. In no other way than under some one of these laws can a citizen of the United States make any use of the public forests. To show the results of the timber-planting act, it need only be stated that of the thirty-eight million acres entered under it, less than one million acres have been patented. This means that less than fifty thousand acres have been planted with stunted, woebegone, almost hopeless sprouts of trees, while at the same time the government has allowed millions of acres of the grandest forest trees to be stolen or destroyed, or sold for nothing. Under the act of June 3, 1878, settlers in Colorado and the Territories were allowed to cut timber for mining and educational purposes from mineral land, which in the practical West means both cutting and burning anywhere and everywhere, for any purpose, on any sort of public land. Thus, the prospector, the miner, and mining and railroad companies are allowed by law to take all the timber they like for their mines and roads, and the forbidden settler, if there are no mineral lands near his farm or stock-ranch, or none that he knows of, can hardly be expected to forbear taking what he needs wherever he can find it. Timber is as necessary as bread, and no scheme of management failing to recognize and properly provide for this want can possibly be maintained. In any case, it will be hard to teach the pioneers that it is wrong to steal government timber. Taking from the government is with them the same as taking from nature, and their consciences flinch no more in cutting timber from the wild forests than in drawing water from a lake or river. As for reservation and protection of forests, it seems as silly and needless to them as protection and reservation of the ocean would be, both appearing to be boundless and inexhaustible.

The special land agents employed by the General Land Office to protect the public domain from timber depredations are supposed to collect testimony to sustain prosecution and to superintend such prosecution on behalf of the government, which is represented by the district attorneys. But timber thieves of the Western class are seldom convicted, for the good reason that most of the jurors who try such cases are themselves as guilty as those on trial. The effect of the present confused, discriminating, and unjust system has been to place almost the whole population in opposition to the government; and as conclusive of its futility as shown by Mr. Bowers, we need only state that during the seven years from 1881 to 1887 inclusive, the value of the timber reported stolen from the government lands was $36,719,935, and the amount recovered was $478,073, while the cost of the services of special agents alone was $455,000, to which must be added the expense of the trials. Thus for nearly thirty-seven million dollars' worth of timber the government got less than nothing; and the value of that consumed by running fires during the same period, without benefit even to thieves, was probably over two hundred millions of dollars. Land commissioners and Secretaries of the Interior have repeatedly called attention to this ruinous state of affairs, and asked Congress to enact the requisite legislation for reasonable reform. But, busied with tariffs, etc., Congress has given no heed to these or other appeals, and our forests, the most valuable and the most destructible of all the natural resources of the country, are being robbed and burned more rapidly than ever. The annual appropriation for so-called "protection service" is hardly sufficient to keep twenty-five timber agents in the field, and as far as any efficient protection of timber is concerned these agents themselves might as well be timber.[1]

That a change from robbery and ruin to a permanent rational policy is urgently needed nobody with the slightest knowledge of American forests will deny. In the East and along the northern Pacific coast, where the rainfall is abundant, comparatively few care keenly what becomes of the trees so long as fuel and lumber are not noticeably dear. But in the Rocky Mountains and California and Arizona, where the forests are inflammable, and where the fertility of the lowlands depends upon irrigation, public opinion is growing stronger every year in favor of permanent protection by the federal government of all the forests that cover the sources of the streams. Even lumbermen in these regions, long accustomed to steal, are now willing and anxious to buy lumber for their mills under cover of law: some possibly from a late second growth of honesty, but most, especially the small mill-owners, simply because it no longer pays to steal where all may not only steal, but also destroy, and in particular because it costs about as much to steal timber for one mill as for ten, and, therefore, the ordinary lumberman can no longer compete with the large corporations. Many of the miners find that timber is already becoming scarce and dear on the denuded hills around their mills, and they, too, are asking for protection of forests, at least against fire. The slow-going, unthrifty farmers, also, are beginning to realize that when the timber is stripped from the mountains the irrigating streams dry up in summer, and are destructive in winter; that soil, scenery, and everything slips off with the trees: so of course they are coming into the ranks of tree-friends.

Of all the magnificent coniferous forests around the Great Lakes, once the property of the United States, scarcely any belong to it now. They have disappeared in lumber and smoke, mostly smoke, and the government got not one cent for them; only the land they were growing on was considered valuable, and two and a half dollars an acre was charged for it. Here and there in the Southern States there are still considerable areas of timbered government land, but these are comparatively unimportant. Only the forests of the West are significant in size and value, and these, although still great, are rapidly vanishing. Last summer, of the unrivaled redwood forests of the Pacific Coast Range, the United States Forestry Commission could not find a single quarter-section that remained in the hands of the government.[2]

. . .

The redwood is the glory of the Coast Range. It extends along the western slope, in a nearly continuous belt about ten miles wide, from beyond the Oregon boundary to the south of Santa Cruz, a distance of nearly four hundred miles, and in massive, sustained grandeur and closeness of growth surpasses all the other timber woods of the world. Trees from ten to fifteen feet in diameter and three hundred feet high are not uncommon, and a few attain a height of three hundred and fifty feet or even four hundred, with a diameter at the base of fifteen to twenty feet or more, while the ground beneath them is a garden of fresh, exuberant ferns, lilies, gaultheria, and rhododendron. This grand tree, Sequoia sempervirens, is surpassed in size only by its near relative Sequoia gigantea, or Big Tree, of the Sierra Nevada, if, indeed, it is surpassed. The sempervirens is certainly the taller of the two. The gigantea attains a greater girth, and is heavier, more noble in port, and more sublimely beautiful.

These two Sequoias are all that are known to exist in the world, though in former geological times the genus was common and had many species. The redwood is restricted to the Coast Range, and the Big Tree to the Sierra.

As timber the redwood is too good to live. The largest sawmills ever built are busy along its seaward border, "with all the modern improvements," but so immense is the yield per acre it will be long ere the supply is exhausted. The Big Tree is also, to some extent, being made into lumber. It is far less abundant than the redwood, and is, fortunately, less accessible, extending along the western flank of the Sierra in a partially interrupted belt, about two hundred and fifty miles long, at a height of from four to eight thousand feet above the sea. The enormous logs, too heavy to handle, are blasted into manageable dimensions with gunpowder. A large portion of the best timber is thus shattered and destroyed, and, with the huge, knotty tops, is left in ruins for tremendous fires that kill every tree within their range, great and small. Still, the species is not in danger of extinction. It has been planted and is flourishing over a great part of Europe, and magnificent sections of the aboriginal forests have been reserved as national and State parks,— the Mariposa Sequoia Grove, near Yosemite, managed by the State of California, and the General Grant and Sequoia national parks on the Kings, Kaweah, and Tule Rivers, efficiently guarded by a small troop of United States cavalry under the direction of the Secretary of the Interior. But there is not a single specimen of the redwood in any national park. Only by gift or purchase, so far as I know, can the government get back into its possession a single acre of this wonderful forest.

The legitimate demands on the forests that have passed into private ownership, as well as those in the hands of the government, are increasing every year with the rapid settlement and up-building of the country, but the methods of lumbering are as yet grossly wasteful. In most mills only the best portions of the best trees are used, while the ruins are left on the ground to feed great fires, which kill much of what is left of the less desirable timber, together with the seedlings, on which the permanence of the forest depends. Thus every mill is a centre of destruction far more severe from waste and fire than from use. The same thing is true of the mines, which consume and destroy indirectly immense quantities of timber with their innumerable fires, accidental or set to make open ways, and often without regard to how far they run. The prospector deliberately sets fires to clear off the woods just where they are densest, to lay the rocks bare and make the discovery of mines easier. Sheep-owners and their shepherds also set fires everywhere through the woods in the fall to facilitate the march of their countless flocks the next summer, and perhaps in some places to improve the pasturage. The axe is not yet at the root of every tree, but the sheep is, or was before the national parks were established and guarded by the military, the only effective and reliable arm of the government free from the blight of politics. Not only do the shepherds, at the driest time of the year, set fire to everything that will burn, but the sheep consume every green leaf, not sparing even the young conifers, when they are in a starving condition from crowding, and they rake and dibble the loose soil of the mountain sides for the spring floods to wash away, and thus at last leave the ground barren.

• • •

It is not generally known that, notwithstanding the immense quantities of timber cut every year for foreign and home markets and mines, from five to ten times as much is destroyed as is used, chiefly by running forest fires that only the federal government can stop. Travelers through the West in summer are not likely to forget the firework displayed along the various railway tracks. Thoreau, when contemplating the destruction of the forests on the east side of the continent, said that soon the country would be so bald that every man would have to grow whiskers to hid its nakedness, but he thanked God that at least the sky was safe. Had he gone West he would have found out that the sky was not safe; for all through the summer months, over most of the mountain regions, the smoke of mill and forest fires is so thick and black that no sunbeam can pierce it. The whole sky, with clouds, sun, moon, and stars, is simply blotted out. There is no real sky and no scenery. Not a mountain is left in the landscape. At least none is in sight from the lowlands, and they all might as well be on the moon, as far as scenery is concerned.

• • •

Notwithstanding all the waste and use which have been going on unchecked like a storm for more than two centuries, it is not yet too late—though it is high time—for the government to begin a rational administration of its forests. About seventy million acres it still owns,—enough for all the country, if wisely used. These residual forests are generally on mountain slopes, just where they are doing the most good, and where their removal would be followed by the greatest number of evils; the lands they cover are too rocky and high for agriculture, and can never be made as valuable for any other crop as for the present crop of trees. It has been shown over and over again that if these mountains were to be stripped of their trees and underbrush, and kept barc and sodless by hordes of sheep and the innumerable fires the shepherds set, besides those of the millmen, prospectors, shake-makers, and all sorts of adventurers, both lowlands and mountains would speedily become little better than deserts, compared with their present beneficent fertility. During heavy rainfalls and while the winter accumulations of snow were melting, the larger streams would swell into destructive torrents, cutting deep, rugged-edged gullies, carrying away the fertile humus and soil as well as sand and rocks, filling up and overflowing their lower channels, and covering the lowland fields with raw detritus. Drought and barrenness would follow.

In their natural condition, or under wise management, keeping out destructive sheep, preventing fires, selecting the trees that should be cut for lumber, and preserving the young ones and the shrubs and sod of herbaceous vegetation, these forests would be a never failing fountain of wealth and beauty. The cool shades of the forest give rise to moist beds and currents of air, and the sod of grasses and the various flowering plants and shrubs thus fostered, together with the network and sponge of tree roots, absorb and hold back the rain and the waters from melting snow, compelling them to ooze and percolate and flow gently through the soil in streams that never dry. All the pine needles and rootlets and blades of grass, and the fallen, decaying trunks of trees, are dams, storing the bounty of the clouds and dispensing it in perennial life-giving streams, instead of allowing it to gather suddenly and rush headlong in short-lived devastating floods. Everybody on the dry side of the continent is beginning to find this out, and, in view of the waste going on, is growing more and more anxious for government protection. The outcries we hear against forest reservations come mostly from thieves who are wealthy and steal timber by wholesale. They have so long been allowed to steal and destroy in peace that any impediment to forest robbery is denounced as a cruel and irreligious interference with "vested rights," likely to endanger the repose of all ungodly welfare.

> Gold, gold, gold! How strong a voice that metal has!
> "O wae for the siller, it is sae preva'lin'!"

Even in Congress a sizable chunk of gold, carefully concealed, will outtalk and outfight all the nation on a subject like forestry, well smothered in ignorance, and in which the money interests of only a few are conspicuously involved. Under these circumstances, the bawling, blethering oratorical stuff drowns the voice of God himself. Yet the dawn of a new day in forestry is breaking. Honest citizens see that only the rights of the government are being trampled, not those of the settlers. Only what belongs to all alike is reserved, and every acre that is left should be held together under the federal government as a basis for a general policy of administration for the public good. The people will not always be deceived by selfish opposition, whether from lumber and mining corporations or from sheepmen and prospectors, however cunningly brought forward underneath fables and gold.

Emerson says that things refuse to be mismanaged long. An exception would seem to be found in the case of our forests, which have been mismanaged rather long, and now come desperately near being like smashed eggs and spilt milk. Still, in the long run the world does not move backward. The wonderful advance made in the last few years, in creating four national parks in the West, and thirty forest reservations, embracing nearly forty million acres; and in the planting of the borders of streets and highways and spacious parks in all the great cities, to satisfy the natural taste and hunger for landscape beauty and righteousness that God has put, in some measure, into every human being and animal, shows the trend of awakening public opinion. The making of the far-famed New York Central Park was opposed by even good men, with misguided pluck, perseverance, and ingenuity; but straight right won its way, and now that park is appreciated. So we confidently believe it will be with our great national parks and forest reservations. There will be a period of indifference on the part of the rich, sleepy with wealth, and of the toiling millions, sleepy with poverty, most of whom never saw a forest; a period of screaming protest and objection from the plunderers, who are as unconscionable and enterprising as Satan. But light is surely coming, and the friends of destruction will preach and bewail in vain.

The United States government has always been proud of the welcome it has extended to good men of every nation, seeking freedom and homes and bread. Let them be welcomed still as nature welcomes them, to the woods as well as to the prairies and plains. No place is too good for good men, and still there is room. They are invited to heaven, and may well be allowed in America. Every place is made better by them. Let them be as free to pick gold and gems from the hills, to cut and hew, dig and plant, for homes and bread, as the birds are to pick berries from the wild bushes, and moss and leaves for nests. The ground will be glad to feed them, and the pines will come down from the mountains for their homes as willingly as the cedars came from Lebanon for Solomon's temple. Nor will the woods be the worse for this use, or their benign influences be diminished any more than the sun is diminished by shining. Mere destroyers, however, tree-killers, wool and mutton men, spreading death and confusion in the fairest groves and gardens every planted,—let the government hasten to cast them out and make an end of them. For it must be told again and again, and be burningly borne in mind, that just now, while protective measures are being deliberated languidly, destruction and use are speeding on faster and farther every day. The axe and saw are insanely busy, chips are flying thick as snowflakes, and every summer thousands of acres of priceless forests, with their underbrush, soil, springs, climate, scenery, and religion, are vanishing away in clouds of smoke, while, except in national parks, not one forest guard is employed.

All sorts of local laws and regulations have been tried and found wanting, and the costly lessons of our own experience, as well as that of every civilized nation, show conclusively that the fate of the remnant of our forests is in the hands of the federal government, and that if the remnant is to be saved at all, it must be saved quickly.

Any fool can destroy trees. They cannot run away; and if they could, they would still be destroyed,—chased and hunted down as long as fun or a dollar could be got out of their bark hides, branching horns, or magnificent bole backbones. Few that fell trees plant them; nor would planting avail much towards getting back anything like the noble primeval forests. During a man's life only saplings can be grown, in the place of the old trees—tens of centuries old—that have been destroyed. It took more than three thousand years to make some of the trees in these Western woods,—trees that are still standing in perfect strength and beauty, waving and singing in the mighty forests of the Sierra. Through all the wonderful, eventful centuries since Christ's time—and long before that—God has cared for these trees, saved them from drought, disease, avalanches, and a thousand straining, leveling tempests and floods; but he cannot save them from fools,— only Uncle Sam can do that.

Notes

1. A change for the better, compelled by public opinion, is now going on,—1901.

2. The State of California recently appropriated two hundred and fifty thousand dollars to buy a block of redwood land near Santa Cruz for a state park. A much larger national part should be made in Humboldt or Mendocino county.

CHAPTER 3

Aldo Leopold's Land Ethic in Forestry

Thus far we have introduced examples of "resourcism" and also "preservationism" in forestry, to use Baird Callicott's language.[1] But, as indicated above, environmental philosophies and ethics have evolved since the days of Fernow, Pinchot, and Muir, and new ideas about forests began to take a foothold in American science during the 1930s. Aldo Leopold took the next jump conceptually in the ethics of forestry when he formulated his famous "land ethic," for this philosophy extends ethical consideration beyond humans and the "higher mammals" to all elements of the earth and forests, not just to those that are of use in our economic system or of value to us aesthetically. Leopold applied his land ethic directly to the agricultural and resource sciences such as forestry, and to conservation problems as he came to understand them, and he sought a greater harmony between humans and the land than existed in his day.

Like Pinchot, Leopold was born to wealthy parents and privileged circumstances, in 1882. But in contrast to Pinchot he was raised closer to the western frontier of North America in Burlington, Iowa, along the then "semiwild" Mississippi River. As a young person he had abundant opportunities to explore the natural surroundings of the area and developed an interest in natural history and the new field of forestry. Educated at the exclusive Lawrenceville School in New Jersey, he went on to Yale in 1905 to complete a bachelor's degree, then in 1909 finished a master's degree in forestry at the Yale School of Forestry. As indicated earlier, forestry was still a new profession in the United States at the time, and newly educated foresters worked mostly for the federal government in the federal forest reserves that had been transferred in 1905 to the U.S. Forest Service under Pinchot's leadership. Federal foresters had large responsibilities to catalogue, protect, and manage millions of acres of public land, and the conservation ideas of Pinchot and Fernow were put to work to accomplish this rather immense task.

Leopold's first job came immediately after graduation; he was hired as a forester by the Forest Service and sent to the southwestern United States, to the Apache National Forest in Arizona Territory. After spending several years learning the ropes in various positions and national

1. J. Baird Callicott, "Current Concepts in Conservation," *Conservation Biology* 12 (1999): 22–35.

forests, in 1912 he was made supervisor of the Carson National Forest in northern New Mexico. He contracted an illness in 1913 and, while recuperating, took the time to read the works of Henry David Thoreau and other naturalists and nature writers, just as Muir had done before him. When he returned to work he was assigned to duties organizing grazing as well as fish and game activities in the Southwestern District, for his personal and professional interests had shifted from forestry proper to the protection of wild game species. After several years in private employment during World War I, he returned to the Forest Service in 1919 as an administrator.

During these early years as a forester, Leopold attempted to apply resource conservation ideas such as "sustained yield" to game and forest issues, and he also developed an interest in the budding science of ecology. A significant accomplishment at this time was getting a half-million acres in the Gila National Forest designated administratively as wilderness, one of the first efforts in wilderness protection on federal lands in the West.[2] In 1924 he was transferred to Madison, Wisconsin, to become the associate director of the U.S. Forest Products Laboratory, then the main research institution of the Forest Service. This job did not particularly suit him, and in 1928 he set himself up as a private consultant in game management, doing game surveys in the upper Midwestern states. By the early 1930s this work earned him high praise as one of the foremost scientific authorities in the country on game and game management. Part of his reputation was based on two publications, *Report on a Game Survey of the North Central States* in 1931 and his famous textbook, *Game Management* in 1933, which was used for many years in wildlife courses in land-grant colleges around the country.[3] He began to think and write seriously about the connections of ethics to ecology and the land community, and also in 1933 he published a well-known and widely-discussed essay, "The Conservation Ethic," in *The Journal of Forestry*.[4] This essay laid down ideas that were important precursors to those in *A Sand County Almanac*, his most well-known, important, and popular publication.

In 1933 the University of Wisconsin offered Leopold the first chair in game management in the United States, and in this position, which he retained until his untimely death in 1948, he flourished as a scientist, teacher, and writer. He served in a variety of other research and professional positions at the university and nationally, directed the work of many excellent graduate students, and became a consultant for federal agencies on conservation research and education. He helped to establish the Wilderness Society in 1935 and also bought a worn-out farm in central Wisconsin on the Wisconsin River that became the setting for some of the sketches in his conservation classic, *A Sand County Almanac*, published posthumously in 1949. He spent many weekends at the farm with his family, working to restore it to a condition of ecological integrity and deepening his understanding of human relationships to nature. During World War II, when his students were away at war, he became very active in professional societies,

---

2. Curt Meine, *Aldo Leopold: His Life and Work* (Madison: University of Wisconsin Press, 1988), chap. 10. Meine argues that the idea of designating parts of the national forests as wilderness first occurred to Leopold in 1913, and Leopold finally proposed it formally in 1921. While wilderness sentiments helped to create the first national parks, the parks were not directed toward maintaining wilderness conditions.

3. Aldo Leopold, *Report on a Game Survey of the North Central States* (Washington, D.C.: Sporting Arms and Ammunition Manufacturers' Institute, 1931); *Game Management* (New York: Charles Scribner's Sons, 1933). Leopold was identified as a "consulting forester" on the title page of *Game Management*.

4. *Journal of Forestry* 31(6) (October 1933): 634–43.

committees, and conservation organizations, talking at conferences and writing for professional journals. In 1947, a year before his tragic death, he was elected an honorary vice president of the American Forestry Association and president of the Ecological Society of America.[5]

Leopold's early conception of forestry was influenced by resource conservation philosophy and was thus quite production-oriented and focused on timber, range, and game management issues. His aim was to enhance the interests of the government and those who used the public lands for extractive purposes, such as ranchers and loggers. However, he eventually came to question this philosophy as he saw how federal forest and range lands were being degraded through shortsighted land practices and inadequate land management by government. His study of ecology prompted him to apply ecological insights to land management, because he was convinced through field study that this science was the key to understanding the conditions of land health and disease. Just as "conservation" had been such an important, synthetic idea to Pinchot in his efforts to relate various land resources, so "ecology" became for Leopold the means for tying together and understanding human land practices.

In time Leopold articulated an alternative to the agricultural conception of forestry that Pinchot advocated, what I would call "biotic forestry."[6] He fashioned a more broadly conceived and humbling idea of forestry as an ecological science and art that adopts a less anthropocentric and utilitarian attitude toward forests in favor of a more "biocentered" philosophical perspective and outcome. Forestry, in his mind, could be freed from its more limited resource conservation and "timber first" roots to become a means of promoting land health and understanding noneconomic values in nature. The land ethic could help foresters work toward a new form of forest conservation that looks at trees and other forest systems and components as integral components of a complicated energy system involving the earth and the sun. His model of forestry made it an applied ecological and aesthetic discipline, above all, with forest health as its goal and economics taking a back seat. He agreed that forests must be used for economic products, and that economic feasibility might set some limits on what we can and cannot do to the land. But he also argued that the ecological capacity of the land limits what humans can do to it, and in any case that forests also serve a whole series of noneconomic functions. They provide wildlife habitat, recreational opportunities, watershed services, wilderness values, aesthetic appreciation, and ecological knowledge and wisdom, among other things. The integrity of forests as ecological and aesthetic systems would take precedence over the extraction of wood and "fibre."[7] Leopold thus provided a foundation for what is now called "ecosystem management" in forestry, a concept that is being applied currently in federal forest management.

The following selection gives a clear picture of Leopold's ideas about the dimensions of this new ecological ethic. "The Land Ethic" is the last section of *A Sand County Almanac* as published

---

5. Most of this information is taken from two sources: Curt Meine, *Aldo Leopold: His Life and Work,* and Susan Flader, *Thinking Like a Mountain: Aldo Leopold and the Evolution of an Ecological Attitude toward Deer, Wolves, and Forests* (Lincoln: University of Nebraska Press, 1978).

6. Peter List, "Biotic Forestry," *Reflections,* Special Issue No. 3, Fall 1998, Newsletter of the Program for Ethics, Science, and the Environment, Department of Philosophy, Oregon State University.

7. Based on Peter List, "The Land Ethic in American Forestry: Pinchot and Leopold," in *The Idea of the Forest: German and American Perspectives on the Culture and Politics of Trees,* eds. Karla L. Schultz and Kenneth S. Calhoon, (New York: Peter Lang, 1996).

in its original edition in 1949. Here Leopold brings together in one place many of his important ethical insights, such as his "key-log" idea that "a thing is right when it tends to preserve the integrity, stability, and beauty of the biotic community."[8] He also formulates his views about how forestry and forestry ethics would be reconceived in his land ethic, separating this technical field into two groups. On the one hand are those like Pinchot who see forestry as a form of agronomy; on the other are those who stress its biotic character. The latter conception is the one Leopold prefers because it embodies an "ecological conscience." Thus, an ethic in forestry must become an ecological ethic; it must promote the management of forests for more than economic profits, emphasize nonmaterial values, and aim at the goal of land health. In this "biotic forestry" foresters will shed a conquering mentality to become more humble, biotic citizens.[9]

8. Whether this principle is still valid in ecology is discussed by Leopold scholar and interpreter J. Baird Callicott in "Do Deconstructive Ecology and Sociobiology Undermine Leopold's Land Ethic?" *Environmental Ethics* 18 (Winter 1996): 353–72. Callicott concludes that this "summary maxim of the land ethic . . . must be dynamized" and proposes a revision that incorporates the current ecological idea of spatial and temporal scale.

9. In my talk "Spiritual Values in Leopold's Land Ethic: The Noumenal Integrity of Forest Ecosystems," I explain Leopold's idea of the "noumenal" value of wilderness and wild species in forest ecosystems, and the general implications of forest noumena for forest management. This talk was published in the *Proceedings of the 1999 Annual Convention of the Society of American Foresters* in Spring 2000. See the Selected Bibliography.

Aldo Leopold

The Land Ethic

When god-like Odysseus returned from the wars in Troy, he hanged all on one rope a dozen slave-girls of his household whom he suspected of misbehavior during his absence.

This hanging involved no question of propriety. The girls were property. The disposal of property was then, as now, a matter of expediency, not of right and wrong.

Concepts of right and wrong were not lacking from Odysseus' Greece: witness the fidelity of his wife through the long years before at last his black-prowed galleys clove the wine-dark seas for home. The ethical structure of that day covered wives, but had not yet been extended to human chattels. During the three thousand years which have since elapsed, ethical criteria have been extended to many fields of conduct, with corresponding shrinkages in those judged by expediency only.

The Ethical Sequence

This extension of ethics, so far studied only by philosophers, is actually a process in ecological evolution. Its sequences may be described in ecological as well as in philosophical terms. An ethic, ecologically, is a limitation on freedom of action in the struggle for existence. An ethic, philosophically, is a differentiation of social from anti-social conduct. These are two definitions of one thing. The thing has its origin in the tendency of interdependent individuals or groups to evolve modes of co-operation. The ecologist calls these symbioses. Politics and economics are advanced symbioses in which the original free-for-all competition has been replaced, in part, by co-operative mechanisms with an ethical content.

The complexity of co-operative mechanisms has increased with population density, and with the efficiency of tools. It was simpler, for example, to define the anti-social uses of sticks and stones in the days of the mastodons than of bullets and billboards in the age of motors.

The first ethics dealt with the relation between individuals; the Mosaic Decalogue is an example. Later accretions dealt with the relation between the individual and society. The Golden Rule tries to integrate the individual to society; democracy to integrate social organization to the individual.

There is as yet no ethic dealing with man's

From *A Sand County Almanac: And Sketches Here and There* by Aldo Leopold. Copyright 1949, 1977 by Oxford University Press, Inc. Used by permission of Oxford University Press, Inc.

relation to land and to the animals and plants which grow upon it. Land, like Odysseus' slave-girls, is still property. The land-relation is still strictly economic, entailing privileges but not obligations.

The extension of ethics to this third element in human environment is, if I read the evidence correctly, an evolutionary possibility and an ecological necessity. It is the third step in a sequence. The first two have already been taken. Individual thinkers since the days of Ezekiel and Isaiah have asserted that the despoliation of land is not only inexpedient but wrong. Society, however, has not yet affirmed their belief. I regard the present conservation movement as the embryo of such an affirmation.

An ethic may be regarded as a mode of guidance for meeting ecological situations so new or intricate, or involving such deferred reactions, that the path of social expediency is not discernible to the average individual. Animal instincts are modes of guidance for the individual in meeting such situations. Ethics are possibly a kind of community instinct in-the-making.

The Community Concept

All ethics so far evolved rest upon a single premise: that the individual is a member of a community of interdependent parts. His instincts prompt him to compete for his place in that community, but his ethics prompt him also to co-operate (perhaps in order that there may be a place to compete for).

The land ethic simply enlarges the boundaries of the community to include soils, waters, plants, and animals, or collectively: the land.

This sounds simple: do we not already sing our love for and obligation to the land of the free and the home of the brave? Yes, but just what and whom do we love? Certainly not the soil, which we are sending helter-skelter downriver. Certainly not the waters, which we assume have no function except to turn turbines, float barges, and carry off sewage. Certainly not the plants, of which we exterminate whole communities without batting an eye. Certainly not the animals, of which we have already extirpated many of the largest and most beautiful species. A land ethic of course cannot prevent the alteration, management, and use of these "resources," but it does affirm their right to continued existence, and, at least in spots, their continued existence in a natural state.

In short, a land ethic changes the role of *Homo sapiens* from conqueror of the land-community to plain member and citizen of it. It implies respect for his fellow-members, and also respect for the community as such.

In human history, we have learned (I hope) that the conqueror role is eventually self-defeating. Why? Because it is implicit in such a role that the conqueror knows, *ex cathedra*, just what makes the community clock tick, and just what and who is valuable, and what and who is worthless, in community life. It always turns out that he knows neither, and this is why his conquests eventually defeat themselves.

In the biotic community, a parallel situation exists. Abraham knew exactly what the land was for: it was to drip milk and honey into Abraham's mouth. At the present moment, the assurance with which we regard this assumption is inverse to the degree of our education.

The ordinary citizen today assumes that science knows what makes the community clock tick; the scientist is equally sure that he does not. He knows that the biotic mechanism is so complex that its workings may never be fully understood.

That man is, in fact, only a member of a biotic team is shown by an ecological interpretation of history. Many historical events, hitherto explained solely in terms of human enterprise, were actually biotic interactions between people and land. The characteristics of the land determined the facts quite as potently as the characteristics of the men who lived on it.

Consider, for example, the settlement of the Mississippi valley. In the years following the [American] Revolution, three groups were contending for its control: the native Indian, the French and English traders, and the American settlers. Historians wonder what would have happened if the English at Detroit had thrown a little more weight into the Indian side of those tipsy scales which decided the outcome of the colonial migration into the cane-lands of Kentucky. It is time now to ponder the fact that the cane-lands, when subjected to the particular mixture of forces represented by the cow, plow, fire, and axe of the pioneer, became bluegrass. What if the plant succession inherent in this dark and bloody ground had, under the impact of these forces, given us some worthless sedge, shrub, or weed? Would Boone and Kenton have held out? Would there have been any overflow into Ohio, Indiana, Illinois, and Missouri? Any Louisiana Purchase? Any transcontinental union of new states? Any Civil War?

Kentucky was one sentence in the drama of history. We are commonly told what the human actors in this drama tried to do, but we are seldom told that their success, or the lack of it, hung in large degree on the reaction of particular soils to the impact of the particular forces exerted by their occupancy. In the case of Kentucky, we do not even know where the bluegrass came from—whether it is a native species, or a stowaway from Europe.

Contrast the cane-lands with what hindsight tells us about the Southwest, where the pioneers were equally brave, resourceful, and persevering. The impact of occupancy here brought no bluegrass, or other plant fitted to withstand the bumps and buffetings of hard use. This region, when grazed by livestock, reverted through a series of more and more worthless grasses, shrubs, and weeds to a condition of unstable equilibrium. Each recession of plant types bred erosion; each increment to erosion bred a further recession of plants. The result today is a progressive and mutual deterioration, not only of plants and soils, but of the animal community subsisting thereon. The early settlers did not expect this: on the ciénegas of New Mexico some even cut ditches to hasten it. So subtle has been its progress that few residents of the region are aware of it. It is quite invisible to the tourist who finds this wrecked landscape colorful and charming (as indeed it is, but it bears scant resemblance to what it was in 1848).

This same landscape was "developed" once before, but with quite different results. The Pueblo Indians settled the Southwest in pre-Columbian times, but they happened *not* to be equipped with range livestock. Their civilization expired, but not because their land expired.

In India, regions devoid of any sod-forming grass have been settled, apparently without wrecking the land, by the simple expedient of carrying the grass to the cow, rather than vice versa. (Was this the result of some deep wisdom, or was it just good luck? I do not know.)

In short, the plant succession steered the course of history; the pioneer simply demonstrated, for good or ill, what successions inhered in the land. Is history taught in this spirit? It will be, once the concept of land as a community really penetrates our intellectual life.

The Ecological Conscience

Conservation is a state of harmony between men and land. Despite nearly a century of propaganda, conservation still proceeds at a snail's pace; progress still consists largely of letterhead pieties and convention oratory. On the back forty we still slip two steps backward for each forward stride.

The usual answer to this dilemma is "more conservation education." No one will debate this, but is it certain that only the *volume* of education needs stepping up? Is something lacking in the *content* as well?

It is difficult to give a fair summary of its content in brief form, but, as I understand it, the content is substantially this: obey the law, vote right, join some organizations, and practice what conservation is profitable on your own land; the government will do the rest.

Is not this formula too easy to accomplish anything worth-while? It defines no right or wrong, assigns no obligation, calls for no sacrifice, implies no change in the current philosophy of values. In respect of land-use, it urges only enlightened self-interest. Just how far will such education take us? An example will perhaps yield a partial answer.

By 1930 it had become clear to all except the ecologically blind that southwestern Wisconsin's topsoil was slipping seaward. In 1933 the farmers were told that if they would adopt certain remedial practices for five years, the public would donate CCC [Civilian Conservation Corps] labor to install them, plus the necessary machinery and materials. The offer was widely accepted, but the practices were widely forgotten when the five-year contract period was up. The farmers continued only those practices that yielded an immediate and visible economic gain for themselves.

This led to the idea that maybe farmers would learn more quickly if they themselves wrote the rules. Accordingly the Wisconsin Legislature in 1937 passed the Soil Conservation District Law. This said to farmers, in effect: *We, the public, will furnish you free technical service and loan you specialized machinery, if you will write your own rules for land-use. Each county may write its own rules, and these will have the force of law.* Nearly all the counties promptly organized to accept the proffered help, but after a decade of operation, *no county has yet written a single rule.* There has been visible progress in such practices as strip-cropping, pasture renovation, and soil liming, but none in fencing woodlots against grazing, and none in excluding plow and cow from steep slopes. The farmers, in short, have selected those remedial practices which were profitable anyhow, and ignored those which were profitable to the community, but not clearly profitable to themselves.

When one asks why no rules have been written, one is told that the community is not yet ready to support them; education must precede rules. But the education actually in progress makes no mention of obligations to land over and above those dictated by self-interest. The net result is that we have more education but less soil, fewer healthy woods, and as many floods as in 1937.

The puzzling aspect of such situations is that the existence of obligations over and above self-interest is taken for granted in such rural community enterprises as the betterment of roads, schools, churches, and baseball teams. Their existence is not taken for granted, nor as yet seriously discussed, in bettering the behavior of the water that falls on the land, or in preserving of the beauty or diversity of the farm landscape. Land-use ethics are still governed wholly by economic self-interest, just as social ethics were a century ago.

To sum up: we asked the farmer to do what he conveniently could to save his soil, and he has done just that, and only that. The farmer who clears the woods off a 75 per cent slope, turns his cows into the clearing, and dumps its rainfall, rocks, and soil into the community creek, is still (if otherwise decent) a respected member of society. If he puts lime on his fields and plants his crops on contour, he is still entitled to all the privileges and emoluments of his Soil Conservation District. The District is a beautiful piece of social machinery, but it is coughing along on two cylinders because we have been too timid, and too anxious for quick success, to tell the farmer the true magnitude of his obligations. Obligations have no meaning without conscience, and the problem we face is the extension of the social conscience from people to land.

No important change in ethics was ever accomplished without an internal change in our intellectual emphasis, loyalties, affections, and convictions. The proof that conservation has not yet touched these foundations of conduct lies in the fact that philosophy and religion have not yet heard of it. In our attempt to make conservation easy, we have made it trivial.

Substitutes for a Land Ethic

When the logic of history hungers for bread and we hand out a stone, we are at pains to explain how much the stone resembles bread. I now describe some of the stones which serve in lieu of a land ethic.

One basic weakness in a conservation system based wholly on economic motives is that most members of the land community have no economic value. Wildflowers and songbirds are examples. Of the 22,000 higher plants and animals native to Wisconsin, it is doubtful whether more than 5 per cent can be sold, fed, eaten, or otherwise put to economic use. Yet these creatures are members of the biotic community, and if (as I believe) its stability depends on its integrity, they are entitled to continuance.

When one of these non-economic categories is threatened, and if we happen to love it, we invent subterfuges to give it economic importance. At the beginning of the century songbirds were supposed to be disappearing. Ornithologists jumped to the rescue with some distinctly shaky evidence to the effect that insects would eat us up if birds failed to control them. The evidence had to be economic in order to be valid.

It is painful to read these circumlocutions today. We have no land ethic yet, but we have at least drawn nearer the point of admitting that birds should continue as a matter of biotic right, regardless of the presence or absence of economic advantage to us.

A parallel situation exists in respect of predatory mammals, raptorial birds, and fish-eating birds. Time was when biologists somewhat overworked the evidence that these creatures preserve the health of game by killing weaklings, or that they control rodents for the farmer, or that they prey only on "worthless" species. Here again, the evidence had to be economic in order to be valid. It is only in recent years that we hear the more honest argument that predators are members of the community, and that no special interest has the right to exterminate them for the sake of a benefit, real or fancied, to itself. Unfortunately this enlightened view is still in the talk stage. In the field the extermination of predators goes merrily on: witness the impending erasure of the timber wolf by fiat of Congress, the Conservation Bureaus, and many state legislatures.

Some species of trees have been "read out of the party" by economics-minded foresters because they grow too slowly, or have too low a sale value to pay as timber crops: white cedar, tamarack, cypress, beech, and hemlock are examples. In Europe, where forestry is ecologically more advanced, the non-commercial tree species are recognized as members of the native forest community, to be preserved as such, within reason. Moreover some (like beech) have been found to have a valuable function in building up soil fertility. The interdependence of the forest and its constituent tree species, ground flora, and fauna is taken for granted.

Lack of economic value is sometimes a character not only of species or groups, but of entire biotic communities: marshes, bogs, dunes, and "deserts" are examples. Our formula in such cases is to relegate their conservation to government as refuges, monuments, or parks. The difficulty is that these communities are usually interspersed with more valuable private lands; the government cannot possibly own or control such scattered parcels. The net effect is that we have relegated some of them to ultimate extinction over large areas. If the private owner were ecologically minded, he would be proud to be the custodian of a reasonable proportion of such areas, which add diversity and beauty to his farm and to his community.

In some instances, the assumed lack of profit in these "waste" areas has proved to be wrong, but only after most of them had been done away with. The present scramble to reflood muskrat marshes is a case in point.

There is a clear tendency in American conservation to relegate to government all necessary jobs that private land-owners fail to perform. Government ownership, operation, subsidy, or regulation is now widely prevalent in forestry, range management, soil and watershed management, park and wilderness conservation, fisheries management, and migratory bird management, with more to come. Most of this growth in governmental conservation is proper and logical, some of it is inevitable. That I imply no disapproval of it is implicit in the fact that I have spent most of my life working for it. Nevertheless the question arises: What is the ultimate magnitude of the enterprise? Will the tax base carry its eventual ramifications? At what point will governmental conservation, like the mastodon, become handicapped by its own dimensions? The answer, if there is any, seems to be in a land ethic, or some other force which assigns more obligation to the private landowner.

Industrial landowners and users, especially lumbermen and stockmen, are inclined to wail long and loudly about the extension of government ownership and regulation to land, but (with notable exceptions) they show little disposition to develop the only visible alternative: the voluntary practice of conservation on their own lands.

When the private landowner is asked to perform some unprofitable act for the good of the community, he today assents only with outstretched palm. If the act costs him cash this is fair and proper, but when it costs only forethought, open-mindedness, or time, the issue is at least debatable. The overwhelming growth of land-use subsidies in recent years must be ascribed, in large part, to the government's own agencies for conservation education: the land bureaus, the agricultural colleges, and the extension services. As far as I can detect, no ethical obligation toward land is taught in these institutions.

To sum up: a system of conservation based solely on economic self-interest is hopelessly lopsided. It tends to ignore, and thus eventually to eliminate, many elements in the land community that lack commercial value, but that are (as far as we know) essential to its healthy functioning. It assumes, falsely, I think, that the economic parts of the biotic clock will function without the uneconomic parts. It tends to relegate to government many functions eventually too large, too complex, or too widely dispersed to be performed by government.

An ethical obligation on the part of the private owner is the only visible remedy for these situations.

The Land Pyramid

An ethic to supplement and guide the economic relation to land presupposes the existence of some mental image of land as a biotic mechanism. We can be ethical only in relation to something we can see, feel, understand, love, or otherwise have faith in.

The image commonly employed in conservation education is "the balance of nature." For reasons too lengthy to detail here, this figure of speech fails to describe accurately what little we know about the land mechanism. A much truer image is the one employed in ecology: the biotic pyramid. I shall first sketch the pyramid as a symbol of land, and later develop some of its implications in terms of land-use.

Plants absorb energy from the sun. This energy flows through a circuit called the biota, which may be represented by a pyramid consisting of layers. The bottom layer is the soil. A plant layer rests on the soil, an insect layer on the plants, a bird and rodent layer on the insects, and so on up through various animal groups to the apex layer, which consists of the larger carnivores.

The species of a layer are alike not in where they came from, or in what they look like, but rather in what they eat. Each successive layer depends on those below it for food and often for other services, and each in turn furnishes food and services to those above. Proceeding upward, each successive layer decreases in numerical abundance. Thus, for every carnivore there are hundreds of his prey, thousands of their prey, millions of insects, uncountable plants. The pyramidal form of the system reflects this numerical progression from apex to base. Man shares an intermediate layer with the bears, raccoons, and squirrels which eat both meat and vegetables.

The lines of dependency for food and other services are called food chains. Thus soil-oak-deer-Indian is a chain that has now been largely converted to soil-corn-farmer. Each species, including ourselves, is a link in many chains. The deer eats a hundred plants other than oak, and the cow a hundred plants other than corn. Both, then, are links in a hundred chains. The pyramid is a tangle of chains so complex as to seem disorderly, yet the stability of the system proves it to be a highly organized structure. Its functioning depends on the co-operation and competition of its diverse parts.

In the beginning, the pyramid of life was low and squat; the food chains short and simple. Evolution has added layer after layer, link after link. Man is one of thousands of accretions to the height and complexity of the pyramid. Science has given us many doubts, but it has given us at least one certainty: the trend of evolution is to elaborate and diversify the biota.

Land, then, is not merely soil; it is a fountain of energy flowing through a circuit of soils, plants, and animals. Food chains are the living channels which conduct energy upward; death and decay return it to the soil. The circuit is not closed; some energy is dissipated in decay, some is added by absorption from the air, some is stored in soils, peats, and long-lived forests; but it is a sustained circuit, like a slowly augmented revolving fund of life. There is always a net loss by downhill wash, but this is normally small and offset by the decay of rocks. It is deposited in the ocean and, in the course of geological time, raised to form new lands and new pyramids.

The velocity and character of the upward flow of energy depend on the complex structure of the plant and animal community, much as the upward flow of sap in a tree depends on its complex cellular organization. Without this complexity, normal circulation would presumably not occur. Structure means the characteristic numbers, as well as the characteristic kinds and functions, of the component species. This interdependence between the complex structure of the land and its smooth functioning as an energy unit is one of its basic attributes.

When a change occurs in one part of the circuit, many other parts must adjust themselves to it. Change does not necessarily obstruct or divert the flow of energy; evolution is a long series of self-induced changes, the net result of which has been to elaborate the flow mechanism and to lengthen the circuit. Evolutionary changes, however, are usually slow and local. Man's invention of tools has enabled him to make changes of unprecedented violence, rapidity, and scope.

One change is in the composition of floras and faunas. The larger predators are lopped off the apex of the pyramid; food chains, for the first time in history, become shorter rather than longer. Domesticated species from other lands are substituted for wild ones, and wild ones are moved to new habitats. In this world-wide pooling of faunas and floras, some species get out of bounds as pests and diseases, others are extinguished. Such effects are seldom intended or foreseen; they represent unpredicted and often untraceable readjustments in the structure. Agricultural science is largely a race between the emergence of new pests and the emergence of new techniques for their control.

Another change touches the flow of energy through plants and animals and its return to the soil. Fertility is the ability of soil to receive, store, and release energy. Agriculture, by overdrafts on the soil, or by too radical a substitution of domestic for native species in the superstructure, may derange the channels of flow or deplete storage. Soils depleted of their storage, or of the organic matter which anchors it, wash away faster than they form. This is erosion.

Waters, like soil, are part of the energy circuit. Industry, by polluting waters or obstructing them with dams, may exclude the plants and animals necessary to keep energy in circulation.

Transportation brings about another basic change: the plants or animals grown in one region are now consumed and returned to the soil in another. Transportation taps the energy stored in rocks, and in the air, and uses it elsewhere; thus we fertilize the garden with nitrogen gleaned by the guano birds from the fishes of seas on the other side of the Equator. Thus the formerly localized and self-contained circuits are pooled on a world-wide scale.

The process of altering the pyramid for human occupation releases stored energy, and this often gives rise, during the pioneering period, to a deceptive exuberance of plant and animal life, both wild and tame. These releases of biotic capital tend to becloud or postpone the penalties of violence.

This thumbnail sketch of land as an energy circuit conveys three basic ideas:

1. That land is not merely soil.
2. That the native plants and animals kept the energy circuit open; others may or may not.
3. That man-made changes are of a different order than evolutionary changes, and have effects more comprehensive than is intended or foreseen.

These ideas, collectively, raise two basic issues: Can the land adjust itself to the new order? Can the desired alterations be accomplished with less violence?

Biotas seem to differ in their capacity to sustain violent conversion. Western Europe, for example, carries a far different pyramid than Caesar found there. Some large animals are lost; swampy forests have become meadows or plowland; many new plants and animals are introduced, some of which escape as pests; the remaining natives are greatly changed in distribution and abundance. Yet the soil is still there and, with the help of imported nutrients, still fertile; the waters flow normally; the new structure seems to function and to persist. There is no visible stoppage or derangement of the circuit.

Western Europe, then, has a resistant biota. Its inner processes are tough, elastic, resistant to strain. No matter how violent the alterations, the pyramid, so far, has developed some new *modus vivendi* which preserves its habitability for man, and for most of the other natives.

Japan seems to present another instance of radical conversion without disorganization.

Most other civilized regions, and some as yet barely touched by civilization, display various stages of disorganization, varying from initial symptoms to advanced wastage. In Asia Minor and North Africa diagnosis is confused by climatic changes, which may have been either the cause or the effect of advanced wastage. In the United States the degree of disorganization varies locally; it is worst in the Southwest, the Ozarks, and parts of the South, and least in New England and the Northwest. Better land-uses may still arrest it in the less advanced regions. In parts of Mexico, South America, South Africa, and Australia a violent and accelerating wastage is in progress, but I cannot assess the prospects.

This almost world-wide display of disorganization in the land seems to be similar to disease in an animal, except that it never culminates in complete disorganization or death. The land recovers, but at some reduced level of complexity, and with a reduced carrying capacity for people, plants, and animals. Many biotas currently regarded as "lands of opportunity" are in fact already subsisting on exploitative agriculture, i.e., they have already exceeded their sustained carrying capacity. Most of South America is overpopulated in this sense.

In arid regions we attempt to offset the process of wastage by reclamation, but it is only too evident that the prospective longevity of reclamation projects is often short. In our own West, the best of them may not last a century.

The combined evidence of history and ecology seems to support one general deduction: the less violent the man-made changes, the greater the probability of successful readjustment in the pyramid. Violence, in turn, varies with human population density; a dense population requires a more violent conversion. In this respect, North America has a better chance for permanence than Europe, if she can contrive to limit her density.

This deduction runs counter to our current philosophy, which assumes that because a small increase in density enriched human life, that an indefinite increase will enrich it indefinitely. Ecology knows of no density relationship that holds for indefinitely wide limits. All gains from density are subject to a law of diminishing returns.

Whatever may be the equation for men and land, it is improbable that we as yet know all its terms. Recent discoveries in mineral and vitamin nutrition reveal unsuspected dependencies in the up-circuit: incredibly minute quantities of certain substances determine the value of soils to plants, of plants to animals. What of the down-circuit? What of the vanishing species, the preservation of which we now regard as an esthetic luxury? They helped build the soil; in what unsuspected ways may they be essential to its maintenance? Professor Weaver proposes that we use prairie flowers to reflocculate the wasting soils of the dust bowl; who knows for what purpose cranes and condors, otters and grizzlies may some day be used?

Land Health and the A–B Cleavage

A land ethic, then, reflects the existence of an ecological conscience, and this in turn reflects a conviction of individual responsibility for the health of the land. Health is the capacity of the land for self-renewal. Conservation is our effort to understand and preserve this capacity.

Conservationists are notorious for their dissensions. Superficially these seem to add up to mere confusion, but a more careful scrutiny reveals a single plane of cleavage common to many specialized fields. In each field one group (A) regards the land as soil, and its function as commodity-production; another group (B) regards the land as a biota, and its function as something broader. How much broader is admittedly in a state of doubt and confusion.

In my own field, forestry, group A is quite content to grow trees like cabbages, with cellulose as the basic forest commodity. It feels no inhibition against violence; its ideology is agronomic. Group B, on the other hand, sees forestry as fundamentally different from agronomy because it employs natural species, and manages a natural environment rather than creating an artificial one. Group B prefers natural reproduction on principle. It worries on biotic as well as economic grounds about the loss of species like chestnut, and the threatened loss of the white pines. It worries about a whole series of secondary forest functions: wildlife, recreation, watersheds, wilderness areas. To my mind, Group B feels the stirrings of an ecological conscience.

In the wildlife field, a parallel cleavage exists. For Group A the basic commodities are sport and meat; the yardsticks of production are ciphers of take in pheasants and trout. Artificial propagation is acceptable as a permanent as well as a temporary recourse—if its unit costs permit. Group B, on the other hand, worries about a whole series of biotic side-issues. What is the cost in predators of producing a game crop? Should we have further recourse to exotics? How can management restores the shrinking species, like prairie grouse, already hopeless as shootable game? How can management restore the threatened rarities, like trumpeter swan and whooping crane? Can management principles be extended to wildflowers? Here again it is clear to me that we have the same A-B cleavage as in forestry.

In the larger field of agriculture I am less competent to speak, but there seem to be somewhat parallel cleavages. Scientific agriculture was actively developing before ecology was born, hence a slower penetration of ecological concepts might be expected. Moreover the farmer, by the very nature of his techniques, must modify the biota more radically than the forester or the wildlife manager. Nevertheless, there are many discontents in agriculture which seem to add up to a new vision of "biotic farming."

Perhaps the most important of these is the new evidence that poundage or tonnage is no measure of the food-value of farm crops; the products of fertile soil may be qualitatively as well as quantitatively superior. We can bolster poundage from depleted soils by pouring on imported fertility, but we are not necessarily bolstering food-value. The possible ultimate ramifications of this idea are so immense that I must leave their exposition to abler pens.

The discontent that labels itself "organic farming," while bearing some of the earmarks of a cult, is nevertheless biotic in its direction, particularly in its insistence on the importance of soil flora and fauna.

The ecological fundamentals of agriculture are just as poorly known to the public as in other fields of land-use. For example, few educated people realize that the marvelous advances in technique made during recent decades are improvements in the pump, rather than the well. Acre for acre, they have barely sufficed to offset the sinking level of fertility.

In all of these cleavages, we see repeated the same basic paradoxes: man the conqueror *versus* man the biotic citizen; science the sharpener of his sword *versus* science the searchlight on his universe; land the slave and servant *versus* land the collective organism. Robinson's injunction to Tristram may well be applied, at this juncture, to *Homo sapiens* as a species in geological time:

> Whether you will or not
> You are a King, Tristram, for you are one
> Of the time-tested few that leave the world,
> When they are gone, not the same place it was.
> Mark what you leave.
> [Edwin Arlington Robinson, *Tristram*]

The Outlook

It is inconceivable to me that an ethical relation to land can exist without love, respect, and admiration for land, and a high regard for its value. By value, I of course mean something far broader than mere economic value; I mean value in the philosophical sense.

Perhaps the most serious obstacle impeding the evolution of a land ethic is the fact that our educational and economic system is headed away from, rather than toward, an intense consciousness of land. Your true modern is separated from the land by many middlemen, and by innumerable physical gadgets. He has no vital relation to it; to him it is the space between cities on which crops grow. Turn him loose for a day on the land, and if the spot does not happen to be a golf links or a "scenic" area, he is bored stiff. If crops could be raised by hydroponics instead of farming, it would suit him very well. Synthetic substitutes for wood, leather, wool, and other natural land products suit him better than the originals. In short, land is something he has "outgrown."

Almost equally serious as an obstacle to a land ethic is the attitude of the farmer for whom the land is still an adversary, or a taskmaster that keeps him in slavery. Theoretically, the mechanization of farming ought to cut the farmer's chains, but whether it really does is debatable.

One of the requisites for an ecological comprehension of land is an understanding of ecology, and this is by no means co-extensive with "education"; in fact, much higher education seems deliberately to avoid ecological concepts. An understanding of ecology does not necessarily originate in courses bearing ecological labels; it is quite as likely to be labeled geography, botany, agronomy, history, or economics. This is as it should be, but whatever the label, ecological training is scarce.

The case for a land ethic would appear hopeless but for the minority which is in obvious revolt against these "modern" trends.

The "key-log" which must be moved to release the evolutionary process for an ethic is simply this: quit thinking about decent land-use as solely an economic problem. Examine each question in terms of what is ethically and esthetically right, as well as what is economically expedient. A thing is right when it tends to preserve the integrity, stability, and beauty of the biotic community. It is wrong when it tends otherwise.

Of course, it goes without saying that economic feasibility limits the tether of what can or cannot be done for land. It always has and it always will. The fallacy the economic determinists have tied around our collective necks, and which we now need to cast off, is the belief that economics determines *all* land-use. This is simply not true. An innumerable host of actions and attitudes, comprising perhaps the bulk of all land relations, is determined by the land-users' tastes and predilections, rather than by their purses. The bulk of all land relations hinges on investments of time, forethought, skill, and faith rather than on investments of cash. As a land-user thinketh, so is he.

I have purposely presented the land ethic as a product of social evolution because nothing so important as an ethic is ever "written." Only the most superficial student of history supposes that Moses "wrote" the Decalogue; it evolved in the minds of a thinking community, and Moses wrote a tentative summary of it for a "seminar." I say tentative because evolution never stops.

The evolution of a land ethic is an intellectual as well as emotional process. Conservation is paved with good intentions which prove to be futile, or even dangerous, because they are devoid of critical understanding either of the land, or of economic land-use. I think it is a truism that as the ethical frontier advances from the individual to the community, its intellectual content increases.

The mechanism of operation is the same for any ethic: social approbation for right actions: social disapproval for wrong actions.

By and large, our present problem is one of attitudes and implements. We are remodeling the Alhambra with a steamshovel, and we are proud of our yardage. We shall hardly relinquish the shovel, which after all has many good points, but we are in need of gentler and more objective criteria for its successful use.

Part II

Two Philosophical Issues in Forestry Ethics

The awareness that American society was in an environmental crisis had been building for some years after World War II but, for the most part, the condition of the environment did not become a significant public worry until 1962 when Rachel Carson's book *Silent Spring* exploded on the national scene and sounded the alarm about the dangers of chemical contamination of our "total environment."[1] Others chimed in, including such prominent public figures as Stewart Udall, Secretary of the Interior under President John F. Kennedy. Udall elaborated on the theme that America was undergoing what he called "the quiet conservation crisis of the 1960s," which meant that we were living in "a land of vanishing beauty, of increasing ugliness, of shrinking open space, and of an overall environment that is diminished daily by pollution and noise and blight."[2] Americans, in short, were fowling their own nest, and the time had come to do something about it. Udall quoted Aldo Leopold and concluded that we needed to develop a new land ethic.

As was the case with other political issues disturbing Americans at that time, many argued that the environmental crisis was not only a crisis in laws, institutions, and behavior, but a spiritual and philosophical crisis, and that the solution to our problems was to develop new philosophies and new interpretations of our religious traditions that could motivate new social and economic behavior. During the 1960s, some religious thinkers took up the idea that Christianity and Judaism needed to be reinterpreted to account for new understandings of human-nature relationships.[3] It also became more and more common to hear talk about the need for changes in society's secular ecological consciousness as well. It is in this kind of social climate, then, that the subjects of environmental ethics and environmental philosophy were born.

1. Rachel Carson, *Silent Spring* (Boston: Houghton Mifflin Company, 1962).
2. Stewart Udall, *The Quiet Crisis* (New York: Holt, Rinehart and Winston, 1963), p. viii.
3. Roderick Nash, *The Rights of Nature* (1989), chap. 4.

One pinnacle of public concern about the environmental crisis was reached during the first Earth Day in April 1970 when many public figures and other observers argued that our society needed some sort of intellectual revolution in our attitudes toward the environment.[4] However, with one or two exceptions, such as the philosopher Charles Hartshorne, it took academic philosophers nearly a decade after *Silent Spring* to turn their professional attention to the environmental crisis and another nine years after Earth Day 1970 for the subject of environmental ethics to blossom into a more full-fledged academic endeavor with the first issue of the new journal *Environmental Ethics*.[5] It took even more time for the environment to be taken seriously as a legitimate philosophical subject in established professional journals, philosophy departments, and philosophy conferences. In short, academic philosophy in North America lagged behind social debate and some other fields of inquiry in turning its focus toward environmental problems.[6] In time, however, discussions of philosophical and practical issues about the environment blossomed into a specialty within academic philosophy in several parts of the world.

It is difficult to identify exactly who first began to seriously discuss environmental issues within academic philosophy. With regard to college education, courses on environmental subjects and environmental studies could be found outside of philosophy curricula well before 1970, but in philosophy the beginning of curricular interest is more realistically the early 1970s. One important figure in this field, J. Baird Callicott, has noted that he was one of the first to teach a course on environmental ethics in the United States, in 1971. However, there were some other philosophers who had an interest in such environmental subjects as wilderness and taught courses on the subject before this date.[7]

---

4. Expressions of concern at the time can be found in such popular books as Garrett De Bell, ed., *The Environmental Handbook* (New York: Ballantine Books, Inc., 1970), which was prepared for the first national environmental teach-in on Earth Day, April 22, 1970, and *Earth Day: The Beginning* (New York: Bantam Books, 1970), a "guide for survival compiled and edited by the National Staff of Environmental Action."

5. Roderick Nash, *The Rights of Nature*, p. 99.

6. Very early philosophy conferences include one held at the University of Georgia in February 1971, which focused on the "environmental crisis" and resulted in the anthology edited by William T. Blackstone, *Philosophy and Environmental Crisis* (Athens: University of Georgia Press, 1974). Another was an interdisciplinary conference at Oregon State University in May 1973 that involved philosophers, social scientists, and historians and centered on economic and environmental issues concerning the quality of life. These conference talks were published in Ronald O. Clarke and Peter C. List, eds., *Environmental Spectrum: Social and Economic Views on the Quality of Life* (New York: D. Van Nostrand Company, 1974).

7. One example is the philosopher John Hammond, now retired from the Philosophy Department at Portland State University in Portland, Oregon, who in the late 1960s taught a course on wilderness philosophies. I was one of three instructors in an interdisciplinary course in environmental studies at Oregon State University in 1972 that dealt with issues of the "rights of nature," among other philosophical topics. In 1975 I began to teach a new course—"The Land Ethic in America"—that eventually was revised and taught as a basic course in environmental ethics. The philosophy curriculum at our university now includes four regular courses on this subject, in addition to related courses in science and policy.

The first controversies in environmental ethics and environmental philosophy in the early 1970s included the following questions: First and foremost, what makes the environmental crisis a moral issue? And, if it is, why do we have moral obligations to protect and preserve natural environments? That is, what arguments can be constructed to bolster such responsibilities? Moreover, if environmental matters are morally important and conservation is a kind of ethical duty, how should that affect the way we conceive of traditional ethics and ethical systems? Can the principles and values in Western ethical systems be used to reflect about nature, or do they need to be amended, overhauled, or even thrown out completely? In short, do we need a "transvaluation of values," a "new" ethic fundamentally different from any system that we have had before in Western culture? Or are there already sufficient intellectual bases for reforming and refashioning ethical concepts in our established philosophical and religious systems?[8] Additionally, what kind of factual and scientific basis should be utilized to properly redefine ethical thinking about the environment or nature? And finally, what changes in our personal behavior and in our social, legal, and political institutions are needed to accomplish this ethical transformation of our society?

These issues revolved around the question of how one might define an environmental ethic or a new environmental philosophy and how one might trace out the implications of this for human life and society. Unfortunately, despite Western philosophy's achievements in providing foundations for other kinds of inquiries in the physical and social sciences over the centuries, and its role in helping to shape the intellectual foundations of Western culture otherwise, it was not very clear that it had the conceptual resources to answer these questions. One philosophical pioneer in this field even argued that Western philosophy had "consistently failed to provide a foundation for environmental thought throughout the course of Western civilization."[9] Surely, then, these fundamental questions were important and would both require and repay serious philosophical attention.

While it would be impractical to include in this anthology samples of philosophical reflections on all of the issues debated in environmental ethics since the early 1970s,

8. This issue was perhaps first broached in academic philosophy by the Australian philosopher Richard Routley in "Is there a need for a new, an environmental, ethic?" *Proceedings of the XVth World Congress of Philosophy*, Varna, Bulgaria, Vol. 1 (1973): 205–10. Along with some philosophers in North America, some Australian philosophers have long had a strong interest in environmental ethics and environmental philosophy.

9. Eugene Hargrove, *Foundations of Environmental Ethics* (Englewood Cliffs, N.J.: Prentice-Hall, 1989), p. 44. However, there have been many efforts in recent years to return to some of the ideas of the leading figures in the history of Western philosophy, to mine them for basic concepts that can support environmental philosophy. Thus, some of the more important European philosophers, such as Martin Heidegger, have been studied with this purpose in mind, but earlier thinkers such as Benedict Spinoza, Aristotle, and even Immanuel Kant have been included as well. David Abram, *The Spell of the Sensuous* (New York: Pantheon, 1996), provides one example of such a reinterpretation. Nonwestern philosophy and nonwestern worldviews have also provided a fruitful source of ideas. A good illustration of this point is J. Baird Callicott, *Earth's Insights: A Multicultural Survey of Ecological Ethics from the Mediterranean Basin to the Australian Outback* (Berkeley: University of California Press, 1994).

several key contributions by philosophers and more philosophically-minded foresters that directly address issues about the ethics of using forests and forestry ethics are anthologized in this and subsequent parts of the book.[10] The selections in Part Two consider the following important philosophical questions with regard to forests and their components: What kinds of values exist in forests? Do trees have intrinsic value? And do they have rights?

These are obviously controversial and contentious issues socially, and environmental philosophers have disagreed about them as well; however, they also represent some of the earliest and most intriguing issues tackled in environmental ethics. Moreover, answers to them lie behind debates about what specific values ought to be promoted, maintained, or preserved in forests, by foresters and forest users. If values deeper than economic values exist in forests—as, for example, Leopold, Muir, and many others have noted—then it would follow that we should take them into account, especially if we seek a more holistic way of relating to forests. If it makes sense to say that the components of forests, including plant and animal species and forest ecosystems, have intrinsic value and also moral or legal rights, it would follow that they are entitled to greater protections and more sensitive use than they have typically received in personal interactions with forests, in management prescriptions, and in legal systems.

---

10. Readers interested in learning more about the broad range of questions addressed in this field and some of the answers given by philosophers should consult some of the standard anthologies in environmental ethics. See the Selected Bibliography at the end of this volume for sources.

CHAPTER 4

Multiple Values in Forests

The idea that the values in forests consist primarily of those that have instrumental and economic significance for humans is, of course, a central feature of the philosophy of resource conservation, as formulated by Fernow, Pinchot, and other foresters. In this view, forests are mostly resources to be used by humans for economic and commercial purposes. However, human societies and foresters have rarely confined their catalogue of forest values to the utilitarian and anthropocentric alone, even when economic values have the highest priority in their value hierarchies or schemes. The tendency to locate more deep and varied values in nature is a common one, and one that has become commonplace as well in contemporary environmental ethics and even in pronouncements about government-directed ecosystem management. As William R. Burch, Jr., a professor of natural resource management at Yale University, noted some years ago, although forests have always had economic and survival value to humans, there is also a "more mysterious, complex, subtle, and intimate relationship between the life of a forest and the life of human society." The social meanings of forests are actually quite diverse and include their use as personal and social metaphors, locales for managing potentially threatening groups of humans, seedbeds of larger social changes, and "leisure settings where the social bond is established and maintained."[1]

Philosophical perspectives about the kinds of forest values thus reveal different levels of breadth; some delimit these values rather narrowly while others more broadly encompass quite a variety of values and valuing behavior. Muir, Leopold, the deep ecologists, and ecofeminists all extend the idea of forest values beyond the utilitarian and merely commercial to include the spiritual, aesthetic, and intrinsic.[2] In the land ethic section of *A Sand County Almanac* Leopold identifies three kinds of value categories in the biotic community: economic, aesthetic, and ecological. He suggests that efforts to find economic value in some parts of the community are bound to be artificial and to fail, but he also argues that, unfortunately, commodification of the

---

1. William R. Burch, Jr., "The Social Meanings of Forests," *The Humanist,* 39(6) (Nov./Dec. 1979): 39–44. For example, recent research by Earl Leatherberry, of the USDA Forest Service, North Central Experiment Station, indicates that forests were refuges for escaped slaves and also safe locations for religious ceremonies of African Americans during the slavery era of U.S. history.

2. Leopold's essay "Goose Music" in *A Sand County Almanac* is a good example of this.

land is the primary means by which the land has been valued in our society, at least before a true land ethic becomes part of our future social evolution. To Leopold, we need to realize that economic value exists and is important, but in a land ethic this kind of value is only one of the values that we should consider in evaluating human actions in and toward the land. As he put it, we should "quit thinking about decent land-use as solely an economic problem. Examine each question in terms of what is ethically and ethically right, as well as what is economically expedient. A thing is right when it tends to preserve the integrity, stability and beauty of the biotic community. It is wrong when it tends otherwise."[3] The point is that a heavy emphasis on economic valuation and values distorts the ethical and ecological consideration of what is best for us to do with regard to the earth. There are other significant values in nature, and some of them should take precedence over the economic, especially when the ecological integrity and health of the land and its components are at stake.

The idea that there are multiple values in nature is now a commonplace belief in environmental studies, the natural resource disciplines, and the applied environmental sciences, and this broader conception of values is present in the writings of one of our foremost figures in environmental ethics, Holmes Rolston III. Rolston is a distinguished professor of philosophy at Colorado State University and author of numerous influential essays on environmental philosophy, including an original and groundbreaking book in the field, *Environmental Ethics*.[4] He is one of the few environmental philosophers in academia to have written extensively about forests and forestry. In the first reading selection below, he applies his formal analysis of the types of values carried by nature generally to forests specifically.[5] In the second selection Rolston characterizes human aesthetic experience in forests as requiring a kind of active engagement that is different than in the case of experiencing human art objects. He describes the "sense of the sublime" that we feel in forests, whether wild or managed, and connects this emotion to a "sacred" value in forests that is "natural." This broader and also deeper approach to forest values and forest valuing reflects the manifold value categories that the American public holds with regard to forests.[6]

---

3. Leopold, *A Sand County Almanac*, p. 224.

4. Holmes Rolston III, *Environmental Ethics: Duties to and Values in the Natural World* (Philadelphia: Temple University Press, 1988). Some of his many illuminating and poetic essays are collected together in another book, *Philosophy Gone Wild: Essays in Environmental Ethics* (Buffalo: Prometheus Books, 1986).

5. Rolston's original analysis is presented in *Environmental Ethics: Duties to and Values in the Natural World* (1988), chap. 1.

6. See, e.g., Brent Steel, Peter List, and Bruce Shindler, "Conflicting Values about Federal Forests: A Comparison of National and Oregon Publics," *Society and Natural Resources*, 7 (1994): 137–53.

Holmes Rolston III

Values Deep in the Woods

In a forest, as on a desert or the tundra, the realities of nature cannot be ignored. Like the sea or the sky, the forest is a kind of archetype of the foundations of the world. Aboriginally, about 60 percent of the Earth's land surface was forested; historically, forests go back 300 to 400 million years. Humans evolved in forests and savannas, where they once had adaptive fitness, and classical cultures often remained in evident contact with forests. In modern cultures, the growth of technology has made the forest increasingly a commodity, decreasingly an archetype. That transformation results in profound value puzzlements. What values lie deep in the forest?

The forest is about as near to an ultimate archetype as we know. I become astonished by the fact that the forest is here, spontaneously generated. There are no forests on Mars or Saturn, none elsewhere in our solar system, perhaps none in our galaxy. But Earth's forests are indisputably here. There is more operational organization, more genetic history in a handful of forest humus than in the rest of the universe, so far as we know. How so? Why? A forest wilderness elicits cosmic questions.

The central goods of the biosphere—hydrologic cycles, photosynthesis, soil fertility, food chains, genetic codes, speciation, reproduction, succession—were in place long before humans arrived. The dynamics and structures organizing the forest do not come out of the human mind; a wild forest is wholly other than civilization. Confronting it, I must penetrate spontaneous life on its own terms. The genius of forestry as a pure science helps us to appreciate the biology, ecology, integrity of the forest primeval. Immersed in a nonhuman frame of reference, foresters know the elements, raw and pure.

Applied forestry, making a commodity out of an archetype, is humane and benevolent at risk of prostituting the primeval. The principles reorganizing the managed forest do come out of the human mind. Seeking goods of their kind, humans modify the natural kinds. A domesticated forest, like a caged wolf, is something of a contradiction in terms. What used to be a forest or wolf is thus reduced to something less. A tract of pine planted for paper pulp is not deep woods. The radical values are gone.

Holmes Rolston III, "Values Deep in the Woods," *American Forests* 94 (5&6) (May/June 1988): 33, 66–69. Reprinted with permission from Holmes Rolston III.

In the forest itself there are no board-feet of timber, BTUs, miles, or acre-feet of water. There are trees rising toward the sky, birds on the wing, and beasts on the run, age after age, impelled by a genetic language almost two billion years old. There is struggle and adaptive fitness, energy and evolution inventing fertility and prowess. There is cellulose and photosynthesis, succession and speciation, muscle and fat, smell and appetite, law and form, structure and process. There is light and dark, life and death, the mystery of existence.

A forest is objectively a community. Only subjectively, with human preferences projected onto it, does it become a commodity. "Forest products" are secondarily lumber, turpentine, cellophane; the forest "produces" primarily aspen, ferns, squirrels, mushrooms. This life is never self-contained but incessantly ingests and eliminates its environment. Trees must photosynthesize, and coyotes must eat. The flora, like the fauna, make resources of soil, air, water, nutrients. Many species have found homes in the forest ecosystem, life-supporting niches into which they are well fitted. This objective satisfaction of life occurs with or without our human experiences. That the forest is able on occasion to satisfy human preferences seems a spinoff from its being able to satisfy biological needs of its own processes.

There can no longer be found about five hundred faunal species and subspecies that have become extinct in the United States since 1600, and another five hundred threatened and endangered species are rarely found. Hardly a stretch of forest in the nation is unimpoverished of its native species—especially those at the top of trophic pyramids: otters and peregrine falcons. We have only scraps of undisturbed once-common ecosystems, such as hemlock forests, and no chestnut forests at all. Acid rain is impoverishing the Adirondacks and the Great Smokies. An area of tropical rainforests the size of West Virginia is being destroyed annually.

All this ought not to be. Rather, forests ought to be optimally rich in native fauna and flora, in community types, and some forest ecosystems should remain intact to support grizzly bears, wolverines, red-cockaded woodpeckers, Chapman's rhododendron. What the forest produces is individuals; but at a deeper level, what the forest has produced is species and ecosystems. Extinction shuts down forever life lines that flowed over the continental landscape long before humans arrived and that might, apart from us—or together with us, were we more sensitive—continue for millennia henceforth.

A pristine forest is a historical museum that, unlike cultural museums, continues to be what it was, a living landscape. A visit there contributes to the human sense of duration, antiquity, continuity, and our own late-coming novelty. The forest—we first may think—is prehistoric and timeless; world history begins with armies and kings. The perceptive forest visitor knows better and realizes the centuries-long forest successions, the age of sequoias or great oaks; he sees erosional and geomorphic processes in rock strata, canyon walls, glacial moraines. The Carboniferous Forests were giant club mosses and horsetails; the Jurassic Forests were gymnosperms—conifers, cycads, ginkgoes, seed ferns. A forest today is yesterday being transformed into tomorrow.

Each forest is unique. Forest types exist only in forestry textbooks; what exists in the world is Mount Monadnock, Tallulah Gorge with its unique colonies of *Trillium persistens,* Mobley Hollow on Sinking Creek. Forests with their proper names and locales—Grandfather Mountain, or Chattahoochee National Forest—always exist specifically, never abstractly. When visited by persons with their proper names, the encounter is valued because it yields distinctive, never-repeated stories—the biography of John Muir in the Sierras, or one's vacation spent hiking the Appalachian Trail.

At least half of what is to be known about forests remains undiscovered. Successive levels of biological organization have properties that cannot be predicted from simpler levels, and the least-known level of organization is that of landscape ecology. Do forests inevitably appear, given a suitable moisture and climatic regime? We are not sure why tree line lies at the elevations it does, or why the balds in southern Appalachians are there. We are beginning to suspect that insect outbreaks sometimes convey benefits to a forest, something like those of fires, and of which we were long unaware.

Does diversity increase over time? Does stability? Do the species at the top of trophic pyramids rise in complexity? In neural power? All this seems to have happened, but why we do not know. Biologists are divided over whether intraspecific or interspecific competition is a minimal or a major force in evolution. Sizable natural systems are the likeliest places to settle such debates. To destroy the relict primeval forests is like tearing the last pages out of a book about our past that we hardly yet know how to read.

Like clouds, seashores, and mountains, forests are never ugly; they are only more or less beautiful; the scale runs from zero upward with no negative domain. Destroyed forests can be ugly—a burned, windthrown, diseased, or clearcut forest. But even the ruined forest, regenerating itself, has yet positive aesthetic properties; trees rise to fill the empty place against the sky. A forest is filled with organisms that are marred and ragged—oaks with broken limbs, a crushed violet, the carcass of an elk. But the word "forest" (a grander word than "trees" in the plural) forces retrospect and prospect; it invites holistic categories of interpretation as yesterday's flora and fauna pass into tomorrow. This softens the ugliness and sets it in somber beauty.

One has to appreciate what is not evident. Marvelous things are going on in dead wood, or underground, or in the dark, or microscopically, or slowly, over time; they are not scenic, but an appreciation of them is aesthetic. The usefulness of a tree is only half over at its death; an old snag provides nesting cavities, perches, insect larvae, and food for birds. The gnarled spruce at the edge of the tundra is not really ugly, not unless endurance and strength are ugly. It is presence and symbol of life perpetually renewed before the winds that blast it.

In the primeval forest humans know the most authentic of wilderness emotions, the sense of the sublime. By contrast, few persons get goose pimples indoors, in art museums, or at the city park. We will not be surprised if the quality of such experiences is hard to quantify. Almost by definition, the sublime runs off scale.

The word *recreation* contains the word *creation*. Humans go outdoors for the repair of what happens indoors, but they also go outdoors because they seek something greater than can be found indoors—contact with the natural certainties. Forests and sky, rivers and earth, the everlasting hills, the cycling seasons, wildflowers and wildlife—these are superficially just pleasant scenes in which to recreate. They are the timeless natural givens that support everything else.

Those who recreate here value leisure (watching a sunset, listening to loons, or to rain) in contrast to working; they value being in a wild world that runs itself and need not be labored over. They value work (climbing, setting up camp) with no paycheck attached; an environment with uncertainties, in contrast to a boring or familiar job. They value an escape, also being drawn to roots. They want to know the weather, protected by minimal cover and shelter so as to leave rain or sun close at hand. They want to submit to the closing day at dusk, to be roused by the rising sun without benefit of clock. They want to know the passing seasons when migrants return, or leaves fall, without benefit of calendar.

People like to recreate in the woods because they touch base with something missing on baseball diamonds and at bowling alleys—the signature of time and eternity.

It is no accident that many organizations that seek to form character use wildlands—Boy and Girl Scouts, Outward Bound, the National Outdoor Leadership School, church camps. Similar growth occurs in individuals independently of formal organizations. The forest provides a place to sweat, to push oneself more than usual, to be more on the alert, to take calculated risks, to learn the luck of the weather, to lose and find one's way. The forest teaches one to care about his or her physical condition. In the forest one has no status or reputation; nobody is much or long deceived; nobody has to be pleased; accomplishment and failure are evident. One is free to be himself or herself, forced to a penetrating sincerity.

Surrounded by politicians and economists, even by foresters at their business, one gets lured into thinking that value enters and exits with human preference satisfactions. Surrounded by the forest, a deeper conclusion seems irresistible. The forest is value-laden. Trees use water and sunshine; insects resourcefully tap the energy fixed by photosynthesis; warblers search out insect protein; falcons search for warblers. Organisms use other organisms and abiotic resources instrumentally.

Continuing this deeper logic, organisms value the resources they use instrumentally because they value something intrinsically and without further contributory references: their own lives. No warbler eats insects in order to become food for a falcon; the warbler defends her own life as an end in itself and makes more warblers as she can. A warbler is not "for" anything else; a warbler is for herself. From the perspective of a warbler, being a warbler is a good thing.

Biological conservation is not something that originates in the human mind, modeled by FORPLAN programs or written into Acts of Congress. Biological conservation is innate as every organism conserves, values its life. Nonconservation is death. From this more objective viewpoint, there is something subjective and naive (however sophisticated one's technology) about living in a reference frame where one species takes itself as absolute and values everything else relative to its utility.

True, warblers take a warbler-centric point of view; spruce push only to make more spruce. But no nonhuman organism has the cognitive power, much less the conscience, to lift itself outside its own sector and evaluate the whole. Humans are the only species that can see the forest for what it is in itself, objectively, a tapestry of interwoven values. Forestry ought to be one profession that gets rescued from this beguiling anthropocentrism through its daily contact with the primeval givens.

"The groves were God's first temples" (Bryant, *A Forest Hymn*). Trees pierce the sky, like cathedral spires. Light filters down, as through stained glass. In common with churches, forests (as do sea and sky) invite transcending the human world and experiencing a comprehensive, embracing realm. Forests can serve as a more provocative, perennial sign of this than many of the traditional, often outworn, symbols devised by the churches. Mountaintop experiences, a howling storm, a quiet snowfall, solitude in a sequoia grove, an overflight of honking geese—these generate experiences of "a motion and a spirit that impels . . . and rolls through all things" (Wordsworth, *Lines Above Tintern Abbey*).

Such values are, it is commonly said, "soft" beside the "hard" values of commerce. They are vague, subjective, impossible to quantify or demonstrate. Perhaps. But what is really meant is that such values lie deep. The forest is where the "roots" are, where life rises from the ground. A wild forest is, after all, something objectively there. Beside it, culture with its artifacts is a tissue of subjective preference satisfactions. Money, often thought the hardest of values, is nothing in the wilderness. A dollar bill has value only intersubjectively; any who doubt this ought to try to spend one in the woods. Dollar values have no significance at all in the forest (and therefore in pure forestry).

The phenomenon of forests is so widespread, persistent, and diverse—appearing almost wherever moisture and climatic conditions permit it—that forests cannot be accidents or anomalies but rather must be a characteristic, systemic expression of the creative process. Forests are primarily an objective sign of the ultimate sources, and only secondarily do they become managed resources. The measure with which forestry can be profound is the depth of this conviction.

Holmes Rolston III

Aesthetic Experience in Forests

I. The Forest as an Archetype

Like the sea or the sky, the forest is a kind of archetype of the foundations of the world. The forest represents—more literally it re-presents, presents again to those who enter it—the elemental forces of nature. Such experience serves well as instance and prototype of the aesthetic appreciation of nature.

Forests bear the signature of time and eternity. Forests take one back through the centuries; or, put another way, they bring the historic and prehistoric past forward for present encounter. This is grander time than most persons usually realize, but that ancient past is subliminally there; confronting forest giants we realize that trees live on radically different scales of time than do we. Trees have no sense of duration, experienced time; they nevertheless endure.

Forests take time by the decades and centuries, compared to the way humans take time by the days and years. The scale is at once of incremental and vast time; in a forest there is seldom any front-page news—perhaps a fire or a storm—but most of life goes on over larger time frames. Trees do not grow overnight; the big oaks in New England were there at the founding of the Republic. The towering Douglas firs in the Pacific Northwest were seedlings when Columbus sailed; sequoias can predate the launching of Christianity.

This becomes deep time. Paleontologically, forests go back three to four hundred million years. Land plants first appeared in the Silurian Period and remained close to the ground, like mosses and liverworts, until the Devonian Period, when we earliest date fossil wood. Considerable evolutionary achievement was required to organize cells, the earliest unit of life, into organisms as rigid and massive as trees. Large, erect plants need the strength of cellulose and also vascular columns up which they can pump water and nutrients.

Dry seasons and winters have to be reckoned with. The cross-fertilization in earlier forms of life had been accomplished in the water. In the tree ferns and in the cycads, which remain yet in Australian and African forests, fertilization still took place in water droplets; only in later conifers do trees work out ways, with insects and wind, to pollinate in the open air. These

---

Holmes Rolston III, "Aesthetic Experience in Forests," *Journal of Aesthetics and Art Criticism* 56(2) (Spring 1998): 157–66. Reprinted with permission from The American Society for Aesthetics.

problems are solved and forests have been persistently present since Middle Devonian times. They have been continuously in place in tropical climates, provided that the landscapes have remained well watered. In temperate and boreal climates forests have tracked ice sheets as they advanced and retreated, the forests returning millennia after millennia.

This deeper sense of time presents an aesthetic challenge. In ways radically unlike the aesthetic appreciation of crafted art objects—whether recently made or surviving from classical centuries—aesthetic interpretation has to reckon with antiquity that is hundreds of orders of magnitude greater. Even where the beholder's knowledge of the details of forest history is rather limited (as is true, more or less, for us all), one knows that this past is there in the shadows—first on the order of centuries, recorded in tree rings and fire scars; and behind that on the order of millennia, recorded in landforms, glacial moraines, successional patterns; and on paleontological scales, as one discovers from fossils and pollen analyses. A forest always comes with an aura of ancient and lost origins.

There is dynamic change in the midst of this antiquity. Seasons pass; the snow melts, birch catkins lengthen, warblers return, the days grow longer, and loons begin to call. Where the season is wet and dry, as in the Amazon, the rains return and the varzea floor floods. These cycles are superimposed on longer range dynamisms not so evident because of their greater scales. Here is vast but passing time; and now one also confronts in nature an element of historical evolution that is, again, radically different from any aesthetic challenge faced with art objects and their cultural history.

Art is sometimes celebrated for its timeless dimensions, despite the fact that art objects themselves age and are reinterpreted from age to age. Sculptors carve forms into stone, and even paint on canvas can persist over centuries. But neither statues nor paintings evolve as do forests. Perhaps there are analogues of classical forms that are enduring in the sweep of the hills or in the symmetries of the conifers. Yet whatever is timelessly recurring is also instantiated in recurrent change.

The forest—we must first think—is prehistoric and perennial, especially in contrast with ephemeral civilizations, their histories, politics, and arts. The perceptive forest visitor realizes also the centuries-long forest successions, proceeding toward climax, yet ever interrupted and reset by fire and storm. One confronts the evolutionary histories of forests tracking climatic changes. One sees erosional, orogenic, and geomorphic processes in rock strata, canyon walls, glacial valleys. The Carboniferous Forests were giant club mosses and horsetails; the Jurassic Forests were gymnosperms—conifers, cycads, ginkgoes, seed ferns. A forest today is yesterday being transformed into tomorrow. A pristine forest is an historical museum that, unlike cultural museums, continues to be what it was, a living landscape. This dynamism couples with antiquity to demand an order of aesthetic interpretation that one is unlikely to find in the criticism of art and its artifacts. Art too is sometimes dynamic, of course, as in music or the dance; but every art form is ephemeral on these scales of time.

In the Petrified Forest in Arizona, tens of thousands of rock logs are strewn across the desert, relics of trees living when the region was tropical forest 225 million years ago. The dominant genus in these great forests was *Araucarioxylon;* the remnant logs are enormous. A living relative is the Norfolk Island pine, *Araucaria heterophylla;* another relative is the monkey puzzle tree, *Araucaria araucana* from South America. Both are tall conifers with a monopodial crown and radial branches, which, because of their beauty of form, are widely planted in subtropical climates today. The genus, with its characteristic form, has persisted through changes. The Petrified Forest is not far from the Grand Canyon, and comparisons give perspective. The Canyon rocks are old, the older the further down one descends; but the Canyon itself was cut in the last five or six million years. So the ancient pines were living long enough ago for the Grand Canyon to be cut and re-cut again some forty-five times over! Their descendants continue today.

John Muir spent most of his life in the California forests, where sequoia trees reach an age of several thousand years: "The forests of America," he exclaimed, "must have been a great delight to God; for they were the best he ever planted."[1] In later life, the aging Muir became interested in the Petrified Forests; through his efforts the forest was declared a National Monument in 1906. Dealing now in millions rather than thousands of years, the sense of antiquity overwhelmed him. "I sit silent and alone from morn till eve in the deeper silence of the enchanted old forests. . . . The hours go on neither long nor short, glorious for imagination . . . but tough for the old paleontological body nearing seventy."[2] Nature has been planting forests a long time.

The sense of time passes over into an archetypal experience of pervasive and perennial natural kind. In the prehuman past, about 60 percent of Earth's land surface was forested, and much of it still is. There is a vast taiga, or boreal forest, in Canada, Siberia, and northern Europe; temperate forest was the historic cover over much of the United States, Europe, and China. There are tropical rainforests, tropical deciduous forests, thorn forests, gallery forests. Australian forests may contain hardly a single species found elsewhere in the world, but still there are the forests, of *Eucalyptus* or *Allocasuarina* rather than oak or spruce. The phenomenon of forests is so widespread, persistent, and diverse, spontaneously appearing almost wherever moisture and climatic conditions permit, that forests cannot be accidents or anomalies but rather must be a characteristic expression of the creative process.

There is also the steppe and the veldt, the tundra and the sea, and these too have their power to arouse a sense of antiquity and of ongoing life. The desert after a rain is a joy to behold in the momentary flourishing of the flora. But forests have more evident and perennial exuberance. The forest is where the "roots" go deep, where life rises high from the ground. Forests convey a sense of life flourishing in more massive and enduring proportions; the vertical contrasts with the horizontal. The biomass is greater than on the grasslands; living things command more space, from canopy through understories down to the underground. The fiber is more solid; the vegetation on the forest floor included annuals and biennials, but the dominants are perennials on scales of decades and centuries. The tropical rainforest is the most complex and diverse ecological community on Earth, with up to three hundred different species of trees in a single hectare.

A characteristic element in the aesthetic experience of nature moves us with how the central goods of the biosphere—hydrologic cycles, photosynthesis, soil fertility, food chains, genetic codes, speciation, reproduction, succession—were in place long before humans arrived. Aesthetics is something, as we shall be saying, that goes on in experiences of the human mind, but the dynamics and structures organizing forest biomes do not come out of the mind. Immersed in a nonhuman frame of reference, one knows the elements primordial.

Subjective though aesthetic experience may be, here we make contact with the natural certainties. Forests and sky, rivers and earth, the everlasting hills, the cycling seasons, wildflowers and wildlife—these are superficially pleasant scenes in which to recreate. At more depth, they are the timeless natural givens that support everything else.

On these scales humans are a late-coming novelty, and that awareness too is aesthetically demanding. Humans evolved out of the forests, although with early *Homo sapiens* that often meant the savanna, the tree-studded but still relatively open-to-view landscape. Our ancestors had descended from the trees and gained upright posture; they needed hands for civilization, spaces through which to hunt, and room for their camps and villages. The gallery forests of Africa are as much forests as Douglas fir in the American Northwest; they too exemplify the forest archetype.

Nor did humans escape their association with forests. There is evidence that we are still genetically disposed to prefer partially forested landscapes.[3] Most of the lands that humans have inhabited, especially as they moved from tropical to temperate climates, were, at the time of human entry, forested; and many of them have remained heavily forested until comparatively recent times. Civilization, especially in Europe and America, created space for itself in the midst of forests, opening these up, making out residential areas more like savannas. Though we felt more comfortable clearing the forest for a pasture, for the farm and the village, we kept the trees throughout the countryside, and along streets and in parks even in our urban environments.

In the back of our minds, we know that all such trees, wherever incorporated into the economics or aesthetics of civilization, are out of the legacy of the forest. We are reminded by them that forests are always there on the horizon of Western culture, part of our life support system, part of our origins. This location—trees amongst us and forest on the horizon of culture—keeps forest there in their wildness as a perennial symbol of an archetypal realm out of which we once came. The forest is where one touches the primordial elements raw and pure. "I went to the woods," remarked Thoreau, "because I wished to live deliberately, to front only the essential facts of life, and see if I could not learn what it had to teach, and not, when I came to die, discover that I had not lived."[4]

No one can live in bare woods alone; civilization too is, for humans, one of the essential facts of life. The town, however, is not so aboriginally archetypal, and that element in life is what is experienced in forests. Were civilization to collapse, the forests would return. The earth would revert to wilderness, because this is the foundational ground. Such aesthetic power of nature stands in strong contrast to classical aesthetic experience of art forms. The creations of sculptors, painters, musicians, and craftsmen always betoken civilization, the critical beholder enjoying the fruits of the labor and leisure of culture. But in the forest the elements are savage; one is not dealing with art or artifact, nor even of artist, but one has penetrated to the archetypes.

There are inanimate natural kinds that nature generates and regenerates over the epochs: mountains, canyons, rivers, estuaries. But the miracle of Earth is that nature decorates this geomorphology with life. Trees evoke this genesis and biological power: Eden with its tree of life, or the shoot growing out of the stump of Jesse, or the cedars of Lebanon—again and again there is life's transient beauty sustained over chaos, life persisting in the midst of its perpetual perishing. A visit to a forest contributes to the human sense of place in space and time, of duration, antiquity, continuity. There one encounters "the types and symbols of Eternity" (Wordsworth).⁵

II. Scientific Appreciation of Forests

En route to such appreciation, one needs the knowledge that scientific forestry can provide. True, one can enjoy forests for their form and color, oblivious to the taxonomic names of the species (*Picea pungens* or *Quercus alba*), much less knowledge of the forest type (montane transition zone to the subalpine, or an oak-hickory forest). The autumn leaves require only an eye for color, with perhaps also a sense of passing seasons, which adds to an ephemeral touch of sadness. This is a lovely Indian summer day, and winter on the way. The hues of spring green, bursting forth upon leafing out, replacing the wintry grays of the trunks and limbs, still set against the darker conifers—one does not need science to appreciate these features. Much less still does one always need paleontological knowledge (that gymnosperms anciently were largely replaced by angiosperms), or ecological explanations (gymnosperms nevertheless dominate in high elevation or latitude climatic regimes).

Still, one cannot adequately enjoy a forest more or less as though it were found art, with admirable form and color. A forest is not art at all; there is no artist. To see the forest landscape as art object is to misunderstand it. Nor is it just some potential materials for aesthetic composition. If we make the forest over into an object of our aesthetic fancy, as we might find a piece of driftwood and display it for its form and curve, then we project onto it our craft and criteria, yet fail to see what is there. Aesthetic experience of nature always demands our realizing that nature itself is a nonartistic object, not designed by any artist for our admiration, not framed or put on a pedestal—all this is much of the secret of nature's aesthetic power, construct though we may the aesthetic categories through which such nature is experienced.

One has to appreciate what is not evident, and here science helps. Marvelous things are going on in dead wood, or underground, or in the dark, or microscopically, or slowly, over time; these processes are not scenic, but an appreciation of them can be aesthetic. The stellate pubescence on the underside of a *Shepherdia* leaf, seen with a hand lens, is quite striking. The weird green luminescence of *Panus stypticus*, a mushroom, discovered on a moonless night, is never forgotten. One experiences how things fit together in the intricate patterns of life. The good of a tree is only half over at its death; an old snag provides nesting cavities, perches, insect larvae, food for birds.

One can enjoy trees, as did Kilmer: "I think that I shall never see, a poem as lovely as a tree."⁶ If one knows, however, that that is a conifer, and those are the pistillate cones and these the staminate cones, and that maples and ashes have opposite leaves, or that willows have only one bud scale, one sees more than poetic beauty in trees. Science requires a closer look at flowers and fruits, their structure and symmetry. There is careful observation to underwrite and support what can otherwise be too impressionistic.

True, those who can count the needle fascicles and get the species right, if they never experience goose pimples when the wind whips through the pines, fail as much as do the poets in their naive romanticism. Nevertheless, only when moving through science to the deeper aesthetic experiences that are enriched by science can the forest be most adequately known. Aestheticians are often not comfortable with this; they want to insist on human capacities to confront nature in relative independence of science.[7] One must be moved, but one needs to be moved in the right direction, where "right" means with appropriate appreciation of what is actually going on.

Trees push toward the sky, and this sense of pressing upward is vital in forest appreciation. There is, of course, a ready scientific explanation for such loft. Given photosynthesis, there is competition for sunlight, and plants that can place their leaves high are the winners in the struggle for survival. The tree has both to invest in structural materials, cellulose, to maintain the heights needed, and also to lift needed nutrients and ground water to such elevations; hence the structure of trunks and limbs. Another of the ecological archetypes is grassland, found extensively where water is too limiting a resource for forests; also there are alpine and tundra ecosystems where the wind and the cold are too limiting.

These survival techniques are the causes of forests, but what is one to make of appreciating the results achieved? This introduces another element in aesthetic challenge that is without precedent in classical art criticism. One seldom requires an appropriate scientific appreciation of an art object for its proper enjoyment. Forests have to be, in a certain measure, disenchanted to be properly enjoyed, although, as we shall insist, forest science need not eliminate the element of the sublime, or even of the sacred. Indigenous and premodern peoples typically enchanted their forests. After science, we no longer see forests as haunted by fairies, nymphs, or gnomes. Forests are biotic communities; we have naturalized them.

Perhaps one can enjoy the riot of autumn colors or the subtle spring hues by lingering over the scene before one's eyes. But a forest cannot be understood simply by looking long and hard at it—whether the understanding sought is scientific or aesthetic. A campfire, for example, built for warmth on an autumn evening, can be enjoyed aesthetically, and perhaps one does not need to know about the oxidation and reduction of carbon to enjoy its flickering light in the twilight, or to welcome its warmth against the cool of the night. But fire cannot really be understood by however careful an observation, trying to see what is taking place. The naturalist Jean Baptiste Lamarck tried that and failed; he thought the aggressive fire was stripping away chromatic layers to find the basic black beneath. Antoine-Laurent Lavoisier gave us the understanding we need with experiments weighing the products of combustion, experiments with animals showing that they could not breath in combusted air. He realized that oxygen is there, that combustion is the oxidation of carbon, with similarities to breathing, the energy driving life.

To understand a forest, one needs concepts, such as carbon bonding, oxidation, oxygen balance, photosynthesis, and knowledge of glucose, cellulose, or nutrients such as nitrogen and phosphorous. Science takes away the colors, if you insist; apart from beholders, there is no autumn splendor or spring green. But science gives us the trees solidly there, photosynthesizing without us, energetically vital to the system of life of which we are also a part. Forestry is usually thought to be an applied science, but it can also, when it gains the perspective of a pure science, help us to appreciate what the forest is in itself. There are trees rising toward the sky, birds on the wing and beasts on the run, age after age, impelled by a genetic language almost two billion years old. There is struggle and adaptive fitness, energy and evolution inventing fertility and prowess. There is succession and speciation, muscle and fat, smell and appetite, law and form, structure and process. There is light and dark, life and death, the mystery of existence.

These figure in aesthetic experience, but there must be science beneath.

III. Aesthetic Engagement in Forests

Science, however necessary, is never sufficient. Forests must be encountered. Forests are constructed by nature, and science teaches us how that is so. Yet forests by nature contain no aesthetic experience; that has to be constructed as we humans arrive. Knowledge of the forest as an objective community does not guarantee the full round of aesthetic experience, not until one moves into that community oneself.

In nature unvisited by humans we incline to think there is no aesthetic experience at all, certainly not in the trees, and hardly in the birds or the foxes. After all, the trees are not even green, much less beautiful, except as we humans are perceiving them. If a tree falls in the forest, and there is no perceiver, there is no sound. The secondary qualities are observer-introduced. *A fortiori*, forests cannot be beautiful on their own. The primary qualities, or the biological functions, or the ecological relationships are there without us. But only when we humans arrive to color things up, to take an interest, is there any experience of beauty; aesthetic experience of forests is an interaction phenomenon during which the forest beauty is constituted.

In the forest itself, there is no scenery, for example; we compose the landscape vista. Subjective experience and objective forests, beauty and trees—this conjoins and juxtaposes opposites: forests undergo no aesthetic experience; trees enjoy no beauty. The beauty is in the eye of the beholder, constituted with our phenomenal experience, whatever forest properties may arouse such sense of beauty. Meanwhile, it is difficult to escape the experience of gratuitous beauty—with autumn leaves, or montane peaks, or with trilliums unexpected along a woodland path.

The aesthetic challenge is to complement the forest dynamics, which have been ongoing over the centuries and millennia, with this novel emergent that does come into being when I arrive. Appropriate aesthetic experience ought to be "up to" the forest, that is, adequate to its form, integrity, antiquity, value; but whether this happens is "up to" me, that is, unless I see that it happens, it does not happen. Aesthetic appreciation would fail if humans, scientists, were to visit and gain nothing but facts about trees.

This demand for adequate response to nature is different from the demand with art. Much more is up to me. Confronting an art object, we realize that there was once an artist, and we may think it significant to recover something of the aesthetic experience of the artist. When we are enjoying a symphony, the musicians are enjoying it too. Aesthetic intent constitutes the arts, and the beholder comes to share, perhaps also to enrich, this intent. But in the forest, surrounded by trees, we alone are the loci of aesthetic life. The challenge is to encounter nonaesthetic trees, mountains, rivers, and awaken to the experience of beauty. It is unlikely that the categories formulated for the human arts will serve for the demands of forest experience.

Aesthetic appreciation of nature, at the level of forests and landscapes, requires embodied participation, immersion, and struggle. We initially may think of forests as scenery to be looked upon. That is a mistake. A forest is entered, not viewed. It is doubtful that one can experience a forest from a roadside pullover, any more than on television. A deer in a zoo is not the experience of wild deer. The cage prevents the reality. Experiencing a forest through a car window differs mostly in that the beholder now is in the cage, which again prevents the reality. You do not really engage a forest until you are well within it.[8]

The forest attacks all our senses—sight, hearing, smell, feeling, even taste. Visual experience is critical. But no forest is adequately experienced without the odor of the pines or of the wild roses; and one catches how much animal senses of smell can exceed our own. The elk I heard, but did not see; they caught my scent. The wind is against me. What is a forest without the wind heard and felt, against which one draws his jacket tighter? Wait, wasn't that a kinglet that called—the first I have heard this season. Art is seldom so multisensory.

Most of all, there is the kinesthetic sense of bodily presence, being incarnate in place. One seeks shelter for lunch, to discover, cooling down after the brisk walk, that there is too much shade, and one moves to the sun, and enjoys the warmth. Hiking in, there are hours of footprints behind me. I have rounded a bend and there before me is the rolling expanse of more forest than that through which I have already come. Where is the next water likely to be? How much more of the trail can I safely do today?

This surrounding and engagement, spontaneity and participatory eventfulness, differs from art, which is typically located and looked upon, as with a framed picture or a statue atop a pedestal. In a forest I have to choose what to consider—how much to integrate, the level of focus—in a place present all around me. A person is immersed in some art, as in a splendid building or a garden. These too have their boundaries: one can see the building from a distance, or circumscribe the garden boundaries. A forest must eventually have boundaries too, but the boundaries are often zones of transition, where one aesthetic challenge passes into another. The boundaries are ample enough that one gets so far in that any discrete borders are gone, especially in large forests. That is, more or less, the test of a forest against a woodlot, or a serious forest against a timber tract: whether one can get at such distance from the boundaries that they disappear from constant consciousness. Such boundaries in art seldom disappear. We need the framing to separate out the artifact and to confine the experience.

There is something amiss about the idea that aesthetics requires disinterest and distance, in contrast to more utilitarian pursuits. This is only half true even for art objects. All art invites participation; the aesthetic experience must have some bite to it. Nevertheless, one walks away from the painting or statue, and gets lunch elsewhere. If the forest is only scenery through a car window, one can plan lunch in town. Deep in the forest one is embodied, surrounded by the elements, and the total sensory, vital participation is more urgent.

True, one can experience the beauty of a forest only if one's more basic needs for food and shelter have been satisfied. One separates out the beauty of the snowflakes, seen at a glance on one's dark jacket sleeve, from the fact that the gathering storm is dangerous, and a few more inches of snow on the winter's snowpack, filling in one's tracks, will obscure the route out. Still, the bodily participation in the forest, the competence demanded and enjoyed there amidst its opportunities and threats, the struggle for location in and against the primordial world—this engagement enriches the aesthetic experience. I am undeniably here, and the forest, for all its aesthetic stimulation, is indifferent to my needs. I am five miles from the trailhead; I am quite on my own. The storm is coming up, the spruce are bending with the wind, supper is not cooked, and it is getting dark.

Gaston Bachelard writes: "We do not have to be long in the woods to experience the always rather anxious impression of 'going deeper and deeper' into a limitless world. Soon, if we do not know where we are going, we no longer know where we are.... This limitless world ... is a primary attribute of the forest."⁹ It is easier to get lost there than in a more open savanna or grassland. Trails give a sense of security. Forests can be dense; they veil space with their trunks and leaves, and one has to take care against disorientation. But that is again to realize our limits, to sense vulnerable embodiment, and to risk engagement with the sublime.

IV. The Forest and the Sublime

In the primeval forest humans know the most authentic of wilderness emotions, the sense of the sublime. By contrast, few persons get goose pimples indoors, in art museums, in fashionable shopping centers, or at the city park. The sublime invokes a category that was, in centuries past, important in aesthetics but is thought to have lapsed in our more modern outlook. Never mind whether the category is currently fashionable. The sublime is perennial in encounter with nature because wherever people step to the edge of the familiar, every world, they risk encounter with grander, more provocative forces that touch heights and depths beyond normal experience, forces that transcend us and which both attract and threaten. Forests are never very modern or postmodern, or even classical or premodern. They explode such categories and move outside culture into fundamental nature.

Almost by definition, the sublime runs off scale. There is vertigo before vastness, magnitude, antiquity, power, elemental forces austere and fierce, enormously more beyond our limits. At an overlook in the mountains, with trees all around, the ground runs right up to your feet and disappears over the horizon, often, in the as-yet-unexplored forest, with a suggestion of space prolonged indefinitely.

The forest's roots, that is, its radical origins, plunge down to depths one knows not where. The trees point upward along the mountain slope, which rises to join the sky, and the scene soars off to heights unknown. The aesthetic situation has gotten out of control because the limits have vanished. The frames and pedestals familiar to cultured aesthetic experience are gone. There are no theatrical stages with actors about to appear, no musical instruments in players' hands, no garden walls or gardeners planting the oncoming season's flowers. One encounters what was aboriginally there in its present incarnation.

But few forests are primeval—the more prosaic aestheticians will protest. Rare is the forest that has not been reshaped by human agency— by cutting up trees with chain saws, by cutting up forests with roads, by fencing forests around and running cattle through them, by intentionally planting more desirable species. There are also the unintended changes, like the chestnut blight, or the understory invaded with honeysuckle.

Still, the forest, shaped by management and mismanagement though it may be, proves more able than the field or pasture to retain the natural element. Nature takes back over and does its thing, if not its pristine activity, then still something relatively wild. Unless the forest, so-called, is only a plantation, impressive wildness remains even in silviculture. Hopefully, the wildlife is there; something of the native biodiversity remains. A National Forest may be a working forest, not a wilderness. Still, a day's hike through it, even if along an old timber road, is more likely to produce the sense of the sublime than is a stroll through the pasture.

In other realms of nature—as we stand awestruck before the midnight sky perhaps, or watching a sunset over arctic ice, or deep in the Vishnu schist of the Grand Canyon— beauty and power are yet lifeless. In a forest the sublime and the beautiful are bound up with the struggle for life. Think, for instance, of windswept bristlecone pines along a ridge in the Sierras. Or of the stunted birch toward the treeline in the Norwegian mountains. The biological element in the sublime is the beauty of life coupled with struggle. The aesthetic challenge is conflict and resolution presented on these awesome scales.

Like clouds, seashores, and mountains, forests are never ugly, they are only more or less beautiful; the scale runs from zero upward with no negative domain. Destroyed forests can be ugly—a burned, windthrown, diseased, or clearcut forest. But even the ruined forest, regenerating itself, still has positive aesthetic properties. Trees rise to fill the empty place against the sky. A forest is filled with organisms that are marred and ragged—oaks with broken limbs, a crushed violet, the carcass of an elk. The gnarled bristlecone at the edge of the tundra is not really ugly, not unless endurance and strength are ugly. It is the presence and symbol of life forever renewed before the winds that blast it.

Forests are full of shadows, and this is metaphorically as well as literally true. The darkness shadowing life is as much the source of beauty as is light or life. The word "forest" (a grander word than "trees" in the plural) forces retrospect and prospect; it invites holistic categories of interpretation as yesterday's flora and fauna pass into tomorrow. Yes, there are fire scars at the bases of these ponderosas, but see how they have healed over. And we were just walking through the lodgepole forest regenerated after that fire two decades back; the stand is already thinning itself and the taller trees overtopping our heads.

Think about it. There is enough power in a handful of these cones to regenerate the forest henceforth for millennia. Yes, giants have fallen, and rotting logs fill the forest floor. And see, here is the humus from which the present forest rises—"the immeasurable height of woods decaying, never to be decayed" (Wordsworth).[10] This softens the ugliness and sets it in somber beauty. When one reaches a high point where the forest dominates the landscape in every direction, and remembers this regeneration of new life out of old on a scale of centuries and millennia, one knows the sense of the sublime.

V. The Forest and the Sacred

When beauty transforms into the sublime, manifest in the perennial vitality of an ancient forest, the aesthetic is elevated into the numinous. "Break forth into singing, O mountains, O forest, and every tree in it!" (Isaiah 44:23). "The trees of the Lord are watered abundantly; the cedars of Lebanon which he planted" (Psalms 104:16). "The groves were God's first temples" (William Cullen Bryant).[11] The forest is a kind of church. Trees pierce the sky, like cathedral spires. Light filters down, as through stained glass. The forest canopy is lofty, far above our heads. There is something about being deep in the woods, with the ground under one's feet and no roof over one's head, that generates religious experience.

Again, just as aestheticians earlier resisted being too indebted to science, now aestheticians may protest that their experiences need not be religious.[12] Nevertheless, the line between aesthetic respect and reverence for nature is often crossed unawares, somewhere in the region of the sublime. In common with churches, forests, like sea and sky, invite transcending the human world and experiencing a comprehensive, embracing realm. Forests can serve as a more provocative, perennial sign of this than many of the traditional, often outworn, symbols devised by the churches.

Mountaintop experiences, the wind in the pines, a howling storm, a quiet snowfall in wintry woods, solitude in a grove of towering spruce, an overflight of honking geese—these generate "a sense sublime of something far more deeply interfused . . . a motion and spirit that impels . . . and rolls through all things. Therefore I am still a lover of the meadows and the woods, and mountains" (Wordsworth).[13] Muir exclaimed, "The clearest way into the Universe is through a forest wilderness."[14]

Were we saying that science has secularized the forest? Yes, if that means that the forest is no longer enchanted. But the forest is strangely resistant to being secularized in the etymological sense of that term, being reduced to "this present age" (Latin *saeculum*), or in any reductionist or profane senses either. Forests do not mechanize well; they are not machines. There is too much that is organic, or, better, too much that is vital, or, better still, too much that is valuable. The spirit of place returns.

Science leaves us puzzled whether the values in the woods are intrinsic or instrumental, and if intrinsic whether they are anthropogenic and projected onto the trees or autonomously intrinsic and found by the forest beholder, whose aesthetic experience tunes him or her in to what is going on. The forest is there, but so also is the person here, trying to figure it all out. The answers seem to lie in terms of what is discovered in the forests, not merely in terms of what preferences we adopt toward it. But when value is discovered there, the forest as archetype, as spontaneously self-organizing, as generator of life, not merely as resource, but as Source of being, the forest starts to become a sacrament of something beyond, something ultimate in, with, and under these cathedral groves.

The forest has a way of spontaneously re-enchanting itself. Forests are not haunted, but that does not mean that there is nothing haunting about forests. Perhaps the supernatural is gone, but here the natural can be supercharged with mystery. Science removes the little mysteries (how acorns make oaks which make acorns) to replace them with bigger ones (how the acorn-oak-acorn loop got established in the first place). Thanks to the biochemists, molecular biologists, geneticists, botanists, ecologists, forest scientists, we know how this green world works. But is this an account that demystifies what is going on?

Photons of light flow from the sun. Some impact leaves and are captured by antenna molecules in the chloroplasts (a half million of them per square millimeter of leaf), relayed to a reaction center molecule where, in Photosystem II, the energy of the photons is used to move electrons up to a high energy perch (at the PS 680 chlorophyll molecule). The electrons then move down a transport chain, cocking an ADP molecule up to its ATP high-energy form, and are passed to the reaction center of Photosystem I. There, with more photons absorbed, the electrons are moved back up to a second high-energy perch (at the PS 700 molecule). They descend another electron transport chain, this time producing a high-energy NADPH molecule.

The two high energy molecules (ATP and NADPH) are then used, in the Calvin cycle, to synthesize sugar. This is a complex series of over a dozen reactions that takes carbon dioxide from the atmosphere and shuttles it around in numerous steps to make, first, three-carbon intermediates and then the six-carbon sugar glucose, as well as other products. That sugar can be stored in the plant as starch, as well as sugar. This is the energy that powers essentially all of life, the fuel for natural history. Or the glucose can be made into another polymer, cellulose, to form the tough and persistent structures of plant and forest life.

Moses thought that the burning bush, not consumed, was quite a miracle. We hardly believe any more in that sort of supernatural miracle; science has made such stories incredible. What has it left instead? A self-organizing photosynthesis driving a life synthesis that has burned for millennia, life as a strange fire that outlasts the sticks that feed it. That is, one could say, rather spirited behavior on the part of secular matter, "spirited" in the animated sense, in the root sense of a "breath" or "wind" that energizes this mysterious, vital metabolism. These bushes in the Sinai desert, these cedars of Lebanon, these forests across America, the best God ever planted—all such woody flora are hardly phenomena less marvelous even if we no longer want to say that this is miraculous.

Indeed, in the original sense of "miracle"—a wondrous event, without regard to the question whether natural or supernatural—the phenomenon of photosynthesis with the continuing floral life it supports is the secular equivalent of the burning bush. The bush that Moses watched was an individual in a species line that had perpetuated itself for millennia, coping by the coding in its DNA, fueled by the sun, using cytochrome c molecules several billion years old, and surviving without being consumed. Remember the magnificent *Araucarioxylon* 225 million years ago in the now petrified Arizona forest, surviving yet in the *Araucaria* of Africa and Australia. To go back to the miracle that Moses saw, a bush that burned briefly without being consumed, would be to return to something several orders of magnitude less spectacular.

The account we have is, if you like, a naturalistic account, but this nature is quite spectacular stuff. Science traces out some causes, which disappear rearward in deep time, and carry on a continuing genesis, and leave us stuttering for meanings. The forest remains a kind of wonderland, a land that provokes wonder. It is not so much that some ultimate or Absolute noumenon eludes us as that the empirical phenomena about which there is absolutely no doubt need more explanation than the secular categories seem able to give. We may doubt that God exists, but here without doubt is this existing forest, and nature lies in, with, and under it. If God is gone, then Nature needs to be spelled with a capital N.

Loren Eiseley, surveying evolutionary history, exclaims, "Nature itself is one vast miracle transcending the reality of night and nothingness."[15] Ernst Mayr, one of the most celebrated living biologists, impressed by the creativity in natural history, says, "Virtually all biologists are religious, in the deeper sense of this word, even though it may be a religion without revelation.... The unknown and maybe unknowable instills in us a sense of humility and awe."[16] The sublime is never really far from the religious, since the sublime takes us to the limits of our understanding, and we wonder at what is mysteriously beyond.

Being among the archetypes, the forest is about as near to ultimacy as we can come in phenomenal experience. It presents us with natural history: a vast scene of sprouting, budding, leafing out, flowering, fruiting, passing away, passing life on. I become astonished that the forest should be there, spontaneously generated. There are no forests on Mars or Saturn; none elsewhere in our solar system, perhaps none in our galaxy. But Earth's forests are indisputably here. There is more operational organization, more genetic history in a handful of forest humus than in the rest of the universe, so far as we know. How so? Why? A forest wilderness elicits cosmic questions, differently from art and artifacts. If anything at all on Earth is sacred, it must be this enthralling creativity that characterizes our home planet. Forests are sacraments of life rising up on Earth. Here an appropriate aesthetics becomes spiritually demanding.

Notes

1. John Muir, *Our National Parks* (Boston: Houghton Mifflin, 1901), p. 331.
2. John Muir, quoted in Robert A. Long and Rose Houk, *Dawn of the Dinosaurs: The Triassic in the Petrified Forest* (Petrified Forest, Ariz.: Petrified Forest Museum Association, 1988), p. 10.
3. Gordon H. Orians and Judith H. Heerwagen, "Evolved Responses to Landscapes," in *The Adapted Mind*, eds. Jerome H. Barkow, Leda Cosmides, and John Tooby (New York: Oxford University Press, 1992), pp. 555–79.
4. Henry David Thoreau, *Walden* in *Walden and Civil Disobedience*, ed. Owen Thomas (New York: W. W. Norton, 1966), p. 61.
5. William Wordsworth, *The Prelude*, Book VI, line 639.
6. Joyce Kilmer, "Trees" (1913), in *Joyce Kilmer: Poems, Essays and Letters* (New York: George H. Doran, 1918), vol. 1, p. 180.
7. In recent discussion, Noel Carroll wants experience of nature "of a less intellective, more visceral sort," p. 245 in "On Being Moved by Nature: Between Religion and Natural History," in *Landscape, Natural Beauty and the Arts*, eds. Salim Kemal and Ivan Gaskell (Cambridge, U.K.: Cambridge University Press, 1993), pp. 244–66; with reply by Allen Carlson, "Nature, Aesthetic Appreciation, and Knowledge," *The Journal of Aesthetics and Art Criticism* 53 (1995): 393–400. See also Holmes Rolston III, "Does Aesthetic Appreciation of Landscapes Need to be Science-Based?" *The British Journal of Aesthetics* 35 (1995): 374–86.
8. Arnold Berleant, *The Aesthetics of Environment* (Philadelphia: Temple University Press, 1992).
9. Gaston Bachelard, *The Poetics of Space* (1958), trans. Maria Jolas (Boston: Beacon Press, 1994), p. 185.
10. William Wordsworth, *The Prelude*, Book VI, lines 624–25.
11. William Cullen Bryant, *A Forest Hymn*, 1825. See also James George Frazer, "The Worship of Trees," in *The Golden Bough*, a new abridgment (Oxford: Oxford University Press, 1994), pp. 82–97.
12. Noel Carroll, "On Being Moved by Nature"; T. J. Diffey, "Natural Beauty without Metaphysics," in Kemal and Gaskell, eds., *Landscape, Natural Beauty and the Arts*, pp. 43–64.
13. William Wordsworth, *Lines Composed a Few Miles Above Tintern Abbey* (1798).
14. John Muir, *John of the Mountains: The Unpublished Journals of John Muir*, ed. Linnie Marsh Wolfe (Boston: Houghton Mifflin, 1938), p. 313.
15. Loren Eiseley, *The Firmament of Time* (New York: Atheneum, 1960), p. 171.
16. Ernst Mayr, *The Growth of Biological Thought* (Belknap Press of Harvard University Press, 1982), p. 81.

CHAPTER 5

The Rights of Trees and Other Natural Objects

If there are multiple values and social meanings in forests and uncountable forest organisms and systems that deserve our respect, how do we determine what our ethical responsibilities are to them? And, do our responsibilities to some forest components take precedence over others? Moreover, if some of these objects and organisms have rights, while others do not, do we have stronger ethical obligations or duties to those that do—for example, stronger obligations to protect them from human disturbances? Rights are important in law and morality, demanding both respect and action on the part of those they are claims against. However, there are different philosophical positions about what these rights are and what they require in the way of human behavior.

Some philosophers argue that attributions of rights are appropriate only within the domain of the human community and human social relationships. They maintain that only humans have rights and only humans deserve the fullest kind of personal or legal respect that having rights implies. In this view, human-centered concerns and interests are paramount in forests, and other organisms and natural systems must be dealt with, conceptually and perhaps even practically, in different ways. Moreover, these thinkers sometimes claim that the concept of rights is such a human-centered one that it is out of place in regard to the other components of nature, such as trees or animal species. A second group of philosophers, particularly those who advocate for animal rights, have argued that the concept of rights can be logically extended to at least the "sentient" part of nature, which includes many species of domestic and wild animals in forests. According to this position, although "nonhuman animals" may not have exactly all of the same rights as humans, they deserve equality of consideration with respect to their comparative species characteristics and natural requirements. A third contingent of thinkers extends rights to additional components of nature—including trees, rivers, species, and ecosystems—and argues for a more substantial respect for those objects and thus a more respectful treatment of the many components of forests, whether they be individuals, communities, or systems.

If the first of these viewpoints about rights holds sway, then humans could logically continue to use and manage forests according to humanly-centered and humanly-biased purposes, values, and goals. Forest management would likely not have to change much from its Pinchotian roots, except perhaps to become more ecologically oriented. However, if either of the last two views were implemented, then the nonhuman elements of forests would deserve more protection, and forest management would have to take this into account. Different forms of management would be needed: in the second case one that elevates the interests and needs of wild animals and other sentient forest creatures beyond their station in Pinchotian forestry; in the third case one that alters management to take account of the special interests and requirements of other forest components as well, including the "nonsentient" and "abiotic" elements such as plant communities and forest streams. The third view would push forestry and forest management further toward "biocentric egalitarianism," to become something like a deep ecology in practice. Some environmental philosophers believe, then, that these questions about rights are not only abstract, academic issues but that answers to them make a difference in how we should formulate forest policies and pursue forest management practices.

This issue of the rights of nonhumans was one of the first debates in the emerging field of environmental ethics in the 1970s. It centered on the foundational question of whether nonhuman animals and organisms including trees have moral and also legal rights, such as standing under the law.[1] The standard view in the tradition of Western philosophy that prevailed in the early 1960s was that humans have rights and perhaps some "higher animals" have certain limited rights, but for the most part no other beings or entities in nature do. This did not necessarily mean that humans could abuse or maltreat objects that lack rights, but it did not give these objects the status and protection of rights-holders.

In modern Western culture this standard theory was challenged in England in the late eighteenth century, with the rise of the anti-hunting and animal rights movement, and by the end of the nineteenth century the idea that animals have rights was no longer taken to be an absurd idea in that country. The animal rights movement ultimately came to North America, most forcefully in the 1970s, under the leadership of such philosophers as the Australian Peter Singer. His book *Animal Liberation*, published in New York in 1975, made clear one philosophical basis for concluding that at least some animals deserve equal consideration with humans, namely those that are "sentient" and can thus feel pleasure and pain.[2]

Singer's arguments were predated by those of the Arizona philosopher Joel Feinberg who, at a philosophy conference on the environment in Georgia in 1971, argued that animals might logically be said to have rights, but not such entities as plants or species. Some philosophers—such as Tom Regan, a prominent animal rights proponent in North Carolina—agreed with Feinberg's conclusion about the rights of animals and developed their own separate arguments in support of this idea.[3]

---

1. The distinction between moral and legal rights is commonly accepted in contemporary philosophy. The idea behind this is that it is one thing to recognize rights in a system of morality or ethics, and another to locate them in a system of public law, though philosophers also often suggest that the latter could not occur without the former since the law is dependent on morality for its injunctions.

2. Peter Singer, *Animal Liberation: A New Ethics for Our Treatment of Animals* (New York: New York Review, 1975).

3. Regan's arguments for animals rights can be found in his book, *The Case for Animal Rights* (Berkeley: University of California Press, 1983). Regan also critically analyzed Feinberg's position, arguing that it was

While other philosophers continued to favor the traditional view on this issue and attacked the idea of the rights of animals as illogical,[4] the idea did not die. In time, the animal rights movement gained considerable visibility and authority in Western societies, and the idea that at least some animals have moral rights that deserve legal protection has become a more accepted article of popular belief.[5] Moreover, the views of Feinberg and Singer paved the way for subsequent consideration of the rights of nonanimals, for some philosophers could see no logical reason why interests and rights should be restricted, conceptually, to humans and animals, and so they extended Feinberg's logic to other components of nature.

The notion that such things as trees and rivers might have legal rights was seriously proposed by a legal philosopher, Christopher Stone, in a groundbreaking book published in 1974, *Should Trees Have Standing? Towards Legal Rights for Natural Objects*.[6] Stone had earlier prepared an article on this subject for a law review journal, hoping to influence the U.S. Supreme Court in its deliberations about the Mineral King Valley case.[7] The case concerned the proposal by Walt Disney Enterprises, using a permit from the U.S. Forest Service, to build a ski resort on federal wilderness land in the Sierra Nevada Mountains in California, and the efforts of the Sierra Club to sue to prevent the development because it believed that this would adversely affect the aesthetic and ecological character of the valley. The federal Ninth Circuit Court had turned down the suit on grounds that the club lacked legal standing to sue, and the club appealed to the Supreme Court. The presumption was that the Sierra Club could show at most a tenuous harm to itself and that no harm could be done to the natural components of the valley by the ski development because natural objects are not legal persons with interests that can be harmed. Stone's law review article made a novel attempt to support the Sierra Club's case by showing why it makes sense to say that natural objects like trees are "jural persons" with identifiable interests. If so, they could be harmed by development and, logically, the law could protect them. Moreover, it also made sense for human beings or human organizations, such as environmental groups, to serve as their legal guardians and to seek redress in court on their behalf—to sue to protect their rights. Stone's theory was supported by three Supreme Court justices, especially by Justice William O. Douglas in his minority opinion, but was rejected by a slim court majority.[8]

Some legal experts have suggested that ideas about the need to protect nonhuman objects such as wild animals are now generally accepted by the federal court system because of the development of new environmental laws in the late 1960s and 1970s that recognize these rights.[9]

---

confused because it both allowed and disallowed the possibility of nonanimal rights. See his article, "Feinberg on What Sorts of Being Can Have Rights," *Southern Journal of Philosophy* 14(4) (Winter 1976): 485–98.

4. For example, R. G. Frey, *Interests and Rights: The Case Against Animals* (Oxford: Clarendon Press, 1980).

5. Bernard Rollin refers to some of the evidence for this in the United States in his book, *The Frankenstein Syndrome: Ethical and Social Issues in the Genetic Engineering of Animals* (Cambridge, U.K.: Cambridge University Press, 1995), pp. 156–57.

6. Christopher Stone, *Should Trees Have Standing? Towards Legal Rights for Natural Objects* (Los Altos, Calif.: Kaufmann, 1974).

7. "Should Trees Have Standing? Toward Legal Rights for Natural Objects," *Southern California Law Review*, 45 (1972): 450.

8. *Sierra Club v. Morton*, 405 U.S. 727 (1972).

9. For example, Robert B. Keiter, "Ecological Policy and the Courts: Of Rights, Processes, and the Judicial Role," in *Human Ecology Review*, 4(1) (Spring/Summer 1997): 2–8.

In particular, the Endangered Species Act of 1973 is thought to be the best example because it extends legal protections not only to endangered and threatened wild species but also to the critical habitats in which they thrive. So ideas like Stone's have, in time, been influential in some parts of United States law and have lost their complete novelty.

One interesting outgrowth of the rights debate in environmental philosophy and law has been the charge that systems of environmental ethics and animal rights are basically incompatible with each other conceptually.[10] In more recent years this charge has been critically evaluated by various philosophers,[11] and the debate about rights has been defused as some environmental philosophers have come to see that there may be better ways to conceive of the philosophical foundations of ethical obligations to natural objects than to assert that such objects, organisms, and systems have rights. Thus, Callicott and Rolston have provided alternatives to this philosophical position.[12] In any case, this debate has in practice not always meant that animal rights advocates and environmentalists disagree on the proper treatment of wild animals and other nonanimal components of forests or about the actual ethical responsibilities that humans have to nonhumans, animals and nonanimals alike.

Robin Attfield, another founding thinker in the field of environmental ethics and a professor of philosophy at Cardiff University in Wales, is one person who has provided a critical antidote to Feinberg's point of view. In Attfield's famous essay on the "good of trees," reprinted in this chapter, he carefully supports the position that trees have rights because they have intrinsic value. However, he suggests that these rights are "overridable" and that the grounds for them are much weaker than the grounds for the rights of other beings. Thus, while he does not discuss the implications of his view for forest management, it is clear that his conclusion does not require the radical alterations in conventional resource management that other rights philosophies would entail.[13]

The view that species and whole ecosystems, such as forests or rivers and not only trees, have

---

10. In 1980 J. Baird Callicott argued for this point in "Animal Liberation: A Triangular Affair," *Environmental Ethics* 2: 311–28; later, in 1989, he considered how the two perspectives could at least sometimes be reconciled in "Animal Liberation and Environmental Ethics: Back Together Again," in *In Defense of the Land Ethic*.

11. For example, Mary Anne Warren, "The Rights of the Non-human World," in *Environmental Philosophy*, eds. Robert Elliot and Arran Gare (Queensland, Australia: University of Queensland Press, 1983).

12. J. Baird Callicott prefers not to utilize the "talismatic power" of the idea of rights in his environmental philosophy, instead focusing on the notion of intrinsic value. See "On the Intrinsic Value of Nonhuman Species," in *The Preservation of Species: The Value of Biological Diversity*, ed. Bryan Norton (Princeton, N.J.: Princeton University Press, 1986). Holmes Rolston finds the idea to be a complex one that is both appealing and tenuous, depending on its application to humans, animals, and the nonanimal parts of nature. He suggests that it is mostly a "term of convenience" that masks other more important issues of what is "right" in our relationships with nature. See chapter 2 of *Environmental Ethics: Duties to and Values in the Natural World* (1988). In his later writings, Stone appears to have backed away from the idea of legal rights for nonhumans, given the difficulties involved. "Standing . . . does nothing but get you through the courthouse door; it does not mean the case on behalf of the environment is won," he says in *Earth and Other Ethics* (New York: Harper and Row, 1987), p. 10. His approach is not to ask whether trees and rivers have rights but what legal status or "considerateness" they intelligibly have, whether they have rights or not (ibid., p. 82).

13. For example, if Christopher Stone's original position on the legal rights of trees were fully enshrined in environmental law, significant changes would result under federal law in regard to the way that forests should be managed, used, and protected.

interests and intrinsic value, and thus should command our deep respect, is supported in the writings of the Australian environmental philosopher Lawrence Johnson.[14] In the brief selections below, Johnson identifies what he calls "well-being interests" in ecosystems and recommends that we develop environmental policy that takes these interests into account. He carefully avoids using the language of "rights," however, and also makes clear that recognizing these interests in resource management and policy has complex implications that will require considerable thought.

---

14. See Lawrence Johnson's wonderfully argued book, *A Morally Deep World: An Essay on Moral Significance and Environmental Ethics* (Cambridge, U.K.: Cambridge University Press, 1991).

Robin Attfield

The Good of Trees

My title can be taken in at least two ways: as "the good of trees" as opposed to "the harm of trees" and as "the good of trees" in the sense of "the value of trees." It might also be taken in the sense of "the use of trees," particularly by those who hold that to speak strictly trees have no good of their own, and are good only for satisfying human interests; this view, however, I consider and reject in the course of Section I after a scrutiny of some writings of Professors Hare and Feinberg, who both seem to hold it. But even if trees have needs and a good of their own, they may still have no value of their own and may still be due no consideration in their own right: in Section II, I examine various proposed moral grounds for preserving trees without finding in them any basis for valuing trees beyond human and animal welfare. The resulting paradox, that trees have interests but no value of their own, is explored in Section III, in which I supply an argument and a thought-experiment to show that trees can after all be of intrinsic value, even though we seldom need to take account of it in practice.

Robin Attfield, "The Good of Trees," *Journal of Value Inquiry* 15 (1981): 35–54. Reprinted with kind permission of Robin Attfield and Kluwer Academic Publishers. Copyright © 1981 Kluwer Academic Publishers.

This essay is not in any way intended to derogate from arguments in support of belief in the rights of animals. Rather I hope it may contribute to the philosophy of intrinsic value and to the philosophy of ecology, and also throw light on the conceptual links between the notions of "purpose" and "interest," between "capacities" and "flourishing," between "diversity" and "good" and between "interests," "value," and "rights." My beliefs about the feelings of trees are unalarmingly traditional; indeed trees are discussed not for the sake of some Arboreal Liberation Campaign, but because they constitute an intriguing test case of several theories in meta-ethics and normative ethics, and because our attitudes toward them are of considerable intrinsic interest.

I: Harm and the Needs of Trees

There is a view held widely among philosophers that, if we speak strictly, the needs of trees and other plants depend wholly on the interests of humans, that plants can only be harmed when actual or possible human desires are frustrated, and that their harm consists precisely in this frustration. This view has been held not only by contemporary writers such as

R. M. Hare[1] and Joel Feinberg[2]; there are some traces of it in the writings of Aquinas,[3] who represents as instruments creatures which, unlike rational agents, do not control their actions, instruments intended solely for the use of agents possessed of intellect; and a similar belief seems to have been held by the ancient Stoics.[4] I shall try to show this view to be a confused one, about which we need to get straight not only for the sake of trees but also so as to become clearer about harm and needs in general. (Some followers of Aquinas and of Kant hold a similar and in my opinion confused view about animals, but this view is contested by Feinberg, who argues in the same paper that some animals have interests and can have rights. While I agree with these conclusions of Feinberg, my own argument about the good of trees can be carried over so as to supplement his account of the interests of animals; for if the good of trees is partially or wholly independent of human interests, there can be little doubt that the same holds good of animals *a fortiori*.)

Hare expresses the basis of his position as follows: "To speak very crudely and inexactly, to say that some act would harm somebody is to say that it would prevent some interest of his being satisfied; and this, in turn, is to say that it would, or might in possible circumstances, prevent some desire of his being realised." This is crude and inexact because "might" lets in too much; nevertheless the conceptual link between "harm" and "interest" is left unqualified, while the link between "harm" and "desire" is presented thus: "I propose to assume for the sake of argument that there is some conceptual link between harm and frustration of prescriptions which are, will or would be assented to."

This dubious assumption leads Hare into a digression on its implications. If the foregoing is granted, Hare remarks, "only creatures which can assent to prescriptions can be harmed in the strict sense. This runs counter to our ordinary way of speaking." Indeed it does, as it yields the conclusions not only that plants and animals cannot be harmed, but also that human embryos and infants cannot be harmed either. But Hare comes to the rescue, at least of plants and animals, by endorsing two analogical extensions of the notion of harm, "once established" for creatures which can assent to prescriptions. First, useful animals like horses and useful plants like apple trees can, like cars, be harmed when something is done to them which prevents their users from realising their prescriptions. Second, even when there is no question of a user, "we can speak analogically of the creature wanting things, and, as in the case of people, treat its goal-directed behaviour as evidence of this (provided that we also pay attention to the dangers in the analogy)."

Talk of such desires is a "pardonable artificiality," but only if we extend the notion of wanting in this way can we reveal the origins of expressions like "good roots"; "the apple tree's good roots, if they are not good for helping it to produce the sort of apples that I want, must be good for helping it to grow into the kind of apple trees that it wants to be—i.e., to achieve the *telos* or end of apple trees by putting on as perfectly as possible their *eidos* or form. If we had not inherited a great deal of this teleological language, we should not speak of good roots in the case of trees not serving a human purpose."

In other words, harm always turns on the frustration of desires and good on their realisation; so, where we talk of good and harm which are unaccompanied by desires, we must be pretending that desires really are present; that desires, so to speak, grow on trees. Our usage, though inherited, must be derivative, and only because of this is it pardonable; if we were strict and consistent non-animists we should not speak at all of the good or harm of useless plants; and what is unpardonable is to suppose that creatures lacking wants have a good of their own which has nothing to do with us.

It may seem unfair to put such emphasis on what Hare himself declares to be a digression; but his whole prescriptivist position over harm turns on it. For, as he himself says, these conclusions about animals and plants follow from his analysis of "harm," and so, by *modus tollens*, their falsity would by the same token imply the falsity of his prescriptivism. Hare has to maintain that our talk about harm to plants and animals is derivative, analogical and barely pardonable, lest we place it at the centre of a naturalist theory on which the nature of harm depends on facts and necessary truths and not on prescriptions. Although I shall not defend such a theory here, the reader who cannot agree with Hare over plants will no doubt draw his or her conclusions.

At all events Hare has to apply his theories to talk of the good of useless or userless trees. This being so, it is difficult to see how he can cope with much of the talk about trees to which Feinberg draws attention. Thus not only can trees grow, blossom and decay; they can thrive and wither, be endangered by fire and be protected from commercial pillage. Now what can thrive, reach maturity, be endangered and be protected, has, I contend, a good itself. How else could we know that it was thriving? Hare might claim that works of art could also be endangered and protected because of their beauty, which humans stand to enjoy, and might go on to claim that trees can only be endangered and protected in this particular sense; if so, he should hold that trees inaccessible to humans and the beauty of which humans do not stand to enjoy cannot be endangered. More plausibly he would fall back on his derivative notion of "harm," and grant that trees can be harmed in a sense beyond that in which statues can. They can be harmed because the realisation of their quasi-aspirations can be imperilled.

But this is to suppose that people who talk of the thriving or endangering of forest trees must ground their talk in what most of them consider a childish and unsubstantiated belief, namely that trees have feelings and purposes, or are indwelt by forms or spirits with conative propensities; or, at best, it is to suppose that they would be willing to acknowledge their talk to be metaphorical, or poetic, or not capable of being taken seriously. Rather than such heroic and implausible suppositions, it would surely be preferable to grant that the good and harm of uncultivated species depend not on any prescriptions, desires, aspirations or wants, but on the capacities of their kind; that it is often open to us to harm them, but not to decide by prescriptions what shall count as their thriving, their decay or their degeneration. Talk of a tree's *eidos* or even of the *telos* it attains at its maturity may well have a place, but the place it has cannot turn on the tree's purposes, or on the belief that it has such.

Hare's remarks about the good of trees do seem to work better for the trees of the orchard, the garden and the plantation; such trees have been selectively bred so that their own fruition corresponds with human purposes. It may still not be the human purposes which make their fruitfulness or their shapeliness elements in their good; this will depend on which general theory of good and harm deserves acceptance. Nevertheless such trees can perhaps be harmed somewhat as Hare's first extension of the notion of harm suggests; their users' purposes can be frustrated if their inbred function is disrupted, somewhat as a car's inbuilt purpose can be nullified by wear and tear. Needless to say, they have a nature of their own in a way that cars do not; yet there is perhaps some analogy. It is rather over the trees, plants and animals of the wilderness that

Hare's theory manifestly breaks down; but if these creatures have a good of their own, it is at least plausible that the same applies to domesticated and cultivated species too.

Feinberg, however, doubts whether trees do have a good of their own, or that they have needs beyond our purposes and the norms which as a result we supply for them. What impresses him is that no one (outside Samuel Butler's *Erewhon*) speaks of plants as having rights. He grants that "plants, after all, are not 'mere things'; they are vital objects with inherited propensities determining their natural growth. Moreover we do say that certain conditions are 'good' or 'bad' for plants, thereby suggesting that plants, unlike rocks, are capable of having 'a good'." But this talk is misleading: paint can be believed bad for the walls of a house in the absence of a belief that the walls have "a good or welfare of their own."

Feinberg's basic point is that trees do not have wants or goals, and hence cannot know satisfaction or frustration, pleasure or pain. As they cannot suffer, we cannot be cruel to them; and as they lack desire and cognition they have no interests, and hence cannot be preserved for their own sakes. Rather when redwood groves are preserved it is for the sake of humans including generations unborn.

I grant Feinberg his premise, that plants lack beliefs and desires, and also, in a strict sense of the term "cruel," that we cannot be cruel to plants. Certainly we can show greater and lesser tenderness in their treatment: different forms of verge-cutting and hedge-cutting, for example, have very different effects on their survival and distribution, while overdoses of fertilisers and pesticides can cause them to wither prematurely. Nevertheless, although they can suffer disease and truncation, they cannot suffer agony or anguish, as perhaps a number of simpler animal species cannot either; and where it is impossible consciously to undergo either pain or the frustration of natural inclinations, cruelty is impossible too (except on the part of those who believe otherwise).

What I do not see, however, is that "desires or wants are the materials interests are made of" and hence that "mindless creatures have no interests of their own." In an earlier passage,[5] Feinberg holds that the explanation why mere things, such as the Taj Mahal or a beautiful natural wilderness, have no good of their own "consists in the fact that mere things have no conative life: no conscious wishes, desires and hopes; or urges and impulses; or unconscious drives, aims and goals; or latent tendencies, direction of growth and natural fulfillments (*sic*). Interests must be compounded somehow out of conations; hence mere things have no interest." And, if so, they have no value in their own right.

Now I have some doubt over classifying latent tendencies as conations; Feinberg's remarks about conations seem out of keeping with what they are intended to summarise. But of the two positions which might be attributed to him here, the fuller statement is preferable: latent tendencies, direction of growth and natural fulfilment do jointly seem, as Feinberg himself apparently suggests, sufficient conditions of having interests. This is not to endow machines or cities (if regarded as material objects) with interests, as they lack natural fulfilment even when built according to a plan; nor are these conditions satisfied by things lacking inherited capacities, such as forests, swamps or even species (as opposed to their members,) though the case of species will be considered again later. It does, however, imply, contrary to Feinberg's subsequent conclusions, that all individual animals and plants have interests. For all have latent tendencies at some time or other, all have a direction of growth, and all can flourish after their natural kind. There is no need to hold that trees have unconscious goals to reach the conclusion that trees have interests; indeed where nothing counts as a conscious goal it is hard to see how anything counts as an unconscious one either. The growth and thriving of trees does not need to be regarded as a kind of wanting, nor trees as possible objects of sympathy, for us to recognise that they too have a good of their own.

Feinberg, however, rejects this construction of our ordinary beliefs about plants. He grants that we talk of their needs, but holds that things only have needs of their own, as distinct from needs for the fulfilment of the goals of some extrinsic agent, when they have a good or interests of their own. Our talk of the needs of trees, however, he holds to resemble that of the needs of cars for oil and petrol: without sunshine and water they "cannot grow and survive; but unless the growth and survival of trees are matters of human concern, affecting human interests, practical or aesthetic, the needs of tress alone will not be the basis of any claim of what is 'due' them in their own right. Plants may need things in order to discharge their functions, but their functions are assigned by human interests, not their own" (p. 54).

Feinberg's readers no doubt experience relief to hear that trees make no claims and have no rights; but this sentiment is really beside the point. Certainly Feinberg has by this stage advanced a theory relating interests and rights; but if both plants have no rights and the theory suggests a close connection between having rights and having interests, then that could as easily be a reason for rejecting or modifying the theory as for concluding that plants have no interests. At all events what is at stake is interests, not rights, and the real argument here has nothing to do with rights, but amounts to the claim that as trees only have needs where human interests require the growth or survival that the needs are necessary for, they have no needs, and hence no good, of their own.

This argument might seem more difficult to controvert than Hare's prescriptivist theory, since any need of a tree which I represent as having no benefit for humans is likely to be regarded as an object of at least my interest; and, even if the play on the meaning of "interest" is remarked, it will be held that objects of my investigative curiosity are also objects of my interests as a source of aesthetic enjoyment. Nevertheless the question which must be faced is whether trees would have needs if there were no humans, and indeed whether they had needs before humans first made their appearance. Once this question is put, the answer is obvious. Indeed Feinberg seems quite mistaken to hold that trees have no needs of their own. Trees had needs before people existed, and cannot be supposed to have lost them.

Feinberg does, however, present a reply to the view that talk of the thriving, flourishing, withering and languishing of trees shows them to have a good or interests of their own. His reply is of an etymological kind, slightly reminiscent of that of Hare over "harm." The original meaning of flourish" was "blossom," but was then extended to "grow luxuriantly, increase and enlarge" and to "thrive." Then it was further extended to persons; about this sense Feinberg says that "When a person flourishes, something happens to his interests analogous to what happens to a plant when it flowers, grows and spreads" (p. 54). (Is not more involved in a person flourishing than the progress of their "interests"?) Finally flourishing is represented as a conscious act or disposition in the claim that "To flourish is to glory in the advancement of one's interests, in short, to be happy" (p. 54), an account which seems not only to degrade happiness, but also to require attitudes not required by flourishing itself.

This etymological account prepares the way for the remark "Nothing is gained by twisting the botanical metaphor back from humans to plants." Feinberg does not expect the senses of "flourish" in the two cases to be telescoped, but he does fear that the re-application of the metaphor to its source will make people believe that plants have interests "in the teeth of our actual beliefs" (p. 55). In Feinberg's eyes, of course, the sense of flourishing tied to interests is also tied to consciousness: and he regards this sense as merely metaphorical, as if there were no common element in the flourishing of people, animals and trees, such as the fulfillment or development of natural propensities. I do not, of course, claim that "flourishing" is used univocally of different natural kinds; but as there does seem to be a common element, I do not see the justification for holding that it is not in the interest of plants to flourish. Truistically they are unaware of their interests; but even creatures with cognition are often unaware of theirs, whether they are flourishing or not.

Nevertheless Feinberg tries to defend his claims by contending that "Some of our talk about flourishing plants reveals quite clearly that the interests that thrive when plants flourish are human, not 'plant interests.'" Sometimes, admittedly, there is a coincidence between our interests and a plant's natural propensities; but there are exceptions, as when we frustrate the natural propensities of a plant by removing dead flowers before the seeds have formed to encourage new flowers, and still talk of its "flourishing"; and what we then mean "is that our interest in the plant, not its own, is thriving" (p. 55). Now plants bred to have large, colourful or exotic flowers do, when they flower, satisfy our interests, even though flowering is only a part of their flourishing as even a cultivated plant. It is probably the overlap between their nature and our purposes which allows us to call this condition "flourishing"; such talk does not however show that whether or not plants flourish turns on our interests rather than theirs. If it were our purpose to hang plastic lanterns on them, we could not claim that their bedecked condition was *ipso facto* one of flourishing; flourishing states have to be states in keeping with a plant's nature (which may, of course, be a cultivated nature).

The real exception, however, to the coincidence of plants' propensities and human interests is not the one which Feinberg believes he finds. What I have in mind is the common and garden experience of unwanted flourishing. Not only do weeds flourish contrary to our interests; so do runaway hedges, trees the roots of which block drains and the shade of which annoys the neighbours, and luxuriant undergrowth which blocks our paths and by-ways; to say nothing of the stings and scratches of plants whose propensities include protection against predators. Often we have good reason to cut back such growth; yet, even as we curse it, we cannot usually deny that the plants are flourishing after their kind—and that in no ironical or animistic sense of "flourishing." But on Feinberg's theory we cannot cut back plants which in any proper sense flourish contrary to our interests, because they are conceptually impossible. Not so easily is paradise regained.

Underlying my criticisms of Hare and Feinberg there is, of course, the Aristotelian principle that the good life for a living organism turns on the fulfilment of its nature. This principle has recently been defended and applied to animals by Stephen Clark,[6] who concludes that it harms creatures to "deprive them, whether they were man or beast, of the proper fulfilment of their genetically programmed potentialities." Clark adds, by way of a *reductio* of his main opponents, the sound point that, if creatures' good is "defined by extrinsic teleology, by their use to man" then it must be held "that it is to a pig's benefit to be killed and eaten," and that it cannot flourish otherwise. But this is absurd. We should not deprive ourselves of a vocabulary in which to talk of creatures' good, or we shall not even be in a position to discuss whether or not we may disregard it.

The same principle can be restated as follows. Let the "essential" capacities of an x be capacities in the absence of which from most members of a species that species would not be the species of x's, and let "x" range over terms for living organisms. Then the flourishing of an x entails the development in it of the essential capacities of x's. I have elsewhere attempted to defend the application of this principle to humans[7]; but, as Clark says of Aristotle's similar argument, the objections which might be invoked against it over humans "do not begin to touch its application in the case of beasts." To this I should add, "or to plants," besides, of course, endorsing his view that the objections to its application to humans are mistaken. But this agreement of Clark and myself about humans is not here at stake, except insofar as the general principle is. This principle is also a principle governing the nature of good and harm, and suggests the kind of theory of harm which I should adopt as against that of Hare. It also implies that trees can be harmed in their own right, and have a "sake" for which acts can be performed, and interests and needs of their own.

What it does not imply, however, is that trees are of value in their own right, have rights, or ought to be shown consideration. To issues like these I now turn, by considering the grounds for preserving trees. Whether the fact that trees have a good of their own is a reason for caring for them is, at this stage, an unanswered question.

II: Grounds for Preserving Trees

Many of the grounds for preserving trees are also, of course, grounds for preserving wild animals and areas of wilderness as well. Of these grounds almost certainly the most important group is associated with the interests of humans. Thus it is important to preserve trees, other wild creatures and their habitats for reasons of scientific research, to retain as wide a gene pool as possible for the sake of medicine and agriculture, and for recreation, retreat and the enjoyment of natural beauty. These grounds, and the extent of their application, are well discussed by John Passmore in *Man's Responsibility for Nature*,[8] and do not need to be discussed in detail here.

Passmore correctly remarks that such considerations will often be overridden by other human interests, and sets out upon a search for other grounds for preservation. This same difficulty has been noticed by Laurence H. Tribe, who observes that, if human interests only are taken into account, the replacement of natural trees by plastic ones would often be justified.[9] His solution is to suggest that forests and other natural objects of beauty such as cliffs might be recognised as having rights which could not easily be overridden. A difficulty here, however, would be the justification of such legal or moral rights, especially where the balance of advantage would favour their disregard. As Robert Nozick[10] urges in the related matter of the treatment of animals, to justify an absolute prohibition on the infliction of pain and suffering we should need a theory of "side constraints" on which the interests of the animal concerned could not be overridden on any ground: a theory of overriding moral rights. But such a theory, requiring as it does the sacrifice on occasion of basic human needs and even of human life in the interest of non-human animals, is so counter-intuitive that it is yet less likely to command acceptance than that of Tribe. Nevertheless our inclination to accept that constraints of some kind are required in the dealings of humans with animals suggests one lesson to be learned about the preservation of wildlife: for the interests of animals, once allowed to count for something, do constitute an additional ground for preserving the plants and the habitats on which they depend; and these interests will occasionally tilt the balance of advantage in favour of preservation.

Another writer who attempts to supplement the arguments from human interests in the cause of preservation, with their acknowledged shortcomings, is Mark Sagoff.[11] His view of the justification for preserving wildlife and wilderness is that they symbolically represent to us values which cannot be satisfactorily expressed without them, and that the loss of significant scenes and places diminishes ourselves. This view does perhaps explain a great part of our interest in nature, and also supplies an extra justification for preserving some tracts of it intact; but it is, of course, another justification drawn from human interests, and, like the counterpart justifications of science, recreation and retreat, is likely to be outweighed on occasion by people's interest in, e.g., food, clothing and shelter.

In order further to assess grounds for the preservation of wildlife and wilderness which go beyond human interests we can conveniently return to Passmore's examination of our moral traditions in this same connection. The themes which he remarks concern the wrongness of causing unnecessary suffering to animals, of extirpating species and diversity, and of vandalism and wanton destruction, while he also touches on the tradition which commends reverence for life as such (and finds it wanting). As I have already acknowledged the moral relevance of animal interests to the preservation of trees, I shall concentrate on the other themes, to see if they require the interests of trees to figure among the grounds of morality.

One of the possible grounds for preserving both individual plants and species of plants is the desirability of diversity. The long history down from Plato's *Timaeus* of the principle that the more diverse a world is the better has been well traced by Lovejoy,[12] and in ecological connections it is an attractive principle because of the important role played by even the humblest member of an ecosystem. But it is less easy to agree that diversity is desirable for its own sake, and that it is because of this that we are required where possible to preserve the manifold species of our planet. It is agreed on most sides that the enjoyment of sentient creatures is desirable for its own sake, and it is an important truth that delight and pleasure are usually fostered by the experience of diversities of sounds, colours, shapes and species, as well as by diversities of social traditions and individual personalities. So it may be that what makes diversity desirable is its enjoyment, together perhaps with the range of desirable activities which it facilitates.

To some, the above theory of the desirability of diversity may seem anthropocentric; in fact, as it takes into account the experiences and activities of non-human species, this impression would be illusory. Nevertheless it makes the diversity of plant species a matter of merely derivative value, at least unless the theory is supplemented in some way; and even if it is supplemented by pointing out the importance of diversity in ecosystems for their stability, the value of diversity remains derivative, depending on the interests of those creatures such as ourselves which benefit from ecological stability.

As this may all sound unsatisfactory, it should be tested. What we have to imagine is a world in which there are no conscious experiences and no activities (at least on the part of creatures); of this imaginary world we must then ask whether it would be any the worse if it became more uniform, e.g., by coming to lack objects of one particular form or composition. Such a thought-experiment may be barely possible until we imagine the agency which might carry out the deprivation. Yet this is the sort of question which it is appropriate to ask, rather than one about, say, whether the loss of one species of plant would impoverish the world. For there may be something intrinsically desirable about plant species not because of their diversity but because they are species of living organisms; and what is at stake is whether diversity is intrinsically desirable, whatever its domain.

The agency which we seem to need to imagine can be introduced by a variation on Richard Routley's "last man" example.[13] The last man knows, in my version of this example, that all life on this planet is about to be terminated by multilateral nuclear warfare. He is, indeed, himself the last surviving sentient organism, and knows that he too will die within a few minutes; but he also happens himself to be possessed of a workable missile capable of destroying all the planet's remaining resources of diamond. The gesture of doing so would certainly be futile, but for himself it has a symbolical significance; and the question with which he is faced, and which we can ask about his projected act, is whether it would do any harm or destroy anything of intrinsic value. If we set aside the possibility that the planet might some day be repopulated with sentient organisms, which would, it seems to me, make a difference, the answer is surely that there is nothing wrong with this act, morally indifferent as I should certainly recognise it to be. The world would not through his act be any the poorer. (Maybe the act deprives God and the company of heaven of the experience of diversity, and is on that ground objectionable; but if so the objection arises because of the loss of valuable experiences rather than because of the value of diversity itself.)

There seems, then, no reason for preferring a slightly more diverse inanimate world to a slightly less diverse one, unless its constituents are objects of someone's or something's experience. In other words, diversity is not intrinsically desirable. If then there is something intrinsically undesirable in losses in the variety of living species, it will turn on their life and not on the loss to diversity as such.

It might here be suggested that it is rather the wrongness of vandalism which accounts for our objections to the elimination of species; indeed that his act was a piece of vandalism might be thought to show after all the wrongness of what was done by the "last man" of the recent example. Now certainly, as Passmore points out,[14] acts of destruction need justification; and certainly dispositions or policies involving the destruction of items of value for its own sake are strongly to be condemned. But even when policies and motives are bad (and this is not clearly true of the last man) the acts which stem from them are not always or necessarily wrong; and besides, vandalism is bad because of the harm habitually or usually done by vandals; so, if we are to hold that the elimination of a species is vandalism (which, I suspect, it often is) we need to show it to do harm or to be undesirable on some such more basic ground. The readiness of people to recognise vandalism may often curtail the need for further argument, as Pete Gunter reports about the tactics of some lumber companies opposed to the declaration of a National Park;[15] yet the recognition of vandalism entails the recognition of the unnecessary perpetration of evils, and it is these evils which constitute the basic objection to it. So we must continue to search for what of value is lost to the world when plants or their species are destroyed, to see whether such losses are all ultimately losses to sentient creatures or not.

The question now becomes whether the

continuation of each living species is valuable in itself. Passmore tells us that according to Aquinas this is the attitude of God, who "in the case of every other species except man . . . cares nothing for the benefit of the individual but does watch over the species as a whole."[16] A partially similar view is taken by Feinberg about animal species: "the preservation of a whole species may quite properly seem to be a morally more important matter than the preservation of an individual animal."[17] But Feinberg grounds this duty in our duty to future humans, rather than to the species concerned as such. And this is one of the grounds for preservation, or rather one class of grounds, taken account of already.

One reason for concern for species is concern for their current members; and when Stephen Clark observes that "Our distress at the destruction of a living tree is not merely at our loss of pleasure in its beauty," he expresses a sentiment which many would echo. Yet concern for species is not the same as concern for the present individual members: it involves the belief that it is desirable that there be elms, etc., and if it is to be an independent ground, that it is intrinsically desirable. Once a species dies out, there will be no more individual members; so either if each life of that kind is valuable in its own right, or if at least it is valuable that there be lives of that kind, the occurrence is a tragedy regardless of the circumstances or consequences.

Now the other tradition discussed by Passmore, that which enjoins reverence for life, has sometimes maintained that each life of any kind is valuable in its own right, and valuable just because it is a life. But, as Jonathan Glover cogently argues,[18] the belief that "all life is sacred" needs drastic modification even when applied to humans: for some lives cease to be worth living, and some never were so; and, we might add, even if some lives which are not in general worth living still include some worthwhile activities and experiences, nevertheless there are some lives which no longer do, and some which never did. And when we turn to other species we find that a great many organisms lack even the capacity to flourish after their own kind, being genetically or accidentally stunted, or having entered the phase of natural decay.

Thus, even if we agree with Feinberg that (some) animals have (some) rights, we are not obliged to hold that every animal life, let alone every vegetable life, is intrinsically valuable. Indeed there is good reason not to hold this at all. Whatever our objections to the destruction of individual trees, it is not the mere fact of their being alive which can justify our reaction; for lives can lack any features which make them worthwhile to anyone or anything, including the creature the life of which is in question.

If so, the intrinsic undesirability of the elimination of a living species cannot turn on the intrinsic value of each and every species member. It could still, in theory, turn on the intrinsic value of there being lives of that kind; but it is hard to see why we should accept this belief, granted that there is nothing intrinsically valuable about diversity in itself. Certainly most species are vital for the continued existence of many others, and certainly we enjoy their variety and might reasonably feel diminished at the extinction of any single one. But this is to acknowledge the importance of each species to other species, not their intrinsic value. It could then be that the tragedy involved in the termination of a species depends on the diminution of the worthwhile activities of members of other species or on the baneful effects is has on such individuals; and these said individuals, to be capable of worthwhile activities, must at least be purposive in a way in which vegetables are not.

The modern understanding of the interdependence of species supplies additional reasons why, to avert harm to humans and animals, almost all species of living creatures should be preserved, together with some of their habitats. Nevertheless the above survey of the grounds for the preservation of wildlife and wilderness suggests that there are few if any grounds to be found beyond the welfare of humans and animals; for neither does mention of vandalism add to the list of basic grounds, nor is there anything intrinsically amiss in losses to diversity, in the extinction of species or in the curtailment of life rather than worthwhile life.

Moreover what is not intrinsically valuable can hardly be thought to have rights; for what has rights must be valuable in its own right. So apparently trees and plants lack rights, even though they are needed by humans many times over—and even though we should literally starve and suffocate without them.

III: The value and rights of trees

The argument so far brings us to a paradox. Trees have needs and a good of their own, yet they have no intrinsic value and no rights of their own. Trees have interests, yet we have no obligation to protect those interests in themselves. And this is a position uncomfortably close to unreason; for, in other cases, what has interests of its own becomes *ipso facto* of moral concern, whereas in this case we are prepared to disregard a large set of interests and treat them as morally irrelevant.

Someone might at this point attempt to disavow the conclusion of Section I, and hold that, e.g., what has no purposes has no interests; but as we there saw, this would be entirely unreasonable. The more tentative conclusions of Section II, however, could more easily be re-examined. Thus it was never established that no tree is of intrinsic value, but only that, as not all lives are worth living,

it could well be that the possible objects of moral concern are confined to the class of the agents of worthwhile activities (and potential activities), and thus that the lives of non-purposive organisms are of no moral significance in themselves. But the premise only shows that some plants are of no intrinsic value, and that not all life is sacred. It could, then, still be true that a full-grown oak is after all morally as important as the crows and the squirrels which shelter in it.

But trees, it will be said, not only lack activity and self-motion but also beliefs, desires and feelings. Squirrels merit moral consideration because they have capacities in some way like our own; trees do not because the similarities are vanishingly few. Granted that it is the capacities of humans which make them morally significant, this analogical argument must be accepted at least as to what it affirms about animals, and as to the commended priority of animals over plants. Yet are the similarities really negligible? Trees, like humans and squirrels, have capacities for nutrition and growth, for respiration and for self-protection; and it is capacities and propensities such as these which determine their interests. If then their interests are partially similar to interests of acknowledged moral relevance (i.e., to our own), can we disregard them totally?

One line of argument which might suggest that plants matter in their own right runs as follows. It is perhaps unimportant that species, regarded abstractly, should continue to have members, and perhaps not all the members matter either. But, regarded concretely as populations, species are often the units which count, and are, at that, units which count a good deal: species such as "Grass" and the "Nitrogen-fixing Bacterium" are, as Clark[19] would have it, "ethically relevant individuals." And Clark is surely correct in claiming that they are "enormously more important to the world at large than any human individual." Members of species, it might be added, are often interdependent, while it is the species as a whole which maintains itself intact against external pressures and competition. Hence, it might be argued, sometimes whole species deserve consideration in their own right.

We should certainly be wary of rejecting all this on the wrong grounds. Thus Passmore concludes that species lack interests because they lack wants and purposes; but, as we have seen, wants and purposes are not necessary in this connection.[20] Indeed it may be that some simple organisms live in colonies which are like individual plants in having latent tendencies, direction of growth and natural fulfilments; and if so these colonies would have interests on the same basis as individual trees. But otherwise the waxing and waning of the populations of species are not, it seems to me, such that we can speak of the fulfilment of natural propensities which they have as species; so the interests which they have must simply be the resultants of the interests of their individual members, a reflection which holds good even of species with interdependent members. And this is as far as the argument about species regarded as populations gets us; for talk of the importance of a species to the world at large does not begin to show it to be of intrinsic value, rather than to be of consequential value.

Admittedly Clark also adduces the contention of Leopold that ecologically interdependent species owe each other consideration as members of a community. Leopold advocates a "land ethic," incorporating the whole terrestrial biotic community in the reference of the term "land." "All ethics so far evolved rest upon a single premise: that the individual is a member of a community of interdependent parts. . . . The land ethic simply enlarges the boundaries of the community to include soils, waters, plants, and animals, or collectively: the land."[21] There is here the suggestion that all interdependence entails mutual obligations. But, as Passmore observes,[22] this is not so. "In the only sense in which belonging to a community generates ethical obligation, they (sc. bacteria and men) do not belong to the same community." Passmore seems to weaken his point by requiring of members of a community that they recognise mutual obligations, a dubious claim which also begs the question against Leopold. But he is surely right that too little is shared and acknowledged by members of the biotic community for it to constitute the basis of obligations to all even on the part of those members to whom they can without absurdity be ascribed.

Is there even so a way at moving from the interests of humans, agreed to be of moral significance, and of sentient animals, increasingly recognised to matter in some degree, to the interests of non-sentient animals and plants so that they too are taken into account? The makings of such an argument begin to appear in Jan Narveson's *Mortality and Utility,* though I should emphasise that Narveson himself is concerned solely with people. What Narveson points out is, in effect, that every agent acknowledges that the satisfaction of his interests is intrinsically good. But if so, every agent must also acknowledge that the satisfaction of every other agent's individual interests is intrinsically good too, unless they can justify regarding others differently. Hence the satisfaction of everyone's interests must be of concern to every consistent moral agent.[23]

Not all the elements in this argument are of current relevance. Thus I do not need to tarry over what people will or will not acknowledge. The argument, regarded as concerned with the intrinsic value of the satisfaction of individual agents' interests, clearly requires us to justify any refusal to take interests into account. I do not begin to see how an adequate justification could be supplied over sentient animals; and even with regard to a refusal over trees it is not clear what the grounds of justification would be, though it is clear that grounds are needed.

One ground might be that trees are not sentient, and thus have radically different interests; if so, the reply is that they share with sentient organisms vegetative interests which are regarded as mattering in other cases; the physical well-being of organisms which have interests is not plausibly a matter of complete indifference, even in cases where the organisms cannot suffer pain or frustration. Another ground might be that trees are not agents, because they lack purposes; if so, the reply takes the form of a request why the interests of non-purposive organisms are not as intrinsically important as the similar interests of purposive organisms, or at least why they are not intrinsically important to some degree. If the answer to this request is that only agents can exercise sanctions, it is not of an appropriate character; if it is that only agents consciously experience frustration, it can be replied that in the case of animals the stunting of natural propensities comprises harm even when it is not understood or sensed as such by the animal affected, and if this harm is an evil, so plausibly is the stunting of organisms lacking sentience.

In all this I willingly grant that the differences in potential between different species are of the very greatest importance. Thus the goods and the harms open to most people because of their essential capacities vastly exceed those open to most animals, and similarly the blessings and sufferings made possible by capacities for purposiveness do indeed make the interests of non-purposive organisms count for less than those of purposive organisms and hence of agents. But this still does not show that the interests of trees count for nothing;

and even if not all lives are worthwhile lives, it still might be that many or even most vegetable lives are worthwhile and of value in themselves. After all, we have still to account for the distress which at least some of us feel at the destruction of a living tree. So the issue of whether trees have an intrinsic value remains at least an open one.

To attempt to test the issue, I revert to a form of Routley's "last man" example closer to his original. So as to discount the value of trees for people and sentient animals, we imagine once again that people and sentient animals are one and all doomed to imminent and inevitable nuclear poisoning, and that this is known to the last surviving human. But this time we imagine him considering the symbolic protest of hewing down with an axe the last tree of its kind, a hitherto healthy elm which has survived the nuclear explosions and which could propagate its kind if left unassaulted. Nothing sentient is ever likely to evolve from its descendants; so the question which he faces, and we can ask about him, is whether there is anything wrong with chopping it down and whether the world would be the poorer for the loss of it. We must suppose further, of course, that he himself will not suffer if he does not cut down the tree; he has enough timber already for firewood and shelter for his own last hours.

This question may seem to raise a problem of method; for it is asked of circumstances about which some would say that we no longer know how to apply our ordinary concepts of value. It is unclear to me how they would claim to know this; I can only invite those who nevertheless make this claim to attend instead to more ordinary cases of the uprooting of healthy trees and our reaction to it. So long, however, as the last man retains his ordinary concepts of value and his capacity to apply them, the question would seem to be both conceptually proper and apposite; and, if so, the problem of method proves illusory.

Most people who face the question would, I believe, conclude that the world would be the poorer for this act of the "last man" and that it would be wrong. He would be unnecessarily destroying a living creature which could have renewed the stock of its own species. (I suspect that a similar reaction would be the typical one to more everyday uprootings, though of course the reasons for such a reaction would often in those cases be mixed ones. I also suspect that the reaction would seldom be different even if the interests of sentient creatures are discounted.) And if, without being swayed by the interests of sentient creatures, we share in these conclusions and reactions, we must also conclude that the interests of trees are of moral significance. Although they rarely come or should come foremost in ethical deliberation, they can and in principle should be considered.

There are, of course, in practice ample grounds for disregarding the interests of trees at most junctures. Human and/or animal interests are almost always at stake, and mere vegetation can be forgotten where those interests would be imperilled. The good of trees might outweigh some of our whims; but it does not outweigh our interests except where our interests depend on it. But this is not to make trees of no ethical relevance in themselves. Very slightly, they have interests mirroring ours; at very many removes they are our living kin. But interests do, it seems, supply reasons for consideration; and there is always the residual possibility of their interests being of greater significance than any others which are at stake.

Theoretically at least, the same applies to other plants, to non-sentient animals, and to those colonies of organisms which function as individuals; although just as among sentient animals so here too there are diversities in the degree of consideration due. There again, the overall grounds for preservation and careful treatment will be supplemented in respect of value to other organisms by enormously diverse amounts, but never more, I suspect, than in the case of trees.

All the same, my conclusion is not without practical significance. It implies among other things that some degree of respect is due to almost all life, even though the main ground for the preservation of natural kinds remains human interests; and it implies that, where natural trees could be replaced without aesthetic loss or other disadvantage to humans, there are still reasons for not doing so. At the more theoretical level it suggests that nothing which has interests is to be viewed wholly instrumentally, and that things which have interests characteristically have some value in their own right. If trees have a good which is not our good, then they also constitute a good; if they have their own form of flourishing, they are thereby of value in themselves.

Do trees have rights? Only what is valuable in its own right has rights; but many trees do now seem valuable in their own right. Yet trees certainly do not have rights in Nozick's sense of there being "side-constraints" prohibiting various forms of treatment whatever the need or the benefits. At best, their interests have to be weighed with those of people and animals.

Need we, however, reject all forms of conceptual tie between interests and rights? The form of connection propounded by Feinberg is as follows. Creatures have rights if and only if they have interests, consideration is due to them, and it is due to them not for the sake of anything else but for their own sake.[24] Interests are necessary since what has rights must be capable of being represented and of being a beneficiary, having a welfare of its own. Feinberg believes, in the light of this condition, that trees lack rights; but, as we have seen, he is mistaken. Now no one would dispute that consideration is often due to trees where this just means that there are grounds for tending or preserving them; what is not usually accepted is that it is due to them for their own sake. If I am right and it is, then, granted Feinberg's conceptual connection of interests and rights, many trees have rights.

Such rights would, however, like all other rights be overridable from time to time; and the grounds for them, the intrinsic value of trees, would be so slender by comparison with the grounds of other rights as to be outweighed most of the time, so much so as to disappear into near oblivion. Yet if some trees have rights, then we should occasionally bear the fact in mind, or unsound theory will lead to misguidedness in action.

Alternatively someone who agrees that trees have interests and are of ethical relevance but cannot accept that they have rights might wish to reject or amend the conceptual tie delineated by Feinberg, such, perhaps, that only purposive or potentially purposive creatures can have rights. To such an amendment I should not object. Rights are not the sole ground of moral reasoning, and it does seem incongruous to represent the treatment of trees as a matter of justice. In any case the grounds for the ascription of rights in Feinberg's unamended sense to trees would remain, and we could show concern for their needs and interests without believing them to have rights. We could, I think, still talk of obligations to them, since if it is sometimes wrong to destroy them for no reason beyond themselves then it is on those occasions obligatory not to do so,[25] and indeed the obligation is due to nothing but the tree, if it is due to anything at all.

"And God said, 'Let the earth pelt forth vegetation, plants yielding seed, and fruit trees bearing fruit in which is their seed, each according to its kind, upon the earth.' And it was so. The earth brought forth vegetation, plants yielding seed according to their own kinds, and trees bearing fruit in which is their seed, each according to its kind. And God saw that it was good."[26] Of course, in Genesis 1 all creation is good; be that as it may, living creatures in any case, it would seem, characteristically have a value of their own.[27]

Notes

1. R. M. Hare, *Essays on the Moral Concepts* (New York: Macmillan, 1972), pp. 98f.

2. Joel Feinberg, "The Rights of Animals and Unborn Generations," in *Philosophy and Environmental Crisis*, ed. William T. Blackstone (Athens: University of Georgia Press, 1974), 43–68, esp. pp. 51–55.

3. *Summa Contra Gentiles*, translated by the English Dominican Fathers, Benziger Brothers, 1928, ch. 112, quoted in *Animal Rights and Human Obligations*, ed. Tom Regan and Peter Singer (Englewood Cliffs, N.J.: Prentice-Hall, 1976), pp. 56–59.

4. See the discussion of the Stoic Balbus in Cicero's *De Natura Deorum* by John Passmore at p. 14 of *Man's Responsibilities for Nature* (London: Duckworth, 1974).

5. Feinberg, "The Rights of Animals and Unborn Generations," pp. 49–50.

6. Stephen R. L. Clark, *The Moral Status of Animals* (Oxford, U.K.: Clarendon Press, 1977), pp. 57–58.

7. Robin Attfield, "On Being Human," *Inquiry* 17 (1974): 175–92; also Robin Attfield, *A Theory of Value and Obligation* (London: Croom Helm, 1987), chaps. 3–5.

8. Passmore, *Man's Responsibilities for Nature*, pp. 101–10.

9. Laurence H. Tribe, "Ways Not to Think about Plastic Trees," *Yale Law Journal* 83 (1974): 1315–48.

10. Robert Nozick, *Anarchy, State and Utopia* (Oxford, U.K.: Blackwell, 1974), pp. 28–42.

11. Mark Sagoff, "On Preserving the Natural Environment," *Yale Law Journal* 84 (1974): 205–67.

12. A. O. Lovejoy, *The Great Chain of Being* (Cambridge, Mass.: Harvard University Press, 1936).

13. Richard Routley, "Is There a Need for a New, an Environmental, Ethic?" in *Proceedings of the Fifteenth World Congress of Philosophy*, Varna, Bulgaria, 1973, pp. 205–10.

14. Passmore, *Man's Responsibilities for Nature*, p. 124.

15. Pete A. Y. Gunter, "The Big Thicket," in Blackstone, *Philosophy and Environmental Crisis*, 117–37, esp. pp. 126–29.

16. Passmore, *Man's Responsibilities for Nature*, p. 117.

17. Feinberg, "The Rights of Animals and Unborn Generations," p. 56.

18. Jonathan Glover, *Causing Death and Saving Lives* (London: Penguin, 1977), ch. 3.

19. Clark, *The Moral Status of Animals*, p. 171.

20. Passmore, *Man's Responsibilities for Nature*, pp. 55f.

21. Aldo Leopold, *A Sand County Almanac* (New York: Oxford University Press, 1949), pp. 203f, quoted by Clark at p. 164.

22. Passmore, *Man's Responsibilities for Nature*, p. 116.

23. Jan Narveson, *Morality and Utility* (Baltimore: Johns Hopkins Press, 1967), pp. 271–75.

24. Feinberg effectively deals with the objection that right-holders must also be capable of making and of waiving claims on their own at "The Rights of Animals and Unborn Generations," pp. 46–49.

25. The claim that it is obligatory not to do what it is wrong to do and the criteria of obligation, wrongness and rightness are discussed more fully in my "Supererogation and Double Standards," *Mind* 89 (1980): 481–99.

26. *Genesis*, ch. 1, vv. 11f, Revised Standard Version.

27. The current chapter first appeared in *Journal of Value Inquiry* 15 (1981): 35–54. I am grateful for comments and criticisms of an earlier draft from David Attfield, John Benson, Robin Downie, Robert Elliot, Thomas McPherson, Mary Midgley, Heather Milne, Peter Singer and members of the Philosophy Seminar of University College, Cardiff, and for bibliographical assistance from Richard Routley. He and Val Routley arrive by another route at some cognate conclusions in "Against the Inevitability of Human Chauvinism," in *Ethics and Problems of the 21st Century*, ed. K. E. Goodpaster and K. M. Sayre (Notre Dame and London: Notre Dame University Press, 1979), pp. 36–59.

Lawrence E. Johnson

Holistic Entities—Species

We have already noted that it is incorrect to construe a species as a collection of individual organisms. A species is a type of ongoing process, the embodiment in organisms, progressively over time, of a genetic lineage. It was further argued that *Homo sapiens*, as distinguished from individual human beings, has morally significant interests. It is only on such a basis that we can properly account for the moral status of humanity. Indeed, it is only on such a basis, if at all, that we can accord direct moral significance to the preservation of any species. However, that species are subject to morally significant injury and, more broadly, that they have morally significant interests is possible only if having morally significant interests does not require sentience or any other feature that species lack. Further consideration led me to conclude that *all* well-being interests are morally significant, and that any entity that has sufficient self-identity for things to go better or worse for it (in its own right) thereby has well-being interests. Accordingly, I concluded species are among those entities having morally significant interests.

Becoming extinct is obviously bad for a species, whereas continuing in equilibrium with its environment is good for it. Survival and equilibrium with its environment facilitate its well-being. Like a wave moving over the water, a species is an ongoing process that is sequentially embodied in different bits of matter. Unlike a wave, however, a species has a cohesive self-identity that defines what is good for it. Some things contribute to the coherence, unity, and viability of a species, and some things detract. Unlike a wave, a species, when healthy, is a process that proceeds in a way serving to maintain its coherence, unity, and viability. As a species flows through the generations, it maintains a form of homeostasis that serves to facilitate its well-being needs, and which also in part serves to define itself and its needs. Geographical dispersion, optimal genetic diversity, optimal reproductive rates, and so forth often serve as centers of homeostasis around which the state of affairs of a species fluctuates. For instance, some species, such as the lion, will lower their reproductive rate during times of

From Lawrence E. Johnson, *A Morally Deep World*, New York: Cambridge University Press, pp. 208–11, 1991. Copyright © by Lawrence E. Johnson. Reprinted with the permission of Cambridge University Press and Lawrence E. Johnson.

scarcity and increase it during times of abundance, which in either case serves to maintain the viability of the species, or at least that of the subpopulation (J. Stevenson-Hamilton 1954). No doubt individual lions tend to preserve their genetic fitness by, through some mechanism, altering their reproductive rates—concentrating or dispersing their genetic resources. By lowering their reproductive rate, as conditions dictate, they would tend to maximize the number of their *living* descendants. Through those individuals the species as a whole maintains its well-being. As well, the genetic diversity maintained by a species, and its various activities, serve to define the species and what is good for it. A species may even change and evolve, developing different requirements and striking a new balance with its environment, arriving at a new self-identity.

Although lions serve the well-being of their species together with their own genetic interests by varying their reproductive rate, it is not always true that the interests of the species are served by the satisfaction of individual genetic interests. In some cases, the welfare of the species is even undermined by things that serve the genetic interests of the individual. In such extreme cases, one would have to say that the species was unhealthy, being in a condition unfavorable to its well-being. An example is the Argus pheasant, whose males have very large secondary wing feathers.[1] These make it difficult for the male to fly properly or to escape predators, and so are quite dysfunctional—save for reproductive purposes. Large and attractive feathers are the primary consideration in the female's selection of a mate. Having long feathers is in the genetic interests of the male, since otherwise he would have no descendants. Mating with a large-feathered male is in the genetic interests of the female, for if she mated with a male with shorter feathers, her male descendants inheriting the trait would have less reproductive success. It would be an advantage for the female to mate with the male that had the largest wing feathers around. By the same token, if a male were blessed with exceptionally large secondary wing feathers, that would be even better for him, if he lived long enough to mate. The species thereby evolves in the direction of ever larger display feathers, all the while being nudged toward extinction by its more effective competitors. In an even more extreme case, the Irish deer was, arguably, driven to extinction by sexual selection favoring huge and otherwise dysfunctional antlers (Stephen Jay Gould 1974). Seven-foot antlers tend to get in the way. Yet, with deer and pheasant alike, reproductive probabilities dictate that it is advantageous for the individual to have attributes and follow mating strategies that are disadvantageous for the species as a whole. So, advantage for the individual does not always yield a functional homeostasis for the species. Yet species have an interest in maintaining their well-being and in not evolving in a way that undermines it. It follows that the interests of the species are not the aggregated interests of the individual species members.

It is still true that the interests of a species often, though not always, coincide with those of its individual species members. In any case, the interests of a species are affected only through those individuals that embody the species at a given time. Individual and species interests are further intertwined with those of other entities, such as ecosystems. The interests of ecosystems and of any other holistic entities are affected only by what happens to their individual organisms. Again, the various interests may or may not coincide. Optional reproductive levels may, for instance, be in the interests of individual, species, and ecosystem alike. In other cases, interests may diverge. Of course, we must first ask whether ecosystems and other holistic entities really do have well-being interests to be considered.

Notes

1. Mentioned by Konrad Lorenz, *On Aggression* (London: Methuen, 1967). Translation of *Das Sogenannte Bose* (Vienna: Dr. G. Borotha-Schoeler Verlag, 1963).

References

Gould, Stephen J. "The Origin and Function of 'Bizarre' Structures." *Evolution* 4 (1974): 191–220.

Stevenson-Hamilton, J. *Wildlife in South Africa* (London: Cassell, 1954).

Lawrence E. Johnson

Ecointerests and Forest Fires

A piece of proverbial wisdom that is actually somewhat true is that there is such a thing as the balance of nature—though we must not take that to mean anything exact or unchanging. Ecosystems display quite a high level of homeostasis. That they do so is virtually a truism, in that they maintain themselves through time in the midst of quite a lot happening. Nor is it a matter of different things remaining more or less stable in parallel. Barry Commoner's "first law of ecology," that "everything is connected to everything else" (1972, 33), is particularly true of ecosystems. Not only do they maintain themselves, they do so with a very high degree of interconnection. Just as we may think of an individual organism as an ongoing life process, manifested in a continually changing combination of material elements, and a species as an ongoing process progressively embodied in different individuals, so may we think of an ecosystem as an ongoing process taking place through a complex system of interrelationships between organisms, and between organisms and their nonliving environment. The organisms change, and the interrelationships may vary somewhat, but there is a continuity to the ecosystem, and a center of homeostasis around which the states of the ecosystem fluctuate, which defines its self-identity. Normally, an ecosystem maintains its stability through an intricately complex feedback system. One example of that is the forage-deer-mountain lion balance, which remains roughly constant through continuous oscillation. However, an ecosystem can suffer stress and be impaired. It can be degraded to lower levels of stability and interconnected complexity. It can have its self-identity ruptured. In short, an ecosystem has well-being interests and therefore has moral significance.

No more than in the case of species or individual organisms are the interests of an ecosystem the aggregated interests of its components, and, as in those cases, the various interests might sometimes be in conflict. It may even be in the interests of an ecosystem for a particular species (or sometimes for particular individuals) to die off, allowing the ecosystem to develop in accordance with its inherent nature. It is often the case that a particular species is a useful component of a given ecosystem only

From Lawrence E. Johnson, *A Morally Deep World*, New York: Cambridge University Press, pp. 216–21, 1991. Copyright © by Lawrence E. Johnson. Reprinted with the permission of Cambridge University Press and Lawrence E. Johnson.

during certain stages of the ecosystem's life cycle. In such a case, the interests of the ecosystem are still the interests of a whole life process that integrally incorporates the problematic component. In some of the valleys of California's Sierra Nevada, for instance, ecosystems often contain a high proportion of junipers, which, in the natural progression, eventually make way for the more slowly growing oaks.[1] Junipers grow rapidly and, being full of sap, are very combustible. Under natural conditions, fires caused by lightening periodically burn out the juniper, preventing it from crowding out the oaks and other plants. After a fire, not only the oaks but the smaller plants and grasses have the opportunity to flourish, and there is an attendant increase in the populations of animals, birds, and insects. If the fires do not come, the juniper, together with a few other species, largely takes over, leading to an ecosystem of reduced diversity and stability. The integrity of the complex whole and its diverse living unity is compromised in favor of an impoverished uniformity.

This is not to say that the juniper is only a weed, one that ought to be exterminated. The juniper has its role in the life of an ecosystem. There should always be a few around so that they may (re)establish themselves in that or a neighboring ecosystem if the conditions should ever become appropriate. When, for instance, there is a total burnout, completely devastating an area, the rapidly growing junipers are very useful in restoring the biotic community and maintaining it until the more slowly growing trees and the other beings of the mature ecosystem again hold sway. Most fires, though, do not devastate an area. They are generally benign. They burn through quickly, removing such things as juniper, and providing growing room for the annuals and other rapidly growing small plants. On the larger scale, they clear the way for the more slowly growing fire-resistant trees. Such trees usually sustain relatively little damage. Minor fires do not burn deeply enough to kill the living soil. When minor fires do not occur from time to time, there is a buildup of undergrowth and debris, and an overgrowth of highly flammable trees such as juniper. Then any fire will be a major one, killing everything including the soil. At certain stages, then, the juniper is helpful to the ecosystem and at others harmful to it. The ecosystem, it would be fair to say, is a life process having a self-identity distinct from that of its component entities, and which may call for juniper at some times and not at others, just as the life process of an oak calls for acorns at some times and not at others.

Homo sapiens, as so often happens, interferes to make a mess of things. When we are not making a mess of things from bad intentions we too often make a mess of things from good intentions. When I was a boy, it was a well-known fact that forest fires were bad. Whatever our attitude toward good and bad might have been, everyone knew that forest fires were bad. The message was preached at us in school and over the media. If it was not the direct content of the message, it was a presupposition. It was drummed into us in the Boy Scouts, and Smokey Bear told us that only we could prevent forest fires. Display posters depicted animal orphans beside burned-out stumps. Forest fires were downright evil. We could no more doubt that than we could doubt that the earth went around the sun—though in both cases we were largely relying on the testimony of experts. No doubt this moral fact led some of the antisocial among us to throw around a few matches. For the most part, we were influenced to be careful not to cause fires accidentally. That was generally to the good, since the frequency of fires that benefit an ecosystem is that which occurs naturally. Ecosystems evolve that way. However, public policy was to extinguish or contain *all* fires, including those of natural origin. As a result, flammable material would accumulate to the point that a very large and very intense fire would utterly destroy an area. Where that did not happen, as in heavily protected Yosemite Valley, the resulting imbalance of species led to a weakened and impoverished ecosystem, with fewer animals, birds, and other species, less complexity and diversity, less stability and less integrity of being.

We cannot give proper recognition to the role of fires in ecosystems if we think only in terms of the welfare of individuals. In general, we can neither understand ecosystems properly nor act properly toward them if we think only in terms of individuals. Consider: Although a fire may contribute to the well-being of an ecosystem, it clearly does not enhance the well-being of each and every individual or species in the ecosystem. Being burned to death is bad for any plant or animal. Still, other individuals gain from improved habitat and decreased competition. Many of the beneficiaries do not yet exist, being future members of increased populations resulting from the fire. For all those affected among individuals that now exist, it would be virtually impossible to weigh up the profits and losses. It may be that the losers outnumber the winners and that their losses outweigh the gains of the winners, but that is only conjecture. It is very nearly irrelevant. It is not entirely irrelevant, since individuals do count, but normally the effects on the species involved and the ecosystem as a whole are weightier and less ambiguous. Species such as the oak, and the animal and small plant species—indeed, most species—largely benefit from periodic small fires in terms of securing and maintaining a viable position in a flourishing ecosystem. (Whether the juniper species suffers is not something I can say for certain. Perhaps it is injured by being periodically decimated, or perhaps it is benefited by the long-term well-being of ecosystems that have a role for juniper. Would an undisturbed ecosystem dominated by juniper be viable in the very long run?) As well as species the ecosystem as a whole flourishes, benefiting in terms of stability and the organic unity of complex interconnection. It flourishes as an ongoing life system. In Yosemite and other areas, I am pleased to note, attempts are now being made to right past wrongs through a program of controlled burning. While I have used fires as my example, we can make similar points concerning adding or eliminating species, or other things that would affect the life process of an ecosystem. We must consider the whole not merely as a collection, but as a whole with its very own interests. Only then can we develop an adequate environmental policy.

Developing a morally adequate environmental policy will not be easy. No one has developed a really convincing account of how we are to measure interest satisfaction and of how we are to balance distribution of benefits against maximization. This is true even on a purely anthropocentric basis, yet the problem is even more complex if we recognize the moral standing of nonhuman individuals, species, and ecosystems. If vastly different beings have vastly different interests, in differing ways to varying degrees, it will be no easy matter, if possible at all, to assign priorities. There arise a great host of issues. To start with, we certainly need a more detailed account of the interests of species and ecosystems. Then there are the more directly moral questions. What consideration is due to a rainforest, for instance, and under what circumstances might its interests be infringed? Some answers are better than other answers, but no general theory is adequate. Even when interests are commensurable, it is no easy matter to settle conflicts of interest, and it may just be that some interests, some benefits and injuries, are not properly commensurable at all. So, what are we to do? How are we humans to pursue a moral career in the natural world?

Notes

1. This material is based on public presentations at Yosemite National Park, California, and on my discussions with the staff there.

Reference

Commoner, Barry. *The Closing Circle*. London: Jonathan Cape, 1972.

Part III

Contemporary Forestry Ethics

Since the blooming of environmental ethics and the increasing volume of environmental criticism of public forestry in the 1970s, various efforts have been made by philosophers and philosophically-minded foresters to evaluate public and private forestry. Much of this has been directed not so much to the techniques and scientific issues in forest management as it has been to its underlying ethical and philosophical assumptions. However, philosophers have also assessed some of the arguments that have been used to bolster certain forms of forest management. Two early examples of the latter include critical evaluations of intensive forest management, one done by an American philosopher, Pete Gunter, and the other by two Australian philosophers, Richard and Val Routley.

In 1972 Gunter, a philosopher at North Texas State University, published *The Big Thicket*, a book that detailed the effects of the exploitation and development of the Big Thicket area of southeastern Texas by large timber companies and land developers.[1] As president of the Big Thicket Association in Texas, Gunter argued that a destructive form of intensive forestry was being practiced in the Big Thicket: not only were too many trees being cut in the interests of industrial tree farming, but the Thicket was losing its unique natural diversity, and its aesthetic and scientific values were being needlessly destroyed.[2] Gunter marshaled biological, historical, and economic arguments for the conclusion that the Thicket should be preserved as a last remnant of the "traditional deep Southern forest."

In the spirit of John Muir, Gunter focused on forest management in a particular region, but his critique of Big Thicket forestry was unique mostly in its geographical

---

1. *The Big Thicket: A Challenge for Conservation* (Austin, Tex.: Jenkins Publishing Company, 1971).
2. *The Big Thicket*, p. 65.

focus and not in its use of philosophical techniques or arguments. Another early and quite thorough review of intensive "tree farm" forestry was done by the Australian environmental philosophers Richard and Val Routley in the 1970s.[3] The Routleys argued that intensive forestry was "the greatest threat to remaining natural forest areas" in developed countries such as Australia. They proceeded to show how the agricultural model of wood production in Australian forestry had detrimental effects on forest values other than wood production and even on the sustainability of long-term intensive wood production itself.[4] They attributed this to the management of forests primarily to provide profits for private industry and argued that what was good for the timber and wood-products industry in Australia was not necessarily good for Australia. Using methods of argument analysis familiar in philosophy, the Routleys explained how advocates of intensive forestry in Australia promoted their case for forest exploitation with a number of "pseudo-ecological arguments." This included the argument that allowing a continued supply of trees is environmentally admirable and that since nature is dynamic it is futile to retain forests in an "unchanging natural state."[5] They concluded that the real conflicts between intensive wood production and other forest values, and the resulting conflict between intensive forestry and forest conservation, could not be smoothed over by these and other rationales used by the lumber industry. Like Aldo Leopold, the Routleys suggested that there are differences in attitudes and ideology that account for these conflicts. Advocates of intensive forestry disagree with their critics about the proper uses of forests, the goals of such uses, and the ways in which forests ought to be controlled by humans. The Routleys asserted that intensive forestry management was in conflict above all with true forest conservation, because of the harmful effects it has on the habitat requirements of a large number of wildlife, on forest soils, and on aesthetic values.[6]

Critiques of intensive forestry have been made by many other individuals as well, both those with and without technical knowledge of forestry and its methods.[7] The point is that philosophers and philosophically-minded foresters have contributed to

3. Richard Routley and Val Routley, *The Fight for the Forests*, 2d ed. (Canberra: Research School of Social Sciences, Australian National University, 1974).

4. Routley and Routley, *The Fight for the Forests*, p. 1.

5. The Routleys discuss a variety of such arguments in chapter 1 of their book. Not surprisingly, versions of many of these arguments are still heard today in debates about public forest management in the United States and elsewhere in the world, where intensive forestry is being practiced.

6. Ibid. For another, more recent assessment by a philosopher of private forest management in a particular locale, in California, see Lisa Newton, "Chainsaws of Greed: The Case of Pacific Lumber," *Business and Professional Ethics Journal* 8(3) (Fall 1989): 29–61. Newton considers in some detail the social and environmental consequences, and also the ethical implications, of Maxxam's hostile takeover of Pacific Lumber Company, in northern California.

7. In addition to the Lisa Newton article, another recent example of such an assessment by a philosopher is Hugh Williams, "What Is Good Forestry? An Ethical Examination of Forest Policy and Practice in New Brunswick," *Environmental Ethics* 18(4) (Winter 1996): 391–410. Williams links moral and philosophical concepts to the ideas of biological diversity and maximizing the public good, and applies this theory to forestry in New Brunswick.

these assessments of intensive forestry by identifying some of the underlying and, they believe, faulty ethical and philosophical assumptions on which this form of forestry has been based.

In this part of the anthology, some examples of efforts by environmental philosophers and foresters to look more specifically at the ethics of contemporary forestry are presented. In chapters 6 through 11, readings are included that consider basic principles in forestry ethics, codes of ethics in several natural resource sciences, the incorporation of a land ethic into the ethics code of the Society of American Foresters, advocacy of new forms of environmental ethics in federal land agencies, ethical issues about global forestry, the ethical focus of new forestry and ecoforestry, and the ethical dialogue in the "war in the woods." The aims of these readings vary: most are intended not merely to criticize existing systems of forestry ethics but to provide some alternative ideas on which modified systems could be based. They seek to clarify the philosophical basis of forestry ethics and thus to reform the practice of intensive forestry.

The viewpoints expressed in these chapters can be related to the ethical systems presented in Part I, since Pinchotian resource management, Leopold's land ethic, and deep ecology provide different directions for ethics in forestry and for current discussions of forester ethics.[8] Many—but not all—of the authors in these chapters recognize the power of Leopold's ideas and of more biocentered forms of ethical thinking. They build on insights from the land ethic to develop alternatives to the dominant paradigm of intensive, industrialized forest management and some of its standard forest practices.[9] The inclusion of these selections affirms that there are powerful philosophical sources arguing for change in forestry, and that many central assumptions of forestry are being seriously challenged.

---

8. Many efforts have been made by foresters to consider the underlying ethical issues in their discipline, and to apply the ideas of the "founding fathers" of forest management in the United States. One excellent example is Alan G. McQuillan, "Is National Forest Planning Incompatible with a Land Ethic?" *Journal of Forestry* 88 (May 1990): 31–37, and there are many others.

9. The idea that intensive, industrial forestry and its assumptions are part of the existing and dominant social paradigm in Western industrial societies has been discussed at length by environmental philosophers, environmental sociologists, and political scientists, among others. Some argue that this dominant social paradigm is shifting and, with it, a new environmental and also new resource management paradigm are emerging. The work of the environmental sociologist Riley Dunlap is important here. See, e.g., "The New Environmental Paradigm," *The Journal of Environmental Education* 9 (1978): 10–19, but also publications of the political scientist, Ronald Inglehart, referred to earlier. The idea of a shift in values and also in resource management has been translated into forestry by David N. Bengston, "Changing Values and Ecosystem Management," *Society and Natural Resources* 7 (1994): 515–33; and Bruce Shindler and Lorie A. Cramer, "Shifting Public Values for Forest Management: Making Sense of Wicked Problems," *Western Journal of Applied Forestry* 14(1) (January 1999): 28–34.

CHAPTER 6

Basic Principles in Forestry Ethics

Kristin Shrader-Frechette, a University of Notre Dame philosopher, and Earl McCoy, a biologist at the University of South Florida in Tampa, have carefully explained how specific kinds of values, such as methodological values, are evident both in the processes of the ecological sciences and in their applications to land management and conservation issues.[1] The same is true for forestry, fisheries, and other applied natural resource sciences; they are not driven by science and scientific concerns alone but are value-laden activities, and their applications in land management are also deeply affected by values and value judgments. In this regard they are no different than other "professional" disciplines; they not only generate and utilize scientific information, but they also embody ethical norms and norms of professional practice. These norms are articulated, reinforced, and criticized in the "culture" of scientific disciplines and the relationships of scientists—that is, in processes of "socialization" and in the personal experiences that take place in their organizations and work environments. In forestry this includes colleges of forestry, professional forestry groups, the public and private companies and agencies in which foresters work, and the interactions foresters have with other foresters, clients, forestry students, the public, and forests themselves. The sources of these norms are partly social and partly personal; they can be located in applicable laws, bureaucratic mandates, educational principles, codes of professional ethics, and business directives, among other things, but also in personal reflection and interpretation of ethical issues by foresters in particular cases and situations. Some of these values have to do with the goals of forest science and management, others with the scientific and practical techniques involved, and still others with the particular responsibilities that professionals impose on each other. The values are not always visible or even acknowledged to exist by scientists and resource professionals but are present nevertheless and are an integral part of the way they conduct their work.

---

1. "How the Tail Wags the Dog: How Value Judgments Determine Ecological Science," *Environmental Values* 3 (1994): 107–20, and *Method in Ecology: Strategies for Conservation* (Cambridge, U.K.: Cambridge University Press, 1993). These ideas are based in part on recent analyses in the philosophy of science; e.g., on the work of Helen Longino, *Science as Social Knowledge* (Cambridge, U.K.: Cambridge University Press, 1990).

Insofar as forestry and the other applied environmental sciences are professions, the members of those professions seek to serve a beneficial public need through their technical expertise and their organizations, and thus have certain obligations to society.[2] Forestry professionals have many ethical responsibilities that follow from this, including responsibilities to other professionals and coworkers; to the agencies and corporations that employ them; to the human communities and broader public they serve; and, according to recent systems of environmental ethics, to forests, forest organisms, and forest systems themselves. A profession by definition adopts norms, canons, or principles of professional practice that embody these various obligations, and these norms are typically identified in their written ethics codes.

As Shrader-Frechette and McCoy indicate, however, some values and norms may bias the procedures and outcomes of applied science, while others may not. Possessing values, then, as a component of one's scientific or management activities, is not something to reject as inappropriate but instead should be recognized and understood for what it is. Foresters and other applied scientists need to become more aware of what their values are and how they apply them in their work; they should determine what kind of values they possess then critically evaluate and change them, as the occasion requires. This is the general drift of the reading selections on forestry ethics that follow. They ask: What particular values, ethical principles, or norms exist in forestry? And, given the social changes toward more environmentalism, deeper environmental concern, and increasing interest in environmental ethics, how should these values be redefined? In the first reading selection below, Michael McDonald, a distinguished philosopher who holds the Maurice Young Chair in Applied Ethics at the University of British Columbia, examines the basic ethical features of the profession of forestry, as they are present in several Canadian forestry sources, such as the code of ethics of the Association of British Columbia Professional Foresters. His approach is designed to reinforce the importance of ethical values in this profession, and to explain what they mean for foresters. He elaborates some difficulties in interpreting these values, such as the forester's obligations to clients, the public, and future generations.

As indicated in earlier chapters, Gifford Pinchot had much to do with defining some of the basic ethics of forestry in the United States, and the orientation of his resource ethic was primarily human-centered or "anthropocentric." It emphasized the centrality of human wants and desires with regard to forests, and of human roles and uses of forest systems. It also fit into the economic resource and agronomic model of the forestry disciplines and assumed, for example, that forest organisms exist primarily to serve human ends, in fact that these resources should promote the greatest good for the greatest number of humans. However, the selection in this chapter by the Canadian professional forester Paul M. Wood argues that this utilitarian forestry ethic is flawed for a number of reasons, not the least of which is that it reserves the definition of what is good to forestry professionals instead of to the public. A more adequate ethic would not define the good solely in terms of maximizing utility, he concludes.[3] James Coufal then goes

---

2. There are many definitions of a profession among the technical disciplines, but they generally follow sociological models of professions, mention certain common elements, and place service to society at the core of a profession. See, e.g., D. Allan Firmage, *Modern Engineering Practice: Ethical, Professional, and Legal Aspects,* "The Definition of a Profession" (New York: Garland STPM Press, 1980).

3. J. E. De Steiguer argues that Pinchot's utilitarian goal of providing the greatest good for the greatest number, which Pinchot and others borrowed from the utilitarian philosophers Jeremy Bentham and John Stuart Mill,

one step further than McDonald and Wood by interpreting the basic outlines of an applied environmental ethic for foresters. Coufal is a well-known forester in the Society of American Foresters, serving as its president in 1999, and a long-time and now retired professor of forestry and environmental studies at the State University of New York, College of Environmental Science and Forestry at Syracuse. He looks at the meaning of environmentalism for forestry and considers the anthropocentric, biocentric, and ecocentric perspectives in ethical thinking. He defines six basic criteria that an adequate ethic for foresters should satisfy, then suggests that this system is a modification of Pinchot's utilitarianism.

As also indicated earlier, Pinchotian resource ethics is being challenged today by more biocentric ethical systems, influenced by thinkers such as Aldo Leopold and the founder of deep ecology philosophy, Arne Naess. These systems question the "anthropocentric bias" in forester ethics and invite foresters and other forest users to see themselves as more integral parts of nature and as members of one species among many whose roles are important and significant in forests. But how can this new, more ecological perspective, this new environmental ethic, be incorporated into forestry and forestry ethics? One answer to this question can be found in what deep ecology implies about forest management. Devall and Sessions assert that this philosophy rejects the approach of Pinchotian resource conservation in favor of what they call "Muir's righteous management" or "biocentric ecological management."[4] As they see it, this form of management encourages forest managers and property owners to "flow with" rather than to force natural processes in forests. Ecoforestry is oriented to local communities in particular bioregions rather than to the aims of large and intensive, industrially-based forest corporations. The practical dimensions of this kind of forest management have been explained in detail by supporters of ecoforestry, and the "Ecoforestry Declaration of Interdependence" in this chapter indicates its general directions. As indicated earlier, this approach is a product of the Ecoforestry Institute founded by Alan Drengson, a professor of environmental philosophy at the University of Victoria in British Columbia. More information about the meaning of ecoforestry for forest management practices can be found in Chapter 11.

---

involves an inherent logical fallacy that makes its achievement illusory in forestry. See his article "Can Forestry Provide the Greatest Good for the Greatest Number?" *Journal of Forestry* 92(9) (September 1994): 22–25.

4. Bill Devall and George Sessions, *Deep Ecology: Living as if Nature Mattered* (Salt Lake City: Peregrine Smith Books, 1985), chap. 8.

Michael McDonald

First Principles for Professional Foresters

1. The member will, in all aspects of his work, regard as his first responsibility the maintenance of the integrity of the forest resource; the protection and enhancement of the productive capacity of the resource; its perpetuation of its utility and value to society.
2. By embracing the ethic of ENHANCED STEWARDSHIP British Columbians can achieve the full potential of all values in our forests of the future. This means intensive, integrated management for all values on the largest forest land base possible. In this way:

    the forests of British Columbia will provide for the economic, environmental, and spiritual well-being of all British Columbians through successive generations.

    Acceptance of this vision requires change. We must cooperatively manage our forests in a truly integrated fashion that considers all values that society deems important.

3. Foresters need help from ethicists in rethinking their professional code right from first principles.

Introduction

I begin with three quotes. The first is from Section 1(a) of the Code of Ethics for the Association of British Columbia Professional Foresters. The second comes from the report entitled "The Future of Our Forests," produced in April 1991 by the Forest Resources Commission, chaired by Sandy Peel (Forestry Resource Commission 1991, p. 7).

The third quote comes from one of the B.C. foresters I met in 1988 when I was doing a cross-Canada study on applied ethics (McDonald and Pullman 1988). The comment about first principles was made in the context of a discussion of the ethical challenges posed by the environmental movement, in particular recent disputes about logging the Clayoquot Sound area on the West Coast of Vancouver Island.

I have taken this request for assistance very seriously in preparing my remarks for this symposium. I see my role here as assisting your discovery and reflection on the first principles

---

Michael McDonald, "First Principles for Professional Foresters," *Ethical Challenges for Foresters, Proceedings of a Symposium to Discuss Ethical Issues in the Management of Forest Resources.* Vancouver, B.C.: University of British Columbia, September 27–28, 1991, pp. 1–18. Used with permission of Michael McDonald.

of your profession's ethics. I will provide assistance in three ways: first, by reminding you of the main ethical features of your profession; second, by making some comparisons to other professions and occupations; and third, by offering some ethical observations on the profession of forestry in British Columbia. In offering these remarks on the ethical foundations of forestry, it might help to lessen anxieties if I tell you about who my role models are and who they are not. I am not here like a Moses to bring down sacred tablets from the mountain of truth. Nor am I here like a Jeremiah to admonish you to repent. My models are not these biblical models of rectitude and moral certainty, rather I would aspire to the less threatening and more useful model suggested by Socrates— that of being an intellectual midwife—helping people give birth to ideas. I come here then fully conscious of the fact that forestry is your chosen profession. I take it as a given that you are proud of being foresters and value the good name and integrity of your profession.

But there may be some who are skeptical. Why should you worry about professional ethics; "If it ain't broke, why fix it?" This is a legitimate question, so let me offer a serious response. First, this is a question that has been faced by a number of professions, and increasingly those professions are taking a long hard look at their own ethics. Take medicine and nursing as examples; nurses as caregivers and physicians as researchers have turned to biomedical ethics to address important issues in medical ethics. Most of our major teaching hospitals have ethics committees. At a number of Canadian hospitals there are now ethics rounds and ethicists who are professionally consulted on difficult cases and policy decisions. Health research institutions are required by the Canada's research councils to have research ethics boards. The Royal College of Physicians and Surgeons, which establishes accreditation standards for Canadian medical schools, now requires education in biomedical ethics at both the undergraduate and graduate levels.[1] I can also attest from personal experience that interest in health care ethics is high—classes in biomedical ethics are oversubscribed every term at the University of British Columbia, and the demand for talks on ethics from the health care sector continues to grow.

In engineering, a number of major Canadian faculties have instituted special courses in ethics for engineers—our first presenter in this symposium, Professor J. T. Stevenson, wrote a major ethics text specifically for Canadian engineering students (Stevenson 1987). In April 1991, I was at a major symposium on accounting ethics which brought together leading members of professional accounting associations and university faculty. And to back good words with good deeds, the $500,000 worth of fines that the Alberta accounting association had exacted from negligent accounting firms in the collapse of major Alberta financial institutions has just been committed to a major programme at the University of Waterloo to develop new materials in accounting ethics.

Why are these and other professions increasingly concerned about ethics? Scandals have played their part. The failure of accountants to warn about the financial instability of firms they audited cost many investors and sometimes taxpayers a great deal of money. It was excesses in medical research that lead to the major crises in the mid-1960s about medical ethics. Researchers were found to have performed dangerous and sometimes useless research on patients who were utterly helpless—in some cases infants, small children, and incompetent elderly persons in large institutions—without any proper consent (Beecher 1966). The collapse of buildings, Bhopal, Three Mile Island, and the Challenger rocket explosion undermined confidence in professional engineers (Martin and Schinzinger 1989).

But it was more than just scandals:

Reasons for concern about professional ethics
1. Scandals
2. Public assertiveness; the emphasis on rights
3. New Technologies
4. Uncertainty about fundamental social values

Let me discuss the last three major factors: (2) increased public assertiveness about rights reflected in diverse rights movements, including campaigns for women's rights, children's rights, gay rights, patients' rights, animal rights, environmental rights, and the rights of minority stockholders; (3) new technologies that pose unprecedented moral problems in such areas as life-sustaining treatments, new reproductive technologies, and new modes of harvesting lands, forests and the seas; and (4) increasing questioning in society concerning basic values. Professional groups, as well as private and public sector institutions and organizations, including traditional pillars of moral respectability like churches and universities, are under pressure both from without and from within. From without, professions face an increasing skeptical public and outspoken public interest groups. Trust is much more easily lost today and, as the forest industry shows, not easily regained once lost. From within, we find in professional and business life a number of individuals who are willing to blow the whistle on their bosses and their colleagues. Moreover, such whistle-blowing activity is encouraged by the media and in some jurisdictions protected by law.

To all this, it may be tempting to respond defensively by charging that politicians and media people are manipulating public opinion for self-serving ends. Those under fire will often feel hurt and both individually and collectively injured by such accusations. You may well ask, "Why should all of us in the profession be blamed for what a few bad characters have done?" or, "Why doesn't the public give us credit for trying to act with integrity and honour?" In such a defensive mood, it is easy for a beleaguered profession to see the situation as a public relations crisis rather than an ethics crisis.

I would suggest that professionals under fire need to get beyond this defensiveness. For one thing, even if there is a public relations problem here, the best public relations device over the long run is the truth (and, I would tongue-in-cheek suggest, a public relations firm with an unblemished record).[2] For another, the best defense is a good offense; it is better for professions to take an active rather than a re-active stance. But the main point I would stress is that at the core of professional life is ethics; ethics has to be the bottom-line for professionals!

To make my case for the centrality of ethics to professional life generally and forestry specifically, I would like to take you on a quick tour of the main characteristics of professions:[3]

Marks of a profession

A. A knowledge base
   1. Skills based on esoteric, theoretical knowledge
   2. Special training and education
   3. Testing for competence

B. Providing a valuable service— a primary good

C. Organization as a profession
   1. Code of professional behaviour
   2. Self-regulation and discipline
   3. Licensed monopoly
   4. Work autonomy
   5. Rewards: status and income

D. The social contract between professions and society: with privileges come special responsibilities.
   1. Altruism—concern for the public good, the good of clients, and unrepresented stakeholders
   2. Competence—both individual and collective

(A) *A knowledge base*. The first thing to notice about professions like law, medicine, engineering is that every professional group lays claim to a specialized knowledge-base: a body of knowledge and reliable ways of acquiring and increasing that knowledge. This knowledge base is usually inaccessible without special training and education. Thus, in section 1 of the Forester's Act, the "practice of professional forestry" is defined with receiving fees or remuneration for:

> ... performing or directing works, services or undertakings which, because of their scope and forest management implications require specialized knowledge, training and experience ...

It is vitally important to the existence of a profession that a firm intellectual base is claimed for professional knowledge. Being a professional in the know isn't just a matter of serendipitous discovery or insider information; hence, having professional knowledge is not just a matter of happening to know something about a particular subject but also having the intellectual skills to identify gaps in one's knowledge and move to learn more. There is then a disciplinary base for law, medicine, engineering, and of course forestry. Lacking that disciplinary base, there is no real claim to professionalism; so alchemists and phrenologists should not be counted as professionals today.

I have described the knowledge-base as "esoteric" because it is out of the ordinary and if not strictly speaking inaccessible to ordinary people or at least quite hard to access without a substantial investment of time, energy, and intelligence. Silviculture just isn't part of the ordinary Jack or Jill's intellectual repertoire. This difference in the intellectual skills of the professional and the lay person means that there is an imbalance of power between the professional and those the professional serves. The physician should know more about my health than I do. Similarly, you should know more about forests than I do.

But notice here that even though there is standardly this imbalance in knowledge between professional and client, I as the client have significant and legitimate interest in the quality of the service provided by professionals: My well-being is vitally affected by what the professional does or fails to do for me. Indeed, with respect to my general well-being, I am the expert and not the professional. While a physician can offer me advice about a life-saving medical procedure or a lawyer can tell me about my chances of winning a given suit, I know better whether I want my life saved (e.g., I may just be prolonging the misery) or the suit launched (e.g., to win the case I alienate my best friend). So a professional is an expert that I may need, but the professional is not necessarily an expert on my needs. Ordinarily then the professional is neither (a) in an intellectual position, or (b) in a moral position, to substitute her judgment of what is in my interest for my own judgment of my best interests.[4]

So in these two important respects, the client should remain in the driver's seat in the professional-client relation. This is reflected in recent changes in typical professional-client relationships. These changes can be most graphically seen in medicine where there has been a clear move away from a paternalistic relation between doctors and patients—the "trust the physician" model—towards a relation that emphasizes the dignity and decision-making power of the patient—a "respect for patient" model. In the former, the patient was seen as simply a passive recipient of health care services, in a way as a kind of child who should be kept in the dark about treatment modalities. On the latter, the respect for patients model, the patient is seen as having the right to be given the information she needs to make decisions about her own treatment and to play in many cases an important role in that treatment. It is also reflected in the publication of statements of patient's rights, the creation of patient's rights advocates, and increased litigation on the part of patients. Now this move to a partnership relation away from a paternalistic one has not been easy for some physicians to make. It isn't easy to unlearn being the god-like physician and acquiring appropriate communication skills, in particular learning to listen to and communicate with the patient in a clear nontechnical way.

Later on, I will say something about applying these lessons to the far more complex situation that foresters face in which the client is not a single person but the body politic. But for the moment, let us note that in our contemporary context the possession of skills based on an esoteric and theoretically grounded knowledge base requires special training and education. The option of learning by apprenticeship is not that distant in time for foresters and their predecessors, forest engineers.[5] In this connection, though, it is worth noting that until the late 1940s legal training in Canada generally worked on an apprenticeship system as well. Becoming a professional takes time. In recent years as most professional schools raise educational requirements, it also requires an increasingly more advanced set of background intellectual skills. Thus, in fields as diverse as law and veterinary medicine it is rare to find individuals being admitted to professional schools without a bachelor's degree. Moreover, in most professions, the knowledge base has been increasing rapidly in recent decades. There just is a lot more to know about silviculture, agricultural sciences, dentistry, and engineering than there was even a decade ago. So in universities we test these students on their professional knowledge. As well, the professions do this with professional qualification examinations. Testing is appropriate because there is something here to be tested: knowledge and skills to be demonstrated before one can really count as having a sufficient grasp of the field to be counted as a professional (*Foresters Act*, s. 7(e)).

Because professional credibility depends on the possession of knowledge and intellectual skills, professions and their members have special reasons to promote the growth of knowledge in their areas. So professionals should prize and not despise learning and research. There should be a close and symbiotic relationship between professionals and professional schools. Beyond this, professions should be careful not to stifle thoughtful discussion and even spirited questioning of received professional wisdom. One of the ways a body of knowledge grows is through vigorous discussion. To be sure, ultimately a line may have to be drawn between the responsible and irresponsible questioning of disciplinary paradigms—between an invigorating iconoclasm and sheer quackery. In drawing that line you must be quite certain you are protecting the public's interests in professionalism and not just the profession's interest in peace and quiet. Hence, an important challenge is to avoid the stultifying and chilling effects of enforced intellectual orthodoxy while still maintaining professional standards.

A final remark concerning the knowledge base of forestry is in order before I move on to the next feature of professionalism. If I am right in contending that the bottom line for professionals has to be ethics, then it seems to me that your profession and a number of other professions should give serious thought to including ethics in the required knowledge base for members of your profession. It is not enough to simply include questions about the Code of Ethics in Registered Professional Foresters (RPF) examinations. Yet when I look at the "Enrolment and Registration Guidelines" of the Association and the Calendar requirements of the Faculty of Forestry here at the University of British Columbia, I see a long list of science requirements but very little on the normative side of the equation—including ethics, politics, law, and economics. I do not see how the profession expects wise and good decisions to be made unless it builds into the professional knowledge base a significant ethics component. And, of course, what I am saying here about the requirements for becoming a forester applies as much to in-service, continuing education for practicing professionals.

(B) *A valuable service.* Professionals claim more than knowledge-based skills. They claim that what they know and can do with their skills is valuable and useful. While there are "professional," in the sense of "paid," baseball, football, and hockey players, it is inappropriate to think of these people as members of professions in the sense that I am discussing in this presentation. What "professional" athletes offer—amusement to spectators—simply isn't in the same valuable and vital category as what lawyers, physicians, and other professionals offer. Justice and health are significant and, outside the Garden of Eden, essential goods; hence, law and medicine count as professions in a way that hockey and boxing do not. The goods that professionals purport to provide are indispensable goods in the sense that clients will see these goods as significant or important to their lives, no matter what sorts of lives they lead. Health certainly is like that and so is justice. One can be a poor man, rich man, beggar man, or thief and want health, and with the possible exception of the thief, also want justice.[6]

What about forestry as a profession that provides such significant, or, what the philosopher John Rawls calls, "primary goods" (Rawls 1971, 90)? A strong case can be made for forestry as profession in jurisdictions like British Columbia if we broaden our notion of primary goods in two ways. First, we should include needs of groups of people as well as the needs of individual persons. Second, we also should think about the technologies and professions our society needs to survive and prosper. If we make both extensions, we can see why the goods offered by a number of professions today are seen as extremely significant. For example, in our complex economy, there is the need for the services of auditors to attest to the veracity of financial statements, and there is a need to have engineers design and supervise the production of significant parts of our technological infrastructures, like roads and computers. Forestry in British Columbia promises an extremely important set of goods for British Columbians—to quote again the Forestry Resources Commission: "the forests of British Columbia will provide for the economic, environmental, and spiritual well-being of all British Columbians through successive generations" (Forestry Resource Commission 1991, 7). According to the Association's 1986 position paper, "British Columbia Land Use "Strategy," "Some 81.5 million hectares of (or 86 percent of the province's total area) is within Provincial Forests." Of course one couldn't make the same case for the importance of forestry as a profession for Saudi Arabia or Prince Edward Island, but here in British Columbia and in much of Canada forests are a major economic and noneconomic resource.

(C) *Organization and recognition as a profession.* Professionals are not just an unrelated group of people who happen to have a common training and offer similar services. Farmers, bankers and auto mechanics fit that description, but do not enjoy professional status. Professionals see themselves and are seen by the public as different than other workers. A lot of the difference is in how professions are organized and in how that organization is socially recognized. With respect to their organization, professions like other corporate bodies have constitutions, goals, rules, a structure of governance, with executive, legislative and adjudicative capacities, a set of members, and common assets or property. Unlike businesses, professional organizations or bodies fall into the not-for-profit sector in having noneconomic ends as their reason for being. But unlike charities and hospitals, professions are recognized as regulating the behaviour of nonmembers as well as members. In particular, professions have a legally recognized monopoly over an occupational area so that they can determine who shall or shall not practice in that area.

In its "Guidelines for the Interpretation of the Code of Ethics," the Association of British Columbia Professional Foresters says that being recognized as a profession provides the profession with two significant privileges: (1) Members of the profession are ultimate authority in their field. (2) Their group is self-governing and self-disciplining (ABCPF 1991, 34).

Legally, professions like the Association of British Columbia Foresters have a number of powers including:

- establishment and monitoring of admission standards
- professional education
- ensuring continuing competence of members
- conferring of a professional designation on members (e.g., RPF)
- establishment and enforcement of standards of conduct and practice
- discipline of members who fail to meet prescribed standards
- public information
- development and promotion of forest policies
- review of public or private policies relating to the profession to ensure compliance with professional standards (Curtis 1991, 330)

As foresters in British Columbia, you enjoy a status that obtains only here and in Quebec; for your professional association acts a licensing body, while in the other provinces, forestry associations only have the right to certify or register members. The difference is very important. In a certification scheme, nonmembers are simply prohibited from using the professional designation; a certified group is like the holder of a trademark. However, nonmembers are not prohibited from offering the same services as members of the profession (Curtis 1991, p. 331). In a licensing scheme, nonprofessionals are legally prohibited from offering services in the area of licensure.[7]

Two questions present themselves. First, an organizational question, why should members of a profession want to put themselves under professional standards and discipline, for this involves a limitation of their freedom to practice as they please? Second, a question of social recognition, why should a free society recognize a monopoly in a given occupational area?

I ask both these questions against the normal ground rules we have in free and democratic societies with respect to occupational life. Basically, these rules require us to meet certain unconditional and conditional negative and positive norms: do not harm, cheat, or lie to others; keep your word; treat others with at least minimal decency.[8] While these rules set limits on how one may compete with others, for example, I may not burn down a competitor's store or poison his livestock. But these moral rules do not require me to refrain from competition within these rules, for example, by underpricing them. Thus, in most other occupations, people do not enjoy the powers professions do. Used car sales people, electronic repair people, hairdressers, bankers, and undertakers possess special skills but (a) they do not have to join any organization to practice their trade and (b) their organizations do not enjoy monopoly powers. They get a job or set up shop for themselves and succeed or fail as their employer or the market dictates. They are of course subject to basic moral rules. They can be sued for damages, arrested for theft, and subject to public censure for serious or even trivial moral faults. Hence, if we are to justify the power professions have over both their own members and nonmembers, the onus is on the profession to provide a convincing case.

(D) *The contract between society and the professions*. We cannot then describe the powers that professions enjoy as rights; they are privileges. This is nicely put in the "Guidelines for Interpretation of the Code of Ethics":

> It is obvious that privileges granted by the public, through Legislation, can also be taken away by the public. It follows that a profession will only maintain its privileges as long as the public maintains confidence in the profession. It is essential to the development of our profession that the work we do leaves no doubt in the mind of the public that foresters are capable, are truly in charge of their profession, and that they are putting the public interest first. (ABCPF 1991, 5)

Why does society extend such legal privileges as self-governance and self-discipline to professions as well as the very real social rewards of status, economic reward, and autonomy in determining conditions of work? Recall what I said earlier about professions being charged with the delivery of highly valuable services—goods that are quite central to a good life—and about professions having a specialized and esoteric knowledge base. If we put the two features together we can see the basis of a social contract between a society and each of its professions. I see our society as reasoning in the following way.

As individuals and as a group, we very much want the goods that professions provide. But most of us are not in a position to make many of the essential judgements with regard to minimal competence, let alone excellence, in each of the various areas in which professions practice. We are then likely to be duped by charlatans and injured by incompetents. We believe that by giving over a realm of authority to a self-governing and self-disciplining group we will do better than with the standard arrangements of the market backed by the authority of civil and criminal law. We will let the profession act on our behalf in securing for us, individually and severally, the services we so much need and value. In return, we give the profession the powers to carry out these tasks for the good of society as a whole and the members of society who are its clients. These powers carry with them the advantages attendant upon control over the practice of a specific occupation. These powers are not given for mere self-aggrandizement or the exploitation of clients.

Society then takes a calculated risk or a gamble that it will be better off with professions than without them. Or to put the matter positively, there is an act of trust in competence and ethical performance of the profession and its members. The profession and each professional takes responsibility for acting altruistically—with the welfare of others as the first goal—and competently, at or above minimum standards of professional competence. These obligations of altruism and competence involve both individual and collective responsibility. In a profession, you should be your fellow professional's keeper. Since professions exist in part to deal with the failure of individual professionals to act responsibly, professionals collectively have an important role in ensuring professional responsibility.

This is why I describe the relationship between society and the profession as a social contract. In exchange for special privileges both official and nonofficial, professionals both individually as practitioners and collectively as a profession are to use these privileges for the benefit of designated stakeholder, whether specific clients or the public as a whole. The social contract is breached if either society or the profession fails to live up to its part of the bargain.

Society can fail to live up to the contract by demanding the fulfillment of responsibilities while denying the possibility of rewards. Society can also fail to give a profession the powers it needs to meet its socially imposed obligations. A question to be asked here is whether British Columbia foresters are given sufficient legal and social protections to live up to their responsibilities as professionals. I am particularly concerned here about the lack of legal protection for professionals who might put their jobs and even careers on the line in order to meet their professional obligations. Society can also fail to live up to its part of the social contract if it fails to specify in enough detail what it expects of a profession or it places upon a profession conflicting obligations. Both may well be the case with foresters in British Columbia and elsewhere in Canada.

How might a profession fail to live up to its part of the bargain? One way is for the profession to put the interest of its members ahead of and at the expense of designated beneficiaries. If engineers sign off on unsafe buildings or accountants issue false or misleading financial statements, then the individual professional has failed to live up to his part of the bargain (Gaa [n.d.]). If the profession as a self-regulating group fails to make reasonable effort to discover and discipline such individuals, then there is a significant collective failure to keep the contract with society. It is very apparent that society will no longer allow professions to take a passive role with respect to policing and disciplining members. By this I mean to say that there are important and, I believe, legitimate pressures on professions to (a) not only act on complaints from designated stakeholders regarding unprofessional conduct, but also (b) to take a proactive stance in maintaining professional ethical standards. This includes some or all of the following:

- Building into the qualification process, licensing, and continuing professional education a significant ethics component
- Engaging in practice reviews of professional work by having a committee examine the work of practicing professional at random and not just in response to complaints
- In areas where the complaint system appears inadequate to take proactive stance, as the College of Physicians and Surgeons has done in Ontario with regard to sexual harassment by medical practitioners.

It is very important here that the professions both meet these responsibilities and be seen to meet them. I think the period of time in which professional discipline was an essentially closed-door matter is ending. To be seen to live up to the social contract involves open discipline processes following confidential investigation. From my own experience as a lay member of the discipline committee for the 14,000-member Institute of Chartered Accountants of Ontario, I would strongly suggest that professions consider adding lay people to discipline committees to ensure that the stakeholder's point of view is represented not just by advocates appearing before the committee but in the very structure of the discipline committee itself. I would commend the Association of British Columbia Professional Foresters (ABCPF) for moving towards having a lay member on the Discipline and Ethics Committee.

If a profession fails to take effective and, in appropriate cases, visible steps to live up to their professional responsibilities, there is little or no reason for society to continue to grant to the profession the privilege of self-regulation.

Identifying Benefits and Beneficiaries. In describing the contract between a society and a profession, you will naturally want to know what obligations are specifically placed on the profession and its members. To determine this, you need look for claimants, those to whom a professional is responsible or answerable, and beneficiaries, those for whom a professional is responsible. Claimants and beneficiaries are often one and the same. If I promise to take you to lunch, then you occupy both the claimant and beneficiary roles. But sometimes claimants are distinct from beneficiaries. This usually is found in trust or fiduciary relationships. If you set up a trust fund for your minor children, then with respect to the administrator of that fund you stand as a claimant but it is your children who are the intended beneficiaries of the fund. This separation of claimant from beneficiary in trust relationships will be important in understanding the "enhanced stewardship" concept that the Forest Resources Commission advocates.

I would now suggest looking at the ABCPF's *Code of Ethics* in order to identify claimants and beneficiaries of obligations that fall upon foresters individually and collectively. The Code list four responsibilities that members of the Association have as professional foresters (ABCPF 1991):

RPF Responsibilities
1. Public
2. Profession
3. Client or Employer
4. Other Members (ABCPF 1991, 1–3)

If you adopt the social contract view I have just advocated, a strong case can be made for treating responsibilities (2) and (4) as ancillary to responsibilities (1) and (3). This is because privileges of self-regulation and self-discipline are primarily granted in order to advance the interests of those outside the profession and only secondarily for the interest of those in the profession. In any case, responsibility (2) is spelled out in terms of exemplifying a high standard of conduct (ABCPF 1991, s. (2) (a)), contributing to the growth of knowledge in forestry (ABCPF 1991, s. (2)(b) and (2)(d)), professional honesty (ABCPF 1991, s.(2)(c)), and proper use of the professional seal (ABCPF 1991, s. (2)(d)). None of these identifies the stakeholders for whom these activities are to be undertaken. Responsibility (4) prescribes various professional courtesies. While these used to be at the core of professional codes of ethics, they are inadequate to justify society's granting an occupational group the privileges of self-discipline and self-regulation. Quite the contrary, these might be seen by the public as attempts to restrict trade and deny outsiders access to occupational status.

This leaves two responsibilities. As spelled out in the *Code of Ethics*, (3) indicates a duty of loyalty to one's client or employer. I think it is ethically uncontroversial that there is such a duty. The ethically significant question is about the limits of loyalty to client or employer. If the professional is thought of as the client or employer's agent, what are the ethical limits to such agency (Michalos 1983; Poff 1987)? Agency is best thought of in terms of a delegation of rights, particularly powers and immunities, by a principal to a person who acts on the principal's behalf. The old mediaeval dictum, *nemo dat god non habet*—one cannot give what one doesn't have—offers us a good clue about the ethical limits of agency. If a principal does not have the right to do something, say, injurious to a third party, then neither does his agent.

But there is very little in your *Code of Ethics* about the ethical limits of loyalty to clients or employers. While most professional codes are not very helpful in this regard, yours is less helpful than others. For example, the *Code* indicates that the forester will

> not subjugate his professional principles to the demands of employment and will advise his client or employer of the consequences of any contemplated course of action which in his opinion is not sound forestry practice. (ABCPF 1991, s. (3)(e))

But what if the employer persists? The *Code* is not only silent, but the *Guidelines* seem to recommend compliance with the employer's or client's wishes:

> While RPFs should be accountable for forestry decisions, it is important to make the distinction between professional forestry decisions and management prerogative. Managers are responsible for and accountable for administrative decisions which based on political, social or economic constraints and administrative budgetary priorities, may sometimes result in deferral or modification of prescribed actions. (ABCPF 1991, p. 8)

Compare this to the advice that the Certified General Accountants of Canada recommends to its members on those "rare occasions (in which) there (is) conflict between the requirements of employment and professional ethics" (CGA Canada 1990, 6). *CGA-Canada Guidelines* recommend discussing the conflict with one's employer, should discussion to resolve the matter fail, then the accountant is told:

> But if the employed accountant finds himself irreconcilably at odds with his employer on a matter of professional ethics, a very difficult situation. Unlike the accountant in public practice, he cannot withdraw his services without surrendering what is probably his sole means of support. If, however, he is satisfied that his view is the only tenable one and that the issue is sufficiently grave, resignation may be his only option. In reaching his decision on such very difficult questions, so long as there is no breach of confidentiality, the CGA Lacy find it helpful to seek advice from the Association. (CGA Canada 1990, 6)[9]

This indicates that there are limits to the duty of loyalty to employers (and clients). When those limits are seriously breached, the professional must dissociate herself from the client or employer. Moreover, the Association indicates that it is willing to offer advice on these difficult questions. Still, quiet dissociation or resignation may not be enough. There may be an obligation on the part of the professional to blow the whistle and, perhaps also, publicly resign (Elliston 1982). I would also suggest that there is an obligation on the part of profession to provide at least moral support for members faced with such cruel choices (Brunk 1985). There is room for improvement in defining and delimiting duties to clients and employers not only within forestry, but also in other professions.

Nonetheless, I think it is reasonable to say forestry faces special problems particularly because the concept of "sound forest practices" depends crucially on the forester's obligations to the general public. And here there is a notable lack of consensus. The Code states that

> the member will, in all aspects of his work, regard as his first responsibility the maintenance of the integrity of the forest resource; the protection and enhancement of the productive capacity of the resource; its perpetuation of its utility and value to society. (ABCPF 1991, s. (1))

At first glance, this provision seems like the emphasis in Canadian engineering codes; thus, the Ontario Engineers Code proclaims that "A professional engineer shall regard his duty to public welfare as paramount" (APEO 1977, s. 2(a); Stevenson 1987, 333–63). These statements of paramount responsibility are, to put it mildly, rather general. They raise the question of how the individual professional is to determine what specifically his or her obligations are with regard to either "public welfare" or "maintaining the integrity of the forest resource." Both codes offer some help to professionals in interpreting their responsibilities in terms of some specific duties, such as not making misleading or exaggerated claims about qualifications and experience either to clients or in the witness box.[10] But it has to be said that the Ontario professional engineer will have an easier time of figuring out her paramount obligation to public welfare than the British Columbia Forester for maintaining the integrity of the forest resource. The main reason for this is I think that there is much more social consensus about cashing out the engineer's paramount responsibility in terms of safety (APEO 1977, s. 2(e)) than there is about determining what counts as "maintaining the integrity of the forest resource." The same I think could be said about professions like medicine and nursing where the patient's health is paramount. Indeed, in health care, duties are prioritized with the first obligation being not to harm (*Primum non nocere* or above all do no harm).

The greater degree of specificity is along two dimensions in engineering and the health care professions. First in these professions, there is a focus on obligations to specific persons. For engineering, it is those directly affected by the engineer's work; for health care, it is the patient. For law, to cite another example, it is the client. Second, a specific aspect of the welfare of that person is singled out. For engineering, it is safety. For nursing and medicine, it is the patient's health. But for British Columbia foresters it is different along both dimensions. First, the beneficiaries are general and not specific. Second, kinds of benefits are left wide open. Thus, the Code says that the forest resource is to be maintained for "its utility and value to society" (APEO 1977, s. (1)(a)).

First with regard to beneficiaries, the Forest Resource Commission identifies the intended beneficiary of British Columbia's forests as "all British Columbians through successive generations" (Forestry Resource Commission 1991, p. 7). But as innocuous as this sounds, the limitation of beneficiaries to British Columbians is controversial. Critics who describe British Columbia as the Brazil of North America are not speaking from the perspective that it is only the interests of this province's citizens that are at stake in our use of provincial forests. Morally, it seems to me that a very strong case can be made that it is wrong to use our resources in ways that harm others. Thus, even if Iraq had set its own oil wells on fire and not those of its neighbor Kuwait, the resulting oil fires were wrong because they harmed Iraq's neighbors.

Even if nonharmful use is taken as a moral prerequisite for the use of any property, it has to be said that the range of designated beneficiaries of British Columbia's publicly held forest lands—"all British Columbians through successive generations"—is very large indeed. What would be required is the fair consideration of the interests of all British Columbians at any time and over time. The charge to consider the interests of all citizens at all times raises the question of whose interests today are ignored in the use of British Columbia forests. Given this province's shameful record with regard to the recognition of aboriginal rights, I venture to suggest that native people's interests are probably much under rated.

The second charge—to consider interests over time—raises the question, "What is the split of the resource between present and future generations?" This is not an idle question to be addressed only by philosophers; it is a major issue especially for professions like yours that have a major stewardship role. I also noticed that in a recent survey of Canada's professional foresters, 47 percent of British Columbia foresters felt that the prospects of sustaining the current supply of harvestable wood as poor (Omnifacts 1991, 2). At the same time, the perspective of British Columbia foresters is described as closer to that of the forestry industry than those of foresters in other parts of the country (Omnifacts 1991, 4). Assuming there is an obligation to future generations of British Columbians, then it looks like there is either a gap between what foresters preach and what they practice or there is a fairly restrictive interpretation of the obligation to future generations amongst British Columbia foresters.

I turn now to the second kind of vagueness in the way the Code spells out responsibilities to the public. The Code does say something concrete about the kinds of values that foresters ought to regard as paramount—these are use or utilitarian values. That is, the forest resource is not regarded as having value apart from the interests of human beings; so it looks like foresters are being told that they cannot be deep ecologists. Indeed, one can see in a wide variety of forest practices in British Columbia a fundamental commitment to purely economic values. Certainly, at various points in its history, the Association of British Columbia Professional Foresters looked like it placed economic values as paramount, in, for example, various position papers on land use, pesticides, and wilderness. Yet if the Forest Resources Commission reflects values foresters would generally espouse, the scope of utilitarian benefits is wider than purely economic ones, since the Commission talks about providing for "the economic, environmental, and spiritual well-being of all British Columbians through successive generations." Moreover, the Code itself and the *Foresters Act* leave open the question of what makes forests valuable; the Code mentions "utility and value to society" (APEO 1977, s.(1)(a)) and the Act mandates "the integration and optimum realization of their total resource values" (APEO 1977, s.(1)(a)) without specifying that these values are purely economic.

Even though there is this vagueness about which values are paramount, all of us could agree that for the implementation of these values it is essential to have accurate information about the state of British Columbia's forests. In this connection, I would remark that it is quite disturbing to read a newspaper report which indicates that "almost all forest service staff are concerned that the current processes that lead to the establishment of AAC (allowable annual cut) overestimate timber supply" (Parfitt 1991, 1). This quotation is from an internal document circulated in the Ministry of Forests and signed by "two of the ministry's top civil servants." What the report indicates is that the Ministry lacks the information necessary to provide a complete inventory of British Columbia's forest resources. Surely, this is a matter that should be of great concern to you as professional foresters, for it undercuts in a significant way the claims to intellectual authority that you can validly make. It is as if your physician were to tell you, "I want to do major surgery, but I have only a very partial and incomplete idea of your current state of health."

Earlier I spoke about fiduciary relationships involving a separation of claimants from beneficiaries: those who stand to benefit by the trust relation are distinct from those charged with provision of the benefits. Surely, with regard to "successive generations" of British Columbians the split of claimants from beneficiaries is extremely significant. Only present generations can speak or act for future generations. Even with regard to the present generation, there is the question in the case of public resources of whether all the interests of all stakeholders are fairly served. Here, there is a serious question of the commensurability of values being served. While with some fiddling and often with serious distortions we can measure economic output, it is not possible to provide an algorithm or formula to weigh economic against noneconomic values. One of the problems in trying to weigh such diverse values is that the lack of quantifiable information about noneconomic values tends to push the discussion away from these values toward economic values. This seems to be an instance of a more general human proclivity to force problems into the mould of existing methodologies rather than sacrifice those methodologies.[11]

So what can your profession do when its avowed first responsibility is so vague and conflict-filled? Let me mention three *unattractive* alternatives.

(a) One possibility would be to simply eschew the responsibility by tossing the ball back into society's lap. But as you know this society is divided in what it wants. It may be a long time before a consensus emerges or, perhaps, worse the consensus that emerges may be based on faulty information and misconceived values.

(b) An alternative would be to take the view that you are simply hired guns doing the bidding of today's regulators. If tomorrow's regulators have contrary wishes then a professional forester will simply adapt her practices to what her new political masters demand. But this turns the professional into a mere tool or instrument in the hands of politicians. It is, if anything, even worse than drawing no ethical limits around the obligation of loyalty to one's client or employer.

(c) A third alternative would be to claim that in the absence of public consensus each forester is to follow his or her own conscience. This may be unobjectionable at a personal level, but it is not very helpful in either deciding what you conscientiously believe or in coordinating your ethical decision-making with others.

So none of these alternatives is very attractive. Each involves an abdication of individual and collective responsibility as depriving the public of the advice of well-informed professionals. Each alternative also obscures the many ways in which foresters can and do have a say in the determination of policy.

You may ask then if there are any morally attractive alternatives. I would suggest that such alternatives would involve a process of dialogue between professional foresters and the other forest stakeholders. This requires, as the Forest Resource Commission suggests, a process of public participation in forest planning and management (Forestry Resource Commission 1991, p. 40). I agree with Jordan Tanz, one of the organizers of this Symposium, that such participation has to go beyond the open-house mode and into active citizen involvement and control in terms of policy-making (Tanz and Howard 1990, 127).[12] In its "Five Year Strategic Plan 1990–1991," the Association strikes the right chord when it sets as the Association of British Columbia Professional Foresters' mission statement:

To contribute our expertise to the process of protecting the public's interest by ensuring that forest land is expertly managed for a multitude of uses, and that our members conduct themselves in a reputable, proficient and trustworthy manner. (AFCPF 1991, 7)

The notion of contributing to a "process of protecting the public's interest" is worth emphasizing. Here, foresters might well look to a variety of other professions, particularly health care professions, in which the process of protecting interests is seen to involve direct participation by those whose interests are involved or, if they are unable to participate, their surrogates. I would suggest that the profession needs to enter a dialogue with diverse stakeholders in order to find mutually acceptable modes of public participation.

Let me close by saying that British Columbia foresters face a number of critical ethical challenges today. Given the pressures upon you—from the public, employers, clients, and regulators, it is important to recognize and deal with these challenges as ethical ones, not just public relations issues. I would strongly urge you to do as you are doing today—devoting your time and energy to ethical issues. Ethics should be an integral part of the education of foresters. Crucially, I think foresters in this province need to work on acquiring more professional independence. While in the short run the search for greater independence may increase conflicts with employers, clients, and even part if not all of the general public, it will in the longer run lead to better serving the needs of all who have a stake in the integrity of British Columbia's forests.

Notes

1. The Royal College of Physicians and Surgeons of Canada, "Postgraduate Biomedical Ethics Teaching," March 1, 1989, p. 2; "General Standards of Accreditation," [n.d.], p. 6.

2. For those following the fortunes of the Forest Alliance, it is also important to make sure that when you hire a public relations firm you think about the firm's ethical track record. See Stephen Hume's columns [op-ed pages] on the Forest Alliance's hiring of Burston-Martseller for public relations. *Vancouver Sun*, 19, 22, 24, and 26 July 1991. Judy Lindsay, the *Vancouver Sun's* business columnist, responded to these criticisms on 20 July 1991, C5.

3. My list of characteristic features of professions is fairly standard though with some minor modifications and regroupings. I have added the second item, providing a valuable service, which I think is an important addition.

4. Incapacity and diminished capacity provide problems in both medical and legal ethics which we usually dealt with by some form of surrogate consent.

5. See RPF *Roots*, pp. 1–19; also the "Association History," *Professional Manual*, pp. 1–2.

6. Plato put forward the counterintuitive view that punishment was good for the unjust because it restored the soul's health.

7. It is worth noting here that though there is a sharp distinction to be drawn between certification and license schemes, there are often important differences among licensed professions. Licenses can be broad or narrow, and professions can be highly turf protecting or not. So while medicine and law tend to be at one end of the spectrum here, professions like engineering and forestry are at the other end, much more open, for example, to the development of para-professionals and less monopolistic.

8. The main unconditional negative norm is not to harm others, which includes not physically injuring them, not taking their belongings, or lying to them; it includes as well some specific and limited positive obligations: like showing at least a minimum respect for others and coming to the aid of others in dire necessity. Negative unconditional obligations are more extensive and pervasive than positive unconditional obligations, but the positive ones, despite libertarian protests to the contrary, are

essential to a civilized and humane social existence. Unconditional obligations will not carry us very far towards such an existence for they can be satisfied with quite minimal human interaction. Conditional obligations carry us a good deal further; these are basically obligations about keeping voluntarily made agreements: keep your contracts and live up to your oath of office or professional code. Conditional obligations are central to business and occupational life.

9. While the APEO does not contain this sort of provision, it does expect that professional engineers will risk unemployment in order to report unsafe engineering practices. See the APEO film, *The Truesteel Affair.*

10. ABCPF Code, (1) (d) and (e). APEO Code 2 (b) and (d).

11. In saying this, I think I am at odds with one of the proposals stated in the Association's 1986 paper on land-use: "a cost/benefit system should be developed which recognizes the social values of the nonconsumptive uses of Crown lands as well as the economic value of consumptive uses" (p. 4). See also the remarks of the Forestry Resource Commission (1991) on p. 27 of their report with respect to forest values: "Values for nonindustrial activities—recreation, wildlife, etc.—cannot be reliably quantified with existing information." One wonders what additional information would allow the quantification of such values, and more importantly, whether such quantification would help make sounder judgements about potentially conflicting uses of British Columbia's forests.

12. Tanz and Howard rightly point out that parts of the public may also have an important role to play in policy-implementation as well (p. 128).

Forestry References

ABCPF. 1991. Association of British Columbia Professional Foresters, *Professional Manual*, 7 February 1991, Vancouver, British Columbia.

Baskerville, G. L. 1988. "Management of Publicly Owned Forests," *The Forestry Chronicle*, June 1988, pp. 193–98.

———. 1990. "Canadian Sustained Yield Management—Expectations and Realities," *The Forestry Chronicle*, February 1990, pp. 25–28.

Benson, C. A. 1990. "The Potential for Integrated Resource Management with Intensive or Extensive Forest Management: Reconciling Vision with Reality—The Extensive Management Argument," *The Forestry Chronicle*, October 1990, pp. 457–60.

Bishop, Chuck, and Frances Bishop. 1988. RPF *Roots: An Historical Survey of the Association of British Columbia Foresters, 1947–1987.* Association of British Columbia Foresters.

Curtis, David S. 1990. "Foresters and the Law of Professional Negligence," *The Forestry Chronicle*, August 1990, pp. 336–40.

———. 1991. "Professional Regulation and Accountability in Forestry," *The Forestry Chronicle*, August 1990, pp. 328–35.

Forestry Resource Commission. 1991. *The Future of Our Forests: Executive Summary*, A. L. Peel, Chairman, Forest Resources Commission, Victoria, British Columbia, April 1991.

Hägglund, Bjorn. 1990. "Sustained-Yield Forest Management: The View from Sweden," *The Forestry Chronicle*, February 1990, 29–31.

Jakes, Pamela, Hans Gregerson, Allen Lundgren, and David Bengston. 1990. "Emerging Issues in Forest Management and Use," *The Forestry Chronicle*, April 1990, pp. 25–28, 34.

O'Keefe, Timothy. 1990. "Holistic (New) Forestry: Significant Difference or Just Another Gimmick?" *Journal of Forestry*, April 1990, 23–24.

Omnifacts Research Limited. 1991. "Survey of Professional Foresters in Canada," Executive Summary from the Final Report to Forestry Canada, January 1991.

Ontario's Registered Professional Foresters. [n.d.] *The Professional Forester*, various numbers.

Parfitt, Ben. 1991. "Forest overcut, report claims." *Vancouver Sun*, Wednesday, September 11, 1991, A1–A2.

Reed, F. L. C. 1990. "Canada's Second Century of Forestry: Closing the Gap Between Promise and Performance," *The Forestry Chronicle*, October 1990, pp. 447–53.

Society of American Foresters. 1990. "Forest Policies of the Society of American Foresters," *Journal of Forestry,* March 1990, 35–38.

Tanz, Jordan S., and Andrew F. Howard. 1990. "Meaningful Public Participation in the Planning and Management of Publicly Owned Forests," *The Forestry Chronicle* 67(2) (April 1990): 125–30.

Wood, Gene W. "The Art and Science of Wildlife (Land) Management," *Journal of Forestry,* March 1990, pp. 8–12.

Other References

APEO. 1977. Association of Professional Engineers of Ontario, *Code of Ethics.* Reprinted in Stevenson, pp. 336–39.

Beecher, H. K. 1966. "Ethics in and Clinical Research," *The New England Journal of Medicine,* 274 (1966): 1354–60.

Brunk, Conrad G. 1985. "Professionalism and Responsibility in the Technological Society," in Poff and Waluchow, pp. 122–37.

CGA Canada (Certified General Accountants of Canada). 1990. *Code of Ethics and Rules of Professional Conduct,* Vancouver, British Columbia.

Elliston, Frederick A. 1982. "Anonymity and Whistleblowing," in Poff and Waluchow, pp. 244–54.

Gaa, James C., and Charles H. Smith. (n.d.). "Auditors and Deceptive Financial Statements: Assigning Responsibility and Blame," in Poff and Waluchow, pp. 138–55.

Martin, Mike W., and Roland Schinzinger. 1989. *Ethics in Engineering,* 2d ed. (New York: McGraw Hill).

McDonald, Michael, Marie-Helene Parizeau, and Daryl Pullman. 1988. *Towards a Canadian Research Strategy for Applied Ethics,* Canadian Federation for the Humanities (CFH), 151 Slater, Suite 407, Ottawa K1P SH3.

Michalos, Alex C. 1983. "The Loyal Agent's Argument." In Poff and Waluchow, pp. 236–941.

Poff, Deborah C. 1987. "The Loyal Agent's Argument Revisited," in Poff and Waluchow, pp. 242–43.

———, and Wilfrid J. 1991. *Business Ethics in Canada,* 2d ed., (Scarborough, Ontario: Prentice-Hall Canada).

Rawls, John. 1971. *Theory of Justice* (Cambridge, Mass.: Belknap Press).

Stevenson, J. T. 1987. *Engineering Ethics: Practices and Principles* (Toronto: Canadian Scholars' Press).

Paul M. Wood

"The Greatest Good for the Greatest Number": Is This a Good Land-Use Ethic?

Introduction

As foresters, we are often involved in land-use decisions. As professionals, we are also guided by ethical principles. An important question for both foresters and the public, therefore, is: What ethical principle guides foresters when they recommend or make land-use decisions?

For decades, foresters in North America have been struggling with the ethics of forest land-use. The central theme, however, has not changed. One author has suggested that "professional forestry has not changed its fundamental perceptions in more than 200 years" (Behan 1990, 12). There have been changes in emphasis, from economic efficiency to ecological integrity, for example, but the central land-use principle can still be stated in the words of Gifford Pinchot, the first chief forester of the U.S. Forest Service, who said that forests should be allocated on the basis of "the greatest good for the greatest number" (Pinchot 1947).[1]

In view of the fact that heated public controversies over the use of forest land have become commonplace, perhaps it is time to revisit this principle. In this paper I will argue that the forestry profession's ethical perspective pertaining to forest land-use may be part of the problem. It is possible that this principle is outmoded and may be hindering the profession's credibility with the public. However, by realigning its ethical perspective on land-use, opportunities are available for the profession to better serve society and to enhance its credibility.

The argument will take the following format: First, I will point out that the forestry profession, depending on the province or state, enjoys either a legally sanctioned monopoly within its self-defined sphere of expertise, or considerable *de facto* control over the same area of expertise. Second, I will draw attention to

---

Paul M. Wood, "'The Greatest Good for the Greatest Number': Is This a Good Land-Use Ethic?" *Forestry Chronicle* 67(6) (December 1991): 664–67. Reprinted with permission from the Canadian Institute of Forestry.

the fact that the profession has included within its sphere of expertise certain subjects with strong political content. Third, I will claim that the profession's ethical perspectives make it obligatory that foresters adhere to specific political positions. Finally, in combination with these empirical observations, I will make the normative claim that the profession has assumed responsibilities for a portion of the political agenda which should more appropriately be retained within the public domain.

In short, this paper discusses the appropriate distribution of decision-making powers between the forestry profession and the public and will suggest that a re-distribution of power back to the public is ethically justified and may help to alleviate controversy in forest land-use issues, and may help the profession to recover its credibility.

The Role of Professions in Society

It can be expected that in most professions there will be questions concerning what should be included within the substantive "decision-making space" of professional judgment as opposed to what should be regarded as political decisions to be made by the public by way of their elected representatives.

Some decisions are clearly within the domain of professional judgment, whereas others are clearly within the public domain. For example, professional engineers may be retained to design a bridge for a city. Judgments concerning the safety of the bridge are within the engineers' "decision-space" and a large part of the reason for retaining professional engineers is to ensure that the bridge is safely designed. However, judgments concerning whether or not the city wants the bridge in the first place is a political decision. The engineers may help

with this decision by pointing out likely consequences of alternative options, but the decision of whether or not to build the bridge ultimately rests with the public's elected representatives.

For other decisions it is not clear who should be the appropriate decision-maker. Questions concerning which decisions should be included within a profession's sphere of expertise are not simply matters of legal interpretation; they are also ethical issues.

Since the function of professions is to serve basic social values (Bayles 1989, 12), one would expect society to define the ethically acceptable "decision space" for the professions. But professions, including those that have exclusive rights to practise as defined by statute (i.e., those that have a monopoly on specified actions and judgments), usually enjoy a high degree of autonomy. Not only are they self-regulating but they usually have considerable discretionary authority to define, by proclamation, their spheres of expertise (Bayles 1989, 11). In short, what should be included within the ethically acceptable "decision space" for a profession is usually left for the profession to decide.

Professions have argued that "because of the intellectual training and judgment required for their practice, nonprofessionals are unable to evaluate their [professional] conduct properly" (Bayles 1989, 12). But herein lies a source of potential conflict:

> The combined effects of these three features—serving basic social values, monopoly, and self-regulation—are central to the issue of the role of professions in a modern society. Monopoly and self-regulation, if exercised improperly, can be detrimental to society and the quality of human life. . . . Monopolies are created for the benefit of society, and if they do not serve society well, then they are not justified. (Bayles 1989, 12)

The Forestry Profession

In recent years the public's attention on forest land-use issues has been increasing, while at the same time the credibility of the forestry profession has been declining. Public criticism of the profession prompted a recent president of the Association of B.C. Professional Foresters to state that "foresters are in jeopardy of losing their right to practise . . ." (Zak 1989, 2).

Like other professionals, foresters have been trained to be technically competent in their chosen field and, in a number of provinces and states, have been granted the legally exclusive right to practise in exchange for their assurance of competent performance. In British Columbia, for example, the *Foresters Act* gives professional foresters exclusive rights of practice (i.e., licensed practice), but the Act is worded to give the profession a degree of flexibility in defining its own sphere of expertise.[2] This is also true in the province of Quebec and a few of the American states. But even for those jurisdictions which do not grant statutory rights of practice to foresters, foresters usually have considerable *de facto* control over natural resources, and usually adhere to codes of ethics prescribed by professional forestry organizations with voluntary membership.[3]

With considerable freedom to define for themselves what should be included within their sphere of expertise, professional foresters have grown accustomed to making certain decisions that have political content. In effect, they have assumed that they have the right to make certain political decisions on behalf of society, although they may not recognize that these decisions have political content. One author, for example, has expressed concern that the U.S. Congress is resolving issues that he feels should more appropriately be resolved by professional foresters (Madden 1990, 36). From a similar perspective, a recent president of the Association of British Columbia Professional Foresters has simply stated that "Forestry is an environmental and political issue—not a technical or scientific issue!" (Zak 1989, 2). Certainly, the most contentious issues within the forestry profession are not technical, but political.

In order to help clarify the difference between technical and political decisions in forestry, it is useful to note the distinction between a land-use decision on the one hand and a management decision on the other. The first involves a decision about the purpose(s) for which an area of forest land will be used and the second involves a decision about how to manage for, or how to achieve, the designated purpose. In a liberal democracy it is axiomatic that decisions concerning the intended use (i.e., purpose) of public land should be made by the public's elected representatives, or their designates. Public land-use issues are also inherently political because they are debatable public issues involving competing interests among persons in society.

While it is true that the major land-use decisions are usually made by political representatives, professional foresters routinely make land-use decisions regarding public land. For example, in British Columbia, provincial forests[4] are designated by politicians. However, within these major areas, numerous land-use decisions are made by professional foresters. Whether or not an environmentally sensitive area is to be logged, for example, or whether or not an area wildlife winter range is to be set aside—these are land-use decisions made by professional foresters on behalf of the public. In general it is professional foresters employed by the government that approve the final plans, thereby effectively making many land-use decisions. I understand this general procedure is also true in other provinces and states and in the U.S. National Forests. As one forester from the U.S. Forest Service in Washington, D.C., pointed out, "The most troublesome environmental debates of the recent past and foreseeable future center on how to allocate the few remaining untouched forested areas" (Ostby 1989, 31). He then goes on to suggest that it is the role of professional foresters to make these allocations.

There is nothing inherently wrong with this general procedure of government professionals making decisions with regard to public land. The elected representative who is ultimately responsible for these decisions simply cannot be personally involved in all the detailed land-use decisions that must be made. He or she must delegate this responsibility to government employees and for forest land-use decisions, professional foresters are usually the responsible designates. It is at this point, however, that the ethical perspectives of foresters become important because foresters have obligations to conform to their professional codes of ethics when making these land-use decisions.

The Foresters' Current Land-Use Ethic

As discussed above, the forestry profession has implicitly adopted "the greatest good for the greatest number" as a land-use ethic. However, as a professional ethic and as an environmental ethic, it is flawed for several reasons.

First, it conflicts with itself. Note that it is actually two principles. The "greatest good" portion is a principle of aggregation; it demands that the aggregate good be maximized. The "greatest number" portion is a principle of distribution; it demands that the good be maximally distributed. But these two principles can be in conflict with each other. It is impossible to maximize two competing goals at the same time and there is no means for determining how to trade-off utility[5] maximization with maximal distribution. For land-use decisions, this means that the principle does not tell us whether to maximize society's utility, *regardless of to whom it accrues,* or whether to ensure that utility is distributed equally (i.e., maximally) among persons in society, *regardless of whether or not utility is maximized.* For forestry purposes, "the greatest good for the greatest number" is a principle that comes with a built-in land-use conflict.

The second flaw is in its implementation. In practice, foresters do give preference to one of these two competing principles; they emphasize the aggregation of utility over the just distribution of utility. For example, the code of ethics of the Association of British Columbia Professional Foresters explicitly states that the first responsibility of each professional forester is to improve the utility and value of forest resources to society and to prevent any reduction in their utility.[6] Similarly, the Society of American Foresters has emphasized that it is a duty of professional foresters to ensure that "the country's forests yield their fullest contribution to the economic and social welfare of the nation" (Banzhaf et al. 1985, 220). If these tenets could provide guidance for the just distribution of public resources, then there might be little cause to challenge them. But just distribution is not explicitly included and I do not believe that it is implicitly intended. In a drive to maximize the utility of all forest resources, foresters assume that somehow just distribution will be obtained inadvertently. This is the basis of the "trickle-down effect." But as one author has pointed out: "The most difficult moral conflicts, especially in social life, are conflicts between utility and justice

(Raphael 1981, 47). In effect, the land-use ethic adopted by foresters claims that forest land should be allocated so as to maximize utility, regardless of to whom it accrues.

A third problem is the scale of application of this professional tenet. Although not as explicitly stated, many foresters have interpreted this emphasis on utility maximization to mean that each and every area of forest must be devoted to the highest possible use. Terms such as "multiple use" and "integrated forest management" are interpreted by many to mean not that there should be a mixture of various forest uses over a large area, but rather that each small area should be allocated to the use that will yield the maximum utility. The issue here is a matter of scale. If each and every portion of a forest is allocated simply on the basis of maximum utility, then the broad picture may suffer. For example, it may be necessary to forego the logging of some timber in order to preserve a sufficiently large wilderness area. Overall, the public may benefit from this tradeoff. But if each small piece of forest is evaluated in isolation and out of context, and the utility maximization ethic is invoked, then many or most of the smaller areas may be logged and the opportunity to protect a large wilderness area will not be given due consideration. Foresters often make this mistake in British Columbia. They have frequently argued that a specific wilderness area should not be considered for preservation because, they claim, it would then be allocated to a "single use," not "multiple use." Notwithstanding the fact that wilderness preservation accommodates many forest uses including aesthetic appreciation, recreation, and the retention of biological diversity, the "single use" argument reveals a failure to look at land-use issues in context. This myopic concentration on utility maximization at the micro level is flawed because it represents a failure to maximize utility at a broader level. In effect, society's resources are wasted if the "greatest good" ethic is not applied at the appropriate scale.

Finally, as a professional and environmental ethic, "the greatest good for the greatest number" is flawed if the word "good" is given a narrow interpretation meaning either economic benefits or social benefits that can be measured in terms of willingness to pay. Foresters in British Columbia, to their credit, have recognized a need to accommodate intangible and non-consumptive forest uses in land-use planning. But in a proposed "Land-use Strategy" the Association of B.C. Professional Foresters continues to take a cost-benefit approach to land allocations. This approach, once again, implies that each land-use decision should be allocated solely on the basis of maximum utility where utility is measured in terms of willingness to pay. In effect, this approach suggests that land and resources are appropriately allocated if they are distributed to those who are willing to pay the most. As has been frequently pointed out, this approach is naive; it oversimplifies the preferential and ethical values inherent in these political issues (Copp 1987; Dorcey 1986; Kelman 1980; Sagoff 1988).

These are several objections to the foresters' current land-use ethic. But it is important to recognize that overall, this ethic constitutes a political position. It suggests that land-use decisions *ought* to be made on the basis of utility maximization, regardless of the just distribution of benefits among persons in society. When applied to political issues, this position then becomes a political position. Public land-use issues are inherently political because they are debatable public issues involving competing values among persons in society.

The critical issue, therefore, is the juxtaposition of the professional forester's assigned task of making decisions on these political land-use issues and his commitment to his professional obligations. The extent to which professional foresters conform to the "greatest good for the greatest number" ethic when making public land allocation decisions is the extent to which the political process has been compromised. *The foresters' land-use ethic commits them to making decisions that favour their predetermined concept of what is good despite the fact that, in these political issues, what is good is publicly debatable by definition.* To some extent, therefore, the public's ability to influence public land-use decisions has been diverted and substituted with the political choice of one profession.

The key point here is that professional bodies, in the ethical standards they impose on their members, must demand technical and professional competence but must not ask for political alliance. Subtly but clearly, the "greatest good for the greatest number" is an ethic that demands political alliance.

Although to my knowledge this problem has not been explicitly stated before, it is reasonable to surmise that the public has been intuitively aware of this issue. It is likely that heated public controversies over forest land-use issues, involving polarized factions, have been at least partly fueled by the unrecognized and subtle political agenda of the forestry profession.

Foundations for a Revised Land-Use Ethic

The profession's attempts to articulate a forest land-use ethic will be frustrated if it continues to focus on confused concepts of utility maximization. Instead, this ethic must be articulated in terms of liberal democratic principles, whereby the concept of the "good" is not predetermined, but is dependent on political debate.

In the context of a liberal democracy, the public retains the right to choose what is good and exercises this right through elected legislators or by way of various forms of direct public participation. Attempts to divert some of this power to the relatively autonomous forestry profession can be perceived as unjust and may exacerbate the public's lack of confidence in the profession.

There is an opportunity for the profession to avoid these pitfalls by identifying the political content that is inherent in the practice of forestry, and by re-designing an appropriate foresters' land-use ethic. The exact shape that this new ethic should take is a subject that needs thorough discussion among foresters and with the public. But this much is clear: under such an ethic it would be necessary for the profession to concede that when public values are relevant to forestry decisions, the public and its elected representatives know best. The legitimate role of the forester under such an ethic would be to support and assist the public's opportunities and ability to participate in these political decisions.

Notes

A previous version of this paper was presented at: Moral Philosophy in the Public Domain: An International Conference on Applied Ethics in Business, Medicine and Environmental Policy. Vancouver, B.C. 7–9 June 1990.

1. Actually, "the greatest good for the greatest number" was originally made famous by British philosopher Jeremy Bentham in his book, *Introduction to the Principles of Morals and Legislation* (1789). Pinchot was probably aware of Bentham's work.

2. Pers. comm., R. Bronstein, R.P.F., Executive Director, Assoc. of B.C. Professional Foresters.

3. The Canadian Institute of Forestry and the Society of American Foresters are two such organizations that have voluntary membership.

4. Large areas in British Columbia known as Tree Farm Licenses and Timber Supply Areas are similarly designated by political processes.

5. For the purpose of this discussion "good" and "utility" can be used interchangeably.

6. See sections 1 (a) and 1 (c) of the code of ethics of the Association of B.C. Professional Foresters.

References

Banzhaf, W. H., A. F. Burns, and J. Vance. 1985. "Ethics and forestry." *J. For.* (April 1985).

Bayles, Michael D. 1989. *Professional Ethics*, 2d ed. Belmont, Calif.: Wadsworth Publishing Co.

Behan, R. W. 1990. "Multiresource Forest Management: A Paradigmatic Challenge to Professional Forestry." *J. For.* (April 1990).

Copp, D. 1987. "The Justice and Rationale of Cost-Benefit Analysis." *Theory and Decision* 23: 65–87.

Dorcey, A. H. J. 1986. Bargaining in the governance of Pacific coastal resources: Research and reform. Westwater Research Centre, University of B.C.

Kelman, S. 1980. "Cost-benefits analysis and environmental safety and health regulation: Ethical and philosophical considerations." In *Cost-benefit Analysis and Environmental Regulations: Politics, ethics, and methods*, eds. D. Swartzman, R. A. Liroff, and K. C. Crocke (Washington, D.C.: The Conservation Foundation).

Madden, R. B. 1990. "The Forestry Challenge of the Nineties." *J. For.* (January 1990).

Ostby, D. 1989. "A Reviewer Comments" [on the immediately preceding article by J. E. Coufal, "Forestry: In Evolution or Revolution"]. *J. For.* (May 1989).

Pinchot, G. 1947. *Breaking New Ground.* Seattle: University of Washington Press.

Raphael, D. D. 1981. *Moral Philosophy.* New York: Oxford University Press.

Sagoff, M. 1988. "Some Problems with Environmental Economics." *Environmental Ethics.* Vol. 10 (Spring 1988).

Zak, Brian. 1989. "The Presidents Corner." *The B.C. Professional Forester.* October 1989.

James E. Coufal

Environmental Ethics: Cogitations and Ruminations of a Forester

It is clear that forestry is being called upon to change. The recent SAF Task Force on Biological Diversity recognized this by saying that "Conservation of biological diversity is a biological and social issue that will probably require changes in current forest conservation and management practices and plans" (Society of American Foresters 1991, p. 38). The call for change in forestry is not new, and if not continuous it has reached crescendo at various other times in forestry history. What will be new is our response, and how we choose to blend anthropocentric, biocentric, and ecocentric ideas and ideals will play a major part in this response.

Before suggesting that there is a convergence of thought and describing what I believe an environmental ethic for forestry should do, I will describe the clearest challenge for forestry to change that I have heard. At a conference titled "Practicing Stewardship and Living A Land Ethic," two speakers, Mike McCloskey, President of the Sierra Club, and Sam Hays, Professor of History at the University of Pittsburgh, told the assembled group of 150 foresters that forestry is becoming increasingly irrelevant (McCloskey 1991). They did not imply that wood and fiber products were becoming less important, but rather that other uses and values of forests were becoming equally or more important than wood and fiber, and that forestry is not socialized or organized to provide full services to forest ecosystems management, but just to timber management. (Hays even challenged the foresters to imagine, if they could, managing a forest where *no* trees would be cut.) They agreed that even in the area of forest science, environmental groups, opinion leaders, legislators, and decision and policy makers are calling more often on leaders in the new fields of conservation biology and landscape ecology, and less often on foresters. Their saying that this is it doesn't make it so, *but what do you think?*

Excerpts from James E. Coufal, "Environmental Ethics: Cogitations and Ruminations of a Forester," *Ethical Challenges for Foresters, Proceedings of a Symposium to Discuss Ethical Issues in the Management of Forest Resources.* Vancouver, B.C.: University of British Columbia, September 27–28, 1991, pp. 18–26. Used with permission of James E. Coufal.

Hays, who is the author of the highly regarded book *Conservation and the Gospel of Efficiency* (1960), said many things that I agreed with, particularly regarding our "management strategies," our failures in these, and his suggested needed changes. But he added something that is so critical that it might point to the reasons why he and others (see Sample 1991) warn about forestry's decline in relevance. Dr. Hays said, "It is quite possible to argue that the values of foresters do not differ from the values in the society at large and that we face only differences of means, not ends. I do not find this plausible" (Hays 1991, 4). He went on to talk of the intensity of the debate, the language used, including the large role of value laden terms, and the alternative visions advanced of the desirable forest as pointing toward fundamental value differences between foresters and society at large. The implication is that the difference is more basic than foresters believing that managed foresters are "better" than wild forests.

Perhaps the question is simply this: what is a fundamental value or ultimate end? Are the alternative visions of the desirable forest visions of ultimate ends, or of means to reaching something even more fundamental?

I take honesty, integrity, truth and beauty to be fundamental values, and I think that foresters hold these values just as much as the public, or legislators, or environmentalists. Healthy, productive, diverse forests seem to be the ultimate ends of foresters and environmentalists alike, even if their definitions of these, their visions, differ. If foresters hold ultimate ends truly different from those of the public or environmentalists, I believe we will be faced with irreconcilable differences leading to a hopelessness based on a lack of rational ends (see Callicott 1989; Davos 1988; Spittler 1988). We should have no common ground with the public, and forestry would then truly need to be in revolution not evolution.

As significant as the value differences between foresters and the public and environmentalists may seem to be, I believe, like Callicott, that "The apparent conflicts of value that confront us at every turn are differences of opinion about 'matters of fact,' 'cause and effect,' i.e., about best proximate means to achieve our ultimate ends" (Callicott 1987, 287). Let me illustrate. In preparing another paper, I asked nearly 30 foresters across the U.S. to share with me what they, as foresters, value and what they thought that *other* foresters valued. One of my correspondents put the idea of common fundamental values and different means succinctly when she said:

> ... I guess I'd say that the foresters I know value the land, ecosystems, the flora and fauna, natural beauty, a wildflower, an elk, sparkling streams, wilderness, etc. just as much as an "environmentalist." But, foresters may be more pragmatic—they know a forest is dynamic, its resources are renewable ..., they admit that society uses and depends on many products in the forest that are available only by harvesting trees ... and foresters are willing to provide these products to people. (Force 1990)

Such pragmatism is in itself enough to cause difficulties. Foresters and environmentalists might agree on the ultimate value of healthy, productive, sustainable forests, but struggle with definitions of these and with the (apparently) polar extremes of multiple use vs. dominant or distinctive use; multiple use vs. multiple value management; conservation vs. preservation; trees vs. forests vs. ecosystems; intensive vs. extensive management; and others. A third year student of mine wrote a paper where the assignment was to start by saying "I believe forestry is...." In it he said that "Forestry involves working in a gray area of confusion between extremes," a neat description of our current situation (O'Connor 1990, 2). The profusion of facts about which to disagree, and the perceptual screens that filter the facts so that we select the ones to meet the needs of our view rather than looking for the truth in others' views adds to this confusion between the extremes. Unfortunately, "When strong positions have been staked out at the extremes, it is difficult to find a common ground to seek compromise for the common good" (Salwasser 1990, 36). We need to examine what strong positions we foresters have staked out at the extremes, but we do not need to believe that working in that gray area of confusion indicates that we have such different values from society at large that we are truly a breed apart. Environmental ethics for forestry, its discussion and substance, can provide the common ground we seek within the natural resource management community, and to reach out and join, not convince or conquer, the public and environmental groups. Without falling into the trap of *paralysis by analysis,* the discussion of environmental ethics for forestry should provide the remedy for *analysis without synthesis* that we have often been guilty of. Some of this is clearly already happening.

It is encouraging to see a convergence of action, and sometimes of thought, among people and groups holding different ethical perspectives. Varner and Monroe write of captive breeding programs and conclude that "Enlightened anthropocentrists find instrumental value in ecosystems, whereas holists find intrinsic value there, but neither perspective can endorse captive breeding without habitat preservation" (1990, 29). Bill Ticknor believes that both intrinsic and instrumental values will drive us to the same choices of practice in forestry, and that these will be choices protecting the productivity and integrity of ecosystems (1991). Ross Whaley finds that a common concern for a "work-ing landscape" is bringing the forest products industry, environmentalists, preservationists and conservationists together to find "the optimum mix between jobs, management of the natural resource, maintaining of a landscape aesthetic which is typically northeast, and preservation of biological diversity and existing wild places" (1991, 1). A final example of this convergence is the very recent SAF "Task Force Report on Biological Diversity in Forest Ecosystems." It takes a utilitarian and basically anthropocentric approach to describing why foresters should even be concerned with biodiversity, but within its anthropocentrically oriented reasoning is the statement that " . . . biodiversity has values that are independent of human utilization" (Society of American Foresters 1991, 6). This is a recognition of intrinsic values that not too many years ago would not likely have appeared in such a report. Further, the Task Force statement that "Providing the diverse resources that are required of today's forests—while maintaining their productivity—requires managers to make decisions that *maintain options for the future*" (p. 19) may seem like long-standing forestry policy, but the language (italicized here) is straight out of the vocabulary of environmentalists.

Historically, foresters have worked primarily to meet societies' demands for wood and fiber products, and even today foresters seem to be the only professionals with the education, experience, and interest to manage trees as a wood and fiber crop of the land. It is, at least in part, what gives forestry its distinct practical purpose, and is not to be abandoned but to be made eco-complete. Environmental ethics involves, in each case, the need to reconcile moral claims of human freedom, equality, and justice, and the claims of individuals in communities, with human obligations to individual animals, plants, species, and to ecosystems. In the case of forestry, I believe with Bill Ticknor that this means that we need:

> To move toward a more intuitive, multi-dimensional approach, which places a high priority on blending the not inconsiderable scenic, aesthetic and spiritual aspects of forestry with the biological and business aspects. (1990, 4)

This approach has been described elsewhere as "multivalue forest management" that sees "both human society and forest community as the comprehensive environment of commodity" (Rolston and Coufal 1991, 38). If this leads to a "new forestry," it will be old in concept but new in expression and practice. It is a concept of stewardship and service leading to a professing and practice that goes beyond trees, stands, and forests to ecosystems and landscapes; beyond concern for products to concern for processes; beyond multiple use to multiple value management; beyond the what is of science to the what ought to be of ethics; and beyond allowing others to speak for the forest to becoming, once again, the primary spokespeople for forests.

Others have offered opinions on what an environmental ethics for foresters or related professionals, or a stewardship creed, might look like and do (Dustin 1990; Salwasser 1990; Linnartz, Craig, and Dickerman 1991; Hays 1991; Ticknor 1991), and here I offer my ideas. First, I believe that it will not abandon but modify Pinchot's utilitarian tenets and it will therefore take the form of a weak or an enlightened anthropocentrism, and that:

An environmental ethic for foresters should:

1. *Provide a sound philosophical basis for discussion and action.* It should be the focus of the common ground we seek, within the profession of forestry, within the range of natural resource professions, and with the clients and public we serve. It should start with the individual and his or responsibility for the health of the land (health as both a condition to be described and a value to be debated—science and ethics), and lead to a consensus or shared perspective in a statement of a professional land ethic.

It should lead to decisions based on sound science, rational economics, and social acceptability, with due consideration for the uncertainty of each. It should foster wholeness and unity, not a division into those who practice "commodity forestry" and those who practice "environmental forestry" as Hays suggests we seem to have now or are moving towards (1991).

2. *Lead to a set of guiding principles, axioms, or maxims that are enduring and consistent, and provide the basis for decisions and policy making.* Such axioms or maxims will provide the bridge between the more abstract philosophy and the concrete situations that demand actions; they will not provide "the" answer, but taken together will provide guidelines to arriving at an acceptable answer.

What form will these take? The SAF Committee on Ethics provides five "Principles Underlying the Proposed Land Ethic" currently being debated (Linnartz, Craig, and Dickerman 1991, 38), most of which are incorporated in my list. Rolston provides many such maxims, even with one set geared more toward an anthropocentric view and another based on a bio/ecocentric view (1986, 144–179). For example, he offers "The Natural Selection Maxim: Respect an Ecosystem as a Proven, Efficient Economy" (p. 157) leading toward respect for process as well as product; and he offers "The Do-To-Yourself-First Maxim" that suggests that we "Impose on Others Lower Risks Than You Yourself Are Taking" (p. 171).

Salwasser suggests as a first principle "Do no harm," and as a second "Heal the wounds," with brief descriptions of each (1990, p. 36).

Such axioms or maxims will help to enumerate the "don'ts," but even more they should lead to "do's" that are in concert with the basic statement of philosophy. But when it comes to answering questions such as "Is clearcutting good stewardship?" or "Is it good stewardship to use pesticides?" and other similar questions that we face daily, they will be flexible enough to allow for landowner specific, site specific, time specific, and context specific decisions and actions.

3. *It will add a third fundamental client to those traditionally served by forestry; that is, along with serving landowners and society, foresters will take as a third client the land itself.* The result of this may be the sustained production of goods and other resource values based on maintaining and enhancing the productivity and integrity of forest ecosystems, all anthropocentric results. But the goal also calls for valuing the forest ecocentrically, and providing service to the land without thought of recompense because the land itself has value.

By setting forestry in the context of its three clients—landowners, society, and the land—the environmental ethic will establish personal, professional, business and the land ethics as integrally related, not separate ticky-tacky boxes to be used one at a time. Such a juxtaposition will prevent the "Sunday is the day for religion" kind of mentality that seems to have taken hold in Western society; it will be proper to talk of science and ethics in forestry *and* to do so any day of the week.

4. *The environmental ethic, in the continuing process of asking "What do you think?" and in the established, systematized statement that it finally becomes, will bring humility to forestry.* This humility I see as of three kinds.

First, a humility of respect for others by recognizing that as forest scientists we might (should!) know how the forest works, or *what is*, but that we have no more prescience about *what ought to be* than the public or environmentalists, and that, as a matter of fact, we have much to learn from them. This should cause us to seek new ways to involve all, but especially those who will be most impacted by our management practices, in land use decisions. I would not, however, go so far as to concede, as Wood suggests we need to do, "that when public values are relevant to forestry decisions, including all public land-use decision, *the public knows best*" (1990, 5; emphasis added here). To say that the public always knows best is to make the same kind of category mistake as when we say "nature knows best." Further, it would ignore the considerable expertise of foresters and relegate them to the status of technicians.

Second is a humility of history. In one sense this will come about by recognizing that the kinds of forestry traditions we defend—decision making by experts (us!); wood and fiber as primary; efficiency as gospel; forestry as an applied, biological science—come largely from Gifford Pinchot and his era, and were themselves changes from the common practices of the times. History should also teach us that we have been socialized to forestry mores via our education, and taught to think about select problems in select ways (see Fortmann and Fairfax 1989), but our true education should lead us past easy acceptance to ask "Why?" and "What do you think?"

Third, the history of science will likely someday look back at our own times and find them to be a moment of convergence of biological, physical and social sciences to the point that "if we wish to proceed on the scientific path and attempt to make our data lawful, we simply cannot have only one set of principles about how reality works. We need to allow for a number of realities" (Leshan and Margenau 1982, 21). Scientists and philosophers, coming from different traditions, are both concluding that the science that we tend to fall back upon, and that may even lead us in forestry to practice scientism, is not the only valid view of reality. I suggest that this involves not only a *respect* for other ways of viewing the world, but the *incorporation* of them into planning and decision making.

5. *A recognition that forestry is ultimately practiced in the forest.* For all of the importance of legislative halls and boardrooms, of computers and GIS systems, of linear programming or generally accepted accounting principles, or even for the academic discussion of environmental ethics, they are meaningless until applied to the management of particular forest lands. Our land ethic and the axioms/maxims that follow from it should cause changes in the way we operate in the field; for example, in how we classify and categorize our land use, in what we inventory and how we inventory it, or in monitoring for the cumulative effects of apparently minor damages. From the standpoint of a single current forestry issue, biodiversity, we must minimize activities that reduce, fragment, or isolate forest habitats, or that simplify stand structure across a landscape, or eliminate individual species and structural or functional attributes that reduce biological diversity (Society of American Foresters 1991, 19).

How we operate in the field is certainly greatly influenced by how we are organized. As well as causing foresters to look at wildlife, recreation, aesthetics, and other similar uses and values of forests as desired products and values rather than as irksome constraints on wood and fiber production, the discussion of a land ethic and the wholeness it implies should also cause us to look seriously at the competitiveness fostered by functionally-organized, functionality-budgeted operations.

This especially pertains to how we organize to educate foresters, wildlife managers, range managers, and so on.

6. *The land ethic should bring back the idea of forestry as art as well as science and business.* There is no cookbook recipe to the practice of forestry; each solution is site specific and forester specific. Also, if we are to speak for forests, we may find that we will need to speak in metaphors that help us to make sense of our world, and help others to see into what we truly value.

The idea of forestry as art is not as esoteric as it may seem. While much of animal behavior is instinctive, human behavior is often based on knowledge passed on through stories, an art form. Father Thomas Berry, an environmental theologian, makes a case for the idea that the deepest crisis of any society comes at those times when its traditional stories become inadequate for meeting its survival demands, and that we are at such a time in our history (1988). He calls for a new vision, a new *dream of the earth*, and at our level forestry is being called upon to respond with its new vision.

Once again, Aldo Leopold foresaw such a need. While discussing the "conservation esthetic" he said that one of its components is " . . . a sense of husbandry . . . realized only when some art of management is applied to the land by some person of perception" (1966, 292–93), and he talked of the landscape tapestry that foresters create. He also talked of the need and value of being close to the land, perhaps a reminder for those of us who become desk-jockies to get out and smell it, touch it, feel it, and revel in it on frequent occasions, and said that "We foresters and game keepers might logically pay for, instead of being paid for, our job as husbandmen of wild crops" (p. 293). Don't mention this too loudly to your boss, but do let your hair down and tell the public of the joy you find in the dynamics, resilience, and beauty of the forest, and in being a forester.

There are clearly other principles that could underlie a land ethic for forestry, and other things it might do. This is my list, but once again, *what do you think?*

A Metaphorical Conclusion

One of my correspondents in the brief study of what foresters value was very late in replying to my call for help. When he did, he said that "After 5 months of failed attempts to define even for myself what I value I think I can provide an answer" (McGough 1991). After discussing the need for an appreciation for the complexity of life, he said:

> Gingerich characterizes our attempts to describe life through science with the following metaphor: "It is beautiful in the way contrasting patterns and themes are organized into a unified, coherent whole. It is panoramic in its scope, the majestic sweep that covers all of nature from the subatomic particles to the vast outer reaches of space and time. Like a tapestry, it is a human artifact ingeniously and seamlessly woven together. It is not easy to extract one small part without affecting the whole." (McGough 1991)

The metaphor is an expression of ecology but with poetic power; a worldview in a few words, and one reminiscent of Leopold's note of the landscape tapestry that we foresters create. But what is important goes beyond this to what McGough added, which was: "So what does the metaphor have to do with what I value? The *what* I value is very simply, the tapestry" (1991, p. 2). This, I suggest, should be an ultimate value of forestry and foresters.

I believe that the tapestry we weave must be one of demonstrated exemplary stewardship, woven in full concert with all of those neighbors, human and other, who share the loom. If we do this, if in our land ethic we find room for the Lords as well as for Paul Bunyan, forestry will not have to be sold, for it will be actively and passionately sought for the inherent value it offers.

References

Berry, T. 1988. *The Dream of the Earth.* San Francisco: Sierra Club Books.

Callicott, J. B. 1987. "Just the Facts, Ma'am." *The Environmental Professional* 9(4): 279–88.

———. 1989. *In Defense of the Land Ethic.* Albany, N.Y.: SUNY Press.

Davos, C. A. 1988. "Harmonizing Environmental Facts and Values: A Call for Co-Determinism." *The Environmental Professional* 10(1): 46–53.

Dustin, D. L. 1990. "Looking Inward to Save the Outdoors." *Parks and Recreation* 25(9): 86–89.

Force, J. E. 1990. Personal Correspondence. 10/12/90.

Fortmann, L. P., and S. K. Fairfax. 1989. "American Forestry Professionals in the Third World." *Economic and Political Weekly,* August 12, 1989: 1839–1844.

Hays, S. P. 1960. *Conservation and the Gospel of Efficiency.* Cambridge, Mass.: Harvard University Press.

———. 1991. "A Challenge to the Forestry Profession." Paper at conference on *Practicing Stewardship and Living a Land Ethic.* March 26–27, 1991. Pennsylvania State University, Harrisburg, PA.

Leopold, A. 1966. *A Sand County Almanac.* New York: Ballantine Books.

Leshan, L., and H. Margenau. 1982. *Einstein's Space and Van Gogh's Sky.* New York: Collier Books, MacMillan.

Linnartz, N. E., R. S. Craig, and M. B. Dickerman. 1991. "Land Ethic Canon Recommended by Committee." *Journal of Forestry.* 89(2): 30, 38.

McCloskey, M. 1991. "Environmental Ethics: Perspectives from the Sierra Club." Paper at conference on *Practicing Stewardship and Living a Land Ethic.* March 26–27, 1991. Pennsylvania State University, Harrisburg, PA.

McGough, D. 1991. Personal correspondence. March 30, 1991.

O'Connor, P. 1990. "I believe forestry is . . ." Unpublished Paper For. 305, Forestry Concepts and Applications. SUNY, College of Environmental Science and Forestry. October, 1990. Syracuse, N.Y.

Rolston, H., III. 1986. "Just Environmental Business." In *Philosophy Gone Wild*, ed. H. Rolston III. Buffalo, N.Y.: Prometheus Books.

———, and J. Coufal. 1991. "A Forest Ethics and Multivalue Forest Management." *Journal of Forestry* 89(4): 35–40.

Salwasser, H. 1990. "Gaining Perspective: Forestry for the Future." *Journal of Forestry* 88(11): 32–38.

Sample, V. A. 1991. "A Global Climate Change for Foresters." *American Forests* 97(7&8): 6–7.

Society of American Foresters. 1991. *Task Force Report on Biological Diversity in Forest Ecosystems.* Bethesda, Md.

Spittler, G. 1988. "Seeking Common Ground in Environmental Ethics." *The Environmental Professional* 10(1): 1–7.

Ticknor, W. D. 1990. "Practicing Objective Forestry in a Subjective World." Keynote Speech, Conference on *Future of Forestry.* October 16, 1990. Washington, D.C.

———. 1991. "Environmental Ethics—What They Are, Why They Matter." Paper at Conference on *Practicing Stewardship and Living a Land Ethic.* March 26–27, 1991. Pennsylvania State University, Harrisburg, PA.

Varner, G. E., and M. C. Monroe. 1990. "Ethical Perspective on Captive Breeding: Is It for the Birds?" *Endangered Species Update* 8(1): 27–29. Ann Arbor: University of Michigan School of Natural Resources.

Whaley, R. S. 1991. "Improving the Quality of the Debate." Unpublished Manuscript. SUNY, College of Environmental Science and Forestry, Syracuse, N.Y.

Wood, P. M. 1990. "Foundations for a Professional Foresters' Land-Use Ethic." Paper at Conference on *Moral Philosophy in the Public Domain: An International Conference on Applied Ethics in Business, Medicine and Environmental Policy.* June, 1990. Vancouver, B.C.

The Ecoforestry Declaration of Interdependence

Holistic natural selection ecoforestry is the result of applying the principles of the Deep Ecology movement to the use of forests and the practice of forestry. During the latter half of the twentieth century it has become clear that forests throughout the world are being destroyed by agriculturally based industrial forestry. Industrial agriculture itself is destroying the land and soil, as well as rural human communities. In each of its major resource activities the industrial model is having the same effects. The overall stress of industrial culture on the Earth has made it apparent that we must make fundamental changes in our philosophy, values, and life practices. If we are to change these practices in ways that are ecologically responsible, as well as morally and spiritually sound, we must begin by recognizing the intrinsic value of all beings. What does this mean for forestry, fishing, farming, or for other activities we engage in such as recreation and travel?

A new approach to agriculture is being developed by Wes Jackson at The Land Institute. Wes and his associates are developing a new agriculture, a permanent form of natural farming that works with native perennials and processes of natural selection.

In forestry two main lines of theory and practice converge to provide a comprehensive, ecologically responsible approach to the use of forests. No forest resource-based work or community is sustainable unless it practices respect for, and doesn't interfere with, the full functioning integrity of natural forest ecosystems. To achieve this, two major actions must be taken: (1) we must first zone forests, starting at the landscape level, based on the principles of landscape ecology; and (2) at the watershed level, stands from which material can be *selectively* removed must be identified, and all removals must take place with minimum impact, guided by principles of conservation biology and natural selection. (All access systems, whether roads or other types, must be designed to have minimum impact.) All removals must be from the forest's abundance, not from its biological capital. Forests are self-maintaining, evolving ecological communities. In broad per-

---

"The Ecoforestry Declaration of Interdependence." Reprinted from Bill Devall, ed., *Clearcut: The Tragedy of Industrial Forestry* (San Francisco: Sierra Club Books and Earth Island Press, 1993), p. 263.

spective they provide a multitude of values and services to humans and other beings.

The Ecoforestry Institute is working to build a worldwide ecoforestry movement. We love forests and want to protect them, as we pledge in our oath. We love human beings and feel the great tragedies of the destruction of all indigenous peoples and forest-based human communities. We believe that it is ecologically and morally wrong to destroy forests to get trees, and thus we pledge not to interfere with the full functioning of forests while we satisfy our vital needs.

Ecoforestry is perennial forest use, based on respect for the wisdom of the forest. Ecoforestry assumes that Nature knows best how to grow and maintain forests; human activities in relation to forests must respect and learn from this wisdom.

Humans need forests. They do not need us. Without natural forests all of the major terrestrial communities will unravel and with them the marine communities as well.

Tree plantations are not a viable or sustainable alternative. Thus, for spiritual, moral, and practical reasons we must change our practices. In addition, the consequences of our past collective actions give us a responsibility to undo the damage we have done. This can be accomplished through the use of responsible restoration ecology practices to aid the return of fully functioning natural forest ecosystems in landscapes and watersheds where they have been degraded or destroyed by our cultural activities.

We now know that the current industrial forestry practices are wrong, and even some mainstream forestry organizations are seeing this truth.

The Ecoforestry Institute is dedicated to the training and certification of ecoforesters as well as to the certification of ecologically responsible forest use. In this way both producers and consumers of forest products can make wise choices that are ecologically responsible and thus protect and honor the many beings that make up the diverse forest communities. Through ecoforestry we can develop sustainability rather than sustaining mere production for increasing consumption. We can shift toward increasing quality of life and dwelling in states of intrinsic worth. Ecoforestry is the wisdom of dwelling in place and becoming an indigenous being.

CHAPTER 7

Codes of Ethics in Forestry, Fisheries, and Wildlife Biology

Many natural resource scientists and managers believe that a commitment to professionalism, to a professional society, and thus to professional ethics yields certain benefits to them personally and enhances the contributions they can make to society.[1] Part of what it means to be a profession is the adoption of a code of ethics or professional behavior, for a code is typically formalized when an occupation organizes itself into a profession.[2] Medicine is one of the earliest scientific professions and very likely the first, historically, to formulate an ethics code—the Hippocratic oath—and to make it an integral aspect of the professional behavior of physicians. In the twentieth century many other occupations in the United States and elsewhere have followed suit, including technical and scientific disciplines such as engineering and biology, and the applied natural resource occupations as well.[3]

1. Not all of those involved in the forestry, fisheries, or wildlife occupations consider themselves "professionals," and in fact some believe that professionalism is irrelevant to their working situations.

2. For an account of some of the basic elements of a profession, refer to the selection by Michael McDonald in chapter 8. Representative definitions of a "profession" can be found in many sources, such as in D. Allan Firmage, *Modern Engineering Practice: Ethical, Professional and Legal Aspects* (New York: Garland STPM Press, 1980).

3. American foresters began "professionalizing" forestry early in this century, and this process can be traced to a meeting in Gifford Pinchot's office in November 1900 when, under Pinchot's leadership, seven foresters got together to organize the Society of American Foresters (SAF). The purpose of the society was to "further the cause of forestry in America by fostering a spirit of comradeship among foresters, by creating opportunities for a free interchange of views upon forestry and allied subjects, and by disseminating a knowledge of the purpose and achievements of forestry." See Samuel Dana, *Forest and Range Policy*, 1956, pp. 137–38, and Harold T. Pinkett, *Gifford Pinchot: Private and Public Forester*, p. 87. Subsequently, there were many discussions of the idea of a profession and of professional ethics in the SAF led by such prominent forestry figures as Pinchot, Fernow, Henry Graves, F. H. Newell, Herman H. Chapman, T. S. Woolsey, Jr., and Frederick E. Olmsted before and after World War I. Chapman was one of the more effective participants in this ongoing discussion and helped to move the SAF

An ethics code is a set of normative prescriptions about how professionals in an occupation should pursue their ideals collectively. It is usually composed of at least two kinds of prescriptions: (a) norms of professional or business practice that apply to such matters as fee setting, use of advertising services, and criticism of others in the profession, and (b) professional ethics that address such basic values as honesty, integrity, fairness, and mutual support in pursuing one's craft. Codes may be fairly brief and contain very general norms; for example, they may take the form of a simple "oath"; or they may be fairly detailed, spelling out specific responsibilities in several different areas of professional activity.[4] In the latter case, professional societies often provide sample cases to help members interpret how the norms apply to situations that arise in their working lives, and they may have some kind of sanctioning system for enforcing the code.[5] In some professions, such as medicine and engineering, where codes are built into state laws, they are enforced by state-supported boards of practitioners and citizens, and involve formal licensing and disciplinary procedures that are backed by the authority of state government. In other cases professional societies must enforce their codes internally, and the codes do not have the force of law. The most severe sanction may be expulsion from the professional society rather than loss of one's right to practice a profession altogether.

Why do occupations organize themselves this way and adopt such codes? There are many reasons, some having very little to do with the desire to follow ethical norms. For example, some occupational groups believe that their credibility with the public will be enhanced if it appears that they have and follow ethical standards or an ethics code. They are concerned with their public image and believe that their competitive position will be improved if their professional commitments are distinguished from those of other practitioners of their craft who lack such a code. It might seem more evident to their clients or the public that they are more competent in their technical knowledge and skills. However, if an ethical code is understood as a "convention between professionals," this means that a professional group also desires to cooperate with others in serving ethical ideals and can do so better with a code than without.[6] Obviously, then, acquiring the status of a profession and adopting these norms serves the interests of the members of a profession individually, but it does so partly by helping its members serve others, including other professionals and the public, for most professions have public service as an important ethical ideal or canon.

Codes serve other purposes as well. Code norms provide guidelines for what professionals should expect of each other in the pursuit of their professional activities, and also give society a

---

to adopt its first code of ethics in 1948. Chapman's 1923 *Journal of Forestry* article, "The Profession of Forestry and Professional Ethics," was republished during the recent SAF land ethic debate (*Journal of Forestry* 90 [April 1992]: 14–17, 34). Consult A. E. Patterson, *A Syllabus on Professional Ethics as They Relate to the Profession of Forestry* (Washington, D.C.: Society of American Foresters, 1949), for some of the early references.

4. Compare the "ecoforesters oath" below with the SAF code. Another code in forestry, that of the Association of Consulting Foresters, contains some twenty-eight "canons."

5. One example of this is the *Ethics Guide for Foresters and Other Natural Resource Professionals* (Bethesda, Md.: Society of American Foresters, 1996).

6. Michael Davis, "Thinking Like an Engineer: The Place of a Code of Ethics in the Practice of a Profession," *Philosophy and Public Affairs*, 20(2) (Spring 1991): 150–67.

clearer picture as to what kind of conduct to expect from members of the profession. Codes help to assure the public and clients of the professional's commitment to basic ethical values, generate public trust and confidence in professional conduct, promote group identity, and obviously make it possible to distinguish the good and the bad in professional behavior. Having a code and following its prescriptions does not mean that professionals have no other ethical responsibilities in their work, nor does it guarantee that they will behave in an ethically responsible way. However, at a minimum a professional code can define some of the ethical obligations that are important in a technical craft and can provide a public standard against which to judge the behavior of professionals in their work environments.[7] Readers should thus see codes as one source of ethical principles that define what foresters take to be right and wrong in their professional lives.

This chapter introduces a sampling of ethical codes from the natural resource professions, including codes in forestry, fisheries, and wildlife biology—three disciplines that are deeply involved with forests and forestry. As one examines the codes, it becomes clear that there are differences in them with regard to the kinds of responsibilities that natural resource professionals are said to have. For example, the codes are similar to codes in other professions such as engineering in articulating responsibilities of professionals to each other, but some of them go further and identify new obligations of resource professionals not only to humans but also to forests and other components of nature.

The code of the Society of American Foresters (SAF), for example, was revised in 1992 to include a commitment to long-term sustainability that follows ecological principles. While stewardship of the land has been considered a "cornerstone" of the forestry profession by foresters, changing the SAF code to make this commitment explicit was thought to help clarify the responsibility of foresters to care for and nurture the land.[8] However, no specific ethical responsibilities to forests or the components of forests, such as wildlife or streams, are articulated in the revised SAF code.[9] In contrast, in the early 1990s the Oregon Chapter of the American Fisheries Society (AFS) designed a supplement to the code of ethics of its parent organization, the American Fisheries Society, that is forthright and innovative in spelling out the biocentric obligations of fisheries professionals. In addition to the goals of providing responsible nature stewardship and credible science, it includes more specific norms such as maintaining the structure, function, and integrity of aquatic, riparian, and upland ecosystems.

One criterion from environmental ethics by which a code of professional ethics in the natural resource disciplines can be evaluated is the extent to which it incorporates new, more biocentered responsibilities—those that would be emphasized in Leopold's land ethic, deep ecology, and

---

7 There are numerous discussions of the nature and purposes of ethics codes in the literature of applied ethics and of the various professions and professional societies. Some of the discussion here is based on Michael Davis's account of the purposes of an ethics code.

8. Ray Craig, "Land Ethic Canon Proposal: A Report from the Task Force," *Journal of Forestry* 90(8) (August 1992): 40.

9. The SAF is currently rethinking its revised code with the aim of doing a "complete makeover" of the code by the Fall of 2000. See S. J. Radcliffe, "Ethics Committee to Propose New Code of Ethics," *Western Forester*, 44(1) (January/February 1999): 6–7. A draft of the new code was distributed in September 1999 at the national convention of the SAF in Portland, Oregon.

other ecologically-oriented environmental ethics.[10] The final selection in this chapter, "The Ecoforester's Way," is an example of what a more thoroughly biocentered oath would look like in forestry. The code for government service is also included in this chapter because many natural resource professionals are employees of the federal government and are expected to follow its norms. Readers must judge for themselves the significance of the norms and ethical principles in the codes presented in this chapter. They should assess what the codes imply about the behavior of natural resource professionals toward each other, their clients, the public, and the organisms and systems in nature.

---

10. This is based on a comparative analysis of the Leopoldian content of the revised SAF and new AFS (Oregon Chapter) codes as reported in Peter List, "Professional Ethics in Forestry and Fisheries," a paper read at the Association for Practical and Professional Ethics, Fifth Annual Meeting, St. Louis, Feb. 29–March 2, 1996.

Code of Ethics for Members of the Society of American Foresters

Preamble

Stewardship of the land is the cornerstone of the forestry profession. The purpose of these canons is to govern the professional conduct of members of the Society of American Foresters in their relations with the land, the public, their employers, including clients, and each other as provided in Article VII of the Society's Constitution. Compliance with these canons demonstrates our respect for the land and our commitment to the wise management of ecosystems, and ensures just and honorable professional and human relationships, mutual confidence and respect, and competent service to society.

These canons have been adopted by the membership of the Society and can only be amended by the membership. Procedures for processing charges of violation of these canons are contained in Bylaws established by the Council. The canons and procedures apply to all membership categories in all forestry-related disciplines, except Honorary Members.

All members upon joining the Society agree to abide by this Code as a condition of membership.

Canons

1. A member will advocate and practice land management consistent with ecologically sound principles.

2. A member's knowledge and skills will be utilized for the benefit of society. A member will strive for accurate, current, and increasing knowledge of forestry, will communicate such knowledge when not confidential, and will challenge and correct untrue statements about forestry.

3. A member will advertise only in a dignified and truthful manner, stating the services the member is qualified and prepared to perform. Such advertisements may include references to fees charged.

"Code of Ethics for Members of the Society of American Foresters." Reprinted from the *Journal of Forestry* (vol. 96, no. 10, p. 52) published by the Society of American Foresters, 5400 Grosvenor Lane, Bethesda, MD 20814–2198. Not for further reproduction.

4. A member will base public comment on forestry matters on accurate knowledge and will not distort or withhold pertinent information to substantiate a point of view. Prior to making public statements on forest policies and practices, a member will indicate on whose behalf the statements are made.

5. A member will perform services consistent with the highest standards of quality and with loyalty to the employer.

6. A member will perform only those services for which the member is qualified by education or experience.

7. A member who is asked to participate in forestry operations which deviate from accepted professional standards must advise the employer in advance of the consequences of such deviation.

8. A member will not voluntarily disclose information concerning the affairs of the member's employer without the employer's express permission.

9. A member must avoid conflicts of interest or even the appearance of such conflicts. If, despite such precaution, a conflict of interest is discovered, it must be promptly and fully disclosed to the member's employer and the member must be prepared to act immediately to resolve the conflict.

10. A member will not accept compensation or expenses from more than one employer for the same service, unless the parties involved are informed and consent.

11. A member will engage, or advise the member's employer to engage, other experts and specialists in forestry or related fields whenever the employer's interest would be best served by such action, and a member will work cooperatively with other professionals.

12. A member will not by false statement or dishonest action injure the reputation or professional associations of another member.

13. A member will give credit for the methods, ideas, or assistance obtained from others.

14. A member in competition for supplying forestry services will encourage the prospective employer to base selection on comparison of qualifications and negotiation of fee or salary.

15. Information submitted by a member about a candidate for a prospective position, award, or elected office will be accurate, factual, and objective.

16. A member having evidence of violation of these canons by another member will present the information and charges to the Council in accordance with the Bylaws.

Adopted by the Society of American Foresters by Member Referendum, June 23, 1976, replacing the code adopted November 12, 1948, as amended December 4, 1971. The 1976 code was amended November 4, 1986, and November 2, 1992.

Code of Ethics and Standards for Professional Conduct for Wildlife Biologists, The Wildlife Society

Associate and Certified Wildlife Biologists shall conduct their activities in accordance with the Code of Ethics and the Standards for Professional Conduct as prescribed by The Wildlife Society outlined below.

Code of Ethics

Associate and Certified Wildlife Biologists have a responsibility for contributing to an understanding of mankind's proper relationship with natural resources, and in particular for determining the role of wildlife in satisfying human needs. Certified wildlife biologists will strive to meet this obligation through the following professional goals: They will subscribe to the highest standards of integrity and conduct. They will recognize research and scientific management of wildlife and their environments as primary goals. They will disseminate information to promote understanding of, and appreciation for, values of wildlife and their habitats. They will strive to increase knowledge and skills to advance the practice of wildlife management. They will promote competence in the field of wildlife management by supporting high standards of education, employment, and performance. They will encourage the use of sound biological information in management decisions. They will support fair and uniform standards of employment and treatment of those professionally engaged in the practice of wildlife management.

Standards for Professional Conduct

The following tenets express the intent of the Code of Ethics as prescribed by The Wildlife Society and traditional norms for professional service.

Wildlife biologists shall at all times:
1. Recognize and inform prospective clients or employers of their prime responsibility to the public interest, conservation of the

---

"Code of Ethics and Standards for Professional Conduct for Wildlife Biologists, The Wildlife Society." Reprinted with permission from The Wildlife Society, 5410 Grosvenor Lane, Bethesda, MD 20814.

wildlife resource, and the environment. They shall act with the authority of professional judgment, and avoid actions or omissions that may compromise these broad responsibilities. They shall respect the competence, judgment, and authority of the professional community.

2. Avoid performing professional services for any client or employer when such service is judged to be contrary to the Code of Ethics or Standards for Professional Conduct or detrimental to the well-being of the wildlife resource and its environment.

3. Provide maximum possible effort in the best interest of each client/employer accepted, regardless of the degree of remuneration. They shall be mindful of their responsibility to society, and seek to meet the needs of the disadvantaged for advice in wildlife-related matters. They should studiously avoid discrimination in any form, or the abuse of professional authority for personal satisfaction.

4. Accept employment to perform professional services only in areas of their own competence, and consistent with the Code of Ethics and Standards for Professional Conduct described herein. They shall seek to refer clients or employers to other natural resource professionals when the expertise of such professionals shall best serve the interests of the public, wildlife, and the client/employer. They shall cooperate fully with other professionals in the best interest of the wildlife resource.

5. Maintain a confidential professional-client/employer relationship except when specifically authorized by the client/employer or required by due process of law or this Code of Ethics and Standards to disclose pertinent information. They shall not use such confidence to their personal advantage or to the advantage of other parties, nor shall they permit personal interests or other client/employer relationships to interfere with their professional judgment.

6. Refrain from advertising in a self-laudatory manner, beyond statements intended to inform prospective clients/employers of qualifications, or in a manner detrimental to fellow professionals and the wildlife resource.

7. Refuse compensation or rewards of any kind intended to influence their professional judgment or advice. They shall not permit a person who recommends or employs them, directly or indirectly, to regulate their professional judgment. They shall not accept compensation for the same professional services from any source other than the client/employer without the prior consent of all the clients or employers involved. Similarly, they shall not offer a reward of any kind or promise of service in order to secure a recommendation, a client, or preferential treatment from public officials.

8. Uphold the dignity and integrity of the wildlife profession. They shall endeavor to avoid even the suspicion of dishonesty, fraud, deceit, misrepresentation, or unprofessional demeanor.

Code of Practices, American Fisheries Society

Members of the American Fisheries Society (AFS) have an obligation to perform their duties in an ethical manner. First and foremost, members accept the responsibility to serve and manage aquatic resources for the benefit of those resources and of the public, based on the best available scientific data, as specified by the Society's "North American Fisheries Policy." They act ethically in their relationships with the general public and with their employers, employees, and associates, and they follow the tenets of the Society's Equal Opportunity Policy. They strive to preserve and enhance the dignity of the fisheries profession. All members must adhere to the "Standards of Professional Conduct" as herein established.

Section I—*Dignity and Integrity of the Profession*

Members of AFS shall
 1. Avoid actual or apparent dishonesty, misrepresentation, and unprofessional demeanor by using proper scientific methodology, by adhering to the Society's "Guidelines for Use of Fishes in Field Research," by fully documenting technical conclusions and interpretations, and by encouraging these practices in others;
 2. Give just credit for professional work done by others;
 3. Make the fisheries profession more effective by exchanging information and experiences with colleagues, students, and the public via formal publications, reports, and lectures; informal consultations; and constructive interactions with professional societies, journalists, and government bodies;
 4. Approve only those plans, reports, and other documents they have helped prepare or have supervised and with which they agree;
 5. Make professional recommendations and decisions to benefit fishery resources and the public, base them on the best available scientific data and judgments, and clearly give the consequences both of following and of not following them;
 6. Restrict, to the extent possible, criticisms of technical results and conclusions to profes-

---

"Code of Practices, American Fisheries Society." Reprinted with permission from American Fisheries Society, 5410 Grosvenor Lane, Bethesda, MD 20814–2199.

sional forums such as meetings and technical journals;

7. Expose scientific or managerial misconduct or misinformation, including misrepresentation of fisheries information to the public, through established institutional procedures or by informing the president of AFS.

8. Treat employees justly and fairly with respect to recruitment, supervision, job development, recognition, and compensation.

Section II—*Relations with Clients and Employers*

Members of AFS shall

1. Serve each client or employer professionally without prejudice or conflict of interest;

2. Advertise professional qualifications truthfully, without exaggeration, and without denigration of others;

3. Maintain confidential relationships with employers and clients unless authorized by the employer or required by law or due process to disclose information, and refrain from using confidential information for personal gain or the advantage of others;

4. Reject all attempts by employers and others to coerce or manipulate professional judgment and advice, exercise professional judgment without regard to personal gain, and refuse compensation or other rewards that might be construed as an attempt to influence judgment.

Section III—*Relations with the Public*

Members of AFS shall

1. Communicate with the public honestly and forthrightly within constraints imposed by employer or legal confidentiality;

2. Oppose the release of selective, biased, or inaccurate fisheries information that might mislead the public or prevent it from gaining a balanced view of a subject;

3. Express opinions on a fisheries subject only if qualified by training and experience to do so and only if fully informed about the subject;

4. Clearly delineate professional opinion from accepted knowledge or fact in all public communications;

5. Base expert testimony to a court, commission, or other tribunal on adequate knowledge and honest conviction and give balanced judgments about the consequences of alternative actions.

Code of Ethics, Oregon Chapter, American Fisheries Society.

This Code of Ethics[1] provides principles of conduct to guide the members of the Oregon Chapter of the American Fisheries Society in maintaining ethical relations with the natural and cultural communities they serve and to which they belong. As fisheries professionals, we are obligated to provide clear, accurate, and timely information; to encourage open discourse, both professional and public; and to participate in the debate that results in informed choices by the public. We are also obligated to select for ourselves and to recommend to others courses of action we believe will protect the biological diversity and integrity of aquatic ecosystems.

We recognize that the complexity of the physical and biological worlds, compounded by the complexity of social values and conflicting perspectives, often means that all of the alternatives contain costs as well as benefits. Often, none of the alternatives can satisfy everyone, and choosing among them will be difficult and painful to some or all of the interested parties. We recognize that resources are finite, that we share them with all forms of life, and that no one species, no one group can "have it all." We also recognize that human culture and quality of life depend on intact ecosystems. Reaching an appropriate level of global sustainability, although it may be achieved with local excess, requires us to take responsibility for educating, studying, and managing for that level of sustainability.

People expect management decisions to be based on sound reasoning and scientific information, guided by reasoned judgment, in keeping with principles of conservation and rational use of aquatic resources. Accurate scientific information is critical to sound management. Both the relevant science and the limits of scientific knowledge and understanding must be clearly communicated to decision makers and the public. Another primary role of fisheries professionals is to define management options and the likely outcomes of implementing them. Predicting outcomes of alternatives often contains considerable uncertainty; people need to be made aware of this uncertainty when they

"Code of Ethics, Oregon Chapter, American Fisheries Society." Reprinted with permission from Oregon Chapter, American Fisheries Society, 460 SW Madison #7, Corvallis, OR 97333.

evaluate alternatives.

Because our knowledge of changes in ecosystems is often coupled with a high degree of uncertainty, reasonable and competent professionals may disagree about the ecological and social consequences of natural resource decisions. We must therefore recognize that the foremost obligation of the fisheries professional is to ensure open, honest discussion of the benefits, costs, risks, and tradeoffs of alternative management actions in balancing scientific principles with the interests of society.

Achieving the goals of responsible stewardship and credible science requires that ethical standards be followed by all of us. To that end, each Oregon Chapter member agrees to follow the principles outlined below:

I will work toward maintaining the structure, function, and integrity of aquatic, riparian, and upland ecosystems—the physical surroundings and the complex, interconnected web of life on which fish and other aquatic organisms depend.

I will take care in my research to minimize adverse effects to the environment and not kill or injure organisms except when essential for collecting data.

I will insist that any use of the aquatic resource promotes ecological integrity and continuity of ecosystems now and into the future. Because human beings are a part of the interconnected web of life, I will consider human needs and influences as integral to the study and management of these ecosystems.

I will contribute to framing and evaluating alternatives for managing the ecosystems on which fish and other aquatic organisms depend and describe the likely outcomes of each alternative, so that the public, their elected representatives, and resource policy makers can make informed decisions.

I will cooperate with professionals in other disciplines to foster interdisciplinary understanding and to guide research and management toward clarifying the complex interactions that affect fish and other aquatic organisms, as well as the ecosystems on which they depend.

I will speak and write honestly and openly about the results of my work, neither hiding nor exaggerating their implications. I will explicitly acknowledge my own biases, assumptions, and values that are the foundation of my understanding and interpretation of scientific theories and knowledge. I will be open to the ideas of others and evaluate those ideas with clear recognition of the influence of my own values.

In writing and speaking, I will acknowledge the work and ideas of others, whether gleaned from publications, presentations, or conversations.

I recognize that my deeply held, professional convictions may conflict with the interests and convictions of others. I am obligated to be clear and honest in distinguishing between reports of results from rigorous study and my professional opinions based on observations or intuition. My professional opinions—clearly so identified—have value, but must not be put forward as fact. In addition, the temporal, spatial, and contextual limits of my facts and their confidence limits must be clearly acknowledged.

I will distinguish between recommendations based on science and those based on policy, both to avoid confusing the public and to better separate political decisions from aquatic science.

I recognize that my professional convictions may sometimes conflict with the policies of my employer. When such conflict arises, I will provide decision makers with full supporting evidence and sufficient time for study and action before I publicly disclose my views. But my commitment to the profession and to ecosystems, including their human components, may compel me on occasion to speak against policies or actions of my employer.

I will learn from the wisdom of the past, but I will freely and consistently question all information, inferences, and assumptions that could affect aquatic ecosystems.

I will continue to learn throughout my professional life—to read, listen, assimilate, integrate, and apply new information as it becomes available. I will follow advances in related disciplines (other branches of biology, hydrology, geology, sociology, economics, ethics, and politics) that affect fish and aquatic ecosystems so that the value of my expertise does not become irrelevant or overwhelmed by unforeseen influences.

I recognize that diversity among my professional colleagues brings differences in perspective, experience, expertise, style, and values to the profession and that these differences are a source of strength and new ideas. I welcome as colleagues people of both sexes, all ages, races, ethnic backgrounds, nationalities, life styles, religions, and physical conditions.

I will uphold the highest standards of excellence, integrity, and public service of my profession, and I will do my share to return to the profession the full measure of all that I have received. I will speak and write to people outside of the fisheries profession to help increase their awareness of and interest in aquatic ecosystems.

I will serve as a mentor to young people in the profession so that they may learn, care, and contribute. I will teach them, encourage understanding of their own and society's values, and, by my own example, help them to develop high ethical standards for research and rescue management.

Note

1. The Code supplements American Fisheries Society Code of Practices and Ethics, 1994.

A Code of Ethics for Government Service

PL 96–303 Signed by the President on July 3, 1980

1. Put loyalty to the highest moral principles and the country above loyalty to persons, party or government department.
2. Uphold the Constitution, laws, and regulations of the United States and of all governments therein and never be a party to their evasion.
3. Give a full day's labor for a full day's pay; giving earnest effort and best thought to the performance of duties.
4. Seek to find and employ more efficient and economical ways of getting tasks accomplished.
5. Never discriminate unfairly by the dispensing of special favors or privileges to anyone, whether for remuneration or not; and never accept, for himself or herself or for family members, favors or benefits under circumstances which might be construed by reasonable persons as influencing the performance of governmental duties.
6. Make no private promises of any kind binding upon the duties of the office, since a Government employee has no private work which can be binding on public duty.
7. Never engage in any business with the government either directly or indirectly, which is inconsistent with the conscientious performance of governmental duties.
8. Never use any information gained confidentially in the performance of governmental duties as a means of making private profit.
9. Expose corruption wherever discovered.
10. Uphold these principles, ever conscious that public office is a public trust.

The Ecoforester's Way

1. We shall respect and learn from the ecological wisdom (ecosophy) of Nature's forests with their multitudes of beings.

2. We shall protect the integrity of the full functioning forest.

3. We shall not use agricultural practices in the forest.

4. We shall remove from the forest only values that are in abundance and that meet vital human needs.

5. We shall remove individual instances of values only when this removal will not interfere with a full functioning forest; when in doubt, we will let them be.

6. We shall minimize the impacts of our actions on the forest by using appropriate, low impact technology practices.

7. We shall do good work and uphold the Ecoforester's Oath as a duty and trust.

This oath contains several phrases that need explanation, including *good work, appropriate technology,* and *ecological wisdom.*

"The Ecoforester's Way." Reprinted from Bill Devall, ed., *Clearcut: The Tragedy of Industrial Forestry* (San Francisco: Sierra Club Books and Earth Island Press, 1993), p. 265.

Good work:

1. provides for basic material needs (physical sustenance);

2. satisfies the need to work cooperatively with others to realize common values;

3. perfects and actualizes abilities and skills (intellectual and physical development);

4. realizes an increasingly extended sense of identification and commitment to larger patterns of interdependence and relationship (maturity);

5. realizes the ecological self in harmony with other and Nature.

Appropriate technology:

1. is ecologically and thermodynamically sound;

2. is suitable to the problem context;

3. is economically and socially equitable and sustainable;

4. facilitates human self-realization and improvement of quality of life, not just increasing quantities of consumption.

Principles of Ecological Wisdom:

1. Nature knows best.

2. Everything is interconnected.

3. Everything goes somewhere.
4. There is no "free lunch."
5. Community, consciousness, and intrinsic values permeate all of Nature.
6. Nature sustains us; we do not sustain Nature.
7. Nature tends toward abundance and flourishing of diversity.

CHAPTER 8

Adopting a Land Ethic in the Society of American Foresters

Codes of ethics in natural resource groups have existed for many years; they have been a common feature of the process of professionalization that has affected applied scientific occupations for over a century. However, as is evident from the readings in chapter 7, ethical norms that identify responsibilities to nature, natural objects, and natural ecosystems are not a typical feature of such codes. This is not to imply that members of these groups do not accept such obligations, since humans can have deep feelings about what they ought to do and can act in an ethical manner without having formulated explicit guidelines or rules to follow. The articulation of a formal code is often something that occurs only after people have already taken ethical responsibilities seriously in their own lives, and the existence of a stated ethical rule does not necessarily change a person's deeper ethical commitments. Moreover, many individuals would not have become involved in disciplines such as wildlife biology or forest ecology if they lacked a strong attachment to at least some part of the natural environment that they research or manage. However, practitioners of a resource profession do not always have the same attachments to nature, the same degrees of emotional involvement in their work, or the same attitudes about their ethical obligations. In addition, the occupations that fall under a general category like "biology" are really quite diverse. Thus a society such as the Society of American Foresters (SAF) is composed of members from academia, research institutions, government agencies, and private corporations, and many SAF members have very different kinds of forestry occupations and associations with forestry and forests. This is characteristic of most applied scientific professions and is thus true of such occupations as civil engineering, environmental toxicology, stream ecology, or environmental management as well.

The technical and occupational diversity of a group can lead to significant differences of opinion about the nature of a member's ethical responsibilities and can cause interesting internal controversies about the ethical directions of a professional society. This point is well illustrated in the professional domain of forestry, when in 1989 debate broke out about the adoption of a land ethic canon in the ethics code of the SAF. The debate struck at the very core of the values that this professional society represents and for several years became the focal point of intense dissension and also healthy self-examination of the assumptions, goals, and practices of foresters. The resulting discussion generated interest among many members of the SAF, throughout the United States, and still occupies the attention of this professional society as it continues to actively redefine its professional code.

James Coufal, a contributor in chapter 6 and professor emeritus of forestry at State University of New York in Syracuse, shifted the debate into first gear when he suggested in 1989 that the Code of Ethics of the SAF said nothing about a land ethic and that it was time to revise it to include a land ethic principle that would give "major consideration" to Aldo Leopold's ideas.[1] Coufal cited several important Leopoldian ethical notions and invited foresters to discuss his general proposal.[2] Because of his prominence as a resource scientist and conservation thinker, and his long association with forestry, Leopold had made an impression on the thinking of forest scientists and managers about the ethical directions of forestry before he died in 1948, particularly with regard to such topics as game management and wilderness conservation.[3] As noted earlier, the advent of environmental concerns and environmentalism in the 1960s made his influence on environmental thinking more considerable. At the same time, as one forester recently remarked about forestry, " . . . there have been relatively few instances in the past 50 to 60 years where Leopold's ideas were put into practice. . . . Leopold's vision is still awaiting a cadre of natural resource leaders."[4]

---

1. *Journal of Forestry* 87 (June 1989): 23–24.

2. This included the idea that ethical concern should be extended to all components of the land, that humans should not see themselves as conquerors of the land, and that human land actions should be judged on aesthetic and ecological criteria, as well as economic criteria.

3. Leopold's ideas about the land ethic now appear to be more influential in the natural resource sciences than they were during his time, and, as indicated in chapter 3, this has much to do with the rise of environmentalism and the interest in ecology during the 1960s. In the U.S. Forest Service, this influence increased in the administrations of Jack Ward Thomas, a wildlife biologist who was chief of the service until 1996, and Mike Dombeck, the current chief and a fisheries biologist. Thomas often cited Leopold in his remarks about the directions of federal forestry, particularly with regard to its mandate to institute ecosystem management. It is interesting to note that the classic text *Forest and Range Policy: Its Development in the United States* (New York: McGraw-Hill, 1956) by Samuel Dana does not even mention Leopold's name. However Harold Steen identifies Leopold's recent importance in the last chapter of his book, *The U.S. Forest Service: A History* (Seattle: University of Washington Press, 1976). In his article, "Is National Forest Incompatible with a Land Ethic?" (1991), Allan McQuillan, a professor of forestry in Montana, places Leopold into the context of federal forestry when he outlines two opposing philosophies about national forest planning, the Pinchot-Fernow commodity view and the Muir-Marshall-Leopold preservationist view. The respected national parks historian Alfred Runte has also reviewed philosophies of national forest management and argued that Leopold's land ethic ideas were, if not the reality of the national forests, their "historical ideal." See his book, *Public Lands, Public Heritage: The National Forest Idea* (Niwot, Colo.: Roberts Rinehart Publishers, 1991). Leopold's reputation in the early 1930s was noteworthy enough that he was given serious consideration by President Franklin Delano Roosevelt to become chief of the U.S. Forest Service, but he was not selected. On this point, see Steen's *The U.S. Forest Service*.

4. Zane Cornett, "Birch Seeds, Leadership, and a Relationship with the Land," *Journal of Forestry* 93(9) (September 1995): 7. Leonard J. Weber argues that the traditional American social ethic focuses on individuals

In July 1990 the SAF House of Society Delegates voted to recommend that the SAF Council draft a land ethic statement that could be submitted to a vote of the SAF membership, and in 1991 a national Land Ethics Task Force was created to accomplish this. The task force subsequently recommended to the ruling council of the SAF that the SAF code be amended to include a new land ethic "canon."[5] The idea was to open up the proposed canon for further discussion and debate among SAF members so that a revised ethical principle, if necessary, could be submitted to the membership.

The subsequent discussion, analysis, and comment by SAF members, groups, and state organizations was sometimes quite passionate and raised numerous questions about the ethical commitments of the organization and its constituency.[6] The debate took on added meaning because it came in the middle of a larger crisis about forest management on federal lands in the United States that involved direct intervention by federal courts in national forest planning in the Pacific Northwest, under the impetus of lawsuits launched by environmental groups.[7] Because of differences about the interpretation and implications of language chosen by the SAF Ethics Task Force, the proposed canon was revised twice before it was given its final form in August 1992.[8] The preamble of the SAF code was also changed to reflect the commitment of

---

and their economic self-interest rather than on the community and its interests, thus the land-use ethic that results is different and, I would conclude, not very consistent with Leopold's extension of ethics to the whole land community. This, of course, agrees with Leopold's own observations about the evolution of ethical systems in Western culture. See Weber's article, "The Social Responsibility of Land Ownership," *Journal of Forestry* 89 (April 1991): 12–17, 25.

5. *Journal of Forestry* 89 (February 1991): 30, 38.

6. The *Journal of Forestry* published many of these responses during 1991 and 1992. For example, see "Response to SAF Land Ethic Proposal," 89 (May 1991): 25–28; "Land Ethic Responses, Part II," 89 (September 1991): 20–23; plus Alan G. McQuillan, "Student Responses to Proposed Land Ethic Canon," 89 (September 1991): 26–28. For an account of the development of the land ethic canon and some of the responses from foresters in the SAF, read Arthur V. Smyth, "The Evolution of SAF's Land Ethic," *Journal of Forestry* 93(9) (September 1995): 22–25.

7. As indicated in earlier chapters, this crisis has been building for some years and has its immediate roots in the growth of environmentalism and environment concern in American culture during the 1960s. Foresters began to discuss the crisis in the 1970s, but debates about public forest management among foresters really took off in the late 1980s and early 1990s. For example, consult the following in the *Journal of Forestry:* James E. Coufal, "Forestry: In Evolution or Revolution?" 87(5) (May 1989): 27–32; Richard B. Madden, "The Forestry Challenge of the Nineties," 88(1) (January 1990): 36–39; P. Jakes, H. Gregersen, A. Lundgren, and D. Bengston, "Emerging Issues in Forestry Management and Use," 88(4) (April 1990): 25–28, 34; Paul Heilman, "Forest Management Challenged in the Pacific Northwest," 88(11) (November 1990): 16–23; Hal Salwasser, "Gaining Perspective: Forestry for the Future," 88(11) (November 1990): 32–38; Robert T. Perschel, "Pioneering a New Human/Nature Relationship," 89(4) (April 1991): 18–21, 28; and Chris Maser, "Authenticity in the Forestry Profession," 89(4) (April 1991): 22–24. Many critical books and articles have been written about this crisis, mostly by people not associated directly with the profession of forestry; for examples, see note 3 in the preface.

8. As social scientists have observed, differences in the opinions and values of foresters are related to a complex of demographic variables, such as age, gender, tenure and occupation level in forestry, rural and urban background, education, and disciplinary background. In the case of U.S. Forest Service personnel, see, e.g., Ben W. Twight and Fremont J. Lyden, "Measuring Forest Service Bias," *Journal of Forestry* 87(5) (May 1989): 35–41; Catherine McCarthy, Paul Sabatier, and John Loomis, "Attitudinal Change in the Forest Service: 1960–1990," a paper delivered at the 1991 annual meeting of the Western Political Science Association, Seattle, Washington, March 21–23, 1991; Greg Brown and Charles C. Harris, "The U.S. Forest Service: Toward the New Resource

SAF foresters to "stewardship" of the land and to "the wise management of ecosystems."[9] These revisions were finally approved by a membership vote of 3 to 1 in November 1992.

All of the proposed revisions of the canon would have been departures from the preceding SAF code, in which there was no direct reference to a forester's ethical relationship to the land, to forests, or to forest organisms.[10] The adoption of a strongly formulated Leopoldian land ethic canon would especially have produced a substantially different content than in the existing code. Holmes Rolston and James Coufal urged the SAF to adopt a new forest ethic that would encompass a new multiple-values philosophy about forests. And, in the end, the final version of the canon did take a bow to Leopoldian ideas in its support for forest management based on ecological principles, for it gave ecology explicit recognition in professional forest management, as Leopold advocated. Nevertheless, the question remains whether the new canon expresses a stewardship ethic or a land ethic, a distinction that several SAF members mentioned during the land ethic debate. Readers of this anthology will have to judge for themselves how far the canon goes toward incorporating Leopoldian ideas. In my opinion, it takes only a small step toward a Leopoldian land ethic, and much remains to be done in the SAF to implement the final version of the new canon, as SAF leaders are well aware.[11] However, since 1996 the SAF Ethics Committee has been reevaluating the 1992 revision of the code with the idea of proposing a "complete makeover" toward the end of 1999. The product of their efforts was widely circulated at the annual convention of the SAF in Portland, Oregon, during September 1999. This more extensive redraft will undergo close scrutiny in the SAF for over a year, with the intention of adopting a final version in late 2000.[12] In the meantime, the SAF has published an anthology of opinion pieces about the land ethic, in its efforts to get "thoughtful consideration of a subject central to natural resource management,"[13] and a draft of the new code is now being circulated in the SAF.

This chapter includes several selections from the first SAF debate, starting with Coufal's proposal in 1989 and continuing with updates on land ethic discussions in the SAF and the

---

Management Paradigm," *Society and Natural Resources* 5 (1992): 231–45; and Lori A. Cramer, James J. Kennedy, Richard S. Krannich, and Thomas M. Quigley, "Changing Forest Service Values and Their Implications for Land Management Decisions Affecting Resource-Dependent Communities," *Rural Sociology* 58(3) (1993): 475–91. Other researchers, such as Brent Steel, a political scientist at Oregon State University, have argued that the causes are deeper than this, having to do with cultural shifts in advanced industrial societies after World War II. The original basis for this argument can be found in the work of Ronald Inglehart, e.g., in his book *Culture Shift in Advanced Industrial Society* (Princeton, N.J.: Princeton University Press, 1990).

9. Ray Craig, "Land Ethic Canon Proposal: A Report from the Task Force," *Journal of Forestry* 90(8) (August 1992): 40.

10. Society of American Foresters, *Ethics Guide* (Bethesda, Md.: Society of American Foresters, 1989).

11. See Peter List (1996), "Professional Ethics in Forestry and Fisheries," mentioned above. On implementation of the revision, see "Land Ethic Implementation Continues," *Journal of Forestry* 91(4) (April 1993): 12.

12. Samuel J. Radcliffe, "Ethics Committee to Propose New SAF Code of Ethics," *The Forestry Source*, 4(4) (April 1999): 4.

13. Forestry Forum, *The Land Ethic: Meeting Human Needs for the Land and Its Resources* (Bethesda, Md.: The Society of American Foresters, 1998).

version of the code revised and adopted in November 1992. Also included is an analysis of the values that should characterize a forest ethic, written by Holmes Rolston and his forester colleague James Coufal.[14]

14. The geographer James Proctor has argued that SAF foresters inevitably have diverse notions about what a land ethic means and that environmental philosophers such as J. Baird Callicott and Bryan Norton give different readings to Leopold's land ethic. He also asserts that Leopold's land ethic provides no specific moral guidance about how foresters should care for the land; see James Proctor, "Will the Real Land Ethic Please Stand Up?" *Journal of Forestry* 94(2) (February 1996): 39–43. However, this last point clearly depends on what is meant by "specific," and some environmental philosophers would disagree with Proctor on the lack of specificity. While Leopold's ethic is obviously not a blueprint for behavior or the equivalent of a religious catechism, philosophers such as Callicott, for example, have worked out some of its specific ethical implications. See Callicott, "Animal Liberation: A Triangular Affair," in his book *In Defense of the Land Ethic*, 1989. Moreover, Leopold himself made numerous observations about forestry and especially agriculture in his writings, and thus provided many specific ideas about what his land ethic implies for forest land management. Callicott has recently laid out some of these guiding ideas for forestry in "A Critical Examination of 'Another Look at Leopold's Land Ethic,'" *Journal of Forestry* 96(1) (January 1996): 20–26. Leopold himself indicates the general directions of his own thoughts about forestry in his famous "A-B" cleavage in "The Land Ethic" section of *A Sand County Almanac*, presented here in chapter 3.

James E. Coufal

The Land Ethic Question

I suggest that it is time for foresters to include a statement about land ethics in our Society of American Foresters (SAF) Code of Ethics.

More than fifty years ago, in this *JOURNAL*, Aldo Leopold wrote of the need for a conservation ethic. His thoughts on the need for a land ethic were expanded in *A Sand County Almanac*, which clearly has become one of the most influential works of the environmental movement; in the September 1988 issue of the *JOURNAL*, thirteen of twenty-six foresters polled listed *A Sand County Almanac* among the most meaningful books they have read. Leopold believed that ethics were first expressed as codes of conduct between individuals and communities (society). Leopold then suggested, in fact urged, that ethical considerations be extended to relationships between man and his community. The term "land ethic" was used because Leopold included in his definition of community "soil, water, plants, and animals, or collectively, the land." Perhaps now, these many years later, it is time we made some formal response to Leopold's vision.

The SAF Code of Ethics, including the Preamble and the Canons, basically says nothing about a land ethic; our Code remains primarily a statement regarding conduct between individuals and between individuals and society. The closest item to a land ethic is Canon 6, whereby members are asked to report to their employers the possible consequences of deviating from accepted professional standards of forestry operations. That these operations owe something to the health of the land is, at best, implied. If foresters believe in a land ethic, it seems logical to expect that our Code of Ethics should provide a guiding statement, whether in the Preamble or a Canon, that would govern the professional conduct of members in their relations to the land, just as a statement currently guides their conduct with employers, clients, the public, and each other. The way a society treats its natural resources has significant impact on just and honorable human relationships, and our attitudes and ideals relate to how we treat those resources. SAF could take a leadership role, in society and among the resource professions, by formally recognizing a land ethic within its Code of Ethics.

James E. Coufal, "The Land Ethic Question." Reprinted from the *Journal of Forestry* (vol. 87, no. 6, pp. 22–24) published by the Society of American Foresters, 5400 Grosvenor Lane, Bethesda, MD 20814–2198. Not for further reproduction.

Can We Agree?

To suggest adding land ethics to our Code assumes that we can agree on the substance of such an ethic, since additions to the Code can only be made by vote of the membership. Such agreement could be difficult to achieve, but much has been written since Leopold's time and there are many sources of wisdom regarding land ethics. As foresters we should, I believe, give major consideration to Leopold's ideas. One of the thought-provoking pieces that led me to suggest we consider the need for a statement about land ethics in our Code of Ethics is a 1985 *JOURNAL* article by Jay Heinrichs, where he wrote of foresters as "Pinchot's heirs." The idea that foresters are also Leopold's heirs seems inherent in Heinrichs's ideas when he suggests that foresters need to accept preservation as a form of management, and that foresters are too often identified with wood rather than with the forest. Somehow I suspect foresters find it easier to be heirs of the utilitarian Pinchot rather than of the holistic Leopold, but in reality we are heirs of both. Leopold, however, spoke more to the land ethic.

Problems with Leopold

Perhaps foresters have some problem relating to Leopold because his views on preservation and protection seem to have come through so strongly, along with his unabashed love of and respect for the land. These themes endeared him to the public and made him a prophet of environmentalism, something often perceived by foresters as an enemy rather than as an opportunity. But Leopold, as much as Pinchot, believed in managing the land, from preservation to intensive culture, as appropriate and compatible with the land's capabilities. Unlike Pinchot, who favored a scientific, technocratic bureaucracy of experts managing forests, Leopold's land ethic is rooted in landowner responsibility first and government later. The very attitudinal change Leopold hoped for seems to be occurring, and foresters need to look at their leadership role in it.

To Leopold, the unifying feature in all levels of management was taking a holistic view. This included first the "land" as described above, and second a land ethic that "changes the role of *Homo sapiens* from conqueror of the land-community to plain member and citizen of it." Third, the critical item, the one Leopold called the "key-log" to be moved to develop a land ethic, was his call that we "quit thinking about decent land-use as solely an economic problem. Examine each question in terms of what is ethically and esthetically right, as well as what is economically expedient." What is ethically and esthetically right may not be any more cloudy than what is economically right, especially at the extremes. Can we put these and other land ethic ideas into a form acceptable to SAF members for inclusion in our Code of Ethics? Do we want to?

Conclusion

My bias is obvious, though I only hope to open the discussion. If you agree that the SAF Code of Ethics should include something on land ethics, I ask that you write to the *JOURNAL* to say why. If you disagree, whether in principle or because you think it would be too difficult to write anything meaningful or enforceable, I ask that you write to explain why you think so. Let us at least discuss the question of the basic rightness and the timeliness of including a statement on land ethics in our SAF Code of Ethics.

Norwin E. Linnartz, Raymond S. Craig, and M. B. Dickerman

Land Ethic Canon Recommended by Committee

During its fall 1990 meeting, the SAF Council favorably received the recommendation from the Committee on Ethics that the Society's Code of Ethics be amended to include a land ethic canon. Council agreed, as recommended by the Committee, that the proposed land ethic canon be published in the *Journal of Forestry* for consideration and discussion by SAF members before submission to referendum. What follows constitutes the committee's original recommendation and will no doubt be revised after receipt of comments from SAF unites and members.

Background

The land ethic topic has been considered by the Committee on Ethics for several years and has been the subject of articles and letters published in the *JOURNAL* (June 1989, p. 22; September 1989, p. 10; October 1989, p. 4; January 1990, p. 6; July 1990, p. 9). All support the need for a land ethic canon in the Society's Code of Ethics. Finally, the House of Society Delegates passed a resolution during its meeting in Washington last July "that HSD recommends to Council that a statement on land ethics be added to the SAF Code of Ethics." Thus, land ethics was the major topic of discussion at the committee meeting held in conjunction with the annual convention.

The committee discussed several alternatives for a land ethic canon, as well as the need for changes in the Preamble to the Code of Ethics. Principles that should be embodied in a land ethic canon, and insertion in the Preamble of appropriate terminology to introduce the land ethic canon, were discussed. We agreed that the land ethic canon should be the first one, in recognition of its importance to the forestry profession. Subsequent to our meeting in Washington, DC, an amendment to the Preamble, the land ethic canon, and a statement of principles underlying the proposed land ethic canon were written,

---

Norwin E. Linnartz, Raymond S. Craig, and M. B. Dickerman, "Land Ethic Canon Recommended by Committee." Reprinted from the *Journal of Forestry* (vol. 89, no. 2, pp. 30, 38) published by the Society of American Foresters, 5400 Grosvenor Lane, Bethesda, MD 20814–2198. Not for further reproduction.

reviewed, and agreed upon by the Committee on Ethics.

We acknowledge the valuable input provided by James Coufal, State University of New York, Syracuse; former committee members Ann Burns, John Barber, and Bill Banzhaf; and other SAF members who attended our meeting or wrote letters in support of a land ethic.

Our recommendation for amendments to the Code of Ethics is followed by a statement of principles that are the basis for the proposed land ethic canon. Proposed additions are indicated in italics.

Preamble

The purpose of these canons is to govern the professional conduct of members of the Society of American Foresters *in their stewardship of forestlands and associated resources and* in their relations with the public, their employers, including clients, and each other as provided in Article VIII of the Society's Constitution. Compliance with these canons helps to assure *environmental integrity,* just and honorable professional and human relationships, mutual confidence and respect, and competent service to society.

(Paragraphs 2 and 3 of the Preamble remain as currently worded.)

Canons

1. *A member will strive to maintain and enhance the integrity and productivity of forestlands and ecosystems, to provide and implement management alternatives to help landowners reach their objectives, and to assure the appropriate production of goods and other resource values to meet the needs of society. A member will guard against conditions or practices that will endanger the capacity of forestlands and ecosystems to provide benefits to society and shall promptly bring such conditions or practices to the attention of those responsible.*

(Present Canons 1 through 15 would be renumbered 2 through 16.)

Principles Underlying the Proposed Land Ethic Canon

1. A land ethic should encompass all ecological elements of a landscape.

"Land" is the basic resource, but a land ethic should consider the entire forest ecosystem that the land supports, including humans and the water, beauty, etc., associated with forest landscapes. Thus, "forestland and associated resources" and "forestlands and ecosystems" are more inclusive than "forestland" by itself.

2. The proposed ethic should stress maintenance and enhancement of the productivity and integrity of forestland and associated resources over time.

This principle recognizes that the benefits of forestland and associated resources to society are long-term and continuous. This principle also calls on members to maintain the capacity of the land to produce these benefits and thereby enhance the usefulness of forestland to society.

Implicit in this principle is the possibility that forest operations may adversely affect forestland and associated resources. However, if these operations are conducted with care towards the land, these effects are temporary and the integrity of the land and associated resources is maintained.

3. The proposed ethic should include providing viable alternatives to landowners to meet their goals.

This principle recognizes that the most

economic alternative may not be the best option. It encourages members to look at overall stewardship of the land when proposing alternatives.

4. The proposed ethic should address sustainable production of goods and other resource values.

This principle recognizes that forests provide many benefits to society, and the proposed ethic calls for members to ensure that these benefits will continue to be provided.

5. The proposed ethic should place a responsibility on members to bring to the attention of the responsible person any activities of which he or she is aware that endanger the productive capacity of the land.

This principle holds a member responsible for discussion with the appropriate decision-maker (landowner, client, supervisor, etc.) any activity that he or she deems to be potentially detrimental to the long-term integrity and value of forestlands. This discussion should include suggestions for appropriate alternatives or remedial action.

Plan of Action

Council and the Committee on Ethics have agreed on the general process and timetable for review, discussion, receipt and consideration of comments, and revision (if necessary) of the proposed amendments prior to their submission for member referendum in the fall of 1992.

Members of the Committee on Forest Policy have reviewed the proposed amendments, and their comments and suggestions will be considered by the Committee on Ethics. The recommended amendments have also been distributed to the members of the House of Society Delegates for review and comment.

Now it is your turn. Please read and study the proposed land ethic canon and the statement of principles on which the canon is based. Discuss it with your colleagues. Ponder it. Then write a letter to the editor or send your comments to the Committee on Ethics, via the national office. Be assured that your ideas will be duly considered by the committee in drafting the final version of the land ethic canon and amendments to the Preamble to the Code of Ethics.

Holmes Rolston III and James Coufal

A Forest Ethic and Multivalue Forest Management: The Integrity of Forests and of Foresters Are Bound Together

"Quit thinking about decent land-use as solely an economic problem. Examine each question in terms of what is ethically and esthetically right, as well as what is economically expedient. A thing is right when it tends to preserve the integrity, stability and beauty of the biotic community. It is wrong when it tends otherwise" (Leopold 1968, 224–25).

"I believe a paradigmatic shift . . . confronts the profession of forestry today, and we are due for one: professional forestry has not changed its fundamental perceptions in more than 200 years" (Behan 1990, 12).

Worthy aspirations shift subtly over time. The objectives of the Society of American Foresters "to advance the science, technology, education, and practice of professional forestry and to use the knowledge and skills of the profession to benefit society" (Society of American Foresters 1990), reflecting Canon 1 in the SAF Code of Ethics, have served the Society well and remain admirable goals in the context they address: what foresters ought to do to bring scientific, technological, and educational benefits to human society. But foresters have begun to ask whether those objectives cover the entire horizon of professional forestry. Should this forestry ethic for society now become also a forest ethic, what Leopold called a land ethic?

An Extended Focus

Nothing in the present SAF statement restricts consideration to economic benefits; to the contrary, the larger social welfare is envisioned. But Leopold has a further focus: the biotic community. The SAF statement has no explicit concern for this focus. Perhaps this concern is implied so far as benefiting human society requires beauty, integrity, and stability in

---

Holmes Rolston III and James Coufal, "A Forest Ethic and Multivalue Forest Management: The Integrity of Forests and of Foresters Are Bound Together." Reprinted from the *Journal of Forestry* (vol. 89, no. 4, pp. 35–40) published by the Society of American Foresters, 5400 Grosvenor Lane, Bethesda, MD 20814-2198. Not for further reproduction.

biotic communities. The two have entwined destinies: in forestry, you cannot have a sound economy on a sick environment. Still, Leopold does call this a land ethic; he laments that land use is "a matter of expediency, not a matter of right and wrong" (Leopold 1968, 201). He expands ethics into territory not previously thought to be ethical—not at least in the European-American West. "The land ethic simply enlarges the boundaries of community to include soils, waters, plants, and animals, or collectively: the land" (p. 204). "That land is a community is the basic concept of ecology, but that land is to be loved and respected is an extension of ethics" (p. viii–ix).

Leopold contrasted fundamental differences about value in the philosophical sense; today we call this a paradigm shift or change of reference frame. This need not mean that the anthropocentric reference frame is wrong, only that it is relative and that there is another that is just relatively moral: the biotic. A complete professional ethic will not only be an ethic for foresters in their responsibility to human society, but an ethic that incorporates respect for forests as natural systems.

The SAF Council has agreed that it is time to consider such a responsibility in the SAF Code of Ethics. Consider what colleagues are saying: "The term forester has lost much of its former meaning, and an identity crisis exists for the profession" (Duncan et al. 1989). Public concern with below-cost sales on national forests is "the recent manifestation of a broad, deep, and enduring change in public attitude toward the forests" (Shands 1988). Speaking as a forester, Shields (1989) finds that the public is "examining resource issues with the presumption that the resource must be protected from us." "To provide leadership in resources management, foresters must first seek common ground within their own ranks" (Madden 1990). "As representatives of the land we are a house divided" (Wood 1990). The growing interest in New Forestry (Franklin 1989) and "New Perspectives" shifts toward concern for the whole forest and its diverse values. Behan (1990) offers "multiresource forest management" to replace the long-standing paradigm of sustained-yield, multiple-use forest management.

A forest ethic will require an unprecedented mix of science and conscience, applied science and applied ethics. Two issues are joined here. One is already under way: consideration of the nature of the land ethic SAF should adopt. The second, also underway but further off in full implementation, is whether and how forestry should develop its traditional multiple uses into an affirmation of multiple values, and whether these newly affirmed philosophical values can be made operational. In this more complete professional ethic, foresters will profess what they believe about forests as well as about benefits to human society.

Community or Commodity

Where ethics remains concerned exclusively with human community, then the natural environment, outside ethics proper, can only count instrumentally to society, that is, only as commodity or amenity. Ecology describes "the land" as what it is—an ecosystemic community. Leopold moves to what it ought to be by urging respect for the larger biological community, of which the human community is an integral part. Forestry's traditional concept of conservation is not displaced by Leopold's land ethic but is included within it.

Forestry, an applied science, is also a pure science when it describes how forests work, whether or not humans are making any resourceful use of them. A forest is originally and objectively a community. Only with human needs and preferences projected onto it does a forest become a commodity. "Forest products" are secondarily lumber, turpentine, paper, cellophane; what the forest "produces" primarily is oak trees, ferns, warblers, squirrels, mosquitoes. The first-order, natural production precedes and supports any second-order, humanistic production.

Resource use exploits the natural productivity of forests and redirects it to benefit human society. But resource use that ignores how the commodity is related to the larger biotic community is in trouble; the usual result is degradation of the biotic and ultimately the human community. A holistic forest ethic affirms the forest as resource, but denies that it is only a resource. In the first stage of the expanding ethic, foresters will move past short-term economic criteria to longer-term "uses"; in the second stage they will move beyond forests merely as a human resource. They will understand their relationship with the beauty, integrity, and stability of the biotic community throughout public and private forests (though perhaps in differing degrees in designated wilderness and intensively managed forests).

The Present Code

The existing SAF code remains at Leopold's first level, relating persons to persons and persons to society. How might it be enlarged?

1. The Preamble reads: "The purpose of these canons is to govern the professional conduct of members of the Society of American Foresters in their relations with the public, their employers, including clients, and each other." Such an interpersonal code says nothing about biotic community; it is about forestry as a practice, not about forests as natural systems. Revealingly, the word "forests" does not occur in the code, only "forest resources." The Code of Ethics and Professional Conduct for the American Institute of Certified Planners urges, "A planner must strive to protect the integrity of the natural environment" (American Institute of Certified Planners 1989, 1). In the shift of reference frame we recommend, the SAF code will urge, "A forester must strive to protect the integrity of forest communities in the natural environment."

2. In a summary of its responsibilities, SAF places first the "enhancement of public understanding and appreciation of forest resources." A more complete responsibility will be to seek "enhancement of public understanding of forests and forest resources." The second responsibility SAF claims is "stewardship of forestry's public and professional image." Perhaps SAF should be less concerned about forestry's image and work to produce foresters deeply concerned about healthy biotic and human communities and about optimizing their values, confident that the image problem will be resolved through what SAF president Whaley calls "demonstrated exemplary stewardship of the resources" (Whaley 1990). The second responsibility could thus become "stewardship of public and private forests."

3. SAF states its "national involvement in natural-resource policy," declaring "the sole objective is to define resource problems and offer scientifically based solutions embodying the best judgment of forestry professionals." A broader, community-oriented perspective would have foresters analyze values available on forested lands, based on a scientific understanding of forest and human systems and embodying the best judgment of forestry professionals, then recommend solutions that optimize these values. The deep natural-resource problem is as philosophical as it is technical. The problem lies in treating as mere resource that toward which one ought to have a land

ethic. The solution is to see both human society and forest community as the comprehensive environment of commodity.

Multiple Values

Multiple use is a commodity model, treating forests expediently as nothing but resource. Multiple value is a community model, respecting both human and forest communities and seeking an integrated appreciation and development of values provided by forests. In 1976 Congress declared that, on public lands, consideration ought to be given to the relative "values" and not necessarily to the "uses" that provide the greatest economic return (Federal Land Policy and Management Act of 1976, P.L. 94–579). That not only moves past economics to noneconomic uses; it moves past "uses" to "values." In an expanded land ethic, a comprehensive analysis of the multiple values carried by natural systems will enrich the model of multiple use.

Multiple use asks of a thing, What is it good for? What use does it have? Unsurprisingly, the question is often answered economically, seeking maximum exploitation of resources. There are no ethical issues regarding the commodities and amenities as such; the ethical issues deal with just distribution of benefits within the community of persons.

Multiple value asks, What values are present intrinsically (in the forests regardless of humans) as well as instrumentally (in forests used as human resources)? How can this richness be optimized? The community model seeks to optimize not only human uses for recreation, timber, range, and watershed but also beauty, integrity, and stability in the biotic community.

Value-based, community-oriented professional ethics will result in SAF objectives that urge foresters to use their skill so that society can enjoy the multiple values its forests provide. Almost as if to anticipate an expanded ethic for forestry, The Wildlife Society, for comparison, seeks to "increase awareness and appreciation of wildlife values" and "undertake an active role in preventing human-induced environmental degradation." It believes "that all forest management must be designed to maintain healthy functioning ecosystems, that wildlife is an integral part of each forest ecosystem, and that to be ecologically acceptable forest management must include consideration and action for wildlife" (The Wildlife Society 1988).

SAF should lead the way for foresters by stating that forests, in their many forms, are a basic component of human culture and then insist that foresters have the responsibility to (1) increase awareness and appreciation of forest values and (2) take an active role in preventing human-induced forest degradation. All forest management ought to be designed to maintain healthy functioning ecosystems—a genuine land ethic.

Adding Values

The five statutory multiple uses are recreation, timber, range, watershed, and wildlife and fish. Expanding these, ten categories could integrate human and biotic values and emphasize realms that multiple use often neglects.

1. Life support values. Underlying all economic values are the timeless natural givens that support everything else—forests, sunshine, wind, rain, rivers, soils, the cycling seasons, flora and fauna, trophic pyramids, succession. There can be no healthy human community unless it is integrated with some land community. Indeed, "land" in Leopold's sense is the source of all life.

2. Economic values. Civilization as we know

it would have been impossible without wood (Perlin 1989). The nation needs wood, fiber, cellulose, and all the commodities that can be derived from its forests. This fundamental utility is so well established that there is no need to emphasize it.

3. Scientific values. At least half of what there is to know about forests remains undiscovered, especially at the ecosystem level. The least understood level of biological organization is regional landscape ecology.

4. Recreational values. Recreation in the forest takes place in the context of creation. Humans leave the reasoned, manufactured, cultured environment to seek something wild and primeval. People recreate in forests to show what they can do, so they like a trail to hike, a mountain to climb, game to shoot. But they also like to be let in on nature's show, to find warblers migrating in the spring, to view the wildflowers, to gain a different perspective. Forests are recreational theaters as well as gymnasiums, and this runs past "uses" to appreciating "values."

5. Esthetic values. Forests are never ugly, they are only more or less beautiful; the scale runs from zero upward with no negative domain. Even the "ruined" forest, regenerating itself, has positive esthetic properties, when trees rise to fill the space against the sky. The word "forest" invites holistic interpretation. In the forest humans experience a sense of the sublime, a benefit seldom enjoyed elsewhere in society.

6. Wildlife values. Life is Earth's great miracle. Life occurs in society, but, prior to that, life takes place in biotic communities. Wildlife is already a designated "use" but we do not always ask what use we can make of a wild animal; we value wildlife for its inherent value. We move past commodity or even amenity use to respect for life in itself, which is always life in community.

"Wild" is not always a negative term, as when we say that a field or a child has gone wild. A wild forest is a negative only from the perspective of present applied forestry; a "weed tree" is a wild element in a managed stand. Managed though forests may be, we also want the "wild" because life on Earth transcends human will, control, and use.

7. Biotic diversity values. About 500 faunal species and subspecies have become extinct in the United States, and another 500 taxa are of concern. Even where not nationally in danger, once-frequent species are locally extinct or rare. Perhaps 3,000 floral taxa are at risk out of 22,000, about one in seven, many on forested land. Hardly a forest is not impoverished of its native species. A forest ethic will optimally conserve the values in native flora and fauna.

8. Natural history values. A pristine forest is prime natural history, a relic of the way the world was for vast stretches of time. The forest as a tangible preserve in the midst of a human culture contributes to our sense of duration, antiquity, continuity, and identity. Educated forest visitors realize the centuries-long scope of forest regeneration, the interplay of ecology and evolution, of erosional, orogenic, and geomorphic processes.

9. Spiritual values. "The groves were God's first temples" (Bryant 1883). In Latin, the consecrated groves of trees of the Romans were called templum. The Celts before them worshipped among the "sacred oaks." Trees pierce the sky like cathedral spires. Light filters down as through stained glass. Forests seem to be transcendent, not just symbols of transcendence invented by people. A wild forest is a sacred space, yet most foresters have been reluctant to profess this publicly or to manage for such a value.

10. Intrinsic values. Surrounded by politicians, citizens, customers, planners, economists, and surrounded by the manufactured

environments of human culture, one is lured into the superficiality of anthropocentrism. Value enters, exists, and exits with the fashions of human perception and preference. Nothing counts until humans count it. Surrounded by the forest, this anthropocentric conclusion seems even more superficial. Rather, the forest itself is value-laden.

The Wider View

Biological conservation in the deepest sense is not something that originates in the human mind, is modeled by Forplan, or is written into acts of Congress. Biological conservation is innate as every organism conserves its life. Biological conservation is life; nonconservation is death. The practice of conservation by foresters emulates this because it respects the original biological conservation.

From this viewpoint, there is something naive (however sophisticated one's technology) about a reference frame where one species takes itself as absolute and values everything else in nature relative to its utility. Forestry ought to be one profession that gets daily rescue from this beguiling anthropocentrism through its contact with the original givens. Foresters ought to liberate society from a narrow humanism that puts ourselves at the center of everything. Foresters ought to help us gain fuller humanity by transcending the overly human interests and helping us to conserve a value-laden world. Scientific forestry is an empirical and theoretical study of forests; philosophical forestry goes further to reform human character in encounters with the natural, the drama of natural history. This is not a burden that forestry bears, but an opportunity it owns. This deeper appreciation of forests could be forestry's greatest benefit to society.

The integrity of forests and of foresters are bound together. The present SAF code speaks admirably of loyalty to other persons, to an agency, to a company. Further virtues that ought to be embraced are loyalty to a land— to the nation and its residents on their native landscapes, the human community entwined with the biotic community. Being concerned for the land does not displace concern for humanity or for a profit, although it will call for new definitions and resolution to do the right thing as opposed to simple applications of accounting principles. It is not only what a nation does to its poor, its minorities, its handicapped, that reveals the character of a people, but also what it does to its wildlife, flora, soils, rivers, landscapes, forests, its home.

A land ethic should enrich rather than impoverish the values in our social, economic, political, and biotic systems. Foresters, led by SAF, can help most in the environmental decade ahead by forging a land ethic.

References

American Institute of Certified Planners. 1989. Code of ethics and professional conduct. Am. Inst. Certif. Plann., Washington, DC.

Behan, R. W. 1990. Multiresource forest management: a paradigmatic challenge to professional forestry. *J. For.* 88(4): 12–18.

Bryant, W. C. 1883. A forest hymn. P. 9 in *The life and works of William Cullen Bryant*, vol. III, ed. Park Goodwin (New York: D. Appleton & Co.).

Duncan, D. P., R. A. Skok, and D. P. Richards. 1989. Forestry education and the profession's future. *J. For.* 87(9): 31–37.

Franklin, J. F. 1989. Toward a new forestry. *Am. For.* 95(11&12): 37–40.

Leopold, A. 1968. *A Sand County Almanac* (New York: Oxford University Press).

Madden, R. B. 1990. The forestry challenge of the nineties. *J. For.* 88(1): 36–39.

Perlin, J. 1989. *A Forest Journey: The Role of Wood in*

the Development of Civilization (New York: W. W. Norton).

Shands, W. E. 1988. Beyond multiple use: managing national forests for distinctive values. *Am. For.* 94(3&4): 14–15, 56–57.

Shields, W. 1989. Outlook: The public and natural resources. *Am. For. Counc. This Month* (October): 7.

Society of American Foresters. 1990. SAF constitution and bylaws. *Soc. Am. For.*, Bethesda, MD.

Whaley, R. S. 1990. Securing a future resource: What is the future and how do we reach it? Unpubl. pap., presented at NY Soc. Am. For. state soc. mtg., Oriskany, NY, Jan. 17.

Wildlife Society, The. 1988. Conservation policies of The Wildlife Society. The Wildl. Soc., Bethesda, MD.

Wood, G. W. 1990. The art & science of wildlife (land) management. *J. For.* 88(3): 8–12.

Raymond S. Craig

Further Development of a Land Ethic Canon

The important question before the Land Ethic Committee and the SAF membership is: What should a Society of American Foresters' land ethic say, and what form should it take? This article updates the work and thoughts of the Land Ethic Committee on the development of a land ethic statement. It provides background information, identifies alternatives that were considered, and concludes with the group's recommendation. The goal is to encourage SAF members to focus on this important question, to help them form their ideas and comments, and to provide feedback to the committee.

Background

The SAF has a Code of Ethics. The original code was adopted in 1948, amended in 1971, and replaced by the current version in 1976. Canon

Raymond S. Craig, "Further Development of a Land Ethic Canon." Reprinted from the *Journal of Forestry* (vol. 90, no. 1, pp. 30–31) published by the Society of American Foresters, 5400 Grosvenor Lane, Bethesda, MD 20814–2198. Not for further reproduction.

4 was amended in 1986. The current code contains canons that address the conduct of SAF members relating to society, other members, and employers.

In recent years, various leaders and members have discussed adding a land ethic canon to the SAF Code of Ethics. This discussion intensified in 1989 and 1990. In 1989, several articles on the land ethic issues appeared in the *Journal of Forestry*. In 1990 the House of Society Delegates unanimously recommended that the SAF Council adopt a land ethic. At least one state society included in its strategic plan a suggestion that members begin looking into possible land ethic statements it might adopt. The SAF Committee on Ethics developed draft canon language and underlying principles, which appeared in the February, May, and September 1991 issues of the *JOURNAL*. The Council asked the Committee on Ethics to continue its work on developing a draft canon.

In 1991, the land ethic issue was discussed during several local and regional workshops. Proponents discussed the need for a process that SAF could use to develop this statement. During its April 1991 meeting the Council adopted a process, and president Ross Whaley appointed an ad hoc Land Ethic Committee to help SAF members articulate their own personal land ethic and to facilitate the debate. The Council further decided to target final adoption of a land ethic statement for 1992.

The issue was considered during the 1991 annual convention in San Francisco. The House of Society Delegates endorsed the process identified by the Land Ethic Committee to complete the development of a land ethic statement. In addition, the *Journal of Forestry* sponsored a forum on the issue during the convention. A number of SAF chapters and state societies devoted meetings to the land ethic issue in 1991, and others indicated they will do the same in 1992.

Alternatives

The Land Ethic Committee considered several alternative forms through which the land ethic statement could be expressed. One option, which would not affect the Code of Ethics, is the adoption of a Forester's Creed. Under this selection, SAF members would sign a statement, take an oath, or otherwise acknowledge that they had read the creed, understood it, and agreed to abide by it. A possible variation is that only new members need sign the creed.

All the other alternatives that were considered involve the Code of Ethics. The committee considered distinguishing between a land ethic and a stewardship ethic. Under this option, a land ethic, which would be a broad philosophical statement about how foresters think and feel about the land, would be placed in the Preamble of the Code of Ethics. A stewardship ethic—a statement on how foresters treat the land—would be in a canon in the Code of Ethics. Another alternative the committee considered was to include a land ethic statement in the Preamble of the Code of Ethics. Under this option the statement is not a canon and therefore is not enforceable, as are other canons.

The land ethic may take any number of forms. However, the Land Ethic Committee is focusing on adopting a land ethic canon. The preferred option of the committee includes amending the Preamble of the Code of Ethics, adopting a land ethic canon, and strengthening references to a land ethic in other SAF guiding documents. Under this option, the land ethic statement is Canon 1. It is enforceable, like all other canons. The committee believes that there is strong member support for such a canon, and believes this is the form the land ethic statement should take. The language recommended by the committee follows (additions are italicized; "ensures" in the third sentence replaces the original phrase "helps to assure").

PREAMBLE
Stewardship of the land is the cornerstone of the forestry profession. The purpose of these Canons is to govern the professional conduct of members of the Society of American Foresters in their relations with *the land,* the public, their employers, including clients, and each other as provided in Article VIII of the Society's Constitution. Compliance with these canons *ensures the wise management of forest resources,* just and honorable professional and human relationships, mutual confidence and respect, and competent service to society.

CANON 1
A member will manage land for long-term sustainability using ecologically sound principles.

Conclusion

The committee believes a separate canon makes a strong statement about the importance placed by the Society of American Foresters on land ethics. This statement may enhance SAF's credibility with publics, federal and state legislators, and nonmembers. Publics can relate the conduct of foresters to the canons.

The committee believes that a good long-term strategy to complement and enhance the SAF land ethic is to add or strengthen references to a land ethic in other SAF guiding documents, such as the SAF Mission Statement, the Constitution and By-Laws, *Forest Policies,* the SAF Strategic Plan, SAF letterhead, and other documents. Under this option, references to the SAF land ethic would be either added or enhanced.

Using this strategy, SAF makes many strong statements on the importance the organization places on a land ethic, and the statements appear in many places that are highly visible to members and publics. The land ethic would permeate the soul of the organization. It becomes a part of all that professional foresters represent and what they say. Adopting this strategy results in SAF adding or enhancing references to a land ethic in guiding documents, as well as adopting a land ethic canon.

The committee believes a strong land ethic canon is important to the forestry profession. We can make a strong statement on what professional foresters represent. The canon has the potential to bring renewed vigor to the profession. The committee urges all SAF members to consider the above recommendations and return any comments to the *Journal of Forestry* as soon as possible.

Raymond S. Craig

Land Ethic Canon Proposal: A Report from the Task Force

The Land Ethic Task Force was created in 1991 to recommend a land ethic canon for inclusion in the Society of American Foresters (SAF) Code of Ethics. During its spring 1992 meeting, Council accepted and unanimously endorsed the following recommendations of the task force:

— amend the Preamble of the Code of Ethics to read (text in bold is recommended new language):

Stewardship of the land is the cornerstone of the forestry profession. The purpose of these Canons is to govern the professional conduct of members of the Society of American Foresters in their relations with *the land,* the public, their employers, including clients, and each other as provided in Article VIII of the Society's Constitution. Compliance with these Canons *demonstrates our respect for the land and our commitment to the wise management of ecosystems, and* ensures just and honorable professional and human relationships, mutual confidence and respect, and competent service to society.

— adopt the following as Canon 1 of the Code of Ethics:

A member will advocate and practice land management consistent with ecologically sound principles.

— place these proposals on the 1992 ballot for referendum vote of the SAF membership; and
— renumber the current canons as 2 through 16 if the land ethic canon passes.

Council also agreed to place the proposed land ethic canon and Preamble amendment in a referendum to the membership this fall.

Background

A land ethic canon has been under intense discussion since 1989. It included various meetings and actions of the House of Society

---

Raymond S. Craig, "Land Ethic Canon Proposal: A Report from the Task Force." Reprinted from the *Journal of Forestry* (vol. 90, no. 8, pp. 40–41) published by the Society of American Foresters, 5400 Grosvenor Lane, Bethesda, MD 20814-2198. Not for further reproduction.

Delegates, Council, standing and ad hoc committees, land ethic workshops, local societies, and articles and letters in the *Journal of Forestry*. The task force considered all these members' comments as it developed the final recommendations.

The task force spent many hours discussing alternative ideas on how to amend the code to include a land ethic canon. Throughout its deliberations, the task force applied the following guiding principles:

Principle 1. The task force believes SAF members want a strong land ethic canon.

Principle 2. The task force believes the Code of Ethics must be considered as a whole. This means members must be guided by the entire code when they are planning or carrying out actions. It also means that all the canons must be considered collectively by the Society as it resolves cases alleging ethic violations.

Principle 3. The task force believes members have a responsibility to consider at least two factors when making ethically difficult professional decisions. The first is to follow the guidance offered in the Code of Ethics, taken as a whole. The second is to disclose all deviations from accepted professional standards to the member's employer or client, as required by Canon 6.

Principle 4. The task force believes that management consistent with ecologically sound principles mandates that landowners' objectives be implemented without ecological damage, freeing the forester to use a broad spectrum of management practices. It does not require that all land use decisions be determined by a narrow view of "sound ecology."

Preamble

The task force believes that the proposed new first sentence of the Preamble, "stewardship of the land is the cornerstone of the forestry profession," emphasizes the importance the Society places on caring for the land. The task force understands that the Preamble provides overall justification for the Code of Ethics. Therefore, it believes the addition to the compliance sentence "demonstrates our respect for the land and our commitment to the wise management of ecosystems" provides the foundation for the land ethic canon.

Canon 1

The task force wanted a clear, concise, and encompassing land ethic canon; it believes the recommended language meets those criteria. A number of members raised issues with the term "long-term sustainability" used in a preliminary recommendation because the term has not been clearly defined by the profession. The task force therefore removed the phrase from its recommendations.

After considerable discussion, the task force decided to use the words "advocate and practice" rather than "manage" in the canon. Not all foresters actually work with the land (e.g., researchers, educators, administrators), although they have influence on those who do. By using the words "advocate and practice" in place of "manage," the task force feels the canon will directly apply to all members, making it even stronger.

Frequently Asked Questions

Many observations and concerns were directed to the Land Ethic Task Force during the process of developing land ethic language. The most frequent concerns are discussed below.

"Land ethic language should include a broad philosophical statement."

It is difficult to accomplish this task without making many of our members uncomfortable; at the risk of undue generalization, most foresters aren't comfortable with espousing philosophy! We don't usually use words like "respect" and "love" in our everyday work. Yet foresters invariably use these words when asked to explain how they feel about the forest, particularly when discussing the reasons that led them to choose this profession. So, even with our discomfort, we are most honest with ourselves and others if we openly state the basis of our relationship with the land. Stewardship connotes nurturing; our desire to nurture comes from the respect and love we hold for the land.

"We have to get away from the perception that we only manage forests for commodity production."

This is true, yet it is also true that a significant portion of our responsibilities to society include commodity production. The challenge lies in expanding our role beyond commodity production to embrace management in consideration of other values. Aldo Leopold was articulate and eloquent in his expression of land ethic concepts, yet those concepts never precluded management of the land for production. His charge was to care for and respect the land while using its resources, and to acknowledge that we are a part of the communities in which we work. He admonished us to value all components of ecosystems, without regard to their usefulness to humans, because all components have intrinsic values. As we manage lands, those values must be considered in our decisions.

"I'm afraid that people will use this canon against us."

SAF's Code of Ethics governs the conduct of its members; each member agrees to abide by its canons. The code is not executed in courts of law (although it is conceivable that it could be used in legal proceedings). As specified in SAF's Constitution and Bylaws, a member can be expelled from the Society if ethics charges are upheld by Council. However, just as in our legal system a member is not guilty simply on the basis of being charged with an ethics violation. The charges are reviewed and investigated by the Ethics Committee and, if necessary, a special investigative committee, which makes a recommendation to council. Council has the final decision.

The Land Ethic Task Force has discussed the implications of frivolous charges based on a land ethic canon, concluding that those concerns should not prevent SAF from articulating and incorporating land ethic values in our Code of Ethics and other documents. We acknowledge that humans make mistakes, and that those mistakes may lead to poor forest management. The motives and intention of a member's actions are critical to the review and conclusions reached in cases of alleged violations of the canons.

"This canon conflicts with the existing canons."

Many members are troubled by the inherent conflict between a land ethic canon and existing canons that demand loyalty to employer and clients. "Ethical" conduct frequently involves difficult decisions. However, the inclusion of a land ethic canon in the Code of Ethics does not create this ethical dilemma, because it already exists. There are inherent conflicts between several of the existing canons, and how a member decides to resolve those conflicts is a matter of personal responsibility. However, priority is implied in the order of the canons; thus the 1990 House of Society Delegates was explicit in its recommendation to Council that a land ethic be adopted as the first canon in our Code of Ethics, not the 16th.

A land ethic canon may actually assist in resolving ethical conflicts because it will document that the profession considers land ethics to be of paramount importance in the practice of forestry. Using one's professional Code of Ethics to support a decision not to conduct certain management practices can also provide a starting point in discussing alternatives with the landowner.

When all factors are taken into consideration, ethical decisions are complex and difficult, and abiding by a land ethic canon will be no different. SAF publishes an *Ethics Guide* that addresses some potential conflicts and provides guidance for resolution. Ultimately, though, the decision always lies with the individual.

"What do we mean by 'long-term sustainability'?"

"Long-term sustainability" was the most frequently questioned phrase from the language reported in the January *JOURNAL*. While we have yet to reach consensus on a definition of the term, most foresters generally agree with the concept. However, questions arise about what we will sustain over the long term. Commodity production? Ecosystems? All species? Rural communities?

The task force has removed that phrase from the recommended land ethic canon because of lack of clarity. Long-term sustainability, regardless of the definition ultimately agreed on, will only be accomplished and protected using management that is consistent with ecologically sound principles.

"What do we mean by 'ecologically sound principles'?"

Management consistent with ecologically sound principles does not require that all land use decisions be determined by a narrow view of "sound ecology." Rather, it mandates that landowner objectives be implemented without ecological damage, freeing the forester to use a broad spectrum of management practices.

Change is fundamental to ecosystems. However, when management accelerates the rate of change to the point that ecological processes are severely disrupted, or where reversal of the "normal" direction of change (e.g., soil erosion versus soil development) occurs, sustainability will be detrimentally impacted.

"What happens if a landowner doesn't want to manage land for forest uses, and wants instead to convert the land to some other use?"

The land ethic canon is not intended to determine highest and best use of the land; thus members are not prohibited from participating in converting land to other uses. "Stewardship of the land" and demonstration of "our respect for the land" do require that land-use conversions be conducted in an environmentally sensitive manner.

Conclusion

Because SAF developed an open process to involve members in the development of a land ethic canon through workshops, a "town meeting," the *Journal of Forestry*, correspondence, and other means, the task force believes members are now ready to embrace the proposed language. If the SAF membership approves these amendments to the Code of Ethics, the Committee on Ethics stands ready to incorporate the land ethic, the guiding principles, and other appropriate discussion of the canon in the *Ethics Guide* and other SAF documents.

The task force urges you to exercise your vote on this issue vital to the future of the Society and the profession. Contact any member of the Land Ethic Task Force via the national office if you have questions about these recommendations.

CHAPTER 9

Advocating New Environmental Ethics in Public Natural Resource Agencies

Chapters 7 and 8 make clear that some environmental scientists and managers in forestry, fisheries science, and wildlife biology belong to professional groups and commit themselves to a professional code of ethics as a guide to their professional behavior and working situations. This implies that it is more than technical standards and standards of professional courtesy that foresters and other resource scientists should uphold; if they are professionals, they should engage in conduct that reflects ethical responsibilities to each other, to society, and to the natural organisms and systems they work with. However, as noted in the introduction to chapter 5, there are some differences of opinion among scientists, politicians, and others about whether it is the responsibility of scientists to make value judgments in their professional capacities, and, if it is, under what kinds of circumstances. Thus some environmental scientists in the Pacific Northwest have been accused by representatives of the timber industry of going over the line and losing their scientific credibility in their zeal to protect and preserve old growth forests and forest species, such as Northern Spotted Owls and Marbled Murrelets. In this view, scientists have become biased, environmental advocates making improper judgments about the desirability of habitat and species protection at the expense of human concerns and interests, rather than "objective" or "neutral" observers and factual interpreters of natural systems. Such critics argue that it is the obligation of public ecological scientists to provide the research and scientific information on which public decisions about the environment should be based. By explaining the scientific aspects of nature and its component elements and systems, they can help natural resource agencies and organizations, businesses, public interest groups, and the public determine what the biophysical and ecosystem consequences are of different natural resource decisions. But they should not promote particular environmental decisions based on their own ethical beliefs or substitute their own environmental value judgments for those of the organizations in which they work or of the policy makers, politicians, and the public that they serve; this is not their legitimate role. Instead they should remain silent in the arena of public environmental decision-making and assist decision-makers to understand what the accepted science is behind natural resource decisions. They can serve society best by providing scientific information about the effects that different policy options have on ecosystem and human health.[1]

This "engineering technician model" about the role of environmental scientists presupposes the truth of the philosophy of positivism, which as noted earlier declares that there is a wide gap between science and values, scientific thinking and value judgments.[2] Positivism has been interpreted to mean that there is also a logical gap between explaining science to society and advocating for the rights of nature or human communities. In this view, scientists should not cross a clearly definable line between facts and values to become policy advocates or advocates of particular environmental choices, no matter how deeply they may personally believe in the need to conserve species and natural systems.

Others disagree and believe that it is perfectly legitimate for scientists to be advocates of ethical positions on conservation options in their work. This is their professional responsibility, in part because of their expertise as scientists and the unique knowledge they have of natural systems, something that nonscientists do not possess. In this view, while environmental and natural resource scientists should be open about their environmental values and should not arrogate to themselves the exclusive right to express and promote these values and to make value or policy judgments on issues of resource conservation, preservation, or management, they have as much right to do so as other groups and individuals in the public policy process. In fact, they should think of themselves as involved in a joint or shared process with other scientists, resource managers, politicians, members of interest groups, and the public in which all have important contributions to make. On this "shared decision-making model," scientists are still in the best position to provide the scientific knowledge that society needs to make natural resource decisions, but they should work with these other participants to develop consensual ethical judgments that

1. This position is an old one, but it is still accepted by many scientists and nonscientists. It was expressed recently in the Pacific Northwest, after more than two hundred leading and reputable scientists, many of them employed by public agencies and organizations, sent a letter to the Clinton Administration in early 1999 expressing doubts that current salmon recovery efforts would be sufficient to restore runs of Snake River salmon listed as threatened with extinction under the Endangered Species Act. The scientists argued that returning the Snake to swift-flowing, pre-dam-era conditions would offer the best promise of reversing salmon decline, and thus that four lower Snake River dams should be breached if the public wants salmon runs restored. On hearing of the letter, spokespeople for several Northwest politicians immediately criticized the scientists for acting improperly, mentioning that it was inappropriate for them as government employees to take a public position on this disputed resource issue. Not only were the scientists wrong about the science, one political spokesperson said, but their job is to inform the public and leave the decision making to elected leaders. He argued that once scientists go beyond advising policymakers on what is "good science" and take a stand, they go beyond their purview as scientists (*Portland Oregonian*, March 27, 1999, pp. D4 and D7).

2. I call this the "engineering technician model," because in some respects it makes the scientist a kind of technician responsible for understanding, explaining, and repairing natural systems but not deciding much of anything else. I outline this and other models in "Environmental Scientists as Advocates for Nature: Some Medical Models," a paper read by the annual conference of the Society for Philosophy in a Contemporary World, Estes Park, Colorado, August 1994.

support particular land management decisions. They can present and advocate environmental ethics in private and public contexts but also should understand that their value judgments are not superior just because they are scientists.

The fact is that in some cases if environmental and resource scientists did not take ethical stands on conservation issues, public decisions could be made that would be unfavorable to the maintenance of such goals as ecosystem health or ecological sustainability. This can happen because of the way in which a resource decision process is structured from the outset or because of the way it is conducted over time. For example, natural resource policy processes can be scientifically biased, either subtly or blatantly, by political or bureaucratic decision rules and procedures that already favor less desirable environmental outcomes, even before scientific research is done or scientific opinion is mined for its relevancy to the decision. This can lead to practical decisions that do not fully promote such policy goals as environmental protection, the conservation of biodiversity, the preservation of human health, or the long-term sustainability of human communities.[3]

This chapter introduces this issue of the advisability of advocacy by environmental scientists, including scientists in forestry. First comes a selection from Kristin Shrader-Frechette, a distinguished philosopher at the University of Notre Dame and long-time contributor to the field of environmental ethics. Professor Shrader-Frechette concludes that environmental advocacy by scientists, researchers, and other scholars is not only "permissible but perhaps ethically mandatory." She bases her conclusion on a carefully constructed argument that considers the consequences of environmental neutrality in a world in which environmental abuses and harms are occurring. She weighs some of the considerations in favor of and against environmental advocacy, then proposes a number of concrete reasons why it is justified, under certain conditions, and why remaining silent or avoiding advocacy may result in unfortunate consequences. While her argument is directed at academic "scholars" in the "ivory tower," and thus at academic scientists, it applies as well to any scientist in the environmental and natural resource fields such as forestry, fisheries, and wildlife who works for a public organization.

The chapter then turns to selections that focus on the issue of scientists speaking out for nature in natural resource agencies such as the U.S. Forest Service and the Bureau of Land Management. Readings are included from *Inner Voice*, a publication of the Association of Forest Service Employees for Environmental Ethics (FSEEE), the most visible advocacy group connected to the federal lands bureaucracy.[4] This association was formed in 1989 by several dissatisfied

---

3. The skewing of the science and thus the public ethics involved in environmental decision processes has been studied and analyzed effectively and in detail by Kristin Shrader-Frechette in several of her writings. She clearly illustrates this in the case of the federal government's Yucca Mountain nuclear waste repository decision process in Nevada. Read her articles, "Unsafe at Any Depth: Geological Methods, Subjective Judgments, and Nuclear Waste Disposal," in *Artifacts, Representations and Social Practice*, eds. C. C. Gould and R. S. Cohen. (The Hague: Kluwer Academic Publishers, 1994), pp. 501–24; "Science, Environmental Risk Assessment, and the Frame Problem," *Bioscience* 44(8) (September 1994): 548–51; and "High-level Waste, Low-level Logic," *The Bulletin of the Atomic Scientists* 50(6) (November/December 1994): 40–45. The theoretical philosophy of science on which part of her analysis is based can be found in Naomi Oreskes, Kristin Shrader-Frechette, and Kenneth Belitz, "Verification, Validation, and Confirmation of Numerical Models in the Earth Sciences," *Science* 263 (February 4, 1992): 641–46. She discusses the processes by which such risk assessments are conducted in environmental situations in her book, *Risk and Rationality* (Berkeley: University of California Press, 1991).

4. Since late 1996 this group has been called "Forest Service Employees for Environmental Ethics" (FSEEE) and is headquartered in Eugene, Oregon.

Forest Service scientists—including Jeff DeBonis, author of one of the selections—who were concerned that timber production was overruling all other goals in national forest planning and land management. These public employees believed that the purposes of protecting biodiversity and sustaining species and ecosystems on national forest lands were being shoved aside by the single-minded desire to "get out the cut." The chapter includes several descriptions from *Inner Voice* of cases in which environmental scientists, mostly employed by the U.S. Forest Service, became advocates for resource ethics within their agencies, speaking out or "blowing the whistle" on resource agency decisions that they believed were wrong.

The situation of Bill Shoaf, a veteran Forest Service employee and team leader in the Tongass National Forest in southeast Alaska, is reported in two of the selections. In 1993 Shoaf objected to plans for harvesting old-growth trees in a Forest Service timber-sale proposal in the Ketchikan area of the Tongass, on the Central Prince of Wales Island. As *Inner Voice* reported, Shoaf concluded that the proposal was not based on the biotic capacity of the land to provide for sustained timber yields over time, because it used unrealistic and exaggerated levels of timber harvest and flawed data. Shoaf believed that Tongass managers were violating federal law and harming the public and its forests. The effects of this mismanagement on local communities would be disastrous in the long run, he predicted, when the timber supply ran out sooner than projected. After questioning the sale process, Shoaf's official duties were reduced, he was forbidden to speak with members of the press, and he received "unacceptable" performance ratings for the first time in his career. However, Shoaf contacted FSEEE for help, and FSEEE asked Dr. K. Norman Johnson, a forestry professor at Oregon State University and developer of the computer plan that the Forest Service used to set timber targets for the Tongass and other national forests, to review and comment on Shoaf's findings. Late in 1994, Johnson supported Shoaf's perspective on overestimates of sustainable harvest levels in the Tongass timber sale.[5] Subsequently, in June 1995, Shoaf was awarded the 1995 Cavallo Prize for Moral Courage in Business and Government in Washington, D.C., for speaking out on the Tongass.[6]

Students and readers may wish to discuss these cases, for it is instructive to consider both what happened in them and how scientists described their commitments to new forms of natural resource ethics. Readers should familiarize themselves with the facts of the cases, keeping in mind that the cases are presented through the eyes of the scientists and sympathetic supporters. They might wish to analyze how scientists behaved and what consequences they faced because of their ethical advocacy, and also what might have occurred if they had remained "neutral" or failed to make their judgments known. Readers might then apply the ethical values and principles that they think are relevant in thinking about the ethical issues in these cases. They could evaluate the adequacy of these ethical ideas in order to understand the actions of the scientists and to think about what they would do if they were in the shoes of the environmental scientists in each case. This exercise can be useful for sharpening one's understanding of the relevance of ethical codes and principles, and other moral values, in examining the applications of environmental ethics, and also for becoming more clear about one's own environmental and personal values.

5. *Inner Voice*, 6(6) (November–December 1994): 3.
6. *Inner Voice*, 7(4) (July–August 1995): 3. Shoaf has written about his story in his book *The Taking of the Tongass: Alaska's Rainforest* (Sequin, Wash.: Running Wolf Press, 2000).

Kristin Shrader-Frechette

Ethics and Environmental Advocacy

One of the most difficult *theoretical* problems in normative ethics is understanding and resolving conflicts over collective responsibility for global environmental crises. It is difficult both because the precise contribution of each member of a collectivity (a group, nation, or planet) in causing and alleviating planetary problems is hard to determine and because environmental goods are both public and indivisible. One of the most difficult *practical* problems in normative ethics is how to achieve authentic collective responsibility. It is problematic both because international laws and sanctions are difficult to formulate and enforce and because the tragedy of the commons and the appeal of being a "free rider" are typically more powerful motivators than ethical suasion. I shall address the second, more practical, problem.

Apart from devising legal, governmental, and institutional strategies for creating and enforcing solutions to problems of the global environmental commons, the other main strategy for environmental action (a noninstitutional strategy) is education and advocacy, especially through nongovernmental organizations. Advocacy of any kind, however, is viewed as inimical both to objectivity in general and to the academy in particular. In this essay I argue that environmental advocacy by scientists, philosophers, and other intellectuals is not only permissible but perhaps ethically mandatory. My conclusion is based on at least four premises for which I shall argue: (1) because decision making in industry, government, and the academy is highly partisan and often contrary to environmental interests and fair play, alleged neutrality (rather than advocacy) actually serves the status quo; (2) scholarly objectivity regarding environmental issues is not achieved by neutrality; (3) provided certain conditions are met, there are sound deontological arguments for scholars assuming positions of environmental advocacy; and (4) provided certain conditions are met, there are sound consequentialist arguments for scholars assuming positions of environmental advocacy.

In sum: the world has grown too small and too troubled to be served by an ivory tower, if, indeed, it ever served us. The ivory tower

---

Kristin Shrader-Frechette, "Ethics and Environmental Advocacy," originally published as "An Apologia for Activism: Global Responsibility, Ethical Advocacy, and Environmental Problems," in *Ethics and Environmental Policy*, Frederick Ferre and Peter Hartel, eds. (Athens: University of Georgia Press, 1994), pp. 178–94. Reprinted with the permission of Kristin Shrader-Frechette.

model of objectivity is clearly wrong, in part because there is no tower, but instead there is an academic and industrial playing field heavily tilted against environmental interests, against fair play, and against open exchange. This is illustrated easily by a recent experience of Peter Singer.

The Playing Field Is Tilted

In May 1991, Peter Singer was standing in an auditorium at the University of Zurich, about to give a lecture on animal rights. Before he could begin, a massive group of leftists and anarchists—including a large number of disabled persons in wheelchairs—disrupted his lecture. They accused Singer, because of one chapter in his *Practical Ethics*, of advocating active euthanasia for severely disabled newborn infants. Singer said that one-third to one-fourth of the auditorium began to chant "Singer *'raus*! Singer *'raus*!" in a deafening roar. As he rose and tried to speak, one of the euthanasia protesters came up from behind him, tore Singer's glasses off his face, threw them to the floor, and broke them.[1]

Part of the Singer case is similar to that of other advocates, including my own—in having my phone bugged and in being threatened, intimidated, and harassed by industry and government groups who have tried to stop some of my writing and speaking on nuclear power and hazardous waste. Although I won't discuss these experiences here, they, like Singer's, illustrate that environmental or ethical advocates, especially those who "rock the boat," are often subject both to the disapproval of the academy and to the violence of vested interests. Yet, the very violence and power of these vested interests is precisely one of the reasons why advocacy, especially environmental advocacy, is so needed in the academy if we are to solve our global environmental problems.

What is environmental advocacy? It is taking a stand, in a partisan sense, in one's professional writing or speaking; taking a stand on a specific, practical issue and defending that stance as rational and ethical rather than merely pointing out the assets and liabilities of alternative positions, rather than merely maintaining a stance of informed neutrality. Environmental advocacy might be exemplified by taking a stand in favor of a solar economy or unilateral disarmament or against commercial nuclear fission or deep geological disposal of hazardous wastes.

Because the justifiability of normative and partisan stances in one's research is proportional to the degree to which the research game is already played in an ideological and highly partisan way, it is important to know something about who controls academic research. Academia is no longer an ivory tower, if indeed it ever was. Adam Smith has co-opted it. In 1981, for example, the West German pharmaceutical company Hoechst gave $70 million to Harvard's Department of Molecular Biology in exchange for rights to market all discoveries made in the department and to exclude all funding and research that interfered with Hoechst's proprietary position. In the same year, Jack Whitehead gave MIT $125 million in exchange for MIT's relinquishing control over patent rights, finances, hiring, and choice of research at its biotechnology research center. Likewise, at Carnegie Mellon, 60 percent of the research funds are from the U.S. Department of Defense.[2] Hence, any environmentalist who takes a particular stand against certain uses of biotechnology or military technology is already speaking within a highly partisan framework created by special interest groups.

Part of the reason for the power of special interest groups, particularly those that are antienvironment, is that of all corporate monies given to United States universities, one-third is provided by only ten corporations, and one-fifth of all industry funds—millions of dollars—is provided by only two corporations.[3] Faculty in molecular biology at Harvard are indentured servants to Hoechst. MIT biotechnologists are hired hands of entrepreneur Jack Whitehead; at Carnegie Mellon, they comprise a branch of the army and the air force.

Universities appear to be selling their integrity in much the same way as medieval churches sold pardons and indulgences. Typically, they give the most power and internal support to departments that have the most corporate monies behind them. As noted Harvard biologist Richard Lewontin put it when he heard about Harvard's deal with Hoechst: "What about the rest of us who are so foolish as to study unprofitable things like poetry, Sanskrit philology, evolutionary biology and the history of the chansons? Will the dean have time to hear our pleas for space and funds between meetings with the university's business partners?"[4] Indeed, will academic administrators even give such researchers a "fair shake" if their scholarship leads them to question the research methods, assumptions, and politics of the government and industry groups, typically antienvironment groups, that funnel their money into the university?

In universities dominated by narrow technical, governmental, and industrial concerns and driven by extramural funding from corporate sources, environmental awareness is almost nonexistent, and liberal education has become progressively more narrow. As Nobelist Isidore Rabi warned, this narrowness is paving the way for a repetition of what happened in Germany during the 1930s when the rise of militaristic nationalism, fueled by the dominance of narrow technical and professional training, eroded ethical values and liberal university education, thus laying the foundation for Hitler's rise. Given such a restrictive conception of the university and scholarship, it was no accident that in 1937 the Prussian Academy of Sciences condemned Albert Einstein because he criticized the violations of civil liberties in the Nazi regime. (The academy said that he should have remained silent, neutral, and objective.) Once an Einstein, or any disinterested academic, is condemned for speaking out in the public interest, then the narrowing of the ivory tower begins to strangle democracy as well. No country can survive the theft of its universities' capacity to criticize. Democratic institutions are fed by the free flow of information and criticism, and government and science, as well as the public, require universities to provide this independent perspective. Otherwise government must blindly choose the answers offered by individuals and corporations, who are by nature self-interested. Because they are self-interested, they cannot be trusted to judge what is in the common interest. Democracy needs the Socratic gadfly, the detached observer, and the social critic. Neither society nor the university can afford to become the whore for special interest groups.[5] The way to avoid their domination by antienvironmental industrial or militaristic special interest groups is for scholars themselves to take partisan stands and advocate positions that are ethically defensible, especially when the positions run counter to those of the interest groups.

Objectivity Is Not Achieved by Neutrality

One reason why scholars so often fail to engage in environmental advocacy through their speaking and writing is probably that they have accepted the antiquated positivistic model of objectivity as neutrality. A corollary of the outmoded positivist tradition of research is that whatever scholarship is not neutral is also subjective in a reprehensible way. If it makes sense for philosophers and other scholars to be advocates and partisans, however, and not merely neutral observers of society, then obviously the acceptability of advocacy presupposes that neutrality is not objectivity. Thanks to Thomas Kuhn, Michael Polanyi, Stephen Toulmin, Paul Feyerabend, and others, we now know that complete objectivity is impossible and that there is no value-free inquiry, at least not free from cognitive or methodological values.[6]

Philosophical analysis, moreover, can show that not all methodological and ethical values deserve equal respect, and therefore not all values are subjective in a reprehensible way. Not all values deserve equal respect—or disrespect, as the positivists would have it—because formulation of any scientific theory is incompatible with the avoidance of methodological values, because there is no fact-value dichotomy, and because values alone never determine all the facts or all aspects of the facts. Just as there are rational reasons, short of empirical confirmation, for accepting one theory over another—reasons such as simplicity and heuristic power—so also are there rational reasons—such as consistency or equal treatment—for accepting one value over another.[7]

If not all ethical and methodological values are subjective in a reprehensible way, then advocating some values and being a partisan on their side is philosophically defensible on both epistemological and ethical grounds.[8] In other words, objectivity does not equal neutrality, for at least six reasons:

1. Failure to criticize indefensible or questionable values gives implicit assent to them in practising ethics or public policy. Hence, once one admits that methodological and ethical values are unavoidable in all research, including scientific research, then not to assess those values is to become hostage to them or at least implicitly to sanction them. Hence, to avoid uncritical acceptance of status quo values one must criticize values rather than remain ethically neutral in all cases.

2. Not all ethical and methodological positions are equally defensible. If they are not, then real objectivity requires one to represent indefensible positions as indefensible and less defensible positions as less defensible.

3. To represent objectivity as neutrality in the face of a great hazard or threat is simply to serve the interests of those responsible for the threat.

4. To represent objectivity as neutrality is also to encourage persons to mask evaluational and ethical assumptions in their research and policy and hence to avoid public disclosure of, and control over, those assumptions.

5. To represent objectivity as neutrality is also to presuppose that objectivity is somehow delivered from on high rather than negotiated and discovered socially through the give-and-take of alternative points of view, point and counterpoint.

6. Most disturbing of all, to represent objectivity as neutrality is to sanction ethical relativism and therefore injustice. This is exactly what happened during World War II when some anthropologists from Columbia University were asked about their position on the actions of the Nazis. They said that because conflicts between the Nazis and others represented a controversy over value systems, they had "to take a professional stand of cultural relativity"; they said that they had to be "skeptics" with respect to all judgments of value.[9]

At least three groups in contemporary society would agree that the Columbia University anthropologists should have been skeptics with respect to judgments of value. They would support a resounding no to the question of whether philosophers should be advocates: (1) the fashionable "deconstructive" postmodernists who have tried to destroy the foundations of ethical, social, and epistemological criticism; (2) the unfashionable positivists who nevertheless lurk in the closets of most natural scientists; and (3) the relativist social scientists who have confused silence with objectivity and neutrality. Someone else can have the task of telling how and why these three positions go wrong. For now, I'd like to provide several consequentialist arguments, followed by a number of contractarian or deontological arguments, for advocacy and partisanship in selected cases of environmental scholarship.

Consequentialist Arguments for Advocacy

One of the most powerful consequentialist arguments in favor of environmental advocacy is that without it greater harm would occur, more persons would be hurt, and more important values would be sacrificed. Although it would be difficult to prove, for example, it is arguable that the Nazis' experimentation on prisoners and brutality against Jews, gypsies, and leftists could have been stopped or at least hampered had the Columbia University anthropologists and other scholars taken a different ethical stance and condemned the atrocities. Likewise, it is reasonable to believe that environmental abuses such as global warming, destruction of the ozone layer, and pollution of air and water could be stopped or at least hampered if scholars would take a partisan stance against them.

Of course, the obvious objection to taking a partisan stance on environmental or other issues is that such stances are often wrong and that careful, conservative scholars ought never move beyond the facts. If knowing that one were correct were a necessary condition for taking a position of advocacy, however, then many evils would be so advanced that it would be impossible to stop them. Moreover, in a situation of uncertainty, advocacy encourages counterarguments and public discussion and hence is often itself an important way to resolve uncertainties.

In other words, an important consequentialist argument in favor of environmental advocacy on specific issues is that such advocacy would help to educate the public. Even if particular scholars were wrong in advocating certain courses of action, the advocacy itself would draw out public debate, analysis of the issues, and a will to know the truth. Environmental advocacy would also help to reverse a status quo dominated by the vested interests of industry, greed, big government, and the military. Without such advocacy, our silence or neutrality likely would serve the status quo, especially what is ethically and environmentally indefensible in the status quo. As Abraham Lincoln put it: Silence makes men cowards. Silence or neutrality makes us cowards in telling the truth about the evils that surround us, and therefore our silence sanctions those evils. Scholars' failure to adopt positions of environmental advocacy also might encourage the consequence that less educated persons, some serving their own vested interests, would dictate public policy debate. If scholars and those most lacking in self-interest do not become advocates, then the advocacy will become the prerogative of the worst elements of society, just as a volunteer army has often become the prerogative of ne'er-do-wells and politics has often become the prerogative of the corrupt.

Environmental advocacy is also defensible on largely prudential grounds. If environmental hazards are threatening our lives and well-being, then a purely prudential argument in favor of scholars adopting positions of environmental advocacy is that such advocacy would lead to better protection of human and environmental welfare. It is arguable, following this line of reasoning, that environmental advocacy is justifiable on the grounds of self-defense. We have the obligation to do whatever is necessary to defend our lives and welfare. Therefore, as a consequence, we have the obligation as scholars to engage in environmental advocacy. In other words, one consequence of our acting as environmental advocates is that we would be better able to protect human rights to bodily security and equal protection, both of which are threatened by environmental degradations.[10]

Deontological Arguments for Advocacy

There are also good deontological reasons for believing that those who oppose the advocacy of scholars are wrong. For example, by virtue of their positions the anthropologists who failed to oppose Hitler were being neither objective nor neutral. It is not objective to say that committing atrocities is neither right nor wrong. It is not objective to say that one should be neutral regarding experimentation on prisoners without their consent. It is not objective to be neutral in the face of systematic discrimination against persons on the basis of their religion or race. Genuine objectivity requires calling a spade a spade. An important deontological argument for ethical advocacy of scholars is that objectivity does not require treating a questionable ethical position and a more reasonable one the same. Indeed, as Aristotle recognized, equal treatment does not mean the same treatment; equal treatment means treating equals the same. By virtue of trivializing and treating morally different positions equally, proponents of alleged neutrality actually discriminate and practice bias.

Failure to practice advocacy often amounts to bias. "Telling it the way it is" frequently requires us to take a stand precisely because certain governmental, political, and economic interests are taking either a reprehensible stand or no stand at all against great evils. Vested interests often exercise a highly questionable sort of advocacy, and our raising questions about their stances typically amounts to advocacy for the other side. No one can evaluate the social science methodology of risk perception studies done near the proposed Yucca Mountain radioactive waste site, for example, without examining and condemning the massive, one-sided advertising campaign mounted against the citizens of Nevada by every nuclear utility in the country. When the nuclear industry spends $5.5 million per year (in ratepayer funds) in one state in an attempt to control the results of social science surveys, the students of social science methodology cannot ignore that fact.[11] Scholars need to condemn such bias. In doing so they act as advocates for alternative action.

One reason researchers need to act as advocates for alternative action is that, often, researchers are the only people with the requisite information to make an informed decision about the rights and wrongs of a particular situation. In other words, an important deontological reason for scholars acting as environmental advocates is that they often have the ability to make a difference; they have a "responsibility through ability." Following the reasoning of moral philosophers such as Peter Singer, if we have the ability to make a difference, and if it would cause us no serious hardship to do so, then we have the duty to attempt to make a difference.[12]

We also have a responsibility through complicity. We have a responsibility to act as environmental advocates because often we have benefited from environmental harm. Frequently, for example, we are responsible for correcting environmental harms because we have paid less for goods produced by manufacturers who fail to curb their pollution. Hence, our monetary benefits have been purchased at the price of harms to the environmental commons. Scholars in developed, Western nations bear a special responsibility through complicity because our standard of living and luxuries frequently are made possible only through environmental degradation and through our using a disproportionate share of environmental resources. Hence, we have a responsibility through complicity to help reverse the environmental damage from which we have profited.[13]

Even if scholars had no responsibility through complicity to act as environmental advocates, we would clearly have a responsibility by virtue of third-party professional obligations. Professional ethics dictates that by virtue of the benefits professionals receive from society, we have an obligation to the public to protect its interests and serve its welfare. Indeed, professionals' obligations to third parties often supersede obligations to first and second parties. In the case of employees of state universities, this third-party obligation is particularly strong and is, indeed, even a first-party obligation, because the people—the taxpayers of the state—are literally our employers. Hence, we have an obligation to protect their interests, a main part of which includes environmental well-being.[14] And if we have an obligation to protect the interests of the public in environmental well-being, then we may have an obligation to engage in environmental advocacy.

Restrictions on Advocacy

Admittedly, of course, if one takes a position of advocacy, then one is bound to provide equal consideration of all relevant interests and to answer all relevant objections of "the other side." This is perhaps the greatest failing of applied philosophers and environmental scholars who take positions of advocacy. They sometimes are more interested in preaching to the converted than in examining both sides, in order to show which is ethically or methodologically preferable. A corollary to presenting alternative sides and to answering relevant objections is to put one's own methodological and ethical judgments up front to determine whether they can bear scrutiny. This again seems to me to be a common failing of applied philosophers working in environmental ethics. They sometimes are more interested in speculative, and often undefended, metaphysics and ethics than in the epistemological justifications for their positions.

Another necessary condition for environmental advocacy is that we meet William Frankena's criterion for discrimination: it must lead to greater overall equality and good, over the long term, for everyone. Otherwise, any discriminatory or partisan arguments, even for environmental goods, are not justifiable and may merely use other persons and their positions as means to our own partisan ends.[15] But herein lies the problem. Those who want to build the Yucca Mountain radioactive waste repository and jeopardize our descendants in perpetuity, or those who want to continue destroying thousands of species per day, typically *agree* with principles of equal consideration of interests and with achieving greater equality and good, over the long term. Usually, however, they disagree with us over the facts. They disagree over whether Yucca Mountain will leak over tens of thousands of years, whether species extinction is a natural process, or whether humans can accommodate themselves to increasing numbers of carcinogens. Therefore, one of the most important tasks of the environmental advocate is to understand and defend the factual assumptions that he or she makes.[16]

Indeed, Paul Gomberg argues quite persuasively that moralists can be advocates and even partisans whose killing of others can be ethically justified provided that certain factual and ethical considerations are satisfied.[17] The factual conditions for justifiable advocacy (according to Gomberg) have to do with the gravity of the physical threat and the guilt of those responsible for it.[18] The gravity of the physical threat is an especially important condition in justifying advocacy regarding a particular environmental situation because the graver the threat, all things being equal, the more justified is a partisan position against it. This is why, for example, in his *Just and Unjust Wars,* Michael Walzer claims that "the survival and freedom of political communities . . . are the highest values of international society," and therefore we can countenance even the killing of civilians when the existence of a nation is up for grabs.[19]

But what about Earth First!'s actions? Is one justified in being an advocate and a partisan if one's goal is to protect a greater environmental good—survival of the planet and its resources? If civil disobedience is justifiable, and I think that there are occasions when it is, then analogous arguments might reveal when philosophical disobedience to the alleged norms of disinterested scholarship is likewise justifiable. Also, if Walzer is correct, then one could argue analogously that if the survival of the earth and its inhabitants is the highest of all values, then even the most extreme forms of advocacy and partisanship, such as killing civilians, can be countenanced when survival is at stake. Obviously, advocating killing is an extreme position. Equally obviously, it is justified only in the gravest of situations. Hence, much of the key to the justification of scholarly advocacy is the factual context in which it takes place.

Although he did not write about philosophical partisanship, John Locke appears to justify the partisan conception of human relationships when he says: "One may destroy a man who makes war upon him, or has discovered an enmity to his being, for the same reason that he may kill a wolf or a lion, because they are not under the ties of the common law of reason, have no other rule but that of force and violence, and so may be treated as a beast of prey."[20]

Few, if any, of us are likely to find ourselves in situations in which, because others are making war on us, we therefore have the right to destroy them or to advocate their destruction. Nevertheless, those who justify Earth First!'s actions appear to believe that they are in such a situation. Partisan scholarship and advocating particular ethical and policy positions, both amounting to a form of coercion, are obviously more justifiable to the degree that they are necessary to prevent some greater evil. The greater the evil needing to be prevented, the greater the justification for the coercive or partisan scholarship. Although I have doubts about whether he succeeded, that is how Garrett Hardin, for example, attempted to justify the highly coercive measures he defends in "The Tragedy of the Commons" and "Living on a Lifeboat."[21]

One could probably say, however, that the views of persons like Garrett Hardin and Edward Abbey—who said that he would sooner shoot a man than a snake because snakes are important members of ecological communities—and Earth First! members are highly ideological. Because they are highly ideological, one would probably argue that they are incapable of being justified by means of the numerous causal inferences necessary to show that some personal or environmental catastrophe is at stake.

Indeed, epistemological conservatism keeps most of us from assenting to, much less joining in, the actions of Earth First!. We also believe that the environmental world is not quite so simple as Earth First! members believe, just as the political world is not so simple as Marxist revolutionaries claim; neither worldview obviously and easily justifies highly partisan actions. It does not seem to be the case, for example, as R. P. Dutt claims,[22] that fascist deeds and acts of war are inevitable under capitalism, because there is never any pure capitalism. Fascism sometimes exists with some degree of democracy because many acts of war are at least partially justifiable. Likewise, I believe that there are few totally unjustifiable acts of environmental degradation. Rather, many environmental actions often involve uncertainty regarding their causal effects, or, if the effects are certain but harmful, their proponents sometimes justify them by appealing to the greater good. In other words, in many cases of environmental controversy there are no "smoking guns."

Although I believe strongly in environmental advocacy, it is not always obvious or provable that environmental catastrophe is inevitable unless we engage in partisan scholarship and activism to promote particular causes, for example, stopping use of all potential carcinogens. We simply do not have that great a fix on the causal chain that results in various environmental damages. Because we don't, our advocacy is never wholly or easily justifiable. For example, recent news reports tell us that there is a cluster of primary brain cancers among residents near the Los Alamos National Laboratory in New Mexico, where nuclear weapons research is conducted. We know radiation causes cancer, and we have a dose-response curve to measure the effects of radiation exposure. We also know that there is a statistically significant increase in the disease rate in the Los Alamos area. The epidemiological studies are inconclusive, however, because we cannot link the effect, cancer, to the alleged cause, radiation exposure, in all cases. For one thing, cancer typically has a latency period and takes several years to show up, because the exposed population often is not studied for a long period of time. Moreover, researchers frequently cannot rule out intervening factors and alternative causes of the cancer, even though increases in the cancer are statistically significant.[23] In other words, many environmental situations are characterized by massive scientific uncertainty. This means that in order to justify environmental advocacy in such a case, one must justify choosing the environmental actions least likely to cause the most serious harm. One must defend a personal rule of scholarship that is based on maximin decisions rather than on utilitarianism or on average expected utility. I shall not take the time to defend such a maximin ethics, both because I have done so elsewhere and because John Rawls has given persuasive arguments that seem to me to be convincing. For both of us, however, perhaps the main key to the acceptability of advocacy directed at maximin choices is the severity of the environmental catastrophe we face. In other words, the key is the factual situation:[24] the greater the catastrophe we face, the greater is the acceptability of advocacy to prevent catastrophe.

If we do engage in partisan scholarship—work that defends and examines only one side of an issue—independent of the correct factual situation, then we should recognize that such coercive tactics may not lead to environmental education. Instead, they may lead to bias, to an inability to engage in rational analysis, and, ultimately, to diminished autonomy and decreased civil liberties for those who seek to be heard on all sides of an issue. Often, the first casualty of those who seek to preserve us from a great social or political evil is civil liberties. Likewise, the first casualty of those who seek to preserve us from a great environmental evil may be loss of autonomy and the ability to rationally analyze a situation.

From a consequentialist point of view, it is possible to defend both partisanship and avoidance of partisanship. Partisan scholarship could lead to the consequences (1) that we as a society lose the ability to engage in rational analysis of a situation, and (2) that because we lose part of our rational abilities, we lose some of our autonomy and some of our capacity for free, informed consent both to environmental hazards and to government actions. Partisan scholarship could also lead to the consequence (3) that from a pragmatic and prudential point of view, experts whose warnings about environmental disaster are proved wrong thereby lose their credibility. Such a loss of credibility would hurt not only society but the profession as a whole.

Avoidance of advocacy and partisan scholarship, on the other hand, could also lead to dangerous consequences. For example, the U.S. Office of Technology Assessment claims that up to 90 percent of all cancers are environmentally induced and theoretically preventable,[25] and we know that one in three persons will die of cancer. Had more people spoken out to advocate reduction of suspected environmental carcinogens, these rates might not be what they are today. Had more moral philosophers argued about the ethical constraints of behavior in a situation of scientific uncertainty, then the carcinogens might not have been so easily accepted. Other consequences of avoiding advocacy might be that those in a position to correct environmentally catastrophic situations would not do so.

For example, when the Chernobyl accident took place, officials in the former USSR said (and continue to say) that only 31 casualties occurred as a result of the accident. They ignored all nonimmediate fatalities, and they forbade medical doctors from inscribing the cause of death on the death certificates of those killed by radiation-related causes. Even the U.S. Department of Energy has admitted that Chernobyl fatalities are likely to go as high as 28,000, and academics at the University of California, Berkeley, have argued that once the statistical casualties are counted, the fatalities could go as high as 475,000.[26] Failure to address the silence of the nuclear industry in such a situation, and failure to be an advocate for the four million persons living near Chernobyl, whose premature deaths could be prevented, were they moved out of contaminated areas, is reprehensible. Environmental advocacy seems required of every scholar who knows the situation.

Sometimes we also might be able to justify our advocacy or our partisanship on the grounds that totally objective dialogue or argument is impossible. The argument here is that those who need to hear nonpartisan analysis would not listen to it, and some of those at fault in situations of environmental degradation have not listened for a long time. This is the same justification suggested by John Locke, who believed that it cannot be taken for granted that two human beings are bound by the same morality or common law of reason. Not all human beings are capable of listening to each other. Rather, a common bond of morality depends on the actual relationships among people, including their intentions toward each other.[27]

In other words, in order to treat "persons on the other side" as being responsible for their actions and able to change, we must believe in their susceptibility to ethical dialogue.[28] If I engage in ethical dialogue with another, I treat the other as ethically responsible. Dialogue both helps to establish and is presupposed by a moral community of agents seeking agreement. Hence, if we understand ascriptions of moral responsibility as entailing the belief that some persons can be affected by dialogue and criticism, then we need to know whether these persons can be so affected. This is a factual question. If they cannot be so affected, and if rational persuasion is impossible, then, presumably, one is not required to present totally neutral, nonpartisan rational arguments in order to persuade them. As Paul Gomberg puts it, if fascist brutality and fascist mindsets are inevitable, then morality is useless.[29]

According to the partisan conception of morality, there may be others with whom one does not share a morality and to whom one's moral duties are limited. This may be why, for example, the quadriplegics and paraplegics who helped to attack Peter Singer in Switzerland did not believe that they shared a common morality with him, whereas they were convinced that he was their enemy, a person whose ideas about euthanasia could result in their destruction. Conversely, persons who were convinced that others did share a common morality with them would not be likely to behave like those who disrupted Singer's talk because they would see no causal connection between a philosopher's beliefs about euthanasia and exterminating the disabled. If one is committed to a universalist morality, one would have trouble believing that another person is "out to get one" or has a design on one's life. In Reuben Ainsztein's words, "Because [Jews] . . . believed in progress and the perfectibility of man, they were the last to realize how bestial the Germans were."[30]

The obvious questions are whether actions are bestial or not and whether people can be written off or not. The obvious problem with environmental advocacy is the epistemological question of whether the factual situation is catastrophic enough to justify advocacy. On the one hand, because most of us do not understand fully the factual conditions around us, we often cannot determine whether or not advocacy is justified. On the other hand, factual uncertainty requires ethically conservative actions, actions not likely to harm either persons or the environment. Hence, factual uncertainty can be grounds for advocating ethically conservative actions.

Because we believe in progress and the perfectibility of humans, we likewise are often too slow to recognize the need for advocacy or the extremity of the environmental catastrophe that we face. This is somewhat like what Kris Kristofferson (the same Kristofferson who wrote "Me and Bobbie McGee" and "Help Me Make It Through the Night") said of his own transformation. He went from being an army brat and volunteering for Vietnam to being a Rhodes scholar, a longtime antiwar activist, a supporter of the United Farm Workers, and an opponent of United States policy in Central America. His own idealism about both humans and the government, however, kept him from recognizing the severity of the military and environmental dangers around him and therefore from taking a position of advocacy. He says: "Growing up, I was never aware of the fact that only white males who owned property were covered in the Constitution and could vote, and the whole country was built on genocide, the murder of natives. I've often thought that the more I read, the more I realized that our Government may never have stood for the things I believe in. But they made a mistake. Somewhere along the line they taught me that's what we stood for, and now I demand it."[31] We must demand it as well.

Notes

1. Peter Singer, "On Being Silenced in Germany," *New York Review of Books* 38, August 15, 1991, 36–42.
2. Kristin Shrader-Frechette, "Helping Science Serve Society," in *Hoe Toonaangevend is de Universiteit?* ed. H. de Ward (Groningen, Netherlands: University of Groningen Press, 1989), 75, 78.
3. Shrader-Frechette, "Helping Science Serve Society," 79.
4. Shrader-Frechette, "Helping Science Serve Society," 77–78.
5. Shrader-Frechette, "Helping Science Serve Society," 78.
6. See Helen Longino, *Science as Social Knowledge* (Princeton: Princeton University Press, 1990); also Shrader-Frechette, *Science Policy, Ethics, and Economic Methodology* (Boston: Reidel, 1984), 73. Finally, see Shrader-Frechette, *Risk and Rationality* (Berkeley: University of California Press, 1991), 40ff.
7. Shrader-Frechette, *Science Policy*, 73–74.
8. Shrader-Frechette, *Science Policy*, 183.
9. Shrader-Frechette, *Science Policy*, 88.
10. A. Gewirth, *Human Rights: Essays on Justification and Applications* (Chicago: University of Chicago Press, 1982), 181ff.
11. Yucca Mountain PR expenditures were revealed through the investigative reporting of D. Olinger, in "Nuclear Industry Targets Nevada," *St. Petersburg Times*, December 1, 1991, D1, D5.
12. Shrader-Frechette, *Risk*, 160–62.
13. Ibid., 162–63.
14. See Michael Bayles, *Professional Ethics* (Belmont, Calif.: Wadsworth, 1981), 92–109.
15. William Frankena, "The Concept of Social Justice," in *Social Injustice*, ed. R. Brandt (Englewood Cliffs, N.J.: Prentice-Hall, 1962), 15; see also Shrader-Frechette, *Risk*, chap. 8, for discussion of this argument.
16. Paul Gomberg, "Can a Partisan Be a Moralist?" *American Philosophical Quarterly* 27 (January 1990): 71.
17. Gomberg, "Partisan," 71–79. Following Gomberg, I take *partisan* to mean "a division of human beings into those on my side, whose interests or judgments count positively, and my enemies" (p. 75).
18. Gomberg, "Partisan," 72–73. What principle of proportionality is relevant to justify partisanship and advocacy? Clearly what is not appropriate is partisanship and advocacy that somehow exceed the gravity of the harm arising from the situation one advocates. What is not appropriate is what Hersh Smoliar, a leader of partisans from the Minsk Ghetto, describes: "Each one of them had his own account to square. . . . Two eyes for one, the whole mouth for one tooth" (quoted in Gomberg, "Partisan," 73). This attitude bespeaks revenge rather than impartial justice; presumably such revenge is appropriate only in the most extreme cases in which one's enemy is outside one's moral community and is bent on annihilation.
19. Michael Walzer, *Just and Unjust Wars* (New York: Basic Books, 1977), 254.
20. Quoted in Gomberg, "Partisan," 75.
21. See Garrett Hardin, "The Tragedy of the Commons," *Science* 162 (1968): 1243–48; and Hardin, "Living on a Lifeboat," *BioScience* 24 (1974): 561–68.
22. R. P. Dutt, *Fascism and Social Revolution* (Chicago: Proletarian Publishers, 1978), 16ff., 44ff., 91, 296ff.
23. J. M. Cousteau, "Nuclear Weapons Testing Casts a Deadly Shadow on the Environment," *Calypso Log* 18 (October 1991): 3.
24. See Shrader-Frechette, *Risk*, chap. 8.
25. See Shrader-Frechette, *Risk*.
26. Cousteau, "Nuclear Weapons Testing," 5.
27. Cited in Gomberg, "Partisan," 75.
28. See Lawrence Stern, "Freedom, Blame, and Moral Community," *Journal of Philosophy* 71 (1974): 72–84.
29. Gomberg, "Partisan," 75.
30. Quoted in Gomberg, "Partisan," 76.
31. Rosa Jordan, "Kris Kristofferson," *Progressive* 55 (September 1991): 36–38.

Inner Voice

- Are you a frustrated Forest Service Employee because your resource ethics conflict with your job?
- Are you afraid to speak out for what you know is ecologically right?
- Do you feel isolated and alone because of your resource ethics?
- Do you think the Forest Service needs to become a more ecologically sensitive organization?
- Would YOU like to help promote this kind of change within the Agency???

Who Are We?

We started out with two people. On a hot Saturday afternoon last September, a timber sale planner and a wildlife biologist were hiking through the Three Sisters Wilderness on the Willamette National Forest. We were discussing the frustration of being a Forest Service employee. The frustration over the agency's resource exploitation and its resulting contribution to world-wide environmental degradation and loss of bio-diversity. The frustration over the fact that as an agency, we could be LEADERS for a new resource ethic, instead of being followers of an out-dated, short-sighted agenda of the past. Frustration at the agency's attitude that our main mission is to supply raw wood products at any environmental cost to an industry that has already depleted its own resources in the quest for the fast buck and good stock reports. We wondered out loud whether we should quit and go to work for a more socially and environmentally aware organization. We realized, however, that becoming just another "outside entity" trying to force change on the agency would be relatively ineffective. But we recognized how hard it is for individuals to speak out because of the fear of persecution and possible loss of jobs. We also realized how ineffective lone voices can be. Then THE IDEA occurred to us that the *most effective* thing we could do right now would be to organize a committed cadre of dedicated activists working from the INSIDE in a POSITIVE way, toward the new vision of the Forest Service! In this way, we would have a STRONGER, MORE EFFECTIVE VOICE if we had a UNITED VOICE. At that point we began our quest to form a united group of like-minded individuals, a group of individuals

---

"Inner Voice," *Inner Voice* 1:1 (Summer 1989): 1, 3. Reprinted with permission from *Inner Voice*, P.O. Box 11615, Eugene, OR 97440.

we knew existed within the agency in great numbers.

What Is Our Vision?

- We believe the value system that presently dominates the Agency in terms of how we manage the land is in need of immediate change.
- We believe that biological diversity and sustainability is more important than "managing" for fiber forests and short-term political expediency, especially on public lands!
- We believe that we should be totally honest with the public, Congress, and especially ourselves in terms of divulging and admitting the extent of resource degradation that has occurred as a result of two decades of excessive timber cutting, road building, and other activities with little regard for other resources values.
- We believe the Forest Service should become the leader in the quest for a new resource ethic based on an economically and ecologically sustainable future for the 21st century. To this end, the agency should promote an alliance with the global environmental movement and distance themselves from the short-sighted agenda of resource exploitation interests.
- We believe it's time for a change in philosophy and strategy: let's start meeting the SPIRIT and LETTER of NEPA, NFMA, The Endangered Species Act (and our other resource protection statutes) instead of meeting the politically-mandated, inflated timber "harvest" levels. To this end, we need to act in *defense* of NFMA, NEPA, The Endangered Species Act, biological diversity, and spotted owl habitat instead of the reverse.
- We believe it's high time our agency stopped being an embarrassment to itself: we want our agency to take its rightful place as a LEADER toward a sustainable, livable 21st century!
- We believe timber harvesting and other resource "management" activities are appropriate on public lands, but NOT at the expense of other resource values or public subsidies, which means NOT at the current and planned inflated levels.
- We believe we should be designing and implementing land management policies which reflect TRUE stewardship and an ecologically sustainable economic base.
- We believe in putting the values of wildlife, fisheries, clean water, continued soil productivity, and aesthetics on *AT LEAST* an equal footing with commodity outputs.
- We believe in promoting line officers based on their understanding and *MEETING THE INTENT and* SPIRIT of our land stewardship laws like NFMA, NEPA, and the Endangered Species Act, instead of getting promoted on how well they get the cut out.
- We believe the current political and organizational structure of the agency requires those of us within the agency at all levels to start speaking out, for a new resource ethic based on an ecologically sustainable future, and send a message to our congressional and agency leaders that it's TIME FOR A CHANGE!

What Are Our Working Objectives?

We want to become agents for change, to accelerate the agency toward a new resource ethics, by:

- expression: Providing a mode of expression for facts, thoughts, and feelings contrary to the "agency line" in order to provide a forum for ideological diversity. The newsletter the INNER VOICE will provide this forum.

Anonymity will be provided to encourage this expression.
- support system: Providing a support system for those of us who now feel isolated because our value system "doesn't fit," and to provide a united, strong voice for change instead of isolated, single voices easily subject to reprisals.
- lobbying: Become a lobbying force at the local and national level for more environmentally sound resource management within the agency.
- education: Educate each other on ways we can work for and promote a change in values on our day-to-day jobs.
- examples: Spotlight people/projects that are making changes toward this new vision.

Who Can Become Members?

- We don't think any particular series, grade or employment status has a corner on visionary thinking. To that end, we welcome *ANY* Forest Service employee, permanent, seasonal, professional, technician, former or retired.
- Although we are not specifically targeting other agencies, other public resource management personnel are welcome to become involved, including BIA, BLM, State Fish and Game agencies, etc. We hope to eventually grow diverse enough to include the interests and issues of these other resource agency personnel as well.

How Can You Participate?

- Submit ideas, articles, editorials, art work, photographs, cartoons, examples/ideas of visionary employees or projects leading the way toward a new resource ethic.
- Design and submit a front page banner for the INNER VOICE—something that captures the spirit of our quest for a new vision. Any creative ideas/artists out there?
- Provide articles and information which "blow the whistle" on such things as resource sacrifice to development interest, hypocrisy, short-sighted management at the expense of the resource, attempts to stifle outspoken employees, etc. Include an example of how the particular situation could be handled in a positive way to edge us toward the new vision.
- Volunteer to be an editor/article reviewer for a particular resource specialty.
- Volunteer to be a network coordinator, someone who would collect articles, promote membership, provide status reports for your forest/region/etc. We would eventually like a network coordinator on each unit.
- Promote organization of "think tanks" or information/technical groups at your unit-level. Address issues of concern to your local area, such as sustainable economics in your community, or specific resource issues on your forest or district. Network with like-minded employees and research broader issues, such as employees' free speech rights within a government agency, and how the Forest Service should address it. Or, how agency wildlife biologists and other specialists are isolated and pressured to conform, and how this can be dealt with. Remember, we will publish the "unabridged" version of your reports anonymously! Keep us informed of working groups as they are formed, and we can keep similar groups in contact with each other.
- Make copies of this newsletter and pass it along to co-workers!
- Help support us financially with this effort. Obviously we will not be able to support this effort (alone) financially for long, so donations will be gratefully accepted and applied toward future membership dues.

- Give us your thoughts and suggestions on how we should organize this association. We are presently considering becoming a nonprofit organization, having a board, steering committee, etc. We are looking into two similar organizations of Federal Employees for ideas. Any suggestions, ideas or expertise would be greatly appreciated.

Nuts and Bolts

- Submitting items for publication in the INNER VOICE: Please send us your letters and comments, articles from other journals and newspapers, your own personally written stories, cartoons, art work, etc. The most efficient way for us to include your material is for you to type it out on an IBM/IBM compatible, mail it on a disk or via telephone (503-896-3985) if you have a modem. Otherwise, anything LEGIBLY written or typed will be accepted! Remember, your anonymity is respected if that is what you want.

On Anonymity

- The INNER VOICE is not an "underground" newsletter. One of the strengths of this organization will be "telling it like it is." I have discussed the idea and our intent to proceed with many people, including Forest Supervisors, Regional and Washington Office Staff Directors, and sent the initial Association flyer to numerous other officials, including the Chief.
- In order to promote maximum participation, while recognizing the reality of the agency's current posture toward "speaking out," you may choose to remain anonymous. If you decide on anonymity, just say so when you submit something for publication. You must include your name, address and phone # to the editor so we can check to make sure you are who you claim to be, but will print the submission with any closing you desire, such as "F.S. Employee in Region X."

The Bottom Line

- We need to hear from you! We need your support, your ideas, your energy. We MUST make this work, because things are not getting better; we are still moving nowhere under the present administration. As a united voice for a new resource ethic, speaking from the inside, we can make a difference! Let's sound a loud message to the upper management and development interests that the Forest Service of the past is being moved out and the new, visionary Forest Service with a new resource ethic for the 21st century is taking over!!!

AFSEEE Vision: Strategy for Forest Service Reform

Forge a socially responsible value system for the Forest Service based on a land ethic which ensures ecologically and economically sustainable management.

AFSEEE Philosophy:

The value system that presently dominates the Forest Service and its land management programs is in need of immediate change.

We believe the current political and organizational structure of the Forest Service obligates those within the Forest Service at all levels to speak out for a new resource ethic, one that takes into account the state of our forests and our world today.

The Forest Service must recognize and acknowledge to the public, Congress, and especially to itself, the extent and causes of resource degradation.

We believe that sustaining biological diversity, resource sustainablity, and the integrity of interrelated ecosystems are more important than managing for commodity production and political expediency. The Forest Service must base all its land management decisions on state of the art ecological understanding.

A Forest Service's priority must be to meet the intent and spirit of resource protection laws such as the National Forest Management Act, the Endangered Species Act and the National Environmental Policy Act.

We believe that land is a public trust, to be passed with reverence from generation to generation. Humankind has no right to abuse the land.

Timber cutting, grazing, mining and other resource management activities may be appropriate use of public lands, when they do not compromise or foreclose other resource values and options. Such extraction activities must be restrained through conservation for future generations and must not distort markets or public expectations through the use of subsidies.

"AFSEEE Vision: Strategy for Forest Service Reform," *Inner Voice* 3(1) (Winter 1991): 13. Reprinted with permission from *Inner Voice*, P.O. Box 11615, Eugene, OR 97440.

The Forest Service must distance itself from short-sighted resource exploitation interests and cooperate with individuals and organizations that promote sustainable, ecologically sound management.

The Forest Service and other public agencies must follow in Aldo Leopold's footsteps and become leaders in the quest for a new resource ethic, working toward an ecologically and economically sustainable future. This quest involves reaching out to all segments of the public to develop strategic visions for forest management in harmony with society's evolving value systems.

AFSEEE Strategies

EXPRESSION: Provide an open forum for expression of facts, thoughts, and feelings about the management of our public lands in order to encourage ideological diversity. The newsletter, the *Inner Voice*, will provide this forum. Anonymity will be provided.

SUPPORT SYSTEM: Provide a support system for Forest Service employees who now feel isolated because their land management ethics "don't fit," while providing a united, strong voice for change instead of isolated, single voices.

ACTIVISM: Act as a force at the local and national levels for environmentally sound resource management within the Forest Service through nonviolent and nondestructive means.

EDUCATION: Act as an educational force to foster public awareness of what is happening to our public lands, while promoting a more environmentally sound resource ethic within the Forest Service. Educate Forest Service employees on effective ways to work for and promote a change in values and ethics in the day-to-day job. Spotlight good land management practices.

Jeff DeBonis

Speaking Out: A Letter to the Chief of the U.S. Forest Service

Dear Mr. Dale Robertson,

I am writing to you personally because I feel very strongly about the future and health of our National Forests, this Nation, the planet, and the future role of the Forest Service in addressing this issue. I am speaking from my heart, and thus may sound extremely candid. But I feel it is time for all of us, especially within the Forest Service, to start speaking out more honestly on the reality of what we are doing to our forests and the role the Forest Service is going to play in addressing this reality as we approach the 21st century.

Before I get into the heart of my message, I would like to give you some information about myself, so you will have a sense of my experience and perspective, and my credibility. I am currently a timber planner on the Blue River Ranger District of the Willamette National Forest, in three Regions. I have worked in all aspects of timber management, from sale planning and preparation, to timber sale contract administration. In addition, I was a Peace Corps volunteer in El Salvador and a contractor for U.S. Aid for International Development in Ecuador. My international experience spanned the gamut from working with the problems of deforestation of tropical rainforests in the headwaters of the Amazon Basin, to reforestation and soil conservation projects in the mediterranean climate of El Salvador. This international perspective has perhaps given me an advantage in seeing through the scotomas (blind spots) that many in our agency seem to be burdened with when it comes to seeing the necessity for quick and effective change.

Our basic problem right now is that we (the Forest Service) are much too biased towards the resource-extraction industries, particularly the timber industry. We support their narrowly focused, short-sighted agenda to the point that we are perceived by much of the public as being dupes of, and mere spokespeople for the resource extraction industries. In the remainder of this letter, I will try to explain to you why I believe this is true, give you examples supporting my assertion, tell you

---

Jeff DeBonis, "Speaking Out: A Letter to the Chief of the U.S. Forest Service," *Inner Voice* 1(1) (Summer 1989): 4–5. Reprinted with permission from *Inner Voice*, P.O. Box 11615, Eugene, OR 97440.

what I think we need to do as an agency, and what top management needs to do to move us into the 21st century as *leaders* of a new resource ethic instead of unwilling participants being dragged along by the chain of 9th Circuit Court of Appeals decisions.

We are over-cutting our National Forests at the expense of other resource values. We are incurring negative, cumulative impacts to our watershed, fisheries, wildlife and other non-commodity resources in our quest to meet our timber targets. This is especially evident in Region 6, on "big-timber" forests like the Willamette, but is also occurring on most other timber forests as well. On every forest I have worked on I can give you numerous on-the-ground examples of "getting the cut out" at the expense of other resource values.

Examples include moving spotted owl habitat areas (SOHA) boundaries and allowing fragmentation of these areas to accommodate timber sales; exceeding recommended cover/forage ratios on big game winter range; ignoring non-game wildlife prescriptions, such as snag and green replacement trees guidelines exceeding watershed/sediment "threshold values of concern" in areas with obvious, cumulative damage, etc. We rarely, if ever, exceed our objectives in non-timber resources, even though these objectives are set at the absolute minimum we can legally "get away with." These practices are so common-place they are the standard operating procedure. They are the norm, and we scarcely think twice about them, until some concerned citizen or one of our own specialists dares to challenge us and we become indignant at their audacity. At the planning level, we have built our Forest Plans from the "top down" instead of the "ground up." In other words, we have taken the politically mandated timber harvest level and manipulated the Forest Plan data to support the cut level, rather than build the plan up from the bottom, letting the harvest level be determined by sound biological and ecological considerations mandated by our resource protection laws.

A simple example of this took place on one Forest Plan I am familiar with. This Plan used an average volume per acre of 25 MBG, instead of the real figure of 17 MBF per acre determined by the past 6 or 7 years of actual harvest from the "big timber" districts. This was done when it was discovered that the politically mandated harvest level was too high to be biologically supported by the actual number of acres available for harvest at the real volume per acre. In other instances, Forest Plans don't account for reduced timber volume lost via resource protection guidelines built into the plans, for example in green replacement "wildlife tree" prescriptions or riparian protection prescriptions. This builds over-harvesting into the Plan as unrealistically high timber harvest levels are striven for.

In the case of yet another Forest Plan, the Forest has avoided developing adequate standards and guidelines to protect wildlife or assess the increasingly obvious cumulative effects occurring in many of the watersheds, even though there are a few examples of the Forest Plans which have adequately addressed these issues. They are avoiding it because they know it would reduce their cut. I could give you many more examples of this from Forest Plans I am personally familiar with, as well as accounts from other co-workers who have encountered similar situations on Forests across the U.S. I don't mean to point fingers at any particular Forest Plan, but it serves as an example that we always seem to choose to meet inflated timber cut levels in lieu of protection of other resource values. Other examples of our bias towards "getting the cut out at all costs" include:

1. the numerous ways we find to try to circumvent NEPA;

2. how we view "environmentalists" as our "enemy" in "getting the job done";
3. how we often isolate and pressure our wildlife biologists and other resource specialists to conform and be "team players" so as not to interfere with "getting the cut out." We do this to the point that they refer to themselves as "combat biologists" on many of the heavy-cut forests. And the sad fact of the matter is that the combat they are referring to is with their own supervisors, Rangers, and Forest Management Teams. A final example concerns the recent Record of Decision for the Final E.I.S. for the spotted owl. In this case, we decided to continue our accelerated harvest rates at 95% of the harvest level that would be available if no action were taken! Habitat areas will only comprise 9% of the current spotted owl habitat, and a full 50% of the remaining existing habitat will be open to continued harvesting and fragmentation. This is being proposed in the face of an almost unanimous agreement in the scientific community that the spotted owl is either crashing towards extinction or very close to it.

As an agency, we support and at times publicly reiterate timber industry's smoke screens of jobs vs. environment, jobs vs. the spotted owl, and help promote the impression that we will all be living in cardboard shacks below some freeway overpass if we don't cut the last grove of old-growth. The disinformation being promoted by the timber industry is too long a subject to get into in this particular letter, so I have taken the liberty of enclosing an additional article I wrote (which you may have already seen) pertaining to some specifics on that particular subject. To put this issue in perspective in a general way, however, we should ask ourselves these questions: Are we, as an agency, going to continue to support the current global epidemic of destruction of our biosphere's ecological diversity and survival, for short-sighted, short-term economic "security"? Are we going to continue to parrot the timber industry's propaganda that turning out National Forests into industrial tree farms is necessary for "jobs," when this very industry exported over 5 billion board feet of raw logs last year from Oregon and Washington alone? Are we going to sacrifice the *public's* National Forests while private industry liquidates their lands at an unprecedented rate because Wall Street views standing timber as "under-valued" (and a leveraged buy-out opportunity)? We are not talking about tourism versus ugly clearcuts. We are talking about corporate greed versus a priceless national treasure.

The question occurs to me: why *are* we so biased in favor of the timber industry? I believe it can be partly explained by the homogenous nature of the Forest Service "culture" which promotes a certain mindset. Some of the characteristic beliefs commonly held by this mindset are:

1. If we just believe we are doing "right," we are right;
2. Two decades of accelerated resource extraction/timber harvest which was viewed as "right";
3. That somehow there are no negative cumulative effects resulting from our accelerated rates of timber harvest because we are doing "right," we "care about the land," and we are all good people working in a respected agency;
4. As long as we "get the job done," and keep producing then things will be O.K., and will somehow get worked out;
5. That somehow we are safely "in the middle" between the two opposing equally-weighted special interest groups repre-

sented by the timber industry and the environmentalists; and
6. If we throw enough money at a problem we can "have it all," that all our resource problems are solvable by creative budgeting.

In the interest of space, I don't want to address the fallacy of all of these beliefs here, but I would like to comment on a few of them.

Point 1: The signs of negative, cumulative impacts to our global ecosystems are becoming more and more obvious every day. I don't need to enumerate them here; we read about new environmental disasters every day. We all agree that problems like rain forest deforestation must be stopped. And yet these same symptoms are occurring in our country, in our National Forests. We rightly become indignant over the fact that 50% of the tropical rain forests have been destroyed, but hardly seem to notice that we, as an agency, have contributed to the destruction of 95% of the temperate and near-temperate rain forests of this continent. Replacing an ecosystem as complex and diverse as our old growth temperate rain forests with a monoculture of "genetically improved" Douglas fir is ecologically unconscionable and totally contrary to NEPA, which states that we "preserve important natural ecosystems and maintain an environment which supports diversity." We are currently risking the extinction of this entire ecosystem, as evidenced by the status of our indicator species the spotted owl, by our continued insistence on logging most of the remaining 5% of the temperate rainforests, the bulk of which is on National Forests. And we are doing this in the face of unprecedented unanimous agreement of federal agency biologists that the owl is in fact endangered due to continued logging on public lands.

This stubborn, get-the-cut-out mindset we tend to embrace as an agency blinds us to the actual destructive results of our actions. We see only what we want to see. As the negative impacts of our actions become more and more obvious, we try to pretend it's not happening. And yet at some subconscious level we know that we are over-cutting. When I talk to co-workers about this subject, it is almost universally agreed that we are, in fact, over-cutting. But most of them fail to make the connection that we, in our agency, are contributing to the global environmental onslaught. I have observed this apparent paradox from sale preparation foresters through District Rangers, S.O. timber staff officers and Forest Supervisors. Most of these people stop short of admitting that we are seriously damaging the resource or our credibility with the public. A few of us do see the global perspective and realize the damage we're doing, but still insist that we can not make the needed changes in our management or resource ethic practices "at this level of the organization," whatever level we happen to be in. Our scotomas are held firm by our mindset. We march blindly on to the tune of continued resource extraction at any cost, and refuse to accept the reality of the destructive results of our actions.

Point 2: We delude ourselves into thinking that we are somehow in the "middle" between the environmentalists and timber industry. The fact that we think the environmentalists have "equal weight" with timber industry as just another "special interest group" is a fallacy. One cannot logically weigh the motives of environmentalists with those of the timber industry. It's like comparing apples and oranges. Timber industry's motive is short-term, quick profits, and tends towards short-sighted economic gain. They have a very narrow focus. The environmental community, on the other hand, has a long-range perspective. They are promoting a vision of a sustainable future, both economically and ecologically. Their motives are altruistic, not exploitative. Unfortunately, we ally ourselves with timber industry and think that the "environmentalists" are somehow obstructing us with their numerous appeals and lawsuits. Industry's disinformation campaign has the public believing that these appeals are frivolous and counterproductive. The fact is, environmentalists are winning appeals and court cases because *we* have broken the law. The only frivolous action going on is our agency's disrespect for environmental preservation and ecological diversity. We are the obstructionist, in our insistence on promoting the greedy, insatiable appetite of the large corporate timber industry we serve so well.

An even more poignant example of our bias towards timber industries' agenda concerns how we react after environmentalists do win their lawsuits against us. In many instances, environmental organizations have won on principle in court, but end up losing "on the ground," often with our compliance and help. Instead of accepting the obvious merits of their case and rethinking our action or attitudes, we find ways to circumvent the rulings and continue our business as usual activities. Examples include the National Wildlife Federation and Sierra Club Legal Defense Fund's case against the Mapleton District of the Siuslaw National Forest in which they won in court, only to have a congressional rider attached to allow buy-back, and eventually new sales to continue to be sold and logged as usual, allowing us to essentially disregard the court injunction. Congressional riders are being used ever more frequently to avoid judicial review by concerned publics so we can continue our accelerated timber liquidation program. Another example is the loss of the "Millennium Grove" of ancient Douglas fir on the Willamette National Forest where environmental organizations would have been able to get a court injunction to stop the logging had the Forest Service, in good faith, not waited three days to notify them that negotiations with Willamette Forest Industries had broken down. Other examples of our industry bias include promoting oil and gas exploration and drilling on the Rocky Mountain Front despite the fact that it threatens the grizzly bear; our support of delisting the grizzly on the Flathead National Forest in Region 1 so we can make our timber cut; etc. etc. The point is, we already have the National Environmental Policy Act, the National Forest Management Act, the Endangered Species Act, the Clean Water Act, and other resource protection laws we could use to promote truly integrated resource management on the National Forests, but choose not to. We choose instead to violate the spirit and intent of these laws to do the bidding of large corporate interests.

Point 3: Creative budgeting is not going to solve the resource problems created by over cutting. We cannot "have it all" when "all" means keeping up the furious rate of harvest the last decade has seen on our National Forests, as well as protecting other resource values like clean water, anadromous fisheries, and old-growth dependent species. Your recent comment in Eugene at the "Oregon's Forests in 2010" conference concerning "making the pie bigger" simply promotes this fallacy. More money for "mitigation" is no substitute for simply avoiding the damage of accelerated management activities in the first place. We are going to have to drastically reduce the current and planned timber cut levels on most of our forests, or accept continued, accelerated resource degradation, loss of biological diversity, and extinction of many species and ecosystems.

Part of the problem in initiating change, or even making people aware of the need for change in any organization, is that the organizational system tends to perpetuate itself of rewarding those who serve the system.

The Forest Service is particularly resistant to change since it is such a tightknit, homogeneous family. Those people who believe in the "mindset" and successfully promote system values get promoted to positions of power and authority. The higher you go, the more vested interest you have in the system, and the less likely you will be to actually "see" new problems with the value system which needs changing. Rocking the boat becomes a threat to your own security and value system, as well as the organization's. Once you become part of the system, it becomes difficult for you to change it. That is why we, in the Forest Service, have such a hard time identifying with what the environmentalists are saying. They are threatening our firmly held value system, our mindset, which keeps telling us we are "doing good," we are "in the middle," we are not hurting the land, we are "caring" for it. All the facts in the world produced by the environmental community can be dismissed as so much propaganda, while timber industry's disinformation is accepted since it supports our mindset. We allow our managers to take some risks, in areas we deem "safe," but we don't violate the major tenet of our faith, which is "get the cut out" (or the AUM's or whatever product we are managing for). Unfortunately, this often translates into doing it at any cost to the non-commodity resources. I realize I am not telling you anything new about organizations, or the difficulty in changing them. You are struggling admirably with getting change initiated in our work force, promoting cultural diversity by 1995. We are not, however, seeking change as aggressively in our resource value system, which is as important to our mission as cultural diversity within the workforce.

When I talk with co-workers about the need for change one of the most often used excuses for not trying to initiate change in the system is the feeling that "we can't effect change in how we manage the resources at this level, Congress must do something." I have heard this from people who work at many levels in the organization, as I said before. The truth is, we *have* all the necessary legislation and legal authority right now to move towards a new vision of truly integrated resource management. The fact that our actions are so often appealed, and that we have lost so many of those appeals in court should have made it obvious to us by now that we are often times simply *not* meeting the letter or spirit of NFMA, NEPA, the Endangered Species Act, and other resource protection laws already available to us. The sad fact is we have chosen to avoid the opportunity to become leaders in a new vision of truly sustainable, rational resource management. We have the legal authority, the personnel, the research facilities, the facts and data to promote and make the needed changes to our value system, and the way we manage our forests. We could be taking the lead on the "moral high ground," forging an alliance with the world-wide environmental movement, instead of being associated with trying to maintain the excessively exploitative practices of the past. We should be associating ourselves with the long-range, holistic, and altruistic motives of the environmental community, which are more in line with our mission as a public resource management agency than the short-sighted, narrowly focused motives of the timber industry.

The "realists" would have us believe this kind of a change in values and practices would not be wise, that it would alienate our traditional power base (the resource extraction industries) and we would lose our support. It would certainly be a major confrontation, but it is something which has to be done. The time is right for this type of realignment. We could generate support with the public and the world-wide environmental community. The time is now for a fresh start with a new admiration, to assert a more rational, conservative, sustainable environmental philosophy. We need to have the courage to move away from our past which placed the political expediency of resource extraction at any cost above resource protection, ecological diversity, and truly integrated resource management.

I would like to list a few specific actions which I believe we as an agency could do to help start initiating the needed changes within our organization. We should:

- Encourage ideological diversity and support the existing "agents for change" currently within the organization, like our wildlife biologists and other specialists.
- Support those courageous managers who are willing to risk their careers and take on the power base in order to promote the new vision, men like Tom Kovalicky, Supervisor of the Nez Perce National Forest.
- Insist on absolute support of the spirit and letter of our resource protection laws with as much energy as you have supported cultural diversity in our workforce.
- Support lowering the existing and planned timber harvest levels substantially throughout the National Forest System. Demand a moratorium on any new development of currently unroaded areas, as well as any harvesting in old growth until we have done a thorough ecological inventory of our lands. In the meantime, if we are worried about jobs, let's support a ban on ALL exports of logs, cants, chips, etc. from ALL lands, public and private.
- Let us start erring on the side of resource protection instead of resource extraction. Let's go to court defending the environmental "moral high ground."
- Support Forest Planning from the "bottom up" rather than the current "top down" approach.
- Demand realistic, specific, and meaningful Forest Plan standards and guidelines which truly protect other resource values, and accurately display the inevitable cumulative effects which will occur if the currently inflated timber harvest levels are actually implemented. Again, the Nez Perce plan is the best example of good standards and guidelines I have seen, and the Willamette's Draft Plan is a good example of what we should be avoiding.
- Have the courage to aggressively move our agency away from the political expediency of the past in our alignment with the resource extraction industries. Move away from the philosophy of constantly expanding the exploitation of our resources which has/is/will result in unacceptable, continued resource degradation which we can no longer afford, and
- Forge a new resource ethic by publicly endorsing an alignment with the world-wide environmental community, aggressively endorse the search for a sustainable future, and demand an attitude change to move our agency away from its current perception that the environmental community is the "enemy" in "getting our job done." We must start perceiving the environmental community as our allies in moving towards an enlightened, ecologically sane 21st century.

In summary, man's greed, ignorance and the political expediency of the past is directly responsible for the deteriorating condition we find our planet in today. Our ecological knowledge has now improved to the point that ignorance is no longer an excuse for our actions. It is unproductive at this point to try and fix blame between North and South, environmentalists and industry, good guys and bad. It is time for us all to accept the fact that change is needed, and needed now. The unfortunate truth is that future generations, if there are any, will look back at the last few decades of history with a mixture of amazement, incredulity and disgust that we allowed such an unprecedented slaughter of our natural ecosystem during this era of massive exploitation for so *little* real long-term value. Wouldn't you like to be able to look back and say the Forest Service was a world leader in the quest for a new vision of a truly sustainable society for the 21st century?

Because this new vision is so important to me, I am sending copies of this letter to some members of Congress, as well as selected Forest Supervisors and Regional Foresters. I am doing this in the hope that, as a concerned citizen, this letter will have maximum impact for change.

F. Dale Robertson

Chief Robertson Responds

Editor's note: This response is to my letter to the Chief, printed in the first issue of *Inner Voice*.

Mr. Jeff DeBonis
Willamette National Forest
Blue River Ranger District

Dear Jeff:

Thanks for your letter. Sorry I haven't answered sooner, but I just have not had time to focus on the many ideas you included in your letter.

First, I guess I should say that I disagree with many of your points, especially your size up of the attitude of the Forest Service. It does not represent my attitude nor that of the people I work with and know best. It seems to me that your letter was one-sided and did not appropriately take into account the interest and needs of the American people in the Forest. We in the Forest Service have to keep a more balanced view of the world under our multiple use mandate. I think one of the things we have to guard against is getting caught up in the rhetoric of either the timber industry or the environmental groups and start believing it without putting some balance into it.

Having said that, you brought up several good ideas that the Forest Service must move forward on, such as more ecologically sensitive forestry. The Blue River Ranger District is a leader in this area, and I commend the District for that and you for your part in it.

My testimony at the Senate oversight hearings this week represents my views on several points related to your letter. So, rather than restate it, I am enclosing a copy of my testimony, along with the recently published old growth policy statement.

I believe in participatory management. I encourage Forest Service employees to speak up and let their views be known as we go about making decisions. Otherwise, we lose many of the advantages of a diverse work force. I hope you continue to work cooperatively within the Forest Service to help us change and be responsive to new thinking and emerging needs of the American people.

Jeff, I hope I can count on you to bring about constructive change in the Forest Service—change that is sensitive to both the environment and the people who are affected by our

---

F. Dale Robertson, "Chief Robertson Responds," *Inner Voice* 2(1) (Winter 1990): 3. Reprinted with permission from *Inner Voice*, P.O. Box 11615, Eugene, OR 97440.

decisions. I hear good things about the job being done on the Blue River Ranger District and hope to get a chance soon to see your good work on the ground.

Sincerely,
F. Dale Robertson
Chief

On Speaking Out: Fighting for Resource Ethics in the BLM

United States Government
Department of the Interior
Bureau of Land Management
MEMORANDUM

TO: California State Director
DATE: September 20, 1976
FROM: Resource & Planning Staff Professionals of the Riverside District, Desert Plan Program, California State Office, and Other Bureau Offices

SUBJECT: Concerns Regarding Bureau of Land Management Programs and Relations with Staff Professionals

PURPOSE: We wish to bring to your attention some serious problems regarding planning and management of the California Desert,

---

"On Speaking Out: Fighting for Resource Ethics in the BLM," *Inner Voice* 1(2) (Fall 1989): 7. Reprinted with permission from *Inner Voice*, P.O. Box 11615, Eugene, OR 97440.

[*This is an excerpt from a 5-page official BLM memo AFSEEE recently received. It was signed by 16 BLM resource professionals—ed.*]

in the hope that by working together in an atmosphere of mutual trust and understanding these problems can be solved.

INTRODUCTION: A growing discontent during past months among staff professionals concerned with the management of the California Desert prompts this unusual, but necessary, direct expression of concern. Our discontent derives from our belief that in the management of California Desert lands the Bureau has not kept faith with the American public, whom it is charged to serve, but has often served itself and special interest. This organizational self-aggrandizement and special-interest catering has had serious effects upon fragile desert resources, which the Bureau, as a public steward, is required to protect. At the same time it has severely eroded the confidence and morale of a highly qualified assemblage of resource professionals.

Our concerns fall into several categories:
1. Break-down in relationship between Management and Resource Staff Professionals; failure to utilize the expertise and talent in

the resource staffs; break-down in communications; derogatory and negative attitudes held by managers.

2. Non-compliance with the National Environmental Policy Act: issuing of SLUPs for off-road events and allowing these events to occur without signed Environmental Analysis Reports; back-dating of EARs; predetermining recommendations and decisions of EARs prior to accumulating, reading, and evaluating the data in EARs.

3. Special interest group catering: immersion of the Desert Ranger force in motorcycle race management and paperwork; allowing CORVA to enter the "closed" Kelso Dunes; suppression and displacement of non-ORV users by motorcyclists and dunebuggyists; failure to use available scientific data in analysis of ORV impacts.

4. Failure to follow the U.S. Government Code of Ethics for Government Employees.

At the root of all of these concerns is a basic lack of openness and honesty in management's interactions with staff and the public.

Each one of these problem areas is outlined below, and most are documented with some examples from our collective experience. Further documentation and additional examples are available in our files.

We consider ourselves loyal and dedicated employees of the Bureau of Land Management. We affirm this because it has been our collective experience that criticism of the Bureau by employees is frequently regarded as disloyalty. We believe that only through internal, constructive criticism can this organization remain viable and fulfill its highest purposes. We reject the prevalent notion that what is good for the Bureau is good. We further reject the concept of the "family" so often articulated by BLM managers, which in effect says, "Do whatever the manager says, don't ask questions, and you will be taken care of." As professionals, we are deeply offended by this traditional patronization. Rather, we feel guided by the United States Government Code of Ethics, which requires all federal employees to place allegiance to country, the public interest, and morality above loyalty to any agency. We have seen and continue to see acts that are wrong and that violate the Code of Ethics. We believe that we would be wrong if we failed to bring these matters to your personal attention. We are encouraged in this endeavor by your memorandum CSO 76–2, concerning Executive Order 11391 (Labor-Management Relations Policy).

We also want to preface our complaint with an explanation of our view of the Bureau, and of our role in it. We believe that the Bureau was established to manage National Resource Lands for the public benefit, and to sustain the values and resources of these lands for as long as possible. The Bureau is a steward of the land, not an agent that parcels it out for consumption only. The function of resource professionals is to provide management with expert advice on the various resources, in order that management decisions best serve the public good.

Resource professionals believe in multiple use. We recognize the country's need for meat, minerals, and energy, and believe that National Resource Lands can provide these resources for centuries to come. We also recognize the public need for beauty, space, and wildness. We believe that these intangible values can be compatible with consumptive uses. We are deeply concerned about the Bureau's general lack of sensitivity toward these values in view of the American public's high regard for them.

Our view of the "public interest" differs substantially from the attitudes of our managers. However, it does not differ substantively from the Bureau's own directives and policy. Our view is idealistic and we take pride in this, because it is our conviction that idealism is essential to the framework of sound natural resource management.

Many of us have appealed to the best senses and judgments of our superiors over a considerable period of time and on many occasions in hope of correcting the concerns we submit here. Our individual expressions have had little effect, and we have reached the common conclusion that at best, management has insufficiently availed itself of the expertise, opinions, and recommendations of its staff in arriving at critical resource management decisions. At worst, management has treated its resource specialists as internal obstacles somehow to overcome in achieving preconceived objectives and decision.

Catering to special interest groups. Paramount among our concerns is the relationship of the Bureau to its clientele groups. The Bureau began as a special interest rather than as a public-serving agency, and it has yet to outgrow the traditions of its past. Much about the Bureau is geared toward special rather than public interests: the backgrounds of its management personnel; selection of management personnel; the composition of Advisory Boards; and the public participation process. In the California Desert, stockmen and off-road vehicle recreationists elicit special considerations which are excessive in terms of resources degraded or lost, expenditures of Bureau effort, and services foregone to other programs and other desert users.

We, the undersigned, concur with the memorandum to the State Director, Bureau of Land Management, titled "concerns Regarding Bureau of Land Management Programs and Relations with Staff Professionals," dated September 20, 1976.

Whistleblower Spills Beans on North Kaibab

A federal investigation is underway regarding timber theft on national forest lands adjacent to the Grand Canyon. The Office of Inspector General (OIG) is looking into allegations that Kaibab Forest Products, an Arizona-based timber company, harvested, perhaps, millions of board feet of old growth ponderosa pine trees illegally on the North Kaibab District of the Kaibab NF.

A spokesman for the OIG said the Office has been probing into the illegal cutting of trees on the Kaibab for the past year, yet agents working on the case have not been at liberty to talk while the investigation is in progress. The Office, the investigative arm of the Department of Agriculture, is only called in by the Forest Service when the value of timber thefts exceed $50,000 or if there is any suspected employee misconduct.

The investigation may also include probes into contract fraud by Kaibab Forest Products. Stephen Carr, a former North Kaibab District employee, says he blew the whistle on the company when he discovered the government had paid for road improvements which had never been done. Carr, who was an engineering technician on the district, says that Kaibab Forest Products "didn't put in one out of every three drainage features that the Kaibab (NF) had paid for." Carr estimates that the cost to the government could add up to thousands of dollars from engineering contract violations.

A spokesman for the timber company denies that any serious violations have taken place. He told reporters that because of a mechanical tree cutting machine, some trees which were marked by the FS to be left standing may have been accidentally cut. He said loggers who sit high up off the ground while driving the machine may not see the marks on some of the trees, and that there are bound to be "some mistakes." The company further denied that any contract fraud had taken place on Forest Service road projects.

Yet Carr, who was "booted out" of engineering after he blew the whistle on the contract violations, was later given the job of measuring and surveying trees that had been illegally cut

"Whistleblower Spills Beans on North Kaibab," *Inner Voice* 4(5): (September/October 1992): 3. Reprinted with permission from *Inner Voice*, P.O. Box 11615, Eugene, OR 97440.

by Kaibab Forest Products. He says he found "plenty of trees that were hand-cut," and that it is a "fabrication or lie" to blame all of the illegal cutting on a machine.

Carr, who worked on the district for 14 years, but now works as an environmental lobbyist in Maryland, spent his last summer with the Forest Service verifying tree thefts on timber sales logged by Kaibab Forest Products. He said his surveying revealed illegally-taken trees in almost every cutting unit, many of which were old growth ponderosa pine as large as 30-inches in diameter. Carr says up to millions of board feet of stolen timber could be involved in the on-going theft.

The former employee does not suspect overt collusion by Forest Service employees in the timber theft. He said that as soon as the North Kaibab district Timber Management Assistant discovered *one* illegally-cut tree, he called for an internal Forest Service investigation. Carr assisted in the "ground-pounding" which then ensued, checking every unit in the sale and discovering the logged "leave trees" especially near unit boundaries away from roads. "It was obvious that somebody was trying to defraud the federal government," Carr said.

Many are asking how the illegal activity could have taken place right under the noses of district officials. Carr blames it on the "incestuous relationship" between local timber workers and North Kaibab district employees, "many of whom have the same last names." However, the collusion may have been more benign neglect than overt complicity. On the North Kaibab, says Carr, "they have been building roads and harvesting timber the way they wanted to for over 40 years and they all tend to trust one another." District timber inspectors rarely walk all of the units to see that everything is in order, Carr adds, encouraging a system that is geared towards "sweetheart deals" for Kaibab Forest Products.

Carr says attitudes on the district were also "part and parcel of an entire mind-set" on the Kaibab NF that has "handed over the last great belt of ponderosa pine forest left in the Southwest." Lying just north of the Grand Canyon in northern Arizona, the district is isolated from large population centers and environmental scrutiny. In the 1980s, after years of moderate logging by local timber operators, the timber targets on the Kaibab were suddenly boosted up with little protest from the public since "everybody worked for either the FS or Kaibab Industry," says Carr. "The Regional Office kept asking for more timber, and employees had to get the cut out."

The Forest has been harvesting 75 to 80 million board feet (mmbf) per year off the Forest in the last decade, which Arizona Game & Fish (AZGF), Northern Arizona School of Forestry, and many environmentalists believe to be 50 to 60 mmbf annually that shouldn't have been cut over the past decade. In fact, sources say that North Kaibab District timber managers had repeatedly pleaded with the Forest Supervisor, during Forest planning, to keep the allowable sale quantity at a sustainable level—no more than 30 to 35 mmbf for the district. However, political pressure has kept the cut too high on the North Kaibab. Now with the collapse of volume levels due to past over-cutting and harvest acreage withdrawn in favor of goshawk nesting areas, there is tension among locals and government officials.

Kaibab Forest Products reportedly issued a massive Freedom of Information Act (FOIA) request to the Arizona State Game and Fish agency, in hopes of compiling evidence that the agency was "closely aligning itself with extreme environmental groups." Referred to inside AZGF as a "witch hunt," the FOIA was sent after rumors surfaced about the mysterious "Kaibab Gang"—FS employees who had briefed Game and Fish officials about the Forest Service's mismanagement on the North Kaibab.

Kaibab Industry's political connections, inter-agency disagreements, and the state of the Southwestern economy may all play into the pending decision of OIG. Carr believes investigators are sorting out the motivations and relationships behind the two types of fraud and verifying their extent—basically "getting all their ducks in a row" before issuing a decision.

He hopes the government will hear the case before a grand jury and fully prosecute those parties guilty of defrauding the American taxpayers.

A Combat Biologist Calls It Quits: An Interview with Al Espinosa

Fisheries Biologist Al Espinosa, a 19-year veteran of Idaho's Clearwater NF, took an early retirement from the Forest Service on January 1, 1993.

Espinosa struggled to protect fisheries on the Clearwater for years against political efforts to maintain high levels of timber harvesting and road-building. Perhaps this caused him to coin the term "combat biologist" to describes the battles he faced everyday at his job. We asked him about how the agency could better incorporate science into its decision-making.—c.b.

IV: Tell us about the work you were doing on the Clearwater.
A.E.: I was a Forest fisheries biologist there for 19 years and fourth months. I ran the fisheries program. We had about 11 biologists on the Forest who did various things like timber sale coordination, monitoring, fish habitat restoration, and survey and inventory work. The Clearwater traditionally had a strong timber program, and I'd say 40 to 50 percent of our job was dealing with that program.

"A Combat Biologist Calls It Quits: An Interview with Al Espinosa," *Inner Voice* 5(1) (January/February 1993): 5. Reprinted with permission from *Inner Voice*, P.O. Box 11615, Eugene, OR 97440.

IV: Why did you take an early retirement from your job?
A.E.: Basically, I'd had enough of the whole scheme of things. I'd had enough of the bureaucracy, enough of the conflict, enough of the battles, and I didn't see the agency turning around at all. I didn't see management really changing. When they got rid of [former Northern Rockies Regional Forester John] Mumma, we took a definite step backwards. With [present Region 1 Forester] coming in, with a background as a timber beast, I see Region 1 trying to get the program back up to what it's traditionally been—a timber program. So on that basis, I said 20 years is enough, rolled it up, and that was it.

IV: You were involved with some studies done on the Clearwater regarding the streams and the fisheries. What were the results?
A.E.: Those were part of the Changed Conditions Analysis which is supposed to have been done at the fifth year of Forest plan implementation. Along with a hydrologist, a biologist, and other field biologists, as the planning team we came up with an assessment looking at mainly our developed drainages—the ones we've been [logging and road-building] in for the past 30 years. We found that 71 percent

of the developed drainages were below Forest Plan standards.

IV: Generally, what did your work show about overall conditions on the Forest?

A.E.: Basically we had too much sediment in our streams that we've been in for the past 30 years. We've been roading them too much. They haven't really cut them any slack and gotten out of there with our development programs so the streams could have time to recover and get back to complying with our Forest Plan standards. Basically, too much activity, too much development over time—habitat had been degraded.

IV: How did the agency respond to the findings of you and your colleagues regarding the effects of timber harvesting and development on Forest resources?

A.E.: Really, they already had known most of it. We'd been telling them for years. We knew it for years that our developed areas just had too many impacts and too much activity. Initially the Forest thought they could use that as an anchor point to amend the Forest Plan. Well, they went to the Regional Office with it, and that's where they had a barrier. They were told that they couldn't make any significant amendments to the plan like change the ASQ (allowable sale quantity) or deal with standards or any of the other controversial issues in the Plan that we'd highlighted in the five-year review. It is not being championed as a good inventory. I think the R.O. is just going to bury it.

IV: The Clearwater and other Forests in Region 1 have not been able to meet their timber targets in the last few years. Why?

A.E.: I think we're running out of trees and watersheds, and they're running up against a lot of constraints, such as old-growth, sensitive species, TES species. I think that the decision space is really narrowed down, so everything they put up is controversial, has a big potential conflict, and it's not easily resolved. The public is appealing a lot of the sales. They're even going to lawsuits on the Montana side. I think the program is crashing. I think it's pretty obvious.

IV: We've been reading in the news about certain pressures placed on employees on the Clearwater. What types of pressures do you see being placed on resource managers?

A.E.: Resource specialists in '92 probably had a big influence on half of the volume that didn't make it out of the building. And on that basis, they've been identified as barriers to the program, getting the program back up to 75 to 90 million board feet.

They've been intimidated, they've been threatened with their jobs, and they've been earmarked for removal because of this. I think that resource people are really under a lot of pressure and stress right now, and I think they're being used as scapegoats. It's obvious that resource conditions have really been responsible for the precipitous drop in the ASW.

The Forest knew this long ago. They should have been making mid-course corrections. They saw the iceberg moving up in the horizon long ago, but the tradition and the lack of guts led them back to the iceberg and they hit it and they sunk. And now they're just looking for scapegoats and sacrificial lambs, and they picked the resource specialists.

I think the Regional Office has a gun to [Forest Supervisor's] head, and they're telling him to tap dance like hell.

IV: I'd like to get to some questions, generally, about science, and scientists in the agency. Do you think in general the Forest Service listens to its specialists or its scientists?

A.E.: Oh, to the extent it doesn't interfere with the reward system and getting the cut out, if you're on a timber forest. They listen, but it goes in one ear and drops out the other. Generally, when there's a conflict with getting the cut out—meeting your targets—I think the agency doesn't want to hear that they're not complying with the Forest Plan or they've been in that drainage too long or they've put too many impacts on the fish and wildlife resources. If you're on a range Forest, you deal with cattle. Anyplace where you've had a significant commodity program, the scientists and specialists are going to have problems getting heard and having their input have some influence.

I think that it has an influence of modifying some projects, that sort of thing. But when it comes down to cutting to the quick, whether the Forest Service is going to have a project or should have a project in an area—frequently scientists are just not listened to.

IV: Some people say that Ecosystem Management is not about science, but about listening to changing political forces in society, such as urban environmentalists. Do you agree?
A.E.: I don't know, it's too new. I see Ecosystem Management as just a lot of rhetoric right now and spin-doctoring. The version I've heard of it, in Region 1, is kind of a ruse to get in there and cut more—take out buffer strips and blend in one clearcut with another and call it "simulating Mother Nature" because Mother Nature burns this country every hundred years or so in a devastating manner. I think that's a lot of bunk right now. You show me one watershed that the Forest Service has managed over time that hasn't become dysfunctional for other resources. If you could show me that, then I might have a little belief in their ability to do Ecosystem Management. But right now, to me it's like selling a bad used car from some car salesman in Encino, California.

IV: How do you think that the agency can best incorporate science into its decision-making?
A.E.: I think the Forest Service is basically a Titanic II right now. It's hit several icebergs; it's listing heavily without a rudder. It's going to hit that final one, I think, because it doesn't learn anything from its mistakes—like the spotted owl controversy. So, it's going to hit that final one and probably go down.

At that point, it needs to be restructured—dismantled completely and restructured to a point where you don't have the allowable cut mandate and management-by-intimidation pervading the whole agency. Until you can remove those concepts from the agency, you're not really going to have good science and good management because the whole system gets distorted and perverted by those concepts.

IV: So you're saying hard targets are contrary to—
A.E.: They drive the system. The reward system is based on getting your cut out, regardless of what happens out there in terms of good science or good management. People sell out to that system. Until you can start rewarding managers for a good land ethic, a good resource ethic, quality management, a balanced program, a diversified program, and a real true Ecosystem Management philosophy, you're not going to have it.

IV: Can you think of a way that the agency could promote this sustainable forestry or sustainable resource management?
A.E.: Yeah, they can drop this allowable cut mandate and management-by-intimidation, this target-mania and quit rewarding managers for just getting wood out. Reward them for meeting their Forest Plan standards and meeting water quality standards and all the other laws that we're supposed to be managing by.

IV: How do you think the agency can protect the integrity, ethics, and principles of resource managers like yourself and other folks who are out there in the trenches every day, trying to uphold standards for good resource management?
A.E.: That's the real disconcerting thing about the whole thing. You live in a democratic society, yet you get hired to do something, and once you start to do it they come down on you because the system doesn't want to hear it or allow it.

I think the only way that's going to change is when you get good leadership in the agency which is sensitive to people's needs. Leadership that will implement a program that cares for people and doesn't try to intimidate and remove them when they don't fit the system.

My belief is that if the Forest Service is going to abuse resource specialists, then it shouldn't even have them, shouldn't even hire them. I think what they ought to do—if they want Stepford wives and lobotomized specialists—they ought to contract their fish and wildlife and hydrology work, take the information, and do what they want with it. But don't hire scientists and then try to beat them up for the next 20 years, because they're just trying to do their job.

Tongass Employees Speak Out

Several Tongass National Forest employees have become outspoken about the suppression of the study "A Strategy for Maintaining Well-Distributed, Viable Populations of Wildlife Associated with Old-Growth Forests in Southeast Alaska" (see *IV*, Nov/Dec '92). The study warns that several species of wildlife could disappear from parts of southeast Alaska if present logging practices continue. Lowell Suring, the Forest Service biologist who headed the team, has come out publicly along with other state and federal employees about the suppression of this study by officials. Suring is leaving the Alaska Regional Office to take a position on the Chugach NF due to the Forest Service's treatment of the report.

Another Tongass biologist, Duane Fisher, received the worst performance evaluation of his life after he tried to incorporate the findings of the viability study into the Tongass's Plan revision. His supervisor, an engineer, was quoted as saying that while wildlife prefer to live in old growth, they are able to survive elsewhere. "Humans will live in northeast Washington there behind the Capitol and survive and even reproduce, but that isn't their preferred habitat. They'd much rather live in Georgetown. Wildlife are much the same way," went the *Marie-Antoinette-ian* logic.

In addition, the leader of the interdisciplinary team for the Central Prince of Wales long-term timber sale proposal warned that planned harvest levels on the Island may result in future shortages to timber-dependent communities.

The draft plan calls for cutting over 20,000 acres of old-growth during the next decade to meet the terms of a 50-year contract with Ketchikan Pulp Co. Bill Shoaf, the ID team leader for the draft environmental impact statement, objected that the task given his team "was purely a management decision and was not based on the biotic capability of the land to provide timber on a sustained yield level."

House Interior Committee Chairman Rep. George Miller (D-CA) has asked Mike Espy, the new Secretary of Agriculture to launch an investigation into management attempts to silence wildlife biologists and to monitor the agency's treatment of the concerns of planners regarding future timber shortfalls.

"Tongass Employees Speak Out," *Inner Voice* 5(1) (January/February 1993): 4. Reprinted with permission from *Inner Voice*, P.O. Box 11615, Eugene, OR 97440.

Cheri Brooks

Enough Is Enough! A Tongass Timber Beast Puts His Foot Down

A 15-year Forest Service veteran has blown the whistle on Tongass National Forest managers. The disclosure to the Office of Special Counsel (OSC)—an independent government agency which evaluates whistleblowers' complaints—shows that predicted levels of timber harvest for the Ketchikan Area of the Tongass NF are not sustainable. The OSC found a "substantial likelihood" that the charges were correct and ordered Secretary of Agriculture Mike Espy to investigate.

Bill Shoaf, Interdisciplinary (ID) Team leader for long-term sale projects in the Ketchikan Area, has been a dedicated and loyal Forest Service employee and has always received "Fully Successful" or "Outstanding" performance evaluations in all categories. But after a year of working on the Central Prince of Wales (CPOW) timber sale, Shoaf began to question the wisdom and legality of Forest Service management activities in southeast Alaska.

The project area for the sale—Prince of Wales Island—is the fourth largest island in the US and the source of much of the biggest and most valuable southeast Alaskan timber. The massive CPOW timber sale is intended to supply timber to Ketchikan Pulp Company (KPC), one of two large, multi-national companies which hold 50-year contracts with the Forest Service guaranteeing them a long-term supply of timber from the Tongass.

Overestimating the Timber

Within the central Prince of Wales project area, the Tongass Land Management Plan (TLMP) Revision concluded that 99.8 percent of the land allocated to timber harvest was in fact harvestable, despite such factors as steep and unstable slopes, high hazard soils, unmapped stream courses, caves, cultural resources, economic constraints, infeasible logging, and high elevation areas where it would be difficult if not impossible to regenerate stands. This assumption led the Forest Service to set very high timber targets (ASQ or allowable sale quantity) in the Preferred Alternative of the TLMP DEIS (418 million board feet/year).

"Enough is Enough! A Tongass Timber Beast Puts His Foot Down," *Inner Voice* 5(5) (September/October 1993): 6. Reprinted with permission from *Inner Voice*, P.O. Box 11615, Eugene, OR 97440.

The Alaska Regional Guide requires that a Multi-Entry Layout Plan (MELP) be prepared to assist in timber sale planning. Shoaf and his team of Forest Service employees conducted an 8-month MELP study which looked at the actual conditions on large parts of the Ketchikan Area. The MELDATA was based on site-specific information, aerial photos, and field input from logging engineers, soil scientists, landscape architects, fishery and wildlife biologists, and silviculturists.

Using MELP data, Shoaf's team concluded that only 44 percent of the land in the Prince of Wales sale area was actually harvestable rather than the 99.8 percent predicted by TLMP. The other 56 percent of the timber base couldn't be logged because of concerns for other resources such as fish, wildlife, and oils, as well as infeasible logging, and economics. The MELP data showed that other project areas on the Forest had been projected for unsustainable harvest levels as well (e.g., Control Lake is only 43 percent harvestable and Lab Bay only 58 percent harvestable).

Phantom Forests

The TLMP predictions of future timber harvest were based on a complex Forest Service computer model for optimizing resource outputs call FORPLAN. TLMP never designed a single unit, looked at a single aerial photograph, or verified any data on the ground. It based the amount of predicted volume on clearcutting as the exclusive means of harvest, even though Forest Service Chief Dale Robertson had directed the decrease of clearcutting in favor of other silvicultural systems.

The Irland Group, a forestry consulting company contracted by the Alaska Region of the Forest Service, has also expressed strong concerns about the timber projections found in TLMP. Their report stated that without site-specific information, planners can not accurately predict future harvest volume. It said that yield predictions found in TLMP's Preferred Alternative were overestimated by at least 22 percent. Instead of listening to these concerns, however, Tongass Forest managers ordered Shoaf to ignore the MELP data and prepare timber sales on Prince of Wales Island using the less accurate assumptions of TLMP.

"The prevalent management posture," disclosed Shoaf, "seemingly is to disregard or discredit any information which would lead to a reduction of ASQ calculations, because this would expose the unsustainable level of harvest which local Forest Service managers seem determined to perpetuate for as long as possible."

This perpetuation of unsustainable levels of harvest violates the Multiple Use Sustained Yield Act and misleads local timber dependent communities into believing that more harvest can occur than is legally possible under environmental laws.

"People in my community are making critical decisions about whether to invest in homes, equipment, and local businesses," said Shoaf. "By projecting exaggerated and unrealistic levels of timber harvest based on flawed TLMP data . . . the Forest Service is setting many people up for financial and emotional disaster in the longer term when the timber supply runs out sooner than projected."

Falling Down

"Falldown" refers to the difference between the amount of timber that an environmental impact statement predicts will be cut and how much is actually cut. Shoaf's team found that the 1989–94 long-term timber sale EIS for KPC had significantly over-estimated the amount of timber that could be harvested from the project area. In order to compensate for this falldown, harvest units had been systematically expanded to include significant areas of the Forest that were not intended to be parts of the units and therefore were not authorized to be harvested.

Out of the 30,011 acres planned for harvest by KPC in the current operating period, only 21,086 were actually harvested—a falldown of 30 percent. To make up for this falldown, 5,047 acres were cut outside the boundaries listed in the Record of Decision. This acreage was clearcut without a cumulative effects analysis and without the public having been informed or afforded the opportunity to comment.

Aside from seriously violating the National Environmental Policy Act, unit expansion by the Forest Service can lead to "highgrading" in violation of the Tongass Timber Reform Act, jeopardize other resources—such as fisheries habitat—and compromise the Forest Service's ability to plan for future timber sales. Projections of future timber supply are often exaggerated because it turns out that these projections include timber which has already been harvested through unit expansion.

Misleading the Public

The intent of the Central Prince of Wales (CPOW) timber sale project is to offer 290 million board feet (mmbf) of timber to KPC under the terms of the long-term contract. NEPA requires publication of a Notice of Intent before preparing an EIS. The Notice of Intent for the CPOW project was published with a map which indicated that the 290 mmbf would be harvested from an area covering 600,000 acres; however, the text read that the timber would be extracted from only 320,000 acres.

For four months, Shoaf's ID team was under verbal direction to disregard the inconsistencies in the Notice of Intent and prepare an EIS based on harvesting timber from 600,000 acres on Prince of Wales Island. But later, the team received written orders to limit all alternatives in the DEIS to the primary sale area (320,000 acres) and to include timber harvest in old-growth retention areas—which had previously been excluded from consideration.

This new direction, according to Shoaf, violated a "good faith agreement" with the Alaska Department of Fish and Game, as well as with the public, that these old-growth retention areas were to be permanently set aside from harvest to provide wildlife habitat.

The CPOW Notice of Intent has never been revised. Tongass Forest managers violated NEPA by misleading the public about the full scope of the CPOW project and are attempting to squeeze an unsustainable volume of timber from an already over-harvested area.

Shoaf also found that the Forest Service was surveying logging roads and laying out harvest units for the central Prince of Wales project as well as other projects before an official decision was made.

Such predecisional activities, focusing strictly on a preferred alternative, also violate NEPA and commit resources (staffing and budget) to one course of action, therefore biasing the decision-maker and limiting the choice of other reasonable alternatives (which may be more environmentally sound). The agency is, in effect, using the EIS to justify a decision already made rather than to inform the decision-maker of the environmental impacts of his or her decision.

Targeting the Whistleblower

As a result of his questioning of these Forest Service activities, Shoaf became subject to a campaign of discrimination, intimidation, and harassment which continues to this day. Especially after the arrival of current Ketchikan Area Forest Supervisor Dave Rittenhouse, Shoaf has seen the reduction of his official duties, has been forbidden from speaking with members of the press (even on his own time), and has received "Unacceptable" performance ratings for the first time in his Forest Service career.

Instead of listening to the concerns of Shoaf and other employees, Tongass Forest managers have taken the attitude that federal environmental regulations are obstacles, or at best constraints, that must be overcome in order to perpetuate the desired harvest level.

On June 14, 1993, Shoaf's immediate supervisor, Dave Arrasmith, issued a written direction that he not tell the public about the MELP information and instead include the inflated timber supply estimation of TLMP preferred alternative—which Shoaf's team had documented as unsustainable. This order is what caused Shoaf to decided to file his disclosure of illegality and gross mismanagement with the Office of Special Counsel.

"I love the Forest Service," says Shoaf, "and it breaks my heart to observe local managers not abiding by major environmental laws passed by Congress to govern forest management. I have strong loyalty to the agency, but also take very seriously my role as public servant. I simply can't condone these violations of Federal law, because it is my professional opinion that the violations will ultimately harm the American public and our beloved forests."

Hanging in the Balance

Congress is now deciding how much money to appropriate the Forest Service for timber sales on the Tongass next year. Alaskan Senator Ted Stevens is lobbying hard to keep Tongass timber targets at a very high level (420 mmbf/yr).

The Alaska Region is completing the final revised Tongass Land Management Plan. But there are many unanswered questions about sustainable harvest levels Forest-wide as well as about what is needed to maintain viable, well-distributed populations of wildlife in southeast Alaska.

The Record of Decision for CPOW has been signed, and logging is scheduled to begin in mid-September. But Shoaf says, "If southeast Alaska is to avoid the kind of community disruption and human suffering which now plague the Pacific Northwest, harvest levels on the Tongass National Forest must be reduced immediately."

CHAPTER 10

Ethical Issues in Global Forestry

The "riches of the forests" were the foundation of the American colonial economy, so much so that New England was called a "timber economy" in the seventeenth and eighteenth centuries.[1] Until the early nineteenth century, much of the lumber and other forest products from American forests were consumed in local markets for use in farming, construction, ship building, manufacturing, and heating. However, these forests were also used by the British navy as a source of masts, spars, planking, and other wood products (such as pitch, tar, turpentine, and resins), and New England businesses exported to England sawed planks and boards, staves and shingles, as well as potash, tar, pitch, and charcoal. Local demand for lumber was thus relatively low in the seventeenth and eighteenth centuries, but the domestic lumber trade blossomed in the mid-nineteenth century because of the rising pace of industrialization in the United States.[2] From mid-century on, as the demand for wood increased, the wave of lumbering and lumber production spread first from New England to the Great Lakes states, then, by the early twentieth century, to the South and Pacific Northwest.[3] Along with this growth in the domestic wood business came an increase in foreign trade in wood and wood products. For example, after the gold rush in California during 1849, West Coast traders sought new markets for lumber in the Pacific Rim, including Australia, Hawaii, Chile, and other countries in northern Latin America, even before West Coast lumber began to be shipped back east for domestic use.[4] Much of the wood from West Coast states was eventually consumed in the national timber economy and was shipped to markets inside the country. In time, however, foreign trade in U.S. timber and wood products began to grow dramatically, particularly after World War II, and in the past forty years the global market for American timber has expanded tremendously.[5] For close to two hundred years, then,

1. Williams, *Americans and Their Forests: A Historical Geography*, chap. 4.
2. Ibid., chaps. 4 and 6.
3. Ibid., chap. 7.
4. Ibid., chap. 9.
5. M. Patricia Marchak, *Logging the Globe* (Montreal: McGill-Queen's University Press, 1995), p. 4.

markets for wood and wood products outside of the United States have been an important economic motivator for the American timber business, although certainly much more so in the twentieth century.

The United States timber industry has consequently become a key participant in the globalization of the timber and wood products business.[6] American timber companies like Weyerhauser and Boise Cascade have eagerly sold logs and dimensional lumber from their own lands to buyers in other parts of the world, such as Japan. They have also sought new sources of timber supply elsewhere, in places like Siberia and Mexico, and in some cases have moved some of their operations outside the United States altogether. As a result, the philosophies and methods of industrial forestry are being exported from the United States as well as from other large timber-producing countries.

Much of the global trade in wood and wood products takes place between "developed" industrial countries in North America, Asia, and Europe,[7] and these countries are also the major purchasers of imported timber and wood products from the "less developed" nations of the world. Still, timber companies in the major northern forest countries are not the only participants in the global timber trade. Companies from New Zealand and Chile sell logs and wood products in the United States, for example, and large corporations and governments in Southeast Asia and Latin America are active organizers of economic activities related to timber. The logging and clearing of original forests in Asia, Latin America, Central America, and some parts of Africa is obviously not carried out only by corporations from the "industrial" or "developed" nations. In short, the globalization of the wood business is now as much a fact about the current world economy as it is for other natural resource and consumer commodities, and it is safe to conclude that this process will continue and will intensify.

A significant factor in this growth in the world's timber business is that it has occurred alongside the development of a "full-scale, mass-production forest industry based on temperate-zone coniferous (softwood) forests" in the northern forest countries.[8] This means that the technological and organizational ability to extract timber and produce wood products in industrial countries has also expanded rapidly in the twentieth century,[9] and the political and economic power that accompanies this is enormous. Moreover, the economic sophistication and the environmental consequences of the timber business raise the prospect that John Perlin's thesis about extensive forestry in the ancient world now applies to the earth as a whole and not just to particular subregions. If demand for timber and wood products continues to grow on a per capita basis worldwide, along with increases in population and consumer intensive lifestyles, then we may be seeing the end not only of most of the unreserved, ancient, and original forests of North America but of ancient forests all over the planet.[10] Plantation forestry and agroforestry,

---

6. United Nations Environmental Program, *Environmental Data Report* (Oxford, U.K.: Blackwell, 1991).
7. A. T. Durning, *How Much Is Enough?* (London: Earthscan, 1992).
8. Marchak, *Logging the Globe*, p. 4.
9. Ibid.

10. Per capita consumption of wood products in the United States has fallen in half during this century, from approximately 160 cubic feet in 1900 to about 80 cubic feet in 1995. In the same period the total consumption of wood rose from about 12 billion cubic feet to close to 18 billion cubic feet, even while population expanded dramatically, in fact four-fold fourfold. Correlatively there is much less waste in the wood products manufacturing

where they are economically and politically feasible, may become the new order of the day internationally, just as plantation forestry has come to dominate industrial forestry operations in the northern forest countries.[11]

These developments in global forestry are only part of the picture, however, for as noted earlier in this anthology environmentalism as a political force in American and European forestry has also become much more significant since World War II, and environmental movements and groups are making themselves heard on forest issues in other parts of the world as well. Forest activists, activism, and protest of forest practices and policies is now quite visible in countries like Brazil, Chile, Thailand, and Malaysia, and concerns about the destruction of forests and forest-dependent species and cultures in Southeast Asia and South America are widespread.[12] The academic discipline of environmental ethics is also slowly spreading from countries such as America, England, India, and Australia to universities and colleges in other parts of the world, such as China, and ethical discussions of forest management and forest practices are now evident in most parts of the world. Environmentalists, scientists, and others from Western countries have participated in some of these non-Western forest disputes, either directly or as observers, and the ethical "dialogue" about forestry is flourishing now in the northern and southern hemispheres of the globe.

Ethics and ethical norms are a pervasive aspect of human cultural systems, and the introduction of ethical considerations into forest resource disputes internationally is as inevitable as the introduction of economic and biological criteria. At the same time, just as there is complexity in social and biological systems, so also are there some underlying complexities in the global dialogue about timber management and the timber trade. This includes complexity in such things as the characteristics of forests and their ecological values in different regions of the world, local patterns of land ownership, the scientific and technological capacities of countries, the economic and political systems within countries, and the ethical, religious, and cultural values of citizens abroad. Moreover, there is complexity in ethical, political, and environmental decision-making globally, nationally, and individually, as this relates to forests and the timber

---

process, and so U.S. forest product output per unit of "roundwood" input has also increased significantly from approximately 8 pounds per cubic foot in 1900 to about 22 pounds per cubic foot in the early 1990s. In short, while total demand for wood products in the United States has risen steadily in the twentieth century and is quite high compared to other countries, the harvesting and manufacturing of wood has also become much more "efficient" because of such factors as advances in technology and increases in the value of "stumpage" or uncut timber. This data was supplied to me in 1997 by David J. Brooks, USDA Forest Service economist.

11. Plantations are forest stands primarily composed of trees established through planting or artificial seeding. While they may provide for nonproduction and nontimber values, the typical idea in this case is to grow trees on short rotations for timber production. Helms, *Dictionary of Forestry*, p. 137.

12. One of the most celebrated and tragic cases of forest activism internationally is that of Chico Mendes, the founder of the Brazilian rubber tapper's union, who in December 1988 was murdered by assassins hired by a group of ranchers and politicians in Acre, Brazil. Mendes had won international acclaim for his role in a nonviolent campaign to protect the Amazon rainforest so that rubber-tappers and others could continue to have an economic livelihood. Read *Fight for the Forest: Chico Mendes in His Own Words*, with additional material by Tony Gross, 2d ed. (London: Latin America Bureau, 1992). A well-known case of cultural destruction as a consequence of logging in rainforests is that of the Penan forest people of Sarawak, Eastern Malaysia, referred to in the Alastair Gunn article in this chapter.

trade. Environmental decisions are made in different ways, are typically grounded in somewhat different sources—whether religious, philosophical, economic, political, or scientific—and can legitimately produce different outcomes. The fact is that the way people arrive at and implement their environmental values about forests can differ dramatically among cultures and societies.[13] In light of this, judgments about the ethical aspects of the global timber trade and its environmental and social consequences must be evaluated carefully.

The character of some of the dialogue about the timber trade can be illustrated in the following overview. North American environmental groups have argued that the level and type of timber harvesting in tropical rainforests destroys ecologically critical habitat and thus contributes to a loss of global biodiversity as well as to a variety of other negative environmental effects. They link these changes to the destruction of communities and cultures, especially those of the remaining, indigenous forest peoples. They advocate that governments in other countries impose internal regulations on timber harvesting and the timber trade to ensure that these fragile and disappearing ecosystems and forest-dependent cultures are sustained by forest management and timber production over long-term periods.[14] The result, they conclude, will be long-term biodiversity protection and equitable attention to the interests and values of their citizens. On the other hand, some critics of domestic forest policies in countries like the United States, especially policies that reduce and restrict timber production in the developed countries, argue that such reductions unfairly shift the environmental burden of commodity production to the developing forest countries. They suggest that a responsibility to produce should accompany a propensity to consume, and that institutions, technologies, and decision-making processes in developed countries are better able to minimize the negative environmental consequences of timber commodity production than are those in developing nations. A continuation of timber harvests at recent high levels in the United States and other industrial forest countries is thus seen as more equitable than harvesting excessive amounts of timber in the third world. It is also asserted that this will reduce harmful environmental impacts in critical third world ecosystems.[15]

These kinds of viewpoints about the ethics of the global timber trade are reflected in the readings in this chapter from James Bowyer, Alastair Gunn, and Doug Daigle. Bowyer is a professor in the Department of Wood and Paper Science at the University of Minnesota. He argues that proposals for "marked reductions" in timber harvest from American forests, while based on important values like biological diversity or aesthetics, are limited by too local an environmental perspective. If the impacts of timber harvest are considered on a global scale,

13. Peter List and David J. Brooks, "Issues of Equity and Ethics in the Pacific Rim Timber Market," in *Proceedings of Forests and Society: Implementing Sustainability, A Workshop, December 5–7, 1997* (Triangle Lake: Oregon State University, 1998), pp. 19–30.

14. Some environmental groups were quite vocal in opposing new "free trade" policies being considered at the November 1999 Seattle meetings of the World Trade Organization. The groups argued that increasing "liberalization" of global trade in wood products in the form of a proposed "free logging agreement" would have disastrous environmental consequences for the remaining, original forests in countries like Malaysia. They predicted that there would be serious acceleration in logging as a result, and that the environmental policies of individual nations and international conventions in sustainable forestry could be negated by free-trade mechanisms.

15. List and Brooks, "Issues of Equity and Ethics."

restricting harvest in industrial countries that have "well-stocked forests" like the United States or Canada can mean "irresponsible and unethical regional environmentalism" in which environmental impacts are transferred to other parts of the world. Consequently, Bowyer recommends that environmentalists and forest preservationists in forest-rich but also heavy resource-consumption countries should rethink forest protectionism from a more global point of view. Alastair Gunn, a well-known environmental philosopher in New Zealand, also raises some acute questions for Western environmentalists who seek to preserve rainforests in other countries in order to protect biological diversity and maintain a source of valuable food, drugs, and other products. He first formulates some of the standard environmentalist objections to the logging and clearing of such forests, particularly in regard to Brazil, Malaysia, and Indonesia. He then counters that such arguments are often too simply constructed and irrelevant to the lives and desires of people "in the South." Northern environmental critics are seen to have "dirty hands" and not to deserve any standing as critics of forest development in southern countries, unless and until they make significant changes in their own trade policies and their extravagant, high-consumption lifestyles. The question of moral hypocrisy on the part of critics in industrial countries must be dealt with first, they imply, before Western environmentalists are accepted as credible witnesses against third world forest destruction.[16]

Finally, Doug Daigle, an environmental advocate and environmental ethicist with the Coalition to Restore Coastal Louisiana, evaluates some of the market shifts in the globalization of the timber trade and identifies some ethical issues related to these changes. He notes that the global timber business is becoming increasingly centralized in the hands of a small group of transnational timber companies and that this has occurred in tandem with the recent industry move from tropical to temperate and boreal forests. He argues that institutional arrangements between governments and the timber industry facilitate industrial exploitation of forest lands and that governments undervalue forests and their benefits. This results in the loss of irreplaceable biodiversity and ecosystems and has harmful effects on indigenous communities. He concludes that institutional resolution of these problems is limited in its effectiveness, and thus individuals must take upon themselves the task of resolving the problems by reducing their own wood consumption, becoming involved in wood recycling, and using alternative sources of fiber. In short, solutions to the social and environmental problems of the global timber trade can best result from taking responsible personal action in one's local wood market. Daigle advocates a consumer-based approach in which people individually pursue ethical actions where they already live. Through these kinds of behavior, more sustainable global forestry will result.

I would observe that while it may be true that individuals can be effective in changing wood markets on a local scale and that if enough consumers took such action significant changes would

16. An interesting argument made in Southeast Asia is that countries in that part of the world are currently much further along with regard to forest conservation and forest management than were Western industrialized countries when the latter destroyed and cleared their forests in past centuries. The conclusion inferred from this is that residents of the Western industrialized countries should thus not be quick to criticize the timber policies and practices of the newly industrializing nations. Of course, the difficulty with this argument is that the rate of forest destruction and conversion in the latter may still overwhelm conservation and management efforts, at least in some cases. But it also puts ethical criticism that crosses borders into a clearer historical context.

occur, the institutional barriers to sustainability must still be tackled as well. Institutional factors in the timber trade and large timber companies operate at a social and economic scale that can overwhelm individual practices and also lead to significant new opportunities for desirable individual behavior. Sometimes very small modifications of these barriers can more quickly bring about far-reaching and beneficial change.

James L. Bowyer

Responsible Environmentalism: The Ethical Features of Forest Harvest and Wood Use on a Global Scale

Proposals calling for a marked reduction in the harvest of wood from domestic forests are increasingly common. Such proposals are almost always based on concern for the environment and are frequently promoted as part of what is described as a new ethical standard for forest management. Arguments for restricting the domestic harvest of timber range from aesthetic issues, wilderness values, and tourism, to concerns about water quality and biological diversity, to the long-term sustainability of the timber harvesting enterprise itself.

Yet as important as these concerns are, the answer may not be as simple as reducing domestic timber harvest levels. If the impacts of timber harvest are viewed in a global, rather than a strictly local context, one is led to some rather sobering conclusions. What, for instance, is the global environmental impact of not harvesting domestic timber when harvesting could be done on a sustained basis? A careful examination of issues related to this question suggests that restrictive protection of local resources without considering global consequences can translate to irresponsible and unethical regional environmentalism, characterized by a transfer of environmental impacts to other regions, and even net negative environmental impacts for the world as a whole.

Population Growth and Raw Material Demand

Any effort to address environmental issues must be based on rational thinking and realistic assumptions, not the least of which are growing populations and the inevitable associated growth in raw material demand. Birth rates worldwide are declining, continuing a long-term trend. However, the current average difference in birth and death rates is substantial (28 vs. 10 per 1000 respectively), translating

James L. Bowyer, "Responsible Environmentalism: The Ethical Features of Forest Harvest and Wood Use on a Global Scale," *Forest Perspectives* 1(4) (Winter 1991): 12–14. Reprinted with permission of James L. Bowyer.

to a high rate of world population growth. Even assuming a significant further decline in birth rates, the current world population of 5.4 billion is expected to double within the next 100 years. Most of the increase will occur in developing regions of the world: Africa, Asia (excluding Japan), and Latin America. While the rate of population growth in the United States is relatively low, it is important to remember that populations continue to increase. With a current annual growth rate of 0.9 to 1.0 percent, some 2.3 to 2.5 million people are added to the U.S. population each year, creating the equivalent of an additional Los Angeles every three years.

While generally conscious that populations are growing both at home and abroad, there is much less awareness of the current situation regarding raw material sources and use. The United States economy is based on consumption of vast quantities of industrial raw materials. Moreover, the U.S. is a net importer of the majority of raw materials used to sustain the economy, and often by a substantial margin; the suppliers are frequently developing nations. Recent trends indicate that the level of importation is increasing.

Wood and wood fiber is used in very large quantities in the U.S., both in familiar forms such as poles, timbers, lumber, and plywood, and in less-known products such as moulded interior panels for autos, adhesives, paints, food additives, clothing, draperies, tires, and even ping-pong balls. Perhaps the most effective way to illustrate the importance of wood is to examine how much is used in relation to other materials. Annually, the U.S. uses roughly as much wood by weight as all metals, plastics, and Portland cement combined. In total, some 16.5 billion cubic feet of wood was consumed in the U.S. in 1987, representing consumption of 80.1 cubic feet per capita, continuing a steady upward trend in domestic wood use (Figure 1). Despite this magnitude of consumption, net growth in U.S. forests exceeds harvest by over 30 percent.

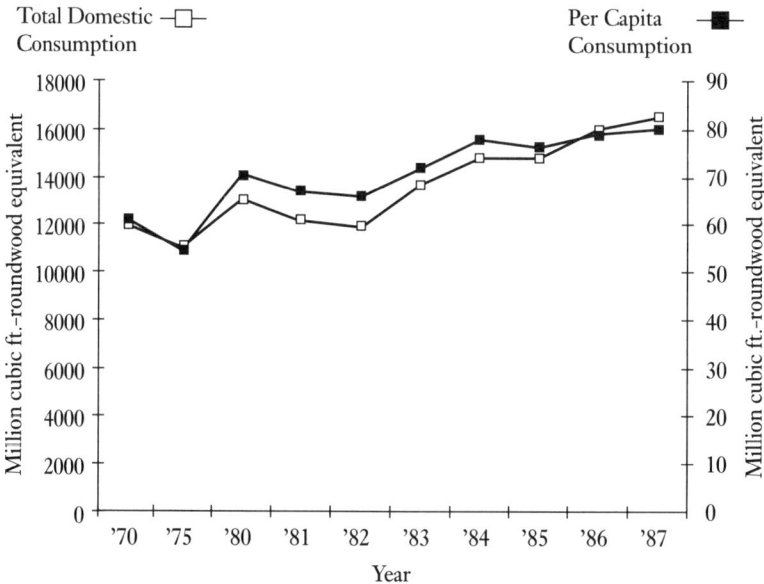

Figure 1: U.S. Consumption of Timber Products for Selected Years

Harvest Options for Domestic Forests

In view of the above figures, any decision to reduce the domestic harvest of timber has a number of economic, environmental, strategic, and ethical implications. It is important that various options for harvesting domestic timber, and the consequences of these options, be carefully considered. Four such options are explored below.

Shift to Nonwood Raw Materials

Given the tremendous quantities of wood used, any substitution of materials in order to reduce timber harvest will have to be massive.

Moreover, the materials substituted will be largely imported and nonrenewable, and in general, the gathering and processing of these substitute materials will result in the use of larger quantities of energy and more severe environmental impacts than will the use of wood. When materials are compared in relation to energy consumed in gathering, processing, and fashioning into a final product, wood compares very favorably with other materials. An evaluation of energy inputs involved throughout the process, from raw material extraction to finished product, is on the order of 70 times higher for aluminum than for an equal weight of lumber, and 17, 3.1, and 3 times higher for steel, brick, and concrete block respectively, than for wood.

A shift to nonwood raw materials is largely unacceptable, not only from an environmental perspective, but also from economic and equity perspectives. An increase in raw material imports would adversely affect the trade deficit as well as raise strategic questions—i.e, whether a world which has twice the current population will be willing to continue to export the level of resources it now does to the United States. With regard to equity, it is important to realize that when we, by design or default, elect to have raw materials gathered and processed elsewhere, we are in effect exporting the associated environmental impacts.

Use Wood—But Import Raw Material Needs

When considering this option, questions must be asked about where substitute wood might come from. Substitute wood could be obtained from one or more of several regions that have relatively abundant supplies: Canada, the Soviet Union, Central and South America, and Oceana.

Of these regions, only Canada, the Soviet Union, and Central and South America have large areas of well-stocked natural forests. There are also relatively small but expanding areas of plantation forests around the world which could (and likely will) supply part of our future wood needs.

Because of issues surrounding the harvest of tropical forests and the environmental stresses now felt in tropical regions, it is unlikely that the natural forests of Central or South America will contribute substantially to future U.S. demand for wood. Canada possibly could supply more of U.S. needs, though there are signs that production limits are being approached in at least some Canadian forests. It is the forests of the Soviet Union that are the most likely candidate as a source of supply, and these will undoubtedly be tapped by U.S. manufacturers in the future.

Importation of timber may be acceptable as a strategy for achieving some reduction in domestic timber demand. However, the same ethical and economic implications that are connected with increased use of imported nonwood materials largely apply to this option as well.

Reduce the Rate of Raw Material Consumption

When considering the rate of U.S. raw material consumption, it is easy to conclude that a reduction in the consumption rate, through taxation, voluntary conservation, or other means, will reduce pressure on the world's raw materials. Some reduction in domestic per capita consumption may be possible, but not likely. Additionally, it is important to remember that the U.S. population is still growing.

A likely doubling of world population in the next 70 to 100 years; a desire on the part of large segments of the world population for greater, rather than lesser, consumption of durable goods (e.g., eastern Europe); and the fact that even modest increases in the standard of living for people now without adequate shelter and other basic necessities will translate to relatively larger increases in raw material demand mean that the likelihood of reduced raw material use on a global scale is even less likely.

It can be argued that improved technology leading to more efficient processing and increased recycling will serve to reduce future raw material demand. Gains in both areas are likely. In order to maintain consumption of raw materials at current levels, however, it will be necessary to have current per capita consumption, assuming a doubling of world population.

Increase Recycling Activity

An increase in recycling of solid waste holds great promise for reducing demand for virgin raw materials. Recycling generally reduces impacts on the landscape and significantly reduces the amount of energy consumed in processing raw materials. Yet despite these advantages, the impact on current levels of raw material demand may be less than a cursory examination might indicate.

In the case of paper, the U.S. now recycles 29 to 31 percent of total consumption. The paper industry has set 40 percent as a recycling target by 1995, and it is widely believed that this target is achievable through large investments of capital and technological development. To reach a 50 percent recycling level will require considerable technology and systems development in collection, separation techniques, sheet formation, etc. Further, as the 50 percent level of recycling is approached, questions arise as to how many times a fiber can be recycled. From initial work at the University of Minnesota and elsewhere, it appears that for some products, a large proportion of virgin raw material will continue to be needed. For other products, fibers may be recyclable as many as four to nine times, and perhaps more. One thing that is clear is that each time a fiber is recycled it is degraded. Given current technologies, this progressive degrading of fiber likely means lower yields each time through the recycling loop as well as a secondary material use pattern that will divert fiber to a less demanding application with each reuse. This problem, and the extent to which it can be dealt with technologically, will define the limits to the recycling rate.

In any event, consider for a moment the impact of recycling 50 percent of paper. Because the current U.S. paper recycling rate is approximately 30 percent, the effect of a 50 percent rate would be to reduce pulpwood demand about 25 percent (20/70 with some decrease in yields due to increased recycling). Should twenty years be required to reach the 50 percent recycle rate, then expected increases in domestic population will blunt the favorable impact upon pulpwood demand. Under this scenario, and assuming no change in basic weights of paper, per capita consumption, or in net import figures, demand for virgin wood fiber should be about 12 to 13 percent lower twenty years hence than it is now at a 50 percent recycling rate.

As we struggle with what the appropriate levels of U.S. timber harvesting should be, we are faced with the fundamental question of whether a U.S. policy designed to create a pristine domestic environment through continued and increasing reliance on other regions of the world for heavy industrial activity is ethically and morally defensible. With respect to forests and the harvest of timber specifically, it is perhaps easy to conclude, in the absence of global or comprehensive thinking, that domestic harvest levels should be significantly reduced. Consideration of raw material options, and associated environmental impacts logically leads, however, to a much different conclusion.

When seeking to protect the environment, the lack of a global perspective can and does lead to what amounts to irresponsible and unethical regional environmentalism. As we enter what has been called a new era of forestry, we need to totally rethink our positions and approach to environmental issues with a global and comprehensive view. To do otherwise will ill serve both the world's environment and its people.

Alastair S. Gunn

Environmental Ethics and Tropical Rain Forests: Should Greens Have Standing?

Almost everyone in the developed world wants the logging of tropical rain forests to stop. Like Antarctica, they are said to be much too important and much too valuable to be utilized just for development and are said to be part of a global heritage. However, it is not that simple. People in the developing world consider our criticisms to be ill-informed, patronizing, and self-serving. We are seen as having "dirty hands." They hold that we neither have nor deserve moral standing as critics until we change our trade policies, rhetoric, and extravagant lifestyles.

Introduction

Almost everyone in the developed world (hereafter "the North") wants the logging of tropical rain forests to stop. Environmentalists argue

Alastair S. Gunn, "Environmental Ethics and Tropical Rain Forests: Should Greens Have Standing?" *Environmental Ethics* 16(1) (Spring 1994): 21–40. Reprinted with permission from Alastair S. Gunn and the Center for Environmental Philosophy, University of North Texas, Denton, Texas.

that at present rates of felling there will be no major tropical forests left within a few decades, that these forests contain most of the world's biological diversity, that they are the sources of many existing and potential foods, drugs, and other products, that millions of species are becoming extinct before they are scientifically described, that governments corruptly hand out logging concessions to relatives and friends, that the cultures of traditional peoples are being destroyed, and their standard of living greatly reduced, that the economic benefits of logging go primarily to elites, that the agriculture created on deforested land is unsustainable, and that tropical forests are needed to slow down climate change. Like Antarctica, they are said to be too important and valuable to be utilized just for development and are said to be part of a global heritage.

Brazil, Malaysia, and Indonesia especially have been the targets of criticism and, sometimes, protest. The Penan people of Sarawak, Eastern Malaysia, have become a symbol of the worldwide situation of hunter-gatherers. The Swiss environmentalist Bruno Manser, star of the movie *Blowpipes and Bulldozers*,[1] has been instrumental in bringing the Penan to world attention; in addition, pop star Sting has toured the world with an Amazonian tribal leader raising money and support to save Amazonian forests. The case against continued logging seems overwhelming to many in the North.

However, it's not that simple. For instance, much of the criticism presented by environmentalists is irrelevant to the lives and aspirations of people in the South, the vast majority of whom would be more at home living in San Diego or Sydney than in a rain forest: there are probably only a few hundred hunter-gatherers remaining in Asia. In this paper, I am concerned not so much with the truth of the claims made in the opening paragraph. True or not, it doesn't follow that publicizing them will change the world, largely because the governments and individuals in the North have "dirty hands" and neither have *nor deserve* standing as critics of the development process in the South until they change their trade policies, their rhetoric, and their extravagant lifestyles.

Ignoring the South

In late 1991, I spent three months in Southeast Asia, including a three-week visit to Malaysia; I concentrate in this paper on Sarawak because it has been a focus of anti-logging protest.[2]

Part of what I mean by "ignoring the South" is the fact that during a six-week visit to the United States in spring 1992 I presented versions of this paper several times and discussed the ideas in it with many people, all of whom were very opposed to the logging of tropical rain forests. When I asked them to specify *which* areas they were especially concerned about, apart from Amazonia, many mentioned Sarawak, yet very few had any idea at all of the location of Sarawak or any other areas of Southeast Asia where rain forest logging is taking place.

The view from Southeast Asia is very different from the view of the North, which to Asian people often seems ignorant, biased, hypocritical, patronizing and self-serving. We[3] are seen as having no concern for their affairs except when our self-interest is affected.

To illustrate, in the second half of 1991, a thick haze developed in areas of Sarawak and Sumatra, eventually spreading through much of Southeast Asia. Initially the haze was thought to be caused by forest fires in Sumatra and Kalimantan, though there seem to have been several factors. Some airports were closed for weeks, ships were lost at sea, and at times in the worst areas visibility was down to a few hundred meters. Although there was no natural cloud, I did not see the sun at all for three weeks in Kuala Lumpur and Singapore. Because the amount of sunlight reaching the ground was only about one third of normal, growth of rice and vegetable crops was reduced by about 20 percent. Some Malaysian hospitals registered marked increases in bronchial asthma and pneumonia in children and conjunctivitis in adults. Yet this disaster was almost completely ignored by the overseas media.

The Malaysian Prime Minister, Dr. Mahathir, stated at the opening of the ASEAN Economic Ministers' meeting in Kuala Lumpur on 7 October 1991 that the fires were causing much more damage than the controlled extraction of timber, while providing no benefits whatsoever; yet, "There has not been one squeak of protest from environmentalists of the North." Why, he asked, if the governments of rich countries are so concerned to save rain forests, did they not send teams of experts and heavy equipment that the poor countries of the region cannot afford? Where were the experts who had put out the oil fires in Kuwait with such skill and at such profit? "Perhaps it is because the haze does not spread to their countries. Perhaps it is because they cannot sound noble as they do when they champion the Penan." In response to what a television reporter called "a cynical question," whether Malaysia had asked for aid, Mahathir replied:

> We did not ask the people of the North to come to Malaysia to champion the cause of the Penan, but they came anyway. If they want to save the forests from burning they won't wait to be asked.[4]

Cynical or not, it got results. Almost immediately, the Indonesian government appealed for help in fighting the fires and eventually received offers from several countries.

Whose Version of the Facts?

A necessary condition of having standing to make moral judgments on any issue is a knowledge of the situation being judged. It is unfortunate that ignorance is often no barrier to people having opinions, in environmental as in other matters. The proper opinion for the ignorant is no opinion. However, the facts about rain forests are not easy to come by: a major problem in evaluating the arguments over logging is evaluating the conflicting factual claims on which they are founded. For instance, even Malaysian environmentalists[5] acknowledge that national parks are properly protected and that on paper both Federal and Sarawak State government forest management plans are some of the best in the world. Officially, the policy is rigidly enforced, and one independent study of an area in Malaysia showed that 91 percent of mammal and 77 percent of bird species persisted after selective logging had occurred.[6] However, critics charge that, in practice, logging is highly destructive because little attempt is made to enforce the policy, and that if present rates of cut are continued, "we can expect the primary forests in Sarawak to disappear in five to ten years' time."[7] Whom should we believe? How should we *decide* whom to believe?

Apart from selectively logged production forests, considerable areas are also clear-cut for conversion to palm oil and rubber plantations, orchards, and agriculture. The Malaysian government maintains that these uses are sustainable, just like the rice, softwoods, or dairy products grown in Bali, Canada, or New Zealand. In contrast, critics say that the plantations, especially, are environmentally damaging and not sustainable.

How are we to evaluate these claims? Despite the huge and growing literature on sustainability, there is no agreement on what precisely it means.[8] In fact, it ought to be possible for reasonable people to agree on a general account of sustainability in terms of types of land uses that can be continued without reducing the overall options for future generations. On this basis, experience has shown beyond all possible doubt that cattle ranching is unsustainable in former rain forests in Amazonia: by 1986, *all* the ranches established between 1965 and 1978 had been abandoned.[9] It is equally clear that rice and vegetable growing can continue indefinitely in deforested areas of Java and Bali. Presumably by now there is experience relevant to resolving the conflicting claims made about plantations. Whatever the conclusion, it is important to point out that removing forest to make land suitable for agriculture has happened everywhere. All over the world both sustainable *and* nonsustainable agriculture have just one thing in common: the land which it uses has been massively altered from its original state, whether forest, scrub, prairie, swamp, or estuary.

Meanwhile people have to live, and if logging were stopped immediately, the economies of Kalimantan and Sulawesi in Indonesia and Sarawak and Sabah in Malaysia would collapse. In Sarawak, which has a population of only 1.8 million, the state economy earned about $1 billion[10] in 1990 from log exports alone. However, critics charge that the economy in its present form provides relatively few benefits to ordinary people, and that native people such as the Penan, Kasan, Iban, and others suffer severe deprivation due to the destruction of their traditional resource base.

The Malaysian government's Federal Land Development Agency has settled hundreds of thousands of unskilled landless people on plantations. Again, the foreigner is at a loss to evaluate the success of this policy. For many years, the projects have provided an income comparable to that of middle-income urban workers as well as the opportunity for settlers to own their land and homes. Critics claim that housing and pay are poor and conditions dangerous. Certainly a great deal of pesticide is used, mostly paraquat. But even finding out who is at risk is difficult. According to one source,[11] 80 percent of the sprayers are women but an expatriate Malaysian (who asked not to be named) told me that he doubted this figure: because of an acute labor shortage, many plantation workers are illegal immigrants, nearly all of whom are male.

Who is the expert, and when experts disagree, who can decide between them? Governments of the South are constantly receiving advice from overseas. But what works here may not work there, and projects funded by outside agencies have often turned into expensive economic, environmental, and social disasters, such as the Aswan High Dam. There are lots of less dramatic examples.

Environmental experts from rich countries frequently generalize about life in the South in ways that they would not dream of generalizing about life in their own countries. For instance, a recent book from the highly respected Worldwatch Institute refers to "the wattle-and-daub villages and urban shanty towns where most of the Third World lives,"[12] a clause that cries out for deconstruction.

More generally, and perhaps on the basis of such confident stereotypic generalizations, we often set ourselves up as expert diagnosticians of the South's problems. The Worldwatch Institute in 1992 listed six "unmet human needs." Presumably calling them "*human* needs" is meant to indicate that they are universal. In addition to child malnutrition, lack of safe drinking water, preventable fatal childhood disease, and preventable fatal reproductive health problems in women, the list includes the facts that about 1 billion adults cannot read or write and that more than 100 million children of primary school age are not in school.[13] These are "needs" only within certain cultural contexts; yet we are meant to rate them on the same scale of urgency as conditions that are life-threatening, not just to humans, but to any animal.

I believe that we should generally accept that on social and environmental questions, local people know best; nevertheless, the selection of local experts is not a straightforward matter. Local people sometimes disagree with the development policies of their own governments. For instance, the New Zealand-assisted reafforestation project in Bukidnon, in the Philippines, is bitterly opposed by some locals; among other reasons, they fear that many small farmers will have their land confiscated, leaving them no option but to work as laborers in industrial forestry plantations.[14] Clearly there are different views about the appropriate direction of development. Critics argue that plantations destroy traditional life, force people into a cash economy, and lead to greater dependence on foreign markets. The Malaysian economy, they argue, should be self-sufficient, which means replanting forests, not industrial plantations.

The Sarawak State Government claims that the Penan are better off living a "modern" lifestyle in settled communities than as nomads. The Dayak leader, Dr. Patau Rubis, who is himself a minister in the State Government, believes that moving into the cash economy has saved his people from "self-destructive habits," and the headman of a Penan village, Kampung Jambatan Suai, is quoted as saying that his people "have been seeking a better life ever since they moved out of the jungle 70 years ago."[15] However, an article in *Singapore Business* takes the view that outside the "showplace" settlement near Mulu National Park, "the Penan live in poor conditions."[16] An exhibit on the lifestyles of traditional people in the Kuching Museum, Sarawak, paints a similar picture. Next to an exhibit of traditional longhouse and nomadic life, a notice states without comment that it is now government policy to persuade the Penan to abandon their nomadic lifestyle and become settled: "The series of photographs shows life in a typical Penan village." The forty pictures show a spartan, decrepit village inhabited by listless, sullen, and generally deprived-looking Penan glowering at the camera. Obviously, someone at the museum doesn't rate the policy very highly. Again, as a foreigner whose experience is limited to a brief tourist visit, I have no way of evaluating these views.

The role of shifting cultivators is itself disputed. The Sarawak government claims that slash and burn is practiced over 3.3 million hectares and is the main cause of forest degradation. Evelyne Hong, formerly of West Malaysia's Institut Masyarakat, says that the farmers clear less than 18,000 hectares of primary forest per year and that the practice must be sustainable because it has been going on for centuries.[17] Their role in the fires of 1991, and even the nature of the fires, is unclear. According to Indonesian government figures, 50,000 hectares of forest were destroyed. However, the Australian Rapid Assessment team found no evidence of any extensive fires in the area of East Kalimantan that it was able to visit in October, but rather a series of small fires, all intentionally lit, in forests, plantations, and farmland.[18] There is certainly evidence that major fires have begun as small fires deliberately lit by shifting cultivators, but logging and the 1991 drought (the worst in thirty years) help to create conditions that are conducive to fires getting out of hand, in which a cigarette butt or broken bottle can cause a major fire.[19]

Tropical Forests: Whose Heritage?

The Dutch did their best to suck Indonesia dry. Yet, Java's huge population is largely a legacy of the Dutch who by their extortionate tax system forced the rapid conversion of the island to farmland, thus enabling the population to increase from six million in 1825 to over 100 million today.[20] A friend said wryly that all the Dutch have bequeathed to his 90-percent Muslim country are some Heineken breweries. Now the Netherlands has banned the import of tropical timber. Such moves are often angrily rejected by local people, who claim that we have no business criticizing their policies.

Some people in the South take seriously the view that foreign environmental organizations are secretly funded by producers of softwood and non-timber building materials who hope to remove the cheap competition of rain forest timber. Many more consider anti-development arguments that begin with the premise that tropical forests are part of a global heritage to be attempts to promote Northern economic interests under the pretense of concern about the global environment:

> All sorts of campaigns are mounted by the richer countries against [destroying forests in order to generate] hydroelectricity, which have already developed their hydroelectric potential. Now of course the World Bank will be used to deprive poor countries of cheap hydroelectric power. Can we be blamed if we think that this is a ploy to keep us poor?[21]

They object very strongly to demands that their development strategies should be determined by our concerns about global warming and ozone damage. Most of the damage has been caused, and continues to be caused, by people in rich countries; brown people do not run much of a risk of skin cancer; in the tropics, climate change will be both less marked and less damaging to agriculture than in temperate countries. Yet, we expect people in the South to make sacrifices that are largely for our benefit.

The rhetoric of global heritage is, in fact, highly inappropriate. For there to be a shared heritage, there must be a *community*. A global heritage needs a global community in which resources are shared and decisions made by consensus. This is not how our world operates. If we are to have some say over tropical forests located in other sovereign states, we have to stop expropriating most of the world's resources and effectively excluding the South from decisions about Antarctica and the oceans. In other words, much more must be done than offering to cancel a few hundred million dollars of debt in return for not logging a few hundred square kilometers of forest.

Even when our criticisms are genuinely inspired by a desire to reduce human misery, we may be seen as lacking standing to make such criticisms. For instance, it is true that the economic benefits of development hare not been shared equally by the people of the South, and I share the view of critics, that it is wrong for a few to have immense riches while others are malnourished, homeless, or deprived of basic health care. Nevertheless, it is the colonialist countries themselves, and neocolonialist agencies such as the International Monetary Fund and the World Bank, that are largely responsible for both establishing and enriching the new elites in the South. In any case, many countries of the North present the same contrast *or even greater* contrasts between the enormously rich and the desperately poor. The income of the richest 20 percent of Indonesians is eight times that of the poorest 20 percent—but in the United States the rich earn twelve times more than the poor, and in France, thirteen times.[22] The United States Medicaid program—intended to provide free medical treatment for the poor—covers only 40 percent of the residents of the state of Georgia living below the federal poverty line; yet at any one time, 40 percent of the hospital beds in Georgia are empty.[23] In cities of grace, style, high culture, and enormous wealth—London, Sydney, Seattle, and Washington D.C.—homeless people wander the streets; there are so many beggars in Seattle that the city passed an "Aggressive Panhandling Law" proscribing them from excessively importuning passersby. I was solicited by far fewer beggars in Southeast Asian cities than in the cities just mentioned. Meanwhile, the six largest corporations in the United States, which have a combined market value of $376.41 billion, use up vast quantities of nonrenewable resources, and grossly pollute the Earth and its human inhabitants.[24]

Rich countries, then, are seen as hypocritical. We appeal to countries of the South to reduce their population growth: yet, over his or her lifetime each baby born in the North will consume many times the resources of a baby born in a poor country.[25] Even our environmentalists live fabulously rich lifestyles compared with the 30 million Indonesians who are below the official poverty line of $90 per year, and the millions more who earn less than $1 per day.[26] When Indonesians see foreigners, they see people like me whose idea of economy is a $15 hotel room. Even Malaysians, whose per capita income will be up to the lower end of the OECD nations within twenty years, consider foreigners to be generally rich, and are mostly happy to go along with forest exploitation because they see it as the basis for their increasing prosperity. Malaysia's *Vision 2020* plan calls for the country to become "fully developed" by 2020. Singapore's Strategic Economic Plan calls for a per capita GNP equal to that of the United States by 2030, and even on the lowest growth scenario, the achievement of the level of the Netherlands by 2017. Given our prosperity, any views we might have of their development programs should take account of these aims.

However, it is generally considered in the North that wide-scale industrialized development is impossible. Alan Miller's is a representative view:

> We may ethically [desire] the extension of our own standard of living to less privileged people in the developing world, but the very fact that the 5 percent of the Earth's population now living in North America consumes almost one third of total global resources demonstrates the limitations of such a fantasy of global consumption. If only 15 percent of the total world population consumed food, fiber, energy, and raw materials at the rate that the U.S. Americans and Canadians do . . . virtually nothing would be left for the remaining 85 percent of the world's people. Furthermore . . . capital stocks and mineral resources could never supply the developing world with the same materials infrastructure needed for its rapid development to advanced industrialization. There is simply not enough steel, lumber, mineral resources, and energy available to enable developing nations to replicate the Western systems.[27]

While there is some truth in this view, it takes no account of the reality of the conditions of life in the South: the issue is much more complex than such a simplistic comparison suggests. One cannot just extrapolate without qualification to the South from what is used (and wasted) to provide a given level of material culture for people living in areas with wide seasonal variations in climate, many of whom reside in sprawling, widely separated cities, where the infrastructure and industries are already in place, and are therefore inefficient. True, it seems very likely that our way of life cannot be sustained even within the North for much longer, let alone exported globally. I was born in 1945; perhaps my children and I will be the only generations in the history of the Earth to spend our whole lives in a society where the meaning of life is shopping. But what are we to conclude from this state of affairs? Surely not that we are licensed to tell everyone else what material standard of living they should aim at.

Nations of the South view outside attempts to influence their policies as attempts at recolonization,[28] for example, our restrictive trade practices and our unwillingness to share innovations in science and technology. Former colonial nations are seen as especially lacking in standing because they have caused massive damage both to their own environments and to those of their former colonies in order to enrich themselves. As early as 1839, Darwin noted that "Wherever the European had trod, death seems to pursue the aboriginal."[29] It was the British who introduced the plantation system into Asia, and indeed in some cases the crops: tea in India and rubber in Malaysia. As Dr. Mahathir notes:

> When the British ruled Malaysia they burnt millions of acres of Malaysian forests so that

they could plant rubber. The timber was totally wasted because in those days nobody wanted Malaysian timber. . . . Malaysians got nothing from the felling of the timber. In addition, when the rubber was sold practically all the profit was taken to England.[30]

Yet, Britain now condemns Malaysia for continuing the British policy of converting forest to plantation.

Our reply is often an admission that we made mistakes, that we sacrificed irreplaceable natural wonders in order to pursue economic goals, but that we have now seen the error of our ways. However, this sort of argument tends to be seen as patronizing: "When you're older and wiser like me, you'll be glad I warned you against making the same mistakes as I did." In any case, it is what we do that counts, not what we profess to believe. As Aristotle noted, "Mere wishes or intentions remain in the vague, and even the unjust *pretend* that they wish to act justly."[31] For instance, the United States, where most people eat more protein than their bodies can absorb, annually imports well over $500 million worth of beef from Brazil alone.

It is not as if we rich countries are even now setting a very good example of looking after our own environments. Politicians in the South are struck by our wasteful habits, such as the amount of food thrown away in restaurants, the air conditioning left on when no one is at home, and the depletion of underground water resources in Southern California to maintain golf courses and artificial lakes around luxury hotels. In August 1991, Bruno Manser, who by then was heading an international rain forest organization, chained himself to the top of a utility pole in London. The Malaysian Deputy Prime Minister Ghafar Baba commented:

> Why did he chain himself to an electric pole? It is obvious that there are not many trees in London, nor are there many trees in other similar big cities. So, why should we listen to these Western people who do not themselves practice conservation?[32]

This criticism, to be sure, is not true of serious environmentalists, and many of the same people in the North who want to end logging in tropical forests also want their own forests to be preserved. Still, few developed countries have more than 20 percent of their original forest cover. Japan, alone, far exceeds this percentage, but its citizens' affluent lifestyle is maintained only by massive imports of timber and food, and there is a major worry about the future of its plywood industry as Sarawak phases out exports of raw logs. Millions of tons of topsoil in North America, Europe, and Australia are blown or washed away every year, or poisoned with chemicals. New Zealand is often considered to be a "clean and green" country, and so it is in many ways; yet almost all its sustainably farmed land is former forest or wetland. In Britain, attempts at commercial afforestation are strenuously resisted by the same environmentalists who oppose tropical logging because they do not wish to lose the parklike English countryside. Meanwhile, to meet the ever increasing demand for paper products, Britain imports ever increasing amounts of rain forest timber.[33]

Should Northern Greens Have Standing?

When people in the South reject our criticisms of their policies—usually politely, but sometimes angrily—they are not just saying that they will do as they like and that we should shut up. Their position has a sound moral base, which is that we have no business criticizing their policies.

Questions about the standing of a person to judge morally the actions of others arise in at least three ways. First, I may claim that the behavior in question is not your business because it is part of my private life—for instance, in Mill's sense of behavior that affects no one except the agent, or which has only trivial effects on others. Or it may be the legitimate concern of some other persons, but not of yours: my family or my church have an interest in my religious activities that others do not. That is, it is simply not your place to comment on my religious beliefs or church attendance, unless, for example, they cause nontrivial harm to others. Mill's harm principle is not the only way to draw the line, of course, but only the most authoritarian moralist insists that *every* aspect of the lives of others is his or her business.

If we wish to influence environmental management in the South, we will have to establish standing in this sense. For instance, we could try to show that their policies are unjustifiably causing nontrivial harm to other people. Or we could try to demonstrate to them that they are unjustifiably destroying things of considerable intrinsic value. Or perhaps we could try to convince them that we know better than they do what is in their best interests, even though given the history of colonial exploitation, this approach is unlikely to succeed. Whatever moral basis we may think we have, we need to do more than merely assert that they ought to change their ways.

Second, it may be claimed that our dirty hands disqualify us as moral critics. The vice of hypocrisy consists in advocating or professing a commitment to behavior but not following one's own precepts. A "successful" hypocrite maintains credibility by concealing the discrepancy between what he or she says and does. The story is, of course, more complicated. For instance, an adequate account of hypocrisy needs to distinguish it from socially understood and accepted forms of saying one thing while intending to do something else, as in games of bluff or in societies where it is polite to make extravagant offers of assistance that no one would dream of accepting. However, I firmly resist the temptation to begin with such an account, noting merely that central to hypocrisy is the attempt to deceive. Hypocrisy is wrong for the same sorts of reasons that lying and deception are wrong: it is coercive; it undermines trust; if widely practiced, it is damaging to the social fabric, and so on.[34] Not only are we not morally justified in preaching to the South principles that we do not practice and have no intention of practicing ourselves, but we have a moral obligation to refrain from doing so.

It may be said that I am being too harsh in making such sweeping charges of hypocrisy. Someone may fail to notice the discrepancy between the principles that they preach to others and their own behavior. They may not be aware that the rich countries cause most of the environmental damage, such as ozone depletion and global warming. Perhaps they do not realize that in driving a car to the grocery store to buy a liter of milk they are wasting over 99.9 percent of the energy used. Or they may know these facts, but fail to connect them with their strictures on the behavior of others. Ignorance may be justifiable, or it may be a form of self-deception, as when someone resolutely avoids finding out facts which would be unwelcome. For instance, suppose that a university requires all instructors to have their students complete course evaluations, but allows instructors to design their own evaluation forms. A sexist or racist professor may profess to be very fair in his dealings with students, but it may not seem necessary to him to include a question on fairness, and thus he will not discover that he discriminates. If this omission is genuinely due to ignorance, is it immoral? Whatever we make of this case, I suggest that there is a continuum from honest and excusable ignorance through deliberate hypocrisy and that in educated societies the environmental ignorance mentioned above is near or at the highly culpable end of the scale.

It is true that the acceptability of an ethical view ought to be independent of the sincerity of the person who is presenting it. However, we do not trust people whom we discover to be hypocrites, just as people in the South do not trust rich outsiders. "Unsuccessful" hypocrites lack moral credibility—for instance, parents who drink or smoke while preaching the evils of drugs to their children—because they exhibit precisely the behavior of which they profess to disapprove. Certain high profile American religious leaders who had sought to project a general air of moral righteousness and publicly condemned the sins of others were completely discredited when the details of their sexual behavior were revealed. Such persons, because they have demonstrated a complete contempt for morality, simply have no right to tell others how they should live. They have ruled themselves out of the ethical debate because they refuse to play by its rules. Perhaps their credibility can be rehabilitated if they show clear evidence of moral improvement, though not if it seems to be just a result of getting caught (or getting AIDS).

A third respect in which one might lack standing is a matter of motives. If I advise or exhort you to behave in certain ways because (I claim) it is your duty or in your best interest to do so, you are entitled to assume that my choice of advice or exhortation is based on a sincere conviction about what *really* is your duty or in your interests. If you come to believe that my real motive is to benefit myself, I lose standing. For instance, if I set up business as Acme Computer Consultants, you will expect me to give you independent purchase advice. But if you discover that I am a really a local distributor for a line of products, you will no longer trust me to be impartial.

Romancing the Stone Age

Any ways of life that turn out to be sustainable for people in developed countries will presumably be very much less wasteful than our present ones. However, I know of very few environmental philosophers who make any attempt to live a much simpler life than the average suburbanite, let alone follow Callicott's advice on "the ethical question on what to eat":

> Purists like Leopold prefer . . . to hunt and consume wildlife and to gather wild plant foods, and thus to live within the parameters of the aboriginal human ecological niche. Second best is eating from one's own orchard, garden, henhouse, pigpen, and barnyard. Third best is buying or bartering organic foods from one's neighbors and friends.[35]

To the extent that traditional societies such as hunter-gatherers lived sustainably—and presumably those that have existed for thousands of years must have been sustainable—they have much to teach us. However, it is not their specific skills that we need—who can live off the land in a city?—so much as the principles behind the ways of life in such societies. Whether or not these are articulated and consciously pursued, they will include an appreciation of limits, an acknowledgment of ecological necessities, a willingness to share resources, and a recognition that we are not the owners of the Earth to do with it as we like.

However, environmentalists from rich countries who write in praise of the simple life often come across as deluded Romantics.

Consider this nonsense, written by a teacher who decided to build himself a woodland cabin in Massachusetts:

> My house was decidedly primitive—had no running water or electricity—but there was a satisfying, elemental comfort about life there . . . I was living a sort of "Third World" existence. . . . I came to relish the elemental experience of hauling water, trimming the wicks of oil lamps, and cooking over a camp stove or open fire.[36]

Yet, another European "discovery"! Of course, he continued to work as a teacher, and when he got bored with playing at being poor, he drove off to have showers and meals at friends' houses, or to go to concerts and the ballet in Boston. The family seems to have had an in-built capacity for self-delusion: his brother Hugh "once won an award for a series of poems he wrote about the experiences of a survivor of Hiroshima."[37]

No doubt this example is extreme; still, as one author notes, admiration of a greatly simplified low entropy lifestyle seems to be typically a "post-affluent" phenomenon: "Only those who have been reared in affluent suburbs can rebel against overconsumption and the banality of materialism." In contrast, he quotes a welfare rights organizer, speaking to a group of young ecology radicals: "We will have some difficulty understanding one another, for our welfare mothers want what you are rejecting."[38]

Rather tentatively, I suggest that the type of oversimplistic value distinctions criticized above reflect distinctions at an epistemological level, for instance, the common division of cultures into "Western" and "Eastern." This division is unfortunate, for a number of reasons: I briefly discuss two here.

First, in the writings of many deep ecologists, as Ramachandra Guha notes, "Complex and internally differentiated religious traditions—Hinduism, Buddhism, and Taoism—are lumped together as holding a view of nature as believed to be quintessentially biocentric."[39] This view of Eastern philosophies (and day-to-day cultural practices) is, as he points out, romantic, monistic, and simplistic. I might add that to talk of a monolithic "Western culture" is equally crass. The Basque independence organization ETA has put out a "culture map" of Europe which indicates the many and diverse cultures of the region, the many different languages, artistic traditions, and so on.

It is both intellectually obtuse and insulting to lump all "non-Western" cultures together. The following story, for whose truth I cannot vouch since I was not present, illustrates this point well. A philosopher was presenting a conference paper about the relevance of Native American culture to environmental ethics. At the end of his presentation he was severely criticized by a young woman of Native American extraction. As any introductory anthropology text will make clear, the many groups who had lived in North America before the Europeans came were very diverse, she said, and he had no business talking about "Indian culture." There were hundreds of different languages, religions, and ways of life. There were societies that were patriarchal and some that were matriarchal; some that were peaceful and egalitarian and others that were warlike, who tortured their prisoners of war and took slaves. There were nomads, cliff dwellers, city builders, hunter-gatherers, artisan and trading cultures, and others that depended largely on banditry. They did *not* all spend their time praying to the buffalo and the bear prior to killing and eating them.

More prosaically, what happens outside the North tends to get lumped together by aggregating statistics from dozens of different countries, each regionally diverse, as if they were all collected by identical means and as if all measured the same phenomena by the same measuring stick. According to the Worldwatch Institute, more than one billion people survive on less than $1 a day.[40] Nevertheless, most people—especially poor people—in the South live their lives only partly in the cash economy, and in any case foreign exchange rates are largely irrelevant to poor people, because they are determined by factors such as the price of internationally traded goods and a country's level of indebtedness. The official exchange rates which are used to calculate per capita income are, therefore, not an indication of purchasing power. There is no comparison between the food that a person with "$1" ends up with in Los Angeles and rural Java. Thus, dollar comparisons overemphasize the gap between people on different parts of the Earth.

A second reason for rejecting the simplistic distinction is that it doesn't fit the facts. As one writer notes:

> When people involved in the management of protected areas use these terms [*traditional, native, indigenous*], the distinction they seem to want to make is between those who live harmoniously (in a strictly ecological sense) with their immediate environment and those who don't. In the current management literature it is too often presumed that traditional societies, native peoples, and indigenous peoples do; modern societies, colonists, and other non-indigenous peoples don't.[41]

As I noted earlier, we have much to learn about sustainability from traditional peoples. Nonetheless, the myth of "the primitive conservationist" cannot be sustained in the light of such evidence as wasteful and environmentally destructive Stone Age megafauna hunting practices in North America, Madagascar, New Zealand, and other areas, and the damage caused by tribal peoples' pigs, goats, and sheep.[42]

Is There a Role for Foreigners?

Local people's objections to logging are often said to be a result of improper foreign interference. This claim was a major theme in the Sarawak elections in late September 1991—in which all anti-logging candidates were decisively defeated—with one cabinet minister advising voters to "ignore Westerners instigating natives to set up timber blockades."[43]

Again, it is hard to know how to evaluate these claims—everyone in all countries, given half a chance, tries to blame their problems on foreigners. Penan people themselves certainly reject the claim that their protests are instigated by foreigners: "It is only the foreigners who bother to come and spend time with us."[44]

One thing is quite clear, though: almost no one, least of all Malaysian environmental groups, welcomes public criticism or anti-logging protests by foreign individuals or non-governmental organizations. Such activities are useless, partly because, as a Singapore journalist puts it, "Pressure tactics and western style straight talking and logic do not work in Asia, much less in former colonies."[45] No doubt they are often counterproductive, even in terms of their own objectives. Eight foreign environmentalists entered Sarawak in July 1991, posing as tourists, and then proceeded to stage protests, including chaining themselves to cranes in a log pond. They were all arrested, charged with trespass, and sentenced to short prison terms.

> In the end, what became of the issue? The foreigners were seen as being persecuted by the repressive Malaysian government that violates human rights to protest. The real issues—the rights of native people, the merits

or otherwise of government policy—were pushed into the background.[46]

This case is reminiscent of the moral outrage in Australia and New Zealand at the hanging in Malaysia of two Australians and at the death sentences (later commuted) originally passed on New Zealanders, Lorraine and Aaron Cohen, in all cases for importing heroin. Now it is really impossible for anyone who can read to enter Malaysia (or Singapore) without knowing the penalties for drug offenses—even Australians who may not have noticed the warnings printed in their passports—since they are emblazoned on entry forms, presumably to allow the truly ignorant one last chance to flush their stash down the toilet. However, the fact that Australians and New Zealanders do not regularly protest about Malaysian drug laws presumably suggests to Malaysians that we do not care whether Malaysians are executed or flogged for drug offenses, but that we want foreigners who freely choose to import narcotics into Malaysia to be treated differently.

Local Greens apparently do not share the widespread admiration for Bruno Manser. The Malaysian environmentalist quoted earlier (note 10) said, "He *probably* has good intentions, but he has really become like a white adventurer, a Tarzan." The media emphasis on his role has made it look as if the Penan are the only people affected by logging—in fact, now only about 300 to 400 of the 9,000 Penan live as hunter-gatherers—and has also "made them look stupid" because of the exaggerated leadership role attributed to Manser. The video *Blowpipes and Bulldozers* presents him as a romantic outlaw, dividing his time between playing his panpipes, recording his observations of the picturesque local flora and fauna (including the local people), and organizing the Penan, before being "smuggled out." Presumably the government was prepared to tolerate him up to a point, for it is hard to believe that he was really a fugitive for several years in a state which waged a successful campaign against armed and highly organized Communist guerrillas not so long ago and where Swiss environmentalists—and Australian film crews—stand out.

The major reason why foreign individuals and governments should avoid public ranting, though, is that most people in the South think that we have no business telling them how to run their affairs. National sovereignty is taken very seriously in states that have won their independence only comparatively recently. This distaste for foreign interference may be difficult for people in the rich countries of Europe and the British Commonwealth to understand, since, unlike the United States (where even many Americans seem to have forgotten their revolutionary origins), we did not "win" our independence. Although all the countries of Southeast Asia except Thailand were European colonies and also suffered under Japanese occupation, none were colonial settler states. We should try to imagine how we would feel if we had gained independence only a few decades ago, perhaps after a bloody war, as in Indonesia. We should imagine too that, like Malaysia or Singapore, only thirty years ago our country was desperately poor, but has since made great progress economically; unlike almost everywhere else in the world, people in Southeast Asia enjoy constantly rising living standards as measured by improvements in health, life span, infant mortality, literacy, and per capita income. Finally, we should imagine that about 99 percent of our population is of non-European origin. Then we should consider how we would react to our former rulers telling us how to run our affairs.

There is a lesson here for those countries that are no longer colonies, but whose populations are overwhelmingly of European extraction. There are direct parallels between the rights of the people of a former colony and those of a colonized minority. When Native Americans, Australian Aborigines, or New Zealand Maori demand control over their own resources, they are asserting an identity. The remark by the Chief Minister of Sarawak that "the forests are our heritage and we will use [them] to benefit our people and not because some Western countries are short of oxygen due to their own environmental pollution"[47] will strike a chord with colonized indigenous people everywhere.

Conclusion

As I hope I have made clear, I do not believe that people in the North have any right to dictate environmental policy to people in the South. However, if they do wish to have an influence over the environmental policies of the South, they should certainly not go egotripping off to protest in Sarawak. Rather, they should look at their own responsibilities. International trade is largely dominated by the North. For instance, almost everyone agrees that the world would be a better place if narcotic drugs were not produced. But how much effort do the governments of the North make on the demand side? South American and Asian farmers who produce the raw material for cocaine and heroin would not be growing it if no one were buying. Indeed, cash cropping is itself largely a product of colonialism. If we want the growers—who in any case receive only a tiny fraction of the street price—to stop producing for our markets, we should obviously offer them economically acceptable alternatives, rather than simply assuming that we have a right to dump paraquat all over them from helicopters.

We in the North should also stop preaching a simple life to the South, or if we can't stop preaching, at least live at the level we prescribe for them, and acknowledge that *of course* people in the South have a right to a standard of living equal to whatever level we believe we are entitled to claim for ourselves. We should demonstrate a commitment to global justice by responding to requests from poorer countries for technological and other assistance in ways that they choose, for projects that they see as necessary. We do have a great deal of expertise to offer in areas such as environmental engineering, agriculture, and public health. Although, as I noted above, it is not always easy for foreigners to identify local needs, it is not impossible. The needs of local people can be identified basically by asking them what they want. A good example is the work of the engineers' organization, Water for Survival, which donates technical expertise, materials, and skilled labor for water projects in many areas of the South. These usually involve the provision of safe, conveniently located drinking water supplies at village level and are undertaken in response to requests from local people.

Finally, we should stop making self-serving claims about "global heritage" that amount to a demand that the South stop developing.

Notes

1. Produced by the Australian organization Gaia Films. Mansa lived with the Penan for several years and took part in their protests against logging of the forest areas that had traditionally been their homes. The movie, which is undoubtedly sincerely intended, is almost laughably romantic in places: maidens in sarongs frolic under waterfalls and the sun seems always (in a rain forest!) to be casting dappled patterns of light and shade on the forest floor. It has been criticized by Malaysian environmentalists as giving far too much attention

to Manser's role: see [discussion of Manser later in this essay].

2. Information in this section is drawn from newspapers in Singapore (*Straits Time*), Malaysia (*New Straits Times, Star*), and Indonesia (*Jakarta Post*) September and October 1991, and Malaysian television news, 7 October 1991.

3. Throughout this paper, "we" means "people in the North," unless otherwise indicated.

4. Certainly, the Penan are a sensitive issue. When *Time* ran a cover story on the demise of tribal peoples, a section on the Penan was blacked out in copies sold in Malaysia. Eugene Linden, "Lost Tribes, Lost Knowledge," *Time*, 23 September 1991, pp. 38–46.

5. The views of Malaysian environmentalist organizations are available via books such as Evelyne Hong, *Natives of Sarawak* (Penang: Institut Masyarakat, 1987); S. M. Mohd Idris, ed., *The Battle for Sarawak's Forests* (Penang: Sahabat Alam Malaysia, 1989); Philip Hurst, *Rainforest Politics* (London: Zed Books, 1990); and from newsletters of organizations such as Greenpeace and Friends of the Earth.

6. A. P. Johns, "Tropical Forest Primates and Logging: Can They Coexist?" *Oryx* 17 (1983): 114–18.

7. "Sarawak: Who Are You Fooling?" *Utusan Konsumer* 236 (August 1991): 6. This criticism is echoed by Nirmal Ghosh, "Sarawak and the Environmental Bogey," *Business Times* (Singapore), 5–6 October 1991.

8. One of the referees of this article for *Environmental Ethics* saw a concern with the definition as "a cultural tradition beginning with the shift to literacy." However, an obsession with definition and the supposed difficulties of getting it right seems to me to be an unfortunate legacy of 1950s analytical philosophy, and a worrying sign of the slide of environmental ethics into what John Passmore (personal communication) refers to as scholasticism. Evidently, a balance is needed.

9. R. J. A. Goodland, "Environmental Aspects of Amazonian Development Projects in Brazil," *Interciencia* 11 (1986): 16–24.

10. All figures are in U.S. dollars. Information in this and the following paragraph from A. Balasubramaniam, ed., *Issues in Environmental Education in ASEAN* (Singapore: Friedrich-Naumann-Stiftung, 1986) and Hurst, *Rainforest Politics*.

11. Anonymous Malaysian environmentalist quoted in *ECO Newsletter*, December 1991.

12. Lester R. Brown et al., *Saving the Planet* (New York: W. W. Norton, 1991). The six ASEAN nations—Brunei, Indonesia, Malaysia, Philippines, Singapore, Thailand—which have a population of over 320 million and contain a huge proportion of the Earth's biodiversity, get a total of four references in the index of this book, versus fifteen references to the United States. Indeed, Brunei, Malaysia, and Singapore are not indexed at all, unlike Cleveland, Davis (California), San Jose, and Seattle, each of which gets one mention.

13. Lester R. Brown, *State of the World* 1992 (New York: W. W. Norton, 1992), pp. 4–5.

14. David Robie, "Cloud Over Bukidnon Forest," *New Zealand Listener*, 22 April 1989, pp. 22–23, 35.

15. Kalimullah Hassan, "Not His Uncle's Man," *Straits Times*, 6 October 1991; James Ritchie, "A Better Future for the Penan," *New Straits Times*, 3 October 1991.

16. Nirmal Ghosh, "Jungle Fever in Sarawak," *Singapore Business*, October 1991, p. 36.

17. Ghosh, "Jungle Fever," p. 28.

18. Reported in *Jakarta Post*, 29 October 1991.

19. Dr. S. Martopo, Director, Research Centre for Environmental Studies, Gadjah Mada University, Indonesia, personal communication.

20. For detailed discussion of the points touched on in this section, see *Our Common Future*.

21. Mahathir, quoted in "Boycott of Tropical Timber."

22. Brown, *State of the World*, p. 138.

23. Reported in *Atlanta Journal-Constitution*, 7 April 1992.

24. According to *Financial World*, April 1992, the top six are in the following order: Exxon, Philip Morris, General Electric, Wal-Mart, Merck, and Coca-Cola. The entire external debt of all Asian countries in 1989 was $369.02 billion. In the same year, India's GNP was $287.38 billion, while the GNP

of Indonesia, Malaysia, the Philippines, Singapore, and Thailand together was $251.86 billion. (Figures from World Resources Institute, *World Resources 1992–93* [New York and Oxford: Oxford University Press, 1992]). It is hard to believe that the economies of these Asian countries were less sustainable, more environmentally damaging, and less focused on meeting basic human needs, than Philip Morris, Exxon, and the rest.

25. North Americans are not, of course, the only overconsumers. For instance, "Per capita, Australians and New Zealanders consume about seventeen times as much of the world's resources as people in the poorest nations." Ann Graeme, "Environmental Choice: The Green Dilemma," *Forest and Bird* [New Zealand] 266 (November 1992), p. 19.

26. As I note later, the resources actually available to poor people in the South are not accurately measured by adding up their cash income and translating it into an internationally convertible currency.

27. Alan S. Miller, *Gaia Connections* (Savage, Md.: Rowman & Littlefield, 1991), p. 83.

28. The following quotation from Mahathir is typical: "We hope people do not latch on to causes and crusades in order to justify political and economic re-colonization." "Malaysia's Growth Model a Success," *New Straits Times*, 27 September 1991.

29. *The Voyage of the Beagle*, quoted in Alfred W. Crosby, *Ecological Imperialism* (New York: Cambridge University Press, 1986), p. vii.

30. Letter from Mahathir to D. Abercombie, August 15, 1987, quoted in INSAN, *Logging Against the Native of Sarawak* (Petaling Jaya: Institute of Social Analysis, 1990).

31. Aristotle, *Ethics* X 8.

32. Examples quoted in *New Straits Times:* "States Urged to Draw Up Labour Plan," 25 September 1991; "Boycott of Tropical Timber 'Not the Solution,'" 26 September 1991, "Rich Nations Told to Curb their Consumption," 27 September 1991.

33. Norman Myers, *The Primal Source* (Boulder: Westview Press, 1983).

34. Sissela Bok, *Lying* (New York: Pantheon Books, 1987).

35. J. Baird Callicott, "Animal Liberation: A Triangular Affair," *Environmental Ethics* 2 (1980): 336.

36. John Hanson Mitchell, *Living at the End of Time* (Boston: Houghton Mifflin, 1990), pp. 6–18. As I understand it, the rural women who in many countries spend several hours each day hauling water do not find this "elemental experience" especially rewarding.

37. Ibid., p. 56.

38. Norman J. Faramelli, "Environmental Quality and Social Justice," in Ian G. Barbour, ed., *Western Man and Environmental Ethics* (Reading, Mass.: Addison-Wesley, 1970), p. 191.

39. Ramachandra Guha, "Radical American Environmentalism and Wilderness Preservation: A Third World Critique," *Environmental Ethics* 11 (1989): 76.

40. Brown, *State of the World*, p. 4. Most of the points that follow are taken from Ziauddin Sardor, *Science, Technology and Development in the Muslim World* (London: Croom Helm, 1977).

41. David Harmon, "Cultural Diversity, Human Subsistence, and the National Park Ideal," *Environmental Ethics* 9 (1987): 156.

42. See for instance George Uetz and Donald Lee Johnson, "Breaking the Web," *Environment* 16, no. 10 (December 1974): 31–39.

43. "20 pc Ruling for Sarawak Logger," *New Straits Times*, 25 September 1991.

44. Ghosh, "Jungle Fever," p. 38.

45. Ghosh, "Sarawak."

46. See note 10.

47. "20 pc Ruling."

Doug Daigle

Globalization of the Timber Trade

Regardless of their ecological differences, all of the world's forests are now joined in a single global market. For those concerned with saving native forests, it is vital to understand not only patterns of development that affect ecosystems but also the flows of trade that connect and fuel these patterns. The process of globalization can be seen most clearly in the Pacific Rim, where both the world's fastest growing economies and the bulk of its remaining forests are to be found. (It is understood here that *forests* refers to native forests, which includes both old-growth or virgin forests and second-growth areas that have an indigenous natural character as opposed to an intensely managed one.)

Transformation of the Timber Trade

Two major shifts have occurred as a result of globalization of the timber trade, a process marked by increasing centralization of the

Doug Daigle, "Globalization of the Timber Trade," in *Environmental Ethics and the Global Marketplace*, ed. Dorinda G. Dallmeyer and Albert F. Ike (Athens: University of Georgia Press, 1998), 153–64. Reprinted with permission from The University of Georgia Press.

timber industry into a smaller group of large transnational corporations. The first shift in market dominance has been a replacement of raw logs by wood chips and pulp. Spectacular growth in the wood fiber trade—an increase by more than 300 percent since 1960—has been matched by a surge in pulp processing. In 1960, wood chips amounted to less than 10 percent of the fiber trade; by 1990, that amount had risen to 54 percent (Hagler 1993). Wood chips are particularly advantageous for ocean trade, where the economics of shipping favor pulp and chips over raw logs, even when the latter are ridiculously cheap, as in Canada.

This shift has developed in tandem with the industry's move from tropical to temperate and boreal forests as major sourcing areas. "Substitutability" of wood for pulp and chips allows comparable utilization of different species from different forest types. Nigel Dudley summarized this development in his report, *Forests in Trouble*, compiled for the World Wildlife Fund in 1992: "Changes in the structure and technology of both forestry and timber utilizations are causing major changes to the ways in which forests are used. In general, manufacturers can use a far wider range of species, ages, and qualities of trees, and demand is moving away from timber to pulp and cellulose. The increasingly international market means that new areas of forest are continually being utilized."

The attention of both the timber industry and environmentalists has shifted north to the forests of Canada, Siberia, and the United States, even as the situation in most tropical forests grows more dire. The greatest remaining supplies of timber lie in the boreal Siberian taiga, which alone accounts for 20 percent of global forest cover (Rosencranz and Scott 1992). Temperate forests, covering 2 billion hectares and providing half of global forest cover, are now among the most intensely logged areas in the world.

Substitutability of wood and the increasing ease with which the timber industry can shift the locations of its operations have also fueled fears about the sustainability of forestry and local timber-dependent economies. These trends and the fears that they engender are direct results of the globalization process.

Globalization and the Pacific Rim

In addition to containing the bulk of the world's remaining native forests, the Pacific Rim is home to its fastest growing economies. Most of these, such as China and the southeast Asian "tiger" economies, are responding to their acute timber shortages by rapidly increasing imports of wood products. Two-thirds of world trade in wood fiber takes place in the Pacific region, which is a base of operations for many of the key players in the timber industry.

In the view of timber analyst Alistair Graham (1993), "The economic development patterns in the countries of the Pacific Rim will largely determine the fate of remaining native forests both temperate and tropical, both hardwood and softwood." The forests of the Pacific Rim fall into the three broad global groups—tropical, temperate, and boreal—and, of course, into many more specific categories. A survey of their status vividly demonstrates the impacts of globalization.

Tropical Forests

Tropical forests in the Pacific Rim include those of Indonesia, Malaysia, the Philippines, and Papua New Guinea (PNG). Since the Second World War, the timber industry has been particularly hard on them. Overcutting has turned one nation after another into a supplier of raw logs and then an importer, as its forests have been depleted.

The evolution of timber exploitation in the tropical Pacific, like that of its economic development, has been driven largely by Japan (Nectoux and Kuroda 1989). Japan earned hard currency in the 1950s by importing hardwood logs from the Philippines and exporting processed timber products to the United States. In the Philippines, Ferdinand Marcos made a substantial part of his fortune by selling off his country's rain forests, similar to the way that later timber magnates have enriched themselves in Malaysia and Indonesia.

Japan turned to Indonesia and Malaysia after Philippine forests were depleted during the 1970s and 1980s. With the entry of South Korea and Taiwan into the Pacific Rim timber market, countries with less extensive areas of forest, such as Australia, Vietnam, Thailand, and Myanmar, have suffered significant impacts. Even countries with limited forested areas, such as the Solomon Islands, have come under increased pressure. The volume of logs exported has almost doubled in the last two years ("Eight Years Left" 1994).

Japan and South Korea have now shifted attention to Papua New Guinea. A spectacular worldwide rise in log prices in 1993 led the PNG government to approve a 400 percent increase in log export volumes. Little of the revenues stay there, but the government has nonetheless allocated two-thirds of "operable" forests for harvesting, despite growing local opposition.

The role of Japan and its neighbors in the tropical timber trade essentially has been colonial: areas rich in natural resources are harvested for processing and sale in distant centers of production and demand. This colonial character has been a hallmark of the global timber trade as well.

Temperate Forests

Figures from the U.N. Food and Agriculture Organization suggest that the actual area of temperate forests is holding steady, but this ignores the crucial issue of forest quality: many native forests are being replaced with intensely managed, monocultural tree stands, with a resultant loss in biodiversity (Dudley 1992).

Temperate forests in the United States and Canada have suffered severe impacts over the past decade by the expanding Pacific Rim market in wood fiber, especially for pulp and chips. These forests also have been the scene of some of the most intense social conflicts that have arisen from the timber trade. The largest instance of civil disobedience in British Columbia's history has occurred at Clayoquot Sound on Vancouver Island, one of the last extensive tracts of the coastal temperate rain forest that once reached unbroken from Canada to northern California.

Public attention in the United States was focused on the "owls vs. loggers" issue in the Pacific Northwest, which was, of course, not the real issue at all. Increased mechanization in the timber industry coupled with exports of raw and minimally processed logs caused the number of timber jobs to fall even during periods of record harvest. Timber employment fell 14 percent overall from 1980 to 1988, while production levels increased by 19 percent (Dudley 1992).

Events in the Northwest are also indicative of the fluidity with which the timber industry can move its operations. The domestic American industry has moved much of its production to the Southeast following the depletion of supplies in the Northwest. Even by 1986, the southeastern United States was supplying 47 percent of the nation's timber harvest, compared with 25 percent in the Pacific Northwest (Postel and Ryan 1991). The markets of the Pacific Rim also have reached there: South Korea's Donghae Paper Company has been among the corporations seeking to open chipping mills in Alabama and Tennessee.

Less well known is the growing importance of Chile as a source of wood for the Pacific Rim. By 1989 the Chilean timber industry was already exporting to five major wood-consuming countries: West Germany, Belgium, Brazil, the United States, and Japan, with one-quarter of the exports going to Japan (Hagler 1993). Along with the United States, Australia, and Canada, Chile now accounts for 87 percent of fiber exports to Japan (Dudley 1992). Chilean wood exports have more than doubled since 1983 (Postel and Ryan 1991).

As part of a general push to increase its pulp and paper capacity, Chile has accelerated the conversion of its millennia—old native *alerce* forests to monoculture plantations slated for chipping and export. By 1991, Chile had planted 1.3 million acres of plantations, 85 percent of which contained just one species, the introduced Monterey Pine.

Boreal Forests

The boreal taiga of Siberia and the Russian Far East is considered the "ultimate wild card" in predictions of growth in timber supply in both the Pacific Rim and global markets (Hagler 1993). With the collapse of the centralized Soviet system, local and regional governments have attempted to assert control over natural resources. Timber "mafias" also have come to power, especially in the Far East. Attempts by multinational giants like Weyerhauser and Georgia-Pacific to set up joint ventures have been stalled by political and economic chaos.

Regional governments increasingly have become suspicious of foreign firms. South Korea's Hyundai Corporation has been restricted from logging any more of the Bikin River basin north of Vladivostok. A large-scale joint venture with Japan also has been slowed by fluctuations in supplies and high prices charged by Siberian partners. The nearness of the huge Asian markets of Japan, Taiwan, and South Korea virtually ensures that exports of Siberian timber will increase in the future. A major market for Siberian wood exists just across the border.

The Question of China

Just as Siberia figures prominently in projections of timber supply in the Pacific Rim and beyond, China is becoming a major factor in terms of demand for wood products. Rapid economic growth and overcutting of domestic forests have brought about an acute timber shortage. The economic reforms of the late 1970s led to a jump in demand for wood. Annual harvests almost doubled from 1976 to 1988, and the area of timber-producing forests has shrunk by almost 3 million hectares since 1980 (Postel and Ryan 1991).

At the current rate of consumption, China will have harvested all of its remaining productive forests within a decade, and imports can be expected to rise substantially well before that. China has already become the major importer of plywood from Indonesia (Graham 1993). The government has set a goal of planting 30 million hectares of trees by the year 2000 and has planted an estimated 10 million hectares of plantations in the expectation of doubling domestic wood production (Postel and Ryan 1991).

Shape of the Global Timber Trade: "Institutional Arrangements"

The fragmentation of the Siberian timber industry is a notable exception to the prevailing trends of increased integration and centralization in the global timber industry. An examination of the Pacific Rim timber trade shows two central characteristics: first, all of its forests, whatever their type and location, are tied into one market; and second, that market continues to be basically colonial in character, with centers of demand drawing upon distant sources of supply.

This colonial model of resource use also has shaped what might be called the "institutional arrangements" by which the timber trade has worked with governments to ensure access to wood supplies. In the tropical countries, timber barons often control logging concessions and revenues from export. But "institutional arrangements" are not limited to third world countries. Canada's liquidation of its forests has followed the colonial model as well.

Forest destruction in Canada has proceeded through a provincial tenure system that grants logging companies huge concessions on public lands at bargain prices, which include some of the lowest stumpage fees in the world. Home-grown timber giant MacMillan Bloedel has been given generous terms for logging British Columbia. In Alberta, Mitsubishi Corporation has been allowed to lease an area the size of

Ohio to feed its pulp operations, and Daishowa Pulp Company has built the world's largest disposable wooden chopstick factory among old-growth aspen forests (McInnis 1994a).

When Daishowa Corporations Peace River Pulp Company built a $579 million mill in Alberta in 1988, approximately $70 million of the infrastructure costs were borne by the taxpayers. Similarly Alberta-Pacific Company, 85 percent Japanese-owned, finished construction of the world's largest bleached kraft pulp mill near Athabasca in 1993 with the province paying infrastructure costs of $75 million and with an agreement that the company need not begin repayment until the mill becomes profitable (McInnis 1994a).

This kind of arrangement means that the government is in effect a shareholder in such operations, even though their terms are not voted on by citizens. In British Columbia, the government was until recently an actual shareholder in MacMillan Bloedel, to whom it awarded the largest number of timber concessions. The Canadian taxpayers thus have ended up paying the economic as well as environmental costs of a volatile market: the combination of an oversupply of pulp and intense international competition has led the pulp industry in Canada to lose more than $1 billion in the last three years (McInnis 1994b). The vicissitudes of the wood fiber market have also resulted in longer-term strategies on the part of importers. Japan relies on Australia for over one-third of its imports of wood chips (Graham 1993). This stems from two "chip scares" in 1980 and 1987, which led Japan to broaden its sources of supply (Hagler 1993). Softwood chip prices doubled overnight in 1980, and Japanese importers found themselves completely dependent on U.S. West Coast exporters, with no other sources of supply. After suffering significant losses, they diversified their supply sources by importing from Australia. When Australian supplies of eucalyptus chips were threatened by a proposed pulp mill in 1987, Japan turned to southeastern U.S. suppliers.

While the evolution of the Pacific Rim and global timber trades has proceeded by a combination of accident and design, the second element has been the stronger. Given the shape of the market now—the increased emphasis on pulp and paper, the ability to use many different kinds of wood from a variety of regions, and the ever-growing demand in established and emerging economies—this element of design carries the most serious implications for the survival of native forests. Without changes in national and global policy, temperate forests will be depleted in a manner similar to the way the tropical forests have been, and the industry will move into Siberia in a big way.

Missing from market projections, however, is any accounting for social and environmental consequences. The fact that northern forests are thought to represent a major "carbon pool" which helps to regulate earth's climate, and that widespread depletion of the taiga could accelerate the process of global warming, is only the most dramatic consequence (Rosencranz and Scott 1992).

Equally striking is the fact that industrial logging usually is subsidized to varying degrees by governments of lands possessing timber supplies. The very volatility of the wood products market makes generous institutional arrangements with compliant governments a virtual necessity for the timber industry. As Alistair Graham (1993) puts it, "Despite all this fawning to international capital at the expense of our democracy and native forests, [the industry] still cannot get a competitive investment unless governments come to the party with large chunks of cash infrastructure support, tax holidays, royalty discounts, and accelerated depreciation perks—and so spread the costs across the whole community."

Aside from specific instances of bribery and collusion (which are not uncommon), the motivation of governments to participate in such arrangements may seem unclear. John McInnis (1994a) of the Western Canada Wilderness Committee has framed the basic question: "We should ask why governments are so eager to subsidize the production of more pulp, the liquidation of more taiga resources, more pollution, more incursion into aboriginal homelands." The answer lies partly in a flawed system of valuing forests and quantifying the costs of their destruction that informs the decision-making process in most governments.

Toward a Solution: Revaluing Forests

The natural resources accounting systems traditionally used by governments tend to favor industrial logging and forest liquidation (World Resources Institute 1992–93, 1994–95). On the national level, natural resource accounting policies encourage forest destruction and degradation by *under*valuing forests that are intact. "Value" is typically seen in terms of value as timber. Nontimber goods usually are ignored in economic assessments of forests because they lack conventional commodity value. Yet these very goods—including environmental services (soil conservation, water cleansing, carbon storage), fruits, resins, and oils—often have an economic value that exceeds that of timber. What they lack is the infrastructure support that makes industrial logging possible.

Undervaluing the forest ecosystem goes hand in hand with *over*estimating the economic benefits, both current and projected, of timber harvesting and forest conversion. The benefits of logging are usually calculated without taking into account the environmental and social costs of deforestation. These may be hard to quantify, but the World Resources Institute (1992–93, 1994–95) and a growing number of economists have shown that if just the costs of infrastructure, tax credits, and production subsidies are added in accounts of forest revenues, the anticipated economic benefits of forest conversion may vanish.

The social costs of deforestation also are substantial. In many countries, both forestry laws and indigenous rights and claims routinely are ignored. The effects on tribal peoples have been overwhelmingly negative, especially in tropical countries experiencing rapid population growth. Ecological disaster usually means social disaster, as in the Philippines, where denuded hillsides caused mudslides that killed thousands after extensive flooding. In the United States and Canada, rural employment generated by logging has been manipulated as a political issue, but as indicated above, the industry itself has been eliminating jobs steadily through greater automation in both mills and harvesting technology, and through the export of both raw or minimally processed logs and chips. Industrial logging also ties rural communities to a "boom or bust" economic structure, which decreases economic and thus social stability.

In Canada, the tropics, Siberia, and many national forests in the United States (such as Alaska's Tongass), royalties and taxes from timber concessions also tend to be set at unrealistically low rates. Government revenues are thus only a fraction of what they could be. Subsidies for harvesting and processing compound the loss of timber revenues for national and local governments. Undervaluing the resource thus encourages overuse and depletion.

Correcting this flawed accounting system is fairly straightforward in theory: forest resources need a revaluation that reflects the full costs of their loss. Forest resources and the environmental as well as economic services that they provide have to be seen as capital assets *before* timber harvest, assets whose depreciation has to be incorporated into any adequate accounting system (World Resources Institute 1992–93, 1994–95). In the model proposed by the World Resources Institute, national budgets that strive to incorporate the full value of forests to a country's well-being would eliminate or reduce most timber subsidies. They want to charge logging prices that reflect environmental and social costs of harvests *and* reward sustainable harvest practices through the kind of incentives now available to standard industrial logging.

The Global Imperative

All national reforms, of course, must contend with the size, scope, and momentum of a global timber trade, which has tied all of the world's forests into one market. Not only does demand rise and fall on a global level, but the very structures of economic development are tied to the market: per capita consumption of paper is a central indicator of the level of development. Alistair Graham (1993) paints a grim picture: "Present levels of, and rates of growth of, demand for wood products are so high that the chances of protecting large areas of remaining native forests of high conservation value are low unless major product substitution takes place, demand for virgin fibre is suppressed as much as possible, and rigorous conservation policies are put in place by countries and corporations alike and all very quickly indeed."

Institutional tools for dealing with this situation appear limited. The record of international bodies such as the International Tropical Timber Organization and the U.N. Commission on Sustainable Development in modifying global timber practices is extremely uneven. The scope for national action has become more uncertain with the passage of the Uruguay Round of the General Agreement on Tariffs and Trade (GATT), which directly affects the ability of a country to restrict the flow of natural resources in and out of its borders. The Uruguay Round also could complicate the implementation of key international reforms such as a global system of wood certification based on economic and environmental sustainability.

The most potent tools available for reducing the consumption of and the demand for wood products are found in consumer-driven "demand management" strategies. The minimum recycled-content laws and requirements put in place on both the state and federal levels in the United States have led to a rapid jump in the use, demand, and price of recycled paper. The use of "tree-free" paper made from kenaf and hemp also has had an impact on the wood products market.

Conclusion

The global forest crisis is tied directly to the evolution of a global market for wood products and the internationalization of the timber industry. There are pervasive ethical issues related to these structures: institutional arrangements between governments and industry facilitate industrial logging and exploitation of public lands, and governments tend to rely on flawed accounting systems that undervalue forests and their benefits. These structures also operate in the context of an irreplaceable loss of biodiversity and ecosystems and harmful impacts on local and indigenous communities. In the face of institutional inadequacy for addressing the scope and severity of the problem, consumer-driven demand management strategies involving recycling and alternate fiber materials appear to be the most effective means at hand for catalyzing change on a significant level.

References

Dudley, Nigel. 1992. *Forests in Trouble: A Review of the Status of Forests Worldwide.* Gland, Switzerland: World Wildlife Fund.

"Eight Years Left for the Solomon Islands." 1994. *World Rain Forest Report* 11 (July—September).

Graham, Alistair. 1993. "Wood Flows around the Pacific Rim: A Corporate Picture." *Forestry, Pulp, and Paper,* June.

Hagler, Robert. 1993. "Global Forest." *Papermaker,* May.

McInnis, John. 1994a. "The Great Alberta Giveaway: The Japanese Connection." *Taiga News,* no. 9 (May).

———. 1994b. "Mitsubishi in Canada: The Fiasco Continues." *World Rain Forest Report* 11 (January—March).

Nectoux, Francois, and Yoichi Kuroda. 1989. "Timber from the South Seas: An Analysis of Japan's Tropical Timber Trade and Its Environmental Impact." *World Wildlife International.* Tokyo: Tsukiji Shokan.

Postel, Sandra, and John Ryan. 1991. "Reforming Forestry." In *State of the World 1991,* ed. Worldwatch Institute, 74–92. New York: W. W. Norton.

Rosencranz, Armin, and Antony Scott. 1992. "Siberia's Threatened Forests." *Nature,* January 23.

World Resources Institute. 1992–93. "Forests and Rangelands." *World Resources Institute: Guide to the Global Environment.* New York: Oxford University Press.

———. 1994–95. "Forests and Rangelands." *World Resources Institute: Guide to the Global Environment.* New York: Oxford University Press.

CHAPTER 11

New Forestry, New Forest Philosophies

One of the main messages of this anthology is that although the public and academic debate about forestry and forests has intensified in the past twenty-five years, environmental philosophers and philosophically-minded foresters have been thinking hard about how to redefine some of the philosophical assumptions of traditional forestry and the dominant forms of forestry ethics. However, in the midst of this rich confusion of ideas, a problem for those intimately involved with forestry is how to sift through these varied proposals and adopt alternatives that can satisfy the political, social, economic, commercial, and bureaucratic systems in which forestry exists while also achieving the goals that society has identified as important, such as the preservation of forest biodiversity and the sustainability of forest-dependent human communities. The difficulty for foresters and other applied environmental scientists who seek to make their professions consistent with new philosophies about nature is that they must learn how to rethink their situations within this broader social context while maintaining their distinctive roles as scientists, technical advisers, and managers and enjoying the self-respect that comes from providing useful services to society.

Criticism and reevaluation of a profession and a craft can be debilitating and discouraging, but it can also be stimulating and can unlock new possibilities for theory and practice. Although the most likely outcome of the contemporary debate about forestry in North America is incremental modification of existing ways of doing things and existing ways of thinking—rather than immediate, revolutionary change—forestry and the other natural resource disciplines can still be reformed on a foundation of new ethical attitudes, technical criteria, and philosophical beliefs. The immediate results of this process may be slow in coming, but over the long term the benefits could be significant, environmentally and socially speaking.[1]

1. This conclusion is not likely to be palatable to radical environmental critics of industrial forestry who seek more immediate and dramatic change, but given the realities of our industrial and economic system, in the short term it is more likely that only incremental reforms can occur. The deep ecologists have pointed out that the reform of culture and personality is a worthy goal of reflection and can in time significantly change our personal relationships with natural systems.

This chapter includes three recent efforts to rethink the roots and directions of forestry and forest ethics, one by a philosophically-inclined forester, Alan G. McQuillan of the University of Montana, and two by the environmental thinkers and philosophers Stephanie Kaza, of the University of Vermont, and Alan Drengson and Duncan Taylor of the University of Victoria in British Columbia. First, McQuillan focuses on what is called "new forestry" and its implications for a philosophy of the national forests in the United States, though he makes clear that new forestry is affecting the thinking of foresters about other public and private forests as well.[2] McQuillan proposes in a Leopoldian vein that foresters stop thinking of new forestry so strictly in scientific terms. He recommends instead a "postmodernist" outlook in which forestry is understood as a form of discourse between forests and the public, and the public and its forests.[3] Timber production, the preservation of biodiversity, and an emphasis on forest aesthetics are worthy goals, but forestry must open itself up to an even more "expanded set of criteria for evaluating activities and forest conditions in light of an entire spectrum of forest-centered values." In promoting a Leopoldian land ethic, forestry needs to seek a synthesis of science and aesthetics, of the biological and the beautiful. McQuillan's conclusion is similar to the multiple values approach to forest ethics advocated by Holmes Rolston and James Coufal earlier in this book, and builds on some of the Leopoldian reflections of J. Baird Callicott in his discussions of a new land aesthetic.[4] As McQuillan concludes, forestry can unashamedly accept the value it places on gardening as long as it realizes that gardening can take many different forms, all of which have their place and their utility. Pluralism and diversity are as necessary in new forestry, then, as they are in new politics and social morality.

Kaza outlines some of the major ethical tensions in the debate about the "Northern Forest" of eastern North America.[5] She identifies five ethical polarities in the environmental controversies between users and dwellers in these forest lands, isolates the "power relations" that lie under these polarities, then proposes the idea that ethical deliberation is an effective tool for examining these relations. She ends by proposing six ethical guidelines that participants in the debate would do well to take into consideration as they seek solutions to their problems. She believes that ethical dialogue is essential for breaking the intellectual and personal deadlocks that paralyze forest

---

2. McQuillan is the author of several groundbreaking articles that cross the boundaries between environmental ethics and forest philosophy. Several are mentioned in the bibliography to this volume.

3. The idea of a postmodern environmental ethics is proposed in the writings of Jim Cheney, an environmental philosopher who teaches in Wisconsin. For his formulation of this kind of ethic and critical reviews of its central claims, consult the writings by a variety of environmental ethicists in the anthology by Max Oelschlaeger, ed., *Postmodern Environmental Ethics* (Albany, N.Y.: SUNY Press, 1995).

4. Callicott's "land aesthetic" is presented in his essay "Leopold's Land Aesthetic," which can be found in his book *In Defense of the Land Ethic: Essays in Environmental Philosophy*, 1989. Peter Miller, an environmental philosopher at the University of Winnipeg who has taken an active part in the Canadian dialogue about new forestry, also argues along these lines. See his article "Environmental Ethics and Canadian Forestry Policy: From Locke to Gaia," in *Canadian Issues in Applied Environmental Ethics*, edited by Alex Wellington et al. (Peterborough, Ontario: Broadview Press, 1997). Miller proposes that a "Gaian" form of environmental ethics become part of public forestry.

5. Stephanie Kaza is no stranger to trees and forests, and as a practicing Buddhist and former resident of California has written about her spiritual approach to various California tree species in *The Attentive Heart: Conversations with Trees* (Boston: Shambhala, 1996).

disagreements and, in concert with ecofeminists, argues that this can occur only when many voices—not only the most powerful—participate. This is a key point that echoes the thinking of many other observers of forest management and public attitudes in the United States and elsewhere, including McQuillan. Public participation in forest planning, particularly in public forestry, must be more broadly democratic and genuine in the future.[6] In a sense everyone is a "stakeholder"—not only those local people who benefit or suffer most directly from forest decisions, those with the most economic power or the loudest and most strident voices, or those who have the ear of forest managers. The natural components and organisms in forests must also have standing at the table, to borrow a thesis from Christopher Stone.[7]

In the final selection in this anthology Drengson and Taylor, two Canadian leaders in the ecoforestry movement, outline a comprehensive philosophy for reforming forestry along deep ecology lines. They oppose this philosophical paradigm to the "dominant, mainstream, expansionist model of modernism" in forestry that promotes an anthropocentric perspective on human relationships to nature and emphasizes the idea that nature is a resource to be used to meet the ever-growing material needs of an expanding human population. In contrast, the new ecological paradigm conceives of humans as "participants" in nature and accepts an ethic based on respect for diversity and ecocentric values. The natural world is not only an instrument for human beings but is rich in an inherent value that exists independent of human interests. In short, they identify and outline two different worldviews that are present in the thinking of Gifford Pinchot, on the one hand, and John Muir and Aldo Leopold, on the other, and vigorously reject the former.

To ecoforesters, large-scale industrial practices imposed on the biological processes of the earth are not sustainable. Extensive clearcutting to promote monocultural forests, for example, reduces the productive powers of an original forest to "nearly zero," significantly destroys its biodiversity, requires a long time for natural recovery, and in the meantime creates considerable suffering in the human communities that depend on it.[8] Also in the spirit of Aldo Leopold, they argue that Pinchotian philosophy is thus in need of redefinition. What they recommend in

6. There is considerable social research that shows that the American public thinks very highly of public participation in forest management and planning. Consult Bruce Shindler, Peter List, and Brent Steel, "Managing Federal Forests: Public Attitudes in Oregon and Nationwide," *Journal of Forestry* 91(7) (July 1993): 36–42. Two useful discussions of participation issues can be found in T. B. Knopp and E. S. Caldbeck, "The Role of Participatory Democracy in Forest Management," *Journal of Forestry* 88(5) (May 1990): 13–15, and Bruce Shindler and Julie Neberka, "Public Participation in Forest Planning: Eight Attributes of Success," *Journal of Forestry* 95(1) (January 1997): 17–19.

7. Stone, *Should Trees Have Standing? Toward Legal Rights for Natural Objects*.

8. The anthology edited by Bill Devall, *Clearcut: The Tragedy of Industrial Forestry* (San Francisco: Sierra Club Books, 1993), is a powerful visual effort designed to illustrate the devastation that industrial forest practices have had on North American forests and contains articles by many ecoforesters and philosophers. Of course, one has to keep in mind that the pictures in many cases were taken close to the time when the clearcuts were made, and, since most of these forests were likely either replanted or regenerated naturally, photos of the same areas taken today would in most cases look quite different and not have the same shock value. Nevertheless, the short-term consequences on biodiversity are likely to be devastating, particularly if these clearcuts are large and adjacent to each other. In any case the effects of clearcutting are not only aesthetic and require scientific interpretation, so scientific sources should be consulted as well. An overview of this practice is given in Hamish Kimmins, *Balancing Act: Environmental Issues in Forestry* (Vancouver, B.C.: UBC Press, 1992).

its place is a form of forestry that is consistent with the ways in which natural forests sustain themselves over time, in short an ecologically-based forestry, and they define the basic principles by which this might be accomplished. It is a forestry consistent with an ecosystem approach that was outlined in a 1995 scientific panel report on sustainable ecosystem management in Clayoquot Sound, on Vancouver Island in British Columbia, and in various documents that define ecosystem management in the United States. To Drengson and Taylor, this new form of forestry is now emerging in North America, and it offers hope for promoting community, cultural, economic, and biophysical sustainability. While ecoforestry is still in its infancy, Drengson and Taylor's book *Ecoforestry* includes many past and current examples of ecoforestry practice in North America. Ecoforestry represents an extension of Leopold's biotic forestry except that it includes a more thoroughly explained set of practical guidelines so that foresters can see how this alternative to industrial forestry can work in the forest itself and also how it can work for forest-related human communities.

In the end, the practicability of any form of new forestry, whatever it may be called, rests not only on our ability to put it down on paper, in a formulated philosophy and set of ethical principles, but on its power to help us act in a responsible manner toward each other and the earth, and to exhibit our deep respect for and humility before nature. Written philosophies, technical criteria, and ethical codes are valuable as guidelines for behavior, but it is important to ask of them not only what they say we ought to do but specifically how they would change what we actually do. As foresters often remark about forest management theories and silvicultural methods, the real test is how they are played out "on the ground." The same can be said about new systems of forestry ethics: What do they define as our responsibilities to forests and how would they change the way forestry and the other environmental sciences implement these responsibilities? I have put this anthology together with the aim of making these matters more clear.

Alan G. McQuillan

Cabbages and Kings: The Ethics and Aesthetics of New Forestry

Introduction

Forestry in the last few years has undergone traumatic transformation. Since Forest Service ecologist Jerry Franklin coined the term *new forestry* in 1989,[1] the profession has been in turmoil. His work might have had minimal impact if his ideas had not struck chords that reverberated throughout a disgruntled and melancholic profession. Despite scientific incompleteness, and traditionalist criticism that is not without merit,[2] Franklin's *new forestry* seems to have become firmly rooted in the psyche of practising foresters in North America.[3]

The prime management agency of publicly-owned forestlands in the U.S., the Forest Service, rapidly embraced the concept and developed a policy initiative, *new perspectives*, within which to locate *new forestry*. Today, the terms are becoming interchangeable;[4] the pervasive theme is to redefine forestry in terms of maintaining biodiversity for sustaining ecological systems in a "kindler, gentler" manner, and with regard for aesthetic considerations.[5] *New forestry*, like perestroika, has attained a level of popular support within the profession's public sector from which there can be no retreat.[6] Surprisingly perhaps, this enthusiasm seems to have carried over to professional foresters within the traditionalist bastions of privately-owned forest industry: it appears that *new forestry* combines industry's perceived need for improved public acceptability of its operations with an up-beat rejuvenation of what today's foresters thought forestry was supposed to be about when they first chose the subject in school.

What *new forestry is* is best described by first stating what it is not. *New forestry* is an ending or transcending of the traditional ideal of the "regulated" forest. From its inception in the U.S. almost exactly a century ago, forestry's aim was the conversion of the continent's vast expanses of old-growth, "mixed up messes" of inherited forest canopy, into regulated, regimented, uniform stands of "thrifty" young trees, vigorous producers of wood fiber in perpetuity.[7] This utopian model of forestry was

---

Alan G. McQuillan, "Cabbages and Kings: The Ethics and Aesthetics of New Forestry," *Environmental Values* 2 (1993): 191–222. Reprinted with permission from The White Horse Press, Cambridge, U.K.

imported from Prussia,[8] and reflected I shall argue a truly modernist vision that blossomed from Stoic, Calvinist and utilitarian rootstock.

With *new forestry*, the vision of the perfectly-regulated forest vanished.[9] Management plans that had been painstakingly developed during a decade of hard labour for the nation's 122 national forests, in accordance with crisis-averting legislation known as the National Forest Management Act of 1976 (NFMA), were produced still-born in the late 1980s, as the very premises upon which the plans were based became suddenly null and void.

This was because no one before or during the "planning decade" (that began in 1976), at least no one I know within the forestry profession, seriously considered old growth forests as possessing any redeeming features outside of the preserves known as national parks or designated wilderness areas. Further, forestry viewed as "over-mature" any tree that was beyond "culmination of mean annual increment" or maximum average rate of growth—the floral equivalent of faunal veal. In practical terms in the Pacific Northwest (where the preponderance of old-growth forests remained), this meant the demise of physiologically mature trees—trees that can reach diameters exceeding ten feet (3 m) at ages exceeding 300 years, and their replacement by a regulated forest where most trees would not exceed two feet (0.6 m) at rotation ages of 50 to 100 years, and most of the forest would be stocked with juvenile trees most of the time.

Almost overnight it seemed, sustained high-level timber production as a correlate of the perfectly regulated forest vanished as the ideal. It had dawned on a hitherto unsuspecting public that "sustained yield" of forest production did not equate to a sustained stock of "forests" as the American public had come to know and love them.[10] Indeed, the terms were polar opposites, since, as every forester knew from school, a high-level perpetual (sustained) yield was obtained only when the old growth was at last converted to vigorous and usually homogeneous stands of young timber. Perhaps not surprisingly when viewed historically, the forestry profession had provided the public with no warning that sustained yield (a popularly-accepted term) implied the demise of what came to be known as "ancient forests."

So what is *new forestry*? Classic regulation is abandoned; in its place are generally-stated concerns for biodiversity, ecological system complexity, aesthetics, protection of all indigenous species of flora and fauna (including those that depend on an old-growth habitat), clean air and water, respect for those who find spiritual values in the forest, a re-emerging "ethics of nature," holistic or systems-oriented approaches to management, coupled with older but not abandoned desires for commodity production, economic prudence and humanistic concern for rural communities disrupted by the vicissitudes of a rapidly changing forestry praxis. Along with *new forestry* comes a whole lexicon, "rewriting," as postmodernist critic Fredric Jameson described, "all the familiar things in new terms and thus proposing modifications, new ideal perspectives, reshuffling of canonical feelings and values."[11] If there were a prize for the phrase repeated most often at recent professional forestry meetings it would have to go to "changing values."

Still, *new forestry* cannot be succinctly defined. The desire for biological diversity, ecological system complexity and the continuance of evolutionary processes, in and of itself is insufficient to prescribe any ideal forest of the future. *New forestry* abandons utopian ideals.[12] Its essence lies, paradoxically perhaps, in its eclecticism, its shifting focus, its multifaceted and not necessarily mutually compatible concerns. It has, as another critic, Charles Jencks, ascribed to postmodern culture, "a strong sense of its departure point, but no clear sense of destination."[13] Describing the shifting focus of postmodernism, Jencks continued:

> The ambivalence accurately reflects this double state of transition, where activity moves away from a well-known point, acknowledges the move and yet keeps a view, or trace, or love of that past location. Sometimes it idealizes the security of this point of departure, with nostalgia and melancholy, but at the same time it may exult in a new-found freedom and sense of adventure.[14]

Today's new foresters display some of this freedom and adventure; they frequently concern themselves with creating a data-based image of the "pre-settlement" forest primeval, while exulting in an expanded vision of forestry, choosing from a vast range of "desired future conditions." (It is the approach to selecting "desired future conditions" that is a prime concern of this paper.)

The remarkable congruence of the language of postmodernism with the language of *new forestry* (seen in terms like "diversity," "eclecticism," "plurality," "landscape," "multi-cultural," "multi-faceted" and other "multi-" prefixed words) leads me to suggest the latter is emerging as a concrete expression of the former, that *new forestry* is a postmodern phenomenon. This supposition is strengthened when one realizes the similarly remarkable congruence of traditional forestry with the ideals of modernism (argued below), and how these arose in reaction to and attempted negation of an earlier Romantic Transcendentalist view of nature.

Having made this connection, it becomes possible for new foresters to seek in postmodernist works how Western thought in general and forestry in particular is engaged in the uncertain process of redefining its relationship with nature. The discourse that surrounds and defines this relationship cuts to the very quick of forestry. We have the view expressed by Linda Hutcheson:

> [I]t seems reasonable to say that the postmodern's initial concern is to de-naturalize some of the dominant features of our way of life; to point out that those entities that we unthinkingly experience as "natural" (they might even include capitalism, patriarchy, liberal humanism) are in fact "cultural"; made by us, not given to us. Even nature, postmodernism might point out, doesn't grow on trees.[15]

This interpretation squares off against a popular, though I believe misguided, ascetic environmentalist position which sees nature as a virginal *otherness*, an object of deification, an Eden from which sinful humans must be excluded. A postmodern forestry might seek instead a re-engagement of humankind with the natural world, freeing people to participate without shame in actions or inactions which transform or do not transform the earth. That any transformation should not destroy the earth is axiomatic to survival—a stance necessary for the continuation of the human and, therefore, the postmodern condition also. But Hutcheson is correct in asserting that "the dominant features of our way of life . . . are in fact cultural."[16]

Bringing nature discourse back to focus presents an opportunity to overcome what is currently an impasse for the profession, even given its recent shift toward *new forestry*. This impasse is forestry's concentration on the scientific method to the exclusion of almost all else. Science, like reason, informs but does not itself motivate action.[17] Motivation may be economic, but foresters are now well aware that many values escape the economic net. Ethics considers other forms of value, and it is no accident that *new forestry* coincides with the Society of American Foresters' adoption of a *land ethic* canon.[18] My thesis goes further: while science informs of what is *possible*, and ethics and economics circumscribe what is *prudent*, I believe humans continue to operate largely within the realm of what they *want*. Our wants, both collectively and individually, arise in a cultural context; they are shaped by our sense of aesthetics (in the broadest construction of the word).[19] Only by making room for other established means of academic discourse, such as literary and artistic criticism, can *new forestry* hope to accommodate the expressed concerns of its clientele, the increasingly postmodern American public. Accordingly, my premise is that forestry is first and foremost a *discourse*, a language-based expression of relationships between forests and foresters, between foresters and the public at large, and, not least, between the public and its forests.[20]

The Ethics of Traditional Forestry

If *new forestry* reflects first and foremost a radical shift in values, then it is appropriate to begin with a consideration of ethics in traditional forestry. For many years I have described foresters as adhering unconsciously to what I have called a gardeners ethic: The gardener is a worthy soul who does not count the hours spent doubled over among the rows, back bent to the sky—planting and mulching, weeding and cultivating, caring or tending for the future crop—a walking and breathing definition of the much-loved term *stewardship*. The best gardens have their cabbages in straight rows, disease-, insect- and weed-free; when the cook descends from the kitchen, cabbages most in need of removal are harvested, leaving a beautiful still-ripening crop; and, when summer is over, the entire garden is stripped for winter.

Untold hours are spent in this virtuous toil, so that an accountant with a stopwatch would be most unwelcome; the devoted gardener does not wish to be told that, based on vegetable prices at the local market, his labour returns a bare fraction of minimum wage. This is the wrong scale, he contends, for measuring such valuable work in husbandry of nature. A wilderness advocate would be equally unwelcome: the gardener seeks no wild nature, no overrun wilderness, he seeks only the co-operation of nature in his organization and ordering of nature's productive forces.

Gardeners, when they meet, lament the latest outbreak of insects or disease, argue over use of artificial chemicals, or whether or not a drought is really upon us. They will discuss the relative merits of different tools, crop species, or government restrictions. But, their discourse fits comfortably within the framework of their paradigm; they know, and will defend against all comers, that theirs is a noble task, sweating their brows in the raising of food for human-kind, a challenging, needed and tangibly important position in the great outdoors.

Forestry, as it came to be practiced in the U.S. (by public foresters beginning in the 1890s and by industry foresters beginning in the 1930s) reflects a curious combination of ethical values. Traditional[21] U.S. forestry has often been described as utilitarian, and this is a good starting place. Besides the general orientation of professional foresters to produce utilities, the acclaimed "first U.S.-born forester" and founder of the Forest Service, Gifford Pinchot, adopted as his maxim for forest management, "the greatest good of the greatest number in the long run."[22] This is a minor variant of a phrase canonized by the founder of the utilitarian movement, Jeremy Bentham.[23] Pinchot passionately shared Bentham's humanism, his concerns for alleviating the pains of industrial and rural poverty, and for a social engineering[24] designed to make the material rewards of labour substantial and attainable by all. Furthermore, Pinchot's forestry, like utilitarianism, was teleological, or goal-oriented. Pinchot's goal was to bring the inherited natural forests of the U.S. under productive management, or, as a Society of American Forester's bumper sticker proudly proclaimed in the 1980s, "Happiness is a well-managed forest."

However, in its original conception, utilitarianism's goal was maximization of *pleasure*, and minimization of *pain*. This has been called hedonistic utilitarianism;[25] and, in Bentham's time (1748–1832), when the pain of proletarian life during an early period of the industrial revolution was so obviously acute, the work of social reformers was clearly defined, and arguments concerning the finer points of pleasure were probably redundant. Later, John Stuart Mill refined the telos of Bentham's ethic to maximizing *higher* pleasure and Hastings Rashdall expounded a form of the ethic which recognized a pluralistic concept of pleasure, known as ideal utilitarianism,[26] a forerunner perhaps to the multiple-use doctrine of postwar U.S. forest policy.

Implicit in the utilitarian ethic is the need to quantify and place on a common scale the various *pleasures* and *pains* that make up the collective good,[27] and this is reflected in the historical development of U.S. national forest planning. Pinchot's notion of social good was thoroughly materialistic. The primary good was timber,[28] accompanied by other commodities such as water for irrigation or power, and forage for livestock grazing. These outputs could be readily quantified and valued. As other demands expanded to where they could not be ignored,[29] the utilitarian net was expanded to catch wildlife and recreation, and the "willingness-to-pay" concept[30] was pressed into service so that *dollars* could remain the common currency in which all forest outputs were to be measured and maximized. This "calculus of pleasure" or benefit-maximization dominated forestry management and economic texts in the 1970s[31] and became the pivot of public forest planning methodology during the 1980s.[32]

To suggest however that U.S. forestry *practice* has been characterized by pleasure or benefit maximization, or by any other *telos*, would be to ignore fundamental metatexts that have influenced forestry praxis, and caused abiding resistance to expanding professional concern into such hedonistic subjects as outdoor recreation, caring for non-game wildlife, or leaving things alone (as, for example, in wilderness areas). Even with regard to commodities, the profession has shown more concern for the *exercise* of forestry than for efficient production of outputs.

One of these metatexts, which has important implications for the notion of development *per se*, rotates around the glorification of labour and the repudiation of idleness that has characterized Western life since well before the Enlightenment. It has been well described by Michel Foucault:

> As for that power, its special characteristic, of abolishing poverty, *labor*—according to the classical interpretation—possessed it not so much by its productive capacity as by a certain force of moral enchantment. Labor's effectiveness was acknowledged because it was based on an ethical transcendence. Since the Fall, man had accepted labor as a penance and for its power to work redemption.... "The land had not sinned, and if it is accursed, it is by the labor of the fallen man who cultivates it; from it no fruit is won, particularly the most necessary fruit, save by force and continual labor." ... The theme was constant among Catholic thinkers, as among the Protestants.... Here is Calvin's admonition: "Nor do we believe, according as men will be vigilant and skillful, according as they will have done their duty well, that they can make their land fertile; it is the benediction of God which

governs all things." ... The poor man who, without consenting to "torment" the land, waits until God comes to his aid, since He has promised to feed the birds of the sky, would be disobeying the great law of Scripture: "Thou shalt not tempt the Lord thy God." Does not reluctance to work mean "trying beyond measure the power of God," as Calvin says? It is seeking to constrain the miracle [of productivity], whereas the miracle is granted daily to man as the gratuitous reward of his labor. . . . [I]t is true that idleness is rebellion—the worst form of all, in a sense: it waits for nature to be generous as in the innocence of Eden, and seeks to constrain a Goodness to which man cannot lay claim since Adam.[33]

Forestry, like gardening and farming, has been pursued deontologically as an "endless" opportunity for virtuous labouring. As a labour of love, an avenue of redemption, the action has been seen as more important even than the outputs produced.

Furthermore, it is characteristic of Western life (in contrast to, say, Taoist practice) that evidence of *activity* is necessary to prove concerned engagement with any perceived situation. Once a problem is recognized (impending insect infestation let us say) it is imperative to *do* something about it. The Taoist notion that calculated inaction can be as powerful as action is usually anathema to Western praxis. In national parks, for example, no kudos is given for just "minding the store" or the ecosystem; rewards go to *improvers* who build visitor information centres or engineer rehabilitation of habitat. A corollary is that averters of crisis go unrecognized; recognition comes to those who react to crisis after it has occurred.

Labour's virtue accrues also from its characteristic as a Stoic self-discipline. In this Stoic vein, concern for the simple necessities of life (food, fuel and clothing) is virtuous, while more than passing concern for luxuries is hedonistic even to the point of sinfulness. It is unsurprising that forestry, as a cultural construct of the early twentieth century, developed a distinct hierarchy of supposedly need-based concerns: timber for building, water for consumption and forage for livestock led by virtue of their characteristic as necessity.[34] As the century developed, it mattered little that people did not *need* 2,000 square-foot homes, newspapers that weighed several pounds, irrigated lawns or T-bone steaks from any perspective of survival. Managing wildlife for hunting and recreation as an economic activity had long been on the official books, but were slow to gain the attention of "true-blooded" foresters. Maintaining habitat for fuzzy-feathered owls or other endangered species, unroaded watersheds for their sheer visual delight, and any number of other "luxuries" never were truly embraced within the annals of traditional forestry.

For these reasons, I characterize traditional forestry as *Stoically* utilitarian. This banishes any lingering notion of the Epicurianism inherent in Bentham's *pleasure* maximization, keeps intact the utilitarian attribute of maximized utility production and infuses a deontological, or duty-oriented, element of hard work.[35] There is yet one more concept necessary for this characterization of ethics in traditional forestry: addition of the term *positivism*. This relates to forestry as science.

The philosopher of the Enlightenment David Hume provided the Western world with the foundation of empirical science when he explicated the impossibility of any a priori knowledge of physical being. Knowledge of the real world could be obtained by human beings only through sensory perception, and this sense-based data, operated on by the logical dictates of *reason*, provided us with a powerful empirical science and technology. Unless one wished to invoke religion or extra-sensory perception, physical empiricism was logically undeniable. However, the dazzling achievements of technology (with all the appearance of magic) led some to regard science as a quasi-religion. Logical positivists, who started from a correct Humean premise, went on to believe that in reason (and its physically-oriented correlate, science) a locus of normative value could actually be found. In this, they ignored the essential disinterestedness of science (which posits cause and effect, or predicts likely outcomes without passing judgment) and the necessary disinterestedness of reason (which deals non-normatively with if-then propositions).[36] Indeed, in this disinterestedness of reason had lain a prime virtue of the Enlightenment: a key to release from monarchical or religious tyranny.

Reason, as Hume wrote in 1739, "is perfectly inert, and can never either prevent or produce any action or affection."[37] His famous dictum is: "Reason is and ought only to be the slave of the passions, and can never pretend to any other office than to serve and obey them." Not wishing to soften the *hard stuff* of science with anything as potentially hedonistic as emotions or passions, the positivists chose to ignore Hume and view science as self-justifying (knowledge for the sake of knowledge, engineering in response to intellectual challenge, . . . *because it's there*). Employment was readily available from the utilitarians, who needed technology for achieving their telos, and positivist science was ready, willing and able to assist. The ultimate irony was the degree of passion with which positivists pursued dispassionate objectivity.

In forestry, this was not without consequence. Traditional forestry had a clearly-defined telos: the establishment of regulated forests as described above. During that era, scientific positivism did not often conflict with forestry's *Stoic utilitarianism*. The positivists'

"these trees *need* thinning" or "this herd *needs* culling" coincided nicely with the social goal. However, as soon as a clearly defined telos disappeared with the advent of *new forestry*, positivism has been found standing naked in the open.[38]

The Ethics of New Forestry

With no clearly defined social objective—timber production is a by-product of *new forestry* we are now often told, and *multiple use* never has been sufficiently well defined to make it function as a driving force—scientists have been quick to fill the void. Researching and managing the forest ecological system for maintenance of biodiversity and system stability is today's scientific interpretation of *new forestry*.

Admittedly, it is established that maintenance of biodiversity is conducive to the long-term health (and therefore *sustainablity*) of forested ecosystems. But to manage a forest for biodiversity is akin to devoting one's life entirely to fitness exercises. Presumably, we all wish to remain fit and well in order that we can *do* other things with our lives, or *enjoy* certain things, or carry out some perceived *duty*.[39] Admittedly too, there is benignity in managing a forest to keep it healthy; at least this is not destructive. But human nature abhors a vacuum, and those with other agendas will not stay away. People still want wood products and other commodities, people still want to recreate (some quietly and others noisily), people still wish to protect endangered species of flora and fauna, and people still find intense aesthetic and even spiritual value in the forested landscape. *New forestry* has not diminished these wants (resisting any temptation to write *needs*), and in some cases has probably increased them, by legitimizing diverse values in forestry. Responding to this expanded decision space demands that foresters formulate an expanded set of criteria for evaluating activities and forest conditions in light of an entire spectrum of forest-centred values.

An important metatext of new forestry speaks to the relationship between humans and nature. Unquestionably, the ascendant author on this topic for at least twenty years has been the wildlife biologist, forester, ecologist and ethicist, Aldo Leopold.[40] Leopold's *A Sand County Almanac* and its chapter on *The Land Ethic* have been quoted so extensively by environmentalists seeking to inculcate new or rejuvenated nature-based values as to need almost no repetition. Five brief quotes from the book published in 1949, a year after his death, serve to recapitulate:

> The ordinary citizen today assumes science knows what makes the community clock tick; the scientist is equally sure that he does not. He knows that the biotic mechanism is so complex that its workings may never be fully understood.[41]

> An ethic may be regarded as a mode of guidance for meeting ecological situations so new or intricate, or involving such deferred reactions, that the path of social expediency is not discernable to the average individual. . . . Ethics are possibly a kind of community instinct in-the-making.[42]

> Examine each question in terms of what is ethically and esthetically right, as well as what is economically expedient. *A thing is right when it tends to preserve the integrity, stability, and beauty of the biotic community.* It is wrong when it tends otherwise.[43]

> In short, a land ethic changes the role of *Homo sapiens* from conqueror of the land-community to plain member and citizen of it. It implies respect for his fellow members, and also respect for the community as such.[44]

> A land ethic of course cannot prevent the alteration, management, and use of these "resources," but it does affirm their right to continued existence, and, at least in spots, their continued existence in a natural state.[45]

Leopold's thesis is a sympathetic combination of Oriental humility and community-centring, with Romantic nature-love and transcendence of the teleological-deontological dichotomy.[46] His role for people within the land community, his acknowledgment of the need for man to use resources, in conjunction with the preservation of some "natural" areas, call for a sympathetic engagement of humans with the natural world that is Romantic, in so far as it places humans *within the realm* of nature. As a scientist, Leopold respects the value of empirically-based scientific knowledge, while recognizing the abiding incompleteness of the same. In the interests of survival of the human species, he urges adoption of a conservative ethics- or rule-based cautiousness grounded in love for the land: for example, the first rule of intelligent tinkering, he tells us, is to keep all the pieces—which translates, among other things, to an emphasis on protection of habitat for endangered species. His goal is survival, but given an uncertain science, his means are closer to the deontological than the utilitarian. He despairs of finding sufficiency in economic incentives and urges, therefore, an ethic of conscience.[47]

Leopold's characterizing of ethics as "community instinct in-the-making" harks back to Hume, according to a view shared by authors as diverse as Baird Callicott and Frederic Hayek.[48] This view sees ethics as a cultural trait that can and should be cognitively and rhetorically encouraged in order that it may be "selected for" in a Darwinian process of natural selection.[49] Callicott sees Leopold continuing a lineage from Hume via Darwin, and Hayek views culture as an evolutionary product which lies *between* instinct and reason.[50]

The fleshing out of Leopold's ethic in terms of *integrity, stability and beauty* displays an interesting synthesis of science and aesthetics. For Leopold, natural biological systems organize themselves along increasingly complex lines which humans coincidentally (or sympathetically) find beautiful. This complexity also provides a degree of stability (defined as *resilience* or ability to recover from external disturbance)[51] that has become a cornerstone of *new forestry*. The naturally complex system has *integrity* (internal or self-referential wholeness) that we not only find beautiful, but which we destroy at our peril. The self-organizing nature of nature has found recent explication through the emerging science of *chaos*, with potential avenues for investigation using fractal geometry.[52] Hayek contends that human society is similarly self-organizing and credits Hume's contemporary, Adam Smith, with the early development of this notion.[53]

In Leopold's description of natural biological process we find clear compatibility with a view of life as a negentropic agent, organizing itself as a braking mechanism, slowing the inexorable progress of the Second Law of Thermodynamics. Describing the chronology of transmutation of an imaginary particle of matter, X, that eventually makes its way into an eagle's feather, Leopold continues:

> An Indian eventually inherited the eagle's plumes, and with them propitiated the Fates whom he assumed had a special interest in Indians. It did not occur to him that they might be busy casting dice against gravity; that mice and men, soils and songs, might be merely ways to retard the march of atoms to the sea.[54]

Leopold's ecocentric holism links beauty with integrity and stability in an ethical trilogy. The aesthetic and the scientific have long been joined at a fundamental level: the criteria by which emerging scientific theories are judged admissible are aesthetic by nature.[55] The synchronicity of a stabilizing biological complexity and human-perceived beauty has potential for cutting through the uncertainties of ecology, finding practical application in the *land ethic* by identifying benign courses of action through their aesthetic appeal. Elegance has long been an aesthetic of mathematics, and biologist Edward Wilson has endorsed this synthetic of Leopoldian pragmatism, stating: "Mathematics and beauty are devices by which human beings get through life with the limited intellectual capacity inherited by the species."[56] According to Wilson, even physicists have been guided by beauty in their development of theory.[57] Aesthetics, then, along with ethics and even mathematics, are cultural constructs which have assisted humans in making strategic decisions in the face of an uncertain and ultimately unknowable future.[58]

New forestry is thoroughly Leopoldian. It comes to terms with nature neither by endorsing the Stoic utilitarian, traditionalists' disdain for the undeveloped natural world (and its concomitant desire for objectification of the future), nor by embracing a reactionary disdain for human intervention of any kind—a disdain often espoused by some misanthropic preservationists who have turned Calvinism inside out and seek to prevent humans from any intercourse with nature. The Leopoldian position locates value in proper[59] functioning of biologic process and health of ecologic communities. In so doing, it avoids the arbitrariness of lines drawn within the animal rights movement, which seeks to extend a Kantian emphasis on individual rights to some uncertain point in the domain of living forms.[60] Instead, Leopold seeks to integrate the human with the natural in a context of *respect*, which I would describe as a call for aesthetic participation with nature, *whatever* we perceive nature to be.[61]

Having proposed that science deals with the realm of the *possible*, while ethics (like economics) circumscribes what is *prudent*, and that both make reference to the *beautiful*, it is appropriate to turn our attention to aesthetics and to criticism.

The Forest as Text: Aesthetics in Traditional Forestry

As Ronald Hepburn acknowledged in 1968, "serious aesthetic concern with nature is today rather an unusual phenomenon."[62] He saw the challenge as one of developing a language and a discourse: "If we cannot find sensible sounding language in which to describe them, experiences [of nature] are felt, in an embarrassed way, as off-the-map—and since off the map, seldom visited."[63] As the ship of criticism moves away from modernism, it is hopeful that this discourse will emerge. If Hutcheson is correct in asserting that "even nature ... doesn't grow on trees," then nature can *only* be treated as text. And if the point be contested, nature emerges nonetheless as a focus of critical discourse.[64]

Forestry in the U.S. dates only to the 1890s, but the image of the forest primeval that colours much environmental discourse dates to the Romantic-Transcendentalist artists and writers of the mid-nineteenth century. The essentially secular sympathetic imagination of the English and European Romantics[65] became fused with the intuition of New England Transcendentalists, such as Emerson and Thoreau, to savour nature as a glimpse of Heaven on Earth. Without benefit of automobile, airplane or television, and with the bulls of the American populace concentrated on the east coast, the national image of the great American wilderness was forged by artists who traveled west, alone, with settlers or officially attached to companies of explorers. Cole, Bierstadt, Durand, Moran and others painted the forested landscape from the Hudson River to the Rocky Mountains in the glorious Romantic style.[66] Mountains soar towards the heavens in a blaze of golden sunsets; storm clouds boil across windswept prairies; cataracts tumble as if unleashed by Sophoclean Furies; trees twist and struggle to maintain rooting on precipitous rock-faces. (Despite the aura of naturalism, a viewer might be forgiven for imagining that Watteau could slip in at any moment to add a cherub or two.[67]) Wild animals graze the water's edge with antediluvian innocence, or raise antlers to the sun from rocky promontory, claiming royal domain over vast territories. If the landscape is peopled at all, it is with Rousseauean noble savages,[68] minute Jeffersonian settlers dwarfed amidst a new-found Eden,[69] wagon-laden settlers on pilgrimage of manifest destiny,[70] or erudite aesthetes savoring the fine line of a meandering stream.[71]

Despite perpetuation of these Romantic images in writings of Sierra Club founder John Muir and their abiding symbolism in today's environmental movement, this view of the great Western wilderness began to wane toward the end of the nineteenth century. The Romantic aesthetic came to be associated with privilege, while the interests of the poor city dweller, settler, or homesteader were thought to be better represented by the utilitarian movement of social reform. The new view glorified labour over aesthetic participation; industry and the violence of industrial development over Arcadian languorous harmony. The proletarian became fashionable, as the aristocratic fell increasingly into disfavor. Consider, for example, this description of a garden in Utah published in an 1877 edition of *The Art Journal:*

In some instances, the utilitarian element, being in the ascendant, has boldly brought the vegetable-garden forward into public notice. I like the sturdy self-assertion of those potatoes, cabbages, and string-beans. Why should they, the preservers of mankind, slink away into back-lots, behind a board fence and leave the land-owner to be represented by a set of lazy bouncing-bets and stiff-mannered hollyhocks, who do nothing but prink and dawdle for a living.[72]

It was in this atmosphere of utilitarian ascendancy that Gifford Pinchot, American-born scion of French and English aristocratic stock, heeded his father's advice and became the first native U.S. forester. Returning in 1890, after brief forestry training in France, he set out to destroy the image of lumbering as forest devastation and to establish the practice of forestry as a sustainable and decidedly agricultural activity.[73] He encountered opposition on all sides: lumber and livestock men cried foul as he and the Federal administration moved to stem the uncontrolled exploitation of public forestlands; John Muir and the wilderness preservationists were equally incensed by his emphasis on development. Between 1891 and 1905 the system of National Forests was established, and, although many others were involved, most of the credit traditionally and rightfully goes to Pinchot and his close friend, President Theodore Roosevelt.[74] Pinchot, always politically volatile, was dismissed by President Taft in 1910, but he fought on for decades, and his spirit has continued to energize the forestry profession since the outset.[75] *Conservation*, as he wrote in 1910, had three great principles:

The first principle of conservation is development, the use of the natural resources now existing on this continent for the benefit of the people who live here now. There may be just as much waste in neglecting the development and use of certain natural resources as there is in then destruction.[76]

The second principle was the prevention of waste,[77] and the third was that "natural resources must be developed and preserved for the benefit of the many, and not merely for the profit of a few."[78]

The birth of U.S. forestry coincided with an era of barely-challenged optimism regarding the ability of man to transcend his dependence on nature with the use of technology. Science became more firmly aligned with the positivism of technological development. This ascendency of technology was reflected in art and architecture, which rejected the Romantic in favour of the modern.[79] Industrial architecture was raised in glorification of labour,[80] and scientific application reached new heights with artists like pointillist Georges Seurat,[81] capping a period that Kenneth Clark has dubbed "heroic materialism."[82] Concern for anti-human excesses of the industrial revolution had begun with Romantics such as William Blake and Robert Burns, but Romanticism had escaped into pastoralism, while the cause of the oppressed had been taken up by hard-headed social reformers like Bentham, Engels, and Dickens.[83] It was this tradition that Pinchot sought to emulate.

As the twentieth century proceeded, modern art and architecture moved toward a geometric simplification, a proliferation of Euclidean forms, which accurately reflected industrial evolution and mechanization. This reached its zenith at the Bauhaus school of art, architecture and design in the Germany of the 1920s. The Cubism of pre-World War I Paris, the Constructivism of revolutionary Moscow, and related influential movements led to Bauhaus artists such as Moholy-Nagy, Kandinsky, Feininger, and Klee.[84]

The Bauhaus is perhaps best known for

having given us modern architecture and furnishings. The ubiquitous offices and apartment blocks of simple rectangular glass prisms that are familiar to all came from the Bauhaus founder Walter Gropius, Mies van der Rohe, Le Corbusier, and colleagues; the matching rectangular metal and *formica*-style furniture came from Gropius, Breuer, and others. That the simplified forms of modernism frequently coincided with economies of production is perhaps due to its basing of form in functionality, allied with its essentially proletarian emphasis.

The Bauhaus' aim, true to the cause of Clark's "heroic materialism," was thoroughly humanist. Bauhaus architect Ludwig Hilberseimer designed cubic skyscraper cities which he envisioned as "a way out of the chaotic absence of order and the paralyzing effect on the individual of the vastness of the city."[85] Hilberseimer's city looks exactly like a series of huge match boxes arranged uniformly on graph paper squares.[86] Hans Wingler explains:

> He wanted to reduce the area covered by a building radically in favor of green areas, hence the possibility of communicating with nature.... His guiding principle was always the idea that the city would again have to become an organism able to function, not just technically but also with consideration for the people living in it. In addition, he thought that one of the main tasks of the planner was to take precautions against the danger of the city deteriorating into slums.[87]

Today it is widely acknowledged that green rectangles of close-cropped grassy carpet bear little resemblance to nature, and that the very uniformity, predictability and monotony of these housing projects would likely lead to the very slum conditions that Hilberseimer was so anxious to avoid.[88]

When Hitler drove the Bauhaus out of Germany in 1933, it moved to a receptive Chicago and continued to flourish. Perhaps the greatest flowering of Bauhaus modernism occurred in the post-World War II United States. It was during this post-war period of rapid development that the U.S. Forest Service also came into its own as a supplier of timber and practitioner of modern forestry. Using Veterans Administration monies to build logging roads, harvests soared in the 1950s and 1960s to levels ten times higher than pre-war figures, and the agency was finally able to achieve its utilitarian aspirations.[89] By around 1960 the American forestry paradigm was shared by public and private-sector foresters nationwide.

Given the ubiquitous acceptance of modernism—exemplified by the Bauhaus, its concentration on geometric simplification, its dictum that *form* should follow *function*, its utilitarian humanism and its often convenient economy of execution—it is hardly surprising that the modern forestry paradigm envisaged the ideal forest as a well-managed orchard. Forestry moved in the direction of establishing monocultures of even-aged trees, disease-, pest- and deformity-free, growing in lines, in stands with rectangular boundaries. The triumph of technology over nature's chaos was confidently expected, but the confidence was short-lived. Since the 1970s, public outcry at the superimposition of rectangular grids of clearcuts (along with a zig-zag pattern of logging roads) on the fractally-complex visual landscape of natural mountainsides has constituted the single greatest criticism of traditional forestry.[90]

Although Pinchot started out by advocating selection logging and the Forest Service did not rely heavily on clearcutting before World War II, Pinchot had set the modernist stage in 1910 when he wrote: "Today we understand that forest fires are wholly within the control of men.... The first duty of the human race is to control the earth it lives upon."[91] He instituted a very effective program of fire suppression in U.S. forests. Today, forest ecologists spend considerable time explaining to everyone else how this preoccupation with fire suppression has led to dangerous fuel buildups, stagnated trees, and associated problems with insects and disease. Reinstituting the natural role of fire in U.S. forests is a prime focus of *new forestry*. If there is one difference more than any other, that separates the modern from the postmodern, it is surely the debunking of Hilbersheimer's notion that *order*, in the form of Euclidean geometric simplification, is harmonious (whether for humans or in nature), and the concomitant acceptance that harmony is much more likely to be associated with *complexity*.[92]

For over twenty years now, there has been popular dissent over traditional forestry's apparent absence of aesthetic concern. Surprisingly perhaps, U.S. forestry did not start out this way. In the folklore of American forestry, Pinchot's first success on returning from France in 1890 was to prove the validity of agronomic forestry on the grounds of the Vanderbilt Estate at Biltmore, North Carolina: from this heroic achievement, his rise to fame began. While Pinchot's accomplishments were substantial, the major work of laying out Biltmore was in fact performed by the aging Frederick Law Olmsted, Senior.

Olmsted was the renowned originator and grand master of American landscape architecture. His first achievement had been Central Park in New York City. If Pinchot had been old enough to witness this project,[93] he would undoubtedly have approved: bringing refreshing air and greenery to the trapped masses of an urban desert was certainly beneficial social reform.

At the end of a distinguished career, Olmsted embarked upon the Biltmore project.[94] Three years later, a young friend of Olmsted's distant cousin was sent to see him by the young man's father, James Pinchot. The enthusiastic Gifford was there to sell Olmsted on the idea of trying out *forestry* at Biltmore. Olmsted needed little convincing since he had reached this conclusion several months earlier,[95] but he was unimpressed by Gifford's approach which lacked specificity.[96] He sent him packing, with instructions not to return unless he had a proper plan.

Pinchot set to work immediately and produced a detailed plan. The goal, he wrote, was to "prove selective cutting of mature trees can improve timberland, and at the same time provide a long-range steady income from lumbering."[97] Olmsted hired Pinchot in December as Forester for Biltmore, where he would later adopt the silvicultural practices first tried out by Olmsted in California—tree thinning (in 1886[98]), and tree planting (in 1888[99]). Gifford launched his illustrious career while Olmsted, in failing mind and health, lost control of the Biltmore project in 1895.[100] From this point on, the sympathetic congruency of aesthetics with forestry dissolved rapidly, as the Romantic ideals of Olmsted gave way to the utilitarian pragmatism of Pinchot and other founders of American forestry.[101]

Throughout his life, Olmsted had infused his work with an intense passion for *cultivating* the beautiful.[102] He wrote:

> What artist so noble as he who, with far-reaching conception of beauty and designing power, sketches the outlines, writes the colors, and directs the shadows of a picture so great that Nature shall be employed upon it for generations, before the work he has arranged for her shall realize his intentions.[103]

Elsewhere, Olmsted opined that "inability to appreciate the value of artistic training is the essence of vulgarity."[104] His interest in landscape aesthetics was not especially elitist; his career was devoted to improving the aesthetic lot of all people. Expressing his Romantic naturalism, he railed against the formalism of France and Italy, preferring to find beauty "in commonplace and peasant conditions."[105] But, with utilitarianism's displacement of Romanticism, as Olmsted's biographer summarized, "popular interest in the role that landscape architecture might play in directing and civilizing America's physical development was lacking."[106]

It remained lacking until around 1970, when popular revolt against the "mangy-dog" appearance of spasmodically clearcut hillsides erupted from Montana to West Virginia, from Wyoming to Alaska. For two decades now, the public has been sensitized to aesthetic concerns in the forest; given a lack of language and an almost complete absence of decision-making criteria that embody aesthetic considerations, however, its vocalized concerns have focused on instrumental values such as endangered species or water pollution.

Postmodernist critic Jean Baudrillard has blamed Bauhaus modernism for an annihilation of aesthetics:

> In fact, aesthetics in the modern sense of the term no longer has anything to do with the categories of beauty and ugliness. Contemporary aesthetics, once the theory of forms of beauty, has become the theory of a generalized compatibility of signs, of their internal coherence (signifier-signified) and of their syntax. Aesthetic value . . . simply translates the fact that its elements *communicate* amongst themselves according to the economy of a model, with maximal integration and minimal loss of information. This aesthetic order is a cold order. Functional perfection exercises a cold seduction, the functional satisfaction of a demonstration and an algebra. It has nothing to do with pleasure, with beauty (or horror) whose nature is conversely to rescue us from the demands of rationality. . . .[107]

Although the Forest Service has employed landscape architects for two decades now, they appear to have been rather ineffective in the public eye. Perhaps they adopted a cold, functional, modernist aesthetic that the public found unfitting to the natural landscape. More recently, foresters shifted from a proud stance of "as long as we are practicing good scientific forestry, we have nothing to hide" (aesthetic of functionalism), to defensive attempts to mask management activities whenever possible. Use of visual buffer strips and other simulations maybe represents a transitional state, a *late* or *high* modernism.[108]

Toward an Aesthetic of New Forestry

An examination of articles in the *Journal of Forestry* reveals that, coincident with the birth of *new forestry* about three years ago, there was a broadening of forestry literature to embrace ethics and emotions. One headline asked "Can Foresters Romance a Land Ethic?" and a two-part article examined forests as they were portrayed by the Romantic Transcendentalist artists of the nineteenth century.[109] This would have been unimaginable in the *Journal* five years earlier.

Aldo Leopold had wished for the end of modernism in forestry as far back as the 1940s. Using the gardening analogy, he referred to what he called the *A-B Cleavage:*

> In my own field, forestry, group A is quite content to grow trees like cabbages, with cellulose as the basic forest commodity. It feels no inhibition against violence, its ideology is agronomic. Group B, on the other hand, sees forestry as fundamentally different from agronomy because it employs natural species, and manages a natural environment rather than creating an artificial one. To my mind, Group B feels the stirrings of an ecological conscience.[110]

And Baird Callicott comments:

> Leopold's land *ethic* is yet another set of rules or limitations. It calls for obligation, self-sacrifice, and restraint and thus could be unappealing.... [Leopold's] land *aesthetic*, on the other hand, might be more palatable since it emphasizes [sensual] assets and rewards.[111]

However, Leopold's popularity arises neither from the prohibitions of his land ethic nor from any particular insights in his expository chapter on aesthetics. Throughout the bulk of the *Almanac* Leopold relies on the poetry of his prose and the constructive use of rhetoric. He appeals to a Romantic sympathetic imagination; his calls to reason do not deny this Romanticism (grounded as that is in the early Enlightenment[112]), but his unprecedented popularity among environmentalists lies, I am convinced, in his command of language. His implicit acceptance of ecology as discourse reveals an innate postmodernism.

New forestry is in the throes of defining a new lexicon, assigning signification to new signs. Foresters, like all other human beings, are language-based creatures, and the words chosen for use will have profound effect on the praxis and, thence, on the forest itself. Ever since Heisenberg revealed the uncertainty principle in physics,[113] the essential Human truth has become harder to ignore: that all inquiry pertains not to any pure objectification of form, but to a discursive relationship between observer and observed. Nature is then reopened to the possibility of the "religious, magical, symbolic" as Baudrillard would have it,[114] or to restoration of "compleat garden" from its modernist reduction as "map."[115]

If the language of traditional forestry has been starkly modernist, there have been exceptions: for example, in the area of wilderness management.[116] Society has made explicit aesthetic choices about the style of *gardening* that is admissible in legally protected wilderness areas.[117] I call this *romantic rusticism*. For trail maintenance, the Forest Service allows the use of double-buck hand saws, pack horses and dynamite. Structures such as log bridges and wooden signs are acceptable. We have had few aesthetic qualms about accepting the rustic technology of the nineteenth century, despite the logical arbitrariness of this decision. Technology that was foreign to the wilderness primeval, that arrived only with white settlers, is acceptable because our cultural notion of wilderness was forged by the Romantic artists of the mid-nineteenth century, as explained above. Implicitly at least, we have long recognized that wilderness is text.

Returning to the forest at large, the function of *planning*, concentrating as it does on rational *design*, is an essentially modernist activity.[118] However, if one broadens planning from a strictly reductionist calculus, to embrace the emotional intent of designers like Olmsted, it can yet escape the cold modernist fold. Today's planning technology centers around computer-based Geographic Information Systems (GIS). As little more than electronic means for drawing maps and displaying complex spatial information, this technology is infinitely more flexible and open-ended than the earlier generation of "black box" optimization models used in forest planning.[119] Indeed, an early proponent of the conceptual system embodied in GIS, Ian McHarg, displayed a thoroughly anti-modern, Romantic notion of landscape planning.[120]

Many important questions in *new forestry* have yet to be addressed. For example, biodiversity and complexity have been identified as desirable attributes for maintaining system stability. Stability, in turn, has been equated with resilience (the ability to "bounce back" or recover from disturbance). That the relationship is not always this simple has been pointed out by Mary Clark: ecosystem integrity and function can depend more on the survival of a few key species than on a simple proliferation of diversity *per se*.[121] Despite avowed interest in resilience, it remains true that ecologists are as concerned as the general public with protecting the *delicate* and the *fragile* in the forest. A dilemma arises, since a resilient system cannot depend on the survival of fragile or delicate elements. Concentration on ecosystem resilience will not by itself protect the delicate: the most resilient system might be one that is weed-infested and devoid of anything fragile.[122]

In terms of aesthetics, complexity has been linked to level of interest,[123] and according to Hepburn, "we know also that in all aesthetic experience it is contextual complexity that, more than any other single factor, makes possible the minute discrimination of emotional qualities; and such discrimination is accorded high aesthetic value."[124] Sheer complexity and associated high level of interest, however, do not sufficiently account for aesthetic appeal. There is often need for some particular unique characteristic, focal point, or disequilibriating feature to make an image come alive.[125] The post-glacial landscape of Scotland and other places used to be scattered with *rocking stones*— large boulders perched precariously so that a finger's touch might gently tip and rock several tons of stone. Although they endured for millennia after the ice retreated, few have survived vandalism of the past century. Shoved down the hillside, these boulders now enjoy a more stable and safer resting place, and ecosystem impact has doubtless been minimal; yet, few would deny that interesting and beautiful phenomena have been destroyed.

The importance of fragile, delicate elements might be to represent a system in unstable rather than stable equilibrium, as symbolized, say, by a bottle balanced on its top, or a rocking stone. Safety-oriented stability maximization ignores the aesthetic exquisiteness of systems maintained in unstable or dynamic equilibrium.[126]

Maybe postmodernism can come to the aid of *new forestry* in this regard: Among the principles of postmodernism laid out by Charles Jencks (who roots postmodernism in architecture and art) we find the concept of the "difficult whole," the paradox of "unfinished wholes" or "fragmented unity," and acceptance of dynamic evolution.[127] Other principles of Jencks which might pertain include: cultural and political pluralism, balance (or "urbane urbanism"), "Anamnesis" (which for Jencks is *acceptance* of history and historical continua), "divergent signification" (which allows "multiple readings" through "enigmatic allegory"), and new stylistic formulae which accommodate "paradox, oxymoron, ambiguity, double-coding, disharmonious harmony, amplification, complexity and contradiction."[128] The postmodern aesthetic is unlike any before in that it is not continuous with modernism and Romanticism; it is fragmented and nonutopian, questioning and ironic, yet optimistic. In total, as Jencks states, in "the age of eclecticism, we have the freedom to *choose*."

It is in designing environments for exercise of choice that the role of the architect again enters. Certainly there is an aesthetic of architectural praxis, but, intimately linked to this, there is also an aesthetic of *participation in* the physical environment, whether urban or rural. At least one forester, Bill Ticknor, has pointed out that architecture provides an appropriate role model for *new forestry*,[129] and the preeminent U.S. silviculturalist, David Smith, recently remarked that "silviculturalists manipulating stands of vegetation are like artists painting pictures."[130] Since 1971 or earlier, the Society of American Foresters has defined forestry as both art and science,[131] and fuller acknowledgement of the artistic side of forestry would assist in bridging the rift between arts and science first highlighted by C. P. Snow.[132]

In closing, my aim has not been to develop a cohesive aesthetic of *new forestry*, but rather to suggest that the utilitarians threw out the baby with the bath-water when they so utterly rejected the Romantic-Transcendentalist aesthetic. However, I am not for a moment suggesting that we should set the clock back to the days of Romanticism. Where modernism and modernist forestry repudiated its Romantic past, *new forestry* would be better advised to acknowledge the lingering relevance of its modernist predecessor, which, as Jencks has suggested, is a postmodern trait.

Gardening has developed as a language in the west since mediaeval times.[133] Where modernist forestry has valued only one kind of gardening—utilitarian vegetable gardening— gardening has in fact an entire spectrum of genres. There is nothing *wrong* with vegetable gardening; it is simply not the *only* form of gardening. From the vegetable garden to the orchard; from the tennis court to the lawn; from the formal gardens of Versailles to the informality of an English cottage garden; from the wild mystery of the wilderness garden to the tranquil mystery of a Japanese Zen garden; from the water-lilied pools of Monet to the fast-flowing streams of the mountains . . . And so on.

Postmoderism intends not to debunk modernism but to transcend it; not to replace one narrow aesthetic with another, but to accept the past, to retain as much of the modern as we desire, and to reacquaint ourselves with classical, Romantic and other pre-modern conditions. It is not necessary for *new forestry* to emasculate either traditional forestry or wilderness management. Tree farms can continue to play a primary role in commodity production, just as we still need farms, factories and vegetable gardens. Wilderness, as the minimally-managed nexus to the untamable *wild,* is still important as a referent of the human condition. Rather than eradicating these polar opposites, *new forestry* offers the opportunity to flesh out an entire spectrum of "gardening" styles in between.

The bulk of public forestlands will likely remain neither wilderness nor tree farm. Instead they will be managed eclectically, in accordance with specific conditions and desires. This will require tolerance. Just as we do not expect ourselves, as individuals, to like every piece of art that is produced, we should not expect to like personally every acre of forest.

Traditional forestry avoided aesthetics in part because it was thought to be a chaotic morass, a Hobbesian no-man's-land in which taste is entirely unpredictable. (The commercial world has long known this to be untrue.) This viewpoint arose within a scientific positivism that deemed literary and artistic criticism inadmissible. Aesthetics is a cultural construct that is properly a subject of education and academic investigation; it is no less and no more *real* than science. If *new forestry* is to succeed, I believe, it must acknowledge the natural as cultural, and in doing this, it might find the established discourse of criticism as helpful as the science of ecology.

Perhaps Linda Hutcheon was right, that even nature doesn't grow on trees; or maybe Steinbeck was closer when he wrote in *The Log from the Sea of Conez:*

> We were curious. Our curiosity was not limited, but was as wide and horizonless as that of Darwin or Agassiz or Linnaeus or Pliny. We wanted to see everything our eyes would accommodate, to think what we could, and out of our seeing and thinking, to build some kind of structure in modelled imitation of the observed reality. We knew that what we would see and record and construct would be warped, as all knowledge patterns are warped, first

by the collective pressure and stream of our time and race, second by the thrust of our individual personalities. But knowing this, we might not fall into too many holes—we might maintain some balance between our warp and the separate thing, the external reality.

Not falling into "too many holes" is what *new forestry* is all about.

Notes

An early version of this paper was presented at the *Mansfield Forum,* The Mike and Maureen Mansfield Center, University of Montana, March 31, 1992.

1. Franklin 1989.
2. For example Atkinson 1990.
3. The implicit allusion to Canada is by intention. At least British Columbia, which is a part of the Western Forestry Conservation Association, seems to be affected by the *new forestry* movement.
4. *New perspectives* is described by Salwasser 1990. Technically, Franklin's *new forestry* relates specifically to a new approach to silviculture, while Salwasser's *new perspectives* is the more general term that refers to a new philosophy of forest praxis—one that could mix *new forestry* with more traditional methods. However, as so frequently happens, popular usage has taken to *new forestry* as the general epithet; I shall follow the popular lead. A Forest Service Northern Region pamphlet (R1–92-11) calls *New Perspectives* "a philosophical approach," and cites four principles: three of these are not new (public participation, integrated management and scientific collaboration); the fourth states: "We must sustain ecological systems to maintain the land's resilience and productivity, and to produce desired resource uses and values over time. Our activities must be environmentally sensitive and aesthetically acceptable." A similar publication from the Siskiyou National Forest in Oregon stresses "biological diversity," Aldo Leopold and "ethical land stewardship," and "mimicking nature's change-and-renewal cycle."
5. Since writing the first draft of this paper, the term *new forestry* has evolved once again, and is now known as *ecosystem management.* In summer, 1992, this became official Forest Service policy. (USDA Forest Service 1992. See also memos from Forest Service Chief Dale F. Robertson to Regional Foresters and Station Directors, June 4 and 26, 1992, on "Ecosystem Management" with attachments.)

6. Specifically, I would cite Western Forest Economists' Annual Meeting, Wemme OR, May 1990; Western Forestry Conservation Association Annual Meeting, Coeur d'Alene ID, December 1990; Montana Society of American Foresters Annual Meeting, Missoula MT, March 1991; U.S. Forest Service Northern Region *New Perspectives* Workshop, Missoula MT, October 1991; Wilderness Society *Defining Sustainable Forestry* Workshop, Washington D.C., January 1992; Western Forestry Conservation Association *Seeking Common Ground* Conference, Portland OR, February 1992; and the Montana State Meeting of the Society of American Foresters, Kalispell MT, March 1992.

7. More completely, the regulated forest has timber stands arrayed in a succession of age classes from the youngest up to harvestable age in such a way that "an approximately equal annual or periodic yield of products of desired size and quality may be obtained" (Davis 1966). A simple model is to imagine the forest as a chess board. Each square contains a stand of a different age, with every age represented from one to 64 years. Each year, the oldest square would be logged and new trees regenerated, ad infinitum.

8. German-born and educated Bernhard Fernow is credited with the birth of forestry and forestry education in the U.S. (Robbins 1982). He was appointed head of the Division of Forestry in the U.S. Department of Agriculture in 1886, a post which passed to Gifford Pinchot when Fernow resigned to start the nation's first U.S. university-based school of forestry at Cornell, New York, in 1898. The system of national forest reserves had begun in 1891, but their management did not come under the auspices of the Department of Agriculture until Pinchot and President Theodore Roosevelt together brought this about in 1905.

9. "Forest regulation" has been a mainstay class

in every forestry school for most of this century. Essentially, the task was to calculate optimal timber harvest age, optimal cultural practices and maximum cutting rates so as to stabilize timber production at the highest rate that could be indefinitely maintained (sustained yield).

10. Richard Alston alluded to this notion of sustainability shifting from *flow* to *stock* at the Wilderness Society *Defining Sustainable Forestry* Workshop, Washington D.C., January 1992.

11. Jameson 1991, xiv.

12. It is tempting to suggest a new ideal derived from the Second Law of Thermodynamics: that the optimal ecosystem is that which minimizes the production of entropy. Although this notion has been gaining ground in theoretical biology (for example, Brooks and Wiley 1988), it has not yet made headway in forestry. If it is shown that natural systems evolve so as to minimize entropy production, then it would still be necessary to show that humans should emulate nature in this regard, although a strong case could probably be made in that direction.

13. Jencks 1987, 346. A current preponderance of endings is reflected in recent titles from *The End of History* to *The End of Nature*, including an environmental video called *Evolution's End*. This itself is a postmodern phenomenon (Jameson 1991).

14. Jencks 1987, 346–49.

15. Hutcheon 1989, 2.

16. Reviewing one hundred years of forestry literature, one marvels at the rapidly changing perspective. Stands of trees that take centuries to mature physically nevertheless undergo astounding transformation in the way they are *seen* by foresters and other people every decade or so. See Raup 1979.

17. An incomplete, but nonetheless significant, insight was offered in a *Journal of Forestry* editorial:

> The problem comes in seeking values from science. Because science is not a religion, but rather a technique for attempting to understand cause-and-effect relationships, it can only predict outcomes from specified actions. It cannot tell us whether the results are desirable or not. (Baird 1991)

The incompleteness lies in thinking that only religion can be a source of value. Value can also arise in the market place (economics), in individual passions (as discussed in relation to David Hume), or collectively in culture as in, say, aesthetics.

18. Society of American Foresters' Committee on Ethics 1991.

19. An overwhelming proportion of people's income in the U.S., I would maintain, is spent satisfying what are essentially aesthetic (sensual) desires, from choice of clothes to automobiles, food, entertainment, lifestyle and location. A bowl of rice and some cardboard or plastic sheets would keep us alive, as the homeless or refugees could attest. Obviously, aesthetics is more than the foresters' notion of scenery.

20. Locating *new forestry* (along with Leopold) in the postmodern implies compatibility with an ecofeminist view of intersubjectivity or reciprocity of relationship between humans and nature. In this vein, while forest *management* connotes a dominating band (Latin, manus) of man lording itself over nature, stewardship (Old English, sty-ward) is increasingly offered as a more reverential alternative expressing care and husbandry. However, the paternalism inherent in stewardship has brought this word also under attack, as, for example, in Rowe 1990. Similarly the possessive (as in "the public and its forests") might offend some "Earth Firsters" and ecocentric holists who express an antianthropocentrism and oppose the very notion of land ownership. The existence of such criticism displays the discursive nature of forestry.

21. It could be called simply *U.S. forestry* since there has been no other enduring forestry paradigm in the U.S.; Atkinson (1992) calls it *traditional forestry* to distinguish it from *new forestry*, a practice which I adopt here, although I would be equally inclined to call it *modern forestry*, since its development peaked in the post—World War II era and represented, I maintain, an application of high modernist thinking in the arena of forest management.

22. Pinchot used this clause in several places, including the letter that he wrote to himself for his supervisor's signature when he became first chief of the Forest Service in 1905 (U.S. Government 1978, 138–39).

23. Lockridge 1989, 130.

24. Pinchot was an ardent supporter of Theodore Roosevelt's *new progressivism*.

25. Lockridge 1989, 130.

26. Lockridge 1989, 141.

27. The necessity for and difficulty of *measurement* (particularly on a common scale) to facilitate the goal of maximization is a particular weakness of utilitarianism and of its contemporary offshoot, "benefit cost analysis" (Wenz 1988).

28. Clary 1986.

29. The Multiple Use-Sustained Yield Act was passed at the Forest Service's behest in 1960.

30. The willingness-to-pay concept values goods and amenities for which little or no price is actually charged in the market. Various methodologies exist for assigning dollar values, such as the "travel cost method" and the "contingent valuation method." Validity is still controversial, and the Forest Service is considering dropping this approach to planning.

31. For example, Duerr et al. 1979.

32. The FORPLAN computer model (Barber and Rodman 1990), which was the core analytical tool in Forest Service planning, used an objective function of maximizing discounted "net public benefit."

33. Foucault 1965, 55-56. The reference to the winning of fruit from the land only by "force and continual labor" (which Foucault cites to Bossuet) illustrates the now-criticized notion of the land as "niggardly" and in need of domination by the hand of man. Other critiques of the condemnation of idleness by Western society, and its connection to commerce and colonialism, are found in Russell 1932 and Coetzee 1988.

34. Even while espousing concern for beauty, biodiversity and ecosystem complexity, the Forest Service continues to cling to its language of need; for example, "ecosystem management . . . is a means we will use to meet society's *needs*. . . . " (Chief Robertson's memo of June 26, 1992, p. 2. See note 5 above).

35. Fernow also wanted *every acre* to do its *duty*.

36. An interesting critique of logical positivism is found in Russell 1956.

37. Hume 1978, 458.

38. For example, and despite occasional disclaimers, the Forest Service in its draft Charter for Wilderness Management (October 1992) clearly views wilderness problems as essentially scientific in nature.

39. Conceivably, one might so enjoy fitness exercises as to decide that is all one wants to do, but that at least would be for *pleasure* and not the tautology of staying well for wellness's sake.

40. See generally Nash 1989.

41. Leopold 1970, 240-41. The woeful lack of knowledge of ecosystem complexity was iterated in 1974 (Farnworth and Golley 1974, 145) and reiterated recently (Atkinson 1992). It was a topic for several speakers at the Wilderness Society's *Defining Sustainable Forestry* Workshop, Washington D.C., January 1992. We can be confident of the sustainability of this theme.

42. Leopold 1970, 239.

43. Leopold 1970, 262.

44. Leopold 1970, 240.

45. Leopold 1970, 240.

46. For a discourse on the ethics of Romanticism see Lockridge 1989, generally, and for the argument that Romanticism synthesizes the teleological with the deontological, see particularly p. 149.

47. In this, Leopold differs from some (for example, Wilson 1984, 131) who share his aims but place greater faith in society's ability to invent contractual mechanisms for individualizing the collective good (to capitalize on Adam Smith's "guiding hand of providence," which purportedly brings together the goal of society with that of the individual).

48. Callicott (1989) is an American environmental philosopher who has attempted to formalize the philosophical basis of Leopold (who was writing as an ecologist and concerned citizen rather than from a position of formal philosophy). Hayek (1989) was a libertarian Austrian economist and Nobel laureate. Callicott and Hayek both trace Darwin to Hume and ground ethics in culture.

49. Ethics then is a species survival mechanism of humans, no different than, say, the turtle's shell or the leopard's speed.

50. Hayek argues that the simple dichotomy of *nature* (the physical, instinctual) and *artifice* (product of human cognition and design) is overly restrictive. Culture, he argues, arises within a slow process

of tradition—an evolutionary dialectic, although not Hayek's words—that transcends the dichotomy and is profoundly important in affecting human economic organization.

51. This notion of stability as resilience is generally accepted today and has been attributed to ecologist E. P. Odum (Farnworth and Golley 1974, 124).

52. The fractal mathematics of natural systems has been developed by Mandelbrot 1983. For an example application in forestry, see Zeide and Pfeifer 1991.

53. Hayek 1989. Charles Peirce's synechism is also pertinent to this notion.

54. Leopold 1970, 113. See also note 12.

55. These criteria (or virtues) of the scientific method include *conservatism, modesty, simplicity* and *generality* (Wenz 1988, 261–62).

56. Wilson 1984, 61. Wilson is comfortable with the synthetic basis of beauty: "Elegance is more a product of the human mind than of external reality" (p. 60).

57. Wilson stated: "To a considerable degree science consists in originating the maximum amount of information with the minimum expenditure of energy [a clearly negentropic notion]. Beauty is the cleanness of line in such formulations, along with symmetry, surprise, and congruence with prevailing beliefs. This widely accepted definition is why P. A. M. Dirac, after working out the behavior of electrons, could say that physical theories with some physical beauty are also the ones most likely to be correct, and why Hermann Weyl, the perfecter of quantum and relativity theory, made an even franker confession: 'My work always tried to unite the true with the beautiful; but when I had to choose one or the other, I usually chose the beautiful'" (Wilson 1984, 60–61).

58. For an excellent treatment of uncertainty, see Malte Faber et al., "Humankind and the Environment: An Anatomy of Surprise and Ignorance," *Environmental Values* 1(3) (1992): 217–41.

59. The Wittgensteinian identification of the *proper* (correct) with the *aesthetic* is perhaps appropriate in this context.

60. This criticism of the animal rights movement is not intended to extend to the essentially utilitarian theorists (such as Peter Singer) who follow in Bentham's footsteps. Bentham included all sentient creatures in his concern for reduced suffering, but thoroughly disparaged the notion of natural rights (Wenz 1988).

61. Consistent with Hume, the objectification of nature cannot escape the subjective sphere.

62. Hepburn 1968, 49.

63. Hepburn 1968, 50.

64. This view is shared in biological science by Wilson (1984), for example, who praises the role of the critic (p. 58) and sees cultural discourse as a biological entity: "The mind is biologically prone to discursive communication that expands thought" (p. 74). "Culture in turn is a product of the mind, which can be interpreted as an image-making machine that recreates the outside world through symbols arranged into maps and stories" (p. 101).

65. Lockridge 1989.

66. Tyler 1983.

67. As, for example, in Waneau's *The Pilgrimage to Cythera* (Clark 1969, 232–36).

68. For example, Paul Kane's *Falls at Colville* (c. 1848).

69. For example, Thomas Cole's *Genesee Scenery (Mountain Landscape with Waterfall)*, 1847.

70. For example, Albert Bierstadt's *Emigrants Crossing the Plains*, 1867.

71. For example, Asher Durand's *Kindred Spirits*, 1849.

72. Woodard 1877, 165, quoting Fitzhugh Ludlow.

73. McGeary 1960, 23.

74. A debate arose recently over the relative importance of Fernow and Pinchot (Twight 1990; Miller 1991).

75. Pinchot headed a Society of American Foresters committee investigating "Forest Devastation" in 1919 (Pinchot 1919), and in 1937 he fought to keep National Forests under control of the Department of Agriculture on the grounds that trees are first and foremost an agricultural crop (Pinchot 1937). See also Heinrich 1985.

76. Pinchot 1967, 43.

77. Still today, salvage logging of dead trees can sometimes *only* be justified on the basis of preventing waste.

78. Pinchot, 1967, 46. Pinchot wrote speeches for Roosevelt, fighting the trusts and conglomerates of capitalism, advocating first "New Nationalism" and then Bull Moose Progressivism (McGeary 1960, 192–215). In any other country Pinchot's politics would have been identified with state-controlled socialism. See also note 101.

79. If impressionism formed the transition in Europe, an organicism represented by, say, Frank Lloyd Wright, perhaps better represented the American transition. The influence of Wright on the earlier work of Bauhaus founder Walter Gropius is evident in the "Summerfield House." See Wingler 1978, 224–25 and 239. See also Silverman 1990, 4.

80. Wingler 1978, 226.

81. Britt 1989.

82. Clark 1969, chap. 13.

83. Clark 1969, 327. Silverman (1990, 5) states: "Surely Hegel, Marx, Mill, and Comte are also modern—but they are modern with a twist, or several twists. Dialectic, the utilitarian principle, and positivism give a new look to Kantian critical philosophy."

84. See generally, Wingler 1978 and Britt 1989. The Bauhaus mechanization of the human form, marrying the body with the machine, can be traced to origins as diverse as the cotton mill, the slave ship (Clark 1969, 323) and Bentham's design for the ideal prison (Foucault 1979). This synthesis flourished, particularly in modern dance (Wingler 1978, especially p. 367, also Clair 1991) and was reflected more recently in the popularity of children's *transformer* toys, for example. Where Romantics shunned the machine, moderns embraced it to the point of emulation.

85. Wingler 1978, 496.

86. Wingler 1978, 497.

87. Wingler 1978, 496.

88. The recent film *Straight Out of Brooklyn* comes to mind.

89. Wilkinson and Anderson 1987.

90. As late as the 1970s, fisheries biologists shared with foresters their passion for landscape simplification. They cleared streams, channelized and straightened them, believing this would improve fish habitat, while ignoring their own intuition which took them to complex streams and log-trapped pools when catching fish for recreation. (James Sedell, Research Ecologist for U.S. Forest Service PNW Research Station, Corvallis, Oregon, speaking at Western Forestry Conservation Association *Seeking Common Ground* Conference, Portland OR, February 25, 1992.)

91. Pinchot 1967, 45.

92. Again, the development of fractal geometry comes to mind, with Mandelbrot's finding that Euclidean dimensions are just special cases along an infinitely-divisible spectrum of fractal dimension (Mandelbrot 1983). Also Francis Hutcheson's theory that beauty and harmony arise from direct (inner) sense perception of "uniformity amidst variety" (Hutcheson 1725, 15–18).

93. Pinchot was born in 1865, two years after completion of Central Park (McGeary 1960, 7, and Fabos et al. 1968, 3).

94. Roper 1973, 406.

95. In January 1891, Olmsted recommended to Vanderbilt that since the soils were poor and the trees had been logged "until nothing remained but runts and ruins and saplings," the best disposition of the majority of the acquired property would be as a European-style forest, this being "a hunting preserve for game, mainly with a view to crops of timber" (Roper 1973, 415).

96. White 1957, 82.

97. White 1957, 84.

98. Roper 1973, 410.

99. Roper 1973, 412.

100. Roper 1973, 469–74.

101. Olmsted has been described both as a Romantic engineer (Fabos et al. 1968, 10) and as a "Utopian Socialist"—referring to a movement quite popular among some of New York's social and literary elite (Fein 1972, 16). Pinchot's own sympathy with the underdog is displayed in his description of Biltmore House as a "magnificent chateau.... But in the United States of the nineteenth century and among the one-room cabins of the Appalachian mountaineers, it did not belong. The contrast was

a devastating commentary on the injustice of concentrated wealth" (Fein 1972, 13).

102. Roper 1973, 421–22.

103. This thoroughly Romantic quotation appears in Fabos et al. 1968, 15.

104. Roper 1973, 460.

105. Roper 1973, 433, 464.

106. Roper 1973, 475. In August 1885 (Fein 1972, caption 28 and p. 151), when Olmsted's memory was failing and he was losing control of affairs (Roper 1973, 469), he wrote a letter to the Biltmore horticulturalist Warren Manning (with whom Pinchot and others had been having trouble; see Roper 1973, 465) in which he most uncharacteristically stated: "I want you to recognize . . . that the ruling interest of the estate is not . . . agricultural; it is not landscape gardening; it is simply *industrial forestry;* the management of trees with reference to commercial profit" (Fein 1972, caption 28). Two months later, Olmsted felt that he had been set aside by his partners and had been betrayed in a business coup (Roper 1973, 469).

107. Baudrillard 1981, 188. See also Hepburn 1968, 49.

108. Jencks 1987, 230–33 and 327. "High" modernism is seen, for example, in the "clothes hanger" pediment of the AT&T Headquarters in Manhattan or the garland-festooned walls of the Public Services Building in Portland.

109. Baird 1991; McGrath, 1991.

110. Leopold 1970, 259.

111. Callicott 1989.

112. For the grounding of Romanticism in "sympathetic imagination" and its original compatibility with the Enlightenment see Lockridge 1989. Lockridge sees the overriding thrust of Romanticism as a "will to value."

113. Heelan 1965. Also Gribbin 1984.

114. Baudrillard 1981, 186.

115. Vernon 1973.

116. The very term "wilderness management" has been called an oxymoron (Nash 1978). However, when *wilderness* is understood in a textural sense as symbolic nexus of wild otherness, rather than as absolute form (the closest knowledge can come to the unknowable), the contradiction vanishes. That such an interpretation was intended is clear in the language of the 1964 Wilderness Act (" . . . *protected* and *managed* so as to *preserve* its natural conditions and which [1] generally *appears* to have been affected primarily by the forces of nature, with the imprint of man *substantially unnoticeable* . . .") [emphasis added]. The intervention of man in wilderness preservation harks back as far as the Colonus of Sophocles. Although the Grove of the Furies was "not to be touched, no one may live upon it; Most dreadful are its divinities, most feared, Daughters of darkness and mysterious earth" (Sophocles 1949, 84), authority over access to the sacred grove was nevertheless under control of the state, a matter for the "city government" (p. 84) or the king, Theseus (p. 85). In a strict sense, managed wilderness is truly simulacrum.

117. Within the limits set by law, forest managers and wilderness users work out joint aesthetic and ecological standards on an area-by-area basis through a process known as Limits of Acceptable Change (Stankey et al. 1984).

118. Baudrillard 1981.

119. For example, the FORPLAN linear programming model used by the Forest Service in the 1980s.

120. McHarg 1973.

121. Clark 1992.

122. For example, a mountain meadow vegetated with hard-to-eradicate spotted knapweed will be considerably more resilient in the face of trampling (by hikers or cattle) than the meadow populated with rare and delicate species of alpine flowers.

123. "It remains none the less true that the quest for monistic simplification, whether in a religious and metaphysical or in a scientific, technological and utilitarian guise . . . is utterly antagonistic to interestingness" (Kolnai 1968). There is maybe an exact analog between interestingness as it pertains to aesthetics, and information as it pertains to negentropy.

124. Hepburn 1968, 55.

125. For Roland Barthes, this would be the "punctum" amidst the more general "studium" (Barthes 1981).

126. *Walking* has been described as a process of moving from one point of unstable equilibrium to

another. In walking, one neither wants to stand still nor to stumble. I believe that the process of walking provides for a more acceptable forestry praxis than does the search for stability or "sustainability" of anything specific.

127. Jencks 1987, 329–50.

128. The French landscape architect Louis Benech alluded to such paradox when he said:

> Nothing is more exciting than spontaneity, even if it is deliberately created." (De Gourcuff 1991)

129. Ticknor 1992.

130. Dr. David Smith, Professor Emeritus of Silviculture, Yale University, speaking at the University of Montana, Missoula, October 1991.

131. Ford-Robertson 1971.

132. Snow 1959.

133. Harvey 1981.

References

Atkinson, William. 1992. "Silvicultural Correctness: The Politicalization of Forest Science," *Western Wildlands* 17(4): 8–12.

Baird, Linda. 1991. "Can Foresters Romance a Land Ethic?" *Journal of Forestry* 89(4).

Barber, Klaus, and Susan Rodman. 1990. "FORPLAN: The Marvelous Toy," *Journal of Forestry* 88(5): 26–30.

Barthes, Roland. 1981. *Camera Lucida: Reflections on Photography*. Translated by Richard Howard. New York: Hill and Wang.

Baudrillard, Jean. 1981. *For a Critique of the Political Economy of the Sign*. Translated by C. Levin. St. Louis: Telos Press.

Britt, David, ed. 1989. *Modern Art: Impressionism to Post-modernism*. Boston: Bullfinch Press.

Brooks, David, and E. O. Wiley. 1988. *Evolution as Entropy*. 2nd ed. Chicago: University of Chicago Press.

Callicott, J. Baird. 1989. *In Defense of the Land Ethic*. New York: SUNY Press.

Clair, Jean. 1991. "The 1920s, Age of the Metropolis: Modernism, Mechanization, and the Birth of the Multiple," *The Journal of Art*, October: 10–11.

Clark, Kenneth. 1969. *Civilisation: A Personal View*. New York: Harper and Row.

Clark, Mary. 1992. "Tasks for Future Ecologists," *Environmental Values* 1(1): 35–46.

Clary, David. 1986. *Timber and the Forest Service*. Lawrence: University Press of Kansas.

Coetzee, J. M. 1988. "Idleness in South Africa," *Harper's Magazine*, 276(1655): 22–26.

Davis, Kenneth. 1966. *Forest Management Regulation and Valuation*. 2nd ed. New York: McGraw-Hill.

De Gourcuff, Alain. 1991. "Benech in Bloom," *France Magazine* 20: 22–25.

Duerr, W. A., D. E. Teeguarden, N. B. Christiansen, and S. Gunenberg. 1979. *Forest Resource Management: Decision-Making Principles and Cases*. Philadelphia: W. B. Saunders.

Fabos, Julius, Gordon Milde, and Michael Weinmayr. 1968. *Frederick Law Olmsted, Sr.: Founder of Landscape Architecture in America*. Boston: University of Massachusetts Press.

Farnworth, Edward, and Frank Golley, eds. 1974. *Fragile Ecosystems: Evaluation of Research and Applications in the Neotropics*. New York: Springer-Verlag.

Fein, Albert. 1972. *Frederick Law Olmsted and the American Environmental Tradition*. New York: George Braziller.

Ford-Robertson, F. C., ed. 1971. *Terminology of Forest Science, Technology, Practice and Products*. Washington, D.C.: Society of American Foresters.

Foucault, Michel. 1965. *Madness and Civilization*. New York: Pantheon Books.

———. 1979. *Discipline and Punish*. New York: Vantage Books.

Franklin, Jerry. 1989. "Toward a New Forestry," *American Forests* 95(11&12): 37–40.

Gribbin, John. 1984. *In Search of Schrodinger's Cat: Quantum Physics and Reality*. London: Black Swan Books.

Harvey, John. 1981. *Mediaeval Gardens*. Portland: Timber Press.

Hayek, F. A. 1989. *The Fatal Conceit: The Collected Works of F. A Hayek* 1. Edited by W. W. Bartley III. Chicago: University of Chicago Press.

Heelan, P. A. 1965. *Quantum Mechanics and Objectivity: A Study of the Physical Philosophy of Werner Heisenberg.* The Hague: Martinus Nijhoff.

Heinrich, Jay. 1985. "Pinchot's Heirs," *Journal of Forestry* 83(5): 277–79.

Hepburn, Ronald. 1968. "Aesthetic Appreciation of Nature," in *Aesthetics in the Modern World*, edited by Harold Osborne, pp. 49–66. New York: Weybright and Talley.

Hume, David. 1978. *A Treatise of Human Nature.* 2nd ed. Oxford: Clarendon Press.

Hutcheon, Linda. 1989. *The Politics of Postmodernism.* London: Routledge.

Hutcheson, Francis. 1725. *An Inquiry into the Original of Our Ideas of Beauty and Virtue.* London: John Darby.

Jameson, Fredric. 1991. *Postmodernism, or the Cultural Logic of Late Capitalism.* Durham: Duke University Press.

Jencks, Charles. 1987. *Post-Modernism: The New Classicism in Art and Architecture.* New York: Rizzoli.

Kolnai, Aurel. 1968. "On the Concept of the Interesting," in *Aesthetics in the Modern World*, edited by Harold Osborne, pp. 166–87. New York: Weybright and Talley.

Leopold, Aldo. 1970. *A Sand County Almanac.* New York: Ballantine Books.

Lockridge, Laurence. 1989. *The Ethics of Romanticism.* Cambridge, U.K.: Cambridge University Press.

Mandelbrot, Benoit. 1983. *The Fractal Geometry of Nature.* New York: W. H. Freeman.

McGeary, Nelson. 1960. *Gifford Pinchot, Forester, Politician.* Princeton, N.J.: Princeton University Press.

McGrath, R. L. 1991. "The Tree and the Stump: Hieroglyphics of the Sacred Forest," Parts One and Two. *Journal of Forestry* 89(7): 12–16, and 89(8): 17–21.

McHarg, Ian. 1973. "The Place of Nature in the City of Man," in *Western Man and Environmental Ethics*, edited by Ian Barbour. Reading: Addison-Wesley Publishing.

Miller, Char. 1991. "The Prussians are Coming! The Prussians are Coming!" *Journal of Forestry* 89(3): 23–27.

Nash, Roderick. 1978. *Wilderness Management: A Contradiction in Terms?* Wilderness Resource Distinguished Lectureship Series 2. Moscow, University of Idaho Wilderness Research Center.

———. 1989. *The Rights of Nature.* Madison: University of Wisconsin Press.

Pinchot, Gifford. 1919. "Forest Devastation: A National Danger and a Plan to Meet It," *Journal of Forestry* 17(8): 911–45.

———. 1937. "Old Evils in New Clothes," *Journal of Forestry* 35(5): 435–38.

———. 1967. *The Fight for Conservation*, Americana Library Edition. Seattle: University of Washington Press.

Raup, Hugh. 1979. "Beware the Conventional Wisdom," *Western Wildlands* 5(3): 2–9.

Robbins, William. 1982. *Lumberjacks and Legislators: Political Economy of the U.S. Lumber Industry, 1890–1941.* College Station: Texas A&M University.

Roper, Laura. 1973. *FLO: A Biography of Frederick Law Olmsted.* Baltimore: Johns Hopkins University Press.

Rowe, Stan. 1990. *Home Place: Essays on Ecology.* Edmonton, Alberta: NeWest Limited.

Russell, Bertrand. 1932. "In Praise of Idleness," *Harper's Magazine* 165: 552–59.

———. 1956. *Logic and Knowledge: Essays, 1901–1950.* New York: MacMillan.

Salwasser, Hal. 1990. "Gaining Perspective: Forestry for the Future," *Journal of Forestry* 88(11): 32–39.

Snow, C. P. 1959. *The Two Cultures and the Scientific Revolution.* New York: Cambridge University Press.

Society of American Foresters' Committee on Ethics. 1991. "Land Ethic Canon," *Journal of Forestry* 89(2): 30, 38.

Sophocles. 1949. "Oedipus at Colonus," in *The Oedipus Cycle*, translated by D. Fitts and R. Fitzgerald. New York: Harvest Books (Harcourt, Brace & World).

Stankey, George, Stephen McCool, and Gerry Stokes. 1984. "Limits of Acceptable Change: A

New Framework for Managing the Bob Marshall Wilderness Complex," *Western Wildlands* 10(3): 33–37.

Ticknor, William. 1992. "Sustainable Forestry: Redefining the Role of Forest Management," paper presented at the Wilderness Society *Defining Sustainable Forestry* Workshop, Washington, D.C., January.

Twight, Ben. 1990. "Bernhard Fernow and Prussian Forestry in America," *Journal of Forestry* 88(2): 21–25.

Tyler, Ron. 1983. *American Canvas: The Art, Eye, and Spirit of Pioneer Artists*. New York: Portland House.

USDA Forest Service. 1992. *Taking an Ecological Approach to Management: Proceedings of a National Workshop, Salt Lake City, April 27–30, 1992*. Washington, D.C., USDA Forest Service, Watershed and Air Management, WO-WSA-3.

U.S. Government. 1978. "Letter from Secretary of Agriculture James Wilson to Chief, February 1, 1905," in *The Principle Laws Relating to Forest Service Activities*, Agricultural Handbook 453.

Vernon, John. 1973. *The Garden and the Map: Schizophrenia in Twentieth-Century Literature and Culture*. Urbana: University of Illinois Press.

Weiss, Allen. 1990. "Lucid Intervals: Postmodernism and Photography," in *Postmodernism: Philosophy and the Arts*, edited by H. J. Silverman, pp. 155–72. New York: Routledge.

Wenz, Peter. 1988. *Environmental Justice*, New York: SUNY Press.

White, Dale. 1957. *Gifford Pinchot: The Man Who Saved the Forests*. New York: Julian Messner.

Wilkinson, Charles, and Michael Anderson. 1987. *Land and Resource Planning in the National Forests*. Washington, D.C.: Island Press.

Wilson, Edward. 1984. *Biophilia*. Cambridge, Mass.: Harvard University Press.

Wingler, Hans. 1978. *Bauhaus: Weimar, Dessau, Berlin, Chicago*. First MIT paperback edition. Cambridge, Mass.: MIT Press.

Woodward, J. D. 1877. "Scenery of the Pacific Railway VI," *The Art Journal* 30: 165–68. New York: D. Appleton.

Zeide, Boris, and Peter Pfeifer. 1991. "A Method for Estimation of Fractal Dimension of Tree Crowns," *Forest Science* 37(5): 1253–65.

Stephanie Kaza

Ethical Tensions in the Northern Forest

Forest as home, forest as resource, forest as landscape, forest as community, forest as wilderness—there is no one way to view the Northern Forest. Each person, town, corporate landholder, tree, moose, and salamander has a different perspective of and experience with the Northern Forest. In the struggle for biological and economic survival, some needs are incompatible. Some organisms and landscapes flourish while others perish.

The ethical dilemmas of the Northern Forest arise out of the urgent and motivating desire to survive. Loggers, forest towns, native peoples, paper companies, and the forest itself all have this desire to survive in common.

The conflicts of the Northern Forest are not unique to this biological region. Similar tensions wrack the great conifer belt of the Pacific Northwest, the abundant rainforest of Amazonia, and the oak woodlands of California.[1] They are driven by the overwhelming imbalance of power of humans and human institutions over nonhumans, that is, trees, deer, fish, watersheds. This crushing imbalance raises many moral and ethical questions—What is right and wrong in each particular situation? There is no single answer. Each conflict is far too complex to be reduced to simple moral prescription.

In this chapter, I outline five ethical polarities, pointing out the tensions in each. The pressing situation of the Northern Forest has raised concerns to the point of threat to survival on many fronts. Under the stress of this struggle, as in all environmental conflicts, people tend to take sides, thereby freezing dialogue, cutting off the possibility for genuine moral engagement with each other. These tensions will not likely disappear, no matter what ultimate solutions are agreed upon. They reflect a long history of relations between forests and people and all the political, economic, social, and psychological struggles for power and definition that have determined the fate of the forests over many not-so-peaceful centuries.[2] How these dilemmas are resolved for the Northern Forests will reveal the moral intentions of the current players. It is my hope that this chapter helps to clarify the tensions

---

Stephanie Kaza, "Ethical Tensions in the Northern Forest," *The Future of the Northern Forest*, Christopher McGrory Klyza and Stephen C. Trombulak, eds. (Hanover: University Press of New England, 1994), pp. 71–87, 245–46. Reprinted with permission from the University Press of New England.

and serves to find a way forward that will make sense to the generations to come.

Simplification Versus Complexity

Environmental conflicts are almost always too complicated to manage easily. In an attempt to control the uncontrollable, the human mind often opts for simplification. This tendency can be seen in ecological, economic, and social realms, all of which affect communication and problem solving in the Northern Forest. In contrast, the natural tendency of systems and life forms is to evolve toward complexity. Tensions arise over what stabilizes a system and what destroys or enhances the forest.

Ecologically, the tendency to simplification can be seen in the homogenization of the landscape. Diverse New England forest habitats, once reflecting a checkered history of storms, glaciers, invasions, and migrations, have been altered extensively by successive waves of deforestation, agriculture, and urbanization.[3] Where succession has been disrupted or set back by major natural or unnatural disturbance, the forest stays in an early stage of colonization. Clearcutting reduces a forest to a field, encouraging growth of pioneer plants and aggressive invaders. Changes in microclimate impact soil health and stability, tree growth, and wildlife diversity. Although simplified systems sometimes show temporary increased species diversity, these are only successional species, not the full array of species in a stable ecosystem. In general, human activities of the twentieth century have tended to simplify ecosystems and reduce complexity.

The tendency toward complexity is articulated by those trying to save endangered species or preserve habitat variety across the latitudes of the Northern Forest. Ecological complexity is appreciated by those who understand the details of mycorrhizal root associations or composite acid deposition. Those who value complexity tend to be college-educated resource professionals or environmental activists. Their primary activities in this regard are stopping the acceleration of simplification and designing restoration programs to reintroduce complexity. The urgency of their vision can be offensive to those who explain the forest in simpler terms.

Economically, simplification is well established by current protocols omitting external costs of production. Logging on Northern Forest lands by large timber or paper companies generates additional local costs in utilities, social services, and bureaucracies for forest regulation. Many of these costs are borne by the public. Paper manufacturing and wood products processing generate air and water pollution that affect lakes, rivers, and human health. Breathing bad air and drinking bad water cause increased health and social welfare costs, almost none of which are borne by the originating factory. For decades, it has been convenient for manufacturers to leave the external costs to the community to pick up, thereby increasing their own profits at the expense of the public. A more complex budget would include external costs, shifting the burden of accountability to those responsible.

Large corporations have tended to focus on single goals; foremost is making a profit for company executives and their shareholders. In managing their land assets for short rotations, timber companies have justified heavy cutting and been able to sustain a high profit margin.[4] If company goals are defined primarily by the profit goal, there is little room for the complexity of multiple goals that would serve the region, community, and forest as well as the corporation. Where large companies dominate the local economy as in a number of Maine communities, single-company towns are precariously reliant on a single employer. In the Northern Forest lands debate, the tendency toward complexity is represented by voices for economic diversification and local self-reliance.

Socially, simplification appears in the form of stereotyping and generalization. In the midst of user conflicts, it is common for people to associate certain points of view with simplified labels—logger, activist, local, flatlander, rural resident, corporation, developer, Native American. Generally this leads to some version of polarization, in which generic conversations replace genuine dialogue between those who are actually involved in the local piece of land. Emotional charges ride high on these stereotypes, and can lead to name-calling and even violence. In the Adirondacks, environmental activists have received threatening phone calls and endured mysterious attacks on personal property.[5]

Regions as well as people can be reduced to stereotypes, oversimplifying the complexity of interstate relations. For example, if Maine is perceived as holding back negotiations because of pressure from its large corporate landholdings, or Vermont is seen as inconsequential because of its small piece of the forest, this blocks creative problem solving that depends far more on individuals working together than on state stereotypes.

The social tension of simplification causes a kind of dehumanization of individuals, each of whom cares about the situation from a particular lived experience. No one likes to feel reduced to a label. Unfortunately, it is simpler to make assumptions about others than to actually get to know them and make an effort to hear their concerns. To accept complexity is to recognize the breadth and depth of people's suffering. Few have the deep wellsprings of patience for this.

By definition, complexity includes what we don't know as well as what we do know. The tension between simplification and complexity often carries a perplexing combination of self-righteous knowing and humbling inadequacy. In some cases, the outcomes of simplification are incompatible with complexity. You cannot clearcut a large area and expect to retain ecosystem stability. Those who want to control the outcome of a Northern Forest environmental issue may often opt for simple solutions, precisely because they are more definable and enforceable. They may paint a negative picture of the "opposition" as if it were a uniform enemy. It is far more challenging to recognize the many facets of what is not known that generate true complexity.

Present Versus Future

The tension of present versus future is the tension of weighing short-term gains against long-term gains. Next to the vivid and incessant demands of the present, it is hard to imagine the future to come. Yet the character of the future is determined by choices made in the present. Short-term gains are favored by those in business now, looking to make a profit and achieve economic survival based on current assets. If these are gone in a hundred years, someone alive today cannot assume personal responsibility for these consequences. So who does bear the consequences? Those who have not yet been born.[6]

Economic valuation of the present is based on the market discount rate, which calculates the value of present goods against their worth later in time. Almost always, goods or resources (such as forests) are considered to have their greatest worth at present. Because they are valued at less in the future, the economic incentive is to maximize gain in the present. This is a strong driving force behind the pressure on current resources. A big corporation such as Georgia-Pacific or Boise Cascade planning to maximize profit through wide-scale harvest of Northern Forest trees will gain more financial rewards for accelerated activity now rather than later. There is no counterbalancing financial mechanism to favor the future.

Economic activity such as tree harvesting involves certain risks to workers, companies, and the public. "Acceptable risk" is usually defined in terms of the present, based on what is known about the risk-generating source at the present time. Risk analysis can be applied to pesticide poisoning, leaking radioactive waste, acid deposition, for example. But who defines "acceptable"? Victims of insecticide sprays or polluted water are not statistics; they are real people affected by real risks. Very little is known about how hazards to human and ecosystem health may act synergistically in the future. What appears acceptable now may bioaccumulate over decades or generations, causing greater problems later. It is almost impossible to adequately define "acceptable risk" because of this. Thus, definitions tend to reflect what is expedient and favorable for those defining the term.

It is possible, however, to enumerate some of the legacies being prepared right now for future generations and gain some idea of what they will be facing. For example, in New York and Vermont, children of this generation's children will need to cope with acidified waterways and soil and cumulatively weakened tree roots that may cause forest deaths in years to come. They will inherit pesticide-impacted soils from spraying that has reduced the vitality of naturally occurring microorganisms. They will find dioxin from the use of paper mill sludge as fertilizer now traveling through the food chain. They will see even-aged stands of planted trees instead of complex forests. They may never see some of the insectivorous tropical migrant warblers whose populations have declined from habitat loss. They will inherit an extensive road system, fragmenting wildlife corridors and woodlands across the state.

The tension between present and future arises around the questions: Whose future? Who will continue to exist in the future? Whose lives will be safeguarded or enhanced by Northern Forest decisions? Small private landholders? Large corporations? Transnational companies? Indigenous nations? Children of Euro-American settlers? Sometimes the tension is phrased as: Who will give up what now to make the future possible for whom?

In an age that celebrates speed, it is particularly difficult to stretch the human imagination into the future across the slowness of years.[7] Speed of travel, of communication, of stimulation, of mechanical harvesting limit the attention span to the immediate. Fast camera cuts and quick sound bites shape the modern sense of reality, robbing people of the capacity to look deeply into the past or future. In the demanding effort to just keep up with the enormous pace of change, people are easily overwhelmed. The present, though complex, is still easier to deal with than the not-yet formed future. But as the Northern Forests come under increasing population pressure from urban centers not far away, the future is being determined already. The question is: Knowing what we know about this region, can we choose a more effective, planned-for option that might be sustainable into the future?

Universalization Versus Indigenization

Universalization is the set of processes involved in imposing a standard ideology, power structure, language, or set of cultural norms on an area or group of people. The tendency of universalization is to homogenize, to reduce difference, to establish common values and traditions.[8] With regard to the land, it is the tendency to treat one territory like another, assuming similarity as an operational foundation. Indigenization, in contrast, is the set of processes that reinforces evolution of culture specific to a local region. The tendency of indigenization is toward heterogeneity, diversity, and a range of cultural traditions and expressions. Indigenous cultures reflect the specific limits and histories of living in particular places.

In the Northern Forest, the tendency toward universalization is represented by consolidation of landholdings by large timber and paper corporations who impose relatively uniform management/harvesting strategies on these lands. Another expression of this tendency is the pattern of increasing development, especially for second family homes. To the extent that "flatlanders" or outsiders alter the local community structure when they visit or resettle in Vermont, for example, they tend to bring with them a more uniform urbanized set of values. This can create tension around environmental issues because of the differences in class, education, and wealth between urban immigrants and local residents.

Universalization is experienced differently by those in power who are imposing an ideology or system and by those who are resisting it.[9] Native peoples or locals in New York or Maine who feel their traditions threatened by the industrial growth economy share a feeling of powerlessness of the small up against the large. They also resent their patterns of culture and community being disregarded as insignificant. Those in power justify their activities with claims of benefit to local communities, assuming a trickle-down morality, that what is right for the dominant player is right for all those affected by it. But this is not always the case.

Similar tension results from perceived universalization imposed by government agencies or environmental organizations. This is part of the resistance to "green lining," as if a boundary marked the area that would then be under the control of the dominant power.[10] Fear of increased environmental regulation and taxation for local towns and small landowners reflects a fear of domination by universalization.

The contrasting tendency, toward indigenization, places more value on local self-determination and respect for particular cultures and biological regions. Fifth-generation Adirondack residents undoubtedly know the history and weather patterns of their specific valleys or hillsides far better than newcomers. Native Abenakis still carry alive in their own traditions a lineage of respect and knowledge of Lake Champlain and the Green Mountains. Indigenization takes time. An individual or community must accumulate years or generations of information and experience about how the forest behaves in the place they call home. This kind of information, especially in the context of a shared social culture, is what enables a people to become native to a place. Some have argued that only local people are adequately equipped to know their own local forests. Some have argued that only by becoming native can one come close to being a good land steward.[11]

The speed and scale of universalization easily overcomes the slow pace of indigenization. The resulting power imbalance is sustained by money and institutional weight. The tension of domination and resistance to domination is a major force around the globe in North-South environmental conflicts, free trade agreements, and transnational corporation invasion. It is no surprise that this tension should also be felt and expressed in Northern Forest controversies.

A subtext of this tension is the classic insider/outsider struggle. "Insiders" are traditionally those who have lived in a situation for some time and have established personal relationships with others based on position, turf, and respect. These involve recognition of power and seniority and a common social community. Insiders negotiate social relations by a set of understandings of personal accountability to neighbors or colleagues.[12] Insiders hold status in rural communities and also corporate or government bureaucracies.

"Outsiders" do not recognize the unspoken order of relationships established by insiders and are often perceived as being inconsiderate, ignorant, and aggressive in their attempts to dominate social or environmental relations. This perception complicates Northern Forest dialogue, leading to defensiveness and suspicion as stable insider social relations are thrown off by encounters with strangers or outsiders. Ironically, government and corporate staff "insiders" feel threatened by environmental activists and local community members "outside" their realm of operations, while local "insiders" feel threatened by environmentalist, government, and corporate "outsiders." The insider experience is akin to the indigenous tendency; the outsider experience often represents the universalizing tendency. Forest as commodity is ruled by market forces, by a capitalist economic framework and the rules that sustain that system. Forest products, unprocessed logs, and pulp are moved around according to demand and economic efficiency. In a commodity framework a tree is reduced to a thing. Tree as object is processed to serve the growth economy, on the premise that more growth is better—more houses, more paper, more wood products, more consumption. The gross national product, in fact, measures the rate of growth, acting as a barometer for the scale of buying and trading.

Commodities are traded on the open market where the goal is to make as great a profit as possible. The forest products industry, for example, exports raw materials to Canada, Europe, and Japan where markets pay more for wood than local markets. "Free trade" flourishes when a company can minimize costs of production by access to cheap raw materials, cheap labor, and few environmental restrictions. When forest liquidation becomes too expensive in one state (or country), a company will leave to do business in another state. As Wendell Berry puts it, "The global economy . . . operates on the superstition that deficiencies or needs or wishes of one place may be safely met by the ruination of another place."[13]

For trees to be traded, they must be seen as objects, void of any relationship with humans other than economic. From this point of view, trees are board feet, biomass, or stumpage—objects of specific value on the open market. This view of relationship, however, is somewhat limited and does not account for other roles of trees in human lives.

Commodity implies ownership, and with ownership comes some sense of obligation to what is owned. But what is owned? One may value the trees but not the land, or the tradable options and income but not the forest. The sense of obligation varies substantially from landowner to landowner, depending on size of holdings, cultural traditions, location, and the owner's capacity to pay attention to his or her land. Absentee ownership may be the most precarious in terms of developing moral relations with the forest.

In contrast to forest as commodity is forest as community. Speaking of his native prairies, Aldo Leopold defined community to include "soils, waters, plants, and animals, or collectively: the land." For Leopold, "an individual [tree, person, animal] is a member of a community of interdependent parts."[14] To respond to the forest as community is to see oneself as a member of the forest community. In this experience of relationship, the forest is part of the fabric of the self and the culture, based on mutual bonding and influence over time. A forest as interconnected web of relations is much harder to objectify than a forest as collection of things.

Forest as community carries the implication of forest as home, the land where one lives. Local residents of the Adirondacks whose homes go back many generations place a strong value on home and community as center point of activity. The forest is the context, the backdrop, a key participant in self-definition of individuals and communities. In taking responsibility for forest as home, local people develop shared traditions and morals that reflect relational values.

Tied to home is a sense of belonging, that one is familiar and accepted where one lives. In the forest as home, the local dweller gains a sense of self in place, self in relation, self in community. This is often marked by appreciation and gratitude for being part of what one loves—a sharp contrast to being defined by what one owns.

The tension between forest as community and forest as commodity tends to be expressed by locals versus nonresident landowners, whether corporate or second home. Private small-scale loggers may speak for a middle ground between the two polarities, seeking community-based decision making while still using the forest for commodity trading. Environmentalists may speak up strongly against abuse of commodity but not necessarily be grounded in a local community. In advocating a public form of ownership, they suggest it is possible to care for a forest without necessarily living there. This augments the tension between the two opposite views. In some cases, it is not possible to maintain the forest as part of the community and also clearcut it as commodity.

Private Versus Public Rights

Of the five ethical tensions I have listed here, this is the one that receives the most public attention. However, I have listed it last rather than first, to show the other tensions also riding in Northern Forest conflicts. I believe the private/public rhetoric often carries the weight of these other tensions, confusing the basic principles with other factors. Many volumes have been written on this classic debate over the last several centuries[15]; I will only briefly cover some key aspects of this last polarity.

Private rights imply individual freedom to use one's land as he or she sees fit. In popular perception, this is held as central to the American way of life, as a primary determiner of human activity and moral choices. This sense of individual freedom is based in an ethic of noninterference: that whatever one wants to do is all right so long as it does not harm others. This social contract is based more in the patterns of social relations than environmental relations between neighbors. In the late twentieth century, however, it is now quite apparent that there is very little one can do environmentally to one's land without it affecting adjoining land in some way—silting the creek, poisoning the groundwater with pesticides, creating air pollution from wood stoves, fragmenting wildlife habitat by logging. Ecosystems are not easily bounded by property lines.

Private rights are associated with self-determination, privacy, and autonomy. In Northern Forest issues, resistance to environmental regulation represents a fear of losing one's freedom. From this perspective, "green lining" is seen as drawing a conspicuous boundary around a set-aside area, thereby threatening such freedom. As needs for privacy increase because of population pressures from the urbanized areas, more and more lines are being drawn at local scales to keep people out of the forest.

Private rights also imply the right to be protected from unwanted infringements or intrusions. Irresponsible corporate management practices that create pollution or degrade the biological health of the land interfere with the rights of the local private landowner to environmental safety and stability. These rights, however, tend to be deemphasized in the current debate.

Landowners are not a uniform group across the Northern Forest. They fall into at least four types: (1) small, local landowners who live year-round on their land; (2) small landowners who use their land as a second, vacation home; (3) large corporate and private family landowners who actively harvest and work the land industrially; and (4) large corporate absentee landowners who are keeping the forest as real estate for future development or trading. The two key aspects to these groups are size of holdings and degree of presence. Large-scale landowners represent more money and therefore more power. Small-scale landowners perceive themselves to be relatively powerless next to these Goliaths. The aspect of presence or absence has a strong influence on the nature of decision making. Local people feel the most powerless when a large absentee landowner suddenly liquidates its assets, as in the big Diamond International sale in 1988. In a single monumental action, it seemed as if presence counted for nothing—for local landowners, environmentalists, and state governments. This seems to run counter to the heart of the private rights philosophy—that human beings should carry some weight as individuals, that their presence should count in the world.

Public rights, on the other hand, represent another American tradition of land-use planning and zoning. Public rights derive from common property practices of European tradition, also used by Native Americans before European arrival. National and state forests protect shared watersheds and wildlife, promoting some sense of commonly held trust and protection of the land. Government agencies are assigned the job of serving U.S. citizens by watching over the air, water, and stability of soil and land. Included in this sense of public is the implication that one has the right to security, health, and happiness—not degraded by another's exercise of freedom.

The tension between private and public reflects a tension of independence versus interdependence. Traditional American heroes have placed great emphasis on independent achievement, whether in conquering the Wild West or surviving the cold northern winters. Interdependence requires cooperation and relying on others, which is unpredictable at best and far from central to the American way of life. Yet interdependence is closer to an ecological model of relationships in a forest community.

Other tensions in this polarity are the resistance to limits on one's freedom and the debates around who will define what is private and what is public. The desire to control one's fate can be overrun by those who represent the public good. Thus, the conversation of private and public often reflects a power struggle between those with and those without power. It can easily derail conversation about what is sustainable for the forest. Power relations are rarely dealt with directly in environmental hearings, yet they almost always affect the dynamics of any forest argument where one party feels helpless. However, this does not necessarily mean the debate is about private versus public; it may be more a debate about who has power (in both a perceived and real sense) and who does not.

Power Relations and Questions of Ethics

In reviewing these five ethical tensions, one overriding influence is power. Who has the power to define the issues? To define the forest? Power can be used to manipulate outcomes, to control local economies, to trade resources for livelihoods, to degrade once flourishing forest ecosystems. The Northern Forest controversies represent a historical and ongoing shifting balance of power in New England. Perceptions and responses to power dynamics are central in addressing all environmental problems. The Northern Forest is no exception.

Power dynamics play out at the local community level, at the state and national levels, and within the global context. International environmental politics reflect the pressures of increasing population, a shrinking resource base, excess waste and consumption by the developed world, and a significant power and debt imbalance between the North and the South. State and national politics reflect increasing regionalization of environmental concerns against long-standing state traditions and characters. Local environmental politics suffer from widely diverse educational backgrounds and understanding of environmental issues. Often power players at one level overrule those at another.

Power may be defined in terms of size of landholdings and budget of organizations and corporate companies. However, power may also be expressed as personal presence—the capacity to stand behind one's principles, to speak from depth of experience, to reflect historical and traditional relationship to the land. The two basic types of power may be described as "power over" and "power from within." When these two come up against each other, there is not only environmental conflict, there is ethical conflict.

Trees, moose, trout, and blueberries do not have a voice in these ethical dilemmas. Rather, their lives are at the mercy of human beings whose industrial, economic, political, and social actions have great impact on the natural world. Nonhuman beings are clearly at the very bottom of the power ladder in the human configuration of things at present. Without language, rights, or capacity to communicate, nonhumans can make little contribution to solving environmental problems in the Northern Forest. Human beings are the only ones who can take moral responsibility for their actions.

It is my thesis that ethical deliberation is an extremely effective and appropriate tool for examining power relations. No matter what scale an organization, institution, agency, company, or community is operating on, one can ask—Is it accountable for its actions? Are the individuals in decision-making roles making conscious choices to act ethically with regard to plants, animals, and people? Raising ethical considerations can shed light on the five polarity tensions described earlier, offering a way forward when negotiations seem paralyzed.

I suggest here six guidelines for clarifying controversies within the Northern Forest. They provide one mechanism for challenging current policies and investigating alternatives. Taken together, they perhaps offer support for healing broken relations within communities and with the forest. While these do not address the specifics of environmental regulations or forest management, they do direct attention to those who must live with these decisions and their implications for others and for future generations. Each of these is a suggested direction to heed, not a dogmatic prescription for problem-solving. Each includes the non-human, the ecological, the land community as well as the human. Each provides another way of framing the issues to include ethical dimensions profoundly significant to the way we choose to address the Northern Forest.

Toward Respect

Respect in the dialogue between users and dwellers in the Northern Forest across the various regions can only enhance communication and understanding. This might include examination of stereotypes and education as to the actual jobs and responsibilities of those who are engaged in Northern Forest issues. Do environmentalists have a sense of the lives of loggers? Do absentee corporate landlords have a sense of the people who live in their communities? Do local residents recognize the native people who lived on the land before them? It seems important that forums for communication and problem solving err on the side of being inclusive, with effort made to hear usually overlooked points of view.

Respect for nonhumans requires some examination of the traditional hierarchies of value that place people at the top and soil at the bottom of the biological pyramid. By what ethical principles do trees have less standing?[16] What kinds of actions generate respect for forest systems for forest inhabitants? What are the actual impacts of pesticides, recreational use, logging, real estate development on nonhuman beings? To engage in respectful relations with nonhumans one might err on the side of learning as much as possible about the details of their lives.

Toward Acknowledging Limits

Limits define a problem, an area in trouble, the finite capacity for a forest to respond to distress. The American tendency is to believe optimistically in the resilience of people and systems, as if there were no end to the amount of damage that could be done without serious consequences. The environmental history of the United States is a story of advancing and plundering across the continent, from New England to the Great Plains, across the Rocky Mountains to the California coast. The frontier mentality of the 1800s is no longer helpful in addressing the environmental difficulties before us. Naming the Northern Forest as a region is one way to begin to define the topics under consideration. Within this framework, it will help to be specific about the limits of each individual subregion—to understand the crucial soil differences between northern Maine and southern Vermont in supporting timber species, to trace the histories of Indian nations and white settlers in the Adirondacks, to see corporate real estate deals in terms of international financial limits.

In the human realm, acknowledging limits may help draw the line on abusive environmental practices that cripple local economies or impact community health. By recognizing shared limits, one may be more willing to work with others concerned about forest issues, despite differences of opinion and personality conflicts. One of the most frustrating aspects of environmental problem solving is acknowledging the limits of what is known about local ecosystems. In most cases, one wishes to know more in order to choose how to act. But often one must act anyway, in some degree of ignorance. One can choose to err on the side of humility and allow for what is not known, rather than making false assumptions. As Aldo Leopold stated so succinctly, "An ethic, ecologically, is a limitation on freedom of action in the struggle for existence."[17] All ethics have at their root the principle of restraint. To choose not to kill someone, to not lie, to not steal—in each case, one is choosing to restrain from actions that would harm another. In Northern Forest controversies, people could choose to err on the side of restraint in developing timber cutting plans, in allowing second family home development, in name-calling at community meetings. To lean toward restraint generally allows more time for reconsideration, more options for the future, less damage to undo later.

Restraint has primarily been developed in the world's religious traditions as it pertains to the virtues of individual actions. But restraint in social actions has a place in the Northern Forest debate. Agencies and institutions can stand behind specific ethics of restraint that bear on their area of responsibility. Policies that restrict development from fragile lakeshores or creeksides err on the side of restraint in support of healthy ecosystems. Corporate labor practices that restrain accumulation of wealth at the top to promote economic well-being of laborers at the bottom extend ethical benefits to more people. Environmental groups who make an effort not to be self-righteous increase the possibility for other points of view to be heard. In each case, the group takes responsibility for its actions, cultivating a social ethic of restraint that allows for a wider conversation.

Toward Caring

Biologists often speak about the *carrying capacity* of the land or the forest ecosystem, referring to the number of trees or deer the area can support. A variation on this might be to examine human *caring capacity* relative to the land and communities that support human activities. The capacity to care is the capacity to take actions on behalf of others and oneself that sustain life and promote healthy development. To care for the forest is to take specific actions that sustain the life of the forest, whether that is staying on the trails, logging selectively, or putting up bluebird boxes. In the last 40 years, much human capacity to care has been derailed into consuming (shopping, buying, going to malls), an activity strongly encouraged by advertisers and product manufacturers. But this investment of time in material goods often carries less satisfaction than investing in human or nonhuman relationships.

To err on the side of caring is to choose to become a more caring person, one who is involved in the relationships that support one's life. In the Northern Forest region, this necessarily includes the forest and the forest animals and plants as well as the human neighbors. Caring takes time; care demands for family and community tend to take top priority. I am suggesting here that caring include time spent in environmental education, forest restoration, community organizing, and also time spent listening directly to the land, the trees, the birds, the mountains. To invest time in caring is to invest time in relationships—with neighbors as well as watersheds.

Toward Accountability

Being accountable is being responsible for the consequences of one's choices. This is fundamental to ethical or moral development. Economic accountability does not need to be an exception to this. Though it is arduous work, one can analyze in depth the economics of a corporation or a region to see whether it takes adequate responsibility for its actions. One major effort in this direction is Mitch Lansky's research for *Beyond the Beauty Strip,* a study of Maine's forest economy.[18] Is a corporation accountable for its labor practices? For its real estate transactions? For its environmental impacts? For the role of local industry relative to global transnational trading?

Ecological accountability implies erring on

the side of more rather than less information and assessment of biological communities. Does a state government agency take responsibility for adequate biological monitoring of its forests? Is information available to citizens' groups and concerned environmentalists? Do the assigned agencies actually know what exists in the field that is represented on satellite data maps? Also, one can look at scientific methods used to assess current states of ecological habitats. Are they adequate as a basis for decisions? Are they influenced by who commissions them?

Professional accountability is another area to investigate for degree of care and attention in taking responsibility. Doctors and lawyers are expected to practice according to established codes of ethics, but most environmental professionals have yet to develop similar codes.[19] What does a forester consider good forestry? What does a hydrologist consider ethical hydrology? Those trained in the scientific method generally have little background in ethical issues and have not been taught to regard them as important to their work. However, with environments and communities under pressure, it may be necessary and appropriate for these resource professionals to show specific accountability for their work.

Toward Restoration

Much of the Northern Forest area has suffered from tourist development, unsightly clearcuts, acid deposition, and unplanned growth. Erring on the side of restoration can work to heal the impacts of harvesting and building on the land. Efforts to reverse acidification, erosion, and groundwater pollution, for example, are efforts toward system restoration, assisted by human restraint and regulation. To return the land and forest to a state of health where that health has been broken is good work.[20] This work brings joy to those who engage in it. There are ample opportunities for citizen groups to restore local creeks and watersheds, to clean up pointsource pollution. In the effort to restore health, one invests care in a place, building a loving and satisfying relationship with the local land.

Restoring human relations that have been broken can also be helpful in generating cooperation. Euro-American settlers have work to do in this area with the original native inhabitants whose numbers are now so reduced. In regions torn by controversy over planning dilemmas, such as the Adirondacks, communities may need to restore relations around divisive issues. To err on the side of restoration is to stand for healing rather than harming. Harsh deeds must be acknowledged before healing can happen. But without some movement toward restoration, the damage carries a shadow on the land, felt by all who live there or pass through.

Conclusion

Each of these six directions offers possibility for forward movement from a foundation of ethical consideration. I believe that only ethical dialogue will fully address the power relations that control current Northern Forest issues. The web of interlocking interests, from industry to government, from state to federal agencies, from global economy to local landholdings, is complex and highly evolved. Power dynamics are not simply a matter of one group or individual pitted against another. Today's networks of interest groups working together can easily override cultural checks and balances designed to limit the power of any one group. Direct feedback loops of accountability are possible at the local level because of the scale of interactions and also because of the history of community values and responses to ethical transgressions.

But similar mechanisms of restraint do not apply at the global scale of activity. The links between interest groups are more important than the differences; being part of a network of power is often more important than being ethically accountable. International and national economic pressures affect Northern Forest real estate ownership and forest harvesting decisions. Since global networks of power are not geographically based in any given locality and are not necessarily committed to a local community, they are removed from traditional local restraints based on ethical accountability.[21]

Decisions affecting the future of the Northern Forest will be made by someone. The question is, by whom and how? To the extent that they are ruled by the most powerful voices, it is unlikely that the less powerful will have a full voice in the outcome. Lansky suggests a consensus model drawing on a coalition of representatives of all concerned interests.[22] President Clinton used a version of this model in his April 1993 Forest Summit in the Pacific Northwest.

I believe the six directions for ethical consideration will be best engaged with many voices speaking up. Social ethics regarding the environment are far from being well worked out. As natural landscapes come under increasing pressure for harvest, recreation, and development, environmental ethics are an increasing part of the dialogue. The ethical debate can only be expected to intensify. There may be no one solution that will serve all parties, especially if trees, birds, and wildflowers are taken into moral consideration. But the effort to examine the ethical implications of each decision will surely lead to greater care in living with each other and with the gifts of the land.

Notes

1. For an introduction to these regional forests, see Norse, Elliot A., 1990, *Ancient Forests of the Pacific Northwest*, Washington, D.C.: Island Press; Gradwohl, Judith, and Russell Greenberg, 1988, *Saving the Tropical Forests*, Washington, D.C.: Island Press; and Pavlik, Bruce M., Pamela C. Muick, Sharon Johnson, and Marjorie Popper, 1991, *Oaks of California*, Los Olivos, Calif.: Cachuma Press.

2. Harrison, Robert Pogue, 1992, *Forests: The Shadow of Civilization*, Chicago: University of Chicago Press.

3. Cronon, William, 1983, *Changes in the Land: Indians, Colonists, and the Ecology of New England*, New York: Hill and Wang.

4. For a case study of Maine's forests, see Lansky, Mitch, 1992, *Beyond the Beauty Strip: Saving What's Left of Our Forests*, Gardiner, Maine: Tilbury House.

5. Discussed in "Adirondack Voices," the newsletter of the Residents' Committee to Protect the Adirondacks.

6. Partridge, Ernest, ed., 1981, *Responsibilities to Future Generations*, Buffalo, N.Y.: Prometheus Press.

7. Macy, Joanna, 1991, *World as Lover, World as Self*, Berkeley, Calif.: Parallax Press, pp. 206–91.

8. For a discussion of the universalizing tendency, see Cheney, Jim, 1989, "Postmodern Environmental Ethics: Ethics as Bioregional Narrative," *Environmental Ethics*, II: 117–34.

9. Narayan, Uma, 1988, "Working Together across Differences: Some Considerations on Emotions and Political Practice," *Hypatia*, 3(2): 31–47.

10. See "Whose Common Future?" 1992, *The Ecologist*, 22(4), entire issue on the enclosure of the commons.

11. Snyder, Gary, 1990, "The Place, the Region, and the Commons," in *The Practice of the Wild*, San Francisco: North Point Press, pp. 25–47.

12. "Whose Common Future?" 1993, p. 124 for a description of insider/outsider dynamics in Third World street markets.

13. Berry, Wendell, 1992, "Conservation Is Good Work," *Wild Earth*, Spring, p. 82.

14. Leopold, Aldo, 1949, "The Land Ethic," in *A Sand County Almanac*, New York: Ballantine Books, p. 239.

15. For a new interpretation of corporate responsibility to private rights, see Saxe, Dianne, 1992, "The Fiduciary Duty of Corporate Directors to Protect Environment for Future Generations," *Environmental Values*, 1: 243–52.

16. Stone, Christopher, 1974, *Should Trees Have Standings? Toward Legal Rights for Natural Objects*, Los Altos, Calif.: William Kaufmann.

17. Leopold, 1949, p. 238.

18. Lansky, 1992, pp. 137–62 on industrial management choices, for example.

19. The American Forestry Association has been working on an ethical code for several years; several other codes for biologists and ecologists are in committees.

20. For examples of this healing work, see the journal of the Society for Ecological Restoration, Restoration and Management Notes (Madison: University of Wisconsin Press).

21. "Power: The Central Issue," 1992, *The Ecologist*, 22(4): 157–64.

22. Lansky, 1992, p. 415.

Alan Drengson and Duncan Taylor

An Overview of Ecoforestry: Introduction

Early in the morning on August 9th, 1993, nearly 300 men, women and children, many of them chanting and singing, were arrested and hauled away by the RCMP for protesting clearcut logging in British Columbia's Clayoquot Sound. The morning's confrontation constituted the largest single mass arrest in B.C. history. By the end of the summer the number charged with obstructing the logging bridge across Clayoquot Sound's Kennedy River totalled 800. Many of the protesters arrested that morning had been camped in a clearcut that had become known throughout the province as the Black Hole. The slashed, burned, blackened and eroded hills surrounding the protest camp look down on that part of Highway 4 which divides in opposite directions at the point where it reaches the west coast of Vancouver Island: to the southeast the road ends at the town of Ucluelet, to the northwest it ends at the community of Tofino. The fact that these communities lie geographically at opposite ends of Pacific Rim National Park merely underscores the polarization that has arisen between the residents of Ucluelet and Tofino regarding the future of the 350,000 hectares of coastal temperate old-growth forest in this region.[1]

Since the early 1970s the town of Tofino has become home to an increasing number of people who openly espouse a pro-environmental position with respect to how the forests of this region should be used. Once almost solely dependent on logging and fishing, Tofino now boasts that most of its revenue is derived from purely sustainable forms of wilderness recreation tourism such as kayaking, backpacking and whale watching, which are utterly dependent on maintaining the integrity of the Sound's forests, rivers and inlets. In turn, the native bands belonging to the Nuu-chah-nulth Tribal Council, who live on many of the islands outside Tofino, have laid claim to the Clayoquot Sound region and have let it be known that status quo resource extraction will no longer be tolerated.

Alan Drengson and Duncan Taylor, "An Overview of Ecoforestry: Introduction" in *Ecoforestry*, Alan Drengson and Duncan Taylor, eds. (Gabriola Island, B.C.: New Society Publishers, 1997), pp. 17–24, 27–32. Reprinted with permission from New Society Publishers.

In contrast, on the other side of Pacific Rim National Park the majority of the residents of Ucluelet have remained almost solely dependent on the forest industry for their employment and livelihood. Indeed, in the past decade they have witnessed thousands of forestry workers on Vancouver Island being laid off due to pressure on the forest industry to maintain its international competitiveness. This has led to rapid changes in equipment and mechanization procedures resulting in a downsizing of the labor force. And when uncertainty regarding forest policy and access to harvestable timber in Clayoquot Sound is also factored in, tensions have tended to be projected in terms of simplistic arguments of *jobs* versus *preservation*. However, this dichotomy is not new.

People active in environmental issues over the last two decades have witnessed the polarization of debates raging over the protection of wilderness values by preservation of ancient West Coast forests, versus the economic values of logging. In the United States, particularly in the states of Washington and Oregon, this crystallization has been evident in the *owls vs. jobs* phrases used to describe the way the issues are seen. Here the owls are used to represent the environment, and jobs the workers and business. The polarization between the residents of Tofino and Ucluelet may be seen to characterize the rift that exists between environmentalists and those who are stridently anti-environmentalist and claim that environmentalism undermines human and economic well-being. But while this portrait is true to some extent, it fails to take account of the *conservationist* stance held by many pro-forestry advocates. Consequently, the debate between these towns also reflects a more scholarly debate between supporters of what has been termed the *deep ecology movement* and proponents of *reformist environmentalism*. For some time now, spokespeople from Ucluelet and other forestry-dependent communities have claimed that they are the *real* conservationists—but conservationists who are realistic enough to respect the human benefits that accrue from one of Canada's largest and most economically important industries.

The impression one sometimes gets from these debates is that we must choose between ecologically sound practices and human economic and social welfare needs. In our view, the jobs vs. environment account is a caricature of our situation and options with respect to resolving current conflicts. As long as attention is focused on this narrow account, resolution seems impossible: either we sacrifice the environment for jobs (economic values) in the short term to meet the demands of social justice and human needs, or we sacrifice jobs to save the environment for our long-term interests. This is a no-win situation. However, we believe that there is a win-win solution. This solution is predicated on the recognition that sustainable communities and economies are subsystems of healthy biophysical systems, and not the other way around.

Since the rise of modernity in the 17th century, we have been rapidly converting natural capital to financial capital and changing our ecological systems to meet the imperatives of an ever-expanding consumptive economic system. This has to change. Indeed, for the long-term survival of our own species as well as the many other lifeforms with whom we share this planet, we now need to recognize that our economic system is utterly dependent upon the larger biophysical ecology and that it has to be transformed to meet the imperatives of the latter. In this way we can reach a win-win situation. In this way we can have long-term forestry jobs, healthy communities and a healthy natural ecosystem. The road into Clayoquot goes in opposite directions—indeed, it symbolically points to the choice between two very different worldviews and sets of values.

In the current conflict over forest preservation and logging we can see that there are definitely two different orientations or approaches at issue. One is the dominant, mainstream, expansionist model of modernism, the other is an emerging ecological paradigm. The *first* is based on an *anthropocentric* model of our relation to nature—humans exist apart from and outside of nature; it accepts a utilitarian value system. In the expansionist paradigm, nature is regarded essentially as a storehouse of resources to be utilized for the meeting of ever-increasing material needs by an ever-increasing human population. Consequently, this position equates growth with the progress of development which, in turn, is regarded as a prerequisite for human happiness and prosperity, claiming that any drop in this growth rate must inevitably result in stagnation, mass unemployment and distress. Those who argue for this position claim that new technological advances can be relied upon to increase global standards of living, harness renewable and more environmentally friendly sources of energy, and increase food production and the availability of other biological products through breakthroughs in biotechnology. In turn, more efficient technologies are seen to be able to solve the problems created by previous technologies, to create substitutes for depleted resources and to replace damaged ecosystems.

On the other hand, the ecological paradigm is based on humans as participants in nature; it accepts an ethic based upon respect for diversity and ecocentric values. The two views in question differ in their sense of values that are intrinsic to nature and to human life. Intrinsic or inherent values are cherished for their own sake. We consider them to be good in themselves; they are ends. Instrumental values are pursued as a means to other things and states that are themselves valued. In the case of valuing the natural world, people holding the intrinsic nature view (the deep ecology movement, for example) cherish other beings for their own sake, quite independent of their usefulness or economic value to humans. The instrumentalist nature view (the Shallow Ecology Movement) sees all intrinsic value as vested solely in humans. The result is that the world is valued only as means; its value is as resources to be used for human consumption and enjoyment. The *intrinsic nature* view sees a world rich in inherent values, beings having value in themselves quite independently of human interests. In the *instrumentalist nature* view we have an obligation to manage and control the world to meet human needs and desires. In the *intrinsic nature* view we have an obligation to manage ourselves so as to preserve the beauty and integrity of the planet's ecological processes and functions. *All* beings count; their vital needs must be respected when we design our practices.

Some of the characteristics of this emerging ecological paradigm may be summarized as follows:

- The universe is an interrelated totality, with all of its parts interconnected and interlocked. A corollary to this is the rejection of those dualistic and atomistic categories inherent within the Newtonian mechanistic perspective on which the expansionist paradigm is founded—for example, the epistemological separation of the subjective knower from the objective known, and the radical separation of facts from values.
- Nature is intrinsically valuable; animals, trees or rocks all have worth and value in themselves regardless of what value they may have for human beings. This is essentially an ecocentric and non-anthropocentric perspective and a rejection of the typically

quantitative approach to nature with its emphasis on viewing the natural world primarily in economic and utilitarian terms.
- Nature is both a physical and a symbolic forum from which to stand back from modern society. In nature—and especially in the more wild areas—humans are afforded an opportunity to actualize their own inner spiritual, esthetic, and moral sensibilities. Moreover, physical nature—especially wilderness—is a benchmark against which the state of human society may be judged. Consequently, large areas of the natural world should be preserved and protected from human interference.

Throughout the 20th century environmental debates have been polarized in terms of these two dominant perspectives. For example, the same type of polarization that continues to occur over the ancient forests has also been evident in disputes over industrial fishing and agriculture and their ecological viability. The first famous articulation of the polarized views referred to above surfaced in debates between John Muir (naturalist and essayist and founder of the Sierra Club in 1892) and Gifford Pinchot (U.S. Chief Forester who largely determined President Theodore Roosevelt's conservation program) early in this century.[2]

Anticipating the later work of Aldo Leopold, Muir argued for the adoption of an environmental land ethic, but one that would recognize the inherent value of natural entities and their right to pursue their own destiny, to continue to evolve. He believed we should preserve large areas of wilderness so that it can evolve independent of human manipulation—even if no human ever visits such areas. In doing so, he was rejecting a basic tenet of modernism which had come to view nature primarily in utilitarian and economic terms. Moreover, it was to put him increasingly at odds with his contemporary Gifford Pinchot as well as the values that dominated North American society at the turn of the 20th century.

Conservation as championed by Pinchot, on the other hand, was to be an ally of the expansionist paradigm. In many respects, it was for this reason that it had gained a certain legitimacy by 1908 when President Theodore Roosevelt held the first National Conference on Conservation at the White House. And not surprisingly, John Muir was not invited. By 1909 the Canadian government had established its own Commission of Conservation.[3] Indeed, the *wise use* school of Pinchot in the United States and Clifford Sifton in Canada equated conservation with *sustainable exploitation*. For both men, conservation should work against the wastefulness and environmentally disruptive excesses of a developing society, but not against development per se. For land to be protected or *alienated* from resource development and extractions was seen to be politically and economically naive. Indeed, conservationists argued that land must be utilized in the interests of a growing industrial economy, thereby providing jobs and wealth to the larger society. Ideally, conservation would require that wise *scientific* management procedures be adopted in the utilization of all resources, including forests, soils, waters and wildlife. Moreover, wherever possible, these resources would be harvested in terms of a renewable crop. In this way, Pinchot and others believed that nature's resources could be *used* and *saved* simultaneously and thereby conserved for future human generations.

Pinchot's legacy lives on with those who champion the sustainability of the existing expansionist paradigm. In other words, conservation was to reinforce the dominant industrial expansionist worldview by ideally protecting the ability of the land to provide a limitless supply of resources—hence, *sustainable economic development*. On the other hand, John Muir's position is favored by those proponents of an emerging ecological perspective who believe that we must recognize ecological limits to growth and transform our economies to meet its imperatives—not the other way around. Moreover, it is argued that the products of ecological and evolutionary processes can only be sustained by protecting the integrity of the ecological processes that give rise to them. This necessitates the preservation of large areas of wilderness for the ongoing protection of biodiversity as well as esthetic and spiritual values. In other words, we must ultimately reject the expansionist paradigm and learn to live off the *interest or abundance* of nature while protecting its *biological capital*. Current wise-use strategies consume natural capital and diversity. Hence, the need to go from the current emphasis on models for sustainable economic development to strategies for *developing environmental sustainability*. We would then place our priorities on maintaining biodiversity and ecological processes.

While there is some uncertainty about exact details and specific timetables, people who have knowledge of Earth's ecosystems agree that the large-scale industrial practices, as imposed today upon the biological processes of the planet, are not sustainable. On the other hand, in the modern period most Westerners accept without question modernism's definition of progress, that through science and technology we can have unlimited growth (certainly an unscientific belief), greater and greater wealth, more and more power, more and more speed, and so on. We have partially realized these aims, except for the last several years when the standard of living has not been going up, debt has been increasing, and social problems have multiplied beyond our capacity to find solutions. We tend to look at each of these problems on its own so as to find individual and even individualistic solutions. But the problems, like the debt, have become intractable. Our apparent solutions often create more problems than real solutions. Even as we increase efficiency, cost effectiveness, and competitiveness in forestry (and fishing and farming), and have been cutting greater and greater volumes of timber with fewer workers, at the same time communities based on forestry have had increasingly hard economic times and decreasing employment. The same things have happened in fishing and farming communities. The application of the industrial paradigm of modernism to these resource-based economies has been disastrous, not only for the humans involved, but also for future generations and the ecosystems that produce the needed resources.

Forest ecosystems, for example, produce trees and a great diversity of other organisms and processes beneficial to us. Remove the whole forest by extensive clearcutting and this great productive power is reduced to nearly zero. That area of land will now be recovering for a long time. Recent industrial methods try to turn forests into monocultured agricultural products, and the result of such methods is a dramatic reduction in ecological diversity. This is reflected in the human communities in the reduction from economic diversity to single-industry towns. The methods, scale and economy of industrial forestry lead to depopulation of forest-based communities and to reduced biological, economic and cultural diversity. Ecoforestry maintains and gives rise to greater diversity on many levels. It is based on the recognition that sustainable communities depend on sustainable forest ecosystems.

The expansionist worldview upon which modernism is based reduces all values to a common monetary measure—for example, dollars. If dollars are the only measure widely accepted for evaluating courses of action, then the demands of modern progress (as defined above) will be to use all resources to our maximum ability so as to generate the largest short-term gains. The creation of wealth in this way is often illusory, for it is based not only on increasing public and private debt, but also on increasing social and ecological debts. Even if we took all human interests into account, strove for economic and social justice, and considered the interests and needs of future generations, we would still not be able to resolve our current dilemmas without embracing a larger system of values, a broader, more inclusive understanding of how we participate in local, regional and global ecosystems.

Broader perspectives such as these help us to better understand our whole heritage and the debt we owe to the natural processes that provide us with a rich accumulation of ecological wealth. This accumulation, we can then appreciate, is part of larger sustaining processes that allow abundance to be continually produced. When we look at our problems with a narrower focus, as suggested by the dominant paradigm, we can be led to think that we must sacrifice either jobs or healthy ecosystems. Nothing could be further from the truth; they are interdependent. Thus, if we work within the limits of local ecosystems, but add diversity to our economies, we can produce many levels of value-added activity. The end result will be greater prosperity for all but the few megacorporations that have no interest in preserving local communities or ecosystems.

A solution, then, might be to redefine the wise-use philosophy of Gifford Pinchot. If we consider the needs of future generations of humans over several hundred years, can we not then design practices that take conservation seriously? The crux then will be seen as how to build conservation costs into the system's economics. This approach could buy time. However, in our view it cannot resolve our fundamental problems. We cannot design sustainable practices without a deeper understanding of the relevant values and costs. Any values lost must be figured as costs. In addition, just as a person who is egocentric often fails to perceive community values, so a person who is *anthropocentric* (believes that only humans have inherent value) can have difficulty understanding and perceiving the diversity of ecological values inherent in the forests and Earth. It is not just a matter of short-term versus long-term perspectives, although looking at our situation with a broader temporal perspective certainly helps. It is a matter of a different frame of reference.

The dispute that erupted in the forests of British Columbia in the summer of 1993 over the government/industry decision to clearcut much of the forests of Clayoquot Sound exemplifies the nature of the debate we have been describing. In 1995 the British Columbia government legislated its Forest Practices Code, which promised that forestry would be conducted in an environmentally sound way. To the critics, however, the Forest Practices Code was a band-aid solution that would merely help to prolong the lifespan of a dying industrial forestry status quo. It was still very mainstream, and mainstream thinking is steeped in ideas of sustained yield and cosmetic cuts, for example, those which follow natural contours and boundaries, rather than in understanding whole, natural forest ecosystems with their multitudes of functions, values, beings and processes. Sustaining a steady flow of raw material to be turned into commodities by means of longer rotations and smaller clearcuts could ultimately lead to the same results as the large-scale conversion of diverse natural forests into just a few commercially profitable species and single-age monocultures. This thinking is based on attempting to control and redesign the forest by removing the old forests and replacing them with "superior" desired species which are managed (meaning by the same methods as industrial agriculture, based on machines and external subsidies such as fertilizers, pesticides and petrochemicals).

Our description of the conflicts so far should make it evident that one way to break the impasse would be to change our forest practices so that they are consistent with the ways in which natural forests sustain themselves through diversity, recycling of woody debris, and natural succession and regeneration. If an economy is based on a natural resource and its use, than clearly the elimination of that resource will destroy the economy over time. This has been dramatically shown in the case of much of the Newfoundland fishing industry with the virtual elimination of the northern cod stock.

• • •

Finally, let us consider the main contrasts between conventional industrial forestry and ecologically based forestry. Indeed, it may be observed that while the goals of ecologically based forestry are largely in keeping with the principles of a deep ecology approach, at times they overlap with some of the "wise use management" conservation principles of shallow ecology and Gifford Pinchot. In light of current economic and political realities, this should be expected (see Figure 2).

Methods for Attaining Ecoforestry Goals

Principles of Ecoforestry

1. Retention must be the first consideration in any planned removal of trees from a stand. Emphasize what must be left to ensure the protection of such things as rare species, sites of native cultural significance, riparian zones (that is, watercourses, lakeshores, etc.).

Industrial Forestry	**Ecoforestry**
1. Trees are seen as products	Forests are ecological communities
2. Short-term production goals	Long-term sustainability
3. Agricultural production model	Forest ecosystem model
4. Trees are the only cash crop	Diverse forest products and services
5. Trees' survival dependent on humans	Self-sustaining, self-maintaining, and self-renewing
6. Chemicals	No chemicals
7. Clearcuts	Harvesting surplus wood and selective removal
8. Same-age stands of trees	All ages of trees
9. Monoculture of single or few species	All species of trees
10. Simplified ecosystem	Natural biodiversity and complexity
11. Capital-intensive and corporate-based	Labor-intensive and locally based
12. Redesigning nature	Accepting nature's design
13. Lifespan, 60–100 years	Lifespan, millennia
14. Loss of the sacred	Sense of the sacred and mysterious
15. Older traditions, aboriginal knowledge outdated	Older traditions and aboriginal knowledge are sources of wisdom

Figure 2: Contrasting Conventional Industrial and Ecologically Based Forestry

2. Leave riparian zones intact. No tree removal should take place in the most sensitive areas. Protect water quality by minimizing alterations to natural drainage patterns.

3. Maintain composition and structures to support fully functioning forests. Important forest structures such as large old trees, snags, and large fallen trees are maintained by letting a minimum of 20 to 30 percent of overstory trees (well distributed spatially and by species) grow old and die in any timber extraction area.

4. Use the lowest impact removal methods possible. Avoid building roads and compacting forest soils as much as possible—all roads should be small-scale, contour, low-grade roads requiring a minimum of blasting.

5. Plan in terms of the needs of the larger watershed, even if owner does not control or own the watershed. A watershed zone plan must designate areas where tree removal is not permitted and those where different levels and types of removal are possible.

6. Prohibit clearcutting as currently practised and utilize ecologically appropriate partial cutting methods that maintain the canopy structure, age distribution, and species mixtures found in healthy natural forests of a particular ecosystem type.

7. Select trees as candidates for removal by considering how abundant and redundant their structures and functions are to the rest of the forest as a whole, leaving potential wildlife trees (to become snags and large woods debris).

8. Allow the forest to regenerate trees through seeds from trees in the logged area. Tree planting will generally not be required because a diverse, fully functioning forest is always maintained, assuring natural regeneration.

9. Maintain ecological succession to protect biological diversity. The process of brush control will be avoided. Over time, all forest phases must occupy every forest site, even on sites managed solely for timber.

10. Prohibit slash burning. Fire is an acceptable tool in landscapes that have a history of naturally occurring fires, but use with caution.

11. Prohibit pesticide use. Disease, insects and shrub/herb vegetation are essential parts of a fully functioning forest.

12. Maintain and restore topsoil quality by leaving sufficient large and small debris.

13. Maintain beauty and other natural esthetic qualities in the visual, sound, and odor landscapes.

14. Always look at the forest as a whole and how each part contributes to the needs and health of the whole in which it resides.

15. Rely as much as possible on local people and markets. Engage in full-cost accounting.

16. Remember that wisdom begins with recognizing our limitations and ignorance. When in doubt, don't![4]

While this form of *ecoforestry* is not yet the norm, there are current indications that there is a trend in this direction. In the wake of the Clayoquot Sound protests and arrests in 1993 the British Columbia government agreed to commission a panel of experts in forest ecology and native cultural concerns to investigate the best way that logging could proceed in Clayoquot Sound. In the spring of 1995 the Scientific Panel for Sustainable Forest Practices in Clayoquot Sound released its final report entitled *Sustainable Ecosystem Management* in Clayoquot Sound Planning and Practices. To the delight of some and the shock of others, the findings of the panel, if fully implemented, would turn B.C. forest practices on their head. In short, the report, in terms of its values and practices, is not only a scathing critique of industrial forestry, but it is also a major endorsement of ecologically-based forms of forestry. It emphasizes that we must first consider what must be left in the forest to maintain hilly functioning forest ecosystems, rather than asking how much we can take out for maximum profit. The Scientific Panel starts with a whole systems view of forest communities:

> The world is interconnected at all levels; attempts to understand it entail analyzing its components and considering the whole system.... In developing guiding principles, the Panel has tried to maintain a wholistic view of forest ecosystems, to recognize connections across the landscape, and to draw on both scientific knowledge and the *Nuu-chah-nulth* lived experience. Current forest management standards will be assessed, and new standards developed, in this context. (Report 4, p. 25)

Rejecting the traditional emphasis on purely economic and utilitarian values from the forest, the Panel has advocated the need to protect all forest values and all forestry components—regardless of the value humans may place on them. For example:

> Human activities must respect the land, the sea, and all the life and life systems they support. Living organisms have a place in nature that must be sustained to maintain the health of the system in which they exist. The necessity to maintain natural ecological systems—including the land and sea themselves—supersedes the value that society may place on any individual component of those systems. (Report 4, p. 25)

The Panel has also recognized that the long-term viability of a culture and its economy is utterly dependent on the long-term viability of the ecosystems in which they reside. In other words, the economy must meet the imperatives of the biophysical system, not the other way around:

> Long-term ecological and economic sustainability are essential to long-term harmony.

The Panel views harmony as a stable and healthy relationship between people and the ecosystems that support them. Maintaining harmony is the responsibility of each generation to those who follow. Standards guiding land use and resource management should ensure ecological, cultural, and long-term economic sustainability. Current rates of population growth and resource extraction may not be sustainable or permit the desired harmony. (Report 4, p. 25)

The Panel recommended that an ecosystem approach to planning be adopted, one in which "the primary planning objective is to sustain the productivity and natural diversity of the Clayoquot Sound region. The flow of forest products must be determined in a manner consistent with objectives for ecosystem sustainability" (Report 5, p. 153).

The Report rejects traditional clearcut logging in favor of a *variable-retention* silvicultural system that attempts to mimic the characteristics of natural forests. It states:

> The variable-retention system provides for the permanent retention after harvest of various forest structures or habitat elements such as large decadent trees or groups of trees, snags, logs, and downed wood from the original stand that provide habitat for forest biota. (Report 5, p. 83)

The Variable-Retention Technique —

1. Maintains watershed integrity; maintains the stability and productivity of forest soils; maintains waterflows and critical elements of water quality within the range of natural variability and within natural waterways;
2. Maintains biological diversity; creates managed forests that retain near-natural levels of biological diversity, structural diversity, and ecological function; maintains viable

populations of all indigenous species; sustain the species, populations, and the processes associated with the late-successional forest stands and structures;

3. Maintains cultural values; protects areas and sites significant to First Nations people;
4. Maintains scenic, recreational, and tourism values; and
5. Is sustainable—provides for a sustainable flow of products from the managed forests of Clayoquot Sound. (Report 5, p. 151)

The Panel also emphasizes the need to take the cultural and spiritual needs of the native people of Clayoquot Sound into account. It notes that "indigenous people live within the landscape from which they and the rest of society extract resources. Because of their longer, often closer, connections to nature, the cultural and spiritual relationships of First Nations peoples to their environment are different from those of other cultures. Such cultural and spiritual needs must be accommodated in standards governing land use and resource management" (Report 4, p. 25). The panel also specifically recognizes the ecological knowledge of First Nations in Report 3.

The systemic approach to the forests of Clayoquot Sound taken by the Clayoquot Sound Scientific Panel emphasizes the close interdependencies that exist among community cultural, economic and biophysical sustainability. All too often forest-based communities feel out of control, the decisions for the land being made elsewhere, driven purely by economies of scale. Increasingly, representatives of forest communities have argued for the need to have more control and say over what takes place in their watersheds. This has certainly been the case with regard to the native people of Clayoquot Sound, as well as with respect to the communities of Tofino and Ucluelet. Indeed, there are compelling arguments to be made for increased levels of local control so long as regional and national standards of forest management are maintained.

Current Arguments for Increased Levels of Local Control

1. Community dependence on exports of a single resource leave the local economy vulnerable to external market variations. Long-term stability requires diversification and investment in the local economy. Such development is best accomplished through local initiatives and planning.
2. Outside control of the local resource base often results in surplus revenues being redirected elsewhere. Companies tend to be reluctant to purchase from local suppliers, invest in local manufacturing, or locate head offices and research facilities in the community. Alternatively, it is argued that a community-based forestry would more readily be able to keep revenues within the region.
3. Small-scale forms of ecoforestry can best protect the wide range of economic and environmental values. For example, community-based enterprises are more apt to be sensitive to the protection of water supplies and wildlife habitat, while providing opportunities for tourist and recreational revenue. It is argued that small-scale forestry may be less wasteful and better able to produce a wider variety of specialized wood products through intensive management. Small-scale is *site-specific*, using a variety of harvesting procedures, and is better suited to the practice of a more environmentally sustainable *wholistic* and ecoforestry-based form of management and technology practices.
4. Locally controlled resources are responsive to the changing needs, values, and lifestyles

of the local population. Control over one's resources gives a greater sense of control over one's life.

North Americans are now at a juncture in their history when they are finally beginning to realize that they are living far beyond their economic and environmental means. We have become wealthy because we have been recklessly converting natural wealth into financial capital, but at a cost which is unsustainable. Like the road into Clayoquot Sound that bifurcates, we have now reached a similar fork in terms of how we live and interact with the larger biophysical world upon which we are dependent. The Clayoquot Sound Scientific Panel's Report points in the direction of an emerging ecological paradigm (or as some would say, "worldview"). It argues for a systemic approach to the management of forest ecosystems and for the recognition that sustainable forestry must take into account the full range of values within a given ecosystem as well as respect the cultural values of those who reside within this ecosystem. The B.C. government has promised to abide by the Panel's recommendations. If it does, it will be the beginning of a radical shift in the way that forestry is conducted in Canada's most economically important forest province. The proverbial horse will have been let out of the barn and forest policies elsewhere in the province will eventually have to come in line with practices that the Panel claims are "not only the best in the province, but the best in the world" (Report 4, p. 8). The gauntlet has been thrown down. Do we have the foresight and the political will to make the transition to ecoforestry—i.e., to ecologically responsible forest use?

Notes

1. Phil Carter, "The Summer of Clayoquot," *Borealis* Vol. 5, No. 1, Issue 15 (Spring, 1994): 8–17; Ron MacIsaac and Anne Champagne, eds., *Clayoquot Mass Trials* (Gabriola Island, B.C.: New Society Publishers, 1994); Tzeporah Berman, Maurice Gibbons, et al., *Clayoquot and Dissent* (Vancouver: Ronsdale Press Ltd., 1994); Howard Breen-Needham, Sandy Francis, eds., *Witness to Wilderness: The Clayoquot Sound Anthology* (Vancouver: Arsenal Pulp Press, 1994).

2. Some good discussions of Muir and Pinchot are found in: Roderick Nash, *Wilderness and the American Mind* (New Haven: Yale University Press, 1979): Carolyn Merchant, ed., *Major Problems in American Environmental History* (Lexington, Mass.: D. C. Heath and Company, 1993); Stewart Udall, *The Quiet Crisis* (New York: Avon Books, 1963).

3. Thomas L. Burton, *Natural Resource Policy in Canada: Issues and Perspectives* (Toronto: McClelland and Stewart, 1977).

4. These points are a synthesis of principles found in ecoforestry literature; see such writers as Merv Wilkinson, Orville Camp, Chris Maser, and Herb Hammond in the bibliography.

References

Camp, O. *The Forest Farmer's Handbook: A Guide to Natural Selection Management.* Ashland: Sky River, 1991.

Hammond, H. *Seeing the Forest among the Trees: The Case for Wholistic Forest Use.* Vancouver: Polestar Press, 1991.

Maser, C. *The Redesigned Forest.* San Diego, Calif.: R. and E. Miles, 1988.

———. *The Forest and Primeval.* San Francisco: Sierra Books, 1990.

———, and Sedell, J. *The Forest to the Sea: The Ecology of Wood in Streams, Rivers, Estuaries and Oceans.* Delray, Fla.: St. Lucie Press, 1994.

Wilkinson, M., and Loomis, R. *Wildwood: A Forest for the Future.* Gabriola, B.C.: Reflections, 1990.

EPILOGUE

The following essay is from a recent book of essays written by Kathleen Dean Moore, chair of the Philosophy Department and Professor of Philosophy at Oregon State University. The collection is entitled *Holdfast: At Home in the Natural World*, and was published by The Lyons Press in 1999. Kathleen is a skilled and perceptive nature essayist and also an expert in the philosophy of law. Her scholarly book *Pardons: Justice, Mercy and the Public Interest* was published by Oxford University Press in 1989. Her first collection of nature essays, *Riverwalking: Reflections on Moving Water*, was published in 1995 (Lyons & Burford Publishers) and won a 1996 Pacific Northwest Booksellers Association Award. In different forms her essays have appeared in such locations as *Willow Spring, Northwest Review, North American Review, The New York Times, Field and Stream, Wild Earth, Interdisciplinary Studies in Literature and the Environment, Southern Review, Commonweal, California Wild, Bear Essentials, Canoe and Kayak, River,* and *Inner Voice.* Some of her essays have also been anthologized in *The River Reader,* edited by John A. Murray (published by The Lyons Press, 1998), in *Forest of Voices: Reading and Writing the Environment*, edited by Lex Runciman and Chris Anderson (Mayfield Publishing, 1995), and in a Norton anthology of short fiction edited by Judith Kitchen, *In Brief: Short Takes on the Personal* (1999). Her writing has received high praise from many reviewers and writers, including Rick Bass, Gary Snyder, Robert Michael Pyle, and Terry Tempest Williams. The essay included here recalls her reflections during 1997 on a sojourn along a logging road in the Coast Range of Oregon, and expresses her view that the cut-over lands have become a "landscape of irretrievable loss." With proper management, trees may regrow after extensive logging, but for many generations to come forests thereafter lose some of the wonderful qualities, both human and natural, that make them what they are.

Kathleen Dean Moore

Traveling the Logging Road, Coast Range

I'm driving between banks of forest duff, through a leafy tunnel lined with sword ferns and foxgloves. Morning fog spreads through the trees and along the narrow road, like milk poured in water. I turn on the windshield wipers and swerve to avoid a salamander. Huckleberry bushes and rhododendrons grow thick under cedars reaching over the road. I'm not sure how tall these trees are; their top branches have disappeared in the fog. I don't know how old the forest is either, but along this road, I have seen scars on the uphill sides of cedars, where Siuslaw people peeled strips of bark more than three hundred years ago. In the undergrowth, in the fog, these are trees without beginning, trees without end: an eternity of forest.

The road has only one lane for most of its length, but every mile or so there's a wider space where a driver can pull over to let a log truck past. There are pink plastic ribbons dangling from branches here and there, and sometimes a mileage number on a plastic post. Thickly paved with asphalt and built to last, the road follows its fogline around the shoulders of mountains and along ridge tops in Oregon's Coast Range. It's surprisingly well built for a one-way road that, as far as I can tell from my topographic map, ends on the top of a hill in the middle of nowhere.

Milepost 19

I crest a hill, startle, and hit the brakes. Bare hillside falls away on my left, bare hillside rises sharply to my right, nothing but mud, acres and acres of steep hillside stripped and sodden. A few blackened spars fall across the hill at odd angles, a few more stand upright—each a stake burned to its base. Far up the hillside, a bulldozer is working slowly. I can hear it shifting and wheezing and powering in low gear, gouging into the earth to tear at a root ball. Then shoving the broken end of a tree into a pile of slash. A single strand of smoke rises from a smoldering slash pile and spreads out brown against the bottom of the clouds.

I pull off the road onto a landing littered with tree bark. The tracks of heavy equipment have cut the ground into muddy stripes. Through the clear fans of my windshield, everything has been reduced to shades of gray except, far away,

---

Kathleen Dean Moore, "Traveling the Logging Road, Coast Range," *Holdfast*: At Home in the Natural World (New York: The Lyons Press, 1999), 89–96. Reprinted with permission from The Lyons Press.

the dull orange smudge of the bulldozer. I have seen a landscape like this before, but it takes me a minute to search my memory. It isn't Central America; nothing I have seen in the slash-and-burn agriculture of third-world countries comes close to this kind of devastation, on this scale. Eventually, I pull back to mind a photograph of a scene from Europe—a cloud-shrouded moonscape of burned and broken snags, where even the ground is churned into craters and thrown into pressure waves of mud and slash. In the foreground, a burned-out tank, and below the photograph, the label: "The Forest of Ardennes, 1945."

Fog turns into rain and within minutes gullies are channeling gray water into larger gullies and digging ditches that spill a slurry of mud onto the road. The mud runs under my car, drops off the roadbed, and slides down a ravine toward the river where salmon are pooling up, waiting to move onto spawning beds.

Before I saw the effects of clear-cutting the great Northwest forests, I imagined a romantic picture: Lumberjacks come in and cut down trees, everyone has clean, sharp-smelling lumber for homes and schools, families have jobs and, where there had been a forest, there is a flower-filled meadow, which is nice for the deer and thus for the hunters; and after a time, the forest grows back and the lumberjacks can cut it again. Then I came to Oregon and saw clear-cutting with my own eyes.

Do people know about the bulldozers? Do they know about the fires and poison sprayed from small planes to kill whatever brush may have survived? Do people know about the steepness of the bare hills and the crumbling edges of eroded ravines, the silt in the spawning beds? Do they know about the absolute, ground-zero devastation? Logging companies don't just cut the trees and haul them away. In clear-cuts I have seen, not only the trees, but the huckleberries, ferns, moss, the fuss of the chickadees, the silver whistle of the varied thrush, even the rich forest duff that holds on to winter rains, the nourishing soil itself, are all gone—hauled off, sawed up, starved out, plowed under, buried, compacted, or burned. All that's left after clear-cutting are steep hillsides of churned-up mud, a few half-burned piles of slash, and a high-quality asphalt road.

Milepost 34

On a line drawn as sharply on the landscape as a boundary line on a map, the clear-cut ends and so does the rain. Ahead are steep scrubland hills, steaming in hard light. I pull of the road, pack up my lunch, and push through the brush down a steep grade toward a stream that shows on my map. But after struggling for almost an hour through blackberry canes and nettles, I find myself less than halfway down the hill, stranded on a stump in the middle of a briar patch. I look around cautiously, shading my eyes with my hand. Hot light and harsh shadows make it hard to see. Nothing on this hillside is taller than I am. There are waist-high salmonberry bushes, their stems fuzzy with thorns, Oregon grape as sharp as English holly, and thick tangles of blackberries reaching over everything, like cobwebs.

I jump from the stump onto the root ball of a sword fern and grab for a fir sapling. The fern's roots break free and the whole clump slides ten feet down the slope. I ride it down, landing on my back, my feet out in front of me, one arm wrapped in a blackberry vine that has scraped from my wrist to my shoulder. The hillside buzzes in the sun. I give up on the hike to the stream, and start the climb back to my car.

When I finally push through a last thicket and emerge, hot and wobbly at the top of the slope, I sit down in the only shade on the hillside, shade cast by a wooden sign. The sign reads, TREES: A RENEWABLE RESOURCE. PLANTED IN 1985.

Sure enough, I can see a few young Douglas-fir trees here and there, light green and frothy, about my height. I can also see every alien, invasive, thorned or poisonous plant that ever grew in hot sun on disturbed soil in this part of the country: Himalayan blackberries, Scotch broom, poison oak, tansy ragwort, Russian thistles, nettles. I wonder if people understand that forests don't just grow back. Plants grow all right; plants always grow in Oregon. But what you get is not what you had before—not by a distance, not in a hundred years.

A pickup truck grinds by, slowing as it passes. I wonder what the driver thinks of me, sitting alone in the dirt, glowering at the scrub.

Milepost 39

I pull over next to a grove where I can see nothing but Douglas-firs ranging off in all directions. They grow tall, straight and thin, closely spaced, evenly ranked, each almost the diameter of a fence post. For ten feet off the ground, the branches are bare spikes. Then the trees leaf out into a canopy that exhales piney air and a slow drift of dry needles. The forest has the feel of a park—the light dusty and even, the afternoon simple and silent. I walk deeper into the trees, brushing a few needles out of my hair.

I am well out of sight of the road, not thinking much, when the silence finally catches my attention. I stop walking to listen. Where are the chickadees, the bees, the flies? I look behind me. What happened to the hemlocks, the big-leaf maples, the low salal? I take a step backward. Douglas-firs five inches across, everywhere I look. Ten feet apart. Three hundred trees per acre. This isn't a forest. This is a farm. I am trespassing on a fence-post farm. Poisoned and plowed and planted and fertilized as a wheat field, this lumber will be harvested as routinely as wheat is cut and threshed. I feel like a grasshopper—nervous, scratching one leg against another, tiptoeing across the dusty ground below tall yellow stalks.

It wasn't very long ago that trucks carried one-log loads through my town. Standing in line at the five-and-dime, customers would pass the word. "One-log load goin' by." We would crane our necks and peer past the fabric bolts and Valentine's candy, through the dusty window and, sure enough, a truck would rumble past carrying a section of log so massive, it was all the truck could haul on a single load. I try to remember now what I thought then, and it seems to me that I felt admiration for the log, but had no understanding that in the place where the tree had grown, another like it would not grow in my lifetime, nor my children's, nor my grandchildren's . . . not in fifteen generations.

The five-and-dime is a used-book store now, and the trucks that come by carry thirty, forty logs a load—thin logs, destined for pulp or fence posts. Logs hang out the back and flap up and down whenever the truck hits a bump in the road.

Milepost 46

The road climbs in a spiral around a bare mountain and finally ends at the top of the hill in a broad expanse of gravel. I get out of my car to look around. I'm guessing that a high-line used to work about where I am standing. Although the hill has grown up in brambles, the earth still bears the marks of skid trails where cables pulled logs up the hill to the yard. This high up, I can see all the way to the afternoon sun and the white line that marks the ocean. From the top of the range to the edge of the sea, the landscape is a patchwork of clear-cuts, replants, landings, bare earth, and a few reserves of old-growth cedar and hemlock along the coast.

When I walk to the far edge of the hill, I learn that I am not alone up here. A man sits in the cab of an old pickup truck, staring out over the fading hills, never looking my way. The hair on the back of his neck is gray and curling, the skin moist and brown from the sun. He wears a plaid shirt covered with a quilted vest and his hands, still gripping the steering wheel, are enormous.

What does he hear, listening so intently? Faint on an old wind, the creak of cables maybe, the shriek of the whistle-pig, shouted commands, men calling out, chain saws shaking with power. Trucks gearing up, logs thudding onto huge log-decks, and the cracking, cracking, as a tree falls through the forest, breaking off limbs, rending the long fibers of its trunk, then silence—a long, terrible silence—and a great thud as the tree drives its limbs into the earth, rises once, settles. Faint on an old wind, the smells of lubricating oil, diesel exhaust, coffee, dust, and the sweetness of new-cut cedar, as beautiful as Christmas.

A few patches of forest are left on old homesteads and in locked-up forest reserves on federal land. A few more plots to cut, a couple of lawsuits pending that may release some logs, some salvage logging after burns in the Siskiyous and Cascades. Three years maybe. Maybe four. Then the logging companies will pull up stakes and look for somewhere else to cut. His children will leave then, too; there's no work for timber workers where there's no timber. One son off to the fish-packing plants in Alaska maybe. Another to California. Once the daughter with the new baby leaves—for Portland? Spokane?—what will he hold in those great rough hands?

Both he and I can see clear to the sea. The view from the end of the road is a landscape of irretrievable loss.

Selected Bibliography on Environmental Ethics and Forestry

The International Society for Environmental Ethics maintains a website that includes a "master bibliography" of sources on environmental ethics (http://www.cep.unt.edu/ISEE.html). The bibliography can be searched on many subjects, including "forestry," using key words. Some of the best journals for philosophical discussions of environmental ethics include *Agriculture and Human Values, The Ecologist, Environmental Ethics, Environmental Values, Ethics and the Environment, The Journal of Agricultural and Environmental Ethics,* and *The Trumpeter.*

Anthologies in Environmental Ethics and Philosophy

Adams, Carol, ed. *Ecofeminism and the Sacred.* Maryknoll, N.Y.: Orbis Books, 1992.

Attfield, Robin, and Andrew Belsey, eds. *Philosophy and the Natural Environment.* Cambridge, U.K.: Cambridge University Press, 1994.

Badiner, Allan Hunt, ed. *Dharma Gaia: A Harvest of Essays in Buddhism and Ecology.* Berkeley, Calif.: Parallax Press, 1990.

Blatz, Charles V., ed. *Ethics and Agriculture: An Anthology of Current Issues in World Context.* Moscow: University of Idaho Press, 1991.

Botzler, Richard G., and Susan J. Armstrong, eds. *Environmental Ethics: Divergence and Convergence.* 2nd ed. Boston: McGraw Hill, 1998.

Callicott, J. Baird, ed. *Companion to "A Sand County Almanac": Interpretive and Critical Essays.* Madison: University of Wisconsin Press, 1987.

———, and Fernando J. R. da Rocha, eds. *Earth Summit Ethics: Towards a Reconstructive Postmodern Philosophy of Environmental Education.* Albany, N.Y.: SUNY Press, 1996.

———, and Michael P. Nelson, eds. *The Great New Wilderness Debate.* Athens: University of Georgia Press, 1998.

———, and Roger T. Ames, eds. *Nature in Asian Traditions of Thought.* Albany, N.Y.: SUNY Press, 1989.

Cooper, David, and Joy A. Palmer, eds. *The Environment in Question: Ethics and Global Issues.* London: Routledge, 1992.

Cooper, N. S., and R. C. J. Carling, eds. *Ecologists and Ethical Judgments.* London: Chapman & Hall, 1996.

Costanza, Robert, Bryan G. Norton, and Benjamin D. Haskell, eds. *Ecosystem Health.* Washington, D.C.: Island Press, 1992.

Dallmeyer, Dorinda G., and Alvert F. Ike, eds. *Environmental Ethics and the Global Marketplace.* Athens: University of Georgia Press, 1998.

Des Jardins, Joseph, ed. *Environmental Ethics: Concepts, Policy, Theory.* Mountain View, Calif.: Mayfield Publishing Company, 1999.

Diamond, Irene, and Gloria F. Orenstein, eds. *Reweaving the World: The Emergence of Ecofeminism.* San Francisco: Sierra Club Books, 1990.

Dower, Nigel, ed. *Ethics and Environmental Responsibility.* Avebury, U.K.: Aldershot, 1989.

Drengson, Alan, and Yuichi Inoue, eds. *The Deep Ecology Movement: An Introductory Anthology.* Berkeley, Calif.: North Atlantic Books, 1995.

Elliot, Robert, ed. *Environmental Ethics.* Oxford: Oxford University Press, 1995.

———, and Arran Gave, eds. *Environmental Philosophy: A Collection of Readings.* University Park: Pennsylvania State University Press, 1983.

Engel, J. Ronald, and Joan Gibb Engel, eds. *Ethics of Environment and Development: Global Challenge, International Response.* Tucson: University of Arizona Press, 1990.

Ferre, Frederick, and Peter Hartel, eds. *Ethics and Environmental Policy: Theory Meets Practice.* Athens: University of Georgia Press, 1994.

Gaard, Greta, ed. *Ecofeminism: Women, Animals, Nature.* Philadelphia: Temple University Press, 1993.

Gottlieb, Roger S., ed. *The Ecological Community: Environmental Challenges for Philosophy, Politics, and Morality.* New York: Routledge, 1997.

Gruen, Lori, and Dale Jamieson, eds. *Reflecting on Nature: Readings in Environmental Philosophy.* New York: Oxford University Press, 1994.

Gunn, Alastair S., and P. Aarne Vesilind, eds. *Environmental Ethics for Engineers.* Chelsea, Mich.: Lewis Publishers, 1986.

Hargrove, Eugene, ed. *Beyond Spaceship Earth: Environmental Ethics and the Solar System.* San Francisco: Sierra Club Books, 1986.

———, ed. *Religion and Environmental Crisis.* Athens: University of Georgia Press, 1986.

———, ed. *The Animal Rights/Environmental Ethics Debate.* Albany, N.Y.: SUNY Press, 1992.

Hart, Richard E., ed. *Ethics and the Environment.* Lanham, Md.: University Press of America, 1992.

Lemons, John, Laura Westra, and Robert Goodland, eds. *Ecological Sustainability and Integrity: Concepts and Approaches.* Dordrecht, Netherlands: Kluwer Academic Publishers, 1998.

Light, Andrew, and Eric Katz, eds. *Environmental Pragmatism.* London: Routledge, 1992.

List, Peter, ed. *Radical Environmentalism: Philosophy and Tactics.* Belmont, Calif.: Wadsworth Publishing Company, 1993.

Mayo, Deborah G., and Rachelle Hollander, eds. *Acceptable Evidence: Science and Values in Risk Management.* New York: Oxford University Press, 1991.

Norton, Bryan G., ed. *The Preservation of Species: The Value of Biological Diversity.* Princeton, N.J.: Princeton University Press, 1986.

Oelschlaeger, Max, ed. *The Wilderness Condition: Essays on Environment and Civilization.* San Francisco: Sierra Club Books, 1992.

———, ed. *Postmodern Environmental Ethics.* Albany, N.Y.: SUNY Press, 1995.

Pierce, Christine, and Donald VanDeVeer, eds. *People, Penguins, and Plastic Trees: Basic Issues in Environmental Ethics.* 2nd ed. Belmont, Calif.: Wadsworth Publishing Company, 1995.

Plant, Judith, ed. *Healing the Wounds: The Promise of Ecofeminism.* Philadelphia: New Society Publishers, 1989.

Pojman, Louis P., ed. *Environmental Ethics: Readings in Theory and Application.* 3d ed. Belmont, Calif.: Wadsworth/Thompson Learning, 2000.

Pojman, Louis P., ed. *Global Environmental Ethics.* Mountain View, Calif.: Mayfield Publishing Company, 2000.

Regan, Tom, ed. *Earthbound: New Introductory Essays in Environmental Ethics.* New York: Random House, 1984.

Scherer, Donald, ed. *Upstream/Downstream: Issues in Environmental Ethics.* Philadelphia: Temple University Press, 1990.

Shrader-Frechette, K. S., ed. *Environmental Ethics.* Pacific Grove, Calif.: Boxwood Press, 1981.

Sterba, James P., ed. *Earth Ethics: Environmental Ethics, Animal Rights, and Practical Applications.* Englewood Cliffs, N.J.: Prentice Hall, 1995.

Taylor, Bron Raymond, ed. *Ecological Resistance*

Movements: The Global Emergence of Radical and Popular Environmentalism. Albany, N.Y.: SUNY Press, 1995.

Tobias, Michael, ed. Deep Ecology. San Diego: Avant Books, 1984.

Tucker, Mary Evelyn, and Duncan Ryuken Williams, eds. Buddhism and Ecology: The Interconnection of Dharma and Deeds. Cambridge, Mass.: Harvard University Press, 1997.

———, and John A. Grim, eds. Worldviews and Ecology. Lewisburg, Pa.: Bucknell University Press, 1993.

VanDeVeer, Donald, and Christine Pierce, eds. The Environmental Ethics and Policy Book: Philosophy, Ecology, Economics. Belmont, Calif.: Wadsworth Publishing Company, 1994.

Warren, Karen J., ed. Ecological Feminism. London: Routledge, 1994.

———, ed. Ecofeminism: Women, Culture, and Nature. Bloomington: Indiana University Press, 1997.

Westphal, Dale, and Fred Westphal, eds. Planet in Peril: Essays in Environmental Ethics. Fort Worth, Tex.: Harcourt Brace College Publishers, 1994.

Westra, Laura, and John Lemons, eds. Perspectives on Ecological Integrity. Dordrecht, The Netherlands: Kluwer Academic Publishers, 1995.

———, and Patricia H. Werhane, eds. The Business of Consumption: Environmental Ethics and the Global Economy. Lanham, Md.: Rowman & Littlefield, 1998.

———, and Peter S. Wenz, eds. Faces of Environmental Racism: Confronting Issues of Global Justice. Lanham, Md.: Rowman & Littlefield, 1995.

Zimmerman, Michael E., ed. Environmental Philosophy: From Animal Rights to Radical Ecology. 2d ed. Upper Saddle River, N.J.: Prentice-Hall, 1998.

Some Significant Works in Environmental Ethics and Philosophy

Adams, Carol J. Neither Man nor Beast: Feminism and the Defense of Animals. New York: Continuum, 1994.

Abram, David. The Spell of the Sensuous. New York: Vintage Books, 1997.

Attfield, Robin. The Ethics of Environmental Concern. 2d ed. New York: Columbia University Press, 1991.

———. Environmental Philosophy: Principles and Prospects. Avebury, U.K.: Aldershot, 1994.

———. The Ethics of the Global Environment. Edinburgh, U.K.: Edinburgh University Press, 1999.

Badiner, Allan Hunt, ed. Dharma Gaia: A Harvest of Essays on Buddhism and Ecology. Berkeley: Parallax Press, 1990.

Berry, Wendell. The Unsettling of America: Culture and Agriculture. New York: Avon Books, 1978.

Bookchin, Murray. Toward an Ecological Society. Montreal: Black Rose Books, 1980.

———. The Ecology of Freedom: The Emergence and Dissolution of Hierarchy. Palo Alto, Calif.: Cheshire Books, 1982.

Brennan, Andrew. Thinking about Nature. Athens: University of Georgia Press, 1988.

Caldwell, Lynton Keith, and Kristin Shrader-Frechette. Policy for Land: Law and Ethics. Lanham, Md.: Rowman & Littlefield, 1993.

Callicott, J. Baird. In Defense of the Land Ethic: Essays in Environmental Philosophy. Albany, N.Y.: SUNY Press, 1989.

———. Earth's Insights: A Multicultural Survey of Ecological Ethics from the Mediterranean Basin to the Australian Outback. Berkeley: University of California Press, 1994.

———. Beyond the Land Ethic: More Essays in Environmental Philosophy. Albany, N.Y.: SUNY Press, 1999.

———, and Eric T. Freyfogle, eds. Aldo Leopold, For the Health of the Land: Previously Unpublished Essays and Other Writings. Washington, D.C.: Island Press, 1999.

Clark, John. Renewing the Earth: The Promise of Social Ecology. London: Green Print, 1990.

Des Jardins, Joseph R. Environmental Ethics: An Introduction to Environmental Philosophy. 2nd ed. Belmont, Calif.: Wadsworth Publishing Company, 1997.

Devall, Bill. Simple in Means, Rich in Ends: Practic-

ing Deep Ecology. Salt Lake City: Peregrine Smith Books, 1988.

———, and George Sessions. *Deep Ecology: Living as if Nature Mattered*. Salt Lake City: Peregrine Smith Books, 1985.

Drengson, Alan. *Beyond Environmental Crisis: From Technocratic to Planetary Person*. New York: Peter Lang, 1989.

Elliot, Robert. *Faking Nature: The Ethics of Environmental Restoration*. London: Routledge, 1997.

Flader, Susan, and J. Baird Callicott, eds. *The River of the Mother of God and Other Essays by Aldo Leopold*. Madison: University of Wisconsin Press, 1991.

Foltz, Bruce V. *Inhabiting the Earth: Heidegger, Environmental Ethics, and the Metaphysics of Nature*. Atlantic Highlands, N.J.: Humanities Press, 1995.

Fox, Warwick. *Toward a Transpersonal Ecology: Developing New Foundations for Environmentalism*. Boston: Shambhala, 1990.

Goldsmith, Edward. *The Way: An Ecological Worldview*. Boston: Shambhala, 1993.

Gray, Elizabeth Dodson. *Green Paradise Lost*. Wellesley, Mass.: Roundtable Press, 1979.

Griffin, Susan. *Women and Nature: The Roaring Inside Her*. New York: Harper and Row, 1978.

Hargrove, Eugene. *Foundations of Environmental Ethics*. Englewood Cliffs, N.J.: Prentice Hall, 1989.

Johnson, Lawrence E. *A Morally Deep World: An Essay on Moral Significance and Environmental Ethics*. Cambridge, U.K.: Cambridge University Press, 1991.

Katz, Eric. *Nature as Subject: Human Obligation and Natural Community*. Lanham, Md.: Rowman & Littlefield, 1997.

Kealey, Daniel A. *Revisioning Environmental Ethics*. Albany, N.Y.: SUNY Press, 1990.

LaChapelle, Dolores. *Earth Wisdom*. Silverton, Colo.: Way of the Mountain Center, 1978.

———. *Sacred Land, Sacred Sex: Rapture of the Deep*. Durango, Colo.: Vivaki Press, 1992.

Leopold, Aldo. *A Sand County Almanac*. New York: Oxford University Press, 1949.

Marietta, Don E., Jr. *For People and the Planet: Holism and Humanism in Environmental Ethics*. Philadelphia: Temple University Press, 1995.

Mathews, Freya. *The Ecological Self*. London: Routledge, 1990.

McLaughlin, Andrew. *Regarding Nature: Industrialism and Deep Ecology*. Albany, N.Y.: SUNY Press, 1993.

Meine, Curt, and Richard L. Knight, eds. *The Essential Aldo Leopold: Quotations and Commentaries*. Madison: University of Wisconsin Press, 1999.

Merchant, Carolyn. *The Death of Nature: Women, Ecology, and the Scientific Revolution*. New York: Harper and Row, 1983.

———. *Radical Ecology: The Search for a Liveable World*. New York: Routledge, 1992.

———. *Earth Care: Women and the Environment*. New York: Routledge, 1995.

Naess, Arne. *Ecology, Community and Lifestyle*. Cambridge, U.K.: Cambridge University Press, 1989.

Newton, Lisa H., and Catherine K. Dillingham. *Watersheds 2: Ten Cases in Environmental Ethics*. Belmont, Calif.: Wadsworth Publishing Company, 1997.

Norton, Bryan G. *Why Preserve Natural Variety?* Princeton, N.J.: Princeton University Press, 1987.

———. *Toward Unity among Environmentalists*. New York: Oxford University Press, 1991.

Partridge, Ernest, ed. *Responsibilities to Future Generations: Environmental Ethics*. Buffalo, N.Y.: Prometheus Books, 1981.

Regan, Tom. *All That Dwell Therein: Animal Rights and Environmental Ethics*. Berkeley: University of California Press, 1982.

Reuther, Rosemary Radford. *New Woman, New Earth: Sexist Ideologies and Human Liberation*. New York: Seabury Press, 1975.

Rolston, Holmes, III. *Philosophy Gone Wild: Essays in Environmental Ethics*. Buffalo, N.Y.: Prometheus Books, 1986.

———. *Environmental Ethics: Duties to and Values in the Natural World*. Philadelphia: Temple University Press, 1988.

Sagoff, Mark. *The Economy of the Earth.* Cambridge, U.K.: Cambridge University Press, 1988.

Scriven, Tal. *Wrongness, Wisdom, and Wilderness: Toward a Libertarian Theory of Ethics and the Environment.* Albany, N.Y.: SUNY Press, 1997.

Stone, Christopher D. *Should Trees Have Standing?* Los Altos, Calif.: William Kaufmann, 1974.

———. *Earth and Other Ethics: The Case for Moral Pluralism.* New York: Harper and Row, 1987.

Sylvan, Richard, and David Bennett. *The Greening of Ethics.* Cambridge, U.K.: White Horse Press, 1994.

Taylor, Paul W. *Respect for Nature: A Theory of Environmental Ethics.* Princeton, N.J.: Princeton University Press, 1986.

Thompson, Paul B. *The Spirit of the Soil: Agriculture and Environmental Ethics.* London: Routledge, 1995.

Varner, Gary. *In Nature's Interests?: Interests, Animal Rights, and Environmental Ethics.* New York: Oxford University Press, 1998.

Wenz, Peter. *Environmental Justice.* Albany, N.Y.: SUNY Press, 1988.

Westra, Laura. *An Environmental Proposal for Ethics: The Principle of Integrity.* Lanham, Md.: Rowman & Littlefield, 1993.

———. *Living in Integrity: A Global Ethic to Restore a Fragmented Earth.* Lanham, Md.: Rowman & Littlefield, 1998.

Sources on Environmental Ethics, Forests, and Forestry

Agrawal, Arun. "The Community vs. the Market and the State: Forest Use in Uttarakhand in the Indian Himalayas." *Journal of Agricultural and Environmental Ethics* 9(1) (1996): 1–15.

Arbor, J. L. "Animal Chauvinism, Plant-Regarding Ethics and the Torture of Trees." *Australasian Journal of Philosophy* 64(3) (September 1986): 335–39.

Attfield, Robin. "The Good of a Tree." *Journal of Value Inquiry* 15 (1981): 35–54.

Banzaf, William H., Fred Marshall, James E. Coufal, and Zane J. Cornett. "Ethical Decision-making: A Roundtable Discussion." *Journal of Forestry* 91(4) (April 1993): 10–13.

Booth, Douglas E. "The Economics and Ethics of Old-Growth Forests." *Environmental Ethics* 14(1) (Spring 1992): 43–62.

———. "Preserving Old-Growth Forest Ecosystems: Valuation and Policy." *Environmental Values* 6(1) (Fall 1997): 31–45.

Bowyer, Jim L. "Responsible Environmentalism: The Ethical Features of Forest Harvest and Wood Use on a Global Scale." *Forest Perspectives* 9(4) (Winter 1991): 12–14.

Browder, John O. "Redemptive Communities: Indigenous Knowledge, Colonist Farming Systems, and Conservation of Tropical Forests." *Agriculture and Human Values* 12(1) (Winter 1995): 17–30.

Burch, William R., Jr. "The Social Meaning of Forests." *The Humanist* 39(6) (Nov./Dec. 1979): 39–44.

Callicott, J. Baird. "A Critical Examination of 'Another Look at Leopold's Land Ethic.'" *Journal of Forestry* 96(1) (January 1998): 20–26.

Callicott, J. Baird. "Harmony Between Men and Land—Aldo Leopold and the Foundations of Ecosystem Management." *Journal of Forestry* 98(5) (May 2000): 4–13.

Chapman, Herman H. "The Profession of Forestry and Professional Ethics." *Journal of Forestry* 90(4) (April 1992): 14–17, 34.

Cooper, David. "Human Sentiment and the Future of Wildlife." *Environmental Values* 2(4) (Winter 1993): 335–46.

Coufal, James, and Charles M. Spuches. *Environmental Ethics in Practice: Developing a Personal Ethics. Materials for Natural Resources Management Instructors.* Syracuse, N.Y.: SUNY College of Environmental Science and Forestry, 1995.

Davis, Michael. "The Moral Status of Dogs, Forests, and Other Persons." *Social Theory and Practice* 12 (Spring 1986): 27–59.

De Steiguer, J. E. "Can Forestry Provide the Greatest Good for the Greatest Number?" *Journal of Forestry* 92(9) (September 1994): 22–25.

DeVall, Bill, ed. *Clearcut: The Tragedy of Industrial Forestry.* San Francisco: Sierra Club Books, 1993.

Drengson, Alan R., and Duncan M. Taylor, eds. *Ecoforestry: The Art and Science of Sustainable Forest Use.* Gabriola Island, B.C.: New Society Publishers, 1997.

Ethical Challenges for Foresters. Proceedings of a Symposium to Discuss Ethical Issues in the Management of Forest Resources, University of British Columbia, September 27–28, 1991. (Sponsored by Students for Forestry Awareness, the UBC Faculty of Forestry, and the UBC Centre for Applied Ethics.)

Gunn, Alastair. "Environmental Ethics and Tropical Rain Forests: Should Greens Have Standing?" *Environmental Ethics* 16(1) (Spring 1994): 21–40.

Gunter, Pete A. Y. *The Big Thicket: A Challenge for Conservation.* Austin, Tex.: Jenkins Publishing Company, 1972.

———. "The Big Thicket: A Case Study in Attitudes toward the Environment." In *Philosophy and Environmental Crisis.* Edited by William T. Blackstone. Athens: University of Georgia Press, 1974.

Hargrove, Eugene. "Philosophy, Religion, and American Forests." In *Encyclopedia of American Forest and Conservation History. Volume Two.* Edited by Richard C. Davis. New York: Macmillan, 1983.

Hoch, David, and Robert A. Giacalone. "On the Lumber Industry: Ethical Concerns as the Other Side of Profits." *Journal of Business Ethics* 13 (1994): 357–67.

Irland, Lloyd C., ed. *Ethics in Forestry.* Portland: Timber Press, 1994.

Kaza, Stephanie. "Ethical Tensions in the Northern Forest." In *The Future of the Northern Forest.* Edited by C. M. Klyza and S. Tombalah. Hanover, N.H.: University Press of New England, 1994.

———. *The Attentive Heart: Conversations with Trees.* Boston: Shambhala, 1996.

Kohak, Erazim. "Speaking to Trees." *Critical Review* 6(2&3) (Spring/Summer 1992): 371–88.

List, Peter. "The Land Ethic in American Forestry: Pinchot and Leopold." In *The Idea of the Forest: The Political Culture of Trees in Germany and America.* Edited by K. Schultz and K. S. Calhoon. New York: Peter Lang, 1995.

———. "Leopoldian Forestry and the Ethical Acceptability of Forest Practices." In *Defining Social Acceptability in Ecosystem Management: A Workshop Proceedings.* Edited by M. Brunson et al. USDA Forest Service, Pacific Northwest Research Station, August 1996.

———. "Aldo Leopold: A Critical Celebration of His Land Ethic" and "Biotic Forestry." *Reflections,* Special Issue no. 3 (August 1998). Corvallis, Ore.: Program for Ethics, Science and the Environment, Department of Philosophy, Oregon State University.

———. "Spiritual Values in Leopold's Land Ethic: The Noumenal Integrity of Forest Ecosystems." *Proceedings of the Society of American Foresters 1999 National Convention,* Portland, Oregon, September 11–15, 1999. Bethesda, Md.: Society of American Foresters, 2000.

———, and David Brooks. "Ethics and Equity in the Pacific Rim Timber Market." In *Forests and Society: Implementing Sustainability. December 5–6, 1997.* Workshop Proceedings, Triangle Lake, Ore. Corvallis, Ore.: Oregon State University, 1998.

Loker, William M. "Cowboys, Indians and Deforestation: Ethical and Environmental Issues Associated with Pastures Research in Amazonia." *Agriculture and Human Values* 13(1) (Winter 1996): 52–58.

McQuillan, Alan G. "Is National Forest Planning Incompatible with a Land Ethic?" *Journal of Forestry* 88(5) (May 1990): 31–37.

Miller, Peter. "Integrity, Sustainability, Biodiversity, and Forestry." In *Perspectives on Ecological Integrity.* Edited by Laura Westra and J. Lemons. Dordrecht, The Netherlands: Kluwer Academic Publishers, 1995.

———. "Towards a Forest Policy for Canada: New Directions from Environmental Ethics." In *An Environmental Ethics Perspective on Canadian Policy for Sustainable Development.* Institute for Research on Environment and Economy. Ottawa,

Ontario: University of Ottawa, 1995.

Newton, Lisa. "The Chainsaws of Greed: The Case of Pacific Lumber." *Business and Professional Ethics Journal* 8(3) (Fall 1989): 29–61.

Orton, David. "Informed Consent or Informed Rejection of Pesticide Use: A Concept for Environmental Action." *Philosophy and Social Action* 16(4) (October–December 1990): 31–46.

Plumwood, Val, and Richard Routley. "World Rainforest Destruction—The Social and Economic Factors." *The Ecologist* 12(1) (January–February 1982): 4–22.

Poesche, Jurgen. "Business Ethics in the Choice of New Technology in the Kraft Pulping Industry." *Journal of Business Ethics* 17(5) (April 1998): 471–89.

Rolston, Holmes, III. "Values Deep in the Woods." *American Forests* 94(5&6) (May/June 1988): 33, 66–69.

———. "Does Aesthetic Appreciation of Landscapes Need to be Science-Based?" *British Journal of Aesthetics* 35(4) (October 1995): 374–86.

———. "Aesthetic Experience in Forests." *Journal of Aesthetics and Art Criticism* 56(2) (Spring 1998): 157–66.

———, and James Coufal. "A Forest Ethic and Multivalue Forest Management." *Journal of Forestry* 89(4) (April 1991): 35–40.

Routley, Richard, and Val Routley. *The Fight for the Forests: The Takeover of Australian Forests for Pines, Wood Chips, and Intensive Forestry.* 2nd ed. Canberra: Research School of Social Sciences, Australian National University, 1974.

Shiva, Vandana, and J. Bandyopadhyay. "The Evolution, Structure, and Impact of the Chipko Movement." *Mountain Research and Development* 6(2) (1986): 133–42.

Shrader-Frechette, Kristin. "Island Biogeography, Species-Area Curves, and Statistical Errors: Applied Biology and Scientific Rationality." *Proceedings of the Philosophy of Science Association* (1990): 447–56.

———, and Earl D. McCoy. "Applied Ecology and the Logic of Case Studies." *Philosophy of Science* 61(2) (June 1994): 228–49.

Society of American Foresters. *The Land Ethic, Meeting Human Needs for the Land and Its Resources.* Bethesda, Md.: The Society of American Foresters, 1998.

Thero, Daniel. "The Ethical Challenge of Rain Forest Preservation." *Dialogue* (October 1991): 5–10.

Thompson, Paul, and Steven Strauss. "Biotechnology, Ethics, and Trees: Research Ethics for Molecular Silviculture." Unpublished paper, March 1999.

Umans, Laurent. "A Discourse on Forestry Science." *Agriculture and Human Values* 10(4) (Fall 1993): 26–40.

Van Buren, John. "Critical Environmental Hermeneutics." *Environmental Ethics* 17(3) (Fall 1995): 259–75.

Weber, Leonard J. "The Social Responsibility of Land Ownership." *Journal of Forestry* 89(4) (April 1991): 12–17, 25.

Williams, Hugh. "What Is Good Forestry? An Ethical Examination of Forest Policy and Practice in New Brunswick." *Environmental Ethics* 18(4) (Winter 1996): 391–410.

Williams, Mary. "Discounting versus Maximum Sustainable Yield." In R. I. Siukora and Brian Barry, eds. *Obligations to Future Generations.* Philadelphia: Temple University Press, 1978.

Wood, Paul M. "Biodiversity as the Source of Biological Resources: A New Look at Biodiversity Values." *Environmental Values* 6 (1997): 251–68.

Index

Abbey, Edward, 216
Abenakis, 323
Abram, David, 18
Accountability: ecological, 329–330; ethical, 331; professional, 330
Adirondacks, 321, 323, 330
Advocacy, 206, 209; environmental, 210, 211, 213–214, 215, 217, 218–219
Aesthetics, 82, 294, 301, 302, 309; experience, 83, 83; forested landscapes, 42; of forestry, 74, 84, 86; landscape, 305; postmodern, 308; Romantic, 302
Africa, forest clearing, 6n.17
Afforestation, 271
Agriculture, 64, 66; agronomy, 56; exploitative, 65; industrial, 336; sustainable and nonsustainable, 266
Agricultural model of wood production, 66, 122
Agricultural products, monocultural, 337
Agroforestry, 254–255
Alaska, 7, 250
Amazonian forests, 265. *See also* Brazil
American Fisheries Society, 165, 171
American Forestry Association, 55; ethical code, 332n.19
American way of life, 326
Ancient culture, 5; extensive forestry in, 254
Animal rights movement, 94, 95, 104, 301–302, 313n.60
Anthropocentrism, 194; attitudes about forests, 55; bias in forester ethics, 127; model of our relation to nature, 335
Apache National Forest (Arizona), 53
Aquinas, Thomas, 99, 107
Aristotle, 104, 214, 271
Attfield, Robin, 96
Attitudes about forests: Colonial American, 12; farmers, 67; 19th century American, 12; utilitarian, 55
Australia, 255, 284
Autonomy, 146

Bachelard, Gaston, 87
Bali, 266
Baudrillard, Jean, 306, 307
Bauhaus school of art, architecture, and design, 303
Bentham, Jeremy, 296, 297
Berry, Thomas, 157
Berry, Wendall, 324
Bhopal, 2
Big Thicket, southeastern Texas, 121
Biocentric equality, 17, 94
Biological capital, 337
Biological diversity, 4n.8, 17, 21, 77, 105, 157, 222, 257, 292, 294, 337, 340; conservation of, 152; forest, xiiin.4, xiiin.6, 5, 17,18, 21, 22n; global, 4; loss of, 221, 231, 282, 286; maintenance of, 299; protection of, 337; sustaining, 225, 341
Biological pyramid, 328
Biotas, 64, 66
Biotic capital, 64
Biotic community, 58, 61
Biotic farming, 66
Biotic forestry, 55–56
Biotechnology, 210, 335
Blake, William, 303
"Blow the whistle." *See* Whistleblowing
Bowyer, James, 256–257
Brazil, 255, 257, 264, 271; Amazon rainforest, 4n.9. *See also* Amazonian forests
Britain, Great, 255, 271. *See also* England
British Columbia, 22n, 283–284; forest practices, 340; Forest Practices Code, 338
British Columbia Professional Foresters, Association of, 134, 137, 140, 147; code of ethics, 126, 128, 137, 148; mission statement, 141–142
British Columbia, University of, 133
Buddhism, 274
Burch, William R., Jr., 73
Bureau of Land Management (BLM), 207, 237, 238–239
Burns, Robert, 303
Butler, Samuel, 101

California, 41, 253, 319; Desert, 229, 237
California, Berkeley, University of, 218
Callicott, J. Baird, 15, 70, 96, 153, 183n, 273, 300, 307, 312n.48
Canada, 261, 283; forest destruction in, 283
Capitalism, industrial, 16, 324
"Carbon pool," 284
Carnegie Mellon University, 210–211

Carr, Stephen, 240–241
Carrying capacity, of the land, 65, 329
Carson National Forest (New Mexico), 54
Carson, Rachel, 69
Cash cropping, 277
Central Park (New York), 305
Certification: forest, 8n.25; wood, 286
Chapman, Herman H., 163–164n.3
Cheney, Jim, 290n.3
Chernobyl, 2, 218
Chile, 254, 255, 282
China, 283
Chipko movement, 20, 20n.33; "tree hugging," 20
Civil disobedience, 216; in British Columbia, 282
Civilian Conservation Corps, 60
Clark, Mary, 308
Clark, Stephen, 103–104, 107, 108, 109
Clayoquot Sound (Vancouver Island, B.C.), 22n, 128, 282, 292, 333, 340, 342; local control, 342; native people of, 342; Scientific Panel for Sustainable Forest Practices, 340
Clean Water Act, 231
Clearcutting, 7, 8n.24, 291, 304, 320, 337, 340, 341, 347; of Northern forests, 347. See also Logging
Clearwater National Forest (Idaho), 243
Climate changes, global, 4
Clinton Administration, 22n, 206
Clinton, William, 331
Code of ethics, 126, 167, 163, 330; natural resource groups, 179; professional, 148, 165, 205; U.S. Government Employees, 238
Columbia University, 212, 213
Commission on Sustainable Development, the United Nations, 286
Commodity production, 19n.31, 66, 201, 256
Commoner, Barry, 117
Complexity, 305; aesthetic, 308. See also Ecosystem complexity
Conscience: ecological, 56, 59, 65, 300; social, 61
Conservation, 16, 25, 40, 61, 66, 68, 271, 303; biological, 78, 194; as development, 33; defined by Leopold, 14, 59; education, 63; forest, xv, 23, 24n.5, 41, 122; forest, movement, 12; government, 62; natural resource, 18; new philosophy of, 24; Pinchotian, 14, 34, 336;

principles of, 32, 34; progressive, 43; traditional concept of, 190; waves of, 2
Conservation biology, 160
Conservation movement and conservationists, 32, 33, 58, 66
Costs, external, 320
Coufal, James, 126, 180, 182–183, 187

Daigle, Doug, 257
Dana, Samuel, 180n.3
Darwin, Charles, 300–301
DeBonis, Jeff, 207
Deep ecologists, 15, 73, 274
Deep Ecology, 16, 17–21, 22n, 94, 123, 165, 291, 339; movement, 18, 160, 334, 335
Deforestation, 2, 6; in Ancient societies, 5–6; environmental and social costs of, 285; global, 3–5, 4n.8–9; rain forest, 230
Demand, consumer-driven, 286–287
Dendrology, 31
Devall, Bill, 18
Developed countries, 264, 270, 271, 273
Dirty hands, problem of, 265, 272
Diversity, cultural, 9. See also Biological diversity
Douglas fir, 348; region of western North America, xiii
Drengson, Alan, 18, 127, 290, 291
Dunlap, Riley, 123n.9
Dutt, R.P., 217

Earth Day, 70
Earth First! 16, 22n, 216, 217, 311n.20
Ecofeminism, 16, 19–22, 19n.31, 20n.34–35
Ecofeminists, 73, 291, 311n.20
Ecoforestry, 16, 19, 21, 127, 160, 161, 291, 292, 337, 340, 342, 343; protection of economic and environmental values, 342
Ecoforestry Institute, 127, 161
Ecological diversity. See Biological diversity
Ecological holism, 15, 15n.16
Ecological Society of America, 14, 55
Ecology, 21, 55, 65, 67, 190; science of, 14, 15, 54, 125, 309
Economic benefits: of development, 269, overestimating, 285
Economic determinism, fallacy of, 67
Economic self-interest, 62
Economic valuation, market discount rate, 321
Economic value, 23, 61, 73, 141,

192–193; to humans, 335; lack of, 62. See also Values
Economy, colonial, 253
Ecosystem complexity, 312n.41, 320
Ecosystems, 115–116, 117–120; diversity of, 118; forest, 285; health of, xivn.7, 206, 207; integrity and function of, 119, 160, 225, 308; interests of, 119; ongoing process of, 117; resilience of, 308; stability of, 117; well-being interests of, 117; wise management of, xivn.7, 55, 73, 167, 180n.3, 182, 245, 292. See also Nature
Egleston, Nathanial H., 24n.5
Einstein, Albert, 211
Eiseley, Loren, 91
Emerson, Ralph Waldo, 51, 302
Endangered Species Act, xiii, 206n.1, 222
England, 255
Enlightenment, the, 299
Environmental activism, radical, 21n.37
Environmental change, human causes of, 1n.1
Environmental conflicts, 319, 320; North-South, 323
Environmental crisis, 2, 3, 16, 17, 69
Environmental critics, Northern, 257
Environmental degradation, 214, 217, 221
Environmental ethics, xv, 3, 3n.6, 9, 15n.17, 20, 69–71, 72, 73, 96, 148, 121, 152, 154, 155, 157, 255, 331; postmodern, 290n.3; social, 331. See also Ethics
Environmental groups, xiiin.6, 2, 235, 3
Environmentalism, 1, 2, 3, 16n.21, 19, 127, 180, 255, 334; environmental movement, xi, 14, 16, 21, 222, 232, 233; reformist, 334
Environmentalists, xivn.7, 153, 230–231, 232, 269, 273, 275, 281, 300, 325
Environmental philosophy. See Philosophy
Environmental protests, 21–22n.32
Environmental regulation and taxation, 323, 325
Environmental sciences, xv, 21; applied, xv, 126
Environmental scientists, 206; engineering technician model, 205; shared decision-making model, 206
Environmental values: about forests, 256; of critics, xiii; public, xivn.7. See also Values

Espy, Mike, Secretary of Agriculture, 247
Ethic: ecological, 15, 57; ecological noninterference, 325; forest, 190, 193; for foresters, 190; holistic forest, 191; new ecological, 1, 2, 55; new environmental, 1, 127; new forest, 182; professional, 148, 190; utilitarian, 297
Ethical conflict, 327
Ethical dialogue, 219, 330
Ethical obligations. *See* Obligations
Ethical principles, 328
Ethical systems: biocentric, 127; Western, 71
Ethics, 57, 61, 295–296, 300, 301, 306, 312n.49; biocentric, 15, 123; biomedical, 129; as core of professional life, 130; ecocentric perspective, 335–336; environmental, 255; for engineers, 129; extension of, 58; forest, 16, 290; forest land-use, 60, 145; forestry, 53, 56, 128–129; 142, 289; foundation of, 15; holistic, 15; land, 1 (*see also* Land ethic); medical, 129; new forestry, 8; normative, 209; professional, 129, 163, 164, 192, 215; of professional behavior, xv; of restraint, 329; traditional forestry, 296, 298; Western, 71
Evolution, 63, 64; ecological, 57, 77; social, 68, 73
Evolutionary theory, 13–14
Extinction of species. *See* Species

Facts, separation from values, 335
Federal Land Development Agency, Malaysia, 267
Federal Land Policy and Management Act of 1976, United States, 192
Feinberg, Joel, 94, 98, 99–103, 107, 111–112
Fernow, Bernhard, 12, 23n.3, 24, 25, 41, 42, 53, 163n.3, 310.n8
Feyerabend, Paul, 212
Fire, 340; suppression, 305. *See also* Forest fires
First Nations people, 342
Fisher, Duane, 247
Fisheries: biologists, 314n.90
Fishing, industrial, 336
Flathead National Forest, 231
Forest: as a church, 89; as a commodity, 76, 191, 324; as a community, 76, 190; exploitation, 28; as a historical museum, 76; as a plantation, 88; as a resource, 191

Forest biodiversity, preservation of, 289
Forest conditions, 26, 27, 28; United States, 6–7
Forest cover, 3, 3n.7; loss of, 5; global, 281
Forest crop production, 29, 30
Forest destruction and degradation, 18, 285
Foresters: adhering to gardeners ethic, 296; defined, 29; environmental ethic, 155; ethics and education of, 142; land-use ethic of, 149; professional, xivn.8, 29, 147, 197, 293; professional organizations of, 147; values of, xiii, xiv, 126, 153, 181
Forest ethic. *See* Ethic
Forest ethics. *See* Ethics
Forest fires, 33, 37, 304
Forest management, xiii, xivn.8, xv, 5, 12, 13, 21, 30, 40, 94, 121, 297, 311n.20; effects of, 9; federal, xiii, 55, 181; holistic, 22n; integrated, 149; intensive, 121; multiresource, 190; multivalue, 155; new ethical standard for, 260; Pinchotian roots, 94; professional, 7; public involvement and participation in, xivn.8, 141, 291n.6; practices, xiiin.4, xiv, 8, 19n.31; scientific, xiv; sustainable, 8n.25; United States, 122n.5. *See also* Management
Forest planning, public participation in, 291, 291n.6
Forest practices, changes in, 339
Forest preservation (Chapter 2): movement, 12–13; orientation to, 335
Forest products industry, 324. *See also* Wood and wood products
Forest Products Laboratory, U.S.D.A., 54
Forestry, xi, xin.3, 9, 16, 19, 26, 28, 32, 51, 66, 126, 290, 298; applied, 75; art of, 29, 157, 308; Australian, 122; business of, 29–30; community-based, 342; defined, 29–30; ecologically based, 339; economic point of view, 30; ethics and ethical dimensions of, xv, 56, 72, 126, 129, 189; European, 23, 61; global, 255; intensive, 6, 121, 123, 123n.9; modernism in, 291; philosophy of, 14, 23, 78, 194, 289; Pinchotian, 18, 94, 297; postmodern, 295; private, xv, 121; professional, 23, 145, 180, 189; profession of, 19, 23, 53, 78, 126, 129, 133,

146, 303; "Prussian," 24; public, xv, 19, 121; science of, 28, 29, 75, 84, 85, 190, 194, 295, 308; state-based, xv; sustainable, 8n.25, 245, 256n.14, 343; traditional, 7, 295, 296, 298, 299, 305, 307, 309, 311n.21; United States, xii, xv, 7–9, 16, 23, 24, 296, 302, 305, 296; value questions in, 9, 90
Forestry Commission, United States, 49
Forestry ethics: philosophical basis of, 123; land-use, 150; systems of, 292; utilitarian, 126. *See also* Ethic; Ethics
Forests: 26, 28, 77, 80, 84; American, xi; ancient, 7n.20, 27, 30, 42, 77, 193, 254, 294, 336 (*see also* Old-growth forest); boreal, 3n.7, 4, 83; Canadian, 147, 261, 338; as commodity, 76, 324; as community, 76, 324–325; economics of, 10–11, 13, 25, 55, 285; European, 5–6, 6n.16; evolutionary histories of, 81; frontier, 3n.7, 4; functions of, 28; hardwood, 7n.22; health of, 4, 55; as home, 325; integrity of, 55; as interconnected web of relations, 325; luxury, 27; midwestern, 12; moral relations with, 324; national, xiii, xiin.6, xivn.7, xv, 13, 25, 36–40, 148, 294; native, 2, 4, 5, 7, 21, 77, 280, 284; plantation, 88; primeval, 77; protection of, 27; purposes of, 12; regenerated, 2; Soviet Union, 261; supply, 27; temperate, 82, 281, 282; tropical, 2, 4, 4n.9, 261; use of, 149, 152; utilitarian economic purposes of, 13; value of, 12, 152; virgin, 27, 30; western, 12; wild, 42, 193
Forest Service, U.S.D.A., xivn.7, 35, 54, 221, 222, 223, 224, 225, 226, 227, 232, 234, 235, 240, 241, 243, 244–245, 249, 250, 251; Alaska region, 249; "culture" of, 229; management, xivn.7; principles of, 32; scientists, 207; United States, 14, 18, 22n, 24, 53, 148, 180n.3, 207, 208, 293, 304, 306, 307
Forest Service employees, xivn.7, 181n.8, 248; values and attitudes, xiv
Forest Service Employees for Environmental Ethics (FSEEE), Association of, 207, 208
Forest Summit in the Pacific Northwest, April 1993, 331

Sustainability (*continued*)
336; environmental, 337; forest, 8, 161, 266, 275, 281, 337; forest policies, 22 n, 342; forest-dependent human communities, 289; forested ecosystems, 299; harvest practices, 286; institutional barriers to, 258; long-term, 165
Sustained yield, 54, 190, 247, 294, 311n.9, 338

Taft, Howard, 303
Taiwan, 281
Taoism, 274
Tanz, Jordan, 141
Taylor, Duncan, 290, 291
Technology, 262, 307; advances of, 335; ascendancy of, 303
Technology Assessment, United States Office of, 218
Temperate regions, 3n.7
Thailand, 255
Thirgood, J.V., 5
Thoreau, Henry David, 50, 54, 83, 302
Ticknor, Bill, 154, 155, 308
Timber and Stone Act (1878), 47
Timber blockades, 275
Timber companies, 320; Alberta-Pacific Co., 284; Boise Cascade, 254, 322; Daishowa Pulp Co., 284; Georgia-Pacific, 283, 322; Hyundai Corporation, 283; MacMillan Bloedel, 283–284; Mitsubishi Corporation, 283–284; Weyerhauser, 254, 283
Timber Culture Act (1873), 47
Timber: famine, 12, 12n.7; import of, 268; management, xiii; production, xii, xiii, xivn.7, 8n.24, 37–38, 294, 299; shortage, 23
Timber First, xivn.7, 55
Timber harvesting, 222, 243; domestic levels, 259, 261; global, 3n.7; tropical rainforests, 256; U.S., 256, 263
Timber industry, xiii, xivn.7, 205, 227, 229, 230–231, 232, 235, 281, 284; centralization of, 282; Chilean, 282; internationalization of, 286; mechanization of, 282; move from tropical to temperate boreal forests, 280; U.S., 254
Timber trade, 280; global, 257, 282, 284, 286; Pacific Rim, 283; tropical 282
Tongass National Forest (Alaska), 208, 247, 248, 251, 285; Ketchikan area, 248
Topsoil, 271
Toulmin, Stephen, 212

Tragedy of the commons, 209
Tree farming and farms, 309; industrial, 121, 229
Tree plantations. *See* Plantations
Trees: grounds for preserving, 104; interests of, 111; intrinsic value of, 112; as object, 324; rights of, 111, 112; roles of, in human lives, 324
Tribe, Laurence H., 104
Tropics, 3n.7; countries, 285; forests, 269, 271. *See also* Forests, tropical

Udall, Steven, 69
United Nations, 3n.7; Commission on Sustainable Development, The, 286
United States forestry, birth of, 303. *See also* Forestry
Utilitarianism, 297, 299; aggregation of utility, 148; benefit maximization or "calculus of pleasure," 297; distribution of utility, 148; hedonistic, 297; maximization of utility, 148, 150

Value change in American society, 9n.29
Value differences between foresters and society, 153
Valuers, anthropocentric, 13 n. 12. *See also* Anthropocentrism
Values, 14, 73, 74, 78, 181, 192, 285; aesthetic, 13, 73, 193; anthropocentric, 73; bias in, xiv n. 7, 126; biotic diversity, 193; cultural, 342; deep, 72, 79; ecological, 73, 338; economic, 23, 61, 73, 141, 192–193, 337; environmental, 206; ethical, 149, 164, 212, 296; forest, 73, 156; instrumental, 306, 335; intangible, 238; intrinsic, 72, 73, 78, 96, 106, 107, 108, 110, 154, 160, 193–194, 291, 335; life-support, 192; natural history, 193; in nature, 73; philosophy of, 9, 60, 66; protection of, 337; radical shift in, 296; recreational, 13, 193, 342; resource, 222, 231, 233; scenic, 342; scientific, 125, 193, 212; "soft" and "hard," 79; spiritual, 13, 73, 74, 193, 294; timber, 285; tourism, 342; utilitarian, 73; wildlife, 193; wild nature, 42
Vancouver Island (British Columbia), 22n, 128, 333
Vanderbilt Estate at Biltmore, North Carolina, 305
Van der Rohe, Mies, 304
Varner, G.E., 154
Vermont, 321, 322, 323

Walzer, Michael, 216
Washington, state of, 229, 334
Western culture, 71, 83, 274
Whaley, Ross, 154
Whistle-blowing, 130, 138, 207, 222, 240, 250
Wilderness, 12, 13, 21, 54, 78, 83, 104, 149, 191, 294, 296, 307, 309, 336; emotions, 77; management, 315n.116; North American, 11; noumenal value of, 56; philosophy of, 42; preservation of, 105, 149, 337; recreation tourism, 333; spiritual meaning of, 42; wildlife, 169
Wilderness Society, The, 14, 54
Wildlife biologists, 169
Wildlife management, 14, 169
Wildlife Society, The, 169, 192
Willamette National Forest (Oregon), 231, 235, 228; Blue River Ranger District, 227
Williams, Michael, 6
"Willing-to-pay" concept, 297, 312n.30
Wilson, Edward, 301
Wisconsin, 41, 54
Wisconsin, University of, 14, 16n.20, 54
Wise use, 36, 40
Women, domination of, 19. *See also* Ecofeminism
Wood, Paul M., 126, 156
Wood and wood products, 4n.7, 152; consumption of, 4n.7, 5; demand for, in the U.S., 255n.10, 260–261; fiber, 152; global market for, 286; global trade in, 254, 281; industrial, 4n.7; manufacturing, 10, 11, 31, 37–38; materials substituted, 261, 281; technology, 31. *See also* Timber trade
Woolsey, T.S., Jr., 163n.3
Wordsworth, William, 84, 90
World Bank, The, 269
World Resources Institute, The, 3n.7, 285, 286
Worldview, 16; biocentered, 18; dominant industrial expansionist, 336; minority tradition, 18
Worldwatch Institute, The, 267, 275
Worth, intrinsic, 161. *See also* Values, intrinsic
Wright, Frank Lloyd, 314n.79

Yale University School of Forestry, 14, 23n.3, 24, 53
Yosemite National Park (California), 42
Yosemite Valley (California), 41, 42, 118

Zimmerman, Michael, 18

Primary goods, 133
Prince of Wales Island, 208, 248, 249, 250
Proctor, James, 183n.14
Professional-client relation, 131; duty to loyalty, 137–138; ethical limits of loyalty, 138
Professionals, 164; fisheries, 173–174; resource, 238
Profession, forestry: credibility of, 147; political agenda of, 150
Professions, 146; characteristics of, 130–136, 163n.2; function of, 146; professionalism, 163; social contract, 135. *See also* Forestry
Property, 58; rights, 43
Prussia, 294
Public Interest Groups, xiii
Pulp production, subsidized, 285

Rabi, Isidore, 211
Railroads, land grant and right-of-way, 47
Rain forests, 4n.9, 266; temperate and near-temperate, 230; tropical, 82
Rashdall, Hastings, 297
Rawls, John, 133, 217
Reclamation, 65
Recreation, xii, 40, 77
Recycling, 262, 286–287; paper, 262; solid waste, 262
Reforestation, 5
Regan, Tom, 94
Regeneration, natural, 340
Relativism, ethical, 212
Religion, 61, 89
Resource conservation philosophy, 12, 15, 21, 25, 54, 55, 73
Resource ethics: Pinchotian, 126, 127; New, 222, 223, 224, 225, 226, 228, 233. *See also* Forestry, Pinchotian; Forestry ethics
Resource management: integrated, 232; natural, 239; Pinchotian, 123; sustainable, 245
Resources: degradation of, 225, 231; development of, 34; non-commodity, 228
Respect for: forest systems, 328; land, 201; life, 107; non-humans, 328; Northern Forest, 328; particular cultures and biological regions, 323. *See also* Values
Responsibilities: individual and collective, 141; to natural ecosystems, 179; to natural objects, 179; to nature, 179. *See also* Obligations
Restoration, 330; ecology, 161
Rich countries, France and the United States, 269; rich versus poor, 269
Right and wrong, concepts of, 57. *See also* Ethics
Rights, 72, 93: Aboriginal, 140; concept of, 93; moral and legal, 94n.1, 72, 104; nonanimal, 95; nonhuman, 94; private, 325–326; public, 326
Riparian zones, 340
Risk analysis, 322
Road-building, 243, 340
Roadless areas, xiii
Robertson, Dale, Forest Service Chief, 249
Rolston, Holmes, III, xv, 15, 74, 96, 155, 182–183, 290
Romanticism, 302, 306, 307, 308, 309, 312n.46, 315n.112
Roosevelt, Franklin D., 180n.3, 314n.78
Roosevelt, Theodore, 24, 43n, 303, 310n.8, 336
Rothenberg, David, 18
Routley, Richard, 106, 110, 121, 122
Routley, Val, 121, 122
Rubis, Dr. Patau, 268
Runte, Alfred, 180n.3
Rural communities, 285

Sagoff, Mark, 105
Salwasser, Harold, 156
Sarawak, 265, 267, 271, 277; primary forests in, 266
Schurz, Carl, 24
Science of chaos, 301
Scientists, 206; environmental advocacy by, 207
Second Law of Thermodynamics, 301, 311n.12
Self-deception, 272
Self-determination, local, 323
Sequoia gigantea, 49
Sequoia National Park (California), 42
Sequoia sempervirens, 49
Sessions, George, 18
Shallow ecology, 17, 339; movement, 335
Shifting cultivators, 268
Shiva, Vandana, 19
Shoaf, Bill, 208, 247, 248–249, 250
Shrader-Frechette, Kristin, 125, 126, 207, 207n.3
Siberia, 254, 283; boreal taiga, 281, 282
Sierra Club, 16, 22n, 42, 95; Legal Defense Fund, 231
Sierra Nevada Mountains, California, 41, 118
Sifton, Clifford, wise use school in Canada, 336
Silent Spring, 70
Silviculture, 31; methods, xii; selective harvesting, 7–8; system, variable retention, 341
Singapore, 265, 276
Singer, Peter, 94, 210, 214, 219, 313n.60
Siuslaw National Forest (Oregon), 231
Smith, Adam, 301, 312n.47
Smith, David, 308
Snyder, Gary, 18
Social contract, 136
Society of American Foresters (SAF), 24, 123, 127, 148, 163.n3, 165, 165n.9, 167, 179, 182, 185, 189, 192, 196, 202, 295, 308; Code of Ethics, 180, 181, 182, 184, 186, 190, 191, 196, 199, 201; land ethic, 198; land ethic canon 180, 186, 196, 197, 199; land ethic statement, 197; Task Force, 152
Socrates, 129
Soil fertility, 64
South Asia: nations, 270, 272, 276; people, 271, 277
South Korea, 281
Special interest groups, 210–211
Species: extinction of, 66, 76; interests of, 119; long-term survival of, 334; old-growth dependent, 231; preservation of, 114; type of ongoing process, 114; utility of, 78; welfare of, 115
Spotted owl, 230, 245; habitat areas (SOHA), 222, 228, 229; Northern, 205
Stability, ecological, 77, 105
Standard of living, 270; global, 335
Standing: to make moral judgments, 272, 273; of a person to judge morally, 272
Steel, Brent, 182.n8
Steen, Harold, 180n.3
Stevens, Senator Ted, 251
Stewardship of the land, 158, 165, 182, 188, 311n.20, 323; concept of, 155, 196; ethic, 182, 197; True, 222
Stoicism, 99, 298
Stone, Christopher, 95
Sublime, sense of the, 77, 88, 89
Subsidies for harvesting and processing, 285
Sumatra, 265
Suring, Lowell, 247
Sustainability: communities, 334; ecological, 207; economic, 334,

McInnis, John, 285
McQuillan, Alan, 180n.3, 290, 291
Mean annual increment, 294
Mendes, Chico, 255n.12
Mexico, 254
Miller, Alan, 270
Miller, George, House Interior Committee Chairman Rep., 247
Miller, Peter, 290n.4
Mill, John Stewart, 297; harm principle, 272
Mineral King Valley Case, 95
Mining industry, 38
Minnesota, University of, 262
Monocultures, 230, 304, 338; intensively managed tree orchards, 282
Modernism, 295, 302, 304, 308; definition of progress, 337; expansionist model of, 335; in forestry, 306; industrial paradigm of, 337
Monroe, M.C., 154
Monterey Pine, 282
Morality: anthropocentric, 17; trickle-down, 323
Moral responsibility, ascription of, 219
Mosaic Decalogue, 57, 68
Muir, John, 13, 13n.12, 16n.20, 41, 53, 54, 72, 77, 82, 90, 121, 291, 302, 303; on modernism, 336; on "righteous management," 18, 127
Multiple-use, 149, 238, 299; as a commodity model of forests, 192; doctrine, 24, 297; forest management, 190
Multiple Use Sustained Yield Act, 249
Murrelets, Marbled, 205

Naess, Arne, 17, 18, 127
Narveson, Jan, 109
National Conference on Conservation at the White House (1908), 336
National Environmental Policy Act (NEPA), 222, 225, 228, 230, 231, 232, 237, 250
National Forest Management Act (NFMA), 222, 225, 231, 232, 294
National forests, 36–40, 227, 228, 229, 230, 231, 303; reserves, 51, 53; uses of, 40
National Forest Service, 34. *See also* Forest Service, U.S.D.A.
National Parks, 13, 52, 294, 298
National Park Service, 42
National Wildlife Federation, 231
Native Americans, 277; and environmental ethics, 274

Natural resource profession, 165
Natural resources: development of, 33; waste of, 33; wise use of, 33, 35
Nature: aesthetic appreciation of, 80, 82, 83; balance of, 63; domination of, 20; ecocentric perspective on, 335–336; intrinsic view of, 17, 335; multiple values of, 74; philosophical conceptions of, 12; respect for, 17, 89; as a resource, 18. *See also* Ecosystems
Netherlands, the, 268
Nevada, 214
New ecological paradigm, 291
Newell, F.H., 163n.3
New England, 80, 253, 327
New Forestry, 155, 190, 290, 292, 293, 299, 300, 301, 305, 306, 307, 308, 309, 310, 311n.20, 311n.21; defined, 293–294, 295, 296
New Perspectives, 190, 293, 310n.4
New York, 322, 323
New York State College of Forestry at Cornell University, 23n.3
New Zealand, 254, 267, 271
Nez Perce National Forest, 233
Norms: ethical, 125, 255; of professional practice, 125, 164
Northern Forest of eastern North America, 290, 319, 320, 323, 326, 330, 331; conflicts, 325; controversy, 327, 329; decisions about, 322; lands debate, 321
North Kaibab District, 240. *See also* Kaibab National Forest
Northwest Earth Institute, Portland, Oregon, 17, 17n.23
Norton, Bryan, 183n
Nozick, Robert, 104, 111
Nuu-chah-nulth Tribal Council, 333

Obligations: biocentric, 165; ethical, of the private owner, 60; forester's, to the general public, 139; to land, 60; negative unconditional, 142n.8; positive, 142–143n.8; professional, 149; sense of, 324. *See also* Responsibilities
Odum, E.P., 313n.51
Old-growth forest, xii, xiin.5, 7n.20, 205, 232, 235, 244, 247, 250, 293, 294, 333, 349. *See also* Forests, ancient
Olmstead, Frederick Law, Sr., 13, 163n.3; 305, 307, 314n.95, 314n.101, 315n.106
Oregon, 229, 344, 346–349
Oregon Chapter of the American Fisheries Society, 165, 173
Oregon's Coast Range, 346

Organic farming, 66
Overconsumption, 274

Pacific Northwest, xiiin.4, 19, 80, 83, 181, 205, 206n.1, 251, 253, 282, 294, 319
Pacific Rim, 253, 280, 281, 282, 283, 284; National Park, 333; tropical forests in, 281
Paper industry, 262
Paper, "tree free," 286
Papua New Guinea, 281
Paradigm: dominant social, 123n.9; emerging ecological, 335, 343; expansionist, 336; modern forestry, 304
Passmore, John, 104, 105, 106–107, 109
Penan people of Sarawak, the, 255n.12, 264, 266, 267, 268, 275, 276
Perlin, John, 5, 254
Pesticide use, 340
Petrified Forest in Arizona, 81–82
Philippines, 267, 281, 285
Philosophy, 9, 61; academic, 70; anthropocentric, 17; biocentered, 21, 55; deep ecology, 127 (*see also* Deep Ecology); ecofeminist, 20n.32 (*see also* Ecofeminism); ecological, 98; environmental, xv, 3, 15, 15n.17, 16, 20, 69, 71, 96; Western, 71, 94
Pinchot, Gifford, xv, 12, 13, 13n.12, 18, 21, 23, 23n.3, 24–25, 41, 42, 43n, 46, 55, 56, 73, 126, 145, 156, 163n.3, 185, 291, 296, 297, 303, 304–305, 310n.8, 311n.22, 313n.75, 314n.78, 314n.93, 314n.101, 315n.106, 336, 339; utilitarian tenets, 155; wise use philosophy, 336, 338
Place: becoming native to a, 323; care in a, 330
Plantations, 27, 161, 255n.11, 266, 267; forestry, 254; industrial tree, 5; monocultural, 19n.31
Plato, 142n.6
Polanyi, Michael, 212
Political economy, principles of 31
Population: density, 65; growth, 4n.7, 285, 335, 259, 260; world, 262
Positivistic model of objectivity, 211–212
Postmodernism, 213, 290, 295, 307, 308, 309
Power dynamics, 330; and ethical tensions, 327
Predators, extermination of, 61
Preference satisfactions, 78

Forest uses, intangible and non-consumptive, 149
FORPLAN, 249
Foucalt, Michel, 297
Fox, Warwick, 18
Fragmentation of forest habitat, xiii
Frankena, William, 215
Franklin, Jerry, 293
Free trade, 324; agreements, 323
Frontier mentality, 328
Future generations, 32, 140, 141, 234; legacies of, 322

Game, 40; management, 54
General Agreement on Tariffs and Trade (GATT), 286; Uruguay Round, 286
General Land Office, 48
Geographic Information Systems (GIS), 307
Gila National Forest (New Mexico), 54
Globalization, 269, 277, 280
Global timber trade, ethics of the, 256
Global warming, 284
Glover, Jonathan, 107
Golden Rule, 57
Gomberg, Paul, 216, 219
Grand Canyon, 82, 240, 241
Graves, Henry, 163n.3
Grazing, 39, 42, 43; cattle ranching, 266
"Greatest good for the greatest number," 148
"Green lining," 323, 325
Green Mountains, The (Vermont), 323
Gropius, Walter, 304
Growth economy, rate of, 324
Guha, Ramachandra, 274
Gunn, Alastair, 257
Gunter, Pete, 106, 121

Habitat: New England forest, 320; old-growth, xii; tropical forests
Hammond, John, 70n.7
Hardin, Garrett, 216
Hare, R.M., 98, 99–104
Hartshorne, Charles, 70
Harvesting. *See* Timber harvesting
Hayek, Frederic, 300, 301, 312n.48, 312n.50
Hays, Samuel, 152, 153
Health: biological, 326; forest, 4, 55 (*see also* Forest); human, 206; land (defined in Leopold), 56, 66
Hepburn, Ronald, 302
Hetchy-Hetchy Valley (Yosemite National Park), 42
Hinduism, 274
Hippocratic oath, 163

H.J. Andrews Experimental Forest, Blue River, Oregon, xiii
Homebuilder, 37, 39
Homeostasis of ecosystems, 117
Hough, Franklin B., 23, 24n.5
Hume, David, 298, 299, 300, 301
Hutcheson, Francis, 314n.92

India, 255
Indigenous communities and people, 256, 257, 267, 277, 286
Indonesia, 257, 264, 267, 268, 270, 276, 281, 283; Sulawesi, 267
Industrial forestry, xiii, 19, 123n.9, 160, 254, 292, 293, 315n.106, 337, 340; conventional, 339; practices, 161
Inglehart, Ronald, 182n.8
Integrity: ecological, 74; of the ecological process, 337. *See also* Ecosystems
Intensive forestry, 122, 191
International Monetary Fund, 269
International Society for Environmental Ethics, 351
International Tropical Timber Organization, 286

Jackson, Wes, 160
Japan, 271, 281, 282, 284
Java, 266, 268
Johnson, K. Norman, 208
Johnson, Lawrence, 97

Kaibab National Forest, 240
Kalimantan, 265, 267
Kant, Immanuel, 99
Kaza, Stephanie, 290
Kennedy, John F., 69
Ketchikan Pulp Co., 247
Key-log idea, the, 56, 67, 185
Kilmer, Joyce, 84
King's Canyon National Park (California), 42
Kovalicky, Tom, 233
Kuala Lumpur, 265
Kuhn, Thomas, 212

LaChapelle, Delores, 18
Lake Champlain, 323
Lamarck, Jean Baptiste, 85
Land: as biotic mechanism, 63; as community, 59; cost benefit approach to, 149; as an energy circuit, 63, 64; ethical obligations to, 60; ethical relation to, 67; health, 74, 155, 184; as property, 58
Land ethic, 73, 157, 158, 180, 182, 185, 187, 192, 194, 225, 245; environmental, 336; evolution of, 67–68; expanded, 192; Leopold's, 14–15, 17, 20, 21, 53, 55, 57–68, 69, 109, 123, 165, 180n.3, 182, 183n.14, 184, 189, 190, 196, 290, 301, 307; professional, 155; utilitarian, xivn.7
Land grant colleges, 54
Landowners, 324, 326; large-scale, 326; small-scale, 326
Landscape architecture, 306
Landscape ecology, 77, 160
Lansky, Mitch, 329
Lavoisier, Antoine-Laurent, 85
LeConte, Joseph, 16n.20
Le Corbusier, 304
Leopold, Aldo, 14–15, 53, 57–68, 69, 73, 74, 109, 122, 123, 127, 157–158, 180, 185, 190, 201, 226, 273, 291, 300, 306, 307, 311n.20, 324, 328, 336; biotic forestry, 292; ecosystem holism, 301; model of forestry, 55
Lewontin, Richard, 211
Limits of Acceptable Change Method, 315n.117
Locke, John, 216, 218
Logging, xiii n. 4, 2; highgrading, 250; industrial, 284, 285, 286; on Northern Forest lands, 320; objections, to, 275; practices, 247; private small-scale, 325; protests by foreign individuals, 275; selection, 304; tropical rainforests, 264, 265
Logical positivists, 213, 299
Log, exports, 282
Louisiana, 257

Mahathir, Dr., Mohamed (Malaysian Prime Minister), 265
Maine, 320, 321, 323, 329
Malaysia, 255, 256n.14, 257, 264, 265, 270, 276, 281
Management, 5; even-age, 7, 8 n. 24; holistic, 294; intensive, 4, 6; Muir's righteous, 18; science-based, xv; strategies, 286–287; timber, xiii; uneven-age, 8 n. 24; wilderness, 307; wise, 51, 336. *See also* Forest management
Manser, Bruno, 264, 271, 276
Mariposa Big Tree Grove, 42
Market, 284; shift from raw logs to wood chips and pulps, 280
Marsh, George Perkins, xi, 13, 23, 24
Mathews, Freya, 18
Mayr, Ernst, 91
McCloskey, Mike, 152
McCoy, Earl, 125, 126
McDonald, Michael, 126
McGough, D., 158
McHarg, Ian, 307